MICHAEL COOPER

Buyer's Guide
to New Zealand
Wines

2012

Hodder Moa

A catalogue record for this book is available from the National Library of New Zealand

ISBN 978-1-86971-253-2

A Hodder Moa Book
Published in 2011 by Hachette New Zealand Ltd
4 Whetu Place, Mairangi Bay
Auckland, New Zealand

Designed and produced by Hachette New Zealand Ltd
Printed by Griffin Press, Australia

Reviews of the latest editions

'This in-depth encyclopaedia is the definitive guide.'
— *tvnz.co.nz*

'I admire Michael Cooper for his writing. His *Buyer's Guide to New Zealand Wines*, the twentieth edition to be released later this year, is truly the "Bible" on the subject…'
— *Raymond Chan Wine Reviews*

'Cooper's annual bestseller is considered "the bible of NZ wine" by fellow industry members and consumers alike.'
— Trinity Hill

'The *Buyer's Guide* is an essential book for anyone wishing to cut through the fluff and get a fast, honest appraisal of practically any wine made in New Zealand. If a wine doesn't rate well, Cooper tells you why, and if it gains five stars his praise is lavish… This is a book for the novice and the connoisseur, the wine student and wine professional, the collector and the drinker.'
— *New Zealand House & Garden*

'The indispensable guide for New Zealanders.'
— *Marlborough Express*

'Whenever I stand in front of the Chardonnay section at my local Glengarry's wine store and feel overwhelmed by the hundred or so New Zealand Chardonnays on display there, I wonder how I could ever make a choice if I didn't have with me the current edition of Cooper's invaluable guide. I never buy wine without having it with me. It is totally indispensable and the best guide on the market by a country mile.'
— *Beattie's Book Blog*

'The absolute bible of New Zealand wines.'
— *Newstalk ZB*

Michael Cooper is New Zealand's most acclaimed wine writer, with 36 books and several major literary awards to his credit, including the Montana Medal for the supreme work of non-fiction at the 2003 Montana New Zealand Book Awards for his magnum opus, *Wine Atlas of New Zealand*. In the 2004 New Year Honours, Michael was appointed an Officer of the New Zealand Order of Merit for services to wine writing.

Author of the country's biggest-selling wine book, the annual *Michael Cooper's Buyer's Guide to New Zealand Wines*, now in its twentieth edition, he was awarded the Sir George Fistonich Medal in recognition of services to New Zealand wine in 2009. The award is made each year at the country's largest wine competition, the New Zealand International Wine Show, to a 'living legend' of New Zealand wine. The weekly wine columnist for the *New Zealand Listener*, he is also New Zealand editor of Australia's *Winestate* magazine and chairman of its New Zealand tasting panel.

In 1977 he obtained a Master of Arts degree from the University of Auckland with a thesis entitled 'The Wine Lobby: Pressure Group Politics and the New Zealand Wine Industry'. He was marketing manager for Babich Wines from 1980 to 1990, and since 1991 has been a full-time wine writer.

Cooper's other major works include *100 Must-Try New Zealand Wines* (2011); the much-extended second edition of *Wine Atlas of New Zealand* (2008); *Classic Wines of New Zealand* (second edition 2005); *The Wines and Vineyards of New Zealand* (published in five editions from 1984 to 1996); and *Pocket Guide to Wines of New Zealand* (second edition 2000). He is the New Zealand consultant for Hugh Johnson's annual best-selling *Pocket Wine Book* and the acclaimed *World Atlas of Wine*.

Contents

6

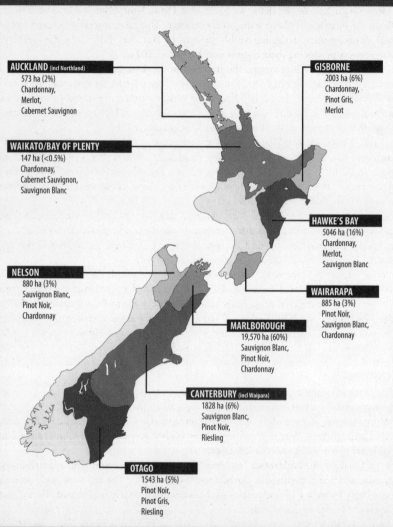

The Winemaking Regions of New Zealand

Area in producing vines 2012 (percentage of national producing vineyard area)

AUCKLAND (incl Northland)
573 ha (2%)
Chardonnay,
Merlot,
Cabernet Sauvignon

WAIKATO/BAY OF PLENTY
147 ha (<0.5%)
Chardonnay,
Cabernet Sauvignon,
Sauvignon Blanc

NELSON
880 ha (3%)
Sauvignon Blanc,
Pinot Noir,
Chardonnay

GISBORNE
2003 ha (6%)
Chardonnay,
Pinot Gris,
Merlot

HAWKE'S BAY
5046 ha (16%)
Chardonnay,
Merlot,
Sauvignon Blanc

WAIRARAPA
885 ha (3%)
Pinot Noir,
Sauvignon Blanc,
Chardonnay

MARLBOROUGH
19,570 ha (60%)
Sauvignon Blanc,
Pinot Noir,
Chardonnay

CANTERBURY (incl Waipara)
1828 ha (6%)
Sauvignon Blanc,
Pinot Noir,
Riesling

OTAGO
1543 ha (5%)
Pinot Noir,
Pinot Gris,
Riesling

These figures (rounded to the nearest whole number) are extracted from the *New Zealand Winegrowers Statistical Annual*, published by New Zealand Winegrowers. During the period 2008 to 2012 the total area of producing vines is projected to expand from 29,310 to 33,600 hectares – a rise of nearly 15 per cent.

Preface

Marlborough Sauvignon Blanc at $6.99 and Pinot Noir from Waipara at $10 ... there's no shortage of cheap wine on the market. This year, several producers closed their doors or were struggling visibly to survive. But that didn't stop the country's winegrowers producing their biggest-ever harvest in 2011.

New Zealand Winegrowers, the industry body, described the huge vintage as a 'response to rising sales of New Zealand wine'. That positive analysis was supported by several producers, although 30 per cent of our exports are of bulk, rather than bottled, wine. The bumper crop — which exceeded the 2010 harvest by 23 per cent — produced an extra 4.3 million cases of wine to sell.

The New Zealand Wine Company, whose key brands include Grove Mill, Sanctuary and Frog Haven, is struggling financially. After reporting a $1.28 million profit in 2009, last year the company suffered a loss of nearly $1.9 million. Its key problems have been the oversupply of New Zealand wine, cheap sales in bulk, and the strength of the New Zealand dollar.

St Helena, Canterbury's oldest winery, founded in 1978, was placed into liquidation earlier in 2011. Matakana Estate, by far the largest producer in the district, which drew grapes from around the country for its Matakana Estate and Goldridge Estate labels, was placed into liquidation late in 2010.

On a more positive note, overseas funds are flowing into the wine industry. Bill Foley, an entrepreneurial American billionaire, snapped up Martinborough's largest vineyard, Te Kairanga, in May. Foley made his first move in New Zealand in 2009, when he bought the New Zealand Wine Fund, whose assets included the Vavasour, Clifford Bay and Goldwater brands and over 100 hectares of Marlborough vineyards.

All eyes are on China. New Zealand's major export markets for wine are still Australia, the UK and the US, but last year sales to China skyrocketed from $6 million to $17 million.

China is widely predicted to be the world's fastest-growing market for wine over the next decade. New Zealand, with its reputation for white wines and screw-cap closures, doesn't fit some of the quality preconceptions — based on classic French reds, sealed with corks — but this country's Free Trade Agreement with China, signed in 2008, has given winegrowers a key boost.

In Guangzhou, Ngatarawa has already opened a showroom where distributors, retailers and restaurateurs can do business while sipping the red-wine style seen as most likely to wow Chinese palates — Hawke's Bay's widely underrated Merlot and Cabernet Sauvignon-based reds.

— Michael Cooper

Vintage Charts 2002–2011

WHITES	Auckland	Gisborne	Hawke's Bay	Wairarapa	Nelson	Marlborough	Canterbury	Otago
2011	3	3	3	4	4	4	4	3
2010	7	6–7	7	6	7	7	6	6
2009	4	6–7	4	5	6	5	6	3–5
2008	5–6	3–4	3–5	5–7	4	2–5	3–6	5–6
2007	6	7	6	4–5	5	5–6	5–6	4–6
2006	6–7	4–5	6	5	5	4–5	5	5–6
2005	7	5	4	3	4	4–5	5	3–4
2004	6	5–6	5–6	5	5	6	3–6	3
2003	5–6	4	3–4	6	5–6	5	4–6	5
2002	6	7	6	6	6–7	4–6	4–7	5–7

REDS	Auckland	Gisborne	Hawke's Bay	Wairarapa	Nelson	Marlborough	Canterbury	Otago
2011	2	2	2	4	3	4	4	3
2010	7	6	6	5	6	6–7	5	5–6
2009	5	6–7	6	5	6	6	6	3–5
2008	5–7	3–4	3–5	5–7	4	2–5	3–6	5–6
2007	3–5	7	6	4–5	5	4–6	5–6	4–6
2006	4–5	4–5	4–5	5	5	4–5	5	5–6
2005	7	5	4–6	3	4	4–5	5	4–5
2004	5–7	6	5–6	5	4	4–5	4–6	3–4
2003	4–6	4	3–4	7	5–7	5	4–7	5–6
2002	6	7	5–6	4	5–7	4–7	3–6	5–6

7 = Outstanding   6 = Excellent   5 = Above average   4 = Average   3 = Below average   2 = Poor   1 = Bad

2011 Vintage Report

'It was a real mixed bag this year, that's for sure,' reported a senior winemaker for one of New Zealand's leading producers. That's how most winemakers drawing grapes from around the country viewed the 2011 harvest.

The industry is still battling its way through oversupply-induced turmoil, but that didn't stop growers from harvesting an unprecedentedly large grape crop in 2011. At 328,000 tonnes, the vintage was 15 per cent bigger than the previous record — set in 2008 and equalled in 2009 — and a 23 per cent leap on 2010.

'It was a typical La Niña vintage,' said New Zealand Winegrowers. Summer brought the strongest La Niña pattern for 30 years, combining extremely high temperatures in many regions with serious floods in the North and South Islands.

In spring, a sunny, dry October — except in Hawke's Bay and Gisborne — was followed by a warm and dry November. At the start of summer, December stayed warm and dry in the eastern North Island regions, but was much damper in the south.

After a wet January in the major North Island wine regions, February was generally warm and dry, but the dampest on record in Central Otago. As the harvest approached, March was drier than usual in Marlborough but very wet in the North Island. In April, the key harvest month, the weather cooled in the eastern areas of both islands, bringing record April rainfall to Hawke's Bay.

Overall, wine regions in the middle of the country — notably Wairarapa, Marlborough and North Canterbury — appear to have fared better than those in Auckland, Gisborne and Hawke's Bay, where New Zealand Winegrowers concedes 'weather issues were a feature'.

In terms of regional production, Marlborough dominated, being the source of over 75 per cent of the national grape crop. The harvest was bountiful in the South Island (exceeding 2010 by 34 per cent in Marlborough and by a whopping 68 per cent in Waipara), but in the North Island, production dropped by 9 per cent in Hawke's Bay and 21 per cent in Gisborne.

Sauvignon Blanc was by far the key variety, accounting for nearly 70 per cent of the total crop. Compared to 2010, the Sauvignon Blanc harvest rose by 29 per cent, Pinot Noir by 32 per cent and Pinot Gris by 39 per cent. All three varieties are grown widely in the South Island. Conversely, such North Island varieties as Syrah and Cabernet Sauvignon declined by 18 per cent and 24 per cent respectively.

The good news is that Marlborough, the industry's engine-room, had a successful vintage. In other key regions, 2011 has provided a stiff test of grapegrowing and winemaking skills.

Northland

Winegrowers in the country's northernmost region harvested just 111 tonnes of grapes — 0.3 per cent of the national total and the smallest crop for a decade.

Spring was favourable, with Kaitaia recording its sunniest-ever October and low rainfall in November. However, the start of summer was warm and wet, with double the normal rainfall in December, and in January eastern Northland received four times its normal rainfall.

A favourably sunny, dry February was followed by a cloudy March. Karikari Estate says the growing season was 'extraordinary. … Those producers who read the conditions … had the best results. Others found out that Northland can be a harsh mistress…'

Auckland

'This vintage is going to be interesting,' noted one of Auckland's top red-wine producers in late January. 'Such a perfect fruit set and early season, then all this rain and more coming.' After the harvest, another top-end producer on Waiheke Island admitted: 'Mother Nature hurled us a tough one.'

At 1464 tonnes, 2011 was an average-sized crop. Puriri Hills, at Clevedon, reported a 'perfect fruit set and early season'. Summer kicked off with a warm, damp December, followed by a warm, wet January (with four times the normal monthly rainfall). February was generally dry and hot, but included a heavy rain 'event' on Waiheke Island.

In autumn, a sunny March led into a wet April, with rainfall well above normal. 'There was plenty of heat for ripeness accompanied by really moist soils, so while we got great ripeness in the fruit, it may end up being a tad dilute in the wines,' Robin Ransom, at Warkworth, told *New Zealand Winegrower*. At Kumeu River, the hand-pickers 'had to work particularly hard to triage [remove] rotten berries,' says Michael Brajkovich.

On Waiheke Island, Te Whau reported 'a tough year, particularly for white varietals'. The 2011 vintage of its Cabernet Sauvignon-based blend, The Point, will be a 'lighter, fruit-forward style, for earlier drinking'.

Waikato/Bay of Plenty

With a tiny crop of 51 tonnes of grapes, growers in the Waikato and Bay of Plenty picked their smallest harvest for a decade — far below the 932 tonnes picked in 2002.

After low rainfall in late spring, in December Mystery Creek reported 'a bonza flowering season, in part due to the dry conditions'. However, January was warm and cloudy, with four times the average rainfall in parts of the region.

One producer has no wine from 2011, 'as the crops were too damaged by a cyclone eight days out from picking'. To the south-west, in Taranaki, Kairau Lodge & Vineyard reported 'a lot of rain and warm, humid conditions, so it's been tough'.

Gisborne

Gisborne growers picked their smallest crop for the past eight years. At 14,450 tonnes of grapes, it was 21 per cent lighter than in 2010, and accounted for less than 5 per cent of the national harvest.

During spring, October was notably wet, with record one-day rainfall at Patutahi. 'With some cooler weather during flowering in early November, the fruit set was a little lighter than previous years,' reported Matawhero.

Summer got off to a good start with a notably dry December, followed by a very cloudy January. 'We had an amazing run into summer,' said Matawhero, 'with unusually hot and dry conditions from mid-December through to the end of January.'

However, humid conditions in February and March created ideal conditions for fungal disease. GroCo, a grower's consortium, reported in March that 'by far the biggest frustration … has been the cloudy, cool days and lack of sunshine'. For April, *New Zealand Winegrower* reported 'heavy downpours right in the thick of harvest'.

One Gisborne winemaker reported widespread rot and 'no red wine this year'. Another was more upbeat, reporting 'a good vintage — but we had to make very heavy [grape] selections'.

Matawhero said that 'in particular the Gewürztraminer and Pinot Gris are looking good', and others enthused about their Pinot Gris, Chardonnay and Viognier. However, Steve Voysey, a vastly experienced Gisborne winegrower, described 2011 as the most challenging vintage for a decade.

Hawke's Bay

At 35,533 tonnes, Hawke's Bay's growers picked 11 per cent of the national grape crop. It was a fairly small harvest — 9 per cent lighter than 2010 and 13 per cent lighter than 2009 — and an exceptionally wet growing season did not enhance the prospects for quality wine.

During spring, frosts were not an issue, but October brought more than double the normal rainfall. Wet weather at flowering prevented a consistent fruit set across all varieties, according to Moana Park. *New Zealand Winegrower* reported a November slip in The Terraces vineyard at Esk Valley, 'triggered by the wettest spring [winemaker Gordon] Russell had experienced at the winery'.

Both summer and autumn were unusually rainy. 'Potential Great for Hawke's Bay 2011 Grape Harvest,' announced Hawke's Bay Winegrowers on 3 March, 'delighted at the clean quality fruit on the vines.' But March proved much wetter than normal and as autumn progressed the weather worsened.

In April, Hawke's Bay was cooler than usual and suffered three times its usual rainfall, setting a new record for the month. When torrential rain in late April triggered widespread flooding and slips, a state of emergency was declared.

Chardonnay, the major white-wine grape, was hit hard in some vineyards: 'We took a bit of a bath with Chardonnay,' admitted Sileni Estate. Merlot was also adversely affected, reported *New Zealand Winegrower*.

In response to forecasts of adverse weather, late-ripening varieties were often harvested earlier than usual. Some fruit of inferior quality was left to rot on the vines. However, Trinity Hill, although unlikely to release its top red, Homage, will produce all of its upper-tier 'black label' range.

'It will be a producer's year, not a regional year,' said Steve Smith, of Craggy Range. 'There will be a few disaster stories and successes. It will be important to look at each wine with an open mind.'

Wairarapa

With 3598 tonnes of grapes, Wairarapa growers picked just 1.1 per cent of the national harvest. According to Wines from Martinborough, 'settled weather with even temperatures through spring was ideal for flowering and vine growth'.

During summer, a dry December was followed by a cloudy January and extremely dry February. On 10 February, Escarpment Vineyard reported the season was 'running a week early and could be a cracker'. At the end of February, Nga Waka reported the lowest spring/summer rainfall on record.

In late March, however, the start of the harvest was postponed by rain, and April was cooler and much wetter than normal. For March and April combined, the rainfall of 188 mm was double the 2006–2010 average of 95 mm.

It was an exceptionally hot growing season, due to high night temperatures, according to Nga Waka. Te Kairanga reported that the warmth meant 'we could pick earlier with the flavour development there earlier than usual'. Martinborough Vineyard said: 'Brixes [sugar levels] were lower, so alcohols will be lower, which is exciting.'

Gladstone Vineyard reported Pinot Noir with 'lovely depth of flavour'. However, the extremely hot growing season and heavy autumn rainfall suggest that 2011 was not a 'classic' vintage.

Nelson

The 2011 vintage was 'more problematic' than 2010 or 2009, especially for Pinot Noir, says Nelson Winegrowers. At 7854 tonnes, the region's winegrowers picked a record crop, 32 per cent bigger than 2010. Over half was Sauvignon Blanc.

In spring, an extremely sunny and dry October set new records. Waimea Estates reported a 'good flowering and fruit set'. Early summer was wet, with double the normal rainfall in December, but during February the weather was dry — and the hottest on record.

At the start of autumn, March brought 'intermittent rain', according to *New Zealand Winegrower*, and April was very cloudy, with lots of rain at the end of the month. At Blackenbrook Vineyard, where the harvest was over early, by the start of April, 'before ferocious rain set in', the prediction is for wines with ripe-fruit flavours and relatively low alcohol levels.

Nelson Winegrowers declared that the wines will reflect how well wineries managed their vineyards. 'Those who had a slightly more leafy canopy, a lower crop and were able to harvest early will produce some fantastic wines.'

Seifried Estate enthused about Gewürztraminer in 'pristine condition'. Rimu Grove, in the *Nelson Mail*, reported some of its best-ever Chardonnay and Pinot Gris, but Pinot Noir on a lower level. Those who picked early probably fared best.

Marlborough

Marlborough, where 60 per cent of the country's vines are planted, enjoyed a relatively favourable vintage. Heavy rain in late December set the scene for a substantial crop, and warm summer weather ensured the harvest would not be late.

With an avalanche of 244,893 tonnes of grapes — exceeding by far the previous record of 194,639 tonnes, set in 2008 — Marlborough produced over 75 per cent of the national harvest. More than 90 per cent of the country's Sauvignon Blanc and over half of the Pinot Noir flowed from the region.

In spring, a very wet September was followed by a sunny, notably dry October and warm, dry November. 'The period from bud-break to flowering was the shortest of the last six vintages, which shows that it was warm,' Brian Bicknell, of Mahi, told *Wine Spectator*.

At the start of summer, December was warm — the hottest since 2005 — but also cloudy and extremely wet. In late December, two major rain storms caused the vines to go 'ballistic,' reported viticultural consultant, Dominic Pecchenino.

'What was unusual about this year,' Dr Mike Trought, of Plant & Food Research, told *New Zealand Winegrower*, 'was that despite the rain experienced during December, temperatures were above average. … There was no water stress on the vines…' By boosting bunch weights and berry sizes, the rain had a direct impact on the potential size of the harvest. A dry, cloudy January was followed by a warm, extremely dry February.

Autumn began with a sunny, dry March which cooled rapidly at the end, bringing snow to the hills. At the beginning of April — the key harvest month — the rainfall for January–March had been only 60 per cent of the long-term average.

Rob Agnew, of Plant & Food Research, enthused: 'The ripening period for Sauvignon Blanc has been very dry and relatively botrytis free.' However, April proved cool, wet and the least sunny since 1995.

'The majority of fruit … was picked at lower sugar levels than usual,' noted *New Zealand Winegrower*. The relatively cool nights in autumn suited Sauvignon Blanc and Pinot Gris, giving wines of 'bright, fresh flavours and nice crisp acidity'.

'Overall, [2011 was] more challenging than 2010,' reported Churton, 'but if you were on top of your viticulture, with open canopies and your crop loads right, it was excellent.' However, due to the tendency to large berries, those growers who cropped heavily risked flavour dilution. 'I do not think 2011 will have the class of 2010,' summarised one of the region's most experienced viticulturists. 'Big berries generally this year.'

Cloudy Bay and Brancott Estate have predicted intensely flavoured wines with slightly lower than normal alcohol levels. Seresin Estate says its Pinot Noir is 'especially exciting'.

Canterbury

Look out for a lot more Canterbury wine. The region's growers reported a 2011 harvest of 9485 tonnes of grapes — well ahead of the previous record, set in 2008, of 6881 tonnes, or the 5870 tonnes picked in 2010.

At Waipara, in North Canterbury, Pernod Ricard NZ reported 'a relatively calm spring. The strong north-westerly winds we normally get at that time didn't occur.' Black Estate was 'rewarded with an incredible spring. Bathers on!'

In summer, a sunny, warm and dry December was followed by a very cloudy

January. Pernod Ricard NZ described its Waipara vines in January as 'looking stunning in terms of vine health, and they have a moderate crop'. Overall, summer was warm, with intermittent rain, says Black Estate.

Following a sunny March and cool April, *New Zealand Winegrower* reported that 'a little more rain than was required during the growing season led to larger bunch weights and volume of fruit available for harvest than normal'. Rain at harvest led to predictions that 2011 would be a good year for botrytis-affected Riesling.

Torlesse reported an early harvest of 'ripe, full-flavoured grapes. ... It will be a very good year.' Greystone described its Pinot Noir and Chardonnay as showing 'less muscle than those of the last couple of years, and more finesse and texture'.

Otago

Otago growers harvested 7104 tonnes of grapes, second only to the bumper 2008 harvest. After an unusually warm, wet growing season, the big crop proved vulnerable to diseases (including, for the first time, powdery mildew). 'I don't think many producers will have been too happy with the vintage,' declared Misha's Vineyard.

Spring was relatively frost-free. At Prophet's Rock, in the Cromwell Basin, October and November were the warmest on record. 'We therefore experienced very rapid spring growth and a very successful flowering.'

However, the favourable weather for flowering and fruit set yielded large, tight bunches of grapes, more susceptible to disease. 'Two months of rain deluged over the last week of December,' reported *New Zealand Winegrower*. 'Coupled with milder temperatures and higher humidity, disease pressure was set to escalate. ... The remainder of summer saw warmer weather, tempered by intermittent periods of rain at just the right times to antagonise viticulturists and excite fungal populations.'

The harvest began early, at Bendigo on 21 February, with Pinot Noir grapes for sparkling wine. A wet March 'did cause concern throughout Otago with the increased risk of powdery mildew and botrytis,' reported Grasshopper Rock.

After battling what *New Zealand Winegrower* described as 'higher tonnages, likelihood of high sugars and the botrytis issue that comes with denser canopies', some vineyards lost their entire crop. Following three frosts in late April, the season came swiftly to a close.

'It was a good year to have grapes off the vines early,' according to Grasshopper Rock. Mount Edward agreed, telling the *New Zealand Herald*: 'If you didn't work hard and didn't pick early, it all turned to custard.'

'I don't think concentration will be a word used to describe [the wines],' Felton Road told *Wine Spectator*. 'Words more like precision, mineral, tension.'

Best Buys of the Year

Best White Wine Buy of the Year

Whitehaven Marlborough Sauvignon Blanc 2011
★★★★★, $17.99–$19.99

Whitehaven is better known in the US – where it is distributed by one of its shareholders, global wine giant E & J Gallo – than in New Zealand. But from one vintage to the next, its Sauvignon Blanc is classy, with rich passionfruit/lime flavours, very fresh, pure and well-rounded. The 2011 vintage of this multiple gold-medal and trophy-winning label, released recently, is right on form – and you can buy a bottle for less than $20.

Whitehaven Marlborough Sauvignon Blanc 2011 (★★★★★) is a classic regional style – mouthfilling, punchy and dry, with crisp, ripe tropical-fruit flavours to the fore, a herbal undercurrent, and lovely poise, delicacy and length. Already very open and expressive, it's the sort of Sauvignon Blanc that draws you back for a second glass … and a third.

Over the years, the wine has won many top accolades, but for such a high-flier on the show circuit, the wine is produced in very large volumes – well over 100,000 cases. *Wine & Spirits* rated Whitehaven Marlborough Sauvignon Blanc last year as the third most popular Sauvignon Blanc served by the glass in American restaurants.

Sue White, the company's co-founder and majority shareholder, believes the key to the wine's quality is Whitehaven's access to grapes from 31 vineyards throughout the Marlborough region. 'Our goal is a wine that reflects the spectrum of flavours achieved in the vineyards and also has a balance of acidity and sweetness to ensure easy drinkability.'

At the winery, the unique flavours in the grapes from each site are retained, by handling each parcel of fruit separately until the final blending. Skin contact is avoided and fermentation is at low temperatures, entirely in stainless steel tanks.

Senior winemaker Sam Smail's description of the 2011 Sauvignon Blanc is spot on: 'The palate is full and vibrant. Fresh nettle, gooseberry and tropical-fruit flavours abound and linger on the long, clean-acid finish.' A dry style (3.5 grams/litre of residual sugar), the wine's subliminal sweetness is balanced by fresh, mouth-watering acidity.

Whitehaven suggests this Marlborough beauty is best enjoyed young and gently chilled, with summer salads, poultry and shellfish.

Best Red Wine Buy of the Year

Wild South Marlborough Pinot Noir 2010
★★★☆, $17.99

A delicious drink-young style, this is a generous, sweet-fruited red, ruby-hued, with good depth of cherryish, plummy flavour, ripe and smooth. At $18 or less, it offers unbeatable value. The judges at the International Wine & Spirit Competition presumably agreed in October 2011, awarding it a silver medal.

'We've never had money for marketing,' says David Mason, who controls Sacred Hill, owner of the Wild South brand. 'The money goes into the wine itself.' The key point is that Wild South Marlborough Pinot Noir 2010 (★★★☆) is just as impressive, in quality terms, as most Pinot Noirs in the $25–$30 price bracket.

And it's consistently a great buy. The 2009 vintage collected a silver medal at the 2010 *Decanter* World Wine Awards, where the judges praised it as 'wild strawberry, beautifully silky and ripe on the palate, with a juicy and elegant length'.

In New Zealand, other reviewers have enthused about the 2010. 'For a young wine, this is showing lovely balance and poise,' stated *FMCG* magazine, 'displaying red/black cherry, spice and a touch of game notes on the nose. The palate is gentle and fruity with supple texture and fine tannins.'

Glengarry Wines promotes Wild South Marlborough Pinot Noir 2010 as delivering 'all that's good about Pinot Noir – complexity, intrigue, glamour – without the associated price tag.' Wild South's 60-hectare estate vineyard lies in the lower reaches of the Waihopai Valley. For the 2010 Pinot Noir, grapes were also purchased from growers in the Marlborough region, including the Awatere Valley, enabling the production of a large-volume wine, about 4000 cases.

Compared to most Pinot Noirs in the sub-$20 category, the Wild South is unusually savoury and complex. How did they achieve that? 'It's a combination of many things,' believes chief winemaker Tony Bish. 'Cold-soaking the skins in the juice, prior to the fermentation, adds complexity and depth, and post-ferment maceration is also important, to achieve the best tannin balance. Oak is employed, and by resting the wine on its yeast lees, without sulphur dioxide, we can add to the "gaminess".'

This bargain-priced red will cellar well for up to five years, but it's already hard to resist.

Other shortlisted wines

Whites
Coopers Creek SV The Limeworks Hawke's Bay Chardonnay 2010 (★★★★☆, $20)
Invivo Marlborough Sauvignon Blanc 2011 (★★★★★, $20)
The Crater Rim Waipara Sauvignon Blanc 2010 (★★★☆, $15)
Twin Islands Marlborough Chardonnay 2010 (★★★☆, $15)

Reds
Thornbury Hawke's Bay Merlot 2010 (★★★★☆, $22)
Trinity Hill Hawke's Bay Merlot 2010 (★★★★, $19.95)
Vidal White Series Cabernet Sauvignon/Merlot 2010 (★★★★☆, $22)

The Twentieth Vintage

If you line them up neatly, the 20 editions of the *Buyer's Guide* fill an entire shelf, each volume growing fatter and fatter. The latest blockbusters, reviewing over 3000 wines, make the slim first edition, published in 1992 with just 800 wines, look cute.

'In the spring of 1991,' the preface to that little book records, 'I embarked on a national vineyard tour, visiting about 100 wineries, from Alexandra to Matakana, and tasting about 1000 wines.' If you tried that today, you'd be gone forever, trying to visit 700 producers and taste 4000 wines.

To keep abreast of New Zealand wine 20 years ago, on most nights I opened 'a couple of bottles at home' (if one was Müller-Thurgau and the other Chardonnay, it's not hard to guess what was set aside for dinner). Today, to keep up with developments around the country, every day you need to taste about 10 wines.

In a section on buying wine, readers of the first edition learned that the arrival of wine on supermarket shelves two years earlier had 'revolutionised' purchasing, but major chains like Liquorland, SuperLiquor and Glengarry were still the dominant wine retailers. No longer — supermarkets now dominate the retail market for wine in New Zealand.

To revive memories of the wine scene 20 years ago, I scanned the fourth (1993) edition of my book, *The Wines and Vineyards of New Zealand*. Montana, the colossus, commanded 40 per cent of the domestic market for New Zealand wine. Under the ownership of Corporate Investments (itself controlled by Peter Masfen), and steered by managing director Peter Hubscher, the company was gearing itself to repel an onslaught of Australian wine under CER.

Snapping at Montana's heels in terms of size was Corbans, part of DB Group, owned by Brierley Investments. With Noel Scanlan as general manager, the company claimed a 38 per cent market share with its popular Corbans, Cooks, Robard & Butler, Stoneleigh and Longridge brands. Villa Maria — owned by the founding Fistonich family and Mangere grape-grower Ian Montgomerie — claimed a 10 per cent share of the market, making it clearly New Zealand's third-largest wine producer.

Nobilo, the country's biggest family-owned winery, was run by brothers Steve, Nick and Mark Nobilo. Nobilo White Cloud — a New Zealand version of Germany's Blue Nun — was a fruity, Müller-Thurgau-based wine, blended with a touch of Sauvignon Blanc, exported in bulk, 20,000-litre stainless steel tanks, and then bottled in Sweden and Denmark.

What about the smaller wineries? Chardonnay wizard John Hancock was still at Morton Estate. Denis Irwin, the founder of Matawhero, was back down Riverpoint Road after a long sojourn in Victoria, fashioning a more subdued style of Gewürztraminer than his high-impact wines of the late 1970s.

In the deep south, the emerging names were Black Ridge, Chard Farm, Gibbston Valley, Rippon, Taramea and William Hill. 'So eye-catching were the top Central Otago Pinot Noirs from the 1990 vintage, with their mouthfilling body, suppleness and cascading fruit flavours,' I wrote in 1993, 'the Wairarapa's Pinot Noir producers surely had a sleepless night or two.'

New wineries were mushrooming — up from 93 in 1984 to 180 in 1993. Attracted by New Zealand's recently proven ability to produce world-class wines, a wave of Australian producers had swept into the industry, including Yalumba (for its Nautilus brand) and Cape Mentelle (Cloudy Bay). Following the runaway success of its debut 1985 and later Sauvignon Blancs, by 1990 Cloudy Bay was majority-owned by the Champagne house, Veuve Clicquot.

Fighting a wave of cheap imported wines, as the government moved to free up the local market, in the early 1990s the industry launched such budget-priced labels as Penfolds Clive River (from Montana), St Aubyns (from Villa Maria) and Corbans White Label. Longer-established cheap wines, some already starting to slide in popularity, included Cooks Chasseur, Corbans Liebestraum and Matua Valley Chablis.

Nobilo Chateau Valley — a simple, berryish, slightly sweet drop — was made, the company declared, 'to introduce white wine drinkers to red'. As consumers grew more and more familiar with wine, many began to switch from light, gently sweet white wines (such as Müller-Thurgau) to dry whites (Chardonnay) and reds (typically Cabernet Sauvignon-based).

Martinborough Vineyard Müller-Thurgau was praised in the 1992 *Buyer's Guide* as being 'about as good as you'll get'. However, the 1992 vintage proved to be the last; the vines were replaced with Pinot Gris.

Have prices soared over the past 20 years? A comparison of the Chardonnays in the 1992 and 2011 editions of the *Buyer's Guide* shows that most wines have risen in price, but by much less than you would expect, given the rate of inflation. Among the biggest movers are Dry River Chardonnay, up from $24 to $52, and Neudorf Moutere Chardonnay, up from $29 to $55.

However, Kumeu River Chardonnay, $30 in 1992, now has a recommended price of $36 and can often be bought for a lot less. Hunter's Marlborough Chardonnay ($24 in 1992) is now actually *cheaper* — $20. Stoneleigh Marlborough Chardonnay and Church Road Hawke's Bay Chardonnay (both $18 in 1992) are now generally purchased on 'promotion' at $14.95.

In terms of grape varieties, the national vineyard has changed radically over the past 20 years. Chardonnay has dropped from 21 per cent to 12 per cent of plantings; Cabernet Sauvignon from 8.6 per cent to 1.6 per cent; and Müller-Thurgau has plummeted from almost 18 per cent to 0.25 per cent.

Meanwhile, Pinot Gris has soared from 0.3 per cent to over 5 per cent of total plantings, and Pinot Noir from 6.6 per cent to over 15 per cent. But Sauvignon Blanc is the key mover, soaring from less than 15 per cent of plantings in 1992 to well over 50 per cent today.

Looking back, many grapes now starting to carve out a niche — with wines on the shelves you can buy — had no retail presence at all in 1992. The white-wine newcomers include Arneis, Flora, Grüner Veltliner, Sauvignon Gris, Verdelho,

Viognier and Würzer. The reds include Carmenère, Chambourcin, Dolcetto, Gamay Noir, Malbec, Marzemino, Montepulciano, St Laurent, Sangiovese, Tempranillo, Zinfandel and Zweigelt.

Even the map of New Zealand winegrowing is hard to recognise from 20 years ago, when Gisborne and Hawke's Bay produced over 60 per cent of the country's wine. In the 2011 vintage, over 75 per cent of New Zealand's wine flowed from a single region, Marlborough.

Canterbury and Otago have enjoyed a big increase in their combined share of the national vineyard (up from 3.5 per cent to over 10 per cent), while Gisborne has plummeted from 27 per cent to 6.5 per cent, Hawke's Bay has slipped from 26 per cent to 16 per cent, and Auckland has slumped from 6 per cent to less than 2 per cent.

Marlborough, of course, has been the runaway success, boasting over 140 wine producers in 2011. The 1993 edition of *The Wines and Vineyards of New Zealand* profiled just 10 wineries based solely in the region: Allan Scott, Cellier Le Brun, Cloudy Bay, Forrest, Grove Mill, Highfield, Hunter's, Merlen, Te Whare Ra and Vavasour. Mentioned briefly were several 'new wineries on the block': Jackson, Nautilus, Wairau River, Cairnbrae, Conders Bend and Lawson's Dry Hills.

Given the wine industry's exhilarating growth over the past 20 years (from 180 wineries in 1992, producing 41.6 million litres of wine, to 672 wineries in 2010, producing 190 million litres of wine), it would be natural to assume that Kiwis are drinking more and more New Zealand wine. In 1992, we drank an average per person of 15.5 litres of wine, including 12.9 litres from New Zealand and 2.6 litres from overseas. By 2010, our wine consumption had jumped to 21.1 litres per capita, but only 13 litres were New Zealand wine. The rest was imported.

The wine industry's vastly increased production of late has been shipped overseas. Wine exports have skyrocketed from 7.1 million litres, worth $34.7 million, in 1992, to 142 million litres, worth $1.04 billion, in 2010.

So what are some of the key wine industry figures from the early 1990s doing now? Nick Nobilo's labour of love is Vinoptima, his tiny vineyard and winery in Gisborne dedicated solely to Gewürztraminer. Peter Hubscher, after his long, illustrious spell at Montana, joined Te Kairanga in a senior managerial role, but is no longer involved. John Hancock, of Morton Estate, co-founded Trinity Hill in 1993 and has since produced some of Hawkes' Bay greatest and most innovative wines.

Many familiar winery names from 20 years ago are gone. In the upper North Island, these include Collards, Pacific, Matakana Estate, Peninsula Estate and de Redcliffe. Further south, do you remember Paritua, Bloomfield, Blue Rock, Chifney, Lintz, Amberley, Daniel Schuster and St Helena?

Crystal ball-gazing, what will New Zealand's wine industry look like 20 years from now? Hugh Ammundsen, of Doubtless Strategic, recently published projections in his *Wine Trends* newsletter, based on key statistics from 2011, 2001, 1991 and 1982.

The country's total area in vines will surge from 33,400 hectares in 2011 to 55,000 hectares in 2031, and the ranks of wine producers from 697 to 975. The value of wine exports will leap from $1.09 billion in 2011 to $2.6 billion by 2031.

Pinot Noir and Pinot Gris will rise from 15 per cent of our wine output to nearly

30 per cent, and the regional importance of Hawke's Bay, Gisborne, Wairarapa, Nelson, Canterbury and Otago will all rise.

Conversely, Sauvignon Blanc will decline from 68 per cent to 45 per cent of the country's production and by 2031 Marlborough will be the source of just 58 per cent of New Zealand wine, down from 75 per cent.

Ammundsen concedes his forecasts are 'completely unable to take account of potentially significant social, cultural, economic or other market factors that could significantly affect the future'. In other words, as he cheerfully admits, they are likely to prove 'woefully wrong'.

This twentieth edition of the *Buyer's Guide* is also the heart of a new website, www.michaelcoopersbuyersguide.co.nz. Launched in November 2011, the website has been designed for wine enthusiasts who turn to the Internet for reviews and wine-buying suggestions. The website also makes the *Buyer's Guide* more accessible to lovers of New Zealand wine around the world.

Classic Wines of New Zealand

A crop of four new Super Classics (Craggy Range Le Sol, Deutz Marlborough Cuvée Blanc de Blancs, Felton Road Block 3 Central Otago Pinot Noir and Johanneshof Marlborough Gewürztraminer), eight new Classics and seven Potential Classics are the features of this year's revised list of New Zealand wine classics.

What is a New Zealand wine classic? It is a wine that in quality terms consistently ranks in the very forefront of its class. To qualify for selection, each label must have achieved an outstanding level of quality for at least three vintages; there are no flashes in the pan here.

By identifying New Zealand wine classics, my aim is to transcend the inconsistencies of individual vintages and wine competition results, and highlight consistency of excellence. When introducing the elite category of Super Classics, I restricted entry to wines which have achieved brilliance in at least five vintages (compared to three for Classic status). The Super Classics are all highly prestigious wines, with a proven ability to mature well (even the Sauvignon Blancs, compared to other examples of the variety).

The Potential Classics are the pool from which future Classics will emerge. These are wines of outstanding quality which look likely, if their current standards are maintained or improved, to qualify after another vintage or two for elevation to Classic status. All the additions and elevations on this year's list are identified by an asterisk.

An in-depth discussion of New Zealand's greatest wines (what they taste like, how well they mature, the secrets of their success) can be found in the second edition of my book, *Classic Wines of New Zealand* (Hodder Moa, 2005), which grew out of the *Buyer's Guide*'s annually updated list of New Zealand wine classics.

Super Classics

Branded and Other White Wines
Cloudy Bay Te Koko

Chardonnay
Ata Rangi Craighall; Clearview Reserve; Clos de Ste Anne Naboth's Vineyard; Kumeu River Estate; Kumeu River Mate's Vineyard; Neudorf Moutere; Sacred Hill Riflemans; Te Mata Elston

Gewürztraminer
Dry River; ***Johanneshof Marlborough; Lawson's Dry Hills Marlborough

Pinot Gris
Dry River

Riesling
Dry River Craighall Vineyard; Felton Road; Pegasus Bay

Sauvignon Blanc
Cloudy Bay; Palliser Estate; Saint Clair Wairau Reserve; Seresin Marlborough

Sweet White Wines
Dry River Late Harvest Craighall Riesling; Forrest Estate Botrytised Riesling; Villa Maria Reserve Noble Riesling

***New Super Classic*

Bottle-fermented Sparklings
***Deutz Marlborough Cuvée Blanc de Blancs

Branded and Other Red Wines
***Craggy Range Le Sol; Esk Valley The Terraces; Stonyridge Larose; Te Mata Coleraine

Merlot
Esk Valley Winemakers Reserve Merlot-predominant blend

Pinot Noir
Ata Rangi; Dry River; ***Felton Road Block 3; Martinborough Vineyard; Pegasus Bay; Villa Maria Reserve Marlborough

Syrah
Te Mata Estate Bullnose

Classics

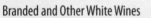

Branded and Other White Wines
**Craggy Range Les Beaux Cailloux

Chardonnay
Babich Irongate; Brancott Estate Ormond 'O' Gisborne; Church Road Reserve; Cloudy Bay; Dog Point Vineyard; Dry River; Esk Valley Winemakers Reserve; Fromm Clayvin Vineyard; Martinborough Vineyard; Pegasus Bay; Seresin Reserve; Te Whau Vineyard Waiheke Island; Vidal Reserve; Villa Maria Reserve Barrique Fermented Gisborne; Villa Maria Reserve Marlborough

Chenin Blanc
Millton Te Arai Vineyard

Gewürztraminer
Stonecroft Old Vine

Pinot Gris
Martinborough Vineyard; Villa Maria Single Vineyard Seddon

Sauvignon Blanc
Brancott Estate [formerly Montana] 'B' Brancott Marlborough; Lawson's Dry Hills Marlborough; Staete Landt Marlborough; Te Mata Cape Crest; Villa Maria Reserve Clifford Bay; Villa Maria Reserve Wairau Valley

Viognier
**Clos de Ste Anne Les Arbres

Sweet White Wines
Glazebrook Regional Reserve Noble Harvest Riesling

Bottle-fermented Sparklings
Deutz Marlborough Cuvée; Nautilus Cuvée Marlborough; Pelorus; **Quartz Reef Méthode Traditionnelle [Vintage]

Branded and Other Red Wines
Babich The Patriarch; **Craggy Range
Sophia; **Craggy Range The Quarry;
Newton Forrest Estate Cornerstone;
Sacred Hill Brokenstone; Unison
Selection

Cabernet Sauvignon-predominant Reds
Brookfields Reserve Vintage ['Gold
Label'] Cabernet/Merlot; Te Mata
Awatea Cabernets/Merlot; Villa Maria
Reserve Cabernet Sauvignon/Merlot

Merlot
Vidal Reserve Merlot/Cabernet
Sauvignon; Villa Maria Cellar

Selection Hawke's Bay Merlot/
Cabernet Sauvignon;
Villa Maria Reserve Hawke's Bay

Pinot Noir
**Dog Point Vineyard Marlborough;
Felton Road Block 5; Fromm Clayvin
Vineyard; Gibbston Valley Reserve;
Greenhough Hope Vineyard; Neudorf
Moutere; Neudorf Moutere Home
Vineyard; Palliser Estate; Pisa Range
Estate Black Poplar Block

Syrah
Mills Reef Elspeth; Passage Rock
Reserve; **Trinity Hill Homage
Gimblett Gravels

Potential Classics

Chardonnay
Corbans Cottage Block Hawke's Bay;
Mission Jewelstone; Ngatarawa Alwyn;
Odyssey Reserve Iliad; Spy Valley
Envoy Marlborough; Trinity Hill
Hawke's Bay [Black Label]; Villa Maria
Single Vineyard Keltern

Gewürztraminer
Cloudy Bay; *Seifried Winemakers
Collection Nelson; Villa Maria Single
Vineyard Ihumatao; Vinoptima
Ormond Reserve

Pinot Gris
Blackenbrook Vineyard Nelson;
Escarpment Martinborough;
*Greystone Waipara

Riesling
Carrick Josephine Central Otago;
Framingham Classic; Muddy Water
Growers' Series James Hardwick
Waipara; Neudorf Moutere; Rippon;
*Valli Old Vine Central Otago

Sauvignon Blanc
Clos Henri Marlborough;
Greenhough Nelson; Highfield
Marlborough; Jackson Estate Stich
Marlborough; *Tupari Awatere Valley
Marlborough; Vavasour Awatere;
Whitehaven Marlborough; Wither
Hills Single Vineyard Rarangi

Viognier
Trinity Hill Gimblett Gravels; Villa
Maria Single Vineyard Omahu
Gravels Vineyard

**New Classic   *New Potential Classic

Sweet White Wines
Cloudy Bay Late Harvest Riesling;
Ngatarawa Alwyn Winemaker's
Reserve Noble Harvest Riesling;
Pegasus Bay Aria Late Harvest
Riesling

Rosé
Esk Valley Merlot/Malbec Rosé

Branded and Other Red Wines
Alluviale; Clearview Enigma;
Clearview Old Olive Block; Clearview
The Basket Press; *Destiny Bay Magna
Praemia; Obsidian; Puriri Hills
Reserve; Te Awa Boundary; Tom;
Trinity Hill The Gimblett

Cabernet Sauvignon-predominant Reds
Babich Irongate Cabernet/Merlot/
Franc; Church Road Reserve Hawke's
Bay Cabernet/Merlot; Mills Reef
Elspeth Cabernet/Merlot; Mills Reef
Elspeth Cabernet Sauvignon; Sacred
Hill Helmsman Cabernet/Merlot

Malbec
Stonyridge Luna Negra Waiheke
Island Hillside

Merlot
Craggy Range Gimblett Gravels; Hans
Herzog Spirit of Marlborough Merlot/
Cabernet Sauvignon; Ngatarawa
Alwyn Merlot/Cabernet; Providence
Private Reserve Merlot/Cabernet
Franc/Malbec

Montepulciano
Hans Herzog Marlborough

Pinot Noir
Akarua Reserve; Amisfield Central
Otago; Bannock Brae Estate Barrel
Selection; Bell Hill; Carrick Central
Otago; Felton Road Bannockburn
Central Otago; Hans Herzog
Marlborough; Kaituna Valley
Canterbury The Kaituna Vineyard;
Mondillo Central Otago; Mt
Difficulty Single Vineyard Pipeclay
Terrace; Muddy Water Slowhand;
Nautilus Four Barriques; Olssens
Slapjack Creek Reserve; Pegasus Bay
Prima Donna; Peregrine Central
Otago; Quartz Reef Bendigo Estate
Vineyard; Quartz Reef Central
Otago Bendigo; Terravin Hillside
Reserve; Villa Maria Cellar Selection
Marlborough; Villa Maria Single
Vineyard Seddon; Wooing Tree
Central Otago

Syrah
Bilancia La Collina; Church Road
Reserve Hawke's Bay; Craggy Range
Gimblett Gravels Vineyard; Kennedy
Point; Passage Rock; Stonyridge
Pilgrim Syrah/Mourvedre/Grenache

Tempranillo
*Trinity Hill Gimblett Gravels

The following wines are not at the very forefront in quality terms, yet have been produced for many vintages, are extremely widely available and typically deliver good to excellent quality and value. They are all benchmark wines of their type – a sort of Everyman's classic.

Chardonnay
Church Road Hawke's Bay; Selaks Winemaker's Favourite Hawke's Bay; Stoneleigh Marlborough

Gewürztraminer
Seifried Nelson

Pinot Gris
Waimea Nelson

Riesling
Hunter's Marlborough; Seifried Nelson; Waimea Classic Nelson

Sauvignon Blanc
Montana Marlborough; Oyster Bay Marlborough; Saint Clair Marlborough; Shingle Peak Marlborough; Stoneleigh Marlborough; Tohu Marlborough; Villa Maria Private Bin Marlborough

Sparkling
Lindauer Brut; Lindauer Special Reserve; Soljans Fusion Sparkling Muscat

Merlot
Church Road Hawke's Bay Merlot/ Cabernet Sauvignon; Te Mata Woodthorpe Vineyard Merlot/ Cabernets; Vidal Hawke's Bay Merlot/ Cabernet Sauvignon

Pinot Noir
Pencarrow Martinborough; Villa Maria Private Bin Marlborough

Cellar Sense

Someone gives you a good bottle of Chardonnay, Riesling, Pinot Noir or Merlot, but it's only a year or two old. Should you drink it or cellar it?

Surveys show that most wine in New Zealand is drunk on the day it is bought and only 1 per cent is cellared for more than a year. Everyone relishes the idea of a personal wine cellar, packed with vintage wines maturing slowly to their peak – but few of us actually do it. Instead, it's three or four bottles in a little rack perched on top of the fridge.

To enjoy many wines at the peak of their powers, you do need to lay them down. Some people keep wine far too long. They *worship* their famous bottles, picking them up from time to time, fondling them, talking about them, but they never get around to opening them – until they are well past their best.

A friend called me over a few years ago to sort out his cellar, acquired in a burst of enthusiasm 20 years earlier. His interest in wine later faded and the bottles had been lying under his house ever since. 'Bring a corkscrew. I can't find mine any more.'

It was hard going. After several bottles, it was clear that most New Zealand wines don't repay keeping for 20 or 30 years. Nor do most of the world's wines. But another tasting revealed that good New Zealand wines can certainly mature well for a decade.

Opened five years ago, 22 highly rated whites from the 1990 to 1994 vintages, although stored in an uncomfortably hot office, yielded some delicious surprises. Most were still alive, nine were enjoyable and four were magical: Matua Valley Reserve Sauvignon Blanc 1994, grown in West Auckland; Neudorf Moutere Riesling 1994; Dry River Craighall Estate Riesling 1994, from Martinborough; and Dry River Gewürztraminer 1994.

The oldest New Zealand wine I've ever tasted was McWilliam's Hawke's Bay Cabernet Sauvignon 1965. I snapped up a bottle for $20 at an auction several years ago, knowing that the wine once acclaimed as New Zealand's greatest-ever red would be well past its best. A mellow, faded conversation-piece, it was still alive – just.

Others have had more exciting experiences. In 1892, William Beetham planted a 1.2-hectare vineyard at Masterton, mostly in Pinot Noir, Pinot Meunier and Syrah. In 1985, Beetham's descendants broached a rare bottle of his Lansdowne Claret 1903. Geoff Kelly, then the wine columnist for *National Business Review*, enthused that the 82-year-old wine was 'alive and well … with the oak standing firm, yet amazing fruit, body and freshness for the age. The finish is superb, long and lingering.'

For my book, *Classic Wines of New Zealand* (second edition 2005), I conducted vertical tastings of over 100 of New Zealand's top wines. In a vertical tasting, several – perhaps all – vintages of a wine are tasted side by side, allowing you to assess the overall quality of a wine, the evolution of its style, the impact of vintage variation and its maturation potential.

One insight from the tastings was that the best South Island Chardonnays age just as well as those from the most prestigious Chardonnay region – Hawke's Bay.

Fromm Clayvin Vineyard Chardonnay, from Marlborough, and Neudorf Moutere Chardonnay, from Nelson, blossom in the bottle for a minimum of five years – every bit as long as such Hawke's Bay classics as Te Mata Elston Chardonnay and Sacred Hill Riflemans Chardonnay.

Another trend in the Chardonnay section was for the wines from cooler vintages to mature better than those from warmer seasons. Crisp, firmly structured Chardonnays may be less seductive in their youth than fleshy, soft models, but they often perform better over the long haul.

Central Otago winemakers sent me a dozen of their 2002 vintage Pinot Noirs to assess, when the wines were more than five years old. How well had they matured?

Overall, pretty well. All of the wines were alive and most were attractive, showing good, bottle-aged complexity. Whether the wines were more enjoyable then than when they were released four years earlier was a matter of debate. Many drinkers enjoy Pinot Noir in its youth, with garden-fresh, vibrant fruit flavours to the fore, while others prefer the savoury, mellow notes that come with maturity.

So which wines most repay cellaring? First, forget the idea that all wines improve with age. Many New Zealand wines are best drunk young.

I suggest drinking fine-quality New Zealand Sauvignon Blancs at six months to two years old. The good news is that screw-caps are preserving the wines' freshness markedly better than corks did, so that Sauvignon Blancs that are several years old can still offer pleasure. Sauvignon Blancs bottled with corks typically tasted past their best before they reached two years old.

Most Pinot Gris, Gewürztraminers and Viogniers are at their best between one and three years old; fine-quality Chardonnays at two to five years old; and top Rieslings at three to seven years old. Some outstanding examples will flourish for longer, but if you buy a case, it pays to check regularly.

Pinot Noirs and Merlots typically drink well at two to five years old. No one knows yet how well Syrah, the hot new red-wine variety, will mature, but the best should reward cellaring for five to 10 years. The top Cabernet/Merlot blends from Hawke's Bay and Waiheke Island are still the safest bet for long-term cellaring.

Cellaring Guidelines

Grape variety	Best age to open

White

Sauvignon Blanc	
(non-wooded)	6–24 months
(wooded)	1–3 years
Gewürztraminer	1–3 years
Viognier	1–3 years
Pinot Gris	1–4 years
Sémillon	1–4 years
Chenin Blanc	1–5 years
Chardonnay	2–5 years
Riesling	2–7+ years

Red

Pinotage	1–3 years
Malbec	1–3 years
Cabernet Franc	2–5 years
Merlot	2–5+ years
Pinot Noir	2–5+ years
Syrah	2–5+ years
Cabernet Sauvignon	3–7+ years
Cabernet/Merlot	3–7+ years

Other

Sweet whites	2–5 years
Bottle-fermented sparklings	
(vintage-dated)	3–5+ years

How to Use this Book

It is essential to read this brief section to understand how the book works. Feel free to skip any of the other preliminary pages, but not these.

The majority of wines have been listed in the book according to their principal grape variety, as shown on the front label. Lawson's Dry Hills Marlborough Sauvignon Blanc, for instance, can be located simply by turning to the Sauvignon Blanc section. Wines with front labels that do not refer clearly to a grape variety or blend of grapes, such as Cloudy Bay Te Koko or Tom, can be found in the Branded and Other Wines sections for white and red wines.

Most entries are firstly identified by their producer's names. Wines not usually called by their producer's name, such as Drylands Marlborough Sauvignon Blanc (from Constellation New Zealand), or Triplebank Awatere Valley Marlborough Pinot Noir (from Pernod Ricard NZ), are listed under their most common name.

The star ratings for quality reflect my own opinions, formed where possible by tasting a wine over several vintages, and often a particular vintage several times. *The star ratings are therefore a guide to each wine's overall standard in recent vintages*, rather than simply the quality of the latest release. However, to enhance the usefulness of the book, in the body of the text I have also given a *quality rating for the latest vintage of each wine*; sometimes for more than one vintage. (Since April 2010 wineries have been able to buy stickers to attach to their bottles, based on these ratings.)

I hope the star ratings give interesting food for thought and succeed in introducing you to a galaxy of little-known but worthwhile wines. It pays to remember, however, that wine-tasting is a business fraught with subjectivity. You should always treat the views expressed in these pages for what they are – one person's opinion. The quality ratings are:

★★★★★	Outstanding quality (gold medal standard)
★★★★☆	Excellent quality, verging on outstanding
★★★★	Excellent quality (silver medal standard)
★★★☆	Very good quality
★★★	Good quality (bronze medal standard)
★★☆	Average quality
★★	Plain
★	Poor
No star	To be avoided

These quality ratings are based on comparative assessments of New Zealand wines against one another. A five-star Merlot/Cabernet Sauvignon, for instance, is an outstanding-quality red judged by the standards of other Merlot/Cabernet Sauvignon blends made in New Zealand. It is not judged by the standards of overseas reds of a similar style (for instance Bordeaux), because the book is focused solely on New Zealand wines and their relative merits. (Some familiar New Zealand wine brands in recent years have included varying proportions of overseas wine. To be featured in this book, they must still include at least some New Zealand wine in the blend.)

Where brackets enclose the star rating on the right-hand side of the page, for example (★★★), this indicates the assessment is only tentative, because I have tasted very few vintages of the wine. A dash is used in the relatively few cases where a wine's quality has oscillated over and above normal vintage variations (for example ★–★★★).

Super Classic wines, Classic wines and Potential Classic wines (see page 21) are highlighted in the text by the following symbols:

Super Classic	Classic	Potential Classic

Each wine has also been given a dryness-sweetness, price and value-for-money rating. The precise levels of sweetness indicated by the four ratings are:

DRY	Less than 5 grams/litre of sugar
MED/DRY	5–14 grams/litre of sugar
MED	15–49 grams/litre of sugar
SW	50 and over grams/litre of sugar

Less than 5 grams of sugar per litre is virtually imperceptible to most palates – the wine tastes fully dry. With between 5 and 14 grams, a wine has a hint of sweetness, although a high level of acidity (as in Rieslings or even Marlborough Sauvignon Blancs, which often have 4 to 6 grams per litre of sugar) reduces the perception of sweetness. Where a wine harbours over 15 grams, the sweetness is clearly in evidence. At above 50 grams per litre, a wine is unabashedly sweet.

Prices shown are based on the average price in a supermarket or wine shop (as indicated by the producer), except where most of the wine is sold directly to consumers from the winery, either over the vineyard counter or via mail order or the Internet.

The art of wine buying involves more than discovering top-quality wines. The real challenge – and the greatest satisfaction – lies in identifying wines at varying quality levels that deliver outstanding value for money. The symbols I have used are self-explanatory:

–V	=	Below average value
AV	=	Average value
V+	=	Above average value

The ratings discussed thus far are all my own. Many of the wine producers themselves, however, have also contributed individual vintage ratings of their own top wines over the past decade and the 'When to drink' recommendations. (The symbol **WR** indicates Winemaker's Rating, and the symbol **NM** alongside a vintage means the wine was not made that year.) Only the producers have such detailed knowledge of the relative quality of all their recent vintages (although in some cases, when the information was not forthcoming, I have rated a vintage myself). The key point you must note is that *each producer has rated each vintage of each wine against his or her highest quality aspirations for that particular label, not against any absolute standard.* Thus, a 7 out of 7 score merely indicates that the producer considers that particular vintage to be an outstanding example of that particular wine; not that it is the best-quality wine he or she makes.

The 'When to drink' (**Drink**) recommendations (which I find myself referring to constantly) are largely self-explanatory. The **P** symbol for PEAKED means that a particular vintage is already at, or has passed, its peak; no further benefits are expected from aging.

Here is an example of how the ratings work:

Felton Road Block 3 Central Otago Pinot Noir   ★★★★★

Grown at Bannockburn, on a north-facing slope 270 metres above sea level, this is a majestic Central Otago wine, among the finest Pinot Noirs in the country. The mature vines are cultivated just in front of the winery, in a section of the vineyard where the clay content is relatively high, giving 'dried herbs and ripe fruit characters'. The wine is matured for 11 to 14 months in Burgundy oak barrels (30 per cent new in 2010), and bottled without fining or filtration. The 2010 vintage (★★★★★) is a very 'complete' wine, dense and youthful in colour, with notably rich cherry, plum, spice and nut flavours. A powerful, finely textured red, already delicious, it's benchmark stuff and a prime candidate for cellaring.

Vintage	10	09	08	07	06	05	04	03	02	DRY $90 AV
WR	7	7	7	7	6	7	7	6	7	
Drink	12-22	11-21	11-20	11-18	11-17	11-18	11-12	P	P	

The winemaker's own ratings indicate that the 2010 vintage is of excellent quality for the label, and is recommended for drinking between 2012 and 2022.

Describes 'Classic' status, ranging from for Super Classic, for Classic to for Potential Classic. This is a wine that in quality terms ranks in the forefront of its class.

Dryness-sweetness rating, price and value for money. This wine is dry in style (below 5 grams/litre of sugar). At $90 it is average value for money.

Quality rating, ranging from ★★★★★ for outstanding to no star (–), to be avoided. This is generally a wine of outstanding quality.

White Wines

Albariño

Coopers Creek's 2011 bottling is the first true example of Albariño from New Zealand or Australia (whose so-called 'Albariño' vines were recently proven to be a French variety, Savagnin). Called Albariño in Spain and Alvarinho in Portugal, this fashionable variety produces light, crisp wines described by Riversun Nurseries at Gisborne as possessing 'distinctive aromatic, peachy characteristics, similar to Viognier'. With its loose clusters, thick skins and good resistance to rain, Albariño could thrive in this country's wetter regions.

Coopers Creek SV Bell-Ringer Gisborne Albariño   (★★★)

Recommended for early drinking, the debut 2011 vintage (★★★) has an inviting, aromatic bouquet, hinting of herbs and spices. A fresh, medium-bodied dry wine (4 grams/litre of residual sugar), it is citrusy and gently spicy, refreshing and moderately characterful. Promising, rather than memorable. Only 250 bottles were made.

Vintage	11
WR	4
Drink	12-14

DRY $20 –V

Arneis

Still rare here – so rare it is not listed separately in the latest *NZ Winegrowers Statistical Annual* – Arneis is one of the most distinctive emerging varieties. Pronounced 'Are-nay-iss', it is a traditional grape of Piedmont, in north-west Italy, where it yields soft, early-maturing wines with slightly herbaceous aromas and almond flavours. The word 'Arneis' means 'little rascal', which reflects its tricky character in the vineyard; a vigorous variety, it needs careful tending. First planted in New Zealand in 1998 at the Clevedon Hills vineyard in South Auckland, its potential is now being explored by numerous producers. Coopers Creek released the country's first varietal Arneis from the 2006 vintage.

Clevedon Hills Arneis
★★★★☆

Estate-grown in South Auckland, the powerful 2009 vintage (★★★★☆) shows excellent freshness and concentration. Attractively scented, it is fleshy and vibrantly fruity, with rich, peachy, spicy flavours, a hint of pineapple, and a dry, rounded finish. The 2010 (★★★★★) is even more impressive. A gently oaked style (40 per cent spent five months in seasoned barrels), it is full-bodied and fleshy, with vibrant, ripe, highly concentrated tropical-fruit flavours, a hint of spearmint, and a long, dry finish. An outstanding, intensely varietal wine, it's delicious now.

DRY $30 –V

Coopers Creek SV Gisborne Arneis The Little Rascal
★★★☆

Top vintages are richly scented, with substantial alcohol and strong, slightly spicy and herbal flavours. The 2010 (★★★☆) is gently sweet (6 grams/litre of residual sugar), sturdy (14.5 per cent alcohol) and fleshy, with ripe, peachy, slightly spicy flavours and a soft, creamy texture. The 2011 (★★★☆) is freshly scented, with very good depth of citrusy, vaguely herbal and nutty flavours, showing clear-cut varietal character. It's enjoyable from the start.

Vintage	10	09	08
WR	7	5	6
Drink	12-15	11-13	11-12

MED/DRY $20 AV

Doctors', The, Marlborough Arneis
★★★★

From Forrest, this off-dry wine is typically floral, fresh and full-bodied, with a basket of ripe-fruit flavours, suggestive of peaches, pears and spices. Delicious from the start, the 2010 vintage (★★★★) is weighty, fleshy and rounded, with ripe, citrusy, spicy flavours showing very good depth.

Vintage	10	09
WR	7	6
Drink	11-13	11-12

MED/DRY $25 AV

Matawhero Gisborne Arneis
(★★★★)

Fleshy and smooth, the 2009 vintage (★★★★) was harvested in the Bell Vineyard, at Hexton, at a ripe 24.2 brix. Delicious young, it's a robust style (over 14 per cent alcohol), with good concentration of peach, pear and lychee flavours, a hint of herbs and a dryish, finely textured finish.

MED/DRY $30 –V

Montana Showcase Series Gisborne Arneis   ★★★★

The debut 2008 vintage (★★★★), grown at Patutahi, is fleshy and slightly minerally, with a dry feel and excellent depth. The 2009 (★★★★) is highly scented, with fresh acidity, strong, very vibrant flavours of citrus fruits and apples, and a hint of nuts. An excellent all-purpose wine.

DRY $24 AV

Trinity Hill Gimblett Gravels Arneis   (★★★★☆)

The tight, youthful, finely poised 2010 vintage (★★★★☆) was hand-picked and fermented and lees-aged for nine months in old barrels. A quietly satisfying wine, it is full-bodied and dry, with strong, citrusy flavours, hints of herbs and nuts, and obvious potential.

DRY $35 –V

Trinity Hill Hawke's Bay Arneis   ★★★★

A consistently good buy. The 2009 vintage (★★★★) was estate-grown and hand-harvested in the Gimblett Gravels, and fermented in tanks and old barrels. The bouquet is fresh, lifted and strongly varietal; the palate is mouthfilling, with ripe pineapple, herb and spice flavours, and an appetisingly crisp, dry finish.

DRY $19 V+

Villa Maria Cellar Selection Hawke's Bay Arneis   (★★★★)

The debut 2010 vintage (★★★★) was hand-picked at three sites and matured on its yeast lees in tanks for two months. Highly fragrant, it is mouthfilling, with fresh, ripe tropical-fruit and spice flavours, and a finely poised, bone-dry finish. The 2011 (tasted prior to bottling, and so not rated), is full-bodied, with ripe tropical-fruit flavours, slightly spicy, dry and smooth.

Vintage	11	10
WR	7	6
Drink	12-14	11-12

DRY $24 AV

Branded and Other White Wines

Cloudy Bay Te Koko, Craggy Range Les Beaux Cailloux, Dog Point Vineyard Section 94 – in this section you'll find all the white wines that don't feature varietal names. Lower-priced branded white wines can give winemakers an outlet for grapes like Chenin Blanc, Sémillon and Riesling that otherwise can be hard to sell. They can also be an outlet for coarser, less delicate juice ('pressings'). Some of the branded whites are quaffers, but others are highly distinguished.

Alluviale Blanc ★★★☆

Very fresh and tight, weighty and restrained in its youth, the 2009 vintage (★★★☆) was grown at Mangatahi, in Hawke's Bay. A blend of Sauvignon Blanc (93 per cent) and Sémillon (7 per cent), partly French oak-fermented, it is ripely scented and mouthfilling, with tropical-fruit flavours, gently seasoned with biscuity oak, and a crisp, dry finish.

Vintage	10	09
WR	6	6
Drink	11-15	11-15

 DRY $24 AV

Alpha Domus The Aviatrix ★★★☆

The 2009 vintage (★★★★) is a blend of Sauvignon Blanc (60 per cent), Chardonnay (27 per cent) and Viognier (13 per cent). Estate-grown in Hawke's Bay and fermented in tanks (60 per cent) and new French oak barrels (40 per cent), it's a skilfully crafted wine, mouthfilling, peachy and smooth, with fresh, ripe, vibrant fruit flavours to the fore and complexity from barrel fermentation and lees-aging. Fleshy and harmonious, it's immediately appealing (4.5 grams/litre of residual sugar). The 2010 (★★★☆) is a good 'food' wine, with generous, ripely herbaceous flavours, oak richness and a slightly creamy texture.

Vintage	10	09
WR	6	6
Drink	11-16	11-15

 DRY $25 –V

Artisan Betty Davis ★★★☆

Grown in the Tara Vineyard at Oratia, in West Auckland, the 2008 vintage (★★★☆) is a barrel-fermented blend of Pinot Gris (85 per cent) and Viognier (15 per cent). Softly mouthfilling, it's a straw-coloured wine with ripe sweet-fruit flavours of peaches, apricots and spices, and very good depth.

 DRY $25 –V

Bellbird Spring Home Block White ★★★★☆

Showing greater complexity than most aromatic whites, the 2009 (★★★★☆) is a single-vineyard, Waipara blend of Pinot Gris, Riesling, Muscat and Gewürztraminer, hand-picked and fermented and lees-aged in old oak barriques. Instantly attractive, it's a weighty, distinctly medium style (32 grams/litre of residual sugar), highly perfumed and full of personality, with rich, peachy, citrusy flavours, showing excellent concentration, complexity and charm, and a deliciously soft finish. The 2008 vintage (★★★★☆), retasted in mid-2011, is maturing well – weighty and rounded, with lovely citrus-fruit, apricot and spice flavours, showing excellent complexity and harmony.

MED $31 AV

Clearview Endeavour   (★★★★★)

New Zealand's most expensive dry white wine is estate-grown at Te Awanga, in Hawke's Bay, and bottled in magnums. Hand-picked from 24-year-old vines and matured for two and a half years in new French oak casks, the 2007 vintage (tasted prior to bottling, and so not rated) is a richly fragrant, powerful wine, sweet-fruited, with highly concentrated flavours of grapefruit, peach and nectarine, and a biscuity, mealy complexity. It should be long-lived.

Vintage	07	DRY $250 (1.5L) –V
WR	7	
Drink	12-15	

Cloudy Bay Te Koko   ★★★★★

Te Koko o Kupe (the oyster dredge of Kupe) is the original name for Cloudy Bay; it is also the name of the Marlborough winery's intriguing, oak-aged Sauvignon Blanc. The 2007 vintage (★★★★★) was grown at five sites around the Wairau Valley and harvested at an average of 22.7 to 23.4 brix. Fermented with indigenous yeasts in French oak barrels (less than 10 per cent new, to ensure a subtle oak influence), it was matured in wood on its yeast lees until September 2008, and all the blend went through a softening malolactic fermentation. Delicious now, it is fleshy and rich, with concentrated, ripe tropical-fruit flavours and a dry, well-rounded finish. A very non-herbaceous style, it is finely textured, weighty, sweet-fruited and harmonious. Te Koko lies well outside the mainstream regional style of Sauvignon Blanc, but is well worth discovering.

Vintage	07	06	05	04	03	DRY $58 AV
WR	7	7	7	6	6	
Drink	11-15	11-13	11-12	P	P	

Craggy Range Les Beaux Cailloux   ★★★★★

Craggy Range's flagship Chardonnay is an unusually complex Hawke's Bay wine with loads of personality and great texture, mouthfeel and depth. Based on low-yielding Gimblett Gravels vines, it is fermented with indigenous yeasts and lees-aged for up to 17 months in French oak barriques (38 per cent new in 2009), with a full, softening malolactic fermentation. The 2009 vintage (★★★★☆) is a youthful, quietly classy wine, still unfolding. Weighty, minerally and creamy, it is very delicate, with peach, pear and grapefruit flavours, mealy, biscuity and nutty, and excellent texture, poise and harmony. Open 2012+.

Vintage	09	08	07	DRY $60 AV
WR	6	7	7	
Drink	11-16	11-15	11-14	

Dada 1   ★★★★☆

Labelled simply as 'a blended, dry white wine from New Zealand', but expensive, Dada 1 2007 (★★★★☆) is from a Hawke's Bay producer. It is not labelled as Sauvignon Blanc because that would 'automatically pigeonhole the wine and the benchmark default to Marlborough Sauvignon Blanc'. Full of personality, it is dry, peachy, spicy and slightly toasty, in a complex style with a long finish. The 2008 vintage (★★★★☆) was grown at Mangatahi and fermented with indigenous yeasts in tanks (60 per cent) and French oak casks (40 per cent). Highly distinctive, it is weighty, rich, ripe and rounded, with tropical-fruit flavours, slightly spicy and biscuity, dry and complex. Alluviale Blanc (above) is from the same winemakers.

Vintage	08	07
WR	6	7
Drink	11-18	11-20

DRY $50 –V

Dog Point Vineyard Section 94   ★★★★☆

Looking for 'texture, rather than rich aromatics', winemaker James Healy and his partner, Ivan Sutherland, fermented and lees-aged their 2009 vintage (★★★★★) Sauvignon Blanc for 18 months in seasoned French oak casks. Hand-picked in the Dog Point Vineyard (for which 'Section 94' was the original survey title) and fermented with indigenous yeasts, it has a complex bouquet, slightly 'funky' and nutty. The palate is tight and concentrated, poised and minerally, with ripe melon, lime and nut flavours, intense and lingering. Drink mid-2012+.

Vintage	09	08	07	06	05	04	03
WR	6	6	5	6	6	5	6
Drink	11-15	11-14	11-13	11-13	11-12	P	P

DRY $33 AV

Hans Herzog Marlborough Heavenly Seven   (★★★★☆)

The 'glorious, mighty' – according to the back label – 2009 vintage (★★★★☆) is a blend of seven varieties (Viognier, Sauvignon Blanc, Pinot Gris, Riesling, Chardonnay, Arneis and Gewürztraminer), late-harvested, co-fermented and matured for a year in French oak puncheons. The bouquet is fragrant and spicy; the palate is full-bodied and dry, with an array of peachy, citrusy, slightly spicy and honeyed flavours, finely textured and concentrated.

Vintage	09
WR	7
Drink	11-14

DRY $44 –V

Hunky Dory The Tangle   (★★★)

From Huia, the 2010 vintage (★★★) is an easy-drinking Marlborough blend of Pinot Gris, Gewürztraminer and Riesling. Full-bodied and smooth, it has decent depth of peachy, citrusy, spicy flavours, hints of ginger and honey, and a gently floral bouquet.

MED/DRY $20 –V

John Forrest Collection The White   ★★★★

With his uniquely diverse blend, winemaker John Forrest is after a 'full-bodied, dry style with fruit intensity and acid definition, but no excess of wood, malolactic fermentation or sugar'. It is billed as an 'uninhibited' marriage of up to seven grape varieties (Viognier, Sauvignon Blanc, Pinot Gris, Chenin Blanc, Riesling, Chardonnay and Gewürztraminer) drawn from Marlborough, Hawke's Bay, Central Otago and the Waitaki Valley. Building up well with bottle-age, the 2007 (★★★★) was made with 'more Chenin Blanc than usual'. It's a fleshy, full-bodied wine with an array of fruit characters, very good flavour depth and a fresh, smooth finish (7 grams/litre of residual sugar).

Vintage	07	06
WR	6	6
Drink	11-15	P

MED/DRY $50 –V

Junction Sideline   (★★★☆)

Grown in Central Hawke's Bay, the 2009 vintage (★★★☆) is a blend of Flora and 'some' Gewürztraminer. Made in a dry style, it's a mouthfilling wine, fleshy and rounded, with very good depth of citrusy, gently spicy flavours.

DRY $20 AV

Kaipara Estate Nine Lakes   ★★★☆

Estate-grown on the South Head Peninsula of the Kaipara Harbour, in Auckland, the 2008 vintage (★★★☆) is a blend of Chardonnay (73 per cent), Pinot Gris (20 per cent), Arneis (5 per cent) and Viognier (2 per cent). Floral and fruity, with fresh flavours of citrus fruits and pears and finely balanced acidity, it could easily be mistaken for a Viognier.

DRY $22 AV

Kidnapper Cliffs Hawke's Bay Solan   (★★★★)

From Te Awa, the debut 2009 vintage (★★★★) is a blend of Sauvignon Blanc (88 per cent) and 'chalky, slaty' Sémillon (12 per cent), fermented in tanks (56 per cent) and barrels. It's an elegant, youthful wine, weighty, with rich, ripe sweet-fruit flavours of melons and limes, and a tight, dry finish.

DRY $35 –V

La Collina White   (★★★★★)

From Bilancia, the debut 2008 vintage (★★★★★) was estate-grown on the terraces and gravels of la collina, in the Gimblett Gravels, Hawke's Bay. A blend of hand-picked Viognier (85 per cent) and Gewürztraminer (15 per cent), fermented with indigenous yeasts and lees-aged for 14 months in seasoned oak casks, it is very weighty, ripe and rounded, with deep peach, apricot and spice flavours. A very distinctive and authoritative dry wine, it reminds me of a Rhône Valley white.

DRY $40 AV

Man O' War Valhalla   ★★★★

This crisp, tautly structured Chardonnay is grown at the eastern end of Waiheke Island. Hand-picked at 24.2 to 25.5 brix, and fermented with indigenous yeasts in French oak puncheons and barriques (20 per cent new), the 2010 vintage (★★★★) has a complex bouquet, slightly toasty, mealy and rich. The palate is tight and youthful, with concentrated, ripe flavours of stone-fruit and spice, but retains firm acid spine. Best drinking 2013+.

Vintage	10	09
WR	7	7
Drink	11-16	11-15

DRY $40 –V

Man O' War Valkyrie (★★★★)

Grown on Waiheke Island, the 2010 vintage (★★★★) was made from Viognier picked at 25 brix and matured for six months in new French oak casks, which had been 'seasoned' with a Chardonnay ferment. A robust wine (14.5 per cent alcohol), it is Chardonnay-like, with vibrant, peachy, slightly spicy and nutty flavours, showing excellent concentration. Best drinking mid-2012+.

DRY $40 –V

Marsden Estate Duo (★★★)

The 2009 vintage (★★★) was made from Flora grapes, grown at Kerikeri, in Northland, and matured for a year in seasoned oak puncheons. Harvested at over 25 brix, it's a fleshy, bone-dry wine with substantial body, lots of peachy, slightly spicy flavour, showing some complexity, and a rounded finish.

Vintage	09
WR	5
Drink	11-12

DRY $20 –V

Paritua Grace ★★★☆

The 2008 vintage (★★★☆) is a medium-bodied Hawke's Bay blend of Sauvignon Blanc and Sémillon, barrel-fermented and oak-aged for 10 months. Crisp and minerally, it is slightly creamy and nutty, with very good depth and complexity, firm acid spine and a tight, dry finish.

Vintage	08
WR	7
Drink	11-13

DRY $30 –V

Pasquale Hakataramea Valley Alma Mater (★★★☆)

Estate-grown at 300 metres above sea level in the Hakataramea Valley, North Otago, the 2010 vintage (★★★☆) was made from co-fermented Pinot Gris and Gewürztraminer, blended with Riesling and given some 'barrel and lees contact'. Fully dry, it is medium-bodied, with fresh acidity and lively, citrusy, peachy, spicy flavours that show very good depth. Worth cellaring.

DRY $32 –V

Richmond Plains Nelson Blanc de Noir ★★★

Certified organic, the 2010 vintage (★★★) is a 'white' (in reality pale pink) wine made from Pinot Noir. Full-bodied, it has fresh, strawberryish, peachy, spicy flavours, a hint of apricot, and a slightly sweet, smooth finish.

MED/DRY $20 –V

Seresin Chiaroscuro ★★★★☆

Certified organic, the 2009 vintage (★★★★★) is a full-bodied, dry blend of Chardonnay (for 'structure'), Pinot Gris (for 'texture'), and Riesling (for 'fruity acidity'). Hand-picked in the Home Vineyard at Renwick, in Marlborough, it was co-fermented with indigenous yeasts in French oak puncheons, oak-aged for 14 months and given a full, softening malolactic fermentation. A robust wine (14.5 per cent alcohol), it is peachy and soft, with instant appeal. Deliciously rich and rounded, it is highly concentrated, peachy and spicy, with hints of apricots and nutty oak adding complexity, and a long, harmonious finish.

Vintage	09
WR	7
Drink	11-16

DRY $65 –V

Terravin Te Ahu ★★★★★

The delicious 2009 vintage (★★★★★) is a single-vineyard Marlborough Sauvignon Blanc, hand-picked on the south side of the Wairau Valley at 24.6 brix and fermented with indigenous yeasts in French oak puncheons. Barrel-aged for nearly a year, it's a 'serious', full-bodied wine with fresh, concentrated flavours of tropical fruits and nuts, showing notable richness and complexity. A powerful wine with a strong presence, it should mature well.

Vintage	10	09	08	07
WR	7	7	5	5
Drink	11-16	11-15	11-12	11-13

DRY $39 AV

Te Whare Ra Toru ★★★★

This Marlborough blend of three ('toru') varieties – Gewürztraminer, Riesling and Pinot Gris – is hand-picked and tank-fermented. It is typically an attractively perfumed, softly mouthfilling wine with ripe pear, spice and slight ginger flavours, a gentle splash of sweetness, and very good texture, harmony and depth.

MED/DRY $23 V+

Ti Point Tess White Merlot (★★★☆)

Estate-grown at Leigh, on the Matakana Coast, the 2011 vintage (★★★☆) is a pale pink wine, handled entirely in tanks. Enjoyable from the start, it is vibrantly fruity, with strong strawberry, spice and apricot flavours and a bare hint of sweetness balanced by fresh acidity.

Vintage	11
WR	5
Drink	11-13

MED/DRY $21 AV

TW Summer CV (★★★☆)

'CV' stands for Chardonnay and Viognier. From Gisborne, the 2010 vintage (★★★☆) is a 50:50 blend of the two varieties, handled entirely in tanks and bottled early. Fleshy and vibrantly fruity, it has plenty of ripe, peachy, slightly spicy flavour in a straightforward, but highly enjoyable, style.

DRY $22 AV

Vynfields Pêche De Noire   (★★★☆)

Estate-grown organically in Martinborough, this dry white is made from Pinot Noir and partly barrel-fermented. The 2009 vintage (★★★☆) is pale pink, with plenty of fresh, peachy, strawberryish, spicy flavour and a hint of apricot, in a crisp, refreshing style.

DRY $26 –V

Waimea Nelson Edel   (★★★★)

The 2009 vintage (★★★★) is a seductive blend of three aromatic varieties – Riesling (47 per cent), Pinot Gris (38 per cent) and Gewürztraminer (15 per cent). Mouthfilling and rich, it's a slightly sweet wine with concentrated, peachy, spicy flavours.

Vintage	10	09
WR	7	6
Drink	11-14	11-12

 MED/DRY $23 V+

White Wire   ★★☆

From Mount George, a subsidiary of Paritua, the 2008 vintage (★★★) was made mostly from Gisborne and Hawke's Bay Chardonnay, blended with Gewürztraminer (5 per cent), Riesling (5 per cent) and Sauvignon Blanc (4 per cent). It's a good, easy quaffer, fruity, tasty and smooth (6.5 grams/litre of residual sugar), with citrusy, peachy, slightly spicy flavours.

 MED/DRY $15 AV

Wooing Tree Blondie   ★★★☆

This is a *blanc de noir* – a white (or rather faintly pink) Central Otago wine, estate-grown at Cromwell. The 2011 vintage (★★★☆) was made from hand-picked Pinot Noir grapes; the juice was held briefly in contact with the skins and fermented in tanks. Mouthfilling and smooth, it's a peachy, slightly strawberryish and spicy wine, with a light touch of tannin. Very fresh and flavoursome, it's already enjoyable.

DRY $25 –V

Breidecker

A nondescript crossing of Müller-Thurgau and the white hybrid Seibel 7053, Breidecker is rarely seen in New Zealand. There were 32 hectares of bearing vines recorded in 2003, but only 7 hectares in 2011. Its early-ripening ability is an advantage in cooler regions, but Breidecker typically yields light, fresh quaffing wines, best drunk young.

Hunter's Marlborough Breidecker ★★★

A drink-young charmer, 'for those who are new to wine'. Grown in the Wairau Valley, the 2011 vintage (★★★) is floral, fresh, light and lively, with a splash of sweetness (12 grams/litre of residual sugar), gentle acidity and ripe, citrusy, slightly peachy and spicy flavours.

Vintage	11	MED/DRY $17 –V
WR	4	
Drink	11-12	

Chardonnay

Do you drink Chardonnay? Sauvignon Blanc is our biggest-selling white-wine variety by far, and Pinot Gris is riding high, but neither of these popular grapes produces New Zealand's greatest dry whites. Chardonnay wears that crown.

It's less fashionable than a decade ago, but Chardonnay is our most prestigious white-wine variety. No other dry whites can command such lofty prices; many New Zealand Chardonnays are on the shelves at $50 or more.

Chardonnay is still highly popular, despite losing ground to Sauvignon. In supermarkets, we are spending almost twice as much on Chardonnay as Pinot Gris – and 10 times more on Chardonnay than Riesling or Gewürztraminer.

However, New Zealand Chardonnay has yet to make the huge international impact of our Sauvignon Blanc. Our top Chardonnays are classy, but so are those from a host of other countries in the Old and New Worlds. In the year to mid-2011, Chardonnay accounted for 3.1 per cent by volume of New Zealand's wine exports (far behind Sauvignon Blanc, with 84 per cent, and also Pinot Noir with 6 per cent).

There's an enormous range to choose from. Most wineries – especially in the North Island and upper South Island – make at least one Chardonnay; many produce several and the big wineries produce dozens. The hallmark of New Zealand Chardonnays is their delicious varietal intensity – the leading labels show notably concentrated aromas and flavours, threaded with fresh, appetising acidity.

The price of New Zealand Chardonnay ranges from under $10 to $250 (for a magnum of Clearview Endeavour). The quality differences are equally wide, although not always in relation to their prices. Lower-priced wines are typically fermented in stainless steel tanks and bottled young with little or no oak influence; these wines rely on fresh, lemony, uncluttered fruit flavours for their appeal.

Recent vintages have brought a surge of unoaked Chardonnays, as winemakers with an eye on overseas markets strive to showcase New Zealand's fresh, vibrant fruit characters. Without oak flavours to add richness and complexity, Chardonnay handled entirely in stainless steel tanks can be plain – even boring. The key to the style is to use well-ripened, intensely flavoured grapes.

Mid-price wines may be fermented in tanks and matured in oak casks, which adds to their complexity and richness, or fermented and/or matured in a mix of tanks and barrels (or even handled entirely in tanks, with oak chips or staves suspended in the wine). The top labels are fully fermented and matured in oak barriques (normally French, with varying proportions of new casks); there may also be extended aging on (and regular stirring of) yeast lees and varying proportions of a secondary, softening malolactic fermentation (sometimes referred to in the tasting notes as 'malo'). The best of these display the arresting subtlety and depth of flavour for which Chardonnay is so highly prized.

Chardonnay plantings have been far outstripped in recent years by Sauvignon Blanc, as wine producers respond to overseas demand, and in 2012 will constitute 12 per cent of the bearing vineyard. The variety is spread throughout the wine regions, particularly Hawke's Bay (where 30 per cent of the vines are concentrated), Marlborough (28 per cent) and Gisborne (28 per cent). Gisborne is renowned for its softly mouthfilling, ripe, peachy Chardonnays, which offer very seductive drinking in their youth; Hawke's Bay yields sturdy wines with rich grapefruit-like flavours, power and longevity; and Marlborough's Chardonnays are slightly leaner in a cool-climate, more appley, appetisingly crisp style.

Chardonnay has often been dubbed 'the red-wine drinker's white wine'. Chardonnays are usually (although not always, especially cheap models) fully dry, as are all reds with any aspirations to quality. Chardonnay's typically mouthfilling body and multi-faceted flavours are another obvious red-wine parallel.

Broaching a top New Zealand Chardonnay at less than two years old can be unrewarding – the finest of the 2009s will offer excellent drinking during 2012. If you must drink Chardonnay when it is only a year old, it makes sense to buy one of the cheaper, less complex wines specifically designed to be enjoyable in their youth.

¼ Acre Wines Hawke's Bay Chardonnay   (★★★★)

From winemaker Rod McDonald, the 2008 vintage (★★★★) was hand-harvested and barrel-fermented. Drinking well now, it's a mouthfilling wine with strong peach and grapefruit flavours, slightly toasty and buttery, and excellent concentration.

DRY $25 AV

3 Stones Hawke's Bay Chardonnay   ★★☆

The 2011 vintage (★★☆) was 40 per cent barrel-fermented. It's a fruity, straightforward wine, peachy and smooth, offering fresh, easy drinking.

Vintage	11
WR	4
Drink	11-15

DRY $19 –V

Akarua Central Otago Chardonnay   ★★★☆

This is consistently one of the region's best Chardonnays. Estate-grown at Bannockburn and fermented and matured in French oak barriques (15 per cent new), the 2009 vintage (★★★☆) is a fresh, racy, fruit-driven style with citrusy, appley flavours, restrained oak influence and a slightly creamy texture.

Vintage	10	09	08	07	06
WR	6	6	6	6	6
Drink	12-15	12-15	11-14	P	P

DRY $25 –V

Ake Ake Chardonnay Reserve   ★★☆

The 2010 vintage (★★) was hand-picked at Kerikeri, in the Bay of Islands, and fermented and matured for a year, with weekly lees-stirring, in tanks and American oak barriques. It lacks charm, with fruit characters overpowered by leesy, yeasty characters.

Vintage	10
WR	5
Drink	11-15

DRY $29 –V

Alexia Hawke's Bay Chardonnay   ★★★

The 2009 vintage (★★★) from Jane Cooper, winemaker at Matahiwi Estate, under her own label, is full-bodied, fruity and smooth, with ripe, peachy flavours offering good, easy drinking.

Vintage	09
WR	6
Drink	11-13

DRY $18 AV

Allan Scott Marlborough Chardonnay   ★★★☆

This label began as a fruit-driven style, but in recent years has shown greater complexity and is now consistently satisfying. Grown at four sites at Rapaura, the 2009 (★★★☆) is a fully barrel-fermented wine (30 per cent new oak), with vibrant, citrusy, peachy flavours to the fore, slightly buttery, toasty notes adding complexity and a smooth, dry finish. It has plenty of drink-young appeal.

Vintage	09	08	07	06
WR	5	5	6	6
Drink	11-14	11-13	11-13	11-12

 DRY $22 AV

Allan Scott Wallops Marlborough Chardonnay   ★★★★☆

This single-vineyard wine is typically rich, creamy and complex. Barrel-fermented with indigenous yeasts and given a full, softening malolactic fermentation, the 2009 vintage (★★★★☆) is a highly fragrant, full-bodied style with a strong presence. A drink-now or cellaring proposition, it is generous, with concentrated, ripe stone-fruit flavours, buttery, toasty notes adding complexity and a lasting finish.

Vintage	10	09	08	07
WR	6	6	7	7
Drink	13-15	11-14	11-14	11-13

 DRY $31 AV

Alpha Domus Barrique Fermented Hawke's Bay Chardonnay   ★★★☆

Fermented and lees-aged for nine months in French (90 per cent) and European oak barrels (20 per cent new), the 2010 vintage (★★★☆) is mouthfilling, fruity and smooth, with citrusy, slightly peachy, mealy and biscuity flavours, in a moderately complex style. Still very youthful, with some elegance, it should be at its best mid-2012+.

Vintage	10	09	08	07	06
WR	7	6	7	6	6
Drink	11-16	11-14	11-13	P	P

 MED/DRY $25 –V

Alpha Domus The Pilot Hawke's Bay Chardonnay   (★★☆)

The 'lightly oaked' 2009 vintage (★★☆) is an off-dry style (5 grams/litre of residual sugar) with mouthfilling body and decent depth of peachy, slightly limey and honeyed flavours.

Vintage	09
WR	6
Drink	11-13

MED/DRY $20 –V

Anchorage Nelson Chardonnay   ★★★

Estate-grown at Motueka, the 2010 vintage (★★★) is a good, drink-young style. Given a full, softening malolactic fermentation and French and American oak-aged, it is fresh and vibrantly fruity, with citrusy, appley flavours and a creamy-smooth texture.

 DRY $19 AV

Anchorage Reserve Chardonnay (★★★☆)

The 2008 vintage (★★★☆) is a Nelson wine, hand-picked from first-crop vines and fermented initially in tanks, then in French oak barrels (100 per cent new). Savoury, with peachy, citrusy, slightly toasty and buttery flavours, and considerable complexity, it shows very good depth.

DRY $22 AV

Anchorage Unoaked Chardonnay ★★☆

From Motueka, the 2009 vintage (★★☆) is a lively Nelson wine, made without oak or malolactic fermentation. It's a straightforward, fruit-driven wine with lemony, appley flavours, dry and crisp.

DRY $16 AV

Aotea Barrique Fermented Nelson Chardonnay (★★★☆)

Formerly labelled 'Seifried', the 2010 vintage (★★★☆) was matured for a year in new and one-year-old American oak barriques. Mouthfilling and creamy-smooth, it is peachy and slightly spicy, with biscuity, toasty notes in a high-flavoured, moderately complex style, for drinking now or cellaring. Verging on four stars.

Vintage	10
WR	5
Drink	11-16

DRY $28 –V

Artisan Kauri Ridge Oratia Chardonnay ★★★★

Still on sale, the fleshy, rich 2007 vintage (★★★★) was grown in the Kauri Ridge Vineyard in West Auckland and fermented in French oak casks (40 per cent new). Maturing well, it is vibrant and sweet-fruited, with excellent depth of ripe grapefruit-like flavours, finely balanced nutty oak, and considerable elegance.

DRY $25 AV

Ascension The Ascent Reserve Matakana Chardonnay ★★★★

Estate-grown and fermented in French oak casks (one-third new), the 2010 vintage (★★★★) is a youthful, tightly structured wine. Mouthfilling, with grapefruit and peach flavours, slightly leesy and biscuity, and a rounded finish, it shows good potential.

DRY $39 –V

Ascension The Druid Matakana Chardonnay (★★★)

A fruit-driven style, the 2010 vintage (★★★) was fermented in a 50:50 split of tanks and American oak barriques (one-third new). Crisp and lemony, it is fresh and lively, with good immediacy.

DRY $29 –V

Ash Ridge Hawke's Bay Cardoness Vineyard Chardonnay   (★★★☆)

From young, low-yielding vines, the 2009 vintage (★★★☆) was fermented in French oak casks (20 per cent new). It's an elegant rather than powerful wine with ripe sweet-fruit characters, citrusy, slightly yeasty flavours and a dry, slightly buttery finish.

Vintage	10	09
WR	6	5
Drink	12-16	11-13

 DRY $23 AV

Ashwell Martinborough Chardonnay   ★★★★

Barrel-fermented, the 2009 vintage (★★★★) is fragrant, with strong peach, grapefruit and toast flavours, creamy-textured and complex. The fleshy, rounded 2010 vintage (★★★☆) has a creamy bouquet and softly mouthfilling palate, with ripe, peachy, buttery flavours, showing considerable complexity. It lacks a bit of acid spine, but has plenty of drink-young appeal.

Vintage	10	09	08	07	06
WR	5	6	6	6	7
Drink	11-16	11-15	11-13	11-12	P

 DRY $28 AV

Askerne Hawke's Bay Chardonnay   ★★★

Estate-grown near Havelock North and fully barrel-fermented, the 2010 vintage (★★★) is a mouthfilling, peachy, slightly toasty wine with generous depth in an upfront style, already enjoyable.

 DRY $20 –V

Askerne Reserve Hawke's Bay Chardonnay   ★★★☆

Estate-grown, hand-picked and barrel-fermented (French, half new), the 2009 vintage (★★★★) is pale yellow, with a complex, slightly oaky bouquet. Mouthfilling and rich, it is finely textured, with concentrated stone-fruit and nut flavours, showing good complexity. Drink now or cellar.

 DRY $30 –V

Astrolabe Voyage Marlborough Chardonnay   ★★★☆

The 2008 vintage (★★★☆) was hand-picked, fermented and matured for 10 months in French and American oak barrels, and given a full, softening malolactic fermentation. A moderately complex style, maturing well, with mouthfilling body and very good depth of citrusy, peachy, toasty flavours, it is fleshy and slightly buttery, with a sweet oak influence.

Vintage	08	07
WR	6	6
Drink	11-12	11-14

DRY $24 AV

Ataahua Waipara Chardonnay ★★★★

From vines over 20 years old, the 2009 vintage (★★★★) is a refined, barrel-fermented wine with substantial body, strong, ripe citrus-fruit flavours, a subtle seasoning of wood (all seasoned French) and fresh acidity. Tight and youthful, with a slightly oily richness, it should be at its best now onwards. The 2010 (★★★★) is similar – full-bodied, with vibrant, citrusy, peachy flavours to the fore, a subtle oak influence and excellent freshness and richness. Open mid-2012+.

 DRY $26 AV

Ata Rangi Craighall Chardonnay ★★★★★

This memorable Martinborough wine has notable richness, complexity and downright drinkability. From a company-owned block of low-yielding, mostly over 20-year-old Mendoza-clone vines in the Craighall Vineyard, it is hand-picked, whole-bunch pressed and fermented in French oak barriques (typically 25 per cent new). The 2009 vintage (★★★★★) has a very fragrant bouquet – peachy, mealy and complex. Authoritative and multi-faceted, it has concentrated, stone-fruit-like flavours, well-integrated oak and excellent depth and harmony. Elegant and finely structured, it's a drink-now or cellaring proposition.

Vintage	09	08	07	06	05	04
WR	7	7	7	7	6	6
Drink	11-17	11-16	11-15	11-12	P	P

 DRY $42 AV

Ata Rangi Petrie Chardonnay ★★★★☆

This single-vineyard wine is grown south of Masterton, in the Wairarapa. It's not in the same class as its Craighall stablemate (above), but the price is lower. The 2009 vintage (★★★★☆) was hand-picked and fermented and lees-aged for seven months in French oak barriques and puncheons (18 per cent new), with 30 per cent malolactic fermentation. The bouquet is citrusy; the palate is tightly structured and dry, with fresh acidity and grapefruit and toast flavours showing excellent delicacy, drive and length.

 DRY $32 AV

Auntsfield Estate Marlborough Chardonnay ★★★★☆

Previously labelled 'Cob Cottage', this is a consistently rewarding wine. Estate-grown on the south side of the Wairau Valley, hand-picked and fermented in French oak barrels (25 per cent new), the 2010 vintage (★★★★☆) is finely fragrant, with substantial body and a complex array of grapefruit, nut and spice flavours, youthful and slightly creamy. The 2009 (★★★★) is also fragrant, weighty, creamy and complex.

 DRY $34 AV

Aurum Central Otago Chardonnay (★★★★)

Estate-grown in the Cromwell Basin, hand-harvested and French oak-fermented, the 2010 vintage (★★★★) is full-bodied and finely balanced. A stylish, youthful wine, it offers strong citrusy and peachy flavours, seasoned with biscuit oak, and a slightly creamy finish. Well worth cellaring.

Vintage	10
WR	6
Drink	11-16

 DRY $28 AV

Awa Valley Chardonnay   ★★★☆

This consistently enjoyable wine is priced sharply. Estate-grown in West Auckland, hand-harvested and barrel-fermented, it is typically full-bodied, with American oak aromas and ripe grapefruit and peach flavours. The 2009 vintage (★★★☆) is mouthfilling and citrusy, with some mealy, toasty complexity and a smooth finish.

DRY $16 V+

Awa Valley Unoaked Chardonnay   (★★★)

Estate-grown at Huapai, the 2009 vintage (★★★) is fresh and lively, with plenty of ripe, peachy, citrusy flavour. Good value.

DRY $15 V+

Awaroa Reserve Chardonnay   (★★★☆)

From a Waiheke Island-based winery, the 2009 vintage (★★★☆) was hand-harvested in the Stell Vineyard at Te Awanga, in Hawke's Bay, and fermented and matured for nine months in French oak casks (mostly new). It's a robust, slightly oaky wine, offering ripe, citrusy, peachy, slightly buttery flavours, showing good richness.

DRY $28 –V

Babich Family Estates Individual Vineyard Gimblett Gravels Chardonnay   ★★★☆

Fermented in tanks (mostly) and casks, this is designed as a fruit-driven style. The 2010 vintage (★★★☆) is mouthfilling, fresh and youthful. Dry, with citrusy, slightly minerally and buttery flavours, showing a sensitive use of oak, it has very good delicacy and depth. Best drinking mid-2012+.

DRY $25 –V

Babich Irongate Chardonnay   ★★★★★

Babich's flagship Chardonnay. A stylish wine, Irongate has traditionally been leaner and tighter than other top Hawke's Bay Chardonnays, while performing well in the cellar, but the latest releases have more drink-young appeal. It is based on hand-picked fruit from the shingly Irongate Vineyard in Gimblett Road, fully barrel-fermented (about 20 per cent new), and lees-matured for up to nine months. Malolactic fermentation was rare up to the 2002, but is now a growing influence. The 2009 (★★★★) is a solid but not memorable vintage. Pale gold, mouthfilling, fresh and youthful, it is sweet-fruited, with good acid spine, finely integrated oak and good intensity of peachy, spicy, toasty, faintly honeyed flavours. The 2010 vintage (★★★★☆) is still a baby, with obvious potential for long-term cellaring. Weighty and creamy-textured, it has strong, ripe, citrusy, slightly spicy flavours, mealy, complex and harmonious. Open 2013+.

Vintage	10	09	08
WR	7	5	7
Drink	12-25	11-15	11-23

DRY $35 AV

Babich Lone Tree Hawke's Bay Chardonnay

Handled entirely in tanks, with 'a bit of malolactic fermentation and lees-stirring' to add complexity, this moderately priced wine is typically finely balanced, with fresh, citrusy flavours. The 2010 vintage (★★☆) has lemony aromas and flavours, in a simple but buoyantly fruity style, fresh, crisp and lively.

DRY $15 AV

Bascand Marlborough Chardonnay

Partly oak-aged, the 2008 vintage (★★☆) is a mouthfilling wine, made in an upfront style with smooth, peachy, slightly buttery and honeyed flavours. With bottle-age, it is becoming distinctly honeyed.

DRY $17 –V

Beach House Hawke's Bay Chardonnay

The barrel-fermented 2009 vintage (★★★☆) has ripe citrus and stone-fruit flavours, a hint of butterscotch and a rounded finish. It's a slightly creamy wine with some elegance and good length.

DRY $24 AV

Bensen Block Chardonnay

The 2008 vintage (★★★) from Pernod Ricard NZ, grown in Gisborne, was made in a fruit-driven style. It's a flavoursome wine, ripe, slightly buttery and creamy, balanced for easy drinking.

DRY $17 AV

Black Barn Barrel Fermented Chardonnay

Grown on the Havelock North hills, hand-picked and barrel-fermented, this is typically a classy wine, in a classic regional style. The 2009 vintage (★★★★) is a powerful, upfront style, weighty and rich, with ripe stone-fruit flavours seasoned with toasty oak and a slightly creamy texture. It's drinking well now.

DRY $33 –V

Black Barn Hawke's Bay Chardonnay

The 2009 vintage (★★★☆) is fragrant and smooth, with ripe citrus-fruit characters to the fore, slightly toasty and buttery notes adding complexity, and mouthfilling body. It's a finely textured wine with good length.

DRY $28 –V

Black Barn Reserve Hawke's Bay Chardonnay

A commanding, refined wine with strong personality, the 2009 vintage (★★★★★) was hand-picked and fermented and matured in French oak casks (50 per cent new). Showing lovely richness, texture and complexity, it is sturdy, with beautifully ripe stone-fruit flavours, finely integrated oak and an enticingly fragrant bouquet. It's already very expressive; drink now or cellar.

DRY $45 AV

Black Estate Omihi Waipara Chardonnay   ★★★★

The 2009 vintage (★★★★) is an upfront style. The bouquet is strong, peachy and toasty; the palate is concentrated, with a hint of butterscotch, fresh acidity and lots of personality. The 2010 (★★★★) was estate-grown, hand-picked at 24 brix from 16-year-old vines, fermented with indigenous yeasts in French oak barriques and puncheons (23 per cent new) and oak-aged for 15 months. Mouthfilling, fresh and citrusy, with a subtle oak influence, it is sweet-fruited, with grapefruit and slight spice flavours to the fore and good intensity, complexity and length.

DRY $33 –V

Blackenbrook Nelson Chardonnay   ★★★☆

The 2009 vintage (★★★) was hand-picked and matured for a year in seasoned American and French oak barriques. Enjoyable young, it is very soft and creamy, buttery and rounded, with plenty of flavour.

Vintage	09
WR	6
Drink	11-13

DRY $24 AV

Blackenbrook Nelson Reserve Chardonnay   ★★★☆

The weighty, buttery 2009 vintage (★★★☆) was estate-grown, hand-picked and matured for a year in new French oak puncheons. Straw-hued, it is a toasty, upfront style, big, rich and slightly creamy, with a strong seasoning of oak.

Vintage	09
WR	6
Drink	11-15

DRY $31 –V

Bloody Bay Gisborne Chardonnay   (★★★)

From wine distributor Federal Geo, the 2009 vintage (★★★) is an enjoyable, drink-young style. It is full-bodied, with ripe, peachy, slightly toasty flavours, showing good depth, and a smooth, dry finish.

DRY $17 AV

Boatshed Bay by Goldwater Marlborough Chardonnay   ★★★☆

Fruity and slightly creamy, with ripe citrusy flavours, the 2008 vintage (★★★) was mostly handled in tanks; 10 per cent of the blend was French oak-aged. It's an enjoyable, easy-drinking style, with a touch of complexity.

Vintage	08
WR	6
Drink	P

DRY $17 V+

Borthwick Vineyard Wairarapa Chardonnay ★★★☆

The 2009 vintage (★★★☆), grown at Gladstone, was fermented in French (65 per cent) and American oak casks (25 per cent new). It's a smooth, easy-drinking wine with good weight and depth of stone-fruit flavours, a hint of butterscotch and a rounded, very harmonious finish.

DRY $25 –V

Bouldevines Marlborough Chardonnay ★★★☆

From the south side of the Wairau Valley, the 2009 vintage (★★★☆) is a single-vineyard wine, fermented in a 50:50 split of tanks and French oak casks (20 per cent new). Bright, light yellow, it is mouthfilling, with fresh, citrusy, peachy flavours, slightly limey and toasty, in a moderately complex style. Drink now or cellar.

Vintage	09
WR	7
Drink	11-15

DRY $25 –V

Boundary Vineyards Tuki Tuki Road Hawke's Bay Chardonnay ★★★☆

Pernod Ricard NZ's wine is grown near the coast, at Te Awanga, fermented in Hungarian oak barriques, and much of the blend is given a softening malolactic fermentation. The 2009 (★★★☆) is generous, ripe and smooth, with tropical-fruit flavours, slightly toasty and creamy, and very good texture and depth.

DRY $20 AV

Brancott Estate Living Land Series Marlborough Chardonnay (★★★☆)

The 2009 vintage (★★★☆) was grown in the Wairau Valley and fermented in tanks (30 per cent) and French oak barrels (70 per cent). It's an easy-drinking wine, mouthfilling, citrusy, smooth (4.9 grams/litre of residual sugar), with buttery and biscuity notes adding complexity and good depth.

DRY $20 AV

Brancott Estate Ormond 'O' Gisborne Chardonnay ★★★★★

Up to and including the 2007, this classic wine was branded Montana, but the 2008 vintage (★★★★☆) is labelled Brancott Estate. The flagship Gisborne Chardonnay from Pernod Ricard NZ, it is made for cellaring. The 2008 is fleshy, with concentrated, ripe, peachy, nutty flavours, showing excellent complexity and harmony. The 2009 vintage (★★★★☆) offers rich, citrusy, mealy, nutty flavours, with a delicious creaminess of texture, and a long finish. It's already drinking well.

DRY $33 V+

Brancott Estate Reserve Gisborne Chardonnay ★★★☆

(Previously branded Montana.) The 2010 vintage (★★★☆) is full-bodied, vibrantly fruity and fresh, with good depth of peachy, slightly mealy and buttery flavours, a subtle oak influence and some complexity. Drink now or cellar.

DRY $23 AV

Brightside Nelson Chardonnay   ★★☆

From Kaimira, the 2010 vintage (★★☆) was given 'light oak treatment'. A creamy-soft wine, it is full-bodied and rounded, with drink-young appeal.

Vintage	10	09	08	07
WR	6	5	5	6
Drink	11-14	11-12	P	P

DRY $16 AV

Brightwater Vineyards Lord Rutherford Barrique Chardonnay   ★★★★

The 2009 vintage (★★★☆) is a single-vineyard Nelson wine, hand-picked and fermented in French oak barriques (20 per cent new). Oak-aged for 11 months, it is vibrantly fruity and moderately complex, with fresh, lemony, slightly toasty flavours and a hint of butterscotch. Worth cellaring.

Vintage	09	08	07	06
WR	6	5	6	6
Drink	11-15	11-14	P	P

 DRY $30 –V

Brightwater Vineyards Nelson Chardonnay   ★★★☆

Fresh and focused, with excellent balance, the 2009 vintage (★★★☆) is a fruit-driven style with lively, citrusy flavours and a gentle seasoning of oak (one-third barrel-fermented) adding a touch of complexity.

DRY $22 AV

Brookfields Bergman Chardonnay   ★★★☆

Named after the Ingrid Bergman roses in the estate garden, this wine is grown alongside the winery at Meeanee, in Hawke's Bay, hand-picked, and fermented and matured on its yeast lees in seasoned French and American oak casks. The 2010 vintage (★★★☆) is mouthfilling and smooth, in an upfront, drink-young style with plenty of ripe, peachy, toasty, creamy flavour.

Vintage	10	09	08	07	06
WR	7	7	7	7	7
Drink	12-14	11-14	11-13	11-12	P

DRY $20 AV

Brookfields Marshall Bank Chardonnay   ★★★★☆

Brookfields' top Chardonnay is named after proprietor Peter Robertson's grandfather's property in Otago. Grown in a vineyard adjacent to the winery at Meeanee and fermented and matured in French oak barriques (50 per cent new in 2009), it is a rich, concentrated Hawke's Bay wine. The 2009 vintage (★★★★☆), oak-aged for eight months, with weekly lees-stirring, is a fresh, elegant wine with a mealy complexity, good texture and strong yet delicate, citrusy, slightly buttery, well-rounded flavours. Best drinking 2012+.

Vintage	09
WR	7
Drink	11-15

 DRY $30 AV

Brookfields Unoaked Hawke's Bay Chardonnay   (★★★☆)

Delicious from the start, the estate-grown 2009 vintage (★★★☆) is scented, with vibrant, ripe stone-fruit flavours, a hint of spice, and a smooth (5 grams/litre of residual sugar) finish. A good example of the unwooded style, it offers very easy drinking.

Vintage	09
WR	7
Drink	11-12

 MED/DRY $19 V+

Brunton Road Gisborne Chardonnay   ★★★

The 2009 vintage (★★★) of this single-vineyard wine was grown at Patutahi and barrel-fermented. Mouthfilling and slightly creamy, it's a moderately complex style, fresh and vibrant, with ripe peach, grapefruit and slight spice flavours, drinking well now.

 DRY $25 –V

Bushmere Estate Classic Gisborne Chardonnay   ★★★★

A good buy. The 2010 vintage (★★★★) is rich, peachy and toasty, in a classic regional style. Fully barrel-fermented, it is slightly oaky at this stage (French, 33 per cent new) but shows excellent richness and complexity, with a creamy-smooth texture. Best mid-2012+.

 DRY $23 V+

Bushmere Estate Gisborne Chardonnay/Viognier   ★★★☆

The 2010 vintage (★★★) is a 2:1 blend, fermented in seasoned French oak barriques. Still unfolding, it is mouthfilling, peachy and moderately concentrated, with a touch of complexity and a smooth, off-dry finish.

 MED/DRY $23 AV

Cable Bay Reserve Waiheke Island Chardonnay   ★★★★☆

The 2009 vintage (★★★★☆) is a single-vineyard wine, grown at Church Bay and matured in French oak barriques. An elegant, complex wine, it shows lovely concentration, delicacy and texture. Still youthful, with a strong, nutty oak influence and deep grapefruit and peach flavours, it shows great potential; open mid-2012+. The 2010 (★★★★☆) has a nutty, complex bouquet. Powerful and concentrated, it is very youthful, with tight peach and grapefruit flavours, slightly minerally and nutty. Built to last.

Vintage	10	09
WR	7	7
Drink	12-22	11-15

 DRY $56 –V

Cable Bay Waiheke Chardonnay   ★★★★☆

Blended from five sites at the western end of the island, this tightly structured wine opens out well with bottle-age. Hand-picked, it is fermented (partly with indigenous yeasts) and matured for 10 months in French oak barriques (around 15 per cent new), with no use of malolactic fermentation. The 2009 (★★★★) is drinking well now. Richly flavoured, it is sweet-fruited, citrusy, slightly spicy, toasty and minerally, with good complexity. The 2010 vintage (★★★★☆) is more open and expressive than its Reserve stablemate (above). Weighty and rich, with ripe stone-fruit, spice and toast flavours, it is tightly structured, elegant and long.

Vintage	10	09	08	07	06
WR	7	6	7	7	6
Drink	12-20	11-20	11-15	11-14	P

DRY $35 –V

Carrick Cairnmuir Terraces EBM Chardonnay ★★★★☆

From a region that has struggled to produce top Chardonnay, this wine is one of the best. The 2008 vintage (★★★★☆), grown at Bannockburn, was fermented and matured for 18 months (EBM means 'extended barrel maturation') in French oak barriques (20 per cent new). Still youthful (when last tasted in mid–late 2010), it is mouthfilling, concentrated and minerally, with grapefruit-like flavours, hints of biscuits and butterscotch, a mealy complexity, and a long, finely balanced finish.

Vintage	08	07	06	05	04
WR	6	7	6	6	6
Drink	11-15	11-15	11-12	11-12	P

DRY $33 AV

Carrick Central Otago Chardonnay ★★★★☆

A tight, elegant, cool-climate style, this wine is grown at Bannockburn, fermented with indigenous yeasts and matured for a year in French oak barriques (15 per cent new). The 2009 vintage (★★★★★), given a full, softening malolactic fermentation, is the best yet. Richly scented, with fresh, ripe grapefruit-like flavours, slightly nutty and creamy, and good acid spine, it is very concentrated, complex and harmonious. A great buy.

DRY $26 V+

Chard Farm Closeburn Chardonnay ★★★

The winery's second-tier Chardonnay is typically a fresh, vibrant Central Otago wine with appetising acidity. Handled entirely in tanks, it offers fresh, crisp, citrusy flavours, with minerally, buttery notes adding interest.

DRY $22 –V

Charles Wiffen Marlborough Chardonnay ★★★☆

Charles and Sandy Wiffen own a vineyard in the Wairau Valley, but their wine is made at West Brook in West Auckland. The 2009 vintage (★★★★), French oak-aged for 10 months, is an upfront style, rich, toasty and creamy. Drinking well currently, it's a peachy, full-flavoured wine with toasty, nutty, buttery notes adding complexity and good length.

DRY $24 AV

Cheeky Little White East Coast Chardonnay (★★☆)

From Babich, the medium-bodied 2009 vintage (★★☆) is fresh and lively, with citrusy, slightly peachy flavours, crisp and dry. A simple, fruit-driven style, it's priced sharply.

DRY $12 V+

Church Road Cuve Chardonnay ★★★★

This label was originally reserved for rare wines, made in 'a more Burgundian, less fruit-driven, less oaky' style of Hawke's Bay Chardonnay than its lush and (at that stage) relatively fast-maturing Church Road Reserve stablemate. However, since 2006 its production has been expanded and the price reduced sharply. The 2008 (★★★★) is a classic regional style, rich and sweet-fruited, with ripe, lemony, peachy flavours, plenty of oak and substantial body. It's a complex, creamy wine with a lingering finish. The 2009 vintage (★★★★☆) was hand-picked and fermented and matured in French oak casks (20 per cent new). It's a very elegant wine, slightly minerally, with strong, citrusy, gently nutty flavours, showing excellent complexity, drive and length.

 DRY $27 AV

Church Road Hawke's Bay Chardonnay ★★★★

This typically mouthfilling, rich wine is made by Pernod Ricard NZ at the Church Road winery in Hawke's Bay. Much of the wine undergoes a secondary, softening malolactic fermentation. The juice is fermented in French (70 per cent) and Hungarian (30 per cent) oak barriques (about one-third new), and the wine is matured for about 10 months on its full yeast lees, with fortnightly stirring. Fleshy and rounded, it has substantial body and ripe stone-fruit flavours showing good texture, complexity and depth. Already drinking well, the 2010 vintage (★★★★) is pale yellow, with a complex bouquet of ripe stone-fruit and toasty oak. Full-bodied, it offers strong, ripe peach and nectarine flavours, slightly nutty, rich and rounded. At its average retail price in supermarkets of around $15, this is a great buy.

Vintage	10	09	08
WR	7	7	5
Drink	11-13	11-12	P

 DRY $27 AV

Church Road Reserve Hawke's Bay Chardonnay ★★★★★

This classy wine is based on the 'pick' of Pernod Ricard NZ's Hawke's Bay Chardonnay crop. It is hand-harvested, fermented with indigenous yeasts in French oak barriques (about 50 per cent new), and stays on its yeast lees for the total time in barrel (up to 14 months), with frequent lees-stirring. In recent years, the wine has become more elegant, less 'upfront' in style, and should mature longer. The 2008 vintage (★★★★★) has a rich, complex bouquet. Full-bodied and concentrated, with deep, stone-fruit flavours, well seasoned with toasty oak, it is powerful and full of personality, with a strong oak influence – but the fruit to carry it. The 2009 (★★★★☆) is mouthfilling and rich, with stone-fruit and toasty oak flavours showing excellent complexity and harmony.

Vintage	09	08	07	06	05	04
WR	6	6	6	7	6	6
Drink	11-13	11-12	P	P	P	P

 DRY $37 AV

Church Road Tom Chardonnay

The debut 2006 vintage (★★★★★) is a great wine – one of the most memorable New Zealand Chardonnays yet. The 2009 (★★★★☆) was hand-harvested in Hawke's Bay, fermented with indigenous yeasts in French oak barriques (35 per cent new), barrel-aged for 14 months on its full yeast lees, with regular stirring, and then matured on light lees in tanks for a further eight months before bottling. Still tight and youthful, it has a very fragrant, complex bouquet. The palate is weighty, rich and rounded, concentrated and smoothly textured, with grapefruit and slight lime flavours, minerally, searching and long. It's less powerful and lush than the 2006, but was released a lot younger (at two rather than three and a half years old).

DRY $70 –V

C.J. Pask Declaration Hawke's Bay Chardonnay

The Hawke's Bay winery's top Chardonnay is grown in Gimblett Road and fermented and matured in all-new French oak barriques, with weekly lees-stirring. The 2008 vintage (★★★★☆) is highly fragrant, with rich stone-fruit flavours, slightly nutty and creamy, and excellent complexity. Pale gold, the 2009 (★★★☆) is fleshy, with ripe, peachy flavours, showing considerable complexity. Toasty, buttery, slightly limey and honeyed, it has very good weight and depth.

DRY $35 –V

C.J. Pask Gimblett Road Hawke's Bay Chardonnay

This second-tier Chardonnay is designed to highlight vibrant fruit characters, fleshed out with restrained wood. The 2008 vintage (★★★) has a hint of oak (25 per cent of the blend was barrel-aged), and fresh, delicate, citrusy fruit flavours shining through.

DRY $19 AV

C.J. Pask Roy's Hill Hawke's Bay Unoaked Chardonnay

Grown in Gimblett Road and handled in stainless steel tanks, the 2009 vintage (★★☆) is a medium-bodied, fruit-driven style with fresh, peachy, slightly limey flavours and a crisp, dry finish. Priced right.

DRY $15 AV

Clearview Beachhead Chardonnay ★★★☆

This Hawke's Bay winery has a reputation for powerful Chardonnays, and top vintages of its second-tier label are no exception – big and rich. The 2010 (★★★★), a powerful, full-bodied wine, estate-grown and hand-picked at Te Awanga, was mostly fermented in seasoned French oak casks. Creamy-textured, with concentrated, peachy flavours, fresh and lively, it has biscuity, toasty notes adding complexity, appetising acidity, and good richness and harmony.

Vintage	10	09	08
WR	7	6	6
Drink	11-16	11-15	11-14

DRY $26 –V

Clearview Reserve Hawke's Bay Chardonnay ★★★★★

For his premium Chardonnay label, winemaker Tim Turvey aims for a 'big, grunty, upfront' style – and hits the target with ease. It's typically a hedonist's delight – an arrestingly bold, intense, savoury, mealy, complex wine with layers of flavour. Based on ultra-ripe fruit (hand-harvested at 24–25 brix from Te Awanga vines, up to 21 years old), the 2009 vintage (★★★★★) is a highly scented, very vibrant wine. Barrel-fermented, it is very poised and elegant, with fresh, rich, grapefruit and peach flavours, seasoned with toasty French (mostly) and American oak (50 per cent new). Weighty and concentrated, with lovely harmony and immediacy, it's still youthful.

Vintage	09	08	07	06	05	04
WR	7	7	7	7	7	7
Drink	11-19	11-18	11-14	11-12	P	P

DRY $35 AV

Clearview Te Awanga Chardonnay ★★★☆

Estate-grown and hand-harvested on the Hawke's Bay coast and mostly handled in tanks, the 2010 vintage (★★★☆) is a delicious, drink-young style. Mouthfilling, it is vibrantly fruity, with strong, ripe, peachy flavours, a subtle seasoning of oak (from a small percentage of barrel fermentation) and a smooth finish.

DRY $21 AV

Clifford Bay Marlborough Chardonnay (★★★)

The 2010 vintage (★★★) is a mouthfilling wine (14.5 per cent alcohol) with strong, lemony, slightly buttery flavours and a fresh, smooth finish. Enjoyable young.

DRY $20 –V

Clos de Ste Anne Chardonnay Naboth's Vineyard ★★★★★

Millton's flagship Chardonnay is based on mature vines in the steep, north-east-facing Naboth's Vineyard in the Poverty Bay foothills, planted in loams overlying sedimentary calcareous rock. Grown biodynamically and hand-harvested, it is fermented in mostly second-fill French oak barrels, and in most vintages it is not put through malolactic fermentation, 'to leave a pure, crisp mineral flavour'. The 2009 (★★★★★) is full of personality. Richly, ripely fragrant, it is mouthfilling, with lovely freshness, delicacy and depth. Highly concentrated, with peach and citrus-fruit flavours, fleshed out with a subtle seasoning of nutty oak, and a fine thread of acidity, it builds to a lasting finish. A notably elegant, 'complete' wine, with its best years ahead, it's well worth cellaring to 2013+.

Vintage	09	08	07	06	05	04	03	02
WR	7	6	7	7	7	7	6	7
Drink	11-21	11-17	11-17	11-16	11-15	11-14	P	11-12

DRY $65 AV

Cloudy Bay Chardonnay ★★★★★

A powerful Marlborough wine with impressively concentrated, savoury, lemony, mealy flavours and a proven ability to mature well over the long haul (at least four years and up to a decade). The grapes, mostly hand-picked, are sourced from numerous company-owned and growers' vineyards in the Wairau and Brancott valleys. All of the wine is fermented (with a high proportion of indigenous yeasts) in French oak barriques (about 20 per cent new) and lees-aged in barrels for up to 15 months, and most goes through a softening malolactic fermentation.

The 2008 vintage (★★★★★) is a powerful yet very elegant, cool-climate style with impressive richness, complexity and harmony. The bouquet is fragrant, biscuity and mealy; the palate is full-bodied, with concentrated, citrusy, slightly buttery and nutty flavours, and good acid spine. Drink now or cellar.

Vintage	08	07	06
WR	5	6	7
Drink	11-16	11-14	11-14

DRY $38 AV

Coniglio Hawke's Bay Chardonnay   ★★★★★

Launched by Morton Estate from 1998, Coniglio is one of New Zealand's most expensive Chardonnays. A Rolls-Royce version of the company's famous Black Label Chardonnay, it is typically an arresting wine, powerful and concentrated. Grown in the cool, elevated (150 metres above sea level) Riverview Vineyard at Mangatahi, Hawke's Bay, it is hand-picked from mature vines and fermented and lees-aged in all-new French oak barriques, with malolactic fermentation according to the season. Harvested at a very ripe 25 brix, the bright yellow 2004 vintage (★★★★★) is a refined wine with a highly fragrant, citrusy, nutty bouquet. Mouthfilling and sweet-fruited, with a fine thread of acidity, it's a rich, elegant wine, maturing gracefully and now probably at its peak. (There is no 2005.)

Vintage	05	04	03	02	01	00
WR	NM	7	NM	7	NM	6
Drink	NM	11-12	NM	P	NM	P

DRY $80 –V

Coopers Creek Cee Vee Chardonnay/Viognier   ★★★

The 2010 vintage (★★★) is full-bodied and fleshy, with ripe, peachy flavours, slightly buttery and soft. It's drinking well now.

Vintage	10
WR	7
Drink	11-12

DRY $17 AV

Coopers Creek Reserve Gisborne Chardonnay   ★★★★

Designed as a 'full-bodied, oak-influenced style', this wine is fermented and matured in French oak barriques (40 per cent new in 2009). The 2009 vintage (★★★★☆) has a fragrant, toasty, mealy bouquet, leading into a complex palate with ripe grapefruit-like flavours. A finely textured wine, it is rich, youthful and well worth cellaring.

Vintage	09
WR	6
Drink	11-12

DRY $25 AV

Coopers Creek SV The Limeworks Hawke's Bay Chardonnay   ★★★★☆

This great value, single-vineyard, Havelock North wine is a 'full-on' style with rich, grapefruit-like flavours, well seasoned with toasty American and French oak (half new) and a creamy-soft texture. The 2010 vintage (★★★★☆) is powerful and youthful. The bouquet is biscuity and oaky, with good complexity; the palate is rich, with well-ripened stone-fruit and nut flavours, good acid spine and a long finish.

Vintage	10	09	08	07	06
WR	7	6	6	5	7
Drink	11-13	11-12	11-12	P	P

DRY $20 V+

Coopers Creek Swamp Reserve Chardonnay   ★★★★☆

Based on the winery's best Hawke's Bay grapes, this is typically a seductive wine with a finely judged balance of rich, citrusy, peachy fruit flavours and toasty oak. Hand-picked in the company's Middle Road Vineyard at Havelock North, it is fermented and matured for 10 months in French oak barriques (up to 50 per cent new). The 2010 vintage (★★★★☆) is youthful and rich, with mouthfilling body and peachy, citrusy, biscuity, toasty flavours, showing excellent complexity, concentration and potential. Best drinking 2013+.

Vintage	10	09	08	07	06
WR	7	6	7	7	6
Drink	11-15	11-14	11-13	P	P

DRY $30 AV

Coopers Creek Unoaked Gisborne Chardonnay   ★★★☆

Coopers Creek no longer matures its popular, moderately priced Gisborne wine in wood, but the recipe still includes maturation on its yeast lees. The 2009 vintage (★★★☆) is full-bodied and vibrantly fruity, with fresh, tight, peachy, citrusy flavours and lively acidity.

Vintage	09	08
WR	6	6
Drink	11-12	P

DRY $17 V+

Corazon Single Vineyard Chardonnay   ★★★★

Grown at Kumeu, in West Auckland, the 2010 vintage (★★★★) is a single-vineyard wine, hand-picked and fermented in French oak casks (30 per cent new). Creamy-textured, it is mouthfilling, with fresh, ripe, citrusy, peachy flavours, seasoned with biscuity oak, good complexity and a rounded finish. Drink now or cellar.

Vintage	10
WR	7
Drink	12-17

DRY $24 V+

Corbans Cottage Block Hawke's Bay Chardonnay   ★★★★★

A consistently classy wine, but this brand is no longer owned by Pernod Ricard NZ. The superb 2007 vintage (★★★★★) was hand-picked in company-owned vineyards, fully barrel-fermented with indigenous yeasts, and matured for a year in French oak barriques (new and one year old). A classic regional style, it showed a fragrant, complex, nutty, creamy bouquet, leading into a generous, finely textured palate with ripe grapefruit and smoky oak flavours, showing lovely delicacy, complexity and length. The 2009 (★★★★☆) is rich and refined, with fresh, tight, grapefruit-like flavours and earthy, nutty, smoky notes adding real complexity.

DRY $36 AV

Couper's Shed Hawke's Bay Chardonnay (★★★)

From Pernod Ricard NZ, the 2009 vintage (★★★) is a fruit-driven style, full-bodied, with plenty of ripe, peachy flavour and a rounded, dryish finish. It has lots of drink-young charm.

DRY $20 –V

Crab Farm Reserve Chardonnay ★★★★

The 2008 vintage (★★★★) from this small Hawke's Bay winery was hand-picked and aged for eight months in new oak barrels. It is mouthfilling and sweet-fruited, with rich, vibrant, peachy, citrusy flavours, oak complexity and good acid spine.

Vintage	08
WR	7
Drink	P

DRY $25 AV

Craggy Range Gimblett Gravels Vineyard Chardonnay ★★★★☆

This stylish Hawke's Bay wine is mouthfilling, complex and savoury, with biscuity, nutty characters from fermentation and maturation in French oak barriques (23 per cent new in 2009). The 2009 vintage (★★★★☆) is a refined, youthful wine, with substantial body and ripe, citrusy flavours, seasoned with biscuity oak. Concentrated, savoury and complex, it's a classy, tightly structured wine, well worth cellaring.

Vintage	09	08	07	06
WR	5	6	6	6
Drink	11-14	11-13	11-13	P

DRY $32 AV

Craggy Range Kidnappers Vineyard Hawke's Bay Chardonnay ★★★★

Made using 'the traditional techniques of Chablis', the 2010 vintage (★★★★) is a very gently oaked style, full of interest. Grown near the coast at Te Awanga, and fermented in a mix of tanks (mostly) and French oak barrels, it is fresh and fruit-focused, with good weight and ripe grapefruit, pear and apple flavours, slightly mealy, finely poised and lingering. It's not showy, but refined and satisfying.

Vintage	10	09	08	07
WR	5	5	6	6
Drink	11-13	11-13	11-13	11-12

DRY $24 V+

Craggy Range Les Beaux Cailloux – see the Branded and Other White Wines section

Crawford Farm Chardonnay ★★★

From Constellation NZ, the 2008 vintage (★★★) is fruity, peachy, slightly buttery and spicy, in a smooth, easy-drinking style.

DRY $22 –V

Croft Vineyard Martinborough Chardonnay ★★★★☆

The 2008 vintage (★★★★☆) is good value. Harvested at 24 brix and fully barrel-fermented (in 30 per cent new oak), mostly with indigenous yeasts, it is elegant, with concentrated peach, grapefruit and nut flavours, showing good complexity, and a finely balanced, long finish.

DRY $24 V+

Crossings, The, Awatere Valley Unoaked Chardonnay (★★)

The 2009 vintage (★★) is a simple wine, fruity and rounded, with citrusy, slightly limey and buttery flavours. Ready.

Vintage	09
WR	4
Drink	12-13

DRY $19 –V

Crossroads Hawke's Bay Chardonnay ★★★☆

A consistently good buy. The 2009 vintage (★★★☆) is full-bodied, peachy and slightly nutty, with generous, ripe-fruit flavours, showing some mealy complexity, and a creamy-smooth finish. The 2010 (★★★☆) is a citrusy, slightly spicy and mealy wine. Fermented mostly in French oak barriques (40 per cent new), but also in tanks (28 per cent), it has a creamy, buttery texture and very good flavour depth.

Vintage	10
WR	6
Drink	11-15

DRY $19 V+

Crossroads Vineyard Selection Kereru Road Hawke's Bay Chardonnay (★★★★★)

Robust, with arresting power, the 2010 vintage (★★★★★) was hand-picked at Maraekakaho and fermented and matured for nine months in French oak barriques (16 per cent new). Very full-bodied, with deep, vibrant peach, pear and spice flavours, a hint of butterscotch and a rich, creamy finish, it is notably concentrated, complex and harmonious. A lovely wine, it's already approachable.

DRY $45 AV

Crowded House Chardonnay (★★★☆)

The 2008 vintage (★★★☆) is a fruit-driven style, blended from Nelson and Marlborough grapes, and 20 per cent fermented in seasoned oak casks. Mouthfilling, smooth and slightly creamy, it has good depth of grapefruit and spice flavours and a faintly nutty, dry finish.

DRY $18 V+

Cypress Hawke's Bay Chardonnay ★★★

The 2010 vintage (★★★) was tank-fermented, with 'some French oak influence', but was not barrel-aged. Fleshy and forward, it's a noticeably high-alcohol style (14.5 per cent), with ripe tropical-fruit flavours, a hint of cashew nuts and a creamy, rounded finish.

Vintage	10
WR	6
Drink	11-13

 DRY $21 –V

Cypress Terraces Hawke's Bay Chardonnay ★★★★

From a sloping, 2-hectare vineyard, the 2010 vintage (★★★★☆) is a barrel-fermented style (French oak, 50 per cent new), very sweet-fruited and softly seductive. Rich, ripe and rounded, it is full-bodied and generous, with peachy, gently nutty, buttery, toasty flavours, a creamy texture, and excellent delicacy and harmony.

Vintage	10
WR	6
Drink	12-14

 DRY $31 –V

Dashwood Marlborough Chardonnay ★★★

Vavasour's lower-tier Chardonnay. The 2010 vintage (★★★) is a fruit-driven style, grown in the Awatere and Wairau valleys. Peachy, ripe and smooth, with a hint of oak and a slightly creamy texture, it's skilfully balanced for easy, early drinking.

 DRY $17 AV

Delegat Hawke's Bay Chardonnay ★★★

For Delegat's lower-tier Chardonnay, the idea is: 'let the fruit do the talking'. Fermented in tanks and barrels, it is typically flavoursome, peachy and citrusy, in a ripe, vibrantly fruity style, creamy-textured, with drink-young appeal.

DRY $17 AV

Delegat Reserve Hawke's Bay Chardonnay ★★★★

Grown in the inland Crownthorpe district and fully barrel-fermented, this is typically an elegant, fragrant wine with citrusy, nutty flavours, fresh acidity, and excellent delicacy and richness.

 DRY $20 V+

Desert Heart Central Otago Chardonnay (★★★★★)

A notably elegant, cool-climate style, the 2009 vintage (★★★★★) was estate-grown at Bannockburn and fermented with indigenous yeasts in French oak casks (10 per cent new). The bouquet is beautifully fragrant, citrusy and slightly nutty; the palate is poised, slightly buttery, lively and racy, with a sustained finish.

Vintage	09	08	07
WR	7	6	7
Drink	11-17	11-16	11-15

 DRY $32 V+

Distant Land Hawke's Bay Chardonnay ★★★

Briefly oak-aged (three months in old barrels), the 2011 vintage (★★★☆) is enjoyable young, with mouthfilling body and generous, peachy, slightly buttery flavours, fresh and lively.

DRY $20 –V

Distant Land Reserve Hawke's Bay Chardonnay (★★★★)

(Note: the word 'Reserve' is only on the back label.) The 2010 vintage (★★★★) was hand-picked in the Dartmoor Valley and matured for a year in French oak. Mouthfilling, it is youthful and very smooth, with ripe, peachy, slightly toasty flavours, showing good richness, and a creamy-textured, harmonious finish. Best drinking mid-2012+.

DRY $29 AV

Dog Point Vineyard Marlborough Chardonnay ★★★★★

This consistently classy, single-vineyard wine is grown on the south side of the Wairau Valley, hand-picked, fermented with indigenous yeasts, matured for 18 to 20 months in French oak barriques (15 to 25 per cent new), and given a full, softening malolactic fermentation. The 2009 vintage (★★★★★) is weighty, very refined and harmonious, with layers of grapefruit, spice and nut flavours, showing excellent delicacy, subtlety and length. It's built for the long haul; open mid-2012+.

Vintage	09	08	07	06	05	04
WR	6	6	6	6	5	6
Drink	11-15	11-14	11-12	11-13	11-12	P

DRY $33 V+

Dolbel Estate Hawke's Bay Chardonnay ★★★★☆

Maturing well, with a nutty, slightly developed bouquet, the generous, sophisticated 2008 vintage (★★★★☆) was estate-grown, hand-harvested and fully barrel-fermented (French, 57 per cent new). It's a sturdy, fleshy wine with concentrated, ripe stone-fruit flavours, dry, savoury and complex, a slightly toasty oak influence and a creamy-smooth finish.

Vintage	08	07
WR	6	6
Drink	11-12	P

DRY $30 AV

Drylands Marlborough Chardonnay ★★★★

From Constellation NZ, this highly enjoyable wine is an upfront style – fragrant, creamy and full of flavour. Fermented predominantly in French oak barriques, it is typically fleshy and smooth, with stone-fruit and citrus-fruit flavours, creamy, toasty and concentrated.

DRY $22 V+

Dry River Chardonnay ★★★★★

Elegance, restraint and subtle power are the key qualities of this Martinborough wine. It's not a bold, upfront style, but tight, savoury and seamless, with rich grapefruit and nut flavours that build in the bottle for several years. Based on very low-cropping (typically below 5 tonnes/hectare) Mendoza-clone vines, it is hand-harvested, whole-bunch pressed and fermented in French oak hogsheads (20 to 25 per cent new). The proportion of the blend that has gone through a softening malolactic fermentation has never exceeded 15 per cent. The 2010 (★★★★★) is a top vintage, revealing lovely harmony and length. Richly fragrant, it is citrusy, sweet-fruited and mealy, with gentle acidity, a very subtle oak influence, and notable poise, delicacy and depth. It's already quite expressive, but best cellared to 2013+.

Vintage	10	09	08	07	06	05	04
WR	7	7	7	7	7	6	6
Drink	13-20	13-20	11-17	12-18	11-14	11-13	P

DRY $52 AV

Elephant Hill Hawke's Bay Chardonnay   (★★★★☆)

Grown near the coast at Te Awanga, in Hawke's Bay, the 2008 vintage (★★★★☆) is rich, complex and full of personality. Hand-harvested, fermented with indigenous yeasts in French oak barriques (50 per cent new) and lees-aged in oak for 10 months, with no use of malolactic fermentation, it's a sophisticated wine with sweet-fruit delights, highly concentrated grapefruit and stone-fruit flavours seasoned with toasty oak, and a fresh, finely balanced finish.

DRY $26 AV

Emeny Road Reserve Chardonnay   ★★★☆

This rare Bay of Plenty wine is grown at Plummers Point, 17 kilometres west of Tauranga. The 2008 vintage (★★★★), oak-aged for eight months, is an elegant wine with good acid spine and generous, ripe grapefruit and peach flavours. Slightly nutty and finely poised, it shows excellent depth and complexity and is drinking well now. Good value.

DRY $21 AV

Escarpment Kupe by Escarpment [Chardonnay]   ★★★★★

From a single Martinborough vineyard 'in the town', rather than at Te Muna, the 2009 vintage (★★★★★) was fermented and lees-aged for a year in French oak barriques (30 per cent new). It's a powerful, mouthfilling wine, deliciously rich and ripe, with concentrated stone-fruit flavours, mealy, nutty notes adding complexity, and a rounded, lasting finish. Drink now or cellar.

DRY $50 AV

Escarpment Martinborough Chardonnay   ★★★★☆

The 2009 vintage (★★★★★) was estate-grown at Te Muna and fermented and matured in French oak barriques (20 per cent new). Delicious now, it is robust and rich, with a fragrant, peachy bouquet and concentrated, ripe stone-fruit flavours, slightly biscuity, well-rounded and long. A top year.

DRY $30 AV

Esk Valley Hawke's Bay Chardonnay ★★★★

Top vintages offer fine value. The 2010 vintage (★★★★) was partly handled in tanks, but 75 per cent of the blend was fermented and lees-aged for eight months in French oak barrels (15 per cent new). Fleshy and smooth, it is rich, ripe and rounded, with sweet-fruit delights and strong, peachy, slightly spicy flavours, showing considerable complexity. Delicious in its youth.

Vintage	10	09	08	07	06
WR	7	6	7	7	6
Drink	12-15	11-12	P	11-12	P

 DRY $24 V+

Esk Valley Winemakers Reserve Hawke's Bay Chardonnay ★★★★★

Often one of the region's most distinguished Chardonnays, this wine was called 'Reserve' rather than 'Winemakers', prior to the 2008 vintage. The 2009 (★★★★) is a blend of grapes from two sites – 92 per cent from Bay View, on the coast (which gives 'lush' fruit characters), and 8 per cent from the Ngakirikiri Vineyard in the Gimblett Gravels (which yields a more 'flinty' style). Hand-picked, fermented with indigenous yeasts and matured for a year in French oak barriques, it has a smoky oak influence (with a hint of 'burnt match'), strong stone-fruit flavours and good, savoury complexity. The youthful 2010 vintage (★★★★★) is highly refined. Concentrated and complex, with rich, citrusy flavours seasoned with nutty oak and a tight, finely balanced finish, it's well worth cellaring; open mid-2012+.

Vintage	10	09	08	07	06	05	04
WR	7	7	7	7	7	7	6
Drink	12-16	12-16	12-14	12-14	12-13	P	11-12

DRY $32 V+

Fairhall Downs Single Vineyard Marlborough Chardonnay ★★★★

Grown and hand-picked in the Brancott Valley, this wine shows rising form and the 2008 vintage (★★★★), still on sale, is one of the best yet. Fermented with indigenous yeasts and matured for 10 months in French oak barriques, it's a very open, expressive and well-rounded wine with mouthfilling body and citrusy, peachy, slightly toasty and nutty flavours, showing good complexity.

Vintage	08	07	06
WR	6	7	7
Drink	11-15	11-13	11-12

 DRY $30 –V

Farmers Market Gisborne Chardonnay (★★★☆)

The attractive 2009 vintage (★★★☆) is a single-vineyard wine, not oak-aged. Medium to full-bodied, it is peachy, ripe and vibrantly fruity, with very good flavour depth and a slightly buttery, rounded finish. Drink now.

DRY $20 AV

Farmgate Hawke's Bay Chardonnay   ★★★☆

From the Ngatarawa winery, this brand is sold directly to consumers via the Farmgate website. The 2008 vintage (★★★) was barrel-aged for 10 months. Full-bodied, with a biscuity bouquet and moderately concentrated flavours, it is peachy and smooth, with a fractionally off-dry finish.

Vintage	08	07	06
WR	7	NM	7
Drink	11-13	NM	P

MED/DRY $22 AV

Felton Road Bannockburn Central Otago Chardonnay   ★★★★☆

Forging ahead in quality, this wine is grown at three sites at Bannockburn and matured in French oak barriques (with limited new oak; 12 per cent in 2010). The 2009 (★★★★☆) is powerful (14.5 per cent alcohol) yet elegant, with fresh, ripe grapefruit, melon and peach flavours, subtle oak, gentle acidity and a very harmonious, well-rounded finish. The 2010 (★★★★☆) is richly scented, with very citrusy aromas and flavours. An intense, elegant, cool-climate style, slightly appley and spicy, with finely integrated oak, it is tight, harmonious, slightly minerally and long. Drink now or cellar.

Vintage	10	09	08	07	06
WR	7	7	6	7	6
Drink	12-22	11-20	11-18	11-13	11-12

DRY $38 –V

Felton Road Block 2 Chardonnay   ★★★★☆

The outstanding 2009 vintage (★★★★★) was grown in a 'special part of the Elms Vineyard in front of the winery', which has the oldest vines, in Central Otago. Strikingly rich, it's a real beauty, with tight, intense, citrusy, peachy, slightly buttery flavours, ripe and long. Likely to be long-lived, it's one of the region's finest Chardonnays yet.

DRY $45 –V

Felton Road Elms Central Otago Chardonnay   ★★★★

The finely poised 2009 vintage (★★★★) is full of interest for Chardonnay lovers. Handled without oak, it is weighty and full-flavoured, citrusy and faintly buttery, with balanced acidity and excellent harmony in a very pleasant style, not at all brash but quietly satisfying, and enjoyable from the start.

Vintage	09
WR	6
Drink	11-17

DRY $24 V+

Fiddler's Green Waipara Chardonnay   ★★★☆

The 2008 vintage (★★★☆) is a distinctly cool-climate style, fermented with indigenous yeasts in French oak barrels (20 per cent new). It offers strong, peachy, citrusy flavours, slightly toasty and honeyed, with good acid spine and some mealy complexity.

DRY $25 –V

Five Flax East Coast Chardonnay   (★★)

The 2010 vintage (★★) from Pernod Ricard NZ is a no-fuss, easy-drinking style, light and fresh, fruity and smooth. Priced right.

Forrest Marlborough Chardonnay   ★★★☆

John Forrest favours a gently oaked style, looking to very ripe grapes and extended lees-aging to give his wine character. It typically matures well. The 2008 vintage (★★★☆) was handled in a 50:50 split of tanks and barrels, and given a full, softening malolactic fermentation. Drinking well now, it is fresh, citrusy and flavoursome, with buttery, toasty notes adding complexity, a crisp, minerally streak and a tight finish.

Framingham Marlborough Chardonnay   ★★★★

Consistently attractive, in a subtle, satisfying style. Grown at several sites in the Wairau Valley, it is fermented in a 50:50 split of tanks and French oak barriques, with lees-aging and some malolactic fermentation. The 2009 vintage (★★★★) was delicious from the start. An elegant wine, it is full-bodied, with vibrant, peachy, citrusy, slightly buttery flavours, showing good richness and harmony, and a rounded finish.

Vintage	09	08	07	06
WR	6	6	6	6
Drink	11-15	11-13	11-12	P

Frizzell Hawke's Bay Chardonnay   (★★★)

Winemaker Rod McDonald set out to make a 'gutsy' style 'but without too much oak'. The debut 2008 vintage (★★★) was given a full, softening malolactic fermentation. A mouthfilling wine, it offered generous, peachy, slightly buttery flavours, with a well-rounded finish. (A 'third bottling', released in 2011, is nutty, creamy and leesy, in a slightly oxidative style, showing considerable complexity.)

Vintage	08
WR	5
Drink	11-12

Fromm Clayvin Vineyard Marlborough Chardonnay   ★★★★★

Fromm's finest Chardonnay is grown on the southern flanks of the Wairau Valley, where the clay soils, says winemaker Hätsch Kalberer, give 'a less fruity, more minerally and tighter character'. Top vintages can mature well for a decade. Fermented with indigenous yeasts in French oak barriques, with little or no use of new wood, it is barrel-aged for well over a year. The 2009 vintage (★★★★★) is rare – only four barrels were made. Youthful and very fresh, it is finely poised, with strong, vibrant grapefruit, peach and nut flavours, revealing lovely delicacy and depth. It's still a baby, but builds across the palate to a lasting finish. Open 2013+.

Vintage	09	08	07	06	05	04
WR	7	NM	7	7	7	6
Drink	11-17	NM	11-15	11-14	11-13	11-12

Fromm La Strada Marlborough Chardonnay   (★★★★)

Not bottled until February 2011, the 2008 vintage (★★★★) was matured for 14 to 16 months in French oak casks (maximum 10 per cent new). Lemon-scented, with slightly biscuity and mealy aromas, it is vibrantly fruity, with fresh, rich grapefruit, lemon, apple and spice flavours, a subtle seasoning of oak, and racy acidity. It's an excellent, distinctly cool-climate style.

Vintage	08	07	06
WR	6	6	6
Drink	11-15	11-13	11-12

DRY $32 –V

Gem Gisborne Chardonnay   ★★★★

Released in 2011, the 2007 vintage (★★★★) from Corey Hall (formerly chief winemaker at Matua Valley) was grown in the Judd Estate Vineyard at Patutahi, hand-picked, and fermented with indigenous yeasts in French oak barriques (one-third new). Bright, light lemon/green, it is stylish, rich and elegant, with peach, grapefruit and toast flavours, savoury and biscuity, and good complexity. Drink now to 2012.

Vintage	07	06
WR	7	6
Drink	12-16	11-15

DRY $30 –V

Gibbston Highgate Estate Heartbreaker Chardonnay   ★★★

The 2009 vintage (★★★) was hand-picked at Gibbston, in Central Otago, and mostly fermented in tanks; a third of the blend was fermented and lees-aged in new and older French oak casks. It is fresh, vibrant and lemony, with a touch of creamy, toasty complexity, a sliver of sweetness (5.8 grams/litre of residual sugar), and firm acid spine.

Vintage	09	08	07	06
WR	5	6	5	6
Drink	12-15	11-15	11-12	11-12

MED/DRY $25 –V

Gibbston Valley Reserve Chardonnay   ★★★★

This is a more complex style than its stablemate under the Greenstone brand (below). Estate-grown in the Chinaman's Terrace Vineyard at Bendigo, in Central Otago, the 2009 vintage (★★★★) was fermented with indigenous yeasts and matured for 18 months in French oak barriques and puncheons (25 per cent new). A mouthfilling, well-rounded wine with plenty of personality, it has a creamy, slightly toasty bouquet, leading into a peachy, buttery palate, with good concentration and complexity.

Vintage	09	08	07
WR	7	7	6
Drink	11-15	11-14	11-12

DRY $32 –V

Giesen Marlborough Chardonnay ★★★

The 2009 vintage (★★★), grown in the Wairau Valley, was 25 per cent tank-fermented; the rest was fermented and matured for a year in barrels. It's a mouthfilling, citrusy wine with a very restrained oak influence, but fresh, crisp and lively.

Giesen The Brothers Marlborough Chardonnay ★★★★

The 2009 vintage (★★★★), fermented and matured in all-new French oak puncheons, has a fragrant, creamy bouquet. Mouthfilling, it is peachy, citrusy, spicy and toasty, with a minerally streak and good complexity. The 2010 (★★★★), handled mostly in new French oak hogsheads, is fragrant and complex, full-bodied and youthful, with stone-fruit, toast and slight butterscotch characters, showing good complexity and richness. Best drinking mid-2012+.

Glazebrook Hand Picked Regional Reserve Chardonnay ★★★★

Ngatarawa's second-tier Chardonnay is named after the Glazebrook family, formerly partners in the Hawke's Bay venture. The 2010 vintage (★★★★) – the first since 2007 – is highly fragrant. Rich and refined, it has concentrated, ripe peach and grapefruit flavours and a well-integrated seasoning of toasty oak. Very harmonious and smooth, it's delicious from the start.

Vintage	10	09	08	07
WR	7	NM	NM	7
Drink	11-15	NM	NM	11-12

Goldridge Estate Gisborne Chardonnay ★★☆

The 2009 vintage (★★☆) was partly barrel-fermented. A single-vineyard wine, it is fresh and lively, in a fruit-driven style with peachy, smooth flavours.

Goldridge Estate Premium Reserve Chardonnay ★★★

The 2010 vintage (★★★☆) is a blend of Hawke's Bay and Gisborne grapes, fermented and lees-aged for 10 months in predominantly French oak barriques. It's an upfront style, full-bodied and creamy, with plenty of peachy, biscuity flavour, ripe and rounded. Enjoyable young.

Goldridge Estate Premium Reserve Hawke's Bay Chardonnay ★★★★

The 2009 vintage (★★★★) is a great buy. A single-vineyard wine, fermented and matured on its yeast lees for 10 months in predominantly French oak barriques (30 per cent new), it has a nutty bouquet leading into a full-bodied palate with peachy, slightly creamy flavours, showing considerable complexity. Fleshy, weighty and well-rounded, it was delicious from the start and is maturing well.

DRY $19 V+

Goldwater Wairau Valley Marlborough Chardonnay   ★★★★

Typically a finely scented, weighty, vibrantly fruity wine with tropical-fruit characters and subtle use of oak in a highly attractive style. Already delicious, the 2010 vintage (★★★★) is attractively fresh and rich, with mouthfilling body and strong, ripe peach and melon flavours. Vibrantly fruity, it has finely integrated, biscuity oak (French, 10 per cent new) and a slightly creamy finish.

Vintage	10	09	08
WR	7	6	6
Drink	11-15	11-13	11-13

DRY $22 V+

Goldwater Zell Waiheke Island Chardonnay   ★★★★☆

Grown in the hillside, clay-based Zell Vineyard on Waiheke Island, this is a rich, complex wine with the ripeness and roundness typical of northern Chardonnays. It is hand-picked, whole-bunch pressed and fermented with indigenous yeasts in French oak casks (30 to 40 per cent new), with full malolactic fermentation in 2008. The 2008 vintage (★★★★★), barrel-aged for a year, is one of the finest yet. A lovely, tightly structured wine, it is highly fragrant, with rich stone-fruit flavours, a hint of butterscotch, and excellent vigour, delicacy and length. It should mature well.

DRY $34 AV

Greenhough Hope Vineyard Chardonnay   ★★★★★

This impressive wine is estate-grown at Hope, in Nelson, hand-picked and fermented and matured for a year in French oak casks (15 per cent new in 2009). The 2009 vintage (★★★★☆) is mouthfilling, youthful and finely poised, with ripe, concentrated flavours of stone-fruit, pears and spices, subtle oak, excellent delicacy and complexity, a fine thread of acidity and a slightly buttery, lasting finish. It's a tightly structured wine, still developing.

Vintage	10	09	08	07	06	05	04
WR	NM	6	6	7	6	6	6
Drink	NM	11-15	11-14	11-14	11-12	11-13	P

DRY $32 V+

Greenhough Nelson Chardonnay   ★★★★

This consistently good wine is fermented and matured in French oak casks (20 per cent new in 2010). The 2010 (★★★★☆) is a top vintage, already delicious. The bouquet is fragrant and complex; the palate is full-bodied and dry, peachy, slightly mealy and nutty, with a hint of butterscotch and lovely harmony. Drink now or cellar. Fine value.

Vintage	10
WR	6
Drink	11-16

DRY $24 V+

Greenstone Central Otago Chardonnay   ★★★

Past vintages were called 'Gibbston Valley Greenstone Chardonnay'. The 2009 (★★★) is an attractive example of 'fruit-driven' Chardonnay – vibrant, with lemony, appley flavours, showing good immediacy.

DRY $24 –V

Greystone Waipara Chardonnay ★★★★

The excellent 2009 vintage (★★★★☆) was hand-picked and mostly (75 per cent) fermented in tanks, but all of the blend was matured in French oak barrels (25 per cent new). A fleshy, weighty, complex wine with rich stone-fruit flavours and a hint of butterscotch, it has lovely texture and depth. The 2010 (★★★★) is also rich, sweet-fruited and harmonious, with deep, peachy, slightly buttery flavours and loads of personality. It's already delicious.

Vintage	10	09
WR	6	7
Drink	11-14	11-14

DRY $34 –V

Greywacke Marlborough Chardonnay (★★★★☆)

The powerful 2009 vintage (★★★★☆) was hand-harvested in the Brancott Valley (mostly in the upper reaches) and fermented and matured for 16 months in French oak barriques (25 per cent new). The bouquet is complex, citrusy and nutty; the palate is very weighty (14.5 per cent alcohol), with concentrated, vibrant, slightly buttery flavours and finely integrated oak. It's still very youthful; open mid-2012+.

Vintage	09
WR	5
Drink	11-16

DRY $38 –V

Grove Mill Marlborough Chardonnay ★★★☆

Typically an attractive, skilfully balanced wine with strong grapefruit and lime flavours, a subtle twist of oak and fresh, crisp acidity. (The 2010 vintage was matured for 10 months in seasoned French oak casks.)

Vintage	10
WR	6
Drink	11-14

DRY $20 AV

Growers Mark Gisborne Chardonnay (★★★)

Grown in the Briant Vineyard, the 2010 vintage (★★★) is full-bodied, with pleasing depth of citrusy, appley, slightly leesy flavours. Enjoyable young.

DRY $25 –V

Gunn Estate Chardonnay ★★★

The 2009 vintage (★★★) is a New Zealand wine, not identified by region and handled without oak. Pale straw, it is mouthfilling, ripe, peachy and smooth, with plenty of flavour and a slightly spicy, rounded, dry finish. Good, easy drinking.

DRY $18 AV

Hans Herzog Marlborough Chardonnay ★★★★☆

At its best, this is a notably powerful wine with layers of peach, butterscotch, grapefruit and nut flavours and a long, rounded finish. The 2009 vintage (★★★★☆) was hand-picked, fermented with indigenous yeasts in French oak puncheons and given a full, softening malolactic fermentation. Pale straw, with a fragrant, mealy, biscuity bouquet, it is full-bodied and well-rounded, with rich, ripe stone-fruit flavours, hints of apricot and butterscotch, and good complexity.

Vintage	09	08
WR	7	7
Drink	11-20	11-19

 DRY $44 –V

Highfield Marlborough Chardonnay ★★★★

Typically a classy wine. The 2010 (★★★★★), fully barrel-fermented, is a top vintage. It has a scented, mealy bouquet. Full-bodied, it is vibrantly fruity, with deep peach, citrus-fruit and nut flavours, finely balanced acidity, and excellent delicacy and harmony. Weighty and creamy-textured, it shows lovely richness and potential.

Vintage	10	09	08	07	06
WR	7	6	5	6	6
Drink	11-15	11-15	11-14	P	P

 DRY $33 –V

Hinchco Barrel Fermented Matakana Chardonnay (★★★)

Hand-picked and fermented and lees-aged in new American oak, the 2008 vintage (★★★) is a peachy, nutty wine with good body and freshness, but less oak would have been better.

 DRY $30 –V

Hitchen Road Chardonnay ★★★☆

The 2010 vintage (★★★☆) is a great buy, like the 2009 (★★★★). Hand-picked at Pokeno, in North Waikato, barrel-fermented and lees-stirred, it has a slightly nutty bouquet. Still unfolding, it is weighty, with fresh, youthful flavours, ripe and peachy, balanced acidity, and very good delicacy and depth. Open mid-2012+.

Vintage	10	09
WR	6	6
Drink	11-12	11-14

 DRY $15 V+

Hitchen Road Pokeno Unwooded Chardonnay (★★★☆)

Priced sharply, the 2009 vintage (★★★☆) was estate-grown at a 'summer-dry' site at Pokeno, in northern Waikato. Fleshy (14.4 per cent alcohol), ripe and rounded, it's a very good example of the unoaked style, with sweet-fruit characters and good depth of stone-fruit flavours, soft and forward.

DRY $15 V+

Huia Marlborough Chardonnay ★★★★

This full-bodied, creamy-textured wine is hand-picked, fermented with indigenous yeasts and matured in French oak casks, developing citrusy, nutty flavours. Understated in its youth, it typically matures well for several years, offering smooth, satisfying drinking. The 2008 vintage (★★★☆) is robust, tight and youthful, with moderately concentrated, grapefruit-like flavours, considerable complexity and a slightly creamy texture. The 2009 (★★★★) is weighty, citrusy, creamy and nutty, with a subtle oak influence and excellent complexity and harmony. Drink now or cellar.

 DRY $34 –V

Hunky Dory Marlborough Chardonnay (★★★)

From Huia, the 2010 vintage (★★★) has drink-young appeal. Full-bodied, it is peachy and citrusy, slightly creamy and smooth, with plenty of flavour and fresh acidity to keep things lively.

 DRY $18 AV

Huntaway Reserve Gisborne Chardonnay ★★★★

This wine (a brand sold by Pernod Ricard NZ in 2010) has been made in a high-impact, creamy-rich style, with fermentation in French oak casks, lees-stirring weekly and a 'huge' percentage of malolactic fermentation. Delicious from the start, the 2009 vintage (★★★★) is full-bodied, with strong, peachy, nutty, slightly buttery flavours, showing excellent ripeness, richness and complexity.

 DRY $24 V+

Hunter's Marlborough Chardonnay ★★★☆

This wine places its accent on fresh, vibrant fruit flavours, overlaid with subtle, mealy barrel-ferment characters. About 40 per cent of the blend is fermented and lees-aged in new French oak barriques (medium toast); the rest is tank-fermented and then matured in one and two-year-old casks. It is a proven performer in the cellar. The 2010 vintage (★★★☆) is fresh and lively, with good depth of peachy, slightly toasty flavours, finely balanced for early drinking or cellaring.

Vintage	10	09	08	07	06
WR	6	5	6	6	6
Drink	11-14	11-13	11-13	P	P

 DRY $19 V+

Hyperion Helios Matakana Chardonnay ★★★☆

The 2008 vintage (★★★☆) was estate-grown, hand-picked and fermented and lees-aged for six months in French oak barriques (one year old). It's a weighty wine with ripe stone-fruit and toasty oak flavours, balanced acidity, fractional sweetness (6 grams/litre of residual sugar) and very good depth.

Vintage	08
WR	6
Drink	11-14

 MED/DRY $27 –V

Indicator Point Marlborough Chardonnay (★★★)

'Produced and bottled for Southpac Liquor...', the 2008 vintage (★★★) is a fruit-driven style with fresh, crisp grapefruit and apple flavours, showing some elegance and depth.

 DRY $17 AV

Ivicevich Signature Reserve Waimauku Chardonnay ★★★★☆

This is West Brook's estate Chardonnay, grown in West Auckland. The 2007 vintage (★★★★☆) is fleshy, with fresh, very delicate pear, grapefruit and spice flavours, gentle acidity and lovely texture.

 DRY $39 –V

Jackson Estate Shelter Belt Marlborough Chardonnay ★★★☆

The 2008 vintage (★★★☆) was estate-grown in the Homestead Vineyard and fully barrel-aged (20 per cent new). Creamy and slightly biscuity on the nose, it is mouthfilling and rounded, with citrusy, peachy flavours, a hint of butterscotch, and very good complexity and depth.

Vintage	08	07	06
WR	6	6	6
Drink	11-14	11-15	11-12

 DRY $23 AV

Johner Wairarapa Chardonnay ★★★☆

Grown at Gladstone, in the northern Wairarapa, the 2011 vintage (★★★☆) was matured for seven months in large, old German oak barrels. Fleshy and smooth, it has youthful, ripe stone-fruit and slight spice flavours, showing very good depth, and a creamy texture.

DRY $24 AV

John Forrest Collection Wairau Valley Marlborough Chardonnay ★★★★☆

Not released until it was more than four years old, the very classy 2006 vintage (★★★★★) was made from clone 95 Chardonnay grapes, grown in the Wairau Valley, and fermented in French oak casks (over half new). Refined and intense, it has highly concentrated, vibrant, citrusy flavours, well-judged, nutty, mealy influences adding richness and complexity, and lovely harmony and flow. Drink now.

DRY $50 –V

John Forrest Collection Waitaki Valley North Otago Chardonnay (★★★★☆)

Fully fermented in French oak barriques (all older) and given a full, softening malolactic fermentation, the debut 2008 vintage (★★★★☆) has a fragrant, creamy bouquet leading into a weighty, citrusy, toasty and buttery wine, with good richness and a rounded finish. It's hard to pin down any distinctive regional characters, but it's a complex wine, maturing well.

Vintage	08
WR	6
Drink	11-12

DRY $50 –V

Julicher Martinborough Chardonnay   (★★★☆)

The very fresh and lively 2009 vintage (★★★☆) was estate-grown and hand-picked at Te Muna, and fermented and matured for 10 months in French oak barrels (20 per cent new). Mouthfilling (14.5 per cent alcohol), it is vibrantly fruity, with ripe grapefruit-like flavours, slightly limey and nutty, and an appetisingly crisp finish.

DRY $21 AV

Junction Corner Post Chardonnay   (★★★☆)

The 2010 vintage (★★★☆) was grown on the Takapau Plains, in Central Hawke's Bay, and fully barrel-fermented. The bouquet is creamy and buttery; the palate is fresh and distinctly citrusy, with toasty, leesy notes adding complexity, very good depth and a dry, crisp finish. Worth cellaring.

DRY $25 –V

Kahurangi Estate Mt Arthur Reserve Nelson Chardonnay   (★★★★)

The robust, powerful 2010 vintage (★★★★) is a high-alcohol wine (14.5 per cent), with fresh acidity and a strong surge of ripe, peachy, toasty flavour. Made in a traditional, upfront style with lots of oak showing, it has real depth through the palate.

DRY $25 AV

Kaimira Estate Brightwater Chardonnay   ★★★☆

Estate-grown in Nelson and fermented and matured for nine months in French oak casks (20 per cent new), the 2009 vintage (★★★) is a fruit-driven style with vibrant, citrusy aromas and flavours and a slightly buttery finish.

Vintage	09	08	07	06
WR	5	5	5	5
Drink	11-12	11-12	11-12	P

DRY $22 AV

Kaipara Estate Nine Lakes Chardonnay   ★★★☆

Estate-grown on the South Head Peninsula of the Kaipara Harbour, Auckland, the 2008 vintage (★★★☆) is mouthfilling, with ripe stone-fruit flavours, slightly buttery notes, a strong seasoning of toasty oak and a rounded finish.

DRY $25 –V

Kaituna Valley The Kaituna Vineyard Canterbury Chardonnay   ★★★☆

Estate-grown on Banks Peninsula, the 2008 vintage (★★★☆) was handled in oak barrels (20 per cent new). Still youthful, it is peachy and slightly toasty, with good freshness and complexity and a soft finish.

Vintage	08
WR	6
Drink	11-13

DRY $22 AV

Karikari Estate Calypso Chardonnay   (★★☆)

The 2010 vintage (★★☆), grown in Northland and Gisborne, is an easy-drinking wine, not complex, but fresh, citrusy and vibrant.

DRY $22 –V

Karikari Estate Chardonnay   ★★★☆

From New Zealand's northernmost wine producer, this sturdy wine often reminds me of a white from the Rhône Valley. The 2009 vintage (★★★☆) was estate-grown and fermented and aged in tanks and French oak barriques (20 per cent new). Ripely scented, it is very smooth, with ripe grapefruit, peach and nut flavours, showing good complexity and richness. Creamy-textured, it's drinking well now.

Vintage	09
WR	6
Drink	11-13

DRY $33 –V

Karikari Estate Wild Chardonnay   ★★★☆

The 2010 vintage (★★★★) is a rare Northland wine (only 75 cases were made), fermented with indigenous yeasts in French oak puncheons. It has a complex, slightly oaky and creamy bouquet. The palate is soft and rich, with good weight and concentrated, ripe, peachy flavours, showing excellent complexity and roundness. It's already delicious.

Vintage	09
WR	6
Drink	11-13

DRY $39 –V

Kawarau Estate Reserve Chardonnay   ★★★★

Certified organic, this consistently excellent, single-vineyard wine is grown at Pisa Flats, north of Cromwell in Central Otago. It is fermented with indigenous yeasts in French barriques, oak-aged and given a full, softening malolactic fermentation. The refined 2008 vintage (★★★★) is lemony and dry, with mouthfilling body, crisp, minerally acidity and nutty oak adding complexity.

DRY $30 –V

Kemp Road Marlborough Chardonnay   (★★★★)

From wine distributor Kemp Fine Wines, the 2008 vintage (★★★★) was hand-harvested and barrel-fermented. The colour is still youthful; the palate is very refined, with ripe, citrusy flavours, slightly minerally and nutty, good concentration and a lingering finish. Drink now or cellar.

DRY $29 AV

Kennedy Point Chardonnay Cuvée Eve   (★★★★)

The debut 2008 vintage (★★★★) was grown in the Oakura Bay Vineyard on Waiheke Island, and fermented (with indigenous yeasts) and matured for 15 months in French oak barriques. It's a full-bodied, rich wine with concentrated, ripe stone-fruit flavours, showing good freshness and complexity.

DRY $38 –V

Kerner Estate Marlborough Chardonnay   (★★★★☆)

Showing strong personality, the 2009 vintage (★★★★☆) was hand-picked, fermented with indigenous yeasts and matured in seasoned French oak casks. Drinking well now but also worth cellaring, it's very full-bodied, with rich, ripe stone-fruit flavours, showing good complexity and persistence, and a creamy-smooth texture.

Vintage	09
WR	6
Drink	11-13

DRY $35 –V

Kerr Farm Thelma Grace Chardonnay   (★★☆)

Made in a 'very lightly oaked' style, the easy-drinking 2009 vintage (★★☆) of this Kumeu, West Auckland wine is pleasantly fruity, with ripe, citrusy, peachy flavours and a smooth finish.

DRY $20 –V

Kidnapper Cliffs Hawke's Bay Chardonnay   (★★★★★)

From Te Awa, the debut 2009 vintage (★★★★★) was estate-grown in the Gimblett Gravels, fermented with cultured yeasts and matured in French oak casks of varying sizes (225 to 500 litres, 15 to 20 per cent new). It's a classy, immaculate wine, weighty and rich, with ripe grapefruit-like flavours and finely integrated, biscuity oak. Built for cellaring, it is very refined, with vibrant fruit flavours shining through and lovely depth, texture and length.

DRY $45 AV

Kim Crawford New Zealand Unoaked Chardonnay   ★★★

Blended from Gisborne, Hawke's Bay and Marlborough grapes, the 2008 vintage (★★☆) is an easy-drinking style with simple, vibrantly fruity, faintly honeyed flavours and a rounded finish. Ready.

DRY $23 –V

Kina Beach Vineyard Reserve Chardonnay   ★★★★☆

This single-vineyard, coastal Nelson wine possesses strong personality. Grown at Kina Beach and fermented and matured in French oak barriques (one-third new), the 2008 vintage (★★★★★) is now developing real complexity. Vibrant and rich, with citrusy fruit characters woven with lively acidity and finely integrated oak, it's an elegant wine, maturing very gracefully. The 2009 (★★★★) is also stylish, with good acid spine and strong, vibrant, citrusy flavours, slightly minerally and toasty.

DRY $30 AV

Kirkpatrick Estate Reserve Patutahi Chardonnay (★★★★)

Grown in Gisborne, the 2009 vintage (★★★★) was barrel-aged for 16 months in oak casks (20 per cent new). Fleshy and smooth, with ripe stone-fruit flavours, slightly buttery and creamy, it's an upfront style with a toasty oak influence and loads of flavour, drinking well from the start.

Vintage	09
WR	5
Drink	11-13

 DRY $28 AV

Kumeu River Coddington Chardonnay ★★★★★

Launched from the 2006 vintage, this wine is grown in the Coddington Vineyard, between Huapai and Waimauku. The grapes, cultivated on a clay hillside, achieve an advanced level of ripeness (described by marketing manager Paul Brajkovich as 'flamboyant, unctuous, peachy'). Powerful, complex and slightly nutty, it's a lusher, softer wine than its Hunting Hill stablemate (below), but the finish is tight-knit, promising plenty of scope for development. The 2009 vintage (★★★★☆) is still youthful, with a fragrant, biscuity, mealy bouquet. Full-bodied, it has generous grapefruit-like flavours, with hints of lime, honey and butterscotch, fresh acidity, a minerally thread and excellent depth.

Vintage	09	08	07	06
WR	6	6	7	7
Drink	11-15	11-14	11-14	11-13

 DRY $43 AV

Kumeu River Estate Chardonnay ★★★★★

This wine now ranks fourth in the company's hierarchy of five Chardonnays, after three single-vineyard labels, but is still outstanding. Grown at Kumeu, in West Auckland, it is powerful, with rich, beautifully interwoven flavours and a seductively creamy texture, but also has good acid spine. The key to its quality lies in the vineyards, says winemaker Michael Brajkovich: 'We manage to get the grapes very ripe.' Grown in several blocks around Kumeu, hand-picked, fermented with indigenous yeasts and lees-aged (with weekly or twice-weekly lees-stirring) in Burgundy oak barriques (typically 25 per cent new), the wine also normally undergoes a full malolactic fermentation. The 2008 vintage (★★★★★) is very open and expressive. Weighty and rich, showing lovely fruit sweetness, it offers highly concentrated stone-fruit flavours, with finely integrated oak and fresh, appetising acidity. Peachy and mealy, with a hint of butterscotch, it's a lush, generous wine, delicious from the start. Still youthful, the 2009 (★★★★) is tighter and crisper, with grapefruit, spice and nut flavours, showing excellent poise, drive and complexity. An elegant wine, it's still developing; open mid-2012+.

Vintage	09	08	07	06	05	04
WR	6	6	7	7	7	7
Drink	11-15	11-14	11-14	11-13	P	P

DRY $36 AV

Kumeu River Hunting Hill Chardonnay ★★★★★

Launched from the 2006 vintage, this single-vineyard wine is grown on the slopes above Mate's Vineyard, directly over the road from the winery at Kumeu. Marketing manager Paul Brajkovich describes the site's Chardonnay fruit characters as 'floral'. A stylish, elegant wine, in its youth it is less lush than its Coddington stablemate (above), but with good acidity and citrusy, complex flavours that build well across the palate. The 2008 (★★★★★) is highly fragrant, with generous grapefruit, peach and nut flavours and a tight-knit finish. A very classy wine, it should be long-lived. The 2009 vintage (★★★★) is leaner. Crisp and minerally, it is citrusy, spicy and nutty, with good complexity. A subtle, age-worthy wine, it has a cooler-year feel.

Vintage	09	08	07	06
WR	6	6	7	7
Drink	11-15	11-14	11-14	11-13

 DRY $45 AV

Kumeu River Mate's Vineyard Kumeu Chardonnay ★★★★★

This extremely classy single-vineyard wine is Kumeu River's flagship. It is made entirely from the best of the fruit harvested from Mate's Vineyard, planted in 1990 on the site of the original Kumeu River vineyard purchased by Mate Brajkovich in 1944. Strikingly similar to Kumeu River Estate Chardonnay, but slightly more opulent and concentrated, it offers the same rich and harmonious flavours of grapefruit, peach and butterscotch, typically with a stronger seasoning of new French oak. For winemaker Michael Brajkovich, the hallmark of Mate's Vineyard is 'a pear-like character on the nose, with richness and length on the palate after two to three years'. The 2008 vintage (★★★★★) is highly fragrant and finely poised, with rich flavours of stone-fruit and toast, showing lovely depth and complexity. The 2009 (★★★★★) is clearly the winery's best Chardonnay of that growing season. In the mould of classic Meursault, it is weighty and complex, with a lovely array of stone-fruit, spice and slight butterscotch flavours, a fine thread of acidity and outstanding concentration. Drink now onwards.

Vintage	08	07	06	05	04
WR	6	7	7	6	7
Drink	11-14	11-14	11-13	P	P

 DRY $50 AV

Kumeu River Village Chardonnay ★★★☆

Kumeu River's lower-tier, drink-young wine is made from heavier-bearing Chardonnay clones than the Mendoza commonly used for the top wines, and is fermented with indigenous yeasts in a mix of tanks (principally) and seasoned French oak casks. The 2009 vintage (★★★☆) is crisp and lively, peachy and vaguely nutty, with a touch of complexity and good body, subtlety and depth.

DRY $18 V+

Lake Chalice Flight 42 Unoaked Marlborough Chardonnay ★★★

Typically a fresh, vibrant wine with good depth of citrusy, appley flavours, balanced for easy drinking. The 2009 vintage (★★★), grown in the Wairau and Awatere valleys, is mouthfilling, slightly buttery and smooth, with fresh, lemony aromas and flavours.

DRY $20 –V

Lake Chalice Marlborough Chardonnay   ★★★☆

This 'black label' wine is fresh, vibrant and creamy, with drink-young appeal. The 2009 vintage (★★★) was fermented in a mix of tanks (70 per cent) and barrels (30 per cent). A strongly 'malo'-influenced style, it is medium-bodied, with a restrained oak influence, gentle acidity and creamy, buttery flavours.

DRY $20 AV

Lake Road Gisborne Chardonnay   (★★☆)

A single-vineyard wine, grown at Patutahi and handled without oak, the 2010 vintage (★★☆) is a fruit-driven style with straightforward, citrusy, peachy flavours, fresh and crisp. Priced right.

DRY $15 AV

Lawson's Dry Hills Marlborough Chardonnay   ★★★★

This is typically a characterful wine with concentrated, peachy, toasty flavours. Released at up to four years old, it gives a rare opportunity to buy a mature Chardonnay, at its peak. The 2007 vintage (★★★☆) is a single-vineyard wine, harvested in the Wairau Valley at a ripe 24 brix, and fermented and matured for nine months in French oak casks (25 per cent new). Light gold, it has crisp, slightly developed grapefruit and toast flavours, showing very good complexity and depth. Ready.

Vintage	07
WR	6
Drink	P

DRY $27 AV

Lawson's Dry Hills Unoaked Marlborough Chardonnay   ★★★☆

Grown in the company-owned Chaytors Road Vineyard in the Wairau Valley, this wine is cool-fermented in tanks, with daily stirring of its yeast lees 'to add a creamy texture', but malolactic fermentation is avoided. The 2009 vintage (★★★) is fresh, crisp and lively, with ripe, citrusy, peachy flavours, showing good depth and some elegance.

Vintage	09	08
WR	6	7
Drink	P	P

DRY $20 AV

Lil Rippa Hawke's Bay Ngatarawa Chardonnay   (★★★)

From Shoestring Wines, the 2010 vintage (★★★) is made from 'nothing but fruit' (read: no oak). It's an enjoyable example of unwooded Chardonnay – mouthfilling, with fresh, ripe, citrusy flavours, showing good depth. Ready to roll.

DRY $17 AV

Locharburn Central Otago Chardonnay   (★★★☆)

Drinking well now, the 2009 vintage (★★★☆) was barrel-fermented and oak-aged. Pale lemon/green, it is full-bodied and creamy, with good depth of citrusy, slightly spicy flavours, some complexity and fresh, lively acidity.

Vintage	09
WR	6
Drink	11-17

DRY $29 –V

Lochiel Estate Mangawhai Chardonnay   (★★★★)

The skilfully crafted, powerful, creamy-textured 2008 vintage (★★★★) was estate-grown in Northland, in the foothills of the Brynderwyn Range, and 80 per cent barrel-fermented (French, 30 per cent new). Light yellow, with a fragrant bouquet mingling ripe-fruit aromas and toasty oak, it is sturdy (14.5 per cent alcohol), with concentrated stone-fruit flavours, good complexity and a rounded finish. A bold, upfront style.

Vintage	08
WR	6
Drink	11-12

DRY $25 AV

Longbush Chardonnay   ★★★

This 'bird series' label is enjoyable young. Grown in Gisborne and French oak-aged for 10 months, the 2008 vintage (★★★) is full-bodied, with a slightly buttery and toasty bouquet, and satisfying depth of peachy, toasty, well-rounded flavour.

Vintage	08	07
WR	6	5
Drink	11-14	P

DRY $18 AV

Longridge Chardonnay   ★★☆

When on special in supermarkets at under $10, Pernod Ricard NZ's wine is a good buy. Partly French and American oak-aged, it is an easy-drinking style, showcasing fresh, ripe-fruit characters. The 2009 vintage (★★☆) is a citrusy, slightly honeyed wine, probably at its best now.

DRY $18 –V

Mahi Marlborough Chardonnay   ★★★★

The top-value 2009 vintage (★★★★☆) was hand-harvested and fermented with indigenous yeasts in French oak barriques. It's a mouthfilling, creamy-textured wine with strong stone-fruit and toast flavours, a fine thread of acidity, a distinct hint of butterscotch and a rich, rounded finish. The 2010 (★★★★) reveals fresh, vibrant citrus and stone-fruit flavours, with a subtle seasoning of oak. Youthful and age-worthy, it is sweet-fruited, with good intensity and elegance.

Vintage	10	09
WR	6	6
Drink	11-16	11-15

DRY $24 V+

Mahi Twin Valleys Vineyard Marlborough Chardonnay   ★★★★☆

Grown and hand-picked in the Twin Valleys Vineyard, at the junction of the Wairau and Waihopai valleys, this wine is fermented with indigenous yeasts and matured up to a year in French oak. The 2009 (★★★★☆) is rich and elegant, with fresh, complex, peach, citrus-fruit and nut flavours, creamy-textured and long. The 2010 vintage (★★★★☆) is similar – very fresh, concentrated, citrusy and nutty, in a tightly structured style with obvious potential. Best drinking 2013+.

Vintage	10
WR	6
Drink	11-17

 DRY $34 AV

Mahurangi River Field of Grace Chardonnay   ★★★☆

Grown at Matakana, the 2009 vintage (★★★★) was fermented and matured for a year in seasoned French oak barrels. Weighty and complex, with generous peachy, slightly spicy flavours, a hint of honey, and a rich, rounded finish, it shows strong personality. The 2008 vintage (★★☆) is also mouthfilling and full-flavoured, but slightly rustic (and now on sale much cheaper). The more enjoyable 2007 (★★★☆) is weighty and complex, but slightly past its best.

Vintage	09	08	07
WR	7	3	7
Drink	11-13	P	P

DRY $39 –V

Mahurangi River Field of Grace Reserve Chardonnay   (★★★)

Grown at Matakana and fermented with indigenous yeasts in all-new French oak casks, the 2009 vintage (★★★) has substantial body and lots of peachy, slightly spicy and honeyed flavour. When tasted in mid-2010, it showed considerable development for a young wine.

Vintage	09
WR	7
Drink	11-14

 DRY $52 –V

Maimai Creek Hawke's Bay Chardonnay   ★★☆

The 2009 vintage (★★☆) is a fruit-driven style, with lemony flavours and mouthfilling body. The 2011 (★★☆) is a full-bodied quaffer, pleasantly fresh and fruity.

 DRY $20 –V

Main Divide Waipara Valley Chardonnay   ★★★☆

The Main Divide range is from Pegasus Bay. The 2008 vintage (★★★☆), the first to be grown at Waipara, was fermented with indigenous yeasts and lees-aged for a year in French barriques (with no new oak). It has fresh acidity and generous, peachy, slightly honeyed flavours, showing considerable complexity and richness.

Vintage	09	08
WR	6	6
Drink	11-16	11-12

 DRY $20 AV

Man O' War Valhalla Waiheke Island Chardonnay
– see Man O' War Valhalla (in the Branded and Other White Wines section)

Man O' War Waiheke Island Chardonnay   ★★★★

Hand-picked at advanced sugar levels (24 to 25.5 brix) and fermented with indigenous yeasts in tanks (70 per cent) and old oak barrels (30 per cent), the 2010 vintage (★★★★) is fresh, flinty, crisp and dry. Tightly structured and elegant, it is a minerally style, with grapefruit and slight lime flavours that linger well. Open mid-2012+.

Vintage	10	09	DRY $28 AV
WR	7	7	
Drink	12-15	11-13	

Map Maker Marlborough Chardonnay Pure   (★★★)

Described by the producer, Staete Landt, as a 'Chablis style', the 2008 vintage (★★★) was grown at Rapaura, hand-picked, fermented in old French barriques and then matured in stainless steel tanks. Mouthfilling, it is citrusy and crisp, with a very subtle oak influence, good vigour and a dry finish.

Vintage	08	DRY $25 –V
WR	6	
Drink	11-12	

Marble Point Hanmer Springs Chardonnay   ★★★☆

Grown in North Canterbury, the 2009 vintage (★★★) was hand-picked at 25 brix and fermented in French oak casks (33 per cent new). It's maturing well, with mouthfilling body and rich, smooth, peachy, slightly buttery flavours, showing good complexity. The 2010 (★★★☆) is fleshy and forward, with peachy, slightly mealy, buttery and toasty flavours and a very rounded finish.

Vintage	10	09	DRY $25 –V
WR	6	6	
Drink	11-15	12-16	

Margrain Martinborough Chardonnay   ★★★☆

The 2009 vintage (★★★★) was fermented and matured for 10 months in French oak casks (10 per cent new). An elegant, cool-climate style, with crisp, lemony, peachy flavours, slightly minerally and tight, it's a subtle, fairly complex, food-wine style that should mature well.

Vintage	09	08	DRY $28 –V
WR	6	6	
Drink	11-13	11-13	

Marsden Bay of Islands Black Rocks Chardonnay ★★★★☆

This Kerikeri wine is outstanding in top vintages – sturdy, with concentrated, ripe sweet-fruit flavours, well seasoned with toasty French and American oak, in a lush, creamy-smooth style. The 2009 vintage (★★★★★) is complex, nutty, rich and creamy, with peachy, spicy, toasty flavours showing excellent depth, complexity and drinkability. The 2010 (★★★★☆) is still very youthful but likely to unfold well, with substantial body and ripe stone-fruit and spice flavours, creamy, nutty, smooth and rich.

Vintage	10	09	08	07	06
WR	6	6	4	5	7
Drink	12-16	11-15	11-14	P	P

DRY $36 –V

Martinborough Vineyard Chardonnay ★★★★★

Mouthfilling, peachy and mealy, this is a powerful, harmonious wine, rich and complex. Made from grapes grown on the gravelly Martinborough Terrace, including the original Mendoza-clone vines planted in 1980, it is hand-picked, fermented with indigenous yeasts and lees-aged for a year in French oak barriques (20 per cent new in 2009). The 2009 vintage (★★★★☆) is well worth cellaring. A sturdy, fragrant wine, peachy, mealy, nutty and slightly creamy, it is weighty and finely balanced, with lovely fruit characters to the fore, excellent concentration and complexity and a lasting finish.

Vintage	09	08	07	06
WR	7	7	7	7
Drink	11-15	11-14	11-13	11-12

DRY $43 AV

Matahiwi Estate Hawke's Bay Chardonnay (★★★☆)

The 2008 vintage (★★★☆) is full-bodied, with strong, citrusy flavours, a gentle seasoning of nutty oak, and a slightly creamy finish. Ready.

Vintage	08
WR	5
Drink	P

DRY $19 V+

Matahiwi Estate Holly Wairarapa Chardonnay ★★★★

The 2009 vintage (★★★★) is a single-vineyard wine, grown near Masterton and fermented with indigenous yeasts (mostly) in French oak casks (35 per cent new). Bright, light lemon/green, with a complex, oaky nose, it is rich and slightly creamy, with crisp grapefruit, lime, toast and nut flavours showing good complexity.

Vintage	09	08
WR	6	6
Drink	11-13	11-12

DRY $26 AV

Matakana Estate Matakana Chardonnay ★★★★

Estate-grown north of Auckland, the 2009 vintage (★★★★) was hand-picked and fermented and lees-aged for 10 months in French oak barriques (35 per cent new). A distinctly northern style, it is fleshy and ripe-tasting, with powerful body, sweet-fruit delights and stone-fruit and nut flavours showing good richness. Ready.

Matawhero Gisborne Chardonnay ★★★☆

The 2010 vintage (★★★) was machine-harvested at Ormond and fermented with indigenous yeasts. An unoaked style, it is mouthfilling, smooth and well-rounded, with plenty of ripe, citrusy, peachy, slightly buttery flavour, but lacks complexity.

Matua Valley Ararimu Chardonnay ★★★★☆

Ararimu ('Path to the Forest') is Matua Valley's premier Chardonnay. It is usually based on low-cropped, hand-picked grapes at Judd Estate in Gisborne, and fermented and lees-aged in French oak casks. The youthful, savoury 2009 vintage (★★★★☆) has a fragrant, toasty, buttery, oaky bouquet. Full-bodied, it possesses strong, ripe peach and grapefruit flavours, with gentle acidity, and excellent complexity and harmony. Best drinking mid-2012+.

Matua Valley Gisborne Chardonnay ★★☆

The 2009 (★★☆), labelled 'Gisborne/Hawke's Bay', is light, with vibrant fruit flavours, citrusy, peachy and smooth. An enjoyable quaffer. The 2010 vintage (★★★), from Gisborne, is lemon-scented and smooth, full-bodied, slightly peachy, toasty and creamy. An easy-drinking wine, it's bargain-priced.

Matua Valley Reserve Release Hawke's Bay Chardonnay ★★★

The 2009 vintage (★★★) is full-flavoured, with a touch of complexity. Pale yellow, it is soft and smooth, peachy, buttery and slightly honeyed. Ready.

Maude Mt Maude Family Vineyard Chardonnay (★★★★)

The fleshy, elegant 2009 vintage (★★★★) was grown in the Mt Maude Vineyard at Wanaka. Matured in seasoned French oak casks, it is fresh and youthful. Creamy-textured, with citrusy, slightly mealy and biscuity flavours, it has very good complexity and potential.

Michael Ramon Matakana Chardonnay (★★★★☆)

Estate-grown, hand-picked and barrel-fermented, the 2010 vintage (★★★★☆) is an elegant wine with a lovely, mealy, nutty complexity. Full-bodied, peachy and toasty, it has a strong French oak influence, but also rich fruit to match.

DRY $45 –V

Michelle Richardson Central Otago Chardonnay   ★★★★☆

The 2010 vintage (★★★★☆) is a superb example of an elegant, rather than 'in your face', style
of Chardonnay ('Chablis with oak' was the style goal). Grown in the Cromwell Basin, it was
mostly (70 per cent) tank-fermented, but 30 per cent was fermented in one-year-old barrels, and
all of the blend was barrel-matured (10 per cent new). Lemon-scented, it is fresh and citrusy,
with a subtle seasoning of oak and lovely poise, delicacy and length. Instantly appealing.

DRY $35 –V

Mill Road Hawke's Bay Chardonnay   ★★

Priced right, Morton Estate's bottom-tier, non-vintage Chardonnay typically offers lively, citrusy
fruit characters in an uncomplicated style, fresh and crisp.

DRY $13 AV

Mills Reef Elspeth Hawke's Bay Chardonnay   ★★★★☆

Mills Reef's flagship Hawke's Bay Chardonnay is consistently rewarding and a classic regional
style. The 2009 vintage (★★★★), labelled 'Gimblett Gravels', is a single-vineyard wine, hand-
picked in Mere Road and fermented and matured for 11 months in French oak barrels (60 per
cent new). Still tight and youthful, it offers concentrated grapefruit, peach and toast flavours,
with a fresh, minerally streak. The 2010 (★★★★☆) is a blend of Gimblett Gravels (80 per cent)
and coastal Te Awanga (20 per cent) grapes. Barrel-fermented (in French oak hogsheads, 76 per
cent new) and oak-aged for 11 months, it is mouthfilling, rich and harmonious, with strong,
ripe stone-fruit flavours, toasty oak and fresh acidity. Well worth cellaring.

Vintage	10	09
WR	7	6
Drink	11-15	11-14

DRY $30 AV

Mills Reef Hawke's Bay Chardonnay   ★★★

Mills Reef's bottom-tier Chardonnay is an easy-drinking Hawke's Bay wine. Grown at Meeanee,
the 2009 vintage (★★★) was mostly handled in tanks, but 43 per cent of the blend was briefly
barrel-aged. It's a mouthfilling, fruity and flavoursome wine, ripe, peachy and smooth (3.7
grams/litre of residual sugar), with a touch of toasty oak and lots of drink-young appeal. (The
2010 is 50 per cent barrel-fermented.)

Vintage	10
WR	7
Drink	11-14

DRY $17 AV

Mills Reef Reserve Hawke's Bay Chardonnay   ★★★☆

Mills Reef's middle-tier Chardonnay. The 2010 vintage (★★★☆) was grown in three vineyards
at Meeanee and fermented and matured for nine months in a 50:50 split of French and
American oak hogsheads (12 per cent new). Pale yellow, it is peachy and toasty, in a moderately
complex, slightly buttery, upfront style. Still developing, it's worth cellaring to mid-2012+.

Vintage	10
WR	7
Drink	11-15

DRY $24 AV

Millton Clos de Ste Anne Chardonnay – see Clos de Ste Anne Chardonnay

Millton Crazy by Nature Shotberry Chardonnay ★★★

Certified organic. This 'glass of Gisborne sunshine' is a fruit-driven style, fermented in tanks (90 per cent) and barrels (10 per cent), with no use of new oak. Very fresh and vibrant, the 2010 (★★★) is full-bodied, citrusy, peachy and smooth (4 grams/litre of residual sugar), with drink-young appeal.

Vintage	10
WR	6
Drink	11-16

DRY $20 –V

Millton Gisborne Chardonnay Opou Vineyard ★★★★

Certified organic, this is Millton's middle-tier Chardonnay. Full of personality, the 2009 vintage (★★★★☆) was hand-picked and fermented with indigenous yeasts in French oak casks (20 per cent new). The bouquet is very fragrant, creamy and inviting; the palate is mouthfilling and rich, with good acid spine and concentrated, ripe-fruit flavours of citrus fruits, peaches and nuts. It's a finely poised wine, for drinking now or cellaring.

Vintage	09	08	07	06
WR	6	6	7	6
Drink	11-16	11-14	11-14	11-12

DRY $27 AV

Millton Gisborne Chardonnay Riverpoint Vineyard ★★★

The 2008 vintage (★★★) was grown organically near the sea, hand-picked and lightly oaked. It's a medium-bodied, easy-drinking wine, fruity and harmonious, with good depth of ripe, peachy flavours, a vague hint of honey and a well-rounded finish.

Vintage	08	07	06
WR	6	6	5
Drink	P	P	P

DRY $20 –V

Mission Hawke's Bay Chardonnay ★★★

Hawke's Bay winemaker Paul Mooney can make Chardonnay taste delicious at just a few months old. However, the 2009 (★★☆) is a lesser vintage. Tank-fermented and lees-aged for a year, it is fresh and citrusy, slightly limey and creamy, in a straightforward, fruit-driven style offering pleasant, easy drinking.

DRY $19 AV

Mission Jewelstone Hawke's Bay Chardonnay ★★★★★

This wine has shone since the super-stylish 2002 vintage (★★★★★), grown in Central Hawke's Bay. The 2008 vintage (★★★★), grown in the Gimblett Gravels, is a stylish wine with mouthfilling body, strong, ripe tropical-fruit flavours, biscuity oak and a tight, crisp finish. The 2009 (★★★★☆) was grown at Ohiti Road, hand-picked, and fermented and lees-aged for

17 months in French oak barrels (40 per cent new). Youthful in colour, it is mouthfilling and rich, with concentrated, grapefruit-like flavours, slightly spicy and nutty, finely integrated oak, a creamy texture and excellent poise and potential.

Vintage	09	08	07	06
WR	7	5	6	5
Drink	12-20	11-16	11-13	P

DRY $34 V+

Mission Reserve Hawke's Bay Chardonnay ★★★★

For Mission's middle-tier Chardonnay, the style goal is a wine that 'emphasises fruit characters rather than oak, but offers some of the benefits of fermentation and maturation in wood'. Hand-picked at Ohiti Road and in the Gimblett Gravels, the 2010 vintage (★★★★) was fermented and lees-aged for 10 months in French oak barriques (25 per cent new). A tight, elegant, finely poised wine, it is citrusy, with strong, grapefruit-like flavours and buttery, nutty notes adding complexity. Worth cellaring.

Vintage	10	09	08	07	06
WR	5	7	7	7	5
Drink	12-15	11-15	11-15	P	P

DRY $25 AV

Mission Vineyard Selection Chardonnay ★★★★

The 2008 (★★★☆) was grown in the Gimblett Gravels, the 2009 (★★★★★) in Central Hawke's Bay. The 2010 vintage (★★★★) was grown in 'several vineyards', 50 per cent barrel-fermented, and lees-aged for 15 months. A stylish wine, it has fresh, ripe grapefruit and peach flavours, slightly mealy and creamy, a fine thread of acidity, and excellent richness and harmony. Consistently good value.

DRY $22 V+

Moana Park Hawke's Bay Chardonnay (★★★)

The 2010 vintage (★★★) was grown at Te Awanga and half tank, half barrel-fermented. Mouthfilling, vibrantly fruity, peachy and smooth, with slightly buttery and toasty notes adding interest, it's enjoyable young.

DRY $19 AV

Moana Park Vineyard Tribute Gimblett Road Chardonnay ★★★★

The impressive 2009 vintage (★★★★☆) was hand-picked in the Gimblett Gravels, Hawke's Bay, and fermented – mostly with indigenous yeasts – in French oak barriques (30 per cent new). A powerful wine, drinking well from the start, it is fragrant and full-bodied, with concentrated, ripe flavours of stone-fruit, butterscotch and nuts, buttery, mealy notes adding complexity, and a rich, rounded finish.

DRY $30 –V

Momo Marlborough Chardonnay

BioGro certified, the 2010 vintage (★★★★) from Seresin was estate-grown in the Home and Raupo Creek vineyards, hand-picked, fermented with indigenous yeasts in seasoned French oak casks, and barrel-aged for 11 months. Youthful in colour, rich, creamy-textured and smooth, it shows unusual complexity and harmony for a $20 Chardonnay. A weighty wine with grapefruit, spice and nut flavours, it is already delicious. A top buy.

Vintage	10
WR	7
Drink	11-15

 DRY $20 V+

Monkey Bay Gisborne Chardonnay

From Constellation NZ, this wine is made without oak or malolactic fermentation, 'to ensure a vibrant, fruit-driven flavour profile'. It's typically an easy-drinking, simple wine with lemony, appley flavours and a very smooth finish.

MED/DRY $17 –V

Monowai Crownthorpe Hawke's Bay Chardonnay (★★★☆)

Grown in inland Hawke's Bay, the 2010 vintage (★★★☆) was handled in a mix of tanks (40 per cent) and French oak casks (60 per cent). Full-bodied and slightly creamy, it shows good weight and roundness, with grapefruit, peach and lime flavours, balanced acidity and a subtle oak influence. Drink now onwards.

Vintage	10
WR	6
Drink	11-16

 DRY $18 V+

Montana Festival Block Gisborne Chardonnay (★★☆)

The 'Festival Block' brand from Pernod Ricard NZ is for 'on-premise' (restaurant) sale only, so is not rated here for price or value. The 2009 vintage (★★☆) is an unoaked style, blended with Viognier (8.5 per cent). It's a fresh and lively, citrusy wine made in a straightforward but enjoyably fruity style.

DRY $? V?

Montana Gisborne Chardonnay ★★☆

From Pernod Ricard NZ, this once hugely popular Chardonnay is made in an undemanding style, fruity and smooth. Tank-fermented, with no use of oak, it's straightforward – crisp, fresh and dry. (Note: at its average price in supermarkets of under $10, it has typically delivered fine value.)

 DRY $18 –V

Morton Estate Black Label Hawke's Bay Chardonnay ★★★★☆

Grown principally in the company's cool, elevated Riverview Vineyard at Mangatahi, this can be a very classy Chardonnay, although some recent releases did not achieve the standard of a decade ago. At its best, it's a powerful wine, robust and awash with flavour, yet also highly refined, with beautifully intense citrusy fruit, firm acid spine and the structure to flourish with age. It is fully barrel-fermented, and given the wine's concentrated fruit characters, the French oak barriques are 100 per cent new. The 2002 was the first to include fruit from Matapiro – over the river from Riverview. The 2007 vintage (★★★★★) is the best since 2002: very elegant, sweet-fruited and finely poised, with rich grapefruit and nut flavours, a minerally thread, and a long, harmonious finish.

Vintage	07	06	05	04
WR	7	5	NM	6
Drink	11-14	11-12	NM	P

DRY $35 –V

Morton Estate Coniglio Chardonnay – see Coniglio Hawke's Bay Chardonnay

Morton Estate Private Reserve Hawke's Bay Chardonnay   ★★★

The 2008 vintage (★★★☆) is the best since 2002. The bouquet is creamy and nutty, with some complexity; the palate is mouthfilling and smooth, with ripe, peachy, nutty flavours, showing good harmony. Ready.

Vintage	08
WR	6
Drink	11-14

DRY $21 –V

Morton Estate Three Vineyards Hawke's Bay Chardonnay   ★★★

The 'three vineyards' include Tantallon, Morton's warmest vineyard, down on the Heretaunga Plains (which gives 'a more tropical, fruit-forward style'), and the cooler Kinross and Riverview vineyards. The 2008 vintage (★★☆) is light yellow, with mouthfilling body and citrusy, slightly honeyed flavours, showing a clear botrytis influence.

Vintage	08	07
WR	6	6
Drink	11-13	11-12

DRY $20 –V

Morton Estate White Label Hawke's Bay Chardonnay   ★★★☆

Morton Estate's best-known Chardonnay is typically a good buy. Fermented and lees-aged in French oak barriques, the 2009 vintage (★★★☆) is drinking well now, with mouthfilling body and fresh, slightly mealy and biscuity flavours, showing good complexity, depth and harmony.

Vintage	09	08
WR	6	6
Drink	11-13	11-12

DRY $18 V+

Mountford Estate Chardonnay   ★★★★☆

Estate-grown and barrel-fermented, the 2008 (★★★★☆) is one of Waipara's finest white wines of the vintage. Light lemon/green, it is fragrant, with impressive body and deep, peachy flavours, very rich and rounded.

DRY $57 –V

Mount Riley Marlborough Chardonnay   ★★★

The 2009 vintage (★★★☆) is an elegant, fruit-driven style, fermented in an even split of tanks and French oak casks. Lees-aged for seven months, it's delicious young, with vibrant, peachy flavours to the fore, a hint of butterscotch and fresh, appetising acidity.

DRY $18 AV

Mount Riley Seventeen Valley Marlborough Chardonnay   ★★★★

The 2009 vintage (★★★★★) is the best yet. Hand-picked, fermented with indigenous yeasts in new and seasoned French oak casks, with extensive lees-stirring and full malolactic fermentation, it is classy and concentrated, with a rich bouquet and lovely depth of ripe, peachy, slightly appley and spicy flavours, a distinct hint of butterscotch, and notable complexity and harmony.

Vintage	09
WR	7
Drink	11-16

DRY $30 –V

Mt Difficulty Central Otago Chardonnay   ★★★☆

Maturing well, the 2008 vintage (★★★☆) was grown at Bannockburn and barrel-aged for nine months. Pale yellow, it is mouthfilling and citrusy, slightly nutty and minerally, with considerable complexity.

DRY $35 –V

Mt Hector Hawke's Bay Chardonnay   ★★☆

From Matahiwi, the easy-drinking 2009 vintage (★★☆) is full-bodied and fruity, with peachy, slightly honeyed flavours, smooth and ready. Priced right.

Vintage	09
WR	5
Drink	11-13

DRY $13 V+

Mudbrick Vineyard Reserve Waiheke Island Chardonnay   ★★★★☆

The outstanding 2010 vintage (★★★★★) was grown at Church Bay and Onetangi, hand-harvested at 25 brix, fermented with indigenous yeasts, and matured in French oak barrels (40 per cent new). Very powerful (15.2 per cent alcohol), it's already delicious, with layers of peachy, figgy, creamy flavour, showing notable ripeness and depth.

Vintage	10	09	08
WR	7	7	7
Drink	12-15	11-13	11-12

DRY $42 –V

Muddy Water Growers' Series Fitzgerald Vineyard Chardonnay   (★★★☆)

Grown at Waipara, hand-picked and fermented with indigenous yeasts in French oak casks (10 per cent new), the 2008 vintage (★★★☆) has firm acid spine, strong, lemony flavours and a subtle oak influence in a distinctly cool-climate, minerally, flinty style.

Vintage	10
WR	6
Drink	11-16

DRY $23 AV

Muddy Water Waipara Chardonnay   ★★★★☆

The 2009 vintage (★★★★☆) was hand-picked at 23–25 brix and fermented with indigenous yeasts in French oak barriques and puncheons (15 per cent new). A classy, minerally wine with rich grapefruit and nut flavours, woven with fresh acidity, it is vibrantly fruity, with good harmony and the prospect of a long life ahead. The 2010 (★★★★☆) is very youthful, with concentrated, ripe stone-fruit flavours, well-integrated oak and excellent richness, ripeness and roundness.

Vintage	10	09	08	07	06
WR	6	7	6	7	7
Drink	11-18	11-22	11-18	11-15	11-12

DRY $32 AV

Murdoch James Blue Rock Chardonnay   ★★★

Grown in Martinborough, the 2009 vintage (★★★) is an unwooded style. Estate-grown in the Blue Rock Vineyard and lees-stirred in tanks, it is fresh and full-bodied (14.5 per cent alcohol), with pleasant, lemony, peachy flavours, crisp underlying acidity and a smooth finish.

DRY $25 –V

Murrays Road Marlborough Chardonnay   (★★★☆)

Lively and fruity, the 2009 vintage (★★★☆) is a moderately complex style with very good depth of ripe, citrusy, peachy flavour and a slightly buttery finish. Drink now.

DRY $26 –V

Nautilus Marlborough Chardonnay   ★★★★☆

This stylish wine has fresh, strong, citrusy flavours and finely integrated oak. The 2010 vintage (★★★★☆) was grown in the Wairau Valley, hand-picked, and fermented and lees-aged in French oak barriques (22 per cent new). An elegant, finely poised wine that should unfold well, it is vibrant, citrusy, peachy and nutty, with barrel-ferment complexity and good richness through the palate. Open mid-2012+.

Vintage	10	09	08	07	06
WR	7	7	7	7	6
Drink	11-15	11-14	11-13	11-12	P

DRY $34 AV

Neudorf Moutere Chardonnay ★★★★★

Superbly rich but not overblown, with arrestingly intense flavours enlivened with fine acidity, this rare, multi-faceted Nelson wine enjoys a reputation second to none among New Zealand Chardonnays. Grown in clay soils threaded with gravel at Upper Moutere, it is hand-harvested from vines up to 31 years old, fermented with indigenous yeasts, and lees-aged, with regular stirring, for a year in French oak barriques and puncheons (38 per cent new in 2009 and 24 per cent new in 2010). The 2010 vintage (★★★★★) has a highly fragrant, complex bouquet. Still a baby, it is full-bodied and vibrant, minerally and poised, with sweet-fruit delights, fresh, highly complex peach, fig and spice flavours, and notable drive and presence. It's crying out for cellaring; open 2013+.

Vintage	10	09	08	07	06	05	04	03	02	
WR	7	7	6	7	7	6	6	7	6	
Drink	11-18	11-17	11-16	11-15	11-16	11-15	11-14	11-13	11-13	

 DRY $56 AV

Neudorf Nelson Chardonnay ★★★★☆

Overshadowed by its famous stablemate (above), this regional blend is a fine Chardonnay in its own right. Grown at Upper Moutere (mostly), but also at Kina, on the coast, and at Brightwater, on the Waimea Plains, it is fermented with indigenous yeasts in French oak casks (20 per cent new in 2010), and given a full, softening malolactic fermentation. The 2010 vintage (★★★★☆) is rich and very vibrant. Youthful, with a distinct hint of butterscotch, it is crisp, peachy and slightly spicy, with finely balanced oak, good acid drive and an invitingly fragrant bouquet. Open mid-2012+.

Vintage	10	09	08	07	06
WR	6	7	6	6	7
Drink	11-17	11-17	11-16	11-15	11-14

 DRY $29 V+

Ngatarawa Alwyn Hawke's Bay Chardonnay ★★★★★

Ngatarawa's premier Chardonnay is based on estate-grown, hand-picked grapes, supplemented with fruit from a neighbouring grower's vineyard. Fermented and lees-aged for a year in French oak barriques, with no use of malolactic fermentation, it is typically an arrestingly bold, highly concentrated wine that takes years to reveal its full class and complexity. Relatively restrained, the 2009 vintage (★★★★☆) is rich, with grapefruit, nut and slight lime flavours to the fore, creamy and finely textured. It's a very subtle and satisfying wine, harmonious and lingering.

Vintage	09	08	07	06
WR	6	NM	7	7
Drink	11-14	NM	11-12	11

 DRY $35 AV

Ngatarawa Silks Hawke's Bay Chardonnay ★★★

The 2009 vintage (★★★) is a typical regional style – mouthfilling, ripe, citrusy and peachy, in a fresh, fruit-driven style with a hint of toasty oak, good depth and a rounded finish.

Vintage	09	08	07	06
WR	6	7	6	6
Drink	11-13	11-12	11	P

 DRY $19 AV

Ngatarawa Stables Hawke's Bay Chardonnay   ★★☆

Ngatarawa's lower-tier Chardonnay is made for easy drinking. The 2010 vintage (★★☆) is a fruit-driven style, peachy, citrusy and straightforward, with a hint of honey and drink-young appeal.

DRY $16 AV

Ngatarawa Stables Reserve Hawke's Bay Chardonnay   ★★★☆

The 2010 vintage (★★★☆) is a sturdy, full-flavoured wine, peachy and slightly toasty, with good balance and considerable complexity. It's likely to be at its best from mid-2012+.

DRY $22 AV

Nga Waka Home Block Chardonnay   ★★★★

This single-vineyard Martinborough wine is based on mature vines and fermented and lees-aged in French oak barriques. At its best, it is an authoritative wine, weighty and concentrated, with grapefruit and toast flavours, a minerally character and great personality. The pale straw 2009 (★★★☆) is fleshy and generous, with rounded, peachy, creamy flavours, showing considerable complexity, but is relatively forward, and lacks the intensity and structure of top vintages.

Vintage	09	08	07	06
WR	7	NM	7	7
Drink	12+	NM	11+	11+

DRY $35 –V

Nga Waka Martinborough Chardonnay   ★★★★☆

Following the launch of the flagship label (above), the price of this consistently rewarding wine was trimmed and it now offers great value and drink-young appeal. The 2010 vintage (★★★★☆) is richly fragrant, with slight butterscotch aromas. Mouthfilling and fleshy, it is sweet-fruited, with stone-fruit flavours showing lovely harmony and richness. Drink now onwards.

Vintage	10	09	08
WR	7	7	7
Drink	12+	11+	11+

DRY $25 V+

Nikau Point Reserve Hawke's Bay Chardonnay   ★★★

The 'One Tree Hill Vineyards' in small print is a division of Morton Estate. The 2008 vintage (★★★☆) has strong grapefruit and peach flavours and a slightly creamy texture. The 2009 (★★☆) is fresh, crisp and lemony, in a simple, but vibrantly fruity and lively, style.

Vintage	09	08
WR	6	7
Drink	11-13	P

DRY $16 V+

Nobilo Regional Collection Gisborne Chardonnay   (★★★)

Tank-fermented and matured 'on' oak, with some malolactic fermentation and lees-aging, the 2008 vintage (★★★) is a creamy-textured wine. Mouthfilling, it is ripe, peachy and slightly buttery, with plenty of flavour and a smooth finish.

 DRY $17 AV

Northfield Frog Rock Waipara Chardonnay   ★★★☆

The 2009 vintage (★★★) has buttery aromas leading into a peachy, slightly honeyed, full-flavoured wine, with a sweet, toasty oak influence and fresh acidity.

 DRY $21 AV

Oak Hill Matakana Chardonnay   (★★★☆)

The fleshy, barrel-fermented 2009 vintage (★★★☆) has a powerful, nutty oak influence (French, one-third new). It offers very good depth of ripe stone-fruit flavours and a well-rounded texture.

DRY $24 AV

Obsidian Waiheke Island Chardonnay   ★★★★☆

The 2009 vintage (★★★★☆) is a single-vineyard wine, hand-harvested and fermented and lees-aged for eight months in French oak barriques (25 per cent new). Refined, full-bodied and finely textured, with peach and grapefruit flavours, it has excellent ripeness, delicacy and freshness, with a slightly creamy richness and lovely harmony. The 2010 (★★★★) is also stylish, with strong, ripe, citrusy, peachy, slightly nutty flavours, showing good complexity. Rich and subtle, it's well worth cellaring.

Vintage	10	09	08	07
WR	7	6	6	6
Drink	11-15	11-15	11-14	11-12

 DRY $35 –V

Odyssey Gisborne Chardonnay   ★★☆

A drink-young style, this is a crisp, fruity, easy-drinking wine. The 2009 vintage (★★☆) was grown in the Kawatiri Vineyard and mostly handled in tanks (10 per cent was fermented in seasoned oak casks). Pale gold, it is mouthfilling and peachy, with a slightly honeyed bouquet and flavours. Ready.

 DRY $19 –V

Odyssey Reserve Iliad Gisborne Chardonnay   ★★★★★

Top vintages represent Gisborne Chardonnay at its finest. Hand-picked from mature vines in the Kawatiri Vineyard at Hexton and fermented and lees-aged in French oak barriques (30 per cent new), the 2010 vintage (★★★★★) has a slightly creamy and toasty bouquet leading into a mouthfilling, rich, sweet-fruited wine. Very elegant, youthful and harmonious, it has concentrated stone-fruit, grapefruit and slight spice flavours, finely integrated oak and a long, poised finish. Drink mid-2012+.

Vintage	10	09	08	07	06
WR	6	6	6	7	6
Drink	11-15	11-13	11-13	11-12	P

 DRY $30 V+

Ohinemuri Estate Reserve Patutahi Chardonnay   ★★★☆

Fermented in barrels (72 per cent) and tanks, and barrel-aged for six months, the 2009 vintage (★★★★) is mouthfilling, with vibrant, ripe stone-fruit and pear flavours. It was slightly oaky in its youth, but powerful and sweet-fruited, with excellent weight, freshness and depth. Tasted prior to bottling (and so not rated), the 2010 looked very promising – full-bodied, rich and soft, with ripe, peachy, citrusy flavours, slightly buttery, fresh and smooth.

Vintage	09
WR	6
Drink	11-15

 DRY $24 AV

Old Coach Road Nelson Chardonnay   ★★★

Tank-fermented and mostly American oak-matured, with lots of lees-stirring, this affordable wine from Seifried Estate is an upfront, high-flavoured style that slides down very easily. The 2009 vintage (★★★) is typically fresh, lemony and flavoursome, with a smooth finish and drink-young appeal.

 DRY $17 AV

Old Coach Road Unoaked Nelson Chardonnay   ★★☆

Seifried Estate's low-priced Chardonnay. The 2010 vintage (★★★), bottled by July, has strong, crisp, citrusy flavours, showing good vigour and freshness.

 DRY $15 AV

Olssens Charcoal Joe Central Otago Chardonnay   ★★★☆

Named after a nineteenth-century goldminer, this wine is hand-picked at Bannockburn, in Central Otago, and fermented and matured in French oak barriques (15 per cent new in 2009). The 2009 vintage (★★★★) is one of the best yet. Fleshy, with ripe grapefruit-like flavours, showing good, oak-derived complexity, it has a hint of butterscotch, a slightly creamy texture and excellent depth. It's drinking well now.

Vintage	09
WR	6
Drink	15-18

 DRY $33 –V

Omaka Springs Falveys Vineyard Marlborough Chardonnay   ★★★

The 2009 vintage (★★★) was estate-grown on the south side of the Wairau Valley and French oak-matured for a year. Mouthfilling and smooth, it's a ripe, citrusy, slightly spicy and creamy wine, with some complexity.

Vintage	09	08
WR	6	7
Drink	11-13	11-12

DRY $17 AV

Opihi Vineyard South Canterbury Chardonnay   (★★☆)

The 2009 vintage (★★☆) is rare – only 44 cases were produced. Hand-harvested and handled without oak, it has some creamy notes, with moderately ripe, appley flavours, fresh acidity and a crisp, dry finish.

DRY $22 –V

Oyster Bay Marlborough Chardonnay   ★★★☆

From Delegat's, this wine is designed to showcase Marlborough's incisive fruit flavours. Fifty per cent of the blend is barrel-fermented, but all of the wine spends six months in casks (mostly French), with weekly lees-stirring. It typically offers ripe grapefruit-like flavours, slightly buttery and crisp, with creamy, toasty elements adding complexity.

DRY $20 AV

Palliser Estate Martinborough Chardonnay   ★★★★

Rather than power, the key attributes of this wine are delicacy and finesse. A celebration of rich, ripe fruit flavours, it is gently seasoned with French oak, producing a delicious wine with subtle winemaking input and concentrated varietal flavours. The 2008 vintage (★★★★) is creamy-textured, with concentrated, citrusy, peachy flavours to the fore, a subtle, biscuity oak influence and excellent harmony.

Vintage	08	07	06	05
WR	7	6	6	5
Drink	11-12	11-12	P	P

DRY $28 AV

Palliser Pencarrow Chardonnay – see Pencarrow Martinborough Chardonnay

Paritua Hawke's Bay Chardonnay   ★★★★☆

The 2009 vintage (★★★★☆) was estate-grown at Maraekakaho, hand-harvested and barrel-aged for 10 months. The bouquet shows good complexity; the palate is slightly creamy, with concentrated grapefruit and nut flavours, rich and rounded. It's delicious now.

DRY $34 AV

Parr & Simpson Limestone Bay Barrique Fermented Chardonnay   ★★★★

From a site overlooking Golden Bay, in Nelson, this wine exhibits strong personality. The 2009 vintage (★★★★☆) was hand-picked at 23.8 brix and fermented and lees-stirred for 10 months in French oak barriques (25 per cent new). It is tightly coiled and concentrated, lemony and mealy, with finely integrated oak, crisp, minerally notes and a dry, long finish. The 2010 (★★★☆) was handled in seasoned French oak casks. Mouthfilling, it is very tautly structured, with lemony, slightly nutty and minerally flavours, woven with steely acidity. A subtle, flinty, age-worthy wine, it's worth cellaring to 2013+.

DRY $23 V+

Passage Rock Barrel Fermented Gisborne Chardonnay   ★★★☆

Sturdy, with ripe, citrusy flavours and considerable complexity, the 2009 vintage (★★★☆) was fermented and aged for six months in French oak barrels. It's a youthful, full-flavoured wine, for drinking now or cellaring.

 DRY $20 AV

Passage Rock Waiheke Island Chardonnay   ★★★★

The 2010 vintage (★★★★) has a nutty, slightly creamy bouquet. Finely textured, it's a sweet-fruited wine with peachy, appley flavours showing very good depth and complexity.

 DRY $40 –V

Peacock Sky Chardonnay   (★★★☆)

Grown on Waiheke Island and matured for five months in new French and American oak casks, the 2009 vintage (★★★☆) is an upfront style with generous, ripe flavours, very toasty and buttery, and a creamy-smooth finish.

Vintage	09
WR	5
Drink	11-12

DRY $30 –V

Pegasus Bay Chardonnay   ★★★★★

Strapping yet delicate, richly flavoured yet subtle, this sophisticated wine is one of the country's best Chardonnays grown south of Marlborough. Muscular and taut, it typically offers a seamless array of fresh, crisp, citrusy, biscuity, complex flavours and great concentration and length. Estate-grown at Waipara, it is based almost entirely on mature Mendoza-clone vines, fermented with indigenous yeasts, given a full, softening malolactic fermentation and matured for a year on its yeast lees in barrels (French oak puncheons, 30 per cent new in 2008). The 2008 vintage (★★★★) is still taut and youthful. Tightly structured, with mouthfilling body and strong, vibrant, grapefruit-like flavours, it is woven with fresh, flinty acidity, with mealy, nutty notes adding complexity.

Vintage	09	08	07	06	05	04
WR	7	6	6	6	6	6
Drink	11-17	11-15	11-16	11-14	11-12	P

 DRY $36 AV

Pegasus Bay Virtuoso Chardonnay   ★★★★☆

The 2008 vintage (★★★★☆) represents the 'five best barrels' made from the company's 24-year-old Mendoza clone vines at Waipara. Fermented with indigenous yeasts, lees-aged for a year in French oak barrels, then matured in tanks on light lees for a further eight months before bottling, it was then bottle-aged prior to its release in 2011. Rich and tightly structured, it has a fragrant, nutty bouquet, with indigenous yeast complexity, and concentrated grapefruit, peach and nut flavours, crisp and minerally. A cool-climate style with real verve and 'drive', it's still unfolding.

 DRY $49 –V

Pencarrow Martinborough Chardonnay   ★★★☆

Pencarrow is Palliser Estate's second-tier label. The 2010 vintage (★★★) is an attractively scented, fruit-driven style, citrusy and smooth. A fresh, youthful middleweight, it shows some leesy complexity and decent depth.

Penny Lane Pure Chardonnay   ★★☆

From Morton Estate, the easy-drinking 2009 vintage (★★☆) is a Hawke's Bay wine, lemon-scented, with fresh, smooth flavours. A pleasant quaffer.

People's, The, Chardonnay   (★★★)

From Constellation NZ, the 2009 vintage (★★★) is a Marlborough wine, made in a buttery, toasty, upfront, rather old-fashioned style. Sweetly oaked, it is lemony and peachy, with lots of flavour.

Peregrine Central Otago Chardonnay   ★★★★

The 2009 vintage (★★★★) was hand-picked and fermented in French oak casks (45 per cent new). Mouthfilling and slightly creamy, with ripe, citrusy, appley, spicy flavours showing good immediacy, it is a finely balanced, subtle wine, crisp, tight and lingering.

Pied Stilt Nelson Chardonnay   (★★★★)

The 2010 vintage (★★★★) is a single-vineyard wine, hand-picked at Motueka and fermented in an even split of tanks and new French oak barrels. Weighty and creamy-textured, with grapefruit and slight spice flavours, showing considerable complexity, it's a powerful wine, still evolving; open mid-2012+.

Poderi Crisci Chardonnay   ★★★

Grown on Waiheke Island, the 2009 vintage (★★★) is crisp and lively, with lemony, appley flavours, showing some complexity. The 2010 (★★★) is light yellow, mouthfilling, fleshy and rounded, with ripe-fruit flavours, some nutty complexity and a smooth finish.

DRY $42 –V

Pukeora Estate Chardonnay   ★★★

Grown in Central Hawke's Bay, this wine was previously sold under the San Hill label. The 2010 vintage (★★★☆) is the best yet – and fine value. Fermented in seasoned French oak barriques (90 per cent) and tanks (10 per cent), it has fresh, citrusy aromas and flavours, in a mouthfilling (14.9 per cent alcohol), fruit-driven style, vibrant and crisp, with a touch of mealy, biscuity complexity.

Vintage	10
WR	6
Drink	11-15

DRY $15 V+

Pukeora Estate Ruahine Range Chardonnay   (★★★★☆)

Grown and hand-picked in Central Hawke's Bay, the 2010 vintage (★★★★☆) was fermented with indigenous yeasts and matured for 10 months in French oak barriques (50 per cent new). It's a very full-bodied wine (14.9 per cent alcohol), sweet-fruited, with deep, ripe stone-fruit flavours, woven with fresh acidity, showing an almost honeyed richness. Drink mid-2012+.

Vintage	10
WR	6
Drink	11-15

DRY $20 V+

Pyramid Valley Vineyards Field of Fire Chardonnay   (★★★★☆)

Estate-grown in North Canterbury, the 2008 vintage (★★★★☆) is a rare wine – only one puncheon was produced. Barrel-aged for 10 months, then matured for a further 16 months in tank, it was bottled unfined and unfiltered. Pale gold, it is highly distinctive, coupling ripe-fruit characters with very crisp acidity. Sturdy and rich, with hugely concentrated peach and apricot flavours, it's a powerful wine with loads of personality.

 DRY $97 –V

Ransom Cosmos Matakana Chardonnay   (★★★)

Enjoyable now, the 2008 vintage (★★★) was fermented in a 50:50 split of tanks and barriques, and all of the blend was barrel-aged. Pale yellow, it is full-bodied, with fresh, citrusy, slightly buttery flavours, showing some complexity and good depth.

DRY $27 –V

Rapaura Springs Gisborne Chardonnay   (★★★)

The 2010 vintage (★★★) is fresh and youthful, with mouthfilling body and ripe, peachy, citrusy, slightly toasty flavours, balanced for easy, satisfying drinking.

DRY $19 AV

Rapaura Springs Marlborough Chardonnay   (★★★★)

The 2008 vintage (★★★★) was barrel-fermented and lees-aged for six months. Mouthfilling and vibrantly fruity, it has generous, sweet-fruit flavours, a subtle oak influence and a rounded, slightly buttery finish.

Vintage	08
WR	5
Drink	11-12

DRY $22 V+

Redmetal Vineyards Hawke's Bay Chardonnay   ★★★☆

Made in an easy-drinking style, the 2010 vintage (★★★☆) is full-bodied and smooth, with very good depth of fresh, ripe, peachy flavours, slightly biscuity and toasty, and a well-rounded finish.

Vintage	10
WR	5
Drink	11-13

 DRY $20 AV

Renato Nelson Chardonnay ★★★★

Estate-grown on the Kina Peninsula, hand-picked and fully barrel-fermented (French, 20 per cent new), the 2010 vintage (★★★★) is a single-vineyard wine, powerful and creamy-textured. Still slightly woody, it is fleshy and full of potential, with strong, ripe stone-fruit flavours seasoned with nutty French oak.

Vintage	10	09	08
WR	6	7	6
Drink	11-15	11-15	11-12

 DRY $24 V+

Richardson Central Otago Chardonnay – see Michelle Richardson Central Otago Chardonnay

Richmond Plains Nelson Chardonnay ★★★

Certified organic, the 2008 vintage (★★★) is a crisp, fruit-driven style with satisfying depth of fresh, dry, citrusy, appley flavours. (The 2009 was mostly handled in tanks, but 20 per cent of the blend was barrel-aged.)

Vintage	09	08	07	06
WR	6	5	6	5
Drink	11-14	11-12	P	P

 DRY $20 –V

Rimu Grove Nelson Chardonnay ★★★★

This wine is always full of personality. Estate-grown near the coast in the Moutere hills and fermented and lees-aged in French oak casks, the 2009 vintage (★★★☆) is a pale straw, full-bodied, slightly creamy wine, with citrusy, peachy flavours, showing very good texture and depth.

Vintage	09	08	07	06
WR	6	6	7	7
Drink	11-18	11-17	11-21	11-20

 DRY $30 –V

Riverby Estate Marlborough Chardonnay ★★★★

This single-vineyard wine is grown in the heart of the Wairau Valley. The 2009 vintage (★★★★), based on 21-year-old, ungrafted vines, was fully fermented in French oak casks (20 per cent new). It's a fragrant, full-bodied wine with rich stone-fruit characters, fresh acidity and an excellent balance of ripe-fruit and nutty oak flavours.

Vintage	09	08	07	06
WR	7	6	7	7
Drink	11-13	11-12	P	P

DRY $29 AV

River Farm Godfrey Road Marlborough Chardonnay   (★★★★)

The full-bodied, creamy-smooth 2009 vintage (★★★★) is a single-vineyard wine, hand-picked at 24.7 brix, fermented with indigenous yeasts in French oak barriques, and barrel-aged for 11 months. It's a weighty, complex wine with concentrated, peachy, biscuity flavours, a hint of butterscotch (from 100 per cent malolactic fermentation) and a dry, finely balanced finish. Worth cellaring.

Vintage	09
WR	6
Drink	11-15

DRY $29 AV

Road Works Waiheke Island Chardonnay   (★★★☆)

The 2008 vintage (★★★☆) is lemon-scented, with substantial body and strong, citrusy, slightly toasty flavours. A sturdy wine with fresh acidity and some oak complexity, it delivers good value.

DRY $19 V+

Rockburn Central Otago Chardonnay   ★★★

Grown at Parkburn, in the Cromwell Basin, and at Gibbston, this is a distinctly cool-climate style with a crisp, minerally streak. The 2009 vintage (★★★☆), hand-picked and mostly handled in tanks (17 per cent of the blend was barrel-fermented), is a fresh, fruit-driven style with lively, citrusy flavours, slightly appley and spicy, and racy acidity.

Vintage	09	08	07
WR	5	5	7
Drink	11-14	11-14	11-14

DRY $25 –V

Rongopai East Coast Chardonnay   ★★☆

From Babich, the 2009 vintage (★★★) is a vibrant, fruit-driven style with ripe melon and peach flavours, showing good depth. Medium-bodied, with fresh acidity, it's finely balanced for easy, enjoyable drinking.

DRY $14 AV

Sacred Hill Halo Hawke's Bay Chardonnay   ★★★☆

The 2009 vintage (★★★★) was hand-picked in the cool, elevated Riflemans Terraces Vineyard and fermented and matured for a year in French oak casks. Fleshy and creamy-textured, it's an elegant, age-worthy wine, ripe and rounded, with peachy, slightly spicy and toasty flavours, showing good complexity.

Vintage	09
WR	6
Drink	11-14

DRY $25 –V

Sacred Hill Hawke's Bay Chardonnay   ★★★

The 2010 vintage (★★★) was estate-grown in the Riflemans Terraces Vineyard and fermented 'with' French oak. A fruit-driven style, it is citrusy and peachy, with plenty of fresh, smooth flavour.

DRY $22 –V

Sacred Hill Riflemans Chardonnay ★★★★★

Sacred Hill's flagship Chardonnay is one of New Zealand's greatest – powerful yet elegant, with striking intensity and outstanding cellaring potential. Grown in the cool, inland, elevated (100 metres above sea level) Riflemans Terraces Vineyard in the Dartmoor Valley of Hawke's Bay, it is hand-picked from 22-year-old, own-rooted, Mendoza-clone vines and fermented with indigenous yeasts in French oak barriques (new and one year old), with some malolactic fermentation. The 2010 vintage (★★★★★) is already highly expressive. The bouquet is very rich and forthcoming, with vibrant fruit aromas coupled with yeast lees and creamy oak notes; the palate is fleshy, with ripe citrus and stone-fruit flavours, dry and tightly structured. A weighty, concentrated wine, it's full of potential.

Vintage	10	09	08	07
WR	7	7	NM	7
Drink	11-17	11-14	NM	11-12

DRY $54 AV

Sacred Hill The Wine Thief Series Hawke's Bay Chardonnay ★★★★

The 2010 vintage (★★★★) was hand-harvested in the Riflemans Terraces Vineyard and fermented in French oak barrels (new and one year old). A subtle, restrained wine in its youth, it is fresh, vibrant and delicate, with citrusy, peachy, slightly toasty flavours, a minerally streak and a lingering finish. It should age well; open mid-2012+.

Vintage	10
WR	6
Drink	11-15

DRY $33 –V

Saint Clair Marlborough Chardonnay ★★★☆

This full-flavoured, very easy-drinking wine is fermented in a 50:50 split of tanks and oak barrels (French and American). The 2010 vintage (★★★☆) is fresh, peachy, slightly spicy and toasty, with good depth and a sliver of sweetness (4.6 grams/litre of residual sugar) adding smoothness to the finish.

DRY $21 AV

Saint Clair Omaka Reserve Marlborough Chardonnay ★★★★☆

A proven show-stopper, this is a fat, creamy wine, weighty and rich, in a strikingly bold, upfront style. It is hand-picked, mostly in the company's vineyard in the Omaka Valley, and fermented and lees-aged in American oak casks, with a full, softening malolactic fermentation. The 2010 vintage (★★★★) is powerful and concentrated, with a strong, sweet oak influence (all American, half new). It offers loads of very fresh, citrusy, spicy flavour, nutty and creamy, in a typically 'in your face' style.

Vintage	10
WR	7
Drink	12-14

DRY $33 AV

Saint Clair Pioneer Block 4 Sawcut Marlborough Chardonnay   ★★★★☆

Grown in the Ure Valley, half-way between Blenheim and Kaikoura, this is a consistently classy wine. The 2009 vintage (★★★★☆) is youthful and refined, with substantial body, concentrated citrus and peach flavours, a subtle oak influence and a long finish. The 2010 (★★★★★) was hand-picked from 12-year-old clone 95 vines, fermented and lees-aged for 10 months in French oak barrels (40 per cent new), and given a full, softening malolactic fermentation. Notably refined, it has rich, citrusy, mealy flavours, with a slightly creamy texture and lovely complexity, delicacy and harmony. It shows good potential, but is already delicious.

DRY $31 AV

Saint Clair Pioneer Block 10 Twin Hills Marlborough Chardonnay   ★★★★☆

This is a single-vineyard, Omaka Valley wine, hand-picked (mostly) and fermented and matured for nine months in French oak casks (partly new). The 2009 (★★★★) is weighty and creamy, with strong, ripe stone-fruit flavours, and mealy, buttery notes adding complexity. The 2010 (★★★★☆) is a powerful wine, very full-bodied (14.5 per cent alcohol), with fresh, rich, peachy, toasty flavours and a hint of butterscotch. Bold and generous, it's slightly wood-dominated at this stage, but has the fruit concentration to match.

DRY $31 AV

Saint Clair Pioneer Block 11 Cell Block Marlborough Chardonnay   ★★★★

Grown in the 'slightly cooler' Dillons Point district, east of Blenheim, the 2009 vintage (★★★★) is a powerful, fleshy wine with strong, ripe peach and grapefruit flavours, considerable complexity and a strong oak influence (French and American, all new). The 2010 (★★★★) was fermented and lees-aged for 10 months in new French oak casks. Youthful, it has concentrated stone-fruit and toast flavours, with a strong oak influence, lively acidity, and good vigour and drive. Open mid-2012+.

DRY $30 –V

Saint Clair Unoaked Marlborough Chardonnay   ★★★

This refreshing wine is cool-fermented in tanks, using malolactic fermentation to add complexity and soften the acidity. The 2009 vintage (★★★) is creamy, with a strong 'malo' influence and restrained, melon-like fruit characters. It's a full-bodied wine, with plenty of flavour and a rounded finish.

DRY $21 –V

Saint Clair Vicar's Choice Marlborough Chardonnay   ★★★

The very user-friendly 2009 vintage (★★★) is a lightly oaked style, full-bodied, with peachy, slightly biscuity and buttery flavours and a fresh, smooth finish.

DRY $19 AV

Saints Gisborne Chardonnay   ★★★

This ripe, creamy-smooth wine has always been enjoyable (but Pernod Ricard NZ sold the brand in late 2010). It has typically been fermented and matured in French (70 per cent) and American oak casks. With its sweet oak aromas, it's an upfront style, peachy, citrusy, toasty and crisp, with moderate complexity and plenty of flavour. (Good value at its average price in supermarkets of $10 to $11.)

 DRY $20 –V

Scott Base Central Otago Chardonnay   (★★★★)

From Allan Scott, the 2009 vintage (★★★★) is a single-vineyard Cromwell wine, fermented with indigenous yeasts in French oak puncheons (25 per cent new) and given a full, softening malolactic fermentation. Fragrant, with fresh, lemony scents, it is full-bodied and elegant, with strong, vibrant, citrusy flavours, slightly nutty and buttery. A stylish wine with good acid spine, it's unfolding well.

Vintage	10	09
WR	5	6
Drink	13-18	11-14

 DRY $31 –V

Sears Road Chardonnay   (★★☆)

From Maimai Creek, this Hawke's Bay quaffer is priced sharply. The 2009 vintage (★★☆) is fleshy and lemony, gutsy and slightly spicy. A no-fuss, drink-young style.

DRY $12 V+

Secret Stone Marlborough Chardonnay   ★★★☆

From Foster's, which also owns Matua Valley, the 2009 vintage (★★★☆) is highly enjoyable. Mouthfilling and smooth, it's a very harmonious, fresh and lively wine with ripe, grapefruit-like flavours, hints of nuts and spices, and a slightly buttery finish.

 DRY $20 AV

Seifried Nelson Chardonnay   ★★★★

Fine value. The 2010 vintage (★★★★), partly fermented and matured in American oak barriques, is a mouthfilling, fresh, fruit-driven wine with strong, vibrant grapefruit and peach flavours, a gentle seasoning of oak, balanced acidity and a slightly buttery finish. Drink now or cellar.

Vintage	10	09	08	07	06
WR	6	6	6	6	6
Drink	11-16	11-16	11-14	11-13	P

 DRY $21 V+

Seifried Winemakers Collection Barrique Fermented Chardonnay   ★★★★

This is always a bold style, concentrated and creamy, with lashings of flavour. The 2009 vintage (★★★★) was fermented and matured for a year in American oak barriques (new and one year old). Pale yellow, it has fresh, strong grapefruit and peach flavours, seasoned with toasty oak, and good acid spine. Worth cellaring.

Vintage	09
WR	6
Drink	11-16

 DRY $28 AV

Selaks Heritage Reserve Hawke's Bay Chardonnay (★★★)

The debut 2010 vintage (★★★) is fresh and mouthfilling, with peachy, slightly honeyed flavours and a restrained oak influence. It's a very easy-drinking style, but lacks the complexity to rate more highly.

 DRY $22 –V

Selaks Winemaker's Favourite Hawke's Bay Reserve Chardonnay ★★★★

This smooth, richly flavoured wine from Constellation NZ is a bargain. The 2009 (★★★★), grown at Bay View and Haumoana, was French oak-fermented – mostly with indigenous yeasts – and 85 per cent of the blend went through a softening malolactic fermentation. A generous wine with ripe stone-fruit flavours seasoned with nutty oak and a hint of butterscotch, it is creamy-textured, with good harmony. The 2010 vintage (★★★★) was estate-grown in the Corner 50 Vineyard, fully barrel-fermented and matured on its yeast lees for nine months. A fleshy, finely structured wine with fresh, vibrant grapefruit and nut flavours and a creamy-smooth finish, it's a generous wine with excellent ripeness and depth.

 DRY $23 V+

Seresin Chardonnay ★★★★☆

This stylish Marlborough wine is designed to 'focus on the textural element of the palate rather than emphasising primary fruit characters'. It is typically a full-bodied and complex wine with good mouthfeel, ripe melon/citrus characters shining through, subtle toasty oak and fresh acidity. The 2008 vintage (★★★★) was hand-picked in the Home and Raupo Creek vineyards, fermented with indigenous yeasts in French oak barriques (25 per cent new), and lees-aged for 11 months, with full malolactic fermentation. A complex style, mouthfilling and concentrated, with strong, ripe stone-fruit flavours, a hint of butterscotch, and a slightly honeyed richness, it's drinking well now.

Vintage	09	08	07	06
WR	7	6	6	7
Drink	11-15	11-15	11-12	P

 DRY $29 V+

Seresin Chardonnay Reserve ★★★★★

Finesse is the keynote quality of this Marlborough wine. Estate-grown in the Home and Raupo Creek vineyards, hand-picked, French oak-fermented with indigenous yeasts and lees-aged in barriques (25 per cent new in 2009) for a year, it is typically a powerful wine, toasty and nutty, with citrusy, mealy, complex flavours of great depth. The 2009 vintage (★★★★☆) offers rich peach and grapefruit flavours, with hints of toast, honey and butter. It's a full-bodied, concentrated wine, worth cellaring to mid-2012+.

Vintage	09	08	07	06	05	04
WR	7	6	7	7	6	7
Drink	11-16	11-15	11-13	11-12	P	P

 DRY $39 AV

Shaky Bridge Central Otago Chardonnay   ★★☆

The 2008 vintage (★★☆) was estate-grown at Alexandra. Hand-picked, it was mostly handled in tanks, then blended with 'a small amount of lightly oaked wine'. It's a fruity, simple wine, smooth, lemony and appley, with crisp acidity and a fractionally off-dry finish.

DRY $20 –V

Shepherds Ridge Marlborough Chardonnay   ★★★☆

From Wither Hills, the 2008 vintage (★★★☆), 60 per cent French oak-aged, is mouthfilling and fruity, with vibrant, citrusy, slightly toasty and buttery flavours, showing a touch of complexity and very good depth.

 DRY $20 AV

Shingle Peak New Zealand Chardonnay   ★★☆

The 2010 vintage (★★☆) from Matua Valley is labelled 'New Zealand', with no individual regions identified. It's a fresh, citrusy, peachy wine, ripe and rounded, offering very easy drinking.

DRY $18 –V

Shingle Peak Reserve Release Marlborough Chardonnay   (★★★☆)

An easy-drinking wine with a touch of class, the 2010 vintage (★★★☆) is vibrantly fruity, with strong, peachy, citrusy, toasty oak flavours, slightly buttery and smooth.

 DRY $26 –V

Shipwreck Bay New Zealand Chardonnay   ★★☆

The 2008 vintage (★★☆) from Okahu Estate is a blend of Gisborne (80 per cent) and Northland grapes. 'Uncluttered by oak', it's a medium-bodied wine, fresh and fruity, with straightforward, lemony, appley flavours and a crisp finish.

 DRY $18 –V

Sileni Cellar Selection Hawke's Bay Chardonnay   ★★☆

Partly French oak-fermented, the 2010 vintage (★★★) is a fresh, fruit-driven style with plenty of vibrant, citrusy flavour and a hint of butterscotch. It offers smooth, easy drinking.

Vintage	10	09	08	07
WR	6	5	4	5
Drink	11-13	11-12	P	P

DRY $20 –V

Sileni Exceptional Vintage Hawke's Bay Chardonnay   ★★★★☆

Sileni's flagship Hawke's Bay Chardonnay. The 2007 vintage (★★★★☆) was fermented in French oak barriques, given a full, softening malolactic fermentation and matured on its yeast lees in oak for 10 months. Mouthfilling and creamy-smooth, it shows excellent complexity, with rich, ripe, peachy, mealy, toasty flavours, a fine thread of acidity and a tight, slightly minerally finish.

Vintage	07
WR	5
Drink	11-12

 DRY $50 –V

Sileni The Lodge Hawke's Bay Chardonnay ★★★★

Estate-grown at the Plateau Vineyard at Maraekakaho and hand-picked, this wine gets the works in the winery. The 2009 vintage (★★★★☆) is a classy wine, fragrant, citrusy and slightly nutty, with substantial body, a subtle oak influence, and excellent delicacy, texture and complexity. The 2010 (★★★★) was barrel-fermented, lees-aged for nine months and given a full, softening malolactic fermentation. A deliciously easy-drinking wine with considerable complexity and richness, it has strong, ripe, peachy flavours, seasoned with toasty oak, and a hint of butterscotch.

Vintage	10	09	08	07	06
WR	6	5	4	5	6
Drink	11-15	11-14	11-12	11-12	P

DRY $32 –V

Soho Carter Waiheke Island Chardonnay ★★★★

The 2010 vintage (★★★★) was fermented and matured in French oak barriques (25 per cent new). Full of promise, it is full-bodied, ripe and rounded. A peachy, sweet-fruited and savoury wine, with good concentration, complexity and texture, it should be at its best from mid-2012+.

DRY $34 –V

Soljans Barrique Reserve Chardonnay ★★★★

The 2009 vintage (★★★★) was hand-harvested in Hawke's Bay and barrel-aged for 11 months. Fresh, weighty and smooth, it's a creamy, finely textured style with peach, pear, spice and toast flavours, showing excellent ripeness, delicacy and depth.

Vintage	09
WR	6
Drink	11-20

DRY $25 AV

Soljans Hawke's Bay Chardonnay (★★★)

The sturdy 2010 vintage (★★★) is a briefly oak-aged wine with ripe, citrusy, peachy, slightly biscuity flavours. Weighty and dry, it shows good depth.

DRY $20 –V

Southern Cross Hawke's Bay Chardonnay ★★★

From One Tree Hill Vineyards, a division of Morton Estate, the 2008 vintage (★★★) is a full-bodied wine with fresh acidity, very satisfying depth of grapefruit and peach flavours and a slightly buttery, creamy finish.

Vintage	08	07
WR	6	6
Drink	P	P

DRY $13 V+

Southern Lighthouse Nelson Chardonnay (★★☆)

From Anchorage, the 2010 vintage (★★☆) is lemony and crisp, in a simple, fruit-driven style, fresh and lively.

DRY $17 –V

Spinyback Nelson Chardonnay ★★★☆

From Waimea Estates, the 2009 vintage (★★★) is a creamy-textured, fruit-driven style with fresh, vibrant, peachy flavours and a crisp finish. Enjoyable young.

Vintage	09
WR	6
Drink	11-12

 DRY $17 V+

Spy Valley Envoy Marlborough Chardonnay ★★★★★

Launched from the 2005 vintage (★★★★★), this distinguished wine is estate-grown in the Waihopai Valley, hand-picked, fermented with indigenous yeasts and lees-aged in French oak barriques (mostly seasoned) for up to 18 months. The 2007 (★★★★★) is very classy – fragrant, citrusy and slightly creamy, with lovely harmony, a fine thread of acidity and a long finish (retasted in 2011, it's maturing superbly). The 2008 vintage (★★★★☆) is enticingly fragrant, fleshy, creamy and soft, with strong, ripe, peachy flavours, showing good complexity, but fractionally less concentrated than the 2007.

Vintage	08	07	06	05
WR	6	7	7	7
Drink	11-14	11-13	11-12	P

 DRY $40 AV

Spy Valley Marlborough Chardonnay ★★★☆

A consistently attractive wine. The 2009 vintage (★★★☆) was hand-picked and fermented and lees-aged for a year in barrels. Drinking well from the start, it's a moderately complex wine with citrusy, nutty flavours, a hint of butterscotch, and good mouthfeel, texture and depth. The 2010 (★★★☆), barrel-fermented and lees-aged for a year, is weighty, with citrusy, slightly mealy and biscuity flavours, fresh, dry and youthful. Open mid-2012+.

Vintage	10	09	08	07	06
WR	7	6	6	6	6
Drink	11-15	11-13	11-12	11-12	P

 DRY $23 AV

Spy Valley Marlborough Unoaked Chardonnay ★★★

The 2009 vintage (★★★☆), estate-grown and lees-aged for five months, is a fruit-driven style, ripely scented, fleshy, fresh and full-flavoured, with good immediacy and a slightly off-dry, smooth finish.

Vintage	09	08	07
WR	7	5	6
Drink	11-12	P	P

 MED/DRY $19 AV

Squawking Magpie Gimblett Gravels Chardonnay ★★★☆

Squawking Magpie is the label of Gavin Yortt, co-founder of the Irongate vineyard in Gimblett Road, Hawke's Bay. The 2009 vintage (★★★☆), fully barrel-aged, is fresh, crisp and slightly minerally, with grapefruit, lime and nut flavours, a hint of honey and some savoury, toasty complexity.

DRY $25 –V

Staete Landt Marlborough Chardonnay   ★★★★

This consistently impressive, single-vineyard wine is grown in the Rapaura district, hand-picked and fermented with partial use of indigenous yeasts in French oak barriques (15 per cent new in 2009). The 2009 vintage (★★★★) is creamy, rich and rounded, with fullness of body and good concentration of stone-fruit and spice flavours, mealy and biscuity.

Vintage	09	08	07	06
WR	6	7	6	6
Drink	11-18	11-17	11-13	11-12

 DRY $29 AV

Stone Bridge Gisborne Chardonnay   ★★★★

The 2007 vintage (★★★★) was impressive – and so is the 2009 (★★★★). French and American oak-aged, it is a youthful, poised wine with citrusy, peachy, nutty, creamy flavours, showing very good depth and harmony. Well worth cellaring.

 DRY $25 AV

Stonecroft Gimblett Gravels Hawke's Bay Chardonnay   (★★★★☆)

The 2010 vintage was grown in the company's Mere Road and Roy's Hill vineyards, hand-picked and matured for nine months in seasoned French oak casks. A wine with a strong presence, it is full-bodied, with ripe stone-fruit flavours, hints of toast and butterscotch, and excellent texture and depth. Weighty, concentrated and complex, with a long, dry finish, it's a good buy.

Vintage	10
WR	6
Drink	12-18

DRY $25 V+

Stonecroft Old Vine Hawke's Bay Chardonnay   ★★★★★

The very refined, harmonious 2009 (★★★★★) was estate-grown in the Gimblett Gravels and fermented and matured for a year in French oak casks (partly new). It is weighty, concentrated and rounded, in a rich, complex style with sweet-fruit delights, generous, peachy, mealy flavours, a hint of butterscotch, and a long, seamless finish. The 2010 vintage (★★★★★) is also a classic regional style – powerful, fleshy, rich and rounded, with gentle acidity and concentrated, peachy flavours, slightly spicy, buttery and toasty.

Vintage	10
WR	6
Drink	12-20

 DRY $45 AV

Stoneleigh Latitude Marlborough Chardonnay   (★★★★)

The debut 2010 vintage (★★★★) is an elegant, tightly structured wine with strong, fresh, citrusy flavours to the fore and finely integrated, nutty oak. It's still youthful; open mid-2012+.

 DRY $25 AV

Stoneleigh Marlborough Chardonnay ★★★☆

From Pernod Ricard NZ, this creamy-rich wine is always enjoyable and top value at its average price in supermarkets of under $15. It is fermented in a mix of tanks (40 per cent) and French oak casks (60 per cent), and bottled with fractional sweetness (4–5 grams/litre of residual sugar). The 2009 (★★★☆) is fresh, lemony and vibrant, with finely integrated oak. It's not highly complex, but shows very good depth and harmony. The 2010 (★★★★) is again fresh, vibrant and citrusy, showcasing attractive ripe-fruit flavours with a subtle seasoning of oak. It's already drinking well.

Vintage	10	09	08	07
WR	7	6	5	6
Drink	11-13	P	P	P

 DRY $22 AV

Stoneleigh Rapaura Series Marlborough Chardonnay ★★★★

Since the 2007 vintage, this wine has moved to a more 'fruit forward' style, involving briefer oak maturation – it is fermented and lees-aged for four months in new and one-year-old French oak casks. The 2010 vintage (★★★☆) is fleshy, with good weight and richness. Fresh, with considerable complexity, it has a sustained, well-rounded finish.

 DRY $27 AV

Stone Paddock Hawke's Bay Chardonnay ★★★

From Paritua, the 2009 (★★★☆) is mouthfilling, with very good depth of fresh, peachy flavours, a hint of oak and a rounded finish. The 2010 vintage (★★☆), 40 per cent barrel-fermented, is an easy-drinking style with straightforward, ripe, peachy flavours and a smooth finish.

 DRY $19 AV

Stop Banks Hawke's Bay Chardonnay (★★★)

From a Marlborough-based producer, the 2008 vintage (★★★) is a fruit-driven style with ripe, peachy flavours, not complex, but vibrant and well-rounded.

 DRY $18 AV

Summerhouse Marlborough Chardonnay ★★★★

This single-vineyard label is worth discovering. The 2009 vintage (★★★★) was fully fermented and lees-aged for 10 months in French oak barriques. It's a full-bodied (14.5 per cent alcohol), well-rounded wine with strong, peachy, gently toasty and buttery flavours. Concentrated, with a slightly oily richness, it's an upfront style, drinking well from the start.

 DRY $27 AV

Takutai Nelson Chardonnay ★★☆

From Waimea Estates, the 2008 (★★☆) is pale gold, with peachy, distinctly honeyed aromas and flavours. Ready. The 2009 vintage (★★★) is good value – with peachy, slightly spicy and nutty flavours, fresh and lively. It's drinking well now.

Vintage	09	08
WR	5	5
Drink	11-13	11-12

DRY $13 V+

Te Awa Chardonnay   ★★★★☆

Top vintages of this Hawke's Bay wine are classy. Hand-harvested in the Gimblett Gravels and fermented and matured in French oak casks, the 2009 vintage (★★★★) is refined and mouthfilling, with ripe grapefruit and subtle oak flavours. Weighty and finely textured, it is likely to unfold well.

 DRY $30 AV

Te Awa Left Field Hawke's Bay Chardonnay   ★★★☆

The fresh, easy-drinking 2009 vintage (★★★☆) is an unoaked style, fermented in small stainless steel 'barrels', lees-aged for six months, and blended with 3 per cent Viognier. Mouthfilling and vibrantly fruity, it is a ripe, peachy, slightly spicy wine, showing good weight, flavour depth and texture.

 DRY $25 –V

Te Henga The Westie Chardonnay   ★★

From Babich, the 2009 vintage (★★) is an easy-drinking North Island wine, fresh and fruity, in a simple style with pleasant, citrusy flavours. The 2010 (★★) is a solid quaffer, full-bodied, lemony and dry.

 DRY $13 AV

Te Kairanga Casarina Reserve Chardonnay   ★★★★

Estate-grown in the Casarina Block at Martinborough, the 2008 vintage (★★★★) was fermented and lees-aged in French oak barriques (50 per cent new). Fragrant, fleshy and rich, with grapefruit-like flavours, plenty of nutty oak, lively acidity, and good drive and length, it's drinking well now.

Vintage	08	07	06	05
WR	7	6	6	5
Drink	11-14	11-13	11-12	P

DRY $29 AV

Te Kairanga Gisborne Chardonnay   ★★☆

This is typically a drink-young style with vibrant fruit characters and restrained oak. The 2008 vintage (★★★) is ripely scented, with fresh, peachy flavours and a crisp finish.

Vintage	08
WR	6
Drink	11-12

DRY $19 –V

Te Kairanga Martinborough Estate Chardonnay   ★★★☆

The pale straw 2009 vintage (★★★) was fermented and matured for 15 months in French oak barriques. Tight, citrusy, limey and peachy, with a crisp, minerally streak, it's a slightly lean wine, with some nutty complexity.

Vintage	09	08	07	06	05
WR	7	NM	6	4	6
Drink	11-13	NM	11-13	11-12	P

 DRY $21 AV

Te Kairanga Runholder Martinborough Chardonnay   (★★★★☆)

The 2008 vintage (★★★★☆) is a powerful, fully barrel-fermented style (nine months in French oak barriques, 30 per cent new), with substantial body and concentrated, ripe peach and grapefruit flavours, mealy, toasty, slightly minerally and complex. It shows excellent weight and richness, with a crisp, dry, long finish.

Vintage	08
WR	7
Drink	11-14

DRY $29 V+

Te Mania Nelson Chardonnay   ★★★

The 2009 vintage (★★★☆) was matured in a 'combination of tank, staves and barrels'. It's an easy-drinking style, creamy-textured, with strong, ripe, peachy flavours, a gentle oak influence and a well-rounded finish.

Vintage	09	08	07	06
WR	6	5	7	6
Drink	11-13	11-12	P	P

DRY $20 –V

Te Mania Reserve Nelson Chardonnay   ★★★★

Typically a powerful wine with heaps of oak seasoning concentrated, ripe-fruit flavours, and a creamy-smooth texture. Still youthful, the 2009 vintage (★★★★) was fermented and matured in French and American oak barriques (30 per cent new). It has a fragrant, biscuity bouquet, with vibrant stone-fruit flavours, seasoned with nutty oak, fresh acidity and a slightly creamy finish.

Vintage	09	08	07
WR	6	5	7
Drink	11-14	11-13	11-12

DRY $28 AV

Te Mata Elston Chardonnay   ★★★★★

One of New Zealand's most illustrious Chardonnays, Elston is a stylish, intense, slowly evolving Hawke's Bay wine. At around four years old, it is notably complete, showing concentration and finesse. The grapes are grown principally at two sites in the Te Mata hills at Havelock North, and the wine is fully fermented in French oak barriques (35 per cent new), with full malolactic fermentation. The 2009 vintage (★★★★★) is very rich, with good acid spine and deep grapefruit, biscuit and slight butterscotch flavours, seamless, complex, rounded and long. Drink now or cellar.

Vintage	10	09	08	07	06	05	04
WR	7	7	7	7	7	7	7
Drink	11-15	11-14	11-13	11-12	P	P	P

DRY $34 V+

Te Mata Estate Woodthorpe Chardonnay   ★★★★

This bargain-priced Hawke's Bay wine is grown in the company's inland Woodthorpe Vineyard in the Dartmoor Valley. Fermented and lees-aged in a mix of tanks (50 per cent) and French oak barrels, it is typically a harmonious wine with ripe grapefruit characters enriched with biscuity oak and very good richness and complexity. The 2009 vintage (★★★☆) is mouthfilling, sweet-fruited and rounded, with fresh, vibrant fruit flavours, a slightly creamy texture, moderate complexity, and very good harmony and depth.

DRY $20 V+

Terravin Chardonnay   ★★★★

The 2010 vintage (★★★★) was grown on the south side of the Wairau Valley in Marlborough and fermented and matured for 15 months in French oak barriques. Bright, light lemon/green, it is fresh, strong and youthful, with citrusy, peachy, slightly spicy flavours, complex and slightly creamy. Best drinking mid-2012+.

DRY $26 AV

Terravin Reserve Chardonnay   (★★★★☆)

Full of potential and very youthful, the 2010 vintage (★★★★☆) was grown on the south side of the Wairau Valley and fermented with indigenous yeasts in three French oak barrels, where it rested for 15 months. Full-bodied, with concentrated peach, grapefruit and toast flavours, showing good complexity, it has fresh acid spine and excellent depth, delicacy and poise. Open 2013+.

DRY $39 –V

Te Whau Vineyard Waiheke Island Chardonnay   ★★★★★

For its sheer vintage-to-vintage consistency, this is Te Whau's finest wine. Full of personality, it has beautifully ripe fruit characters showing excellent concentration, nutty oak and a long, finely poised finish. (At a vertical tasting of the 1999 to 2008 vintages, held in October 2010, the wine showed excellent uniformity of quality and style.) Hand-picked and fermented and lees-aged for a year in French oak barriques (one-third new), the 2009 vintage (★★★★★) has a fragrant bouquet with slightly 'funky', indigenous yeast notes. Rich and tightly structured, it has concentrated stone-fruit and nut flavours, excellent texture and complexity, and a well-rounded finish. An elegant wine with obvious potential, it's maturing very gracefully; open 2012+. The 2010 (★★★★★) is youthful, complex and creamy, with highly concentrated stone-fruit and spice flavours, finely textured and lasting. It should be very long-lived.

Vintage	10	09	08	07
WR	7	6	7	7
Drink	11-16	11-15	11-15	11-12

DRY $70 –V

Thornbury Gisborne Chardonnay   ★★★☆

From Villa Maria, the 2010 (★★★☆) was fermented in tanks and barrels. It's a high-flavoured wine, vibrant, peachy and toasty, with ripe-fruit characters and a smooth, slightly buttery finish. The 2011 vintage (tasted prior to bottling, and so not rated) was grown at Patutahi and Manutuke, and fermented in tanks (80 per cent) and barrels (20 per cent). In its infancy, it tasted crisp and citrusy, with strong, pure Chardonnay fruit flavours to the fore.

Vintage	11	10	09
WR	5	7	6
Drink	11-13	11-14	11-15

DRY $21 AV

Three Paddles Martinborough Chardonnay   ★★★

From Nga Waka, the 2010 vintage (★★★) is a freshly scented, buoyantly fruity wine, citrusy and slightly limey, with lively acidity and lots of drink-young appeal.

Vintage	11	10	09
WR	6	7	7
Drink	11+	11+	11+

 DRY $18 AV

Ti Point Hawke's Bay Chardonnay   ★★★

The 2010 vintage (★★★), grown in the Dartmoor Valley, was mostly fermented with indigenous yeasts in tanks, but 25 per cent of the blend was fermented and matured in seasoned French oak barrels. A good, drink-young style, it is mouthfilling, vibrant and smooth, with fresh, ripe, peachy, citrusy flavours to the fore, and a very subtle seasoning of oak.

Vintage	10
WR	6
Drink	11-20

 DRY $21 –V

Tiritiri Reserve Chardonnay   ★★★★☆

Duncan and Judy Smith's tiny (0.27-hectare), organically managed vineyard is in the Waimata Valley, 25 kilometres from the city of Gisborne. The 2008 vintage (★★★★) is full-bodied and rounded, slightly creamy and nutty, in a fleshy, sweet-fruited style, finely balanced, soft and generous ($39). The 2009 ($49), fermented and lees-aged for 10 months in French oak barriques, should blossom with cellaring. Refined, elegant and youthful, it's a sophisticated, immaculate wine, with grapefruit, peach and subtle oak flavours and a rich, slightly creamy finish.

Vintage	09	08	07
WR	6	4	6
Drink	12-16	12-15	P

 DRY $49 –V

Tohu Gisborne Chardonnay   ★★★

Made in a drink-young style, the 2009 vintage (★★☆) is a light wine with straightforward, fresh, lemony, appley flavours.

 DRY $19 AV

Tohu Marlborough Chardonnay   ★★★

The 2009 vintage (★★★), labelled 'Unoaked', is a drink-young style, mouthfilling and dryish (5 grams/litre of residual sugar). Given a full, softening malolactic fermentation, it is fleshy and fruity, with a slightly creamy texture and a well-rounded finish. The 2010 (★★★), also 'uncluttered by oak', is mouthfilling and creamy, with citrusy, peachy flavours, fresh and lively.

DRY $21 –V

Toi Toi Marlborough Unoaked Chardonnay   ★★★

The 2010 vintage (★★★) is a single-vineyard wine, grown in the lower Wairau Valley. Buoyantly fruity and smooth, with citrusy, appley flavours, showing decent depth, and a slightly creamy texture, it offers good, easy drinking.

 DRY $17 AV

Tolaga Bay Estate Tolaga Bay Unoaked Chardonnay   (★★★)

Enjoyable young, the 2009 vintage (★★★) is a single-vineyard wine from the East Cape, north of Gisborne. Fleshy, it is ripe and rounded, with very satisfying depth of peachy, slightly spicy flavour.

 DRY $18 AV

Torlesse Waipara Chardonnay   ★★★

The 2009 vintage (★★☆) is fresh and lemony, with a slightly honeyed bouquet. It's a very lightly wooded wine (20 per cent oak-aged), fruity and crisp.

Vintage	09	08	07
WR	5	5	5
Drink	12-15	12-15	11-12

 DRY $18 AV

Torea Marlborough Chardonnay   (★★★)

From Fairhall Downs, the 2009 vintage (★★★) is peachy, soft and flavoursome, with distinctly buttery, 'malo' notes. French oak-aged, it's ready to roll.

 DRY $19 AV

Torrent Bay Nelson Chardonnay   (★★☆)

From Anchorage, the 2008 vintage (★★☆) was grown at Motueka and fermented in French and American oak casks. It's a lemony, appley, slightly honeyed wine, with a slightly sweet (6 grams/litre of residual sugar) finish. The 2009 is fully dry.

 MED/DRY $16 AV

Tranquillity Bay Nelson Chardonnay   (★★☆)

From Anchorage, the 2009 vintage (★★☆) was grown at Motueka. It's a lemony, appley wine in a very fruit-driven style, offering fresh, easy drinking.

 DRY $13 V+

Trinity Hill Hawke's Bay Chardonnay [Black Label]   ★★★★★

(Up to and including the 2008 vintage, this wine was labelled 'Gimblett Gravels'.) The winery's flagship Chardonnay, it is typically stylish, intense and finely structured. The 2010 (★★★★☆), a regional blend, was grown in the Gimblett Gravels, at Bridge Pa (Maraekakaho), and in Central Hawke's Bay. Matured for 10 months in French oak casks (20 per cent new), it is rich and elegant, with sweet-fruit delights and impressive delicacy, depth and harmony.

Vintage	10	09	08	07	06
WR	6	7	5	6	6
Drink	12-15	11-14	11-12	11-13	11-12

DRY $35 AV

Trinity Hill Hawke's Bay Chardonnay [White Label]   ★★★☆

The 2010 vintage (★★★☆) was grown in the Gimblett Gravels and mostly handled in tanks, but 10 per cent of the blend was French oak-fermented. It's a mouthfilling wine with fresh peach and grapefruit flavours and gentle, spicy, nutty notes adding a touch of complexity.

Vintage	10	
WR	6	
Drink	11-14	

DRY $19 V+

Tukipo River Estate Fat Snapper Central Hawke's Bay Chardonnay   ★★★

Grown at Takapau, the 2010 vintage (★★★) is an off-dry wine (6 grams/litre of residual sugar), matured in tanks (90 per cent) and barrels (10 per cent). It's a good, fruit-driven style, full-bodied, fresh and vibrantly fruity.

MED/DRY $20 –V

Tukipo River Estate Fat Trout Central Hawke's Bay Chardonnay   ★★★☆

Grown at Takapau, the 2009 vintage (★★★★) is a 'full-on' style, with excellent concentration of stone-fruit flavours, seasoned with toasty oak (40 per cent new). Fleshy and creamy-textured, with balanced acidity and slightly buttery notes, it's drinking well now.

DRY $29 –V

TW Estate Chardonnay   (★★★)

Grown in Gisborne, the 2010 vintage (★★★) is an unoaked style with ripe, peachy, citrusy flavours, enjoyably fresh, vibrant, dry and crisp.

DRY $17 AV

TW Gisborne CV Chardonnay/Viognier   ★★★☆

The 2009 vintage (★★★☆) is a blend of Chardonnay (70 per cent) and Viognier (30 per cent). A drink-young style, it is a fresh, fruity, mouthfilling dry wine with peachy, smooth flavours, showing very good depth.

DRY $20 AV

TW Growers Selection Gisborne Chardonnay   (★★★★)

Hand-picked at 23 brix and barrel-fermented, the 2009 vintage (★★★★) is a weighty, rounded wine with a slightly creamy texture and citrusy, nutty flavours showing good, barrel-ferment complexity.

DRY $28 AV

TW Innocent Chardonnay   (★★★)

The 2010 vintage (★★★) of this Gisborne wine is 'untouched by oak'. Fresh, crisp and lively, it's not complex, but a good example of the 'fruit-driven' Chardonnay style.

DRY $20 –V

TW Summer CV – see the Branded and Other White Wines section

Twin Islands Marlborough Chardonnay   ★★★☆

From Nautilus Estate, this lightly wooded, drink-young style offers top value. The 2009 vintage (★★★☆), fermented in tanks (85 per cent) and barrels (15 per cent), is fruity and smooth, peachy, slightly spicy and buttery, with good vibrancy and texture, and greater complexity than you'd expect in its humble price range. The 2010 (★★★☆) is mouthfilling, fruity and smooth, with lively, citrusy flavours, showing good delicacy and texture.

DRY $15 V+

Two Rivers Clos Des Pierres Marlborough Chardonnay   (★★★★)

From a stony Wairau Valley site ('Clos des Pierres' means 'Place of Stones'), the 2010 vintage (★★★★) is a hand-picked, French oak-fermented wine. Fleshy, rich and rounded, with strong, peachy, nutty flavours, a creamy texture and balanced acidity, it's well worth cellaring.

DRY $30 –V

Two Tracks Marlborough Chardonnay   ★★★☆

From Wither Hills, the 2008 vintage (★★★☆) was mostly handled in tanks, but 20 per cent of the blend was wood-aged. It's a fruit-driven style, crisp and lively, with peachy, slightly toasty flavours, showing very good vigour and depth.

Vintage	08
WR	5
Drink	P

DRY $20 AV

Unison Gimblett Gravels Hawke's Bay Chardonnay   (★★★★)

The debut 2010 vintage (★★★★) was grown in an adjacent vineyard to Unison, hand-picked and fermented in a single French oak puncheon. It's an elegant, youthful wine, mouthfilling, with peachy, citrusy, slightly buttery and toasty flavours, sweet-fruit characters, finely balanced acidity and good harmony. Open mid-2012+.

DRY $35 –V

Vavasour Anna's Vineyard Chardonnay   ★★★★★

Named after Peter Vavasour's late wife, this is the company's top wine, produced intermittently. Released in late 2009, the 2006 vintage (★★★★★) was grown in the original vineyard in the Awatere Valley, hand-picked, barrel-fermented with indigenous yeasts, and lees-aged for 10 months in French oak casks (75 per cent new). A complex style, it's delicious now, with peach, grapefruit and nut flavours. Fragrant, with rich, ripe sweet-fruit characters, it is very pure, silky and finely textured. (The next release is from the 2010 vintage.)

DRY $33 V+

Vavasour Awatere Valley Chardonnay   ★★★★☆

A powerful Marlborough wine, rich and creamy. The 2010 vintage (★★★★☆) was fermented and lees-aged for 10 months in French oak barriques (25 per cent new). Already delicious, it is fleshy, concentrated and complex, with a strong presence. Very full-bodied, it has concentrated, ripe melon and peach flavours, fresh acidity, mealy, biscuity notes and a creamy-smooth texture. Great value.

Vintage	09	08	07	06
WR	6	6	7	7
Drink	11-14	11-13	11-12	11-12

 DRY $24 V+

Vidal Legacy Hawke's Bay Chardonnay   (★★★★★)

(This new flagship Chardonnay has replaced the former Reserve label.) The debut 2010 vintage (★★★★★) was fermented and matured for 10 months in French oak barriques (50 per cent new). It's a very classy, youthful wine with a richly fragrant bouquet, showing indigenous yeast complexity, leading into a tight, elegant palate with concentrated, citrusy, nutty flavours and a long finish. Open mid-2012+.

Vintage	10
WR	7
Drink	11-17

DRY $33 V+

Vidal Reserve Hawke's Bay Chardonnay   ★★★★★

(Note: from the 2010 vintage, this label will be replaced by the new Legacy Series Chardonnay.) At its best, this has been one of Hawke's Bay's finest Chardonnays, with a string of top wines stretching back to the mid-1980s. The 2009 vintage (★★★★★) was hand-picked, mostly in the Gimblett Gravels but also at Maraekakaho and Ohiti, and fermented, entirely with indigenous yeasts, in French oak barriques (45 per cent new). It's a beautifully rich and complex wine, highly refined, with deep, ripe stone-fruit flavours, a slightly creamy texture, and excellent harmony and length.

Vintage	09	08	07	06
WR	7	6	7	7
Drink	11-15	11-13	11-12	11-12

 DRY $32 V+

Vidal Reserve Series Hawke's Bay Chardonnay   (★★★★)

This new, middle-tier label was launched from the 2010 vintage (★★★★). Fermented and lees-aged for 10 months in French oak casks (27 per cent new), it is already delicious, with good weight on the palate, concentrated, fresh and lively peach and nectarine flavours, and a creamy, persistent finish.

Vintage	10
WR	7
Drink	11-15

DRY $24 V+

Vidal [White Series] Hawke's Bay Chardonnay   ★★★☆

Typically a fruit-driven style with a touch of class (future vintages will be labelled as 'White Series'). Mouthfilling, fresh and vibrantly fruity, the 2010 (★★★☆) was grown predominantly in the Keltern Vineyard at Maraekakaho. Fermented in a mix of tanks (17 per cent), seasoned French oak barriques (74 per cent) and new French oak barriques (9 per cent), it's an elegant, youthful wine with grapefruit and slight spice flavours, and some mealy, biscuity notes adding a touch of complexity.

Vintage	10	09	08
WR	7	7	6
Drink	11-13	11-13	P

 DRY $22 AV

Villa Maria Cellar Selection Marlborough Chardonnay   ★★★★

A stylish, good-value wine. The 2010 (★★★★), a blend of Marlborough (89 per cent) and Hawke's Bay (11 per cent) grapes, was fermented and aged for 10 months in oak barriques. It's a fleshy, well-rounded wine with ripe stone-fruit flavours, slightly toasty and creamy notes adding complexity, and good richness and harmony.

Vintage	10	09	08	07	06
WR	6	6	6	6	6
Drink	11-15	11-14	11-14	11-12	11-12

 DRY $24 V+

Villa Maria Private Bin East Coast Chardonnay   ★★★

A drink-young, fruit-driven style. It is mostly grown in the North Island regions of Gisborne and Hawke's Bay, but a small portion of the blend comes from Marlborough. Mostly lees-aged in tanks, but partly barrel-aged, it typically offers fresh, ripe, citrusy flavours, with a touch of buttery, toasty complexity, satisfying depth, and a rounded, dry finish.

 DRY $18 AV

Villa Maria Reserve Barrique Fermented Gisborne Chardonnay   ★★★★★

This acclaimed wine is grown mostly in the company's Katoa and McDiarmid Hill vineyards. The 2009 (★★★★★) – which also includes fruit from the McIldowie Block, a relatively warm site at Patutahi – was hand-picked, given a full, softening malolactic fermentation, and fermented and matured for 10 months in French oak casks (43 per cent new). A very elegant, rich wine, tight and youthful, it is creamy-textured, with grapefruit, peach and nut flavours showing impressive delicacy, complexity and depth. The 2010 (★★★★★) is a blend of McDiarmid Hill (60 per cent), McIldowie (35 per cent) and Katoa (5 per cent) grapes. Hand-picked and fermented and matured for 10 months (with weekly lees-stirring) in French oak barriques (38 per cent new), it's a powerful, youthful wine, fleshy, rich, peachy and slightly buttery, with lovely delicacy and concentration.

Vintage	10	09	08	07	06
WR	7	6	6	7	7
Drink	11-18	11-14	11-13	11-16	11-15

 DRY $38 AV

Villa Maria Reserve Hawke's Bay Chardonnay ★★★★☆

The 2009 vintage (★★★★☆) was grown at Maraekakaho, Te Awanga and in the Gimblett Gravels. Fermented and matured in French oak barriques (43 per cent new), it is fragrant, with peach and butterscotch aromas and flavours. Weighty and finely textured, it's a youthful, elegant wine, best cellared until 2012. The 2010 (★★★★★), grown in the Waikahu, Ngakirikiri and Keltern vineyards, was fermented and lees-aged for 10 months in French oak barriques (44 per cent new). The bouquet is rich and nutty, with indigenous yeast notes; the palate is mouthfilling, with deep, peachy, citrusy, nutty flavours, highly complex, tight, youthful and long.

Vintage	10	09	08
WR	7	7	7
Drink	11-18	11-15	11-14

 DRY $33 AV

Villa Maria Reserve Marlborough Chardonnay ★★★★★

With its rich, slightly mealy, citrusy flavours, this is a distinguished wine, very concentrated and finely structured. A marriage of intense, ripe Marlborough fruit with premium French oak, it is one of the region's greatest Chardonnays. It is typically grown in the warmest sites supplying Chardonnay grapes to Villa Maria, in the Awatere and Wairau valleys. The grapes are hand-picked and the wine is fermented with cultured and indigenous yeasts in French oak barriques (25 per cent new in 2010). The 2008 vintage (★★★★☆) is a sophisticated wine, weighty, with a complex bouquet and rich, citrusy, creamy and nutty flavours. The 2010 (tasted just prior to bottling, and so not rated) looks very classy – elegant and tightly structured, with citrusy flavours showing lovely freshness and depth.

Vintage	10	09	08	07	06
WR	7	7	6	7	7
Drink	11-17	11-15	11-15	11-14	11-13

 DRY $33 V+

Villa Maria Single Vineyard Ihumatao Chardonnay ★★★★☆

This impressive wine is estate-grown at Mangere, in Auckland, and fermented with indigenous yeasts in French oak barriques (35 per cent new in 2010). The 2009 (★★★★☆) is powerful and creamy-textured, with ripe, peachy, nutty flavours, showing excellent complexity and harmony. The 2010 (★★★★★) is a top vintage. Hand-picked and fermented with indigenous yeasts (mostly), it is very rich and creamy, with ripe stone-fruit flavours showing outstanding concentration and complexity. Poised and youthful, it's a lovely wine, already highly expressive, but also an obvious candidate for cellaring.

Vintage	10	09	08	07	06
WR	7	6	6	7	7
Drink	11-18	11-14	11-13	11-14	11-13

 DRY $38 –V

Villa Maria Single Vineyard Keltern Chardonnay ★★★★★

Grown at the Keltern Vineyard, a warm, inland site east of Maraekakaho in Hawke's Bay, this wine is hand-picked, fermented with indigenous yeasts and lees-aged in French oak barriques (45 per cent new in 2010). The 2009 vintage (★★★★☆) is savoury and creamy, with a smoky bouquet and very ripe, peachy flavours, subtle, complex and smooth. The 2010 (★★★★☆) is an elegant, tightly structured wine, citrusy, peachy, nutty and minerally, with a bouquet showing a distinct hint of matchstick. Full-bodied, with impressive complexity and a sustained, slightly creamy finish, it's still very youthful.

Vintage	10	09	08	07
WR	7	6	6	7
Drink	11-18	11-16	11-16	11-17

DRY $38 AV

Villa Maria Single Vineyard Taylors Pass Chardonnay ★★★★

Grown in the company's Taylors Pass Vineyard in Marlborough's Awatere Valley, this wine is hand-picked and fermented and matured for a year in French oak barriques (25 per cent new in 2010). The 2010 has a highly fragrant, creamy bouquet and vibrant, ripe grapefruit and nut flavours that show real concentration. Tasted prior to bottling (and so not rated), it looked extremely promising.

Vintage	10
WR	7
Drink	11-17

DRY $38 –V

Volcanic Hills Hawke's Bay Chardonnay (★★★☆)

From Green Rocket, an Auckland-based company, the 2010 vintage (★★★☆) is an easy-drinking style – fresh and vibrantly fruity, with good depth of ripe, peachy flavours, a subtle seasoning of French oak and a smooth (4.5 grams/litre of residual sugar), harmonious finish.

Vintage	10
WR	5
Drink	11-13

DRY $20 AV

Voss Reserve Chardonnay ★★★★☆

This powerful, richly flavoured Martinborough wine is typically fragrant and mouthfilling, with ripe grapefruit flavours, hints of nuts and butterscotch and a creamy, rounded finish. The 2009 vintage (★★★★) was hand-picked from vines up to 22 years old, and fermented and matured for 10 months in French oak barriques (15 per cent new). Fresh and elegant, with citrusy, mealy flavours, subtle use of oak, balanced acidity and a rounded, dry finish, it's not a 'showy' wine, but has depth and finesse.

DRY $28 V+

Waimarie Waimauku Chardonnay (★★★★)

Estate-grown at Muriwai, in Auckland, and matured for a year in seasoned French oak casks, the 2009 vintage (★★★★) has a fresh, complex, nutty bouquet, leading into a fleshy, soft wine with strong personality. Creamy and nutty, with good concentration, it's drinking well now and offers great value.

DRY $20 V+

Waimata Cogniscenti Chardonnay   (★★★★)

The finely poised 2009 vintage (★★★★) is a fragrant, creamy-textured Gisborne wine, fermented in French oak (25 per cent new) with indigenous yeasts, lees-aged for eight months and given a full, softening malolactic fermentation. It offers rich, citrusy, nutty flavours, showing excellent delicacy and complexity.

DRY $28 AV

Waimea Nelson Chardonnay   ★★★★

The 2009 vintage (★★★★), fully barrel-fermented, is finely balanced, with mouthfilling body, fresh, strong, grapefruit-like flavours seasoned with toasty French oak, and good, nutty, leesy complexity. The 2010 (★★★★) is rich and lemony, slightly buttery and toasty, with loads of flavour. Drink now or cellar.

Vintage	10	09	08
WR	7	6	6
Drink	11-14	P	11-13

DRY $23 V+

Waipara Hills Soul of the South Waipara Chardonnay   (★★★☆)

The 2008 vintage (★★★☆) was grown in the Glasnevin Vineyard, behind the winery, and matured in seasoned oak barrels, with no use of malolactic fermentation. It's an elegant, gently wooded wine with ripe grapefruit and slight spice flavours, showing good concentration, and fresh acidity.

DRY $21 AV

Waipara Hills Southern Cross Selection Waipara Chardonnay   (★★★☆)

Fully fermented and matured for five months in French oak barrels (partly new), the 2008 vintage (★★★☆) was grown behind the winery, in the Glasnevin Vineyard. It's a vibrantly fruity wine with grapefruit, peach and toasty oak flavours, showing very good depth.

DRY $29 –V

Waipara Springs Reserve Premo Chardonnay   (★★★)

The 2008 vintage (★★★) was harvested from 29-year-old vines and French oak-fermented with indigenous yeasts. Maturing solidly, it's a full-bodied wine, showing some complexity, with citrusy, peachy, toasty, slightly honeyed flavours.

DRY $24 –V

Waipara Springs Waipara Chardonnay   ★★★

The 2008 vintage (★★★☆) is a full-flavoured wine, maturing soundly, with peachy, slightly limey and honeyed flavours, showing a touch of complexity, and a crisp finish. Ready.

DRY $19 AV

Wairau River Marlborough Chardonnay ★★★☆

The 2008 vintage (★★★) was mostly handled in tanks, but 30 per cent was oak-aged. It's a fruit-driven style with vibrant, lemony, slightly biscuity flavours, showing good freshness and depth.

Vintage	08
WR	5
Drink	P

 DRY $20 AV

Wairau River Reserve Marlborough Chardonnay ★★★★

Grown at two sites adjacent to the Wairau River, on the north side of the valley, the 2009 vintage (★★★★) was matured for 10 months in seasoned French oak puncheons. Slightly creamy, it's an elegant, gently oaked style with rich, grapefruit-like flavours, nutty, mealy notes adding complexity, and good harmony. The 2010 (★★★★) is similar – rich, rounded and very harmonious, with peachy, distinctly nutty flavours, creamy-textured and already delicious.

 DRY $30 –V

Walnut Block Marlborough Chardonnay (★★★★)

The mouthfilling, creamy-textured 2009 vintage (★★★★) was hand-picked from a single vineyard in the Wairau Valley. Fleshy and youthful, it has peachy, slightly buttery, mealy and toasty flavours, showing excellent complexity and depth. Worth cellaring.

 DRY $28 AV

West Brook Barrique Fermented Marlborough Chardonnay ★★★★

The 2008 vintage (★★★★), fully barrel-fermented, is a powerful, rich wine, finely balanced, with ripe grapefruit and slightly mealy flavours, showing sensitive use of oak, and good complexity and harmony. Fine value.

 DRY $20 V+

West Brook Waimauku Estate Chardonnay ★★★★☆

This stylish, complex wine is estate-grown in West Auckland. Hand-harvested and fermented in French oak casks (35 per cent new), the 2008 vintage (★★★★★) has a very fragrant, slightly smoky bouquet. Creamy-textured, with ripe grapefruit and stone-fruit flavours and finely integrated, nutty oak, it's a deliciously rich, very harmonious wine.

 DRY $29 V+

Whitehaven Marlborough Chardonnay ★★★

The 2009 vintage (★★★) was matured in French oak puncheons (45 per cent new). Enjoyable young, it's a full-bodied wine, citrusy and slightly buttery, with plenty of flavour and some complexity.

Vintage	09	08	07	06
WR	7	5	6	6
Drink	11-14	11-14	P	P

DRY $20 –V

Wild Rock Pania Hawke's Bay Chardonnay   ★★★★

Wild Rock is a division of Craggy Range. Partly barrel-fermented, the 2009 vintage (★★★★) is a mouthfilling, well-rounded wine with a fragrant, nutty bouquet. Sweet-fruited, with ripe stone-fruit flavours, it is peachy, toasty and rich, with an attractively creamy texture.

Vintage	09	08	07
WR	6	7	6
Drink	11-13	11-12	P

 DRY $20 V+

Wild South Marlborough Chardonnay   ★★★

The 2010 vintage (★★★) from Sacred Hill was handled entirely in tanks. Estate-grown in the Wairau Valley, it is mouthfilling and creamy-textured, with fresh, citrusy, appley flavours. A good, drink-young style.

 DRY $19 AV

Wither Hills Wairau Valley Marlborough Chardonnay   ★★★★

This attractive wine was formerly made in a rich, peachy, toasty style and sold at $29, but is now made with less new oak and lees-stirring, in the search for a more refined style. Enjoyable from the start, the 2009 vintage (★★★★) is a fleshy, generous wine with a fragrant bouquet of peachy fruit and a subtle, biscuity oak influence. It's a finely textured wine with good complexity and richness. The 2010 (★★★★) is mouthfilling and sweet-fruited, with generous peach and grapefruit flavours, hints of toast and butterscotch, and a finely poised, dry finish. Good value.

Vintage	10	09	08
WR	7	7	7
Drink	11-15	11-14	11-13

 DRY $20 V+

Wooing Tree Central Otago Chardonnay   ★★★☆

The 2010 vintage (★★★) was hand-picked in the Cromwell Basin and fermented in French oak casks. It's a full-bodied wine with fresh, citrusy, slightly nutty flavours, a minerally streak and strong, buttery notes.

 DRY $28 –V

Wrights Reserve Gisborne Chardonnay   (★★★★)

From an Ormond Valley site under conversion to organic, the 2010 vintage (★★★★) was matured in new French oak barrels and given a full, softening malolactic fermentation. It's a mouthfilling wine with good concentration of ripe stone-fruit flavours, oak complexity and a slightly buttery, smooth finish. Already drinking well, it's a generous wine, rich and rounded.

DRY $35 –V

Chenin Blanc

Today's Chenin Blancs are markedly riper, rounder and more enjoyable to drink than the sharply acidic, austere wines of the 1980s, when Chenin Blanc was far more extensively planted in New Zealand. Yet this classic grape variety is still struggling for an identity. In recent years, several labels have been discontinued – not for lack of quality or value, but lack of buyer interest.

A good New Zealand Chenin Blanc is fresh and buoyantly fruity, with melon and pineapple-evoking flavours and a crisp finish. In the cooler parts of the country, the variety's naturally high acidity (an asset in the warmer viticultural regions of South Africa, the United States and Australia) can be a distinct handicap. But when the grapes achieve full ripeness here, this classic grape of Vouvray, in the Loire Valley, yields sturdy wines that are satisfying in their youth yet can mature for many years, gradually unfolding a delicious, honeyed richness.

Only three wineries have consistently made impressive Chenin Blancs over the past decade: Millton, Margrain and Esk Valley. Many growers, put off by the variety's late-ripening nature and the susceptibility of its tight bunches to botrytis rot, have uprooted their vines. Plantings have plummeted from 372 hectares in 1983 to 47 hectares of bearing vines in 2012.

Chenin Blanc is the country's eleventh most widely planted white-wine variety (behind even Reichensteiner, a bulk-wine variety), with plantings concentrated in Gisborne and Hawke's Bay. In the future, winemakers who plant Chenin Blanc in warm, sunny vineyard sites with devigorating soils, where the variety's vigorous growth can be controlled and yields reduced, can be expected to produce the ripest, most concentrated wines. New Zealand winemakers have yet to get to grips with Chenin Blanc.

Bishop's Head Waipara Valley Chenin Blanc   (★★★)

The 2009 vintage (★★★) was grown in North Canterbury, barrel-fermented with indigenous yeasts and oak-aged for a year. Worth cellaring, it's a clearly varietal wine, citrusy and appley, with fresh acidity and good depth.

DRY $26 –V

Esk Valley Hawke's Bay Chenin Blanc   ★★★★

This is one of New Zealand's few truly convincing Chenin Blancs, with the ability to mature well for several years. A single-vineyard wine, grown at Moteo Pa, the 2009 vintage (★★★★) was partly fermented and lees-aged in tanks, but 55 per cent of the blend was fermented and matured in seasoned French oak barriques and larger, 600-litre *demi-muids*. It's an elegant, medium-bodied wine with tight, lemony flavours, showing some barrel-ferment complexity, and obvious cellaring potential. (The 2011 vintage, only 7.5 per cent barrel-fermented, is basically a dry wine, with only 4.5 grams/litre of residual sugar.)

Vintage	11	10	09	08	07	06
WR	6	6	6	7	7	6
Drink	12-16	11-15	11-14	11-14	11-14	11-12

DRY $24 AV

Farmgate Hawke's Bay Chenin Blanc   ★★★☆

Grown in the Gimblett Gravels and partly barrel-fermented, the 2008 vintage (★★★☆) is a mouthfilling, minerally wine with good depth of pear, citrus-fruit and apple flavours and a crisp, dry finish. Starting to drink well, the 2009 (★★★☆) is full-flavoured, peachy, citrusy and slightly honeyed, with lively acidity. (Sold directly to consumers by Ngatarawa from the Farmgate website.)

Vintage	09	08
WR	6	6
Drink	11-16	11-14

DRY $22 AV

Forrest Marlborough Chenin Blanc ★★★

This is an extremely rare beast – a Chenin Blanc from the South Island. The 2009 vintage (★★★) is an easy-drinking style, grown in the Wairau Valley, with a sliver of sweetness and very decent depth of lemon, apple, slight pear and spice flavours. A medium-bodied, slightly creamy wine, it's fruity and smooth.

MED/DRY $30 –V

Margrain Martinborough Chenin Blanc ★★★★

When Margrain bought the neighbouring Chifney property, they acquired Chenin Blanc vines now around 30 years old. The 2008 vintage (★★★★) is medium-bodied, with good harmony of ripe citrus, melon and pineapple flavours, a splash of sweetness (18 grams/litre of residual sugar) and appetising acidity. It should blossom with cellaring.

Vintage	08
WR	7
Drink	11-19

MED $30 –V

Millton Chenin Blanc Te Arai Vineyard ★★★★★

BioGro certified, this Gisborne wine is New Zealand's best Chenin Blanc. It's a richly varietal wine with concentrated, fresh, vibrant fruit flavours to the fore in some vintages (2007, 2009); nectareous scents and flavours in others (2005, 2008). The grapes are grown organically and hand-picked at different stages of ripening, culminating in some years ('It's in the lap of the gods,' says James Millton) in a final harvest of botrytis-affected fruit. Fermentation is in tanks and large, 620-litre French oak casks, used in the Loire for Chenin Blanc. Still a baby, the 2009 vintage (★★★★) is very fresh, crisp and lively, with no sign of botrytis at this stage. Racy, with a basically dry impression on the palate (7 grams/litre of residual sugar), and a very subtle oak influence, it is minerally and lingering. Open 2013+.

Vintage	09	08	07	06	05	04
WR	6	6	7	7	6	7
Drink	11-21	11-15	11-15	11-20	P	11-14

MED/DRY $28 V+

Sea Level Home Block Nelson Chenin Blanc (★★★☆)

Grown at Mariri and handled entirely in tanks, the 2011 vintage (★★★☆) is very fresh and lively, with citrusy, appley flavours and a minerally streak. Woven with fresh acidity, it's a basically dry style (4 grams/litre of residual sugar), approachable now but well worth cellaring.

Vintage	11
WR	6
Drink	13+

DRY $23 –V

Flora

A California crossing of Gewürztraminer and Sémillon, in cool-climate regions Flora produces aromatic, spicy wine. Some of New Zealand's 'Pinot Gris' vines were a few years ago positively identified as Flora, but the country's total area of bearing Flora vines in 2012 will be just 2 hectares.

Artisan Kauri Ridge Oratia Flora

Estate-grown in the Kauri Ridge Vineyard at Oratia, in West Auckland, the 2009 vintage (★★★☆) is a distinctly medium style (25 grams/litre of residual sugar), medium-bodied, with ripe tropical-fruit flavours, showing very good depth, and a rounded finish. Very gluggable.

MED $20 AV

Ascension The Rogue Flora ★★★

Grown at Matakana, this is typically a floral, weighty wine with grapey, slightly sweet and spicy flavours in an easy-drinking style. The 2010 vintage (★★★), hand-picked and lees-aged in tanks, is lemony, slightly appley and spicy, in a crisp and lively style, offering good summer sipping.

MED/DRY $29 –V

Omaha Bay Vineyard The Impostor Matakana Flora ★★★★

New Zealand has few examples of Flora, but this is clearly the best. The 2009 vintage (★★★★) is a mouthfilling, generous wine, fleshy and ripe, with strong, peachy, spicy, slightly gingery flavours and loads of personality.

Vintage	09	08	07	06
WR	6	6	6	6
Drink	11-14	11-12	11-12	P

MED $27 –V

Gewürztraminer

Only a trickle of Gewürztraminer is exported (34,000 cases in the year to mid-2011, 0.2 per cent of total wine shipments), and the majority of New Zealand bottlings lack the power and richness of the great Alsace model. Yet this classic grape is starting to get the respect it deserves from grape-growers and winemakers here.

For most of the 1990s, Gewürztraminer's popularity was on the wane. Between 1983 and 1996, New Zealand's plantings of Gewürztraminer dropped by almost two-thirds. A key problem is that Gewürztraminer is a temperamental performer in the vineyard, being particularly vulnerable to adverse weather at flowering, which can decimate grape yields. Now there is proof of a strong renewal of interest: the area of bearing vines has surged from 85 hectares in 1998 to 290 hectares in 2012. Most of the plantings are in Marlborough (29 per cent of the national total), Gisborne (28 per cent) and Hawke's Bay (20 per cent).

Slight sweetness and skin contact were commonly used in the past to boost the flavour of Gewürztraminer, at the cost of flavour delicacy and longevity. Such outstanding wines as Dry River have revealed the far richer, softer flavours and greater aging potential that can be gained by reducing crops, leaf-plucking to promote fruit ripeness and avoiding skin contact.

Gewürztraminer is a high-impact wine, brimming with scents and flavours. 'Spicy' is the most common adjective used to pinpoint its distinctive, heady aromas and flavours; tasters also find nuances of gingerbread, freshly ground black pepper, cinnamon, cloves, mint, lychees and mangoes. Once you've tasted one or two Gewürztraminers, you won't have any trouble recognising it in a 'blind' tasting – it's the most forthright, distinctive white-wine variety of all.

Anchorage Nelson Gewürztraminer ★★★

Grown at Motueka, the 2009 vintage (★★★) is a gently perfumed, medium-bodied wine with good depth of fresh lychee and spice flavours, gentle acidity and a dry (2.9 grams/litre of residual sugar) finish.

DRY $20 –V

Aotea Nelson Gewürztraminer (★★★★☆)

(From Seifried, this brand replaces the former Winemaker's Collection label.) The 2011 vintage (★★★★☆) is pale and exotically perfumed, weighty and slightly sweet (20 grams/litre of residual sugar), in a fleshy, intensely varietal style with fresh, concentrated stone-fruit, ginger and spice flavours.

Vintage	11
WR	6
Drink	11-15

MED $23 V+

Askerne Hawke's Bay Gewürztraminer ★★★☆

This winery has a good track record with Gewürztraminer. The 2010 vintage (★★★) was estate-grown, hand-picked and mostly handled in tanks; 15 per cent of the blend was fermented in old French oak casks. Fresh, lemony and slightly spicy, with a dryish finish (5 grams/litre of residual sugar), it has a slightly creamy texture and appealing, rose petal aromas.

Vintage	10	09	08	07	06
WR	7	6	6	7	7
Drink	12-14	11-12	P	P	P

 MED/DRY $20 AV

Astrolabe Voyage Marlborough Gewürztraminer   ★★★★

The richly scented 2009 vintage (★★★★), grown at Grovetown and in the Waihopai Valley, has a gentle splash of sweetness (9.8 grams/litre of residual sugar). Exotically perfumed, it's a rich wine with a slightly oily texture and concentrated flavours of lychees, spices and pears, ripe and rounded.

Vintage	09	08
WR	6	6
Drink	12-13	11-13

MED $24 AV

Ataahua Waipara Gewürztraminer   ★★★★

The 2010 vintage (★★★★) is a medium-dry style, fermented in old oak barrels. The bouquet is spicy and complex, with exotic notes; the palate also reveals good complexity, with strong, spicy, gingery, faintly honeyed flavours. Worth cellaring.

MED/DRY $22 V+

Beach House Hawke's Bay Gewürztraminer   ★★★☆

Grown at Te Awanga, the 2009 vintage (★★★☆) is floral and fresh, with good weight and depth of lychee and spice flavours, leading to a well-spiced, dryish, finely balanced finish.

DRY $22 AV

Blackenbrook Vineyard Nelson Gewürztraminer   ★★★★☆

A consistently delicious wine. The estate-grown, exotically perfumed 2009 vintage (★★★★☆) is an Alsace style, hand-picked very ripe (over 24 brix), with substantial body and just a sliver of sweetness (7 grams/litre of residual sugar). Richly scented, it is mouthfilling, with peachy, spicy flavours showing excellent delicacy and depth, considerable complexity, gentle acidity and a long, spicy finish. (The 2010 is a sweeter style, harbouring 25 grams/litre of residual sugar.)

Vintage	10	09	08	07	06
WR	6	7	7	NM	7
Drink	11-15	11-13	P	NM	P

MED/DRY $26 AV

Blackenbrook Vineyard Nelson Reserve Gewürztraminer   ★★★★☆

The powerful, softly mouthfilling (14.5 per cent alcohol) 2010 vintage (★★★★☆) was harvested at 25.2 brix. It is still youthful, but pure and delicate, with lychee, pear, peach and spice flavours, a slightly oily texture and gently sweet (18 grams/litre of residual sugar), soft, long finish. Best drinking 2012+.

Vintage	10
WR	7
Drink	11-15

MED $31 –V

Bladen Marlborough Gewürztraminer   ★★★★

Hand-harvested in the Tilly Vineyard, the 2010 (★★★★☆) is a top vintage. Made in a medium style (19 grams/litre of residual sugar), it is full-bodied and intensely varietal, with a richly perfumed bouquet and concentrated, peachy, spicy, gingery flavours. Delicious drinking from now onwards.

MED $25 AV

Bouldevines Marlborough Gewürztraminer   ★★★☆

Ripely scented and mouthfilling, the 2009 vintage (★★★☆) is a single-vineyard, finely textured wine with good depth of lychee and spice flavours, gentle acidity and a dryish finish. The 2011 (★★★☆) is a promising wine, pale and youthful, with mouthfilling body, ripe peach, pear and spice flavours and a dryish (7 grams/litre of residual sugar) finish.

Vintage	11
WR	7
Drink	11-13

MED/DRY $25 –V

Brancott Estate 'P' Patutahi Gisborne Gewürztraminer   ★★★★☆

In the past branded as Montana, but since 2009 as Brancott Estate, at its best this wine is full of personality, with a musky perfume and lush lychee and spice flavours. The 2009 vintage (★★★★★) is one of the best – mouthfilling, with a heady fragrance and very rich, citrusy, spicy flavours. It's deliciously weighty, concentrated and well-rounded.

MED $36 –V

Brennan Gibbston Gewürztraminer   ★★★★

Grown at Gibbston, in Central Otago, the 2010 vintage (★★★★☆) has a perfumed, spicy, slightly earthy bouquet, showing good complexity. An Alsace-style, mouthfilling and gently sweet (21 grams/litre of residual sugar), it is intensely varietal, with strong peach, apricot and spice flavours. Oily-textured, with excellent freshness, concentration and harmony, it's already delicious.

MED $28 –V

Brookfields Ohiti Estate Hawke's Bay Gewürztraminer   ★★★☆

Grown in stony soils in Ohiti Road, inland from Fernhill, this is typically a sturdy, soft wine with plenty of character. The 2010 vintage (★★★) is full-bodied, with citrusy, peachy, spicy flavours and a relatively dry (5 grams/litre of residual sugar), smooth finish.

Vintage	10
WR	7
Drink	12-16

MED/DRY $20 AV

Bushmere Estate Gisborne Gewürztraminer   ★★★★

The 2009 vintage (★★★★) is a medium-dry style (8 grams/litre of residual sugar), hand-harvested at 23.5 brix. Exotically perfumed, with good body and concentrated, ripe flavours of peaches, spices, lychees and ginger, it's worth cellaring. Balanced for easy drinking, the 2010 (★★★☆) is ripely scented, with good depth of fresh, citrusy, spicy flavours, a hint of apricot and a slightly sweet finish.

MED/DRY $21 V+

Charles Wiffen Marlborough Gewürztraminer   (★★★☆)

The mouthfilling 2009 vintage (★★★☆) shows some richness of ripe, lemon/spice flavours, fresh acidity and good harmony.

DRY $24 –V

Clearview Beachhead Gewürztraminer   ★★★☆

The richly perfumed, weighty 2010 vintage (★★★★) is from grapes estate-grown at Te Awanga, in Hawke's Bay, blended with fruit 'from another renowned local producer'. Oily-textured, it has concentrated, very ripe lychee, spice, ginger and apricot flavours, with a slightly sweet (11 grams/litre of residual sugar), well-rounded finish.

MED/DRY $21 AV

Cloudy Bay Marlborough Gewürztraminer   ★★★★★

Top vintages of this wine are distinctly Alsace-like – highly perfumed, weighty, complex and rounded. The 2008 (★★★★☆), fermented and matured in old French oak barrels, is full-bodied, rich and complex, in a medium-dry style (8 grams/litre of residual sugar), with concentrated, citrusy, spicy flavours, showing lovely depth and harmony.

Vintage	08
WR	6
Drink	11-13

MED/DRY $30 AV

Coopers Creek Gisborne Gewürztraminer   ★★★★

A consistent bargain. The 2010 vintage (★★★★☆) is another great buy. Richly perfumed, it is slightly gingery on the nose, with a fleshy, concentrated palate. A medium-dry style (7.5 grams/litre of residual sugar), it is ripe and rounded, with a slightly oily texture and lovely poise, delicacy and harmony.

Vintage	10	09	08	07
WR	6	5	NM	6
Drink	12-14	11-12	NM	P

MED/DRY $17 V+

Crossroads Hawke's Bay Origin Vineyard Gewürztraminer   ★★★★

Still on sale, the 2008 vintage (★★★★) offers good value. Handled almost entirely in tanks (3 per cent in old oak barriques), it is still lively, in a mouthfilling, fleshy style with good concentration of ripe lychee and spice flavours, slightly sweet (11 grams/litre of residual sugar) and rounded. It shows good, bottle-aged complexity and is drinking well now.

Vintage	08
WR	5
Drink	11-14

MED/DRY $19 V+

Darling, The, Marlborough Gewürztraminer   ★★★★☆

A single-vineyard wine, grown at Rapaura, the 2010 vintage (★★★★☆) is dry (4 grams/litre of residual sugar) and richly scented, with an oily texture and concentrated citrus-fruit, spice and slight ginger flavours. Handled in tanks (40 per cent) and old oak casks (60 per cent), it shows excellent complexity and potential.

Vintage	10
WR	6
Drink	11-13

 MED/DRY $24 V+

Distant Land Marlborough Gewürztraminer   ★★★★

Bargain-priced, the musky, perfumed 2010 vintage (★★★★) is full-bodied, with strong pear, lychee and spice flavours, hints of oranges and ginger, and a slightly sweet (11 grams/litre of residual sugar), smooth, lingering finish. Grown at Omaka, the 2011 (★★★★) is pale and perfumed, with strong peach, apricot and spice flavours, slightly sweet and rich. Another good buy.

 MED/DRY $20 V+

Dry Gully Central Otago Gewürztraminer   (★★★)

From an Alexandra-based producer, the 2009 vintage (★★★) is mouthfilling and smooth, with satisfying depth of pear, lychee and spice flavours, fresh acidity and a slightly gingery finish.

Vintage	09
WR	4
Drink	11-13

 MED/DRY $20 –V

Dry River Gewürztraminer Dry River Estate   ★★★★★

This intensely perfumed and flavoured Martinborough Gewürztraminer is one of the country's finest. Medium-dry or medium in most years, in top vintages it shows a power and richness comparable to Alsace's *vendange tardive* (late-harvest) wines. Always rich in alcohol and exceptionally full-flavoured, it is also very delicate, with a tight, concentrated, highly refined palate that is typically at its most seductive at two to four years old, although it can mature well for more than a decade. The 2009 vintage (★★★★☆) is mouthfilling (14 per cent alcohol), ripe and slightly sweet, with fresh, pure, intensely varietal flavours of stone-fruit and spices, showing excellent depth and harmony. Drink now or cellar.

Vintage	09	08	07	06	05	04
WR	6	7	NM	6	NM	6
Drink	11-16	11-15	NM	11-12	NM	P

MED/DRY $48 AV

Dry River Lovat Vineyard Gewürztraminer   ★★★★★

Grown in the Lovat Vineyard in Martinborough, a few hundred metres down the road from the winery, the 2010 vintage (★★★★★) was made from 18-year-old vines. Floral and full-bodied, it is very rich and harmonious, with concentrated, well-ripened peach, ginger and spice flavours, a splash of sweetness (17 grams/litre of residual sugar), and a rounded, long finish. A very harmonious wine, it's already delicious.

Vintage	10	09	08
WR	7	7	7
Drink	12-17	11-14	11-15

 MED $44 AV

Ellero Central Otago Gewürztraminer   ★★★☆

From 19-year-old vines at Bannockburn, the 2010 vintage (★★★☆) was fermented and matured in seasoned French oak. Pale, with a lifted, spicy, perfumed bouquet, it is full-bodied and dry, with very good depth of citrusy, spicy flavours.

 MED/DRY $27 –V

Farmgate Hawke's Bay Gewürztraminer   ★★★☆

From Ngatarawa, the 2010 vintage (★★★☆) is medium-bodied, with good varietal character and depth of citrusy, spicy flavour. Made in a slightly sweet style, it is finely balanced, with some complexity.

Vintage	10	09	08	07
WR	6	NM	7	7
Drink	11-14	NM	11-13	P

MED/DRY $22 AV

Forrest The Valleys Wairau Gewürztraminer   ★★★★

The 2009 (★★★★☆) is a top vintage, enticingly scented, with an array of fresh, vibrant, beautifully ripe peach, lychee and spice flavours, a sliver of sweetness and a soft, rich finish.

Vintage	09	08	07	06
WR	7	6	7	7
Drink	11-13	11-12	P	P

 MED/DRY $25 AV

Framingham Marlborough Gewürztraminer   ★★★★☆

This label has shown excellent form of late. A single-vineyard wine, made in a medium style, it is mostly handled in tanks, but part of the blend is aged in old barrels. The 2009 vintage (★★★★★) was 30 per cent barrel-fermented. Exotically perfumed, it is weighty and concentrated, with gentle sweetness (16 grams/litre of residual sugar) and rich peach, lychee, ginger and spice flavours, fresh, vibrant and long. The 2010 (★★★★☆) has an inviting, musky bouquet. A full-bodied (14 per cent alcohol) wine, it is finely textured, with delicious, peachy, spicy, gingery flavours, concentrated and well-rounded.

Vintage	10	09	08	07	06
WR	6	7	7	6	6
Drink	11-15	11-14	11-13	P	P

 MED $28 AV

Gibson Bridge Reserve Marlborough Gewürztraminer

Fleshy and softly textured, the 2009 vintage (★★★★) is a single-vineyard Renwick wine, ripely perfumed, with strong lychee, pear and ginger flavours and a lingering, well-rounded, spicy finish. Still very youthful, the 2010 (★★★) is weighty and slightly sweet, with fresh, delicate pear and lychee flavours, slightly limey and citrusy. Worth cellaring.

MED/DRY $25 –V

Glasnevin Limited Release Waipara Valley Gewürztraminer   (★★★★☆)

From Fiddler's Green, the 2009 vintage (★★★★☆) was harvested at an advanced stage of ripeness (25.4 brix) and fermented and matured for a year in seasoned French oak barriques. Youthful in colour, it is very full-bodied (14.5 per cent alcohol) and richly perfumed, with peachy, spicy flavours showing good complexity. Thought-provoking, with an unusually dry feel and real individuality, it's definitely a 'food' wine.

Vintage	09
WR	6
Drink	11-16

DRY $28 AV

Greenhough Nelson Gewürztraminer   ★★★★

Grown at Hope and Moutere, the 2009 vintage (★★★★) is richly perfumed and mouthfilling, with concentrated peach, lychee and spice flavours, and an off-dry (8 grams/litre of residual sugar), finely balanced finish.

Vintage	09	08	07	06
WR	6	7	6	5
Drink	11-14	11-12	P	P

MED/DRY $22 V+

Greystone Waipara Valley Gewürztraminer   ★★★★★

An emerging star. Exotically perfumed, the 2010 vintage (★★★★★) is a full-bodied (14.5 per cent alcohol), medium style, still youthful but already delicious. It offers rich lychee, pear, ginger and spice flavours, woven with fresh acidity, and shows lovely delicacy, depth and harmony. The 2011 (★★★★★) is another winner. Highly scented, it is mouthfilling, with an oily texture, gentle sweetness and vibrant, peachy, spicy, gingery flavours, impressively rich, finely balanced and lingering.

Vintage	11
WR	7
Drink	11-15

MED $28 V+

Huia Marlborough Gewürztraminer   ★★★☆

The 2009 vintage (★★★★), a single-vineyard wine, is drinking well now – sturdy and rich, with a slightly oily texture and strong peachy, spicy, gingery flavours, dry and rounded. The 2010 (★★★) is currently more restrained, with vibrant, citrusy, spicy, slightly limey and gingery flavours. Open mid-2012+.

DRY $28 –V

Huntaway Reserve Gisborne Gewürztraminer   ★★★★

The Huntaway brand was sold by Pernod Ricard NZ in 2010. This characterful wine has usually been partly barrel-fermented. The 2009 vintage (★★★★) is highly attractive, in a distinctly Alsace style with considerable complexity and rich, soft flavours.

 MED/DRY $24 AV

Hunter's Marlborough Gewürztraminer   ★★★★☆

Hunter's produces a consistently stylish Gewürztraminer, with impressive weight, flavour depth and fragrance. The 2010 vintage (★★★★) is youthful, with fresh, citrusy, spicy flavours, ripe and strong. It has good weight, with a well-rounded, medium-dry finish (12 grams/litre of residual sugar) that lingers well.

Vintage	10	09	08	07	06
WR	5	7	7	6	5
Drink	11-12	11-13	11-12	P	P

MED/DRY $23 V+

Johanneshof Marlborough Gewürztraminer   ★★★★★

This beauty is one of the country's great Gewürztraminers. The 2009 vintage (★★★★★) is a medium style with lovely richness, delicacy and harmony. Finely poised, with gentle acidity, it has beautifully ripe lychee and spice flavours and a heady, musky bouquet. The 2010 (★★★★★) is another winner. Exotically perfumed, with Turkish delight aromas, it is mouthfilling and rounded, with rich, pure flavours of pears, lychees and spices, a splash of sweetness (21 grams/litre of residual sugar), and lovely concentration and harmony.

Vintage	10	09	08	07	06	05	04	03
WR	7	6	6	7	6	7	7	6
Drink	11-20	11-17	11-16	11-17	11-15	11-15	11-14	11-12

MED $30 AV

Junction, The, Side Step Gewürztraminer   (★★★☆)

Grown in Central Hawke's Bay, the 2008 vintage (★★★☆) is a strongly varietal wine with distinctly spicy aromas and a weighty palate with lively, citrusy, well-spiced flavours. It's maturing well.

MED/DRY $26 –V

Kaimira Estate Brightwater Gewürztraminer   ★★★☆

The 2009 (★★★★) is a distinctly medium style (30 grams/litre of residual sugar) from Nelson. Estate-grown at Brightwater, it is very full-bodied (14.5 per cent alcohol), with a strong surge of spicy, gingery flavour. It's delicious now. The 2010 vintage (★★★☆) is much drier (6 grams/litre of residual sugar) and a less 'upfront' style than the 2009, but should reward cellaring, with lychee, pear and spice flavours showing good delicacy and freshness.

Vintage	10
WR	5
Drink	11-16

 MED/DRY $23 –V

Kirkpatrick Estate Patutahi Gisborne Gewürztraminer   ★★★☆

The 2009 (★★★☆) is a medium-dry (10 grams/litre of residual sugar), slightly honeyed wine, peachy and spicy, with good flavour depth and harmony. The 2010 vintage (★★★☆) is fragrant and full-bodied, with soft, ripe flavours showing very good delicacy and richness.

Vintage	09
WR	5
Drink	11-13

 MED/DRY $25 –V

Konrad Marlborough Gewürztraminer   ★★★☆

Hand-picked in the Waihopai Valley, the 2010 vintage (★★★☆) was mostly handled in tanks, but a small portion was fermented with indigenous yeasts in seasoned French oak barrels. Made in a 'deliberately restrained' style, it is ripely perfumed and weighty, soft and dryish (5 grams/litre of residual sugar), with very good depth of stone-fruit and spice flavours.

Vintage	10
WR	6
Drink	11-15

 MED/DRY $19 V+

Lake Road Gisborne Gewürztraminer   (★★★☆)

The 2010 vintage (★★★☆) is a good buy. Harvested at over 24 brix, it is a medium to full-bodied style, finely balanced for easy drinking, with plenty of fresh, slightly sweet, gingery, spicy flavour and an inviting fragrance.

 MED/DRY $19 V+

Lawson's Dry Hills Marlborough Gewürztraminer   ★★★★★

This is consistently one of the country's most impressive Gewürztraminers. Grown near the winery in the Home Block and nearby Woodward Vineyard, at the foot of the Wither Hills, it is typically harvested at over 24 brix and mostly cool-fermented in stainless steel tanks, but a small component is given 'the full treatment', with a high-solids, indigenous yeast ferment in seasoned French oak barriques, malolactic fermentation and lees-stirring. The 2009 (★★★★) is a medium-dry style (9 grams/litre of residual sugar), with substantial body and rich lychee, spice and ginger flavours. It's a generous wine with some exotic notes, slightly sweeter and crisper than the fleshy, soft 2008 (★★★★☆).

Vintage	09	08	07	06	05	04
WR	7	7	7	7	6	7
Drink	11-14	11-13	11-12	P	P	P

MED/DRY $27 V+

Lawson's Dry Hills The Pioneer Marlborough Gewürztraminer   (★★★★★)

The debut 2009 vintage (★★★★★) was estate-grown, harvested at an average of over 25 brix, with some botrytis shrivel, and partly barrel-fermented. The bouquet is rich and highly spiced; the palate is powerful, very soft and concentrated, with deep lychee, spice and ginger flavours, considerable complexity and strong drink-young appeal.

MED $32 AV

Mahi Twin Valleys Marlborough Gewürztraminer ★★★★

The 2010 vintage (★★★★) was grown at the Fareham Lane junction of the Wairau and Waihopai valleys, hand-picked and fermented with indigenous yeasts in tanks (60 per cent) and seasoned French oak barriques (40 per cent). Drinking well now, it's a dry wine (3 grams/litre of residual sugar), ripely perfumed and mouthfilling, with an oily texture and peachy, gently spicy and gingery flavours, showing good complexity.

Vintage	10	09
WR	6	6
Drink	11-16	11-15

 DRY $24 AV

Maimai Creek Hawke's Bay Gewürztraminer ★★★☆

The 2009 vintage (★★★) is a mouthfilling (14.5 per cent alcohol) wine with plenty of spicy flavour and a dryish, gingery finish.

 MED/DRY $20 AV

Matawhero Gisborne Gewürztraminer ★★★☆

The 2009 vintage (★★★☆) is the first for many years under one of the most famous wine brands of the 1970s and 1980s, now under new ownership. Grown mostly in the Patutahi district, inland from Matawhero, it is a full-bodied, dry style with a perfumed, gingery bouquet. Mouthfilling, with plenty of peachy, gingery, spicy flavour, ripe and rounded, it's now showing some bottle-aged complexity, but lacks the magic of the early wines.

DRY $25 –V

Misha's Vineyard The Gallery Central Otago Gewürztraminer ★★★★☆

The 2010 vintage (★★★★) was hand-picked at Bendigo at over 24 brix and mostly handled in tanks, but 12 per cent was fermented with indigenous yeasts in seasoned oak casks. It's a mouthfilling (14 per cent alcohol), medium-dry style (9 grams/litre of residual sugar), aromatic, fleshy and soft, with substantial body, pure lychee and peach flavours, hints of lime and ginger, and excellent freshness, delicacy and harmony.

Vintage	10	09	08
WR	6	6	7
Drink	11-15	11-14	11-13

 MED/DRY $28 AV

Mission Hawke's Bay Gewürztraminer ★★★☆

Typically good value. The 2011 vintage (★★★★) has musky, spicy, Turkish delight aromas. Mouthfilling, with good weight, ripeness and richness, it's an opulent style with a sliver of sweetness (9 grams/litre of residual sugar) and a lingering finish.

 MED/DRY $20 AV

Morton Estate White Label Hawke's Bay Gewürztraminer ★★★☆

The 2009 vintage (★★★☆) is a powerful wine (14.5 per cent alcohol), ripely perfumed, with strong pear, lychee, ginger and spice flavours, quite open and expressive.

Vintage	09
WR	7
Drink	P

MED/DRY $19 V+

Mud House Marlborough Gewürztraminer (★★★☆)

The 2009 vintage (★★★☆) is an easy-drinking, full-flavoured wine, fresh, citrusy, spicy and gingery, with a touch of sweetness and substantial body.

MED/DRY $20 AV

Ngatarawa Stables Hawke's Bay Gewürztraminer (★★★)

A good buy, the easy-drinking 2010 vintage (★★★) is mouthfilling and smooth, with satisfying depth of peachy, spicy flavours and an off-dry (5 grams/litre of residual sugar), soft finish.

Vintage	10
WR	6
Drink	11-14

MED/DRY $15 V+

Ohinemuri Estate Matawhero Gewürztraminer ★★★☆

The 2009 vintage (★★★☆) was grown in Gisborne and mostly fermented in tanks, but 18 per cent of the blend was barrel-fermented. It's a medium style (18 grams/litre of residual sugar), with mouthfilling body and plenty of gingery, spicy flavour, crisp and strong.

Vintage	09	08	07	06
WR	5	6	7	6
Drink	10-13	P	P	P

MED $23 –V

Old Coach Road Nelson Gewürztraminer ★★★☆

The 2010 vintage (★★★☆) from Seifried Estate has an inviting, musky perfume. It is mouthfilling and gently sweet (10 grams/litre of residual sugar), with very good depth of citrusy, spicy flavours and a smooth finish. The 2011 (★★★) is full-bodied, with a fresh, spicy bouquet and plenty of citrusy, spicy, slightly gingery flavour, a little sweet and crisp.

MED/DRY $19 V+

Olssens Central Otago Gewürztraminer ★★★

Estate-grown at Bannockburn, the 2010 vintage (★★★) was fermented in tanks and old, neutral oak barrels. It's an easy-drinking, dryish style (5 grams/litre of residual sugar), with gentle acidity and decent depth of lemon, lychee and spice flavours.

MED/DRY $25 –V

Omihi Road Waipara Gewürztraminer   ★★★★

The 2009 vintage (★★★★☆) from Torlesse is rich, intensely varietal and weighty. Slightly oily, it has concentrated peach, lychee and spice flavours, gentle sweetness (15 grams/litre of residual sugar) and fresh, appetising acidity.

Vintage	09	08
WR	7	6
Drink	12-15	11-12

MED $25 AV

Pasquale Waitaki Valley Gewürztraminer   (★★★★)

Estate-grown at Kurow, hand-picked and fermented and lees-aged in tanks (mostly) and old French oak casks, the 2010 vintage (★★★★) is a medium-dry style (14 grams/litre of residual sugar). Full-bodied, it has excellent depth and texture, with gentle acidity and delicious lychee, pear, spice and ginger flavours. Drink now or cellar.

MED/DRY $30 –V

Pegasus Bay Gewürztraminer   ★★★★★

The memorable 2009 vintage (★★★★★) is from vines planted at Waipara in the 1970s. Hand-picked at 28 brix and fermented with indigenous yeasts in old French barrels, it has a ravishingly full-bloomed bouquet, perfumed and complex, leading into a weighty palate (14 per cent alcohol) with superbly concentrated, spicy, gingery flavours. Made in a medium style (26 grams/litre of residual sugar), it's a commanding, deliciously harmonious wine with a powerful presence.

Vintage	10	09
WR	6	6
Drink	11-14	11-12

MED $32 AV.

Ra Nui Wairau Valley Marlborough Gewürztraminer   ★★★☆

The 2010 vintage (★★★☆) is a dry style (4 grams/litre of residual sugar) with fresh, moderately concentrated flavours of lychees, spices, lemons and apples that linger to a smooth, well-spiced finish.

DRY $24 –V

Rimu Grove Nelson Gewürztraminer   (★★★☆)

Grown in the Moutere hills and handled entirely in tanks, the 2010 vintage (★★★☆) is weighty (14.5 per cent alcohol), with very good depth of ripe lychee and spice flavours, a slightly oily texture and abundant sweetness (45 grams/litre of residual sugar).

Vintage	10
WR	7
Drink	11-18

MED $29 –V

River Farm Godfrey Road Marlborough Gewürztraminer (★★★☆)

The 2009 vintage (★★★☆) was hand-picked at 24.5 brix and a small portion of the blend was fermented with indigenous yeasts in seasoned French oak casks. Mouthfilling (14.5 per cent alcohol), it is tightly structured, with lemon, spice and slight ginger flavours, showing some complexity, and a fully dry finish.

Vintage	09	DRY $20 AV
WR	6	
Drink	11-14	

Rockburn Spitfire Central Otago Gewürztraminer (★★★★)

Estate-grown at Parkburn, in the Cromwell Basin, the debut 2011 vintage (★★★★) is full-bodied and well-rounded, with strong, ripe lychee and spice flavours. Already delicious, it's a gently sweet (30 grams/litre of residual sugar) style, showing excellent richness and potential.

Vintage	11	MED $33 –V
WR	7	
Drink	11-16	

Rossendale Canterbury Gewürztraminer (★★★☆)

The perfumed, strongly varietal 2010 vintage (★★★☆) is a medium-bodied wine with fresh, peachy, citrusy, spicy flavours. Slightly sweet and gingery, it has balanced acidity and a distinctly spicy finish.

MED/DRY $30 –V

Saint Clair Pioneer Block 12 Lone Gum Gewürztraminer ★★★★

Grown in a warm site in Marlborough's lower Omaka Valley, the 2010 vintage (★★★★☆) is an exotically perfumed Alsace style, soft and generous. Already delicious, with a distinct splash of sweetness (20 grams/litre of residual sugar), it has gentle acidity, an oily texture and luscious, concentrated lychee, ginger and spice flavours.

MED $24 AV

Saint Clair Reserve Godfrey's Creek Gewürztraminer ★★★☆

From first-crop vines in the Brancott Valley, the 2008 vintage (★★★★) is a distinctly medium style (24 grams/litre of residual sugar). Fleshy, with strong, peachy, spicy flavours, fresh, ripe and rounded, it is softly structured, oily and lush.

Vintage	08	MED $27 –V
WR	6	
Drink	P	

Saints Gisborne Gewürztraminer ★★★☆

Grown at Patutahi, the 2009 vintage (★★★☆) is a slightly sweet style with strong, ripe flavours of stone-fruit and spice.

MED/DRY $20 AV

Sea Level Home Block Nelson Gewürztraminer   (★★★★☆)

Estate-grown at Mariri, the debut 2011 vintage (★★★★☆) is already delicious. Full-bodied, it's a medium style (19 grams/litre of residual sugar), intensely varietal, with rich ginger, spice and apricot flavours, gentle acidity and lovely harmony.

Vintage	11
WR	6
Drink	13+

 MED $23 V+

Seifried Nelson Gewürztraminer   ★★★★

Typically a floral, well-spiced wine, of excellent quality and value. The intensely varietal 2010 (★★★★) is exotically scented, in a medium style (16 grams/litre of residual sugar), with rich, peachy, gingery, spicy flavours. The 2011 (★★★☆) is fractionally drier (14 grams/litre of residual sugar), with mouthfilling body and fresh, spicy flavours, showing very good delicacy and depth. Finely balanced, it should open out well during 2012–13.

Vintage	11	10	09
WR	6	6	6
Drink	11-15	11-15	11-13

MED/DRY $21 V+

Seifried Winemakers Collection Nelson Gewürztraminer   ★★★★★

This is typically a rich wine with loads of personality. Grown at Brightwater, the 2010 vintage (★★★★☆) is a medium style (22 grams/litre of residual sugar), perfumed, rich and oily-textured, with concentrated stone-fruit and spice flavours, a hint of apricot and real harmony. Delicious from the start.

Vintage	10	09	08	07	06
WR	6	6	6	6	7
Drink	11-15	11-14	11-12	P	P

 MED $23 V+

Seresin Marlborough Gewürztraminer   ★★★★

This wine is hand-picked in the Raupo Creek Vineyard, in the Omaka Valley. The 2009 vintage (★★★★☆) is a medium-dry style (11 grams/litre of residual sugar), partly (15 per cent) fermented in old French oak barriques. Richly perfumed, it's an Alsace style, mouthfilling and complex, with intensely varietal stone-fruit, ginger and spice flavours, finely textured, soft and rich.

Vintage	09	08
WR	7	6
Drink	11-14	11-13

MED/DRY $30 –V

Soljans Gisborne Gewürztraminer   ★★★☆

Drinking well now, the 2010 vintage (★★★☆) is a medium style (17 grams/litre of residual sugar), full-bodied, with peachy, spicy flavours, fresh and strong.

 MED $20 AV

Spy Valley Envoy Marlborough Gewürztraminer ★★★★☆

The outstanding 2009 vintage (★★★★★) was estate-grown in the Waihopai Valley, hand-harvested at 25.6 to 27.8 brix, and fermented in small oak vessels. A distinctly medium style (26 grams/litre of residual sugar), it is fleshy and soft, with ripe aromas and flavours of peaches, pears and spices, showing lovely harmony, complexity and richness.

Vintage	09	08	07	06
WR	7	6	6	6
Drink	11-14	11-13 · 11-12		P

MED $30 –V

Spy Valley Marlborough Gewürztraminer ★★★★

Estate-grown in the Waihopai Valley, this wine is consistently impressive. The 2011 vintage (★★★★) was harvested at 23.4 to 25.2 brix and partly fermented in seasoned oak barrels. Slightly sweet (12 grams/litre of residual sugar), it is an exotically perfumed, full-bodied wine with gentle acidity and loads of spicy, slightly gingery flavour.

Vintage	11	10	09	08	07	06
WR	7	6	7	6	6	6
Drink	11-14	11-13	11-12	P	P	P

MED/DRY $23 AV

Stafford Lane Nelson Gewürztraminer (★★☆)

The 2009 vintage (★★☆) is a medium-bodied wine, fresh, crisp and lively, with decent depth of lemon, apple and spice flavours and an off-dry (6.7 grams/litre of residual sugar) finish.

MED/DRY $19 –V

Stone Bridge Gisborne Gewürztraminer ★★★

The 2010 vintage (★★★) is a medium-dry style (11 grams/litre of residual sugar), invitingly perfumed, with moderately concentrated flavours of lychees, ginger and spice.

MED/DRY $20 –V

Stonecroft Hawke's Bay Gewürztraminer ★★★★

The 2010 vintage (★★★★☆) was partly barrel-fermented (unusual for this wine). Full-bodied, well-spiced and rich, it shows excellent weight and concentration, with deep, ripe, peachy, slightly gingery flavours, an oily texture and impressive complexity. (The 2011 vintage is labelled 'Gimblett Gravels'.)

Vintage	11	10	09
WR	7	7	6
Drink	12-20	11-20	11-20

MED/DRY $25 AV

Stonecroft Old Vine Gewürztraminer ★★★★★

The Gewürztraminers from this tiny Hawke's Bay winery are striking and among the finest in the country. This 'Old Vine' wine, introduced from the 2004 vintage, is made entirely from grapes hand-picked from the original Mere Road plantings in 1983. The 2009 (★★★★★), handled entirely in tanks, makes a powerful statement. An authoritative wine with a voluminous, spicy, gingery, slightly honeyed fragrance, it is weighty and complex, with superbly rich, peachy and spicy flavours, fresh and lasting. The 2010 vintage (★★★★☆) is viewed as a slightly 'lighter' style, so priced lower than the usual $45. Still very youthful, it is full-bodied and gently sweet (10 grams/litre of residual sugar), with concentrated, ripe stone-fruit and spice flavours, finely balanced, rounded and rich.

Vintage	09
WR	6
Drink	11-20

MED/DRY $45 AV

Summerhouse Marlborough Gewürztraminer ★★★☆

The 2010 vintage (★★★☆) of this single-vineyard wine is mouthfilling and soft, with moderately concentrated flavours, showing good texture, delicacy and freshness. The 2011 (★★★☆) is full-bodied (14.5 per cent alcohol), with fresh, youthful pear and spice flavours, slightly sweet (6 grams/litre of residual sugar), ripe, generous and well-rounded. Best mid-2012+.

MED/DRY $25 –V

Te Kairanga Six Sons Gisborne Gewürztraminer (★★★★)

Drinking well now, the 2008 vintage (★★★★) is ripely scented, with mouthfilling body and fresh, finely balanced lychee, ginger and spice flavours. It's a medium-dry style (12 grams/litre of residual sugar), with excellent depth.

Vintage	08
WR	6
Drink	11-12

MED/DRY $21 V+

Te Whare Ra Marlborough Gewürztraminer ★★★★

This was once an arrestingly powerful, hedonistic wine that crammed more flavour into the glass than most other Gewürztraminers from the region. Some of the wines I have tasted in recent years have been less exciting, but the 2009 vintage (★★★★★) is impressive. Very full-bodied (14.5 per cent alcohol), it's in the Alsace mould, with beautifully ripe peachy, citrusy, spicy flavours, finely textured and showing greater complexity than most. A wine of real power and presence, it's delicious now, but should also mature gracefully.

MED $32 –V

Three Miners Earnscleugh Valley Gewürztraminer ★★★

The 2010 vintage (★★★) is a fleshy, barrel-fermented style from Central Otago with 'funky' aromas reflecting a strong indigenous yeast influence. Full-bodied, it has very good depth of peach, lychee and spice flavours and a rounded, dry finish.

DRY $22 –V

Tohu Single Vineyard Nelson Gewürztraminer   (★★★☆)

Hand-picked in the Redwood Valley, the easy-drinking 2011 vintage (★★★☆) is a medium-dry style (10 grams/litre of residual sugar), with good weight and depth of citrus fruit, lychee, ginger and spice flavours, fresh and rounded.

 MED/DRY $22 AV

Torlesse Waipara Gewürztraminer   ★★★★

Fine value. The 2009 vintage (★★★★) is fresh and lively, in an intensely varietal style with a distinct splash of sweetness (16 grams/litre of residual sugar) and spicy, concentrated flavours.

Vintage	10	09
WR	6	6
Drink	12-15	12-15

 MED $18 V+

Villa Maria Private Bin East Coast Gewürztraminer   ★★★★

The 2009 (★★★★) has a perfumed, intensely varietal bouquet of lychees and spices. Weighty and rounded, it has excellent body and depth of fresh lychee, pear and spice flavours, dryish and lingering. The 2011 (tasted prior to bottling, and so not rated) was promising, with a richly scented bouquet and crisp, citrusy, spicy flavours.

Vintage	11	10	09
WR	6	6	6
Drink	12-14	11-13	11-12

 MED/DRY $23 AV

Villa Maria Single Vineyard Ihumatao Gewürztraminer   ★★★★★

Estate-grown in South Auckland, this wine is partly fermented with indigenous yeasts in seasoned French oak barriques; the rest is handled in tanks. The 2010 vintage (★★★★☆), 30 per cent barrel-fermented, has fresh, strong, slightly sweet flavours (7 grams/litre of residual sugar), showing lovely delicacy, purity and length. Open 2012+.

Vintage	10	09
WR	7	5
Drink	11-15	11-13

 MED/DRY $32 AV

Vinoptima Ormond Reserve Gewürztraminer   ★★★★★

This wine, launched from 2003, is from Nick Nobilo's vineyard at Ormond, in Gisborne, devoted exclusively to the variety, and is partly fermented in large 1200-litre German oak ovals. The lovely 2006 (★★★★★) is mouthfilling and rich, with notable delicacy, concentration and harmony. The 2004 (★★★★★) is the other outstanding vintage to date.

Vintage	06	05	04	03
WR	6	5	7	5
Drink	11-17	11-12	11-12	P

MED $99 –V

Waimea Nelson Gewürztraminer   ★★★★

Grown on the Waimea Plains and at Ruby Bay, the 2010 vintage (★★★★) was harvested at a very ripe 24–25 brix. It's a full-bodied, off-dry style (9 grams/litre of residual sugar) with an inviting, floral bouquet, gentle acidity and fresh, concentrated stone-fruit and spice flavours.

MED/DRY $23 AV

Waipara Hills Soul of the South Waipara Gewürztraminer   (★★★★)

Estate-grown in the Mound Vineyard, the 2009 vintage (★★★★) is ripely scented and mouthfilling, fresh and rich, with crisp, vibrant flavours of citrus fruits and spices, excellent delicacy, and a medium-dry (11 grams/litre of residual sugar), finely balanced finish.

MED/DRY $21 V+

Waipara Springs Premo Gewürztraminer   (★★★★☆)

Lovely now, the 2008 vintage (★★★★☆) is a medium style (25 grams/litre of residual sugar), full-bodied and finely textured, with very ripe peach, spice and slight apricot flavours, showing a touch of complexity and impressive concentration, and a well-rounded finish.

MED $24 V+

Wairau River Marlborough Gewürztraminer   ★★★☆

The 2010 vintage (★★★★) is an off-dry style (7 grams/litre of residual sugar), 10 per cent oak-matured. Richly perfumed, with lychee and spice aromas, it is full-bodied (14.5 per cent alcohol), with strong lychee, pear and spice flavours, showing very good delicacy and purity, and a fresh, lingering finish.

Vintage	11	10	09	08
WR	6	6	6	5
Drink	12-15	11-13	11-12	P

MED/DRY $25 –V

West Brook Marlborough Gewürztraminer   ★★★☆

The 2010 vintage (★★★★) is a fleshy, elegant wine, partly (13 per cent) barrel-fermented, with a musky, floral bouquet and refreshing, ripe, gently sweet flavours, showing excellent concentration.

MED $24 –V

Whitehaven Marlborough Gewürztraminer   ★★★★

The 2009 vintage (★★★★) is mouthfilling and soft, with indigenous yeast fermentation in old barriques for part of the blend adding a touch of complexity. It has strong lychee, spice and slight ginger flavours, fresh and ripe, in an off-dry style (9 grams/litre of residual sugar) with lovely texture.

Vintage	09	08
WR	7	5
Drink	11-14	11-12

MED/DRY $20 V+

Wrights Gisborne Gewürztraminer (★★★★)

Grown in the Ormond Valley and partly barrel-fermented, the 2010 vintage (★★★★) is a richly perfumed wine with a spicy, exotic bouquet. Mouthfilling and dry, it has concentrated, peachy, gingery flavours, showing excellent complexity and depth.

DRY $25 AV

Yealands Estate Marlborough Gewürztraminer ★★★

Estate-grown at Seaview, in the Awatere Valley, the 2009 vintage (★★☆) is citrusy, spicy and slightly limey, with green edges, fresh acidity and a slightly sweet (8 grams/litre of residual sugar) finish.

MED/DRY $24 –V

Grüner Veltliner

Grüner Veltliner, Austria's favourite white-wine variety, is currently stirring up interest in New Zealand, from Gisborne to Central Otago. 'Grü-Vee' is a fairly late ripener in Austria, where it yields medium-bodied wines, fruity, crisp and dry, with a spicy, slightly musky aroma. Most are drunk young, but the finest wines, with an Alsace-like substance and perfume, are more age-worthy. Coopers Creek produced New Zealand's first Grüner Veltliner from the 2008 vintage, but according to the latest national vineyard survey, just 1 hectare of Grüner Veltliner vines will be bearing in 2012.

Babich Family Estates Headwaters Organic Block
Marlborough Grüner Veltliner (★★★)

Made in a dry style, the debut 2011 vintage (★★★) is a medium-bodied wine with a floral bouquet and lemony, slightly spicy flavours, fresh and crisp. In its infancy, it's hard to pin down clear-cut varietal characters, but bottle-age (and in later years, vine-age) will surely help.

DRY $25 –V

Coopers Creek SV The Groover Gisborne Grüner Veltliner ★★★☆

The 2010 vintage (★★★★) is the best yet. Mouthfilling and finely textured, it's a basically dry style (4.5 grams/litre of residual sugar), fleshy, ripe, peachy and spicy, with gentle acidity and a well-rounded finish.

DRY $20 AV

Vintage	10	09	08
WR	6	6	5
Drink	12-13	11-12	P

Doctors', The, Marlborough Grüner Veltliner (★★★★)

From Forrest Estate, the debut 2010 vintage (★★★★) was made from infant, two-year-old vines at Renwick, in the Wairau Valley. A weighty, dryish, fruity wine with very good depth of peach, pear, lychee and spice flavours and a rounded finish, it's not highly distinctive, in terms of varietal character, but a delicious mouthful.

MED/DRY $25 AV

Konrad Marlborough Grüner Veltliner (★★★☆)

From first-crop vines, estate-grown and hand-picked in the Waihopai Valley, the 2010 vintage (★★★☆) is a weighty, dry wine (4 grams/litre of residual sugar), fresh and aromatic, with a rounded, slightly spicy finish.

DRY $24 –V

Vintage	10
WR	5
Drink	11-13

Seifried Nelson Grüner Veltliner   ★★★★

The debut 2010 vintage (★★★☆) of a variety famous in Hermann Seifried's homeland was made in a fully dry style. Mouthfilling, with peachy, slightly spicy and lemony flavours, it's a quietly satisfying, vibrantly fruity wine with a rounded finish. The 2011 (★★★★☆) is a big step up. Dry, with excellent intensity and poise, it has gently spicy aromas, fresh, strong, citrusy, spicy flavours and a lasting finish. It's full of personality.

Vintage	11	10
WR	6	5
Drink	11-13	11-13

Tinpot Hut Marlborough Grüner Veltliner   (★★★☆)

Fresh and full-bodied, the 2010 vintage (★★★☆) has ripe, citrusy, slightly peachy flavours to the fore and hints of spices and ginger. It's a finely balanced wine with fresh acidity, good depth and a dry (3.5 grams/litre of residual sugar) finish.

Waimea Nelson Grüner Veltliner   (★★★★)

The debut 2010 vintage (★★★★) is one of the country's top Grüner Veltliners so far. Grown on the Waimea Plains, it is full-bodied and fresh, with very good depth of citrusy, slightly minerally and spicy flavours and a dry (3 grams/litre of residual sugar), persistent finish.

DRY $25 AV

Müller-Thurgau

New Zealand's most common variety 25 years ago, Müller-Thurgau is an endangered species. Most likely a crossing of Riesling and Sylvaner, Müller-Thurgau became extremely popular in Germany after the Second World War, when it was prized for its ability to ripen early with bumper crops. In New Zealand, plantings started to snowball in the early 1970s, and by 1975 it was our most widely planted variety. In 2012, however, there will only be 74 hectares of bearing vines – down from 1873 hectares in 1983. Two-thirds of the vines are clustered in Gisborne.

Müller-Thurgau should be drunk young, at six to 18 months old, when its garden-fresh aromas are in full flower. To attract those who are new to wine, it is typically made slightly sweet. Its fruity, citrusy flavours are generally mild and soft, lacking the crisp acidity and flavour intensity of Riesling.

Corbans White Label Müller-Thurgau ★★☆

This cheap, easy-drinking wine is typically light, lemon-scented and smooth, with fresh, citrusy flavours, gentle sweetness and moderate acidity.

MED $8 V+

Opihi Vineyard South Canterbury Müller-Thurgau ★★★

Estate-grown and hand-picked, the 2009 vintage (★★☆) is light, with lemony, appley flavours, gentle sweetness (9 grams/litre of residual sugar), and crisp acidity keeping things lively.

MED/DRY $16 –V

Muscat

Muscat vines grow all over the Mediterranean, but Muscat is rarely seen in New Zealand as a varietal wine, because it ripens late in the season, without the lushness and intensity achieved in warmer regions. Of the country's 122 hectares of bearing Muscat vines in 2012, 96 hectares are clustered in Gisborne. Most of the grapes are used to add an inviting, musky perfume to low-priced sparklings, modelled on the Asti Spumantes of northern Italy.

Blackenbrook Vineyard Nelson Muscat ★★★★

The debut 2010 vintage (★★★★) is a breakthrough – the South Island's first Muscat. Estate-grown, hand-picked at 23.4 brix and lees-aged in tanks, it's a finely scented – although not overwhelmingly musky – wine, fresh and finely poised, with delicious, citrusy flavours, hints of oranges and spices, gentle sweetness and mouthfilling body. The 2011 (★★★★) is similar – weighty and harmonious, with slightly sweet (12 grams/litre of residual sugar), concentrated peach, spice and orange flavours, fresh, vibrant and already delicious. But watch out for the 'light-hearted' and 'fun to drink' descriptors on the back label – it's a full-bodied wine with 14 per cent alcohol.

Vintage	11	10
WR	7	7
Drink	11-13	11-12

MED/DRY $23 AV

Leaning Rock Central Otago Rosa Muskat (★★★★)

Still on sale, the attractively perfumed 2008 vintage (★★★★), grown at Alexandra, is not a true Muscat, but based on a variety – also called Schönburger – bred by crossing Pinot Noir, Chasselas and Muscat Hamburg. Full of charm, it's a juicy, gently sweet, medium-bodied wine with distinct hints of oranges and pineapples, none of the earthiness typical of most white wines made from Pinot Noir, gentle acidity and very good depth. Worth trying.

MED $20 V+

Millton Te Arai Vineyard Muskats @ Dawn ★★★

Modelled on Moscato d'Asti, this Gisborne wine is handled entirely in tanks and stop-fermented with low alcohol (7.5 per cent in 2010) and plentiful sweetness (66 grams/litre of residual sugar in 2010). It typically has perfumed, Muscat aromas, leading into a light wine with gentle acidity and fresh, lemony, appley flavours, showing good delicacy and liveliness. Easy, summer sipping. SW $20 –V

Tolaga Bay Estate Tolaga Bay Muscat ★★★

Grown on the East Cape, north of Gisborne, the 2009 vintage (★★★) tastes like Asti Spumante – without the bubbles. Light and lively, it's a low-alcohol wine (10 per cent), gently perfumed, with a touch of *spritzig* and fresh, attractive citrus-fruit and orange flavours, slightly sweet and smooth.

MED $20 –V

Pinot Blanc

If you love Chardonnay, try Pinot Blanc. A white mutation of Pinot Noir, Pinot Blanc is highly regarded in Italy and California for its generous extract and moderate acidity, although in Alsace and Germany the more aromatic Pinot Gris finds greater favour.

With its fullness of weight and subtle aromatics, Pinot Blanc can easily be mistaken for Chardonnay in a blind tasting. The variety is still rare in New Zealand, but in 2012 there will be 17 hectares of bearing vines, mostly in Canterbury and Central Otago.

Clayridge Marlborough Pinot Blanc ★★★☆

The 2010 vintage (★★☆) is medium-bodied, with citrusy, appley, spicy flavours, fresh and youthful, and a slightly creamy texture. It's a solid wine, but lacks the richness of some past releases.

DRY $24 –V

Gibbston Valley Central Otago Pinot Blanc ★★★☆

Estate-grown at Bendigo and fermented with use of indigenous yeasts and old French oak casks, this is typically a mouthfilling wine, peachy and dry. The 2009 vintage (★★★★) tastes like a cross of Chardonnay and Pinot Gris. Delicious young, it's fresh and full-bodied, with rich, peachy, slightly spicy and toasty flavours.

DRY $27 –V

Greenhough Hope Vineyard Pinot Blanc ★★★★☆

From vines planted at Hope, in Nelson, in the late 1970s, the 2009 vintage (★★★★★) is engrossing. Fermented and matured in seasoned French oak barriques and produced in a slightly off-dry style (5 grams/litre of residual sugar), it's very full-bodied (14.5 per cent alcohol), weighty, complex and rich, with deep peach, pear and spice flavours, slightly buttery and savoury. Sweet-fruited and highly concentrated, it's a very harmonious wine, for drinking now or cellaring. The 2010 (★★★★☆) oak-aged for 15 months, is very full-bodied (14.8 per cent), fleshy and rounded, with strong peach and pear flavours, slightly spicy and biscuity, and good complexity. A powerful, youthful wine, it's very age-worthy.

Vintage	10	09	08	07	06
WR	6	6	7	7	6
Drink	11-15	11-15	11-13	11-12	11-12

MED/DRY $32 –V

Kerner Estate Marlborough Pinot Blanc ★★★☆

Hand-picked and barrel-fermented with indigenous yeasts, the 2008 vintage (★★★☆) is mouthfilling and creamy-textured, with pear and spice, slightly buttery flavours, showing good depth and complexity. Maturing well, it tastes like a cross of Pinot Gris and Chardonnay.

Vintage	09
WR	6
Drink	11-13

DRY $25 –V

Mt Rosa Central Otago Pinot Blanc   (★★★★)

The 2009 vintage (★★★★) is a dry wine, barrel-fermented and matured on its yeast lees for nine months. Attractively scented, with the confectionery notes typical of this variety, it is fresh, with lively acidity and peachy, gently oaked flavours, showing excellent delicacy and depth.

DRY $22 V+

Pyramid Valley Vineyards Growers Collection
Kerner Estate Vineyard Marlborough Pinot Blanc   ★★★★

Hand-picked in the Waihopai Valley, the 2009 vintage (★★★★☆) is a golden, robust wine (14.9 per cent alcohol), described by winemaker Mike Weersing as having 'intimidating power and presence'. After fermenting for the exceptionally long period of 17 months in seasoned French oak casks, mostly puncheons, it shows less of the freshness and vibrancy typical of the region's whites, but loads of personality. A hedonistic wine, it nevertheless tastes basically dry (11 grams/litre of residual sugar), with bottomless depth of peachy, slightly spicy and honeyed flavour.

MED/DRY $36 –V

Rock Ferry Marlborough Pinot Blanc   (★★★★)

The youthful 2010 vintage (★★★★) is a slightly Chardonnay-like wine, showing excellent complexity. Fermented in tanks (60 per cent) and with indigenous yeasts in seasoned oak casks (40 per cent), it is mouthfilling, with ripe stone-fruit and spice flavours, showing good concentration, and a dryish (5 grams/litre of residual sugar), finely textured, persistent finish. Worth cellaring.

Vintage	10
WR	5
Drink	11-15

MED/DRY $25 AV

Whitestone Waipara Pinot Blanc   ★★★☆

The 2009 vintage (★★★★) is a mouthfilling, partly barrel-fermented wine with good weight and concentrated, ripe citrus-fruit and peach flavours. It's a finely textured wine with a long finish.

DRY $24 –V

Pinot Gris

Pinot Gris' popularity has continued to rise over the past year, with sales in supermarkets soaring by 24 per cent. The wines are also starting to win an international reputation. Almost 300,000 cases were exported in the year to mid-2011 – 10 times the volume shipped five years ago.

At *Winestate* magazine's 2010 Wine of the Year Awards, in Australia, the trophy for champion Pinot Gris was awarded to Greystone Sand Dollar Waipara Pinot Gris 2010. The top five Pinot Gris of the year also included Prophet's Rock Central Otago Pinot Gris 2009 as runner-up; Greystone Waipara Pinot Gris 2009 in third place; Overstone Hawke's Bay Pinot Gris 2010 in fourth; and Villa Maria Single Vineyard Seddon Marlborough Pinot Gris 2009 in fifth.

The variety is spreading like wildfire – from 130 hectares of bearing vines in 2000 to 1764 hectares in 2012 – and accounts for over 5 per cent of the total producing vineyard area. New Zealand's third most extensively planted white-wine variety, with plantings now almost double those of Riesling, Pinot Gris is trailing only Sauvignon Blanc and Chardonnay.

A mutation of Pinot Noir, Pinot Gris has skin colours ranging from blue-grey to reddish-pink, sturdy extract and a fairly subtle, spicy aroma. It is not a difficult variety to cultivate, adapting well to most soils, and ripens with fairly low acidity to high sugar levels. In Alsace, the best Pinot Gris are matured in large casks, but the wood is old, so as not to interfere with the grape's subtle flavour.

What does Pinot Gris taste like? Imagine a wine that couples the satisfying weight and roundness of Chardonnay with some of the aromatic spiciness of Gewürztraminer. As a refined, full-bodied, dryish white wine – most New Zealand versions are fractionally sweet – that accompanies a wide variety of dishes well, Pinot Gris is worth getting to know.

In terms of style and quality, however, New Zealand Pinot Gris vary widely. Many of the wines lack the enticing perfume, mouthfilling body, flavour richness and softness of the benchmark wines from Alsace. These lesser wines, typically made from heavily cropped vines, are much leaner and crisper – more in the tradition of cheap Italian Pinot Grigio.

Popular in Germany, Alsace and Italy, Pinot Gris is now playing an important role here too. Well over half of the country's plantings are concentrated in Marlborough (43 per cent) and Hawke's Bay (21 per cent), but there are also significant pockets of Pinot Gris in Gisborne, Otago, Canterbury, Nelson, Auckland and Wairarapa.

3 Stones Hawke's Bay Pinot Gris (★★☆)

The 2010 vintage (★★☆) is an easy-drinking wine, made in a dry style (4.8 grams/litre of residual sugar) with smooth, slightly spicy and peachy flavours.

DRY $19 –V

3 Terraces Pinot Gris (★★★★)

From Gladstone Vineyard, the 2009 vintage (★★★★) was grown in the northern Wairarapa. A medium-dry style, it shows good richness and harmony, with ripe peachy flavours and a creamy-smooth finish.

MED/DRY $18 V+

36 Bottles Central Otago Pinot Gris ★★★☆

The 2009 vintage (★★★★) was hand-picked at Lowburn. It has good immediacy, with mouthfilling body and vibrant peach, pear and spice flavours in an off-dry style, deliciously strong and lively.

MED/DRY $25 –V

12,000 Miles Wairarapa Pinot Gris   ★★★☆

From Gladstone Vineyard, the 2011 vintage (★★★☆) was tank-fermented and lees-aged. It's a full-bodied wine with very fresh and vibrant, ripe peach, pear and spice flavours, in a dry (4 grams/litre of residual sugar) but well-rounded style, enjoyable from the start.

DRY $22 AV

Akarua Central Otago Pinot Gris   ★★★☆

Estate-grown at Bannockburn, the 2010 vintage (★★★☆) was mostly handled in tanks but 15 per cent was barrel-fermented. Scented and mouthfilling, it is fresh and youthful, with vibrantly fruity flavours of pears, lychees and spices, a sliver of sweetness (10 grams/litre of residual sugar) and some complexity.

Vintage	10	09	08
WR	6	6	6
Drink	11-13	11-12	P

MED/DRY $25 –V

Ake Ake Vineyard Pinot Gris   (★★★★)

The 2010 vintage (★★★★) was hand-picked at 24 brix from first-crop vines at Kerikeri, in Northland, tank-fermented and bottled early. It's an auspicious debut – full-bodied, with strong stone-fruit and spice flavours, showing a touch of lees-aging complexity. Weighty, rich and dry, it's a distinctly northern style, with gentle acidity and a ripe, well-rounded finish.

Vintage	10
WR	5
Drink	11-12

DRY $24 AV

Alexandra Wine Company alex.gold Pinot Gris   (★★★☆)

Grown in Central Otago and fermented in seasoned oak barrels, the 2010 vintage (★★★☆) is a creamy-textured wine with citrus and stone-fruit flavours, spicy and nutty, showing considerable complexity.

DRY $25 –V

Alexia Wairarapa Pinot Gris   (★★★★)

Delicious young, the 2010 vintage (★★★★) was grown in the northern Wairarapa and partly barrel-fermented. Finely scented, it's an instantly attractive wine with mouthfilling body and a sliver of sweetness (9 grams/litre of residual sugar) amid its rich, ripe, peachy flavours, enlivened by fresh, appetising acidity.

Vintage	10
WR	6
Drink	11-13

MED/DRY $18 V+

Allan Scott Omaka Marlborough Pinot Gris (★★★★)

The debut 2009 vintage (★★★★) is an Alsace-style, single-vineyard wine, tank-fermented and matured in old oak barrels, with regular lees-stirring. It's a mouthfilling, off-dry wine (6 grams/litre of residual sugar), with stone-fruit, pear and spice flavours, showing very good delicacy, complexity and depth, and a slightly creamy texture.

Vintage	09
WR	6
Drink	11-14

 MED/DRY $29 –V

Amisfield Central Otago Pinot Gris ★★★★

The 2010 vintage (★★★★) was estate-grown in the Cromwell Basin and mostly handled in tanks, but 30 per cent was fermented with indigenous yeasts in large, seasoned French oak barrels. A good 'food' wine, it is mouthfilling and fleshy, with ripe, peachy, spicy flavours, oak-derived complexity, and a well-rounded, off-dry (7 grams/litre of residual sugar) finish.

Vintage	10	09	08	07	06
WR	7	5	7	5	4
Drink	12-15	11-14	11-20	11-12	P

 MED/DRY $30 –V

Anchorage Nelson Pinot Gris ★★★

The 2009 vintage (★★★) is medium-bodied, with crisp, slightly sweet (11 grams/litre of residual sugar) flavours of lychees, pears and spices, and good depth.

 MED/DRY $18 AV

Anchorage Winemakers Release Nelson Pinot Gris (★★★)

Mouthfilling and creamy-textured, the 2010 vintage (★★★) is a dryish wine (5 grams/litre of residual sugar) with peach, lychee, pear and distinctly spicy flavours, that give it a slightly Gewürztraminer-like feel.

 MED/DRY $19 AV

Ant Moore Marlborough Pinot Gris ★★★★

A dryish style, the 2010 vintage (★★★☆) was grown in the Waihopai and Awatere valleys. Spicy aromas lead into a medium to full-bodied wine with very good depth of ripe, citrusy and peachy flavours, spicy and slightly gingery.

 MED/DRY $23 AV

Archangel Central Otago Pinot Gris (★★★★)

Full of youthful charm, the 2010 vintage (★★★★) is full-bodied and slightly sweet, with fresh, strong stone-fruit, citrus-fruit and spice flavours, showing excellent balance, delicacy and richness. It shows good personality; open mid-2012+.

MED/DRY $29 –V

Arrow Junction Central Otago Pinot Gris (★★★☆)

From wine distributor Federal Geo, the 2009 vintage (★★★☆) is fleshy, with ripe stone-fruit and spice flavours, a slightly creamy texture and a fully dry finish.

DRY $24 –V

Artisan The Far Paddock Marlborough Pinot Gris ★★★☆

The 2009 vintage (★★★★) is a dryish style (5 grams/litre of residual sugar) with substantial body (14.5 per cent alcohol), fresh, strong flavours of peaches and apricots and a strongly spicy finish.

MED/DRY $20 AV

Ashwood Estate Gisborne Pinot Gris ★★★★

The 2009 vintage (★★★★) is the fruit of a partnership between grower Murray McPhail and winemaker Nick Nobilo, of Vinoptima. It's a full-bodied, medium style (15 grams/litre of residual sugar), with ripe flavours of quince, peach and ginger, a distinct spiciness, fresh acidity and excellent depth. A youthful, finely balanced wine, it should mature well.

MED $25 AV

Askerne Hawke's Bay Pinot Gris ★★★☆

The 2011 vintage (★★★) was estate-grown near Havelock North and fermented in tanks (82 per cent) and old French oak barrels (18 per cent). Medium-bodied, it is slightly sweet (10 grams/litre of residual sugar), with balanced acidity, fresh peach and pear flavours, hints of ginger and apricot, and good balance and depth.

Vintage	11	10	09
WR	5	6	6
Drink	12-14	11-12	P

MED/DRY $20 AV

Astrolabe Discovery Kekerengu Coast Pinot Gris (★★★☆)

Grown between the Awatere Valley and Kaikoura, the 2009 vintage (★★★☆) is a floral and fleshy, slightly oily wine with good texture, delicacy and depth of pear, lychee and spice flavours and an off-dry (8.8 grams/litre of residual sugar) finish.

Vintage	09
WR	6
Drink	11-12

MED/DRY $25 –V

Astrolabe Experience The Rocks Pinot Gris (★★★☆)

Still on sale, the 2008 vintage (★★★☆) was grown in the Awatere Valley, hand-picked and barrel-fermented, with frequent lees-stirring. It's a slightly Chardonnay-like wine, fleshy and creamy-textured, with stone-fruit and spice flavours, plenty of toasty oak in evidence (arguably a bit too much) and a dry (4 grams/litre of residual sugar) finish.

Vintage	08
WR	6
Drink	11-12

DRY $37 –V

Ata Rangi Lismore Pinot Gris   ★★★★☆

Grown in the Lismore Vineyard in Martinborough, 400 metres from the Ata Rangi winery, the 2010 vintage (★★★★☆) is scented, mouthfilling (14.5 per cent alcohol) and sweet-fruited, with vibrant, ripe nectarine, pear and lychee flavours, very fresh and rich, a sliver of sweetness (8 grams/litre of residual sugar) and obvious potential.

Vintage	10	09	08	07	06
WR	7	7	6	6	7
Drink	11-14	11-13	11-12	P	P

 MED/DRY $30 –V

Aurum Central Otago Pinot Gris   ★★★★

The 2010 vintage (★★★★) is a youthful, full-bodied wine, estate-grown and hand-picked at Lowburn, tank-fermented and lees-stirred. An intensely varietal wine, it shows excellent purity and delicacy of peach and lychee flavours, with gentle sweetness (8 grams/litre of residual sugar) and a slightly oily richness.

Vintage	10	09	08	07
WR	7	6	5	6
Drink	11-15	11-13	11-12	P

 MED/DRY $25 AV

Babich Black Label Marlborough Pinot Gris   ★★★★

Sold mostly in restaurants, the powerful 2010 vintage (★★★★) was partly barrel-fermented. Richly scented, it is full-bodied and rounded, with strong, ripe stone-fruit and toasty oak flavours, a slightly oily texture and a dry finish.

 DRY $25 AV

Babich Marlborough Pinot Gris   ★★★☆

Grown in the Wairau and Waihopai valleys and partly (15 per cent) barrel-fermented, the 2010 vintage (★★★★) is fleshy and rounded, in a distinctly Alsace style with peach, lychee and spice flavours, a hint of apricots, and good texture and richness.

 MED/DRY $20 AV

Bald Hills Pigeon Rocks Central Otago Pinot Gris   ★★★

From a small block of vines at Bannockburn, in Central Otago, the 2010 vintage (★★★) is a dryish wine (5 grams/litre of residual sugar). It has a distinctly cool-climate feel, with lychee and spice flavours, fresh, crisp and lively.

 MED/DRY $25 –V

Bascand Marlborough Pinot Gris   ★★☆

Faintly pink, the very easy-drinking 2009 vintage (★★☆) is full-bodied, with pear and spice flavours, gentle sweetness (10 grams/litre of residual sugar) and a soft, creamy texture.

MED/DRY $17 –V

Bellbird Spring Block Eight Pinot Gris ★★★★

The 2009 vintage (★★★★) was estate-grown at Waipara, hand-picked, and fermented and lees-aged in old oak casks. Mouthfilling, it's a medium-sweet style (40 grams/litre of residual sugar), with concentrated, ripe lychee, pear, spice and apricot flavours, a hint of oak and a very smooth finish. The 2010 (★★★★) is soft and forward, with good weight and rounded, ripe lychee and spice flavours, showing excellent harmony and complexity. The 2011 (★★★★) is fleshy and rounded, with peachy, spicy flavours, hints of apricots and honey, and good complexity and personality.

Vintage	11	10	09
WR	5	6	6
Drink	11-14	11-14	11-15

 MED $32 –V

Bellbird Spring Home Block Waipara Pinot Gris (★★★☆)

The 2010 vintage (★★★☆) is a distinctive, tight and youthful wine, hand-picked and barrel-fermented with indigenous yeasts. Full-bodied, it has fresh pear and spice flavours, a sliver of sweetness and some complexity.

 DRY $31 –V

Bilancia Hawke's Bay Pinot Gris ★★★★

The 2010 vintage (★★★★☆) was grown at Haumoana, hand-picked and tank-fermented. A good 'food' wine, it is ripely scented, fleshy and soft, in an Alsace style with strong, peachy, spicy flavours, showing excellent texture and richness.

 MED/DRY $25 AV

Bilancia Reserve Pinot Gris ★★★★★

Grown at Haumoana, near the Hawke's Bay coast, this is a vineyard selection of grapes from the most heavily crop-thinned, later-harvested vines. The classy 2008 vintage (★★★★★) is mouthfilling (14.5 per cent alcohol), with deep stone-fruit and spice flavours, gentle acidity, a sliver of sweetness (7 grams/litre of residual sugar), a slightly oily texture and lovely harmony. It's a distinctly Alsace-style wine, for drinking now or cellaring.

Vintage	08
WR	7
Drink	11-16

MED/DRY $35 AV

Bird Old Schoolhouse Vineyard Marlborough Pinot Gris ★★☆

The 2010 vintage (★★☆) was estate-grown in the Omaka Valley. Faintly pink, it's a medium to full-bodied wine with pear and spice flavours, showing moderate depth, and a dryish (5 grams/litre of residual sugar) finish.

 MED/DRY $25 –V

Black Barn Vineyards Hawke's Bay Pinot Gris   ★★★★

Delicious from the start, the 2009 vintage (★★★★) was hand-harvested at two sites in the Te Mata district and briefly lees-aged. Fleshy and finely textured, it's a medium-dry style (12 grams/litre of residual sugar), with very good delicacy and richness of pear, lychee and spice flavours, fresh, pure and vibrant.

MED/DRY $25 AV

Blackbirch Marlborough Pinot Gris   (★★★)

From The New Zealand Wine Company, the 2009 vintage (★★★) is fleshy and smooth, with fresh, slightly sweet, citrusy, peachy, spicy flavours, showing good varietal character. It's drinking well now.

MED/DRY $17 AV

Black Cottage Marlborough Pinot Gris   (★★★)

From Two Rivers, the 2010 vintage (★★★) is a good buy. Mouthfilling, it's a very easy-drinking style with good depth of vibrant, peachy, slightly spicy flavours, gently sweet and smooth.

MED/DRY $15 V+

Blackenbrook Vineyard Nelson Pinot Gris   ★★★★★

An emerging classic. The 2010 vintage (★★★★★) was hand-picked at 25.7 brix. Harbouring 15 per cent alcohol, it is beautifully floral, with fresh, very vibrant peach, pear and spice aromas and flavours, a hint of ginger, slight sweetness (18 grams/litre of residual sugar), and lovely purity, delicacy and richness.

 MED $26 V+

Vintage	10	09	08	07	06
WR	7	6	7	7	6
Drink	11-15	11-12	11-12	P	P

Black Stilt Waitaki Valley North Otago Pinot Gris   ★★★☆

The 2010 vintage (★★★★) was harvested in early May from ultra low-cropping (1 tonne/hectare) vines. Slightly minerally, with excellent delicacy, varietal character and depth, it is richly scented and vibrantly fruity, with strong, slightly sweet flavours of peaches, pears and spices, woven with appetising acidity.

MED/DRY $26 –V

Bladen Marlborough Pinot Gris   ★★★

The 2010 vintage (★★★☆) was estate-grown and hand-picked. An easy-drinking style, it is mouthfilling, with moderately rich, fresh and ripe, peachy, spicy flavours and a well-rounded finish. Good drinking now onwards.

MED/DRY $25 –V

Bloody Bay Marlborough Pinot Gris   (★★★)

From wine distributor Federal Geo, the 2009 vintage (★★★) is a powerful (14.5 per cent alcohol), upfront style with gingery, very spicy, slightly honeyed flavours and a smooth finish.

DRY $17 AV

Boreham Wood Single Vineyard Awatere Valley Pinot Gris   ★★★★

The 2009 vintage (★★★★) is an Alsace-style, fleshy, dryish (6 grams/litre of residual sugar) and well-rounded. It has strong, ripe peach, pear and spice flavours, showing some complexity, and excellent texture, richness and downright drinkability.

Vintage	09	08
WR	7	6
Drink	11-14	11-12

MED/DRY $24 AV

Borthwick Vineyard Wairarapa Pinot Gris   (★★★★)

The finely poised 2010 vintage (★★★★) was fermented in tanks (60 per cent) and seasoned oak barrels (40 per cent). Fleshy and vibrant, with fresh, ripe stone-fruit, lychee and spice flavours, balanced acidity, a touch of complexity and a fully dry finish, it's a cool-climate style with good immediacy.

DRY $24 AV

Bouldevines Marlborough Pinot Gris   ★★☆

The 2009 vintage (★★) has citrusy, slightly appley aromas and flavours, lacking any real richness. The 2011 (★★☆) has fresh, citrusy, slightly spicy flavours, in a dryish (6 grams/litre of residual sugar) style, crisp and refreshing.

Vintage	11
WR	6
Drink	11-13

MED/DRY $25 –V

Boundary Vineyards Paper Lane Waipara Pinot Gris   ★★★☆

From Pernod Ricard NZ, the 2010 vintage (★★★☆) is a weighty, fleshy Waipara wine with fresh stone-fruit and spice flavours, a slightly oily texture and a medium-dry, rounded finish.

MED/DRY $22 AV

Brancott Estate 'F' Fairhall Marlborough Pinot Gris   (★★★★☆)

Mouthfilling, ripely scented and softly textured, the 2010 vintage (★★★★☆) was mostly hand-harvested and then fermented in tanks and wooden cuves. Weighty, with strong pear, lychee and spice flavours, good complexity, an oily texture and excellent harmony, it's a slightly sweet wine (9 grams/litre of residual sugar), enjoyable now but still youthful.

MED/DRY $35 –V

Brancott Estate Living Land Series Marlborough Pinot Gris   ★★★☆

The 2010 vintage (★★★☆), tasted in its infancy, looked highly promising, with satisfying body and ripe, slightly sweet flavours, showing very good depth. The 2011 (★★★☆) is similar, with vibrant pear and spice flavours, fresh and strong.

MED/DRY $20 AV

Brancott Estate North Island Pinot Gris   ★★★

Up to the 2008 vintage, this wine was sold under the Montana brand. The 2009 (★★★) is medium-bodied, with fresh, vibrant pear and spice flavours, showing good balance and drink-young appeal.

MED/DRY $18 AV

Brancott Reserve Hawke's Bay Pinot Gris   (★★★☆)

Often seen on special at $15, Pernod Ricard NZ's 2010 vintage (★★★☆) is attractively scented and vibrant, with citrusy, peachy, spicy flavours, showing good delicacy, a sliver of sweetness and finely balanced acidity. It's a youthful wine, instantly likeable.

MED/DRY $26 –V

Brennan Gibbston Pinot Gris   (★★★★☆)

The 2009 vintage (★★★★☆) was estate-grown at Gibbston, in Central Otago, and partly barrel-fermented. Full-bodied, rich and smooth, it has peachy, spicy, slightly candied flavours, showing good complexity, a slightly creamy texture, and a highly fragrant, complex bouquet. It's delicious now.

MED/DRY $30 –V

Brick Bay Matakana Pinot Gris   ★★★☆

At its best, this wine is weighty, rich and rounded. Hand-picked and lees-aged, it is made in an off-dry style. The 2010 vintage (★★★★) is ripely scented and mouthfilling, with rich, ripe, peachy, slightly spicy flavours, showing excellent freshness, purity and depth. Full-bodied and finely poised, it's unfolding well.

Vintage	10	09	08	07	06
WR	7	7	7	7	7
Drink	11-15	11-14	P	P	P

MED/DRY $32 –V

Brightside Nelson Pinot Gris   ★★★

From Kaimira Estate, the 2010 vintage (★★★) is full-bodied and fresh, with a sliver of sweetness (9 grams/litre of residual sugar) amid its peachy, citrusy, slightly spicy flavours, which show good depth.

MED/DRY $18 AV

Brightwater Vineyards Lord Rutherford Pinot Gris   (★★★★☆)

The rich and oily 2010 vintage (★★★★☆) is highly scented, mouthfilling and gently sweet (13 grams/litre of residual sugar), with ripe citrus-fruit, peach and spice flavours. It's an elegant wine with a touch of complexity, good texture and a long finish.

Vintage	10
WR	5
Drink	11-12

MED/DRY $30 –V

Brightwater Vineyards Nelson Pinot Gris   ★★★★

Scented, with fresh, ripe pear, lychee and spice flavours, the 2010 vintage (★★★★) shows excellent delicacy, harmony and length. It's a distinctly medium style (20 grams/litre of residual sugar), well-rounded and rich. (Grown in the Moutere hills.)

Vintage	10	
WR	5	
Drink	11-12	MED $25 AV

Bronte by Rimu Grove Nelson Pinot Gris   ★★★☆

Rimu Grove's second-tier label. The 2010 vintage (★★★☆) is an off-dry style, mostly handled in tanks; 9 per cent of the blend was lees-aged in old French oak barrels. Full-bodied, with a bouquet showing some 'oxidative' notes, it has stone-fruit and spice flavours, revealing considerable complexity, and good richness and harmony.

 MED/DRY $22 AV

Brookfields Robertson Hawke's Bay Pinot Gris   ★★★

The 2011 vintage (★★★) is a slightly sweet wine (7 grams/litre of residual sugar), full-bodied and fresh, with lively, citrusy, slightly appley and spicy flavours, showing good depth.

Vintage	11	
WR	7	MED/DRY $20 –V
Drink	12-15	

Brunton Road Gisborne Pinot Gris   ★★★

A single-vineyard wine, grown at Patutahi, the 2010 vintage (★★★) is a fresh, lively wine with a sliver of sweetness (6 grams/litre of residual sugar) and good depth of peach, pear and lychee flavours.

 MED/DRY $22 –V

Burnt Spur Martinborough Pinot Gris   ★★★★☆

From Martinborough Vineyard, the 2010 vintage (★★★★☆) was grown in the company's Burnt Spur Vineyard, just south of the township, hand-picked, and lees-aged in tanks. A rich, medium style (15 grams/litre of residual sugar), it has concentrated, ripe flavours of peaches, pears and spices in a full-bodied, finely textured Alsace style with lovely mouthfeel and immediacy.

 MED $23 V+

Bushmere Estate Gisborne Pinot Gris   (★★★)

Mouthfilling and smooth, the 2010 vintage (★★★) has moderately concentrated, ripe pear and spice flavours, with an off-dry (7 grams/litre of residual sugar) finish.

MED/DRY $21 –V

Butterfish Bay Northland Pinot Gris   (★★★☆)

The debut 2009 vintage (★★★☆) was hand-harvested on Paewhenua Island, a peninsula reaching into Mangonui Harbour. It's a medium to full-bodied wine, freshly aromatic, with good depth of ripe peach, pear and lychee flavours, a sliver of sweetness (9 grams/litre of residual sugar) and a well-rounded finish.

Vintage	09
WR	6
Drink	P

MED/DRY $28 –V

Cable Bay Waiheke Island Pinot Gris   (★★★☆)

The 2010 vintage (★★★☆) was handled in tanks, with a 'touch' of barrel fermentation. It's an ideal 'food' wine – citrusy, spicy, crisp and dry (2 grams/litre of residual sugar), with good depth, vigour and freshness. Drink now or cellar.

Vintage	10
WR	7
Drink	11-15

DRY $29 –V

Camshorn Waipara Pinot Gris   ★★★★

Grown in Pernod Ricard NZ's hillside vineyard in North Canterbury, the easy-drinking 2008 vintage (★★★★) is an enticingly scented wine, oily and rich, with strongly varietal pear, lychee and spice flavours, pure, gently sweet and smooth. It's drinking well now.

Vintage	08	07
WR	5	5
Drink	P	P

MED/DRY $26 –V

Carrick Central Otago Pinot Gris   ★★★★

The stylish 2010 vintage (★★★★) was grown at Bannockburn and 30 per cent fermented in very old casks; the rest was handled in tanks. It's a scented, mouthfilling wine (14 per cent alcohol), with just a hint of sweetness (5.7 grams/litre of residual sugar) amid its peach and slight apricot flavours, which show excellent freshness, depth and harmony.

MED/DRY $25 AV

Catalina Sounds Marlborough Pinot Gris   ★★★☆

The 2010 vintage (★★★★) is a refined Waihopai Valley wine, hand-harvested, with some use of barrel fermentation. The bouquet is scented and citrusy; the palate offers pure, vibrant lemon, pear and lychee flavours, with leesy notes adding complexity. Slightly oily, with a dry finish, it's well worth cellaring.

DRY $24 –V

Central Schist Central Otago Pinot Gris ★★☆

The label three times describes the 2010 vintage (★★☆) as 'great', but it's a pleasant quaffer. Smooth, with an obvious splash of sweetness, it's a clearly varietal wine with pear, lychee and spice flavours, showing solid depth.

 MED $18 –V

Chard Farm Central Otago Pinot Gris ★★★★

Hand-picked in Cromwell Basin vineyards, the 2009 vintage (★★★★) is scented, fleshy and well-rounded (6 grams/litre of residual sugar). Full-bodied, with a slightly oily texture, it has vibrant, ripe, peachy, spicy flavours, a hint of honey, and excellent depth and harmony.

 MED/DRY $28 –V

Charles Wiffen Marlborough Pinot Gris ★★★★

The 2009 vintage (★★★★) is medium-bodied, with fresh, ripe stone-fruit and pear flavours, a gentle splash of sweetness and finely balanced acidity. It's a very harmonious wine, delicious from the start.

 MED/DRY $23 AV

Church Road Cuve Hawke's Bay Pinot Gris ★★★★☆

Grown 300 metres above sea level in Pernod Ricard NZ's cool, inland site at Matapiro, the 2008 vintage (★★★★) is a scented, distinctly medium style showing good weight and concentrated, ripe, slightly honeyed flavours. Still available, it's drinking well now. The 2009 (★★★★☆) is even better, with beautifully ripe, peachy flavours, an oily texture and a rich, well-rounded finish.

 MED/DRY $27 AV

Church Road Hawke's Bay Pinot Gris ★★★★

A classic regional style – rich, ripe and round. Estate-grown in Pernod Ricard NZ's cool, elevated, inland site at Matapiro, the 2010 vintage (★★★★) is a full-bodied, peachy, spicy wine with a slightly oily texture, good complexity and richness, and a well-rounded finish.

 MED/DRY $27 –V

C.J. Pask Gimblett Road Hawke's Bay Pinot Gris (★★★☆)

Full-bodied, with ripe, dryish, stone-fruit and pear flavours, the 2010 vintage (★★★☆) is a finely textured wine with slightly nutty notes adding complexity and very good depth.

 MED/DRY $19 V+

Clark Estate Single Vineyard Awatere Valley Marlborough Pinot Gris ★★★☆

Attractively scented, fleshy and full-bodied, the 2010 vintage (★★★☆) is a partly barrel-fermented wine with very good depth of vibrant pear, lychee and spice flavours, slightly sweet and smooth.

 MED/DRY $23 AV

Clayridge Excalibur Marlborough Pinot Gris (★★★★☆)

Still on sale, the 2008 vintage (★★★★☆) was barrel-fermented with indigenous yeasts. It's a powerful, dryish wine (5 grams/litre of residual sugar), with rich, peachy, spicy flavours, notably complex and concentrated, maturing well.

MED/DRY $33 –V

Clifford Bay Marlborough Pinot Gris   (★★★☆)

From Vavasour, the debut 2010 vintage (★★★☆) is mouthfilling, with clear-cut varietal character. Still youthful, it has fresh pear and spice flavours, showing very good depth, and an off-dry, crisp finish.

MED/DRY $20 AV

Clos St William Waipara Pinot Gris   (★★★★)

The 2009 vintage (★★★★) was hand-picked at 25 brix and given some exposure to old oak. Fleshy, it's a medium-dry style with well-ripened pear, spice and stone-fruit flavours, a slightly oily texture, and excellent harmony and richness.

MED/DRY $20 V+

Cloudy Bay Marlborough Pinot Gris   ★★★★

Handled in seasoned French oak barrels and tanks, the 2009 vintage (★★★★) is full-bodied and vibrant, with strong, fresh pear and spice flavours, good complexity and harmony, and a well-rounded, dryish (5 grams/litre of residual sugar) finish.

Vintage	09
WR	7
Drink	11-12

MED/DRY $30 –V

Compassion New Zealand Pinot Gris   (★★☆)

From Spencer Hill, the 2008 vintage (★★☆), released in late 2010, is designed to raise funds for an alliance of charities. Enjoyable now, it's a mouthfilling wine with solid depth of peachy, spicy flavours, dryish and mellow.

MED/DRY $18 –V

Coney Piccolo Martinborough Pinot Gris   ★★★★

The 2009 vintage (★★★★) has rich, vibrant pear, lychee and spice flavours and a crisp, off-dry (6.5 grams/litre of residual sugar) finish. It shows good freshness, weight and concentration, with some cellaring potential.

MED/DRY $24 AV

Coopers Creek New Zealand Pinot Gris   ★★★

A multi-region blend of Auckland, Gisborne and Hawke's Bay grapes, this is an easy-drinking, medium to full-bodied wine with decent depth of citrus-fruit, pear and spice flavours, slightly sweet and crisp. The 2009 vintage (★★☆) has citrusy, slightly spicy flavours, with a touch of sweetness (5.5 grams/litre of residual sugar) and reasonable depth.

Vintage	09	08	07	06
WR	5	6	7	6
Drink	12-13	P	P	P

MED/DRY $17 AV

Coopers Creek SV The Pointer Marlborough Pinot Gris   ★★★☆

The 2009 vintage (★★★☆) is fleshy and slightly creamy, with very good depth of vibrant pear, lychee and spice flavours, slightly sweet, fresh and rounded. The 2010 (★★★☆) is full-bodied and creamy-textured, with peachy, spicy, slightly buttery flavours, smooth (8 grams/litre of residual sugar) and forward.

Vintage	10	09	08
WR	6	6	7
Drink	12-14	11-12	P

 MED/DRY $20 AV

Couper's Shed Hawke's Bay Pinot Gris   ★★★★

The invitingly perfumed 2009 vintage (★★★★) was grown by Pernod Ricard NZ at Matapiro and 35 per cent of the blend was fermented with indigenous yeasts in old French oak barriques; the rest was tank-fermented and lees-aged. It's a full-bodied, medium-dry style (13.2 grams/litre of residual sugar) with ripe stone-fruit, spice and ginger flavours, a slightly oily texture and excellent delicacy and richness. The 2010 (★★★★) is intensely varietal and vibrantly fruity, with slightly sweet pear, lychee and spice flavours, fresh, finely balanced and rich.

 MED/DRY $20 V+

Cracroft Chase Single Vineyard Grey Pearl Canterbury Pinot Gris   ★★☆

Grown in the Port Hills at Christchurch, the 2009 vintage (★★☆) is an off-dry wine (6 grams/litre of residual sugar), lees-aged in tanks. It's a pleasant, Pinot Grigio style, light and lemony, with a slightly spicy, crisp finish.

Vintage	09
WR	6
Drink	11-13

 MED/DRY $15 AV

Cracroft Chase Wood's Edge Pinot Gris   ★★★☆

The 2009 vintage (★★★★) was estate-grown in Canterbury. Fresh, elegant and dry, with good acid drive, it has strong, youthful, lemony and spicy flavours that linger well.

DRY $20 AV

Craggy Range Otago Station Vineyard Waitaki Valley Pinot Gris   ★★★☆

The 2009 vintage (★★★★) is lemon-scented and fleshy, with ripe, peachy, citrusy flavours, fresh and strong, a slightly creamy texture and a harmonious, off-dry (6 grams/litre of residual sugar) finish.

Vintage	09	08
WR	6	6
Drink	11-15	11-14

 MED/DRY $35 –V

Crater Rim, The, Gibbston Valley Central Otago Pinot Gris   (★★★☆)

Still on sale and drinking well now, the 2008 vintage (★★★☆) is a single-vineyard wine, grown at Gibbston. Still youthful in colour, it is mouthfilling and fleshy, with stone-fruit, spice and ginger flavours, showing good depth, and a dryish finish (5 grams/litre of residual sugar).

 MED/DRY $19 V+

Crater Rim, The, Waipara Pinot Gris   ★★★★

The 2010 vintage (★★★★☆) is a single-vineyard wine, fermented with indigenous yeasts and partly barrel-fermented. Straw-coloured, with a slightly honeyed bouquet, it is mouthfilling and rich, with an array of peach, apricot, ginger and spice flavours, showing excellent concentration and complexity. Full of personality, it's a medium style (18 grams/litre of residual sugar), already delicious.

 MED $26 –V

Crossroads Hawke's Bay Pinot Gris   ★★☆

The 2009 (★★☆) is dry, with peachy, slightly gingery flavours. The 2011 vintage (★★☆) is also basically dry (4 grams/litre of residual sugar), with decent depth of lemony, slightly spicy and gingery flavours.

Vintage	11
WR	5
Drink	11-14

 DRY $19 –V

Cypress Hawke's Bay Pinot Gris   ★★★☆

Balanced for easy drinking, the 2010 vintage (★★★☆) was handled entirely in tanks. Full-bodied and smooth, with a ripe, citrusy fragrance, it is creamy-textured, with very good depth and a slightly spicy, soft finish.

Vintage	10	09	08
WR	6	6	6
Drink	11-13	11-12	P

Darling, The, Marlborough Pinot Gris   ★★★★

This single-vineyard wine is grown at Rapaura, in the Wairau Valley, and mostly handled in tanks; 20 per cent is barrel-fermented with indigenous yeasts. The 2010 (★★★★☆) has strong personality. Mouthfilling, with strong peach, lychee and spice flavours, fresh and pure, it is slightly sweet, with an oily texture and excellent depth and harmony. Certified BioGro, the 2011 (★★★☆) is mouthfilling and moderately concentrated, with fresh, citrusy, slightly spicy flavours and a dryish (7 grams/litre of residual sugar) finish.

Vintage	11	10
WR	7	7
Drink	11-14	11-13

 MED/DRY $23 AV

Dashwood Marlborough Pinot Gris ★★★★

A consistently good buy. Grown in the Awatere Valley, the 2011 vintage (★★★★) is an attractively scented, full-bodied wine, vibrantly fruity, with strong pear and lychee flavours, hints of spices and ginger, and a slightly sweet, finely balanced finish.

 MED/DRY $20 V+

Dawn Ghost Central Otago Pinot Gris (★★★☆)

From an Alexandra-based company, the 2009 vintage (★★★☆) is full-bodied, fresh and smooth, with very good depth of peachy, citrusy, slightly spicy flavour.

MED $19 V+

Devil's Backbone Central Otago Pinot Gris (★★★☆)

From Shaky Bridge, the 2010 vintage (★★★☆) was grown at Alexandra and blended with Gewürztraminer (5 per cent). Light, crisp and tangy, it has fresh, citrusy, appley flavours that linger well.

 MED/DRY $20 AV

Devil's Staircase Central Otago Pinot Gris ★★★

From Rockburn, the 2011 vintage (★★★) is a crisp, youthful wine with vibrant, citrusy, appley flavours, a distinct splash of sweetness (15 grams/litre of residual sugar) and appetising acidity.

 MED $20 −V

Distant Land Marlborough Pinot Gris ★★★★

The 2010 (★★★★) is a single-vineyard wine, grown in the lower Wairau Valley and handled without oak. Full-bodied and fresh, it has good concentration of ripe peach, spice and nectarine flavours, showing excellent delicacy and vibrancy, and a finely balanced, off-dry (8 grams/litre of residual sugar) finish. The 2011 vintage (★★★★) is delicious from the start, with strong, vibrant pear, spice and slight apricot flavours, showing excellent delicacy, harmony and length.

MED/DRY $20 V+

Domain Road Vineyard Central Otago Pinot Gris (★★★★)

The 2010 vintage (★★★★) is an excellent debut. Partly (35 per cent) barrel-fermented, it's a medium-dry style (11.5 grams/litre of residual sugar), fresh, mouthfilling and rounded, with ripe peach, pear, lychee and spice flavours, a very subtle seasoning of oak and good texture, complexity and potential.

 MED/DRY $24 AV

Drumsara Central Otago Pinot Gris ★★★★

The 2010 vintage (★★★★), estate-grown at Alexandra, has plenty of personality. Made in a dry style, it is very fresh, vibrant and mouthfilling, with strong, citrusy, slightly peachy flavours, showing good harmony and richness.

Vintage	09	08
WR	6	5
Drink	11-13	11-12

 DRY $29 −V

Dry River Pinot Gris

From the first vintage in 1986, for many years Dry River towered over other New Zealand Pinot Gris, by virtue of its exceptional body, flavour richness and longevity. A sturdy Martinborough wine, it has peachy, spicy characters that can develop great subtlety and richness with maturity (at around five years old for top vintages, which also hold well for a decade). It is grown in the estate and nearby Craighall vineyards, where the majority of the vines are over 25 years old. To avoid any loss of varietal flavour, it is not oak-aged. The 2010 vintage (★★★★★) is outstanding. Intriguingly scented, it has pear, lychee, spice and quince aromas, fresh and intense. A notably ripe wine, it has a delicious array of fruit flavours, including a distinct hint of oranges, unobtrusive sweetness (18 grams/litre of residual sugar), and great delicacy and harmony.

Vintage	10	09	08	07	06	05
WR	7	7	7	7	7	7
Drink	12-20	11-19	11-18	11-17	11-18	11-13

MED $55 AV

Durvillea Marlborough Pinot Grigio (★★★)

From Astrolabe, the 2009 vintage (★★★) is floral, fresh, light and crisp, in a dry, Pinot Grigio style.

DRY $14 V+

Edge, The, Martinborough Pinot Gris ★★★

From Escarpment, the 2009 vintage (★★★☆) is an easy-drinking style, full-bodied and slightly sweet, with fresh, vibrant flavours of lychees, pears and spices, showing very good depth.

MED/DRY $19 AV

Elder, The, Martinborough Pinot Gris (★★★★☆)

Delicious now, the 2010 vintage (★★★★☆) is a single-vineyard wine, grown at Te Muna and fermented in a 50:50 split of tanks and old French oak casks. Fleshy, rich and rounded, it has strong peach and nectarine flavours, gently seasoned with oak, and excellent complexity, texture and depth.

DRY $35 –V

Elephant Hill Hawke's Bay Pinot Gris (★★★★☆)

Estate-grown at Te Awanga, the 2010 vintage (★★★★☆) has an enticingly floral, fragrant bouquet leading into a mouthfilling, very elegant wine with excellent vibrancy, delicacy and richness. It offers very pure pear, lychee and spice flavours that build across the palate to a dryish, lasting finish.

MED/DRY $29 AV

Eradus Awatere Valley Marlborough Pinot Gris ★★★☆

An easy-drinking style, the 2010 (★★★☆) is mouthfilling, with citrusy, peachy, spicy flavours, fresh, vibrant and finely balanced. The 2011 vintage (★★★☆) is mouthfilling and slightly sweet (6 grams/litre of residual sugar), with youthful peach, pear and spice flavours, fresh acidity, and very good balance and depth. Fine value.

Vintage	11
WR	7
Drink	11-13

MED/DRY $18 V+

Escarpment Martinborough Pinot Gris ★★★★★

This distinctive, 'Burgundian-inspired' Pinot Gris is barrel-fermented. The 2009 vintage (★★★★★) was delicious from the start. An authoritative wine, it is fleshy and rich, with concentrated stone-fruit and pear flavours, finely integrated oak and a finely textured, smooth (5 grams/litre of residual sugar) finish. Drink now or cellar.

 MED/DRY $29 V+

Esk Valley Hawke's Bay Pinot Gris ★★★★

A distinctly Alsace style, the 2010 vintage (★★★★) was hand-picked and fermented in tanks and seasoned oak barriques. Weighty and smooth, with strong peach, lychee and spice flavours, it shows very good ripeness and depth, a touch of complexity and an off-dry, softly textured finish. (The 2011 is a dry style, 55 per cent fermented in old neutral casks.)

 MED/DRY $24 AV

Vintage	11	10	09	08	07	06
WR	6	7	7	6	7	6
Drink	12-14	11-13	11-14	11-13	11-12	P

Fairhall Downs Single Vineyard Marlborough Pinot Gris ★★★☆

Estate-grown in the Brancott Valley, the 2010 vintage (★★★★) was fermented in a 50:50 split of tanks and seasoned French oak casks. Still youthful, it's a mouthfilling wine with ripe, peachy, spicy flavours, very fresh and lively, and impressive richness.

DRY $25 –V

Fairmont Estate Gladstone Terraces Pinot Gris (★★★★)

The 2010 vintage (★★★★) is a powerful wine (14.5 per cent alcohol) with ripe stone-fruit and spice aromas and flavours. Peachy and strongly varietal, it is slightly oily, with good freshness and richness.

 MED/DRY $20 V+

Farmers Market Marlborough Pinot Gris (★★★★)

The 2009 vintage (★★★★) was grown in the Awatere and Wairau valleys. Mouthfilling, slightly sweet and honeyed, it's an Alsace-style wine with good concentration of ripe peach, pear and spice flavours.

 MED/DRY $20 V+

Fiddler's Green Waipara Pinot Gris ★★★

The 2009 vintage (★★★) is mouthfilling, with peach and pear flavours, hints of ginger and honey, and a slightly sweet (14 grams/litre of residual sugar) finish. It's a slightly Gewürztraminer-like wine, with a distinct spiciness.

 MED/DRY $23 –V

Vintage	09	08
WR	6	6
Drink	11-12	11-12

Forrest Marlborough Pinot Gris ★★★☆

The 2010 vintage (★★★☆) is an attractive, drink-young style with mouthfilling body and fresh pear, lychee and spice flavours, showing good depth. Hand-harvested at two sites in the Wairau Valley and mostly handled in tanks (5 per cent in old barrels), it is medium-dry, with finely balanced acidity and a smooth finish.

Vintage	10	09
WR	6	5
Drink	11-16	11-15

 MED/DRY $22 AV

Framingham Marlborough Pinot Gris ★★★★☆

The 2010 vintage (★★★★☆) is full-bodied (14.5 per cent alcohol) and gently sweet (9 grams/litre of residual sugar), with strong, citrusy, peachy, spicy, gingery flavours, well-rounded and rich. Intensely varietal and very harmonious, it's already delicious.

Vintage	10	09	08	07	06
WR	6	7	6	7	6
Drink	11-13	11-12	11-12	P	P

MED/DRY $25 V+

Frizzell Pinot Gris (★★★☆)

Grown in Marlborough, the 2009 vintage (★★★☆) was fermented and lees-aged in tanks, with some use of indigenous yeasts. It has fresh, vibrant, pear-like aromas and flavours, a hint of spices, good weight and a crisp, dry finish.

Vintage	09
WR	6
Drink	11-13

DRY $22 AV

Gem Marlborough Pinot Gris ★★★☆

Grown at Rarangi, the 2009 vintage (★★★☆) was mostly tank-fermented, but 18 per cent was barrel-fermented with indigenous yeasts. It's a full-bodied wine with ripe peach and spice flavours, in a dry style with very good depth.

Vintage	09
WR	7
Drink	12-16

DRY $27 –V

Gibbston Highgate Estate Dreammaker Pinot Gris ★★★

The 2010 vintage (★★★) is a single-vineyard Gibbston wine, tank-fermented and made in an off-dry style (14 grams/litre of residual sugar). Medium-bodied, it is slightly Germanic, with crisp acidity woven through its lemony, slightly peachy and appley flavours, which show good depth.

Vintage	10	09
WR	5	4
Drink	11-12	11-12

MED/DRY $25 –V

Gibbston Valley Central Otago Pinot Gris   ★★★★

At its best, this wine is full of personality. The 2009 vintage (★★★★) was grown at Bendigo (principally) and Gibbston, and mostly handled in tanks; 15 per cent was fermented in old oak barrels. Fresh, lively and full-bodied (14 per cent alcohol), it's a finely scented, dry wine with very good depth of pure peach, lychee and spice flavours, cool-climate vivacity and a well-rounded finish. Still very youthful, the 2010 (★★★☆) is freshly scented, with moderately concentrated pear, lychee and spice flavours, a sliver of sweetness (6 grams/litre of residual sugar) and a touch of nutty complexity (from 17 per cent barrel fermentation).

Vintage	10	09	08	07	06
WR	6	7	7	7	6
Drink	11-21	11-15	11-12	P	P

 MED/DRY $28 –V

Gibbston Valley Dulcinee The Expressionist Series Pinot Gris   ★★★★☆

The 2009 vintage (★★★★☆) was estate-grown at Bendigo, in Central Otago. A medium-dry style (8 grams/litre of residual sugar), it is fleshy and concentrated, with a creamy texture and strong, peachy, spicy flavours, showing good complexity and loads of personality. Delicious now onwards.

Vintage	09	08	07
WR	7	7	7
Drink	11-20	12-16	11-15

 MED/DRY $35 –V

Gibson Bridge Cellar Selection Marlborough Pinot Gris   ★★★★

The fleshy and rounded 2010 vintage (★★★★) shows good complexity. Mouthfilling, with fresh, peachy, spicy, vaguely toasty flavours, showing excellent depth, it's a slightly Chardonnay-like wine with a dryish finish.

 MED/DRY $30 –V

Gibson Bridge Reserve Marlborough Pinot Gris   ★★★★

Full-bodied, the 2010 vintage (★★★★) is a single-vineyard wine with good concentration of peachy, slightly gingery and spicy flavours, with a hint of apricot. It has a slightly oily texture, with a dryish, well-spiced finish.

 MED/DRY $29 –V

Gibson Bridge Single Vineyard Marlborough Pinot Gris   (★★★☆)

The easy-drinking 2009 vintage (★★★☆) is full-bodied, with very good depth of stone-fruit and pear flavours, a hint of ginger and a fresh, distinctly spicy, smooth finish.

 MED/DRY $24 –V

Giesen Marlborough Pinot Gris   (★★★)

Ready for drinking, the 2010 vintage (★★★) is a weighty wine (14.5 per cent alcohol), grown at Rapaura, in the Wairau Valley. Peachy, slightly spicy and gingery, it has plenty of flavour and an off-dry (6 grams/litre of residual sugar) finish.

 MED/DRY $19 AV

Gladstone Vineyard Pinot Gris

The 2009 vintage (★★★★☆) is one of the finest yet. Grown in the northern Wairarapa, it was hand-picked and mostly fermented and lees-aged in tanks, but 30 per cent of the blend was fermented and matured in old French barrels. Beautifully scented, it is rich and finely textured, with concentrated stone-fruit and spice flavours, complexity from the subtle oak handling and a deliciously smooth, dry finish (4.6 grams/litre of residual sugar).

Vintage	09
WR	5
Drink	11-13

DRY $25 AV

Glasnevin Limited Release Pinot Gris

From Fiddler's Green, the 2008 vintage (★★★★☆) is a rich Waipara wine, fermented with indigenous yeasts and matured for nine months in French oak barriques (20 per cent new). It's a concentrated wine with peachy, spicy flavours showing excellent complexity, an oily texture, and a finely balanced, dry (4 grams/litre of residual sugar), well-rounded finish. It's drinking well now.

Vintage	08
WR	7
Drink	11-14

DRY $32 –V

Glazebrook Regional Reserve Hawke's Bay Pinot Gris

From Ngatarawa, this wine is grown in The Triangle and tank-fermented to dryness. Pale yellow, the 2009 vintage (★★★) is showing some bottle-aged maturity, with satisfying depth of citrusy, slightly appley and minerally flavours, crisp and dry.

Vintage	10	09	08	07	06
WR	NM	6	5	6	6
Drink	NM	11-12	P	P	P

DRY $20 –V

Golden Hills Estate Nelson Pinot Gris (★★★★☆)

Grown at Richmond, the 2009 vintage (★★★★☆) was hand-harvested and tank-fermented. An intensely varietal wine, it has a sliver of sweetness (8.7 grams/litre of residual sugar) amid its rich stone-fruit and spice flavours, balanced by fresh acidity. Highly fragrant and concentrated, it's a great buy.

MED/DRY $20 V+

Goldwater Wairau Valley Pinot Gris (★★★☆)

Aromatic, fresh and crisp, the 2010 vintage (★★★☆) has good depth of citrusy, appley flavours, a minerally streak and lots of personality.

MED/DRY $22 AV

Greystone Sand Dollar Waipara Pinot Gris ★★★★★

A dry style, the 2010 (★★★★★) has substantial body and deep, peachy, slightly spicy flavours. Fresh, tight and minerally, with lively acidity, it shows excellent concentration. The 2011 vintage (★★★★★) is similar – very elegant, rich, vibrantly fruity and poised, with an oily texture and strong, dry (4 grams/litre of residual sugar), peachy, spicy flavours, just waiting to unfold.

Vintage	11		
WR	7		
Drink	11-14		

 DRY $30 AV

Greystone Waipara Pinot Gris ★★★★★

Beautifully poised, scented and mouthfilling, the 2010 vintage (★★★★★) has concentrated flavours of stone-fruit, lychees and spices and an oily texture. Vibrantly fruity and slightly sweet (14 grams/litre of residual sugar), it shows notable depth and harmony. The 2011 (★★★★★) is also benchmark stuff. Highly scented, it is rich and delicate, with ripe stone-fruit, lychee and spice flavours, showing lovely purity and length.

Vintage	11	10	09
WR	6	6	7
Drink	11-14	11-13	11-13

 MED/DRY $29 V+

Greystone Winemaker's Series Waipara Pinot Gris ★★★★

Fleshy and rounded, the 2009 vintage (★★★★) was fully fermented in seasoned French oak barrels and made in an off-dry style (12 grams/litre of residual sugar). Straw-coloured, it is peachy, gingery and slightly honeyed, with excellent concentration, considerable development showing – and loads of personality.

Vintage	09
WR	7
Drink	11-13

 MED/DRY $32 –V

Greywacke Marlborough Pinot Gris ★★★★☆

The 2010 vintage (★★★★☆) is a single-vineyard, Brancott Valley wine, hand-harvested and fermented in a 50:50 split of tanks and old French barriques; all of the wine was then barrel-aged for four months. Still unfolding, it is mouthfilling, with vibrant peach, citrus-fruit and spice flavours, showing good concentration, fresh acidity and considerable complexity. Made in an off-dry style (8 grams/litre of residual sugar), it should be at its best mid-2012+.

Vintage	10	09
WR	5	5
Drink	11-17	11-16

 MED/DRY $29 AV

Grower's Mark Marlborough Pinot Gris (★★★☆)

From Farmers Market, the 2009 vintage (★★★☆) is attractively perfumed and creamy-textured, with very good depth of lemon, apple and lychee flavours, soft and round.

MED/DRY $25 –V

Gunn Estate Pinot Gris   ★★☆

From Sacred Hill, the 2009 vintage (★★★) is a blend of Australian and New Zealand wines. It's a medium-bodied style (12.5 per cent alcohol), not highly scented, with solid depth of fresh peach, pear and slight spice flavours and a smooth, dry (3.9 grams/litre of residual sugar) finish.

DRY $18 –V

Hans Herzog Marlborough Pinot Gris   ★★★★☆

Grown on the north side of the Wairau Valley, the 2009 vintage (★★★★) was hand-picked and mostly tank-fermented; 20 per cent of the blend was fermented and matured for a year in French oak puncheons. Faintly pink, it is sturdy and bone-dry, with ripe, peachy, spicy flavours, concentrated and complex. It's a 'serious' style of Pinot Gris, in a distinctive, food-friendly style.

Vintage	09	08
WR	7	7
Drink	11-15	11-14

DRY $39 –V

Hawkshead Gibbston Valley Central Otago Pinot Gris   ★★★★

Estate-grown and hand-picked at Gibbston, the 2010 vintage (★★★★) is a tank-fermented wine, mouthfilling, with rich, youthful peach, pear and spice flavours, slightly sweet (7 grams/litre of residual sugar), fresh and lively. Well worth cellaring.

MED/DRY $26 –V

Hell or Highwater Central Otago Pinot Gris   (★★☆)

Grown in the Highwater Vineyard, on the Tarras-Cromwell Road, the 2009 vintage (★★☆) is mouthfilling, with fresh flavours of pears and citrus fruits, moderate depth and an off-dry finish. Pleasant, easy drinking.

MED/DRY $18 –V

Huia Marlborough Pinot Gris   ★★★☆

The 2009 vintage (★★★☆) was grown at two Wairau Valley sites and fermented in tanks and old French oak casks. It's a full-bodied, creamy-textured wine, soft, with generous, ripe stone-fruit flavours, hints of pears and spices, and drink-young appeal. The 2010 (★★★☆) is fresh and mouthfilling, with citrusy, slightly spicy flavours, a touch of complexity and a finely balanced, off-dry finish.

MED/DRY $28 –V

Huntaway Reserve Gisborne Pinot Gris   ★★★

The 2009 (★★★☆) is fleshy, with very good depth of slightly sweet pear/spice flavours, a touch of complexity and a well-rounded finish. The pale straw 2010 vintage (★★★) is weighty, with ripe, peachy flavours, nutty, creamy notes, and drink-young appeal.

MED/DRY $23 –V

Hunter's Marlborough Pinot Gris   ★★★★

An excellent buy. The 2010 vintage (★★★★) is a distinctly Alsace style – sturdy (14.5 per cent alcohol) and gently sweet, with strong, ripe peach and spice flavours, a hint of apricots and a finely textured, rounded finish. The 2011 (★★★★) is mouthfilling, with vibrant peach and spice flavours, hints of ginger and apricot, slight sweetness (8 grams/litre of residual sugar), and excellent freshness, vigour and depth.

Vintage	11
WR	5
Drink	11-13

MED/DRY $19 V+

Hyperion Phoebe Matakana Pinot Gris   ★★☆

Estate-grown north of Auckland, the 2009 vintage (★★★) was fermented in old barrels. It is medium-bodied, with lemon, pear and spice flavours, showing good depth, fractional sweetness (6 grams/litre of residual sugar) and fresh, appetising acidity keeping things lively.

Vintage	09
WR	6
Drink	11-15

MED/DRY $28 –V

Incognito Pinot Gris   (★★★)

The 2009 vintage (★★★) from Gibbston Highgate was estate-grown and hand-picked at Gibbston, in Central Otago, tank-fermented, briefly lees-aged and made in an off-dry (9 grams/litre of residual sugar) style. Medium-bodied, it is fresh, citrusy and slightly appley, with plenty of flavour.

MED/DRY $20 –V

Invivo Marlborough Pinot Gris   (★★★☆)

The 2011 vintage (★★★☆) is an off-dry style, mouthfilling and moderately concentrated, with pear, lychee and spice flavours, showing good varietal character, a slightly creamy texture, and drink-young appeal.

MED/DRY $23 AV

Isabel Marlborough Pinot Gris   ★★★

Freshly scented and full-bodied, the 2009 (★★★☆) is a dryish wine with good depth of vibrant pear, lychee and spice flavours and lively acidity. Faintly pink-tinged, the 2010 vintage (★★) is mouthfilling, with ginger, apricot and spice flavours, but also shows a slight lack of freshness and vibrancy.

MED/DRY $24 –V

Johanneshof Marlborough Pinot Gris Medium   ★★★☆

The 2009 vintage (★★★★) is one of the best yet. Gently sweet (18 grams/litre of residual sugar), it is ripely scented, in a rich Alsace style, softly textured, with excellent concentration.

MED $29 –V

Johanneshof Marlborough Pinot Gris Trocken/Dry   ★★★☆

The slightly pink 2010 vintage (★★★☆) is a distinctive style, unusually dry (4 grams/litre of residual sugar), with fresh strawberry and spice aromas. Fresh and crisp, it has good depth of peachy flavour, a hint of apricots, and a well-spiced finish. (From 2011 onwards, the 'Medium' and 'Trocken/Dry' labels will be combined in a medium-dry style.)

DRY $29 –V

Johner Estate Wairarapa Pinot Gris   ★★★★

Grown at Gladstone, the 2009 (★★★★) is an elegant, rich wine, mouthfilling, with fresh acid spine and peachy, spicy flavours, showing good concentration and harmony. The 2011 vintage (★★★★), matured in 'old, big oak barrels', is delicious from the start. Dry (3 grams/litre of residual sugar) but finely balanced, it is mouthfilling, with fresh, lively acidity threaded through ripe, peachy, slightly spicy flavours, which show good complexity, richness and harmony.

DRY $22 V+

Jules Taylor Marlborough Pinot Gris   ★★★★

From two sites in the Awatere Valley and partly barrel-fermented, the 2010 vintage (★★★★) is a fleshy, rich, finely poised wine in the Alsace style. Mouthfilling, it is peachy, slightly spicy and honeyed, with a gentle splash of sweetness, an oily texture and excellent concentration and harmony.

MED/DRY $20 V+

Julicher Martinborough Pinot Gris   (★★★☆)

The pale pink 2009 vintage (★★★☆) was hand-picked at Te Muna (but not estate-grown), and 25 per cent of the blend was fermented in old French oak casks. It's an easy-drinking style, peachy and slightly spicy, with a hint of strawberries, some complexity and a smooth, dryish (5.6 grams/litre of residual sugar) finish.

MED/DRY $20 AV

Junction Pastime Pinot Gris   ★★★☆

From Central Hawke's Bay, the 2010 vintage (★★★★) has a fragrant bouquet, ripe and peachy. A mouthfilling wine, it is very fresh and vibrant, with rich stone-fruit and spice flavours, creamy-textured and lingering.

MED/DRY $22 AV

Jurassic Ridge Waiheke Island Single Vineyard Pinot Grigio   ★★★☆

Grown at Church Bay and tank-fermented, with extended lees-aging, the 2010 vintage (★★★☆) is a pale gold, full-bodied wine with ripe stone-fruit flavours, peachy and spicy. It shows very good depth, with a dry, well-spiced finish.

DRY $29 –V

Kaimira Estate Brightwater Pinot Gris   ★★★☆

Estate-grown in Nelson and handled without oak, the 2009 vintage (★★★★) is one of the best yet. Richly scented, it is fleshy and mouthfilling, in an Alsace style with fresh flavours of ripe peaches, lychees and spices, showing good harmony and richness, and a finely textured, dry (4.5 grams/litre of residual sugar) finish.

Vintage	09
WR	6
Drink	11-14

 DRY $20 AV

Kaituna Valley Canterbury Summerhill Vineyard Pinot Gris   ★★★

Estate-grown at Tai Tapu, on Banks Peninsula, the 2010 vintage (★★★) is a fleshy, full-bodied wine with spicy, slightly gingery flavours, showing a slight lack of delicacy, but also good richness.

MED/DRY $24 –V

Kalex Central Otago Pinot Gris   (★★★☆)

Straw-coloured, with a hint of pink, the 2010 vintage (★★★☆) is a full-bodied, peachy and distinctly spicy wine, with good concentration and drink-young appeal.

Vintage	10
WR	7
Drink	11-15

MED/DRY $27 –V

Kapiro Vineyard Kerikeri Pinot Gris   (★★★☆)

Hand-picked from two-year-old vines in Northland, the 2010 vintage (★★★☆) is lemon-scented, with mouthfilling body and well-rounded, gently sweet (9 grams/litre of residual sugar), peachy, citrusy flavours, slightly gingery and spicy.

Vintage	10
WR	7
Drink	11-12

MED/DRY $28 –V

Karikari Estate Calypso Pinot Gris   (★★★☆)

Grown at Paewhenua Island, in Northland, the 2010 vintage (★★★☆) is full-bodied (14.5 per cent alcohol), with very good depth of ripe, peachy, spicy flavours, fresh acidity keeping things lively, and drink-young appeal.

MED/DRY $22 AV

Kate Radburnd Sun Kissed Hawke's Bay Pinot Gris   (★★★)

From C.J. Pask, the 2010 vintage (★★★) is a fresh, citrusy, gently spicy wine with a finely balanced, dryish, slightly minerally finish.

 MED/DRY $17 AV

Kerner Estate Marlborough Pinot Gris (★★★★)

A good 'food' wine, the 2009 vintage (★★★★) was hand-picked and fermented in old oak casks. Light yellow, it is fleshy and creamy-textured, with ripe stone-fruit and spice flavours, showing good richness and complexity.

Vintage	09
WR	7
Drink	11-13

 DRY $25 AV

Koura Bay Sharkstooth Marlborough Pinot Gris ★★★☆

Typically a fragrant Awatere Valley wine with good body and depth of flavour. The 2009 vintage (★★★☆) is fresh-scented, mouthfilling and vibrantly fruity, with peach, pear and spice flavours, a sliver of sweetness and lively acidity.

Vintage	09	08
WR	6	5
Drink	11-12	P

 MED/DRY $22 AV

Kumeu River Pinot Gris ★★★★

This consistently attractive wine is grown at Kumeu, in West Auckland, matured on its yeast lees, but not oak-matured. Made in a medium-dry style, it is typically floral and weighty, with a slightly oily texture, finely balanced acidity and peach, pear and spice aromas and flavours, vibrant and rich. Still very youthful, the 2010 vintage (★★★★) is mouthfilling, with vibrant peach, apricot and spice flavours, finely balanced and lingering. Best drinking mid-2012+.

Vintage	10	09	08	07	06
WR	7	7	7	7	7
Drink	11-14	11-13	11-12	P	P

 MED/DRY $27 –V

Lake Chalice Eyrie Vineyard Marlborough Pinot Gris ★★★★

Grown mostly in the Eyrie Vineyard, in the Waihopai Valley, the 2009 vintage (★★★★) is a mouthfilling, vibrantly fruity wine. Made in an off-dry style, it has pear, lychee and spice flavours, showing excellent delicacy and purity. The 2010 (★★★★), partly barrel-fermented, is fragrant and weighty, with strong, peachy, spicy flavours, a touch of complexity, and very good delicacy and harmony.

 MED/DRY $20 V+

Lake Forsyth Banks Peninsula Limited Release Pinot Gris (★★)

The 2010 vintage (★★) is a pale straw, full-bodied wine (14.5 per cent alcohol) with soft, peachy flavours that show a slight lack of delicacy and freshness.

Vintage	10
WR	7
Drink	11-16

MED/DRY $35 –V

Lake Forsyth Banks Peninsula Pinot Gris (★★★★☆)

The fleshy, rich 2009 vintage (★★★★☆) is an Alsace-style wine, grown in Canterbury and lees-aged in tanks and French oak. Full of personality, it has slightly creamy aromas, mouthfilling body, and concentrated stone-fruit and spice flavours, showing good complexity.

Vintage	09
WR	7
Drink	11-15

DRY $32 –V

Lake Hayes Central Otago Pinot Gris ★★★☆

From Amisfield, the 2009 vintage (★★★☆) was grown alongside the cellar door at Lake Hayes and at another site in Gibbston, and lees-aged in tanks. Crisp and vibrantly fruity, it has very good depth of peachy, limey, slightly spicy flavours and a slightly sweet (7.5 grams/litre of residual sugar) finish. The 2010 (★★★), also blended from Lake Hayes and Gibbston grapes, is lemon-scented, with fresh, citrusy, slightly sweet flavours (7 grams/litre of residual sugar), firm acid spine, and a slightly buttery finish.

Vintage	10	09	08
WR	6	5	6
Drink	11-13	11-12	P

MED/DRY $25 –V

Lawson's Dry Hills Marlborough Pinot Gris ★★★★☆

The 2010 (★★★★☆) was grown in the Waihopai Valley, harvested at 23.4 to 24.2 brix, and 18 per cent of the blend was fermented with indigenous yeasts in seasoned French oak casks; the rest was handled in tanks. It's a beautifully scented wine with peachy, spicy flavours, showing considerable complexity, and lovely richness and roundness. The 2011 vintage (★★★★☆) has a fragrant, spicy bouquet, leading into a mouthfilling, rounded wine with strong peachy and spice flavours, hints of ginger and honey, and good complexity. It's a very harmonious wine, already highly expressive.

Vintage	10	09	08
WR	7	7	5
Drink	11-12	P	P

MED/DRY $26 AV

Lawson's Dry Hills The Pioneer Marlborough Pinot Gris (★★★★☆)

The debut 2009 vintage (★★★★☆) was harvested in the Waihopai Valley at 23.5 to 25.4 brix, with some botrytis in the late-picked fruit. Tank-fermented, it's a very harmonious wine with fresh pear and spice aromas and flavours, showing good richness, a sliver of sweetness (12.6 grams/litre of residual sugar) and impressive depth and harmony. Best drinking 2012+.

MED/DRY $32 –V

Lil Rippa Awatere Marlborough Pinot Gris (★★★☆)

Bargain-priced, the 2010 vintage (★★★☆) is fleshy, with slightly sweet, peachy, spicy flavours, showing very good depth.

MED/DRY $17 V+

Lil Rippa Marlborough Pinot Gris   (★★★☆)

A blend of Awatere Valley and Wairau Valley grapes, the 2010 vintage (★★★☆) is full-bodied and creamy-textured, with peachy, spicy flavours, slightly sweet (9 grams/litre of residual sugar), fresh and finely balanced.

 MED/DRY $17 V+

Lime Rock Central Hawke's Bay Pinot Gris   ★★★☆

The 2010 vintage (★★★☆) was grown at Waipawa and partly barrel-fermented. Peachy and spicy, with a slightly oily texture, it's a bone-dry style with good weight, varietal character and depth.

 DRY $23 –V

Limestone Creek Waipara Pinot Gris   (★★★)

From Greystone, the 2011 vintage (★★★) is a medium style (20 grams/litre of residual sugar) with vibrant citrus-fruit, pear and lychee flavours, made in a fruity, very easy-drinking style.

 MED $20 –V

Lobster Reef Marlborough Pinot Gris   (★★★☆)

The 2009 vintage (★★★☆) is full-bodied, with crisp, gently sweet flavours of ripe citrus fruits, pears and spices, showing very good freshness and depth in its youth.

 MED/DRY $19 V+

Locharburn Central Otago Pinot Gris   ★★★

Grown at Lowburn, the 2010 vintage (★★★) was mostly handled in tanks, but 30 per cent was fermented in French oak barrels (one-third new). Made in a dry style (4 grams/litre of residual sugar), it has a slightly creamy, nutty bouquet, firm acid spine and lemony, appley flavours showing a touch of complexity.

Vintage	10	09	08
WR	6	6	6
Drink	11-17	11-12	P

 DRY $25 –V

Longridge Hawke's Bay Pinot Gris   ★★☆

The 2009 vintage (★★★) is a medium-bodied wine with refreshing pear and spice flavours, good varietal character and a finely balanced, smooth, dry finish. The 2011 (★★☆) is light and crisp, with fresh pear, lychee and spice flavours in a pleasant, easy-drinking style.

 MED/DRY $18 –V

MacKenzie's Pardon Pinot Gris   (★★☆)

Grown in Waipara, the 2010 vintage (★★☆) is a single-vineyard wine, freshly scented, with decent depth of citrusy, peachy, slightly spicy flavours and an off-dry finish.

MED/DRY $21 –V

Mahi Ward Farm Marlborough Pinot Gris   ★★★☆

From a single vineyard at Ward, the 2010 vintage (★★★☆) was hand-picked and fermented with indigenous yeasts in French oak barriques. Mouthfilling and dry (2 grams/litre of residual sugar), it's peachy, citrusy, slightly toasty and nutty, with considerable complexity and aging potential. Best drinking mid-2012+.

Vintage	10
WR	6
Drink	11-17

 DRY $24 –V

Maimai Creek Hawke's Bay Pinot Gris   ★★☆

The 2009 vintage (★★★☆) is full-bodied (14 per cent alcohol), with ripe pear and spice aromas and flavours, showing good varietal character, a slightly oily texture and very good depth. In its infancy, the 2011 (★★) is disappointing – peachy, honeyed and smooth, but lacking fragrance and depth.

 MED/DRY $20 –V

Main Divide Waipara Valley Pinot Gris   ★★★★

From Pegasus Bay, this is a top buy. The 2010 vintage (★★★★), barrel-fermented and lees-aged, is fleshy and rich, with a late-harvest feel. It is gently sweet, with concentrated pear, lychee and spice flavours, fresh acidity and lots of drink-young appeal.

Vintage	10	09
WR	6	7
Drink	11-14	11-13

 MED/DRY $20 V+

Main Divide Pokiri Reserve Late Picked Waipara Valley Pinot Gris
– see Sweet White Wines section

Man O' War Ponui Island Pinot Gris   ★★★★

From a small island off the eastern end of Waiheke, in Auckland, the 2010 vintage (★★★★★) was hand-harvested at 25–26 brix and made without oak. A medium style (23 grams/litre of residual sugar), it is fleshy (14.5 per cent alcohol) and rich, with fresh, vibrant peach, pear and spice flavours, a minerally streak, and lovely depth and harmony. A 'complete', highly seductive wine, it's the country's best Pinot Gris to date from north of Hawke's Bay. From a very difficult season, the 2011 (★★★), tasted in its infancy, is a much lighter wine (12 per cent alcohol), attractively scented, with vibrant, peachy, citrusy, spicy flavours, showing good depth.

Vintage	11	10
WR	6	7
Drink	11-13	11-13

 MED $28 –V

Manu Marlborough Pinot Gris   (★★★☆)

From Steve Bird, the 2009 vintage (★★★☆) is a ripely scented, dry wine (3 grams/litre of residual sugar), with mouthfilling body, a slightly oily texture and very good depth of peachy, gently spiced flavours.

DRY $20 AV

Maori Point Central Otago Pinot Gris   ★★★☆

Grown at Tarras, north of Lake Dunstan, the 2009 vintage (★★★☆) is a crisp, dry, minerally wine with lemony, slightly spicy flavours, showing good freshness, vigour and length. It's a Pinot Grigio style, worth cellaring. The 2010 (★★★☆), tank-fermented and lees-stirred, is similar – a medium to full-bodied, dry style with fresh, citrusy, slightly appley and spicy flavours, showing very good vibrancy and length.

Vintage	09	08	07
WR	6	6	6
Drink	11-14	11-12	P

Margrain Martinborough Pinot Gris   ★★★☆

The 2009 vintage (★★★☆) is a full-bodied (14.5 per cent alcohol), bone-dry wine with lemon, peach and spice flavours, crisp and strong. Made in a more austere style than most, it's a good food wine, now starting to soften with bottle-age.

Vintage	09	08	07	06
WR	6	7	7	7
Drink	11-15	11-16	11-13	11-12

Margrain River's Edge Martinborough Pinot Gris   (★★★)

The 2010 vintage (★★★) is a distinctly medium style (19 grams/litre of residual sugar), with fresh, smooth, moderately concentrated pear and lychee flavours, balanced for easy drinking.

Marsden Bay of Islands Pinot Gris   ★★★☆

In favourable seasons, this Kerikeri, Bay of Islands winery produces an impressive Pinot Gris. Drinking well now, the 2010 vintage (★★★☆) is a medium-dry style (9 grams/litre of residual sugar), showing good freshness, purity and length. Full-bodied, it has ripe stone-fruit flavours, hints of pears and spices, gentle acidity and a well-rounded finish.

Vintage	10	09	08
WR	6	5	5
Drink	11-13	11-12	P

Martinborough Vineyard Pinot Gris   ★★★★★

This powerful, concentrated wine is one of the finest Pinot Gris in the country. It is hand-picked and fermented with a high percentage of indigenous yeasts, and lees-aged, partly in seasoned French oak casks (50 per cent in 2009), in a bid to produce a 'Burgundian style with complexity, texture and weight'. The 2009 (★★★★) was produced in a slightly sweeter style (8 grams/litre of residual sugar) than past vintages. Tightly structured, it is mouthfilling and fleshy, with ripe, peachy, spicy flavours, showing good harmony and richness.

Vintage	09	08	07	06
WR	6	7	6	6
Drink	11-14	11-13	11-12	P

MED/DRY $40 AV

Matakana Estate Matakana Pinot Gris   ★★★☆

Estate-grown north of Auckland, the 2009 vintage (★★★☆) is a distinctive wine – fleshy, with peachy, lemony, spicy flavours, hints of toasty oak and good complexity.

DRY $27 –V

Matawhero Gisborne Pinot Gris   (★★★)

Balanced for easy drinking, the debut 2009 vintage (★★★) is a single-vineyard wine, medium-bodied, with a sliver of sweetness (6 grams/litre of residual sugar) amid its ripe, slightly buttery flavours of lychees, ginger and spice, which show good depth.

MED/DRY $30 –V

Matua Valley Gisborne Pinot Gris   (★★)

The 2010 vintage (★★) is a pleasant, light quaffer, with pear and peach flavours, slightly sweet and soft.

MED/DRY $12 AV

Matua Valley Matua Road Pinot Gris   (★★☆)

The 2009 vintage (★★☆), not identified by region, is an easy-drinking style, medium to full-bodied, with decent depth of peachy, spicy flavour and a smooth, well-rounded finish. Priced sharply.

MED/DRY $12 V+

Maude Central Otago Pinot Gris   ★★★☆

The 2011 vintage (★★★★) was grown at Pisa and Wanaka. Highly scented, it's a dryish style (4 grams/litre of residual sugar) with an invitingly floral, spicy bouquet and a full-bodied palate (14.5 per cent alcohol). Very fresh and vivacious, it has peach, lychee, pear and spice flavours, a touch of complexity from partial barrel fermentation, and excellent depth and harmony.

DRY $22 AV

Michael Ramon Matakana Pinot Gris   ★★★

Grown on the Tawharanui Peninsula and fully barrel-aged, the 2009 vintage (★★★) is mouthfilling, with ripe-fruit flavours of stone-fruit and pear, a slightly creamy texture and biscuity oak characters adding complexity.

MED/DRY $30 –V

Michelle Richardson Central Otago Pinot Gris   (★★★★)

Still very fresh and finely poised, the 2010 vintage (★★★★) is a single-vineyard wine, hand-picked in the Cromwell Basin and fermented with indigenous yeasts in tanks (80 per cent) and seasoned oak barrels (20 per cent). Mouthfilling, it offers strong, vibrant flavours of citrus fruits and lychees, a slightly nutty complexity and a dryish (8 grams/litre of residual sugar) finish. Best drinking mid-2012+.

MED/DRY $28 –V

Mills Reef Reserve Hawke's Bay Pinot Gris ★★★☆

The 2011 vintage (★★★★) shows good complexity. Fermented in tanks (35 per cent) and old oak barrels (65 per cent), it is mouthfilling and vibrantly fruity, with ripe peach, pear and spice flavours, a very subtle seasoning of oak, a slightly creamy texture and a dry finish (3 grams/litre of residual sugar). Already enjoyable, it's a good 'food' wine.

Vintage	11
WR	6
Drink	11-13

DRY $24 –V

Misha's Vineyard Dress Circle Central Otago Pinot Gris ★★★★☆

The classy, intensely varietal 2010 vintage (★★★★★) was hand-picked at Bendigo at 24 brix and mostly handled in tanks; 24 per cent of the blend was fermented with indigenous yeasts in seasoned oak barrels. It's a sturdy wine (14 per cent alcohol), mouthfilling, fleshy and concentrated, with a slightly oily texture, vibrant citrus-fruit, lychee and spice flavours, showing lovely richness and roundness, and an off-dry (12 grams/litre of residual sugar) finish. Drink now or cellar.

Vintage	10	09	08
WR	6	7	7
Drink	11-15	11-14	11-13

MED/DRY $26 AV

Mission Hawke's Bay Pinot Gris ★★★

The Mission has long been a standard-bearer for Pinot Gris. The 2010 vintage (★★★) is mouthfilling, with ripe, peachy, spicy flavours, in an easy-drinking style with a smooth, yet dry (3 grams/litre of residual sugar) finish.

DRY $20 –V

Mission Reserve Hawke's Bay Pinot Gris ★★★

The 2010 vintage (★★★☆) was grown at Mangatahi, barrel-fermented and oak-aged for eight months. Mouthfilling and dry, it's a Chardonnay-like wine, creamy-textured, with ripe citrus-fruit and pear flavours, a subtle oak influence, and good complexity.

DRY $27 –V

Mission Vineyard Selection Hawke's Bay Pinot Gris ★★★★

The 2010 vintage (★★★★☆), a dry style (4 grams/litre of residual sugar), is the best yet. A single-vineyard wine, it is ripely scented and mouthfilling, with strong, peachy, spicy flavours, a hint of apricot, a deliciously creamy texture, and excellent harmony and richness.

DRY $22 V+

Moana Park Hawke's Bay Pinot Gris (★★★)

Grown in the Dartmoor Valley and tank-fermented, the easy-drinking 2010 vintage (★★★) is full-bodied, fruity and slightly sweet, with peachy, citrusy, spicy flavours and a well-rounded finish.

MED/DRY $19 AV

Momo Marlborough Pinot Gris

From Seresin and certified organic, the 2010 vintage (★★★★) was hand-picked at two sites, and 60 per cent of the blend was fermented and matured for four months in old French oak barriques. Richly scented, it is very full-bodied (14.5 per cent alcohol), with strong, ripe peach and spice flavours, considerable complexity, gentle acidity and a soft, gently sweet finish. It's drinking well now.

Vintage	10	09
WR	7	6
Drink	11-14	11-13

MED/DRY $23 –V

Moncellier Marlborough Pinot Gris

From winemaker Greg Rowdon and Bill Spence (co-founder of Matua Valley), the 2010 vintage (★★★★) is a single-vineyard wine, grown in the upper Wairau Valley. A dry style (4 grams/litre of residual sugar), it is weighty and finely textured, with stone-fruit, pear and spice flavours, showing excellent delicacy and length. The 2011 (★★★★) is highly scented, with pear, lychee and spice aromas. Dryish (5 grams/litre of residual sugar), it is mouthfilling, with vibrant, delicate, intensely varietal flavours that linger well.

MED/DRY $25 AV

Monowai Crownthorpe Pinot Gris

Grown in inland Hawke's Bay, the 2011 vintage (★★★☆) is a very fresh, medium-bodied wine, clearly varietal, with vibrant pear, spice and lime flavours showing very good depth. Crisper and drier than most Pinot Gris (5 grams/litre of residual sugar), it's an ideal 'food' wine.

Vintage	11
WR	6
Drink	11-14

MED/DRY $22 AV

Montana Living Land Series Waipara Pinot Gris

The floral, full-bodied 2009 vintage (★★★☆) was handled entirely in tanks and made in a medium-dry style (8 grams/litre of residual sugar). Ripely scented, it is fresh and smooth, with a slightly oily texture and peach, pear and spice flavours, showing good depth.

MED/DRY $20 AV

Montana North Island Pinot Gris

Drinking well now, the 2010 vintage (★★★) is a fleshy wine with peach, pear and spice flavours and a rounded finish.

MED/DRY $18 AV

Montana Reserve Hawke's Bay Pinot Gris

Grown at Matapiro, an elevated, inland district, and matured on its yeast lees in tanks, the easy-drinking 2009 vintage (★★★☆) is fleshy and smooth, with fresh acidity and good depth of lively pear and spice flavours.

MED/DRY $24 –V

Morepork Northland Pinot Gris   ★★★

The 2011 vintage (★★★) is from a vineyard named after its two pigs. Hand-picked and made in a medium-dry style (7 grams/litre of residual sugar), it's fresh and full-bodied, in a clearly varietal style with vibrant pear, lychee and spice flavours, balanced for easy drinking.

Vintage	11
WR	6
Drink	11-13

MED/DRY $24 –V

Morepork Northland Rosemary's Reserve Pinot Gris   (★★★★)

The 2010 vintage (★★★★) was grown in the Morepork Vineyard, at Kerikeri. Showing lots of personality, it's a full-bodied, concentrated wine, dryish (7 grams/litre of residual sugar), peachy, spicy and slightly gingery.

Vintage	10
WR	7
Drink	11-12

MED/DRY $25 AV

Morton Estate White Label Hawke's Bay Pinot Gris   ★★★☆

Grown at the company's inland Kinross Vineyard, the 2008 vintage (★★★☆) is scented, with mouthfilling body and good depth of fresh, citrusy, slightly spicy flavours. The 2009 (★★★☆) is fleshy, with strong, peachy, slightly honeyed flavours and a distinctly spicy finish.

Vintage	09	08	07	06
WR	6	6	6	7
Drink	11-12	11-12	P	P

DRY $19 V+

Mount Dottrel Central Otago Pinot Gris   ★★★★

The 2009 vintage (★★★★) from Mitre Rocks is an attractively scented, dry wine (3 grams/litre of residual sugar), with fresh, pure lychee, pear and spice flavours. Grown at Bendigo and Gibbston, and 15 per cent barrel-fermented, it shows excellent vibrancy, delicacy and depth.

Vintage	09	08
WR	6	6
Drink	11-12	P

DRY $23 AV

Mount Fishtail Marlborough Pinot Gris   ★★★

From Konrad, the 2010 vintage (★★★) was fermented in tanks (85 per cent) and French oak casks (15 per cent). It's a medium-dry style (9 grams/litre of residual sugar) with plenty of ripe, peachy, citrusy, spicy, gingery flavour. Enjoyable now.

Vintage	11	10
WR	6	6
Drink	12-16	11-15

MED/DRY $20 –V

Mount Riley Marlborough Pinot Gris ★★★☆

The 2010 vintage (★★★☆) was mostly handled in tanks, but 5 per cent of the blend was barrel-fermented. It's a medium-dry style, mouthfilling and smooth, with very good depth of fresh, pure pear and spice flavours and a ripely scented bouquet.

MED/DRY $18 V+

Mt Beautiful Cheviot Hills Pinot Gris (★★★★☆)

From first-crop vines and 30 per cent barrel-fermented, the 2009 vintage (★★★★☆) of this North Canterbury wine was picked at 26 brix. It's a powerful, fleshy, almost dry wine (5 grams/litre of residual sugar) with stone-fruit and spice flavours, weighty and rounded, and excellent complexity and depth.

MED/DRY $24 V+

Mt Difficulty Central Otago Pinot Gris ★★★★

Estate-grown at Bannockburn, the 2010 vintage (★★★★) was hand-picked and tank-fermented. Full-bodied and fresh, it's a drier style than many (5 grams/litre of residual sugar), with good intensity of citrus-fruit, spice and nectarine flavours, a touch of lees-aging complexity and a refreshingly crisp finish. It's still unfolding.

MED/DRY $26 –V

Mt Difficulty Roaring Meg Central Otago Pinot Gris ★★★☆

The 2009 vintage (★★★☆) is a gently sweet style (9 grams/litre of residual sugar), fresh and vibrant, with crisp acidity, pure varietal flavours of pears and spices, and good delicacy and depth.

MED/DRY $20 AV

Mt Hector Wairarapa Pinot Gris ★★★

From Matahiwi, the 2010 (★★★☆) is good value. It has pear-like aromas and flavours, a hint of spices and a gentle splash of sweetness in a vibrantly fresh, attractive style. The 2011 vintage (★★☆) was grown in the Wairarapa, despite the back label references to 'vineyards across the Hawke's Bay region'. Pleasant young, it has fresh lychee, pear and spice flavours, slightly sweet (12 grams/litre of residual sugar) and smooth.

MED/DRY $13 V+

Mt Rosa Central Otago Pinot Gris ★★★☆

The 2008 vintage (★★★☆) is a scented wine, grown at Gibbston, with mouthfilling body, good depth of peachy, spicy flavours, a touch of complexity and a dry finish. The very easy-drinking 2009 (★★★☆) is fleshy, with slight sweetness and ripe, citrusy, slightly appley flavours, showing good depth.

MED/DRY $26 –V

Mud House South Island Pinot Gris (★★★)

Enjoyable young, the 2009 vintage (★★★) is clearly varietal, with fresh, peachy, slightly spicy flavours, slightly honeyed and smooth.

MED/DRY $19 AV

Murdoch James Blue Rock Pinot Gris ★★★☆

The lively, attractive 2010 vintage (★★★☆) is a single-vineyard Martinborough wine with citrus-fruit, pear and spice flavours, showing very good depth. It's an off-dry style (6 grams/litre of residual sugar), woven with fresh, appetising acidity.

MED/DRY $25 –V

Murrays Road Marlborough Pinot Gris (★★★☆)

Faintly pink-hued, the 2010 vintage (★★★☆) is a single-vineyard wine from the heart of the Wairau Plains. Full-bodied, it has generous, peachy, spicy flavours and a slightly sweet, well-rounded finish.

MED/DRY $26 –V

Nautilus Marlborough Pinot Gris ★★★★

The 2010 vintage (★★★★) was mostly estate-grown and hand-picked in the Awatere Valley, and made with a subtle oak influence (15 per cent fermented in old French barrels). It's an off-dry style (5.8 grams/litre of residual sugar), invitingly scented, full-bodied and well-rounded, with ripe pear, lychee and spice flavours, showing excellent delicacy and harmony. Worth cellaring.

Vintage	10	09	08	07	06
WR	7	7	6	7	6
Drink	11-14	11-13	11-12	11-12	P

MED/DRY $29 –V

Ned, The, Waihopai River Marlborough Pinot Gris ★★★☆

This single-vineyard wine, grown in the Waihopai Valley, is typically finely balanced, with stone-fruit, pear and spice flavours, showing a touch of complexity, fractional sweetness, and fresh acidity keeping things lively.

MED/DRY $17 V+

Neudorf Maggie's Block Nelson Pinot Gris ★★★★☆

Looking for a dry Pinot Gris? Invitingly scented, with pure, vibrant pear, lychee and spice flavours, showing a slightly oily richness, the 2010 vintage (★★★★★) is one of the best dry Pinot Gris ever made in New Zealand. A single-vineyard wine, grown at Brightwater, on the Waimea Plains, it was hand-picked and mostly fermented and lees-aged in tanks; 10 per cent of the blend was French oak-fermented.

Vintage	10	09	08	07
WR	6	6	5	5
Drink	11-15	11-14	11-13	11-12

DRY $25 V+

Neudorf Moutere Pinot Gris   ★★★★★

The 2010 vintage (★★★★★) was hand-picked in the Home Vineyard at over 24 brix and fermented with indigenous yeasts in tanks (85 per cent) and old French puncheons. Medium-dry (12 grams/litre of residual sugar), it is fleshy and finely balanced, in an Alsace style with rich, peachy, spicy flavours, a touch of complexity, good acid spine, and power through the palate. It should be long-lived.

Vintage	09	08	07	06
WR	7	6	7	6
Drink	11-18	11-17	11-17	11-16

 MED/DRY $30 AV

Odyssey Marlborough Pinot Gris   ★★★☆

Estate-grown in the Brancott Valley, the 2010 vintage (★★★☆) was hand-picked, tank-fermented and matured on its yeast lees in old French oak casks. Pale gold, it's a distinctive style, full-bodied, peachy and slightly spicy, with a hint of oak, good complexity and a dry finish (2 grams/litre of residual sugar).

Vintage	10	09	08
WR	6	6	6
Drink	11-13	11-14	11-12

 DRY $25 –V

Ohau Gravels Pinot Gris   ★★★☆

From Ohau, north of the Kapiti Coast, in the Horowhenua, the 2010 vintage (★★★☆) was hand-picked and mostly handled in tanks, with a small percentage of barrel fermentation. Richly scented, it is full-bodied and smooth, with very good depth of fresh citrus-fruit, pear and spice flavours, a hint of honey, and a gentle splash of sweetness (12 grams/litre of residual sugar).

 MED/DRY $24 –V

Old Coach Road Nelson Pinot Gris   ★★★

From Seifried, the 2010 vintage (★★☆), grown mostly in the Redwood Valley, is fruity and smooth, with moderate depth of dryish lemon and spice flavours. The 2011 (★★★) is a very easy-drinking style, with mouthfilling body and fresh, dryish (4 grams/litre of residual sugar), citrusy, spicy flavours, fresh and smooth.

DRY $17 AV

Olssens Tom Logan Central Otago Pinot Gris   ★★★☆

The 2010 vintage (★★★★) was estate-grown at Bannockburn, hand-picked and fermented in tanks and French oak barrels. Scented and finely poised, it's a mouthfilling wine with ripe stone-fruit and distinctly spicy flavours, a touch of complexity, slight sweetness (8 grams/litre of residual sugar), and good concentration.

 MED/DRY $29 –V

Omaha Bay Vineyard Matakana Pinot Gris ★★★☆

The 2010 vintage (★★★★), the finest yet, was handled in old oak casks (80 per cent) and tanks (20 per cent). Mouthfilling and dry, with the roundness typical of northern styles, it has a touch of complexity and excellent depth of peachy, spicy flavours, very fresh and lively. The 2009 (★★★☆) is maturing well, with substantial body and strong stone-fruit and spice flavours.

Vintage	10	09	08	07	06
WR	6	5	6	6	5
Drink	12-15	11-13	11-13	11-12	P

 DRY $30 –V

Omaka Springs Marlborough Pinot Gris ★★☆

Grown in the Omaka Valley, the 2010 vintage (★★★) is a slightly sweet (12 grams/litre of residual sugar) style, peachy, slightly spicy and creamy, with plenty of flavour in an easy-drinking style. The 2011 (★★☆) is fresh and moderately varietal, with pear and spice flavours showing some green-edged, herbal notes.

Vintage	11	10
WR	7	7
Drink	11-13	11-13

 MED/DRY $17 –V

Omihi Road Waipara Pinot Gris ★★★★

From Torlesse, the 2009 vintage (★★★★★) is an enticingly scented, powerful wine, fermented and lees-aged for four months in barriques. Fleshy, with ripe peach and spice flavours, it is fresh and concentrated, with a splash of sweetness (16 grams/litre of residual sugar), a rich, oily texture and lovely depth and harmony.

Vintage	09	08
WR	7	6
Drink	12-15	11-12

 MED $25 AV

Omori Estate Lake Taupo Pinot Gris ★★★

Grown on the south-west shores of the lake, hand-picked and lees-aged in tanks, the 2009 vintage (★★★) is medium-bodied, with fresh, peachy, slightly spicy and honeyed flavours, woven with firm acidity. A slightly austere style with good individuality, it's definitely a 'food' wine.

 DRY $25 –V

Opawa Marlborough Pinot Gris ★★★☆

The 2010 vintage (★★★☆) was made in a 'lighter, crisper' style (think Pinot Grigio) than its Nautilus Estate stablemate (an Alsace style). Hand-picked and tank-fermented, it is floral, full-bodied and dry (3 grams/litre of residual sugar), with citrusy, slightly spicy flavours, showing good delicacy and roundness. The 2011 (★★★★) is the best yet. The bouquet is floral and clearly varietal; the palate is mouthfilling, with strong peach, pear, lychee and spice flavours, showing excellent delicacy, vibrancy and length.

DRY $22 AV

Open House Smooth Marlborough Pinot Gris   (★★★)

From Wither Hills, the 2009 vintage (★★★) is a good buy. Mouthfilling and (yes) smooth, it has good body and depth of fresh, clearly varietal pear and spice flavours, with gentle sweetness giving an easy-drinking appeal.

MED/DRY $15 V+

Opihi Vineyard South Canterbury Pinot Gris   ★★★☆

Grown on a north-facing slope inland from Timaru, in South Canterbury, this is typically a highly attractive wine. Hand-picked and tank-fermented, the 2009 vintage (★★★☆) is a tightly structured, distinctly cool-climate style, fresh and crisp, with dry (3 grams/litre of residual sugar), peachy flavours, woven with lively acidity, and good varietal character and depth.

DRY $24 –V

Ostler Audrey's Waitaki Valley Pinot Gris   ★★★★☆

The 2010 vintage (★★★★★) is arguably the finest white wine yet from the Waitaki Valley. It was estate-grown and mostly tank-fermented, but 30 per cent was barrel-fermented with indigenous yeasts, using large, old oak. Made in an off-dry style (6 grams/litre of residual sugar), it is a powerful wine (14.5 per cent alcohol), finely textured, with a floral bouquet and lovely depth of fresh, vibrant peach, pear, lychee and spice flavours.

Vintage	10	09
WR	6	6
Drink	11-15	11-14

MED/DRY $34 –V

Ostler Blue House Vines Waitaki Valley Pinot Gris   ★★★★

The 2010 vintage (★★★★☆) is a medium-dry style (9 grams/litre of residual sugar), grown in a single vineyard. Showing excellent body, freshness, depth and harmony, it has pear, citrus-fruit and slight passionfruit flavours, a fine thread of acidity, and a slightly oily richness.

Vintage	10	09
WR	6	5
Drink	11-15	11-14

MED/DRY $28 –V

Palliser Estate Martinborough Pinot Gris   ★★★☆

The 2010 vintage (★★★☆) is mouthfilling, with fresh acidity and pure pear, lychee and spice flavours. Slightly sweet, it shows good harmony and potential. Best drinking 2012+.

MED/DRY $24 –V

Parr & Simpson Limestone Bay Pinot Gris   ★★★★

Full of personality. A single-vineyard Nelson wine from Pohara, in eastern Golden Bay, the 2010 vintage (★★★★) was hand-picked at 24 brix and 40 per cent was fermented and matured in seasoned French oak barriques It's a full-bodied, dry wine (3.8 grams/litre of residual sugar) with fresh, strong citrus and stone-fruit flavours, oak richness, balanced acidity, and obvious cellaring potential. An excellent food wine, it should be at its best from mid-2012 onwards.

DRY $23 AV

Pasquale Waitaki Valley Pinot Gris   (★★★★)

Grown in South Canterbury, the 2010 vintage (★★★★) was hand-picked at 23 to 24 brix. Still youthful, it has good body and concentrated, intensely varietal pear/spice aromas and flavours, woven with fresh acidity. An off-dry style (6 grams/litre of residual sugar), it should be at its best from mid-2012 onwards.

MED/DRY $27 –V

Passage Rock Waiheke Island Pinot Gris   ★★★

The 2009 vintage (★★★) is a mouthfilling wine (14 per cent alcohol), easy-drinking, with soft peach, pear and slight spice flavours, fresh, vibrant and smooth.

MED/DRY $23 –V

Paulownia Pinot Gris   (★★★☆)

The 2009 vintage (★★★☆), grown in the northern Wairarapa, is mouthfilling and creamy-textured, with ripe, peachy, slightly spicy flavours and a dryish (10 grams/litre of residual sugar) finish.

MED/DRY $18 V+

People's, The, Pinot Gris   (★★★☆)

From Constellation NZ, the finely balanced 2010 vintage (★★★☆) was estate-grown in the Corner 50 Vineyard, in Hawke's Bay. Ripely scented, it is sturdy, with very good depth of peachy, slightly spicy flavours and a dryish (5 grams/litre of residual sugar) finish. Enjoyable young.

MED/DRY $20 AV

Peregrine Central Otago Pinot Gris   ★★★☆

The 2009 vintage (★★★☆) was harvested in the Cromwell Basin at 24 brix and fermented and lees-aged in tanks. It's a crisp, medium to full-bodied wine with good depth of citrusy, dryish (6.3 grams/litre of residual sugar) flavours.

MED/DRY $25 –V

Peter Yealands Marlborough Pinot Gris   ★★★

The 2010 vintage (★★★★), estate-grown in the Awatere Valley, is the best yet. Attractively scented, it's a delicious drink-young style, very fresh and lively, with good intensity of peach, pear and spice flavours, crisp, slightly sweet (5 grams/litre of residual sugar) and punchy. The 2011 (★★★) is floral and full-bodied, with vibrant, slightly appley flavours, balanced for easy drinking.

MED/DRY $20 –V

Pied Stilt Nelson Pinot Gris   (★★★☆)

Worth cellaring, the 2010 vintage (★★★☆) is a single-vineyard Motueka wine, freshly scented and medium-bodied, with very good depth of lively citrus-fruit, lychee and spice flavours, slightly sweet (10 grams/litre of residual sugar) and finely balanced.

MED/DRY $20 AV

Pisa Range Estate Central Otago Pinot Gris ★★★☆

The youthful, dry 2010 vintage (★★★☆) has very good body and depth of citrusy, peachy, slightly appley and spicy flavours, threaded with fresh acidity. Hand-picked, tank-fermented and lees-aged, it has some cellaring potential.

 DRY $28 –V

Poderi Crisci Pinot Grigio ★★★☆

Grown on Waiheke Island, the 2009 (★★★) was handled in a 50:50 split of tanks and seasoned French oak casks. It's a gently spicy wine, full-bodied, with ripe, peachy flavours and a crisp, bone-dry finish. The 2010 vintage (★★★★) is the best yet. Mouthfilling (14 per cent alcohol), it has concentrated, ripe citrus-fruit, peach and slight spice flavours, a slightly oily texture and excellent depth. The 2011 (★★★) is medium-bodied, with citrusy, slightly spicy and nutty flavours, showing a touch of complexity. It's a Pinot Grigio style, light and lively.

Vintage	10	09
WR	7	7
Drink	11-13	11-12

 DRY $29 –V

Prophet's Rock Central Otago Pinot Gris ★★★★

The 2010 vintage (★★★★) was estate-grown and hand-picked at Bendigo, in the Cromwell Basin. Medium to full-bodied, with stone-fruit and spice flavours, it's a finely balanced, medium-dry wine (12 grams/litre of residual sugar) with very good depth, texture and harmony.

Vintage	10	09	08	07
WR	6	7	6	7
Drink	12-15	11-15	11-14	11-14

 MED/DRY $28 –V

Pukeko Vineyard White Tail Pinot Gris (★★)

The 2010 vintage (★★), grown at Kerikeri, in Northland, is crisp, citrus and appley, but when tasted in early 2011 it was slightly disjointed.

 MED/DRY $22 –V

Pukeora Estate Central Hawke's Bay Pinot Gris ★★☆

Grown at Waipukurau, in Central Hawke's Bay, the 2009 vintage (★★☆) is a dry wine handled entirely in tanks. It's a sturdy, high-alcohol style (14.9 per cent), straw-hued, with ripe, peachy, spicy flavours that show a slight lack of vibrancy. The 2010, 16 per cent barrel-fermented, is a step up. It's not highly scented, but offers good body and depth of peachy, slightly spicy flavours, fresh and lively.

Vintage	10	09	08
WR	6	6	5
Drink	11-13	11-12	P

DRY $20 –V

Q Waitaki Pinot Gris

From young, first-crop vines in the Waitaki Valley, the 2010 vintage (★★★☆) is scented, with fresh citrus-fruit, pear and lychee flavours. It's a vibrantly fruity wine with lively acidity, good depth and a slightly sweet, smooth finish.

MED/DRY $35 –V

Quartz Reef Bendigo Central Otago Pinot Gris

The 2010 (★★★★☆), estate-grown and hand-harvested at Bendigo, was fermented and lees-aged in tanks. The best vintage to date, it is very fragrant and lively, with excellent vibrancy and concentration of citrusy, peachy, spicy flavours, a sliver of sweetness (7 grams/litre of residual sugar) and good acid spine. Drink now or cellar.

Vintage	10	09	08	07	06
WR	7	6	6	6	6
Drink	11-14	11-12	P	P	P

DRY $26 –V

Ransom Clos de Valerie Pinot Gris

Still on sale in 2011, the 2008 vintage (★★★☆), grown at Mahurangi, is a dry wine (3 grams/litre of residual sugar), fermented in tanks (90 per cent) and barrels (10 per cent). Pale yellow, it is drinking well now, in a medium to full-bodied style, citrusy and spicy, with bottle-aged complexity.

DRY $26 –V

Ra Nui Marlborough Wairau Valley Pinot Gris

The 2009 vintage (★★★☆), hand-picked in the Cob Cottage Vineyard, is mouthfilling, with very good depth of peach, pear and slight spice flavours, and a finely textured, dry finish. The 2010 (★★★☆) is full-bodied and ripely scented, with citrusy, slightly spicy and limey flavours and a dry (3 grams/litre of residual sugar) finish.

DRY $24 –V

Rapaura Springs Marlborough Pinot Gris

The bargain-priced 2010 vintage (★★★☆) is a medium-dry style (12 grams/litre of residual sugar), mouthfilling, with fresh, peachy, spicy flavours, balanced for easy drinking, and very good depth. Drink now.

MED/DRY $16 V+

Red Tussock Marlborough Pinot Gris (★★★★)

The 2009 vintage (★★★★) is full-bodied and softly textured, with strong, ripe stone-fruit, pear and spice flavours and a dryish finish. Slightly oily, it shows excellent varietal definition, freshness and depth.

MED/DRY $23 AV

Redoubt Hill Vineyard Nelson Pinot Gris ★★☆

Grown at Motueka, the 2010 vintage (★★★) is scented, with slightly sweet pear and spice flavours, fresh acidity, and good balance and vigour.

 MED/DRY $26 –V

Renato Nelson Pinot Gris ★★★★

Estate-grown at Kina, on the coast, hand-picked and lees-aged, the 2010 vintage (★★★★) is a slightly sweet style (8 grams/litre of residual sugar), ripely scented, with good richness, delicacy and harmony. It has fresh stone-fruit and spice flavours, well-rounded and long.

Vintage	10	09	08	07	06
WR	7	6	7	6	7
Drink	11-15	11-13	11-13	11-13	11-12

 MED/DRY $22 V+

Ribbonwood Marlborough Pinot Gris ★★★☆

From Framingham, the 2010 vintage (★★★☆) is mouthfilling and generous, with ripe, peachy, slightly spicy flavours, showing very good depth, and a rounded, dryish (6 grams/litre of residual sugar) finish.

 MED/DRY $20 AV

Richmond Plains Nelson Pinot Gris (★★★★)

The 2010 vintage (★★★★) is mouthfilling (14.5 per cent alcohol), fleshy, lemony and spicy, in a medium-dry style (7 grams/litre of residual sugar) with good weight, concentration and length.

 MED/DRY $20 V+

Rimu Grove Bronte Pinot Gris – see Bronte by Rimu Grove Pinot Gris

Rimu Grove Nelson Pinot Gris ★★★★

The 2010 vintage (★★★★), grown in the Moutere hills, was mostly handled in tanks, but 15 per cent was lees-aged in seasoned French oak barrels. Mouthfilling, with a slightly oily texture and concentrated, citrusy, spicy flavours, it's a weighty (14.5 per cent alcohol), medium-dry style (12 grams/litre of residual sugar), showing excellent complexity and length.

Vintage	10	09	08	07	06
WR	7	7	7	7	6
Drink	11-18	11-17	11-15	11-12	P

MED/DRY $29 –V

Riverby Estate Marlborough Pinot Gris ★★★

A single-vineyard wine, grown in the Wairau Valley, the 2009 vintage (★★★☆) is fleshy and soft, with mouthfilling body and a gentle splash of sweetness (10 grams/litre of residual sugar) amid its ripe peach, pear and spice flavours, which show very good depth.

 MED/DRY $20 –V

River Farm Godfrey Road Marlborough Pinot Gris ★★★☆

The 2010 vintage (★★★☆) is a single-vineyard wine, hand-picked and partly fermented with indigenous yeasts in seasoned French oak barrels. Sturdy and dry (3 grams/litre of residual sugar), it has substantial body (14.5 per cent alcohol), with fresh, ripe pear and spice flavours and a finely textured, rounded finish.

DRY $20 AV

Vintage	10	09
WR	6	6
Drink	11-14	11-14

Rockburn Central Otago Pinot Gris ★★★

Grown at Parkburn, in the Cromwell Basin, and at Gibbston, the 2010 (★★★☆) was handled in tanks. An off-dry style, it is floral, full-bodied and fresh, with very good depth of lemony, peachy, spicy flavours and a smooth finish. The 2011 vintage (★★★) is very fresh, crisp and appley, in a punchy, medium-dry style (10 grams/litre of residual sugar).

MED/DRY $28 –V

Vintage	10
WR	6
Drink	10-13

Rockface Waipara Pinot Gris (★★★)

From Bishop's Head, the 2010 vintage (★★★) is freshly scented, mouthfilling and clearly varietal, with satisfying depth of peach, pear and spice flavours.

MED/DRY $17 AV

Rock Ferry Central Otago Pinot Gris ★★★★

Full of personality, the 2010 vintage (★★★★) is a single-vineyard wine, grown at Bendigo and mostly handled in tanks; 30 per cent of the blend was fermented with indigenous yeasts in French oak puncheons. Mouthfilling and creamy-textured, it has rich stone-fruit and spice flavours, showing good complexity, with a dryish (6 grams/litre of residual sugar) finish. Drink now onwards.

MED/DRY $29 –V

Vintage	10	09
WR	6	6
Drink	11-15	11-13

Rongopai Marlborough Pinot Gris (★★★☆)

From Babich, the 2010 vintage (★★★☆) is a top buy. Sturdy (14.5 per cent alcohol), it is fresh and vibrantly fruity, with ripe, peachy, spicy flavours, hints of apricot and ginger, and very good depth. It's drinking well now.

MED/DRY $15 V+

Ruby Bay Vineyard Pinot Gris ★★★☆

The 2009 vintage (★★★) is a single-vineyard Nelson wine, hand-picked. Gently aromatic, it's fresh and medium-bodied (12.3 per cent alcohol) with pure, delicate, pear-like flavours and an off-dry (5 grams/litre of residual sugar) finish.

Vintage	09
WR	5
Drink	11-12

 DRY $24 –V

Sacred Hill Halo Marlborough Pinot Gris ★★★★

The 2010 vintage (★★★★) is 'predominantly' from the company's Hell's Gate Vineyard, in the Waihopai Valley. An unusually dry style (3 grams/litre of residual sugar), it has a fragrant, citrusy bouquet, leading into a full-bodied palate with citrusy, appley, spicy flavours, finely balanced and lingering.

Vintage	10
WR	6
Drink	11-13

 DRY $26 –V

Sacred Hill Marlborough Vineyards Pinot Gris ★★★☆

Estate-grown in the Waihopai Valley, the 2010 vintage (★★★☆) is a dry wine (1.4 grams/litre of residual sugar). A crisp, Pinot Grigio style, it is vibrantly fruity, with strong flavours of pears and lychees and a gently spicy finish.

 DRY $21 AV

Saint Clair Godfrey's Creek Reserve Pinot Gris ★★★☆

The 2009 vintage (★★★☆) is an off-dry style (7.5 grams/litre of residual sugar), fleshy, with gentle acidity and ripe peach and nectarine flavours, showing very good depth.

Vintage	09	08	07	06
WR	6	6	6	6
Drink	11-12	P	P	P

MED/DRY $25 –V

Saint Clair Marlborough Pinot Gris ★★★☆

The 2009 vintage (★★★☆) is attractively scented, fresh and lively, with a slightly oily texture and pear, lemon and spice flavours showing very good depth and harmony.

 MED/DRY $21 AV

Saint Clair Pioneer Block 5 Bull Block Marlborough Pinot Gris ★★★☆

From a single vineyard in the Omaka Valley, the 2010 vintage (★★★☆) is a medium wine (19 grams/litre of residual sugar), made in a *tardive* (late-harvest) style. Tank-fermented, it is full-bodied, with plenty of flavour – peachy, well-spiced and soft. Enjoyable young.

 MED $23 –V

Saints Gisborne Pinot Gris ★★★

From Pernod Ricard NZ, the 2009 vintage (★★★) is lemon-scented, with fresh, citrusy flavours, crisp and lively.

MED/DRY $18 AV

Scott Base Central Otago Pinot Gris (★★★☆)

From Allan Scott, the 2009 vintage (★★★☆) is a dryish style (5 grams/litre of residual sugar), ripely scented and mouthfilling, with crisp stone-fruit, pear and spice flavours, fresh and vibrant.

MED/DRY $29 –V

Sea Level Home Block Nelson Pinot Gris (★★★★)

From Sam Smail – senior winemaker at Whitehaven, Marlborough – and his father, Mike, the 2011 vintage (★★★★) is a full-bodied wine with very youthful, pure, delicate pear/spice aromas and flavours. Intensely varietal, it's a refined wine, slightly sweet (7 grams/litre of residual sugar), with obvious potential.

Vintage	11
WR	6
Drink	11-14

MED/DRY $18 V+

Sears Road Pinot Gris (★★)

From Stirling Vines, producers of Maimai Creek, the 2009 vintage (★★) is a Hawke's Bay wine. A full-bodied, lemony, slightly gingery wine with a crisp finish, it's a solid quaffer.

DRY $12 AV

Secret Stone Marlborough Pinot Gris (★★★☆)

From Matua Valley, the 2009 vintage (★★★☆) is ripely scented and mouthfilling, with very good depth of slightly sweet pear, spice and stone-fruit flavours, a slightly oily texture, and good delicacy and harmony.

MED/DRY $20 AV

Seifried Nelson Pinot Gris ★★★

The 2011 vintage (★★★) is mouthfilling and smooth, with a splash of sweetness (11 grams/litre of residual sugar) and fresh, moderately concentrated peach, spice and slight apricot flavours, offering very easy drinking.

Vintage	11	10	09	08
WR	6	6	6	6
Drink	11-12	11-12	P	P

MED/DRY $21 –V

Selaks Heritage Reserve Marlborough Pinot Gris (★★★☆)

From Constellation NZ, the debut 2010 vintage (★★★☆) is full-bodied, with a slightly oily texture and good depth of fresh peach, pear and spice flavours, vibrantly fruity and dryish.

MED/DRY $22 AV

Selaks Winemaker's Favourite Hawke's Bay Pinot Gris   ★★★☆

The 2009 vintage (★★★☆) is mouthfilling, with good depth of clearly varietal, peachy flavours, a slightly oily texture and a lingering, rounded finish.

MED/DRY $21 AV

Seresin Marlborough Pinot Gris   ★★★★★

One of the region's most distinctive Pinot Gris. The 2009 vintage (★★★★★) is notably rich and complex, in a barrel-fermented, Alsace style, full of personality. Beautifully floral, concentrated, ripe and rounded, it has an oily richness and deep stone-fruit flavours, slightly spicy, gingery and long. BioGro certified, the 2010 (★★★★★) was hand-picked in the Home and Raupo Creek vineyards, fermented with indigenous yeasts, and lees-aged for five months in seasoned French oak barriques. It's a dryish wine (6.8 grams/litre of residual sugar) with substantial body (14 per cent alcohol) and ripe peach, apricot and spice flavours, showing excellent complexity and depth. Finely poised, with great drinkability, it has layers of flavour and interest.

Vintage	10
WR	7
Drink	11-15

MED/DRY $30 AV

Seresin Raupo Marlborough Pinot Gris   (★★★★★)

Just 394 bottles were produced of the outstanding 2008 vintage (★★★★★). Hand-picked in the Raupo Creek Vineyard, it was fermented with indigenous yeasts and matured for 15 months in seasoned French oak barrels. Powerful and complex, it has deep pear, lychee and spice flavours, layered with toasty and creamy notes, in an unusually weighty and complex style. Slightly sweet (18 grams/litre of residual sugar), with a rich, lasting finish, it's a wine of real personality.

Vintage	08
WR	7
Drink	10-15

MED $50 AV

Shaky Bridge Central Otago Pinot Gris   ★★★

The 2010 vintage (★★★☆) was estate-grown and hand-picked at Alexandra and made in a dry (3 grams/litre of residual sugar) style. Well worth cellaring, it's fresh and tightly structured, with strong, citrusy, slightly spicy flavours, threaded with appetising acidity.

DRY $25 –V

Shaky Bridge Pioneer Series Pinot Gris   (★★★)

The 2010 vintage (★★★) is fractionally sweeter (6 grams/litre of residual sugar) than its stablemate (above). It's a mouthfilling, creamy wine with good depth of peachy, spicy flavours and a smooth finish.

MED/DRY $18 AV

Shingle Peak Marlborough Pinot Gris   ★★★☆

The 2010 vintage (★★★★) is a great buy. Full-bodied, it is creamy-textured, with peachy, slightly spicy flavours in the Alsace style, showing excellent depth and harmony. The 2011 (★★★) offers easy drinking, with fresh peach, pear and spice flavours, slightly creamy and smooth.

 MED/DRY $18 V+

Shingle Peak Reserve Release Marlborough Pinot Gris   ★★★☆

The 2010 vintage (★★★☆), partly barrel-fermented, is scented and soft, with moderately concentrated, peachy, slightly spicy flavours, gentle sweetness and lots of drink-young appeal.

 MED/DRY $20 AV

Sileni Cellar Selection Hawke's Bay Pinot Gris   ★★★

The 2010 vintage (★★★) was mostly tank-fermented and lees-aged, with a small portion of barrel fermentation. Medium-bodied, with fresh pear and spice aromas and flavours, it's a dry style (3.8 grams/litre of residual sugar), enjoyable young, with good varietal character and harmony.

Vintage	10
WR	6
Drink	11-14

 DRY $20 –V

Sileni Parkhill Hawke's Bay Pinot Gris   (★★★★)

Hand-picked in a coastal vineyard and 50 per cent barrel-fermented, the 2010 vintage (★★★★) is a fresh, richly scented, dryish wine (4.5 grams/litre of residual sugar), with ripe stone-fruit flavours showing some oak/lees-aging complexity, and very good vibrancy, harmony and length.

 DRY $25 AV

Sileni The Priestess Hawke's Bay Pinot Gris   (★★★★)

Grown in The Triangle and 50 per cent barrel-fermented, the 2010 vintage (★★★★) is a full-bodied style with concentrated stone-fruit and spice flavours. A dry style (2 grams/litre of residual sugar), rich, ripe and rounded, with leesy, nutty notes adding complexity, it is drinking well now.

 DRY $25 AV

Soho Jagger Marlborough Pinot Gris   (★★★★)

A generous, fresh-scented wine, the 2011 vintage (★★★★) is full-bodied, with strong yet delicate lychee, pear and spice flavours and a dryish (6 grams/litre of residual sugar) finish. Instantly appealing.

DRY $27 –V

Soho Marlborough Pinot Gris ★★★☆

The 2010 vintage (★★★☆) offers 'unadulterated flavours' – with no definition. A full-bodied, slightly creamy wine, it has off-dry, pear and spice, slightly gingery flavours, and lots of drink-young appeal.

MED/DRY $26 –V

Soho White Collection Marlborough Pinot Gris (★★★)

Faintly pink, the 2011 vintage (★★★) is peachy, spicy and slightly Gewürztraminer-like. Crisp and dry (4 grams/litre of residual sugar), it's a flavoursome wine, ready to roll.

DRY $21 –V

Soljans Kumeu Pinot Gris ★★★☆

The mouthfilling 2010 vintage (★★★☆) is a fresh, finely balanced, easy-drinking West Auckland wine with ripe, slightly sweet flavours (10 grams/litre of residual sugar) of pears and lychees, and a hint of apricot.

MED/DRY $20 AV

Southern Cross Hawke's Bay Pinot Gris (★★☆)

From One Tree Hill Vineyards, a division of Morton Estate, the 2009 vintage (★★★) is a sturdy, dryish style with fresh, ripe flavours of citrus fruits and peaches and a smooth, gently spicy finish.

MED/DRY $17 –V

Spinyback Nelson Pinot Gris ★★★☆

From Waimea Estate, the 2009 vintage (★★★☆) was harvested on the Waimea Plains at 22 to 24 brix, tank-fermented and lees-stirred. Full-bodied (14 per cent alcohol), it has crisp, dryish (5.8 grams/litre of residual sugar) flavours of peaches and spices, showing good depth.

Vintage	09	08	07
WR	7	7	6
Drink	11-12	P	P

MED/DRY $18 V+

Spy Valley Envoy Marlborough Pinot Gris ★★★★☆

The 2009 vintage (★★★★☆) was estate-grown in the Waihopai Valley and fermented and lees-aged in large German oak ovals and old French barriques. It's a fleshy, soft wine with soaring alcohol (14.8 per cent) and very ripe stone-fruit and spice flavours, showing some oak complexity. A beautifully harmonious wine, it is finely textured and rich, with a very rounded finish. The 2010 (★★★★☆), barrel-fermented and made in a medium style (31 grams/litre of residual sugar), is mouthfilling and harmonious, with ripe stone-fruit and spice flavours, a very subtle seasoning of oak, and excellent richness, complexity and roundness.

Vintage	10	09	08	07	06
WR	7	7	6	6	6
Drink	11-15	11-14	11-12	11-12	P

MED $29 AV

Spy Valley Marlborough Pinot Gris   ★★★★

A generous wine with strong personality, the 2010 vintage (★★★★☆) is a great buy. Harvested at 23.3 to 26.5 brix and partly fermented in old oak casks, it's a medium-dry style (10.5 grams/litre of residual sugar), fleshy and forward, with good concentration of ripe stone-fruit and spice flavours, a slightly oily texture and a rich, rounded finish. The 2011 (★★★★) is full-bodied (14.5 per cent alcohol) and finely scented, with fresh, peachy, citrusy, spicy flavours, showing good concentration and balance. Drink now or cellar.

Vintage	11	10	09	08	07	06
WR	6	6	7	6	6	7
Drink	11-14	11-13	11-12	P	P	P

 MED/DRY $23 AV

Staete Landt Marlborough Pinot Gris   ★★★★☆

This single-vineyard wine is hand-harvested at Rapaura and fermented and matured on its yeast lees in old French oak puncheons. It is typically weighty and concentrated, with a slightly nutty complexity. The 2009 vintage (★★★★☆) is bone-dry – unusual for Pinot Gris. Full-bodied, fresh and finely poised, with gentle acidity, it has vibrant stone-fruit and spice flavours, ripe and rich, carrying the dry style perfectly.

Vintage	09	08	07
WR	7	7	6
Drink	11-17	11-13	11-12

 DRY $29 AV

Stafford Lane Nelson Pinot Gris   ★★☆

The 2009 vintage (★★) is light-bodied, with restrained, lemony, spicy flavours and a slightly sweet (8.3 grams/litre of residual sugar) finish.

 MED/DRY $19 –V

Stanley Estates Marlborough Pinot Gris   (★★★★)

The fragrant, mouthfilling 2010 vintage (★★★★) has fresh, pear-like aromas and rich lychee and spice flavour, showing slight sweetness, a touch of oak-derived complexity and good harmony.

 MED/DRY $23 AV

Starborough Awatere Valley Marlborough Pinot Gris   (★★★★★)

The lovely 2011 vintage (★★★★★) is a single-vineyard wine, hand-picked and mostly handled in tanks; 20 per cent of the blend was barrel-fermented. Already delicious, it is rich and vibrantly fruity, with deep pear, lychee and spice flavours, a subtle seasoning of oak and excellent delicacy, balance (6 grams/litre of residual sugar) and length. Drink now or cellar.

MED/DRY $24 V+

Starborough Marlborough Pinot Gris ★★★★

Priced attractively, the 2011 vintage (★★★★) is a blend of Wairau Valley (75 per cent) and Awatere Valley (25 per cent) fruit, mostly handled in tanks, but 10 per cent of the blend was fermented and aged in old oak barrels. Deliciously fresh and vibrant, it has strong, yet delicate pear and spice flavours, and a smooth, finely textured and dryish (6 grams/litre of residual sugar) finish.

Vintage	10
WR	6
Drink	11-13

MED/DRY $21 V+

Stoneleigh Latitude Marlborough Pinot Gris (★★★☆)

The debut 2011 vintage (★★★☆) is designed to celebrate the terroir of the 'Golden Mile' – Rapaura Road. It's a freshly aromatic, full-bodied wine with moderately concentrated flavours of pears and spices. A slightly sweet style (11 grams/litre of residual sugar), it shows good delicacy and depth.

MED/DRY $27 –V

Stoneleigh Marlborough Pinot Gris ★★★★

From Pernod Ricard NZ, the 2010 vintage (★★★★) is attractively scented, with strong, fresh, intensely varietal peach, pear and spice flavours and an oily, rounded texture. A slightly sweet style, balanced for easy drinking, it shows good richness. Tasted in its infancy, just after bottling, the 2011 (★★★☆) showed very good freshness, purity and depth.

MED/DRY $23 AV

Stoneleigh Rapaura Series Marlborough Pinot Gris ★★★★☆

The 2010 vintage (★★★★☆) was on sale within three months of the harvest. Picked at 23 to 24 brix, and aged on its yeast lees in tanks, it's a richly scented, beautifully ripe-tasting wine with concentrated stone-fruit and spice flavours and a slightly sweet, soft, harmonious finish. Delicious from the start, it's still drinking well.

MED/DRY $27 AV

Sugar Loaf Marlborough Pinot Gris (★★★☆)

The 2010 vintage (★★★☆) is a lively, clearly varietal wine, partly barrel-fermented, with fresh peach, pear and spice flavours, showing good depth, and a dryish finish.

MED/DRY $19 V+

Takatu Matakana Pinot Gris ★★★★

Grown on a north-facing hillside, this is a sophisticated wine, fermented and lees-aged in old French oak puncheons. The 2010 (★★★★☆) is a top vintage, with impressive vigour and depth. A good 'food' wine, it is mouthfilling and dry, with peachy, spicy, slightly toasty flavours, showing excellent complexity and potential.

Vintage	10	09
WR	7	7
Drink	11-17	11-15

DRY $35 –V

Takutai Nelson Pinot Gris   (★★★)

From Waimea Estates, the 2009 vintage (★★★) is a great buy. A single-vineyard wine, grown on the Waimea Plains, it has plenty of spicy, slightly sweet (6 grams/litre of residual sugar), smooth flavour, soft and ready.

Vintage	10	09
WR	6	6
Drink	11-13	11-12

 MED/DRY $13 V+

Tatty Bogler Otago Pinot Gris   ★★★★

From Forrest, the 2009 vintage (★★★★) was grown at Bannockburn, in the Cromwell Basin, and the Waitaki Valley (hence the 'Otago' statement of origin on the label, rather than 'Central Otago'). Tasted soon after bottling, it's a powerful, rounded wine, 10 per cent barrel-fermented, with mouthfilling body and strong lychee, pear and spice flavours, finely textured and rounded (7 grams/litre of residual sugar).

Vintage	09	08
WR	6	6
Drink	11-15	P

 MED/DRY $29 –V

Te Henga The Westie Premium Marlborough Pinot Gris   (★★★)

From Babich, the 2010 vintage (★★★) is a sturdy wine (14.5 per cent alcohol), partly oak-aged. Fresh, citrusy, spicy and slightly gingery, it's a flavoursome, off-dry wine, enjoyable now.

 MED/DRY $16 V+

Te Mania Nelson Pinot Gris   ★★★☆

The 2010 vintage (★★★☆) was hand-picked and mostly tank-fermented; 15 per cent was matured in old casks. Full-bodied, with fresh, ripe citrus, lychee and spice flavours, it is softly textured, with pure, clearly defined varietal characters, a touch of sweetness and good length.

MED/DRY $22 AV

Te Mara Central Otago Pinot Gris   ★★★★☆

The 2009 vintage (★★★★) was grown in the Cromwell Basin and handled in tanks. Richly scented, it's a fleshy, ripe-tasting wine, peachy and spicy, with a hint of honey, slight sweetness balanced by fresh, lively acidity, and very good depth and harmony.

MED/DRY $26 AV

Terrace Edge Waipara Valley Pinot Gris   ★★★★☆

Consistently great value. The 2010 vintage (★★★★☆) was hand-picked at over 25 brix and fermented with indigenous yeasts in seasoned oak barrels. Highly scented, with a spicy, gingery bouquet, it is robust (14.5 per cent alcohol), with strong, ripe stone-fruit and spice flavours. Fleshy and powerful, it is fresh and vibrant, with gentle sweetness (15 grams/litre of residual sugar) and loads of personality.

MED $21 V+

Terrace Heights Estate Marlborough Pinot Gris   ★★★☆

Grown in the Wairau Valley, hand-harvested and tank-fermented, the 2010 (★★★☆) is fleshy, with slightly sweet peach, pear and spice flavours, finely balanced for easy drinking. The 2011 vintage (★★★★) is powerful (14.5 per cent alcohol), mouthfilling and creamy, with strong peach, pear and spice flavours and a dryish (7.5 grams/litre of residual sugar) finish.

Vintage	11	10	09	
WR	6	6	6	MED/DRY $22 AV
Drink	11-14	11-13	11-12	

Terravin Marlborough Pinot Gris   ★★★★

Estate-grown in the Omaka Valley, this wine is hand-picked, fermented with indigenous yeasts and lees-aged in old French oak barrels. The 2010 vintage (★★★★) has stone-fruit and spice flavours, fresh and rich, hints of lychees and pears, a subtle seasoning of oak and a gently sweet finish.

 MED $29 –V

Thornbury Waipara Pinot Gris   ★★★☆

The 2010 vintage (★★★★) was mostly handled in tanks; 5 per cent was fermented in old oak puncheons. It's an off-dry style, finely scented, with vibrant pear/spice flavours, showing excellent freshness, depth and immediacy. The 2011 (★★★☆), also fermented in tanks (mostly) and old oak puncheons, is slightly sweet (5 grams/litre of residual sugar), fleshy and soft, with pear and spice flavours offering very easy drinking. (From Villa Maria.)

Vintage	11	10	09	
WR	7	5	7	MED/DRY $22 AV
Drink	11-13	P	11-12	

Three Miners Central Otago Pinot Gris   ★★★

From the Earnscleugh Valley, the 2010 vintage (★★★) is a mouthfilling wine with good depth of fresh, citrusy, gently spicy flavours, balanced acidity and a fully dry finish. It should drink well over the next couple of years.

DRY $22 –V

Tiki Waipara Pinot Gris   ★★★☆

The debut 2010 vintage (★★★☆) is a single-vineyard wine with fresh, lemony, appley aromas and flavours. Medium-bodied, with hints of lychees and spices, a slightly oily texture and gentle sweetness, it's a vibrantly fruity, smooth wine, offering very easy drinking. The 2011 (★★★★) is freshly scented and mouthfilling, with vibrant peach, pear and spice flavours, showing excellent balance and depth. Very finely poised and lingering, it's already delicious.

 MED/DRY $28 –V

Tinpot Hut Marlborough Pinot Gris ★★★★

The 2009 vintage (★★★★☆) was grown in the Awatere and Wairau valleys. Attractively scented, it is mouthfilling and vibrantly fruity, with strong, slightly sweet peach, pear and spice flavours, showing excellent ripeness, harmony and richness.

 MED/DRY $21 V+

Ti Point Marlborough Pinot Gris ★★★★

The 2010 vintage (★★★★), weighty and fully dry, was estate-grown in the Waihopai Valley, blended with a splash of Viognier (5 per cent) and partly (10 per cent) barrel-fermented. Scented and rich, it shows good concentration of grapefruit and peach flavours, fresh acidity and a well-spiced finish.

Vintage	10	09
WR	6	7
Drink	11-20	11-14

 DRY $21 V+

Tohu Nelson Pinot Gris ★★★☆

The 2010 vintage (★★★☆) is a single-vineyard wine, partly barrel-fermented. Dry (2.5 grams/litre of residual sugar), it is a 'serious' style, weighty, with fresh acidity and very good depth of fresh pear and spice flavours. Worth cellaring.

 DRY $22 AV

Toi Toi Brookdale Reserve Marlborough Pinot Gris ★★★

The 2010 vintage (★★★) is a dry style (3 grams/litre of residual sugar), scented and full-bodied, with decent depth of pear and spice flavours, woven with fresh acidity.

 DRY $22 –V

Toi Toi Marlborough Pinot Gris (★★★)

The 2009 vintage (★★★) is medium-bodied, with fresh pear, apple and spice flavours and a rounded (5 grams/litre of residual sugar), lingering finish. An easy-drinking style, it offers good value.

 MED/DRY $17 AV

Torea Marlborough Pinot Gris ★★★☆

From Fairhall Downs, the 2010 vintage (★★★☆) was 50 per cent oak-aged. It's a high-alcohol style (14.5 per cent), attractively scented, with fresh, vibrant, peachy flavours, slightly sweet and smooth. Enjoyable now.

MED/DRY $19 V+

Torlesse Waipara Pinot Gris   ★★★★

The 2009 vintage (★★★★☆) is scented, mouthfilling and finely poised, with vibrant lychee and spice flavours showing lovely purity, richness and roundness. Made in a medium style (16 grams/litre of residual sugar), it's a good buy.

Vintage	09
WR	5
Drink	12-15

MED $20 V+

Torrent Bay Nelson Pinot Gris   ★★☆

From Anchorage, the 2009 vintage (★★★) is a medium-bodied wine with vibrant, crisp flavours of lemons, apples and spices and a splash of sweetness (8.3 grams/litre of residual sugar). It's a fresh, easy-drinking wine, priced right.

MED/DRY $16 AV

Trinity Hill [Black Label] Hawke's Bay Pinot Gris   ★★★★

The 2009 vintage (★★★★☆) was mostly (77 per cent) grown at Haumoana, with smaller parcels of grapes from Southern Hawke's Bay and the Gimblett Gravels. Hand-picked, fermented in tanks and old oak barrels, and blended with Viognier (10 per cent), it's a dry wine (1.5 grams/litre of residual sugar), powerful and fleshy, with concentrated, ripe stone-fruit flavours and hints of ginger, spices and honey. Generous and finely textured, it has a rich, rounded finish.

Vintage	09	08	07	06
WR	6	6	5	5
Drink	11-12	P	P	P

DRY $34 –V

Trinity Hill [White Label] Hawke's Bay Pinot Gris   ★★★☆

The 2009 vintage (★★★☆), blended with Viognier (14 per cent), is mouthfilling and soft, with citrusy, peachy flavours, fresh and pure, very good varietal character and depth, and a dry (3 grams/litre of residual sugar) finish. The 2010 (★★★☆), which also includes a dollop of Viognier (14 per cent), is full-bodied, with peachy, spicy, dryish flavours (4 grams/litre of residual sugar), slightly creamy and soft.

Vintage	10
WR	5
Drink	11-13

DRY $19 V+

Triplebank Awatere Valley Marlborough Pinot Gris   ★★★☆

Pernod Ricard NZ's wine is aromatic and flavourful. The 2010 vintage (★★★☆) is a floral, citrusy wine with cool-climate freshness and vibrancy. Full-bodied, with a touch of sweetness, it has very good depth of lemony, slightly spicy flavours, balanced for easy drinking. The 2011 (★★★☆) is mouthfilling, with fresh, pure, slightly sweet lychee and spice flavours that linger well.

MED/DRY $24 –V

Tupari Marlborough Pinot Gris ★★★★☆

The debut 2009 vintage (★★★★☆) is a single-vineyard wine, grown in the Awatere Valley. It is beautifully scented, with mouthfilling body, pure, peachy, spicy flavours, a slightly oily texture and a well-rounded, very harmonious finish. The 2010 (★★★★★) is even better. Enticingly scented, it is full-bodied (14.5 per cent alcohol), with concentrated stone-fruit and spice flavours, showing lovely vibrancy, delicacy, depth and harmony. Drink now or cellar.

 MED/DRY $29 AV

Turanga Creek Le Pur Pinot Gris ★★★☆

Grown at Whitford, in South Auckland, the skilfully crafted 2009 vintage (★★★★) is fleshy, ripe and rounded, with peach, pear and spice flavours, showing very good freshness and concentration, and a dry finish. The 2010 (★★★☆), the first to be labelled Le Pur ('The Pure'), is mouthfilling and bone-dry, with very good depth of pear/spice flavours and a creamy-soft finish.

Vintage	10
WR	6
Drink	11-14

 DRY $24 –V

Tussock Nelson Pinot Gris ★★★

From Woollaston, the 2010 vintage (★★★) is a lively, medium-dry wine (6 grams/litre of residual sugar), freshly scented and fleshy, with lemony, slightly appley and spicy flavours and a smooth finish.

 MED/DRY $18 AV

Two Rivers of Marlborough Pinot Gris ★★★★

The 2010 vintage (★★★★) was harvested at nearly 25 brix and 10 per cent barrel-aged. A finely scented, fresh, mouthfilling and elegant wine, it shows good richness of pear, lychee and spice flavours, with a tightly structured, dryish (4.9 grams/litre of residual sugar) finish.

 DRY $24 AV

Two Tracks Marlborough Pinot Gris ★★★

From Wither Hills, the 2009 vintage (★★★☆) is fresh and lively, with pure, ripe peach and spice flavours, vibrant, slightly sweet and finely poised.

 MED/DRY $17 AV

Urlar Gladstone Pinot Gris ★★★☆

A distinctive style, the 2009 vintage (★★★☆) was grown in the Wairarapa and fermented and matured for a year in seasoned French oak casks. Slightly Chardonnay-like, it is big-bodied, with grapefruit and peach flavours, slightly toasty and creamy, good ripeness and complexity, and a dry finish.

DRY $28 –V

Vavasour Awatere Valley Pinot Gris

The 2010 (★★★★) was grown in Marlborough's Awatere Valley and mostly handled in tanks, but 10 per cent was fermented and lees-aged in seasoned French oak barriques. Fragrant and full-bodied, it is strongly flavoured, with a subtle seasoning of oak, and good varietal character and harmony. The 2011 vintage (★★★★☆) is richly scented and mouthfilling, with peach, pear and lychee flavours showing excellent depth, delicacy and balance. Slightly sweet, vibrantly fruity and youthful, it has some spicy, gingery notes adding interest and obvious potential.

Vintage	11	10	09	08
WR	7	7	6	5
Drink	11-14	11-14	11-13	11-12

MED/DRY $24 AV

Vidal [White Series] East Coast Pinot Gris

The 2010 vintage (★★★) is a blend of Gisborne (46 per cent), Hawke's Bay, Marlborough and Waipara grapes, and includes splashes of Gewürztraminer (9 per cent), Viognier (2 per cent) and Sauvignon Blanc (1 per cent). It's a dry style (4 grams/litre of residual sugar), fresh and vibrant, with decent depth of pear and spice flavours and a slightly oily texture. A good all-purpose wine.

Vintage	10	09	08
WR	6	6	6
Drink	11-12	P	P

DRY $22 AV

Villa Maria Cellar Selection Marlborough Pinot Gris

Delicious from the start, the 2010 vintage (★★★★), mostly hand-picked in the Awatere Valley, is an almost dry style with rich pear and spice flavours, mouthfilling body and a well-rounded finish. The 2011 (tasted prior to bottling, and so not rated) has strong pear/spice aromas and flavours, with hints of peaches and apricots. Partly (5 per cent) fermented in seasoned French oak casks, it's a slightly drier style than most (5 grams/litre of residual sugar).

Vintage	11	10	09
WR	6	6	7
Drink	11-15	11-14	11-13

MED/DRY $24 AV

Villa Maria Private Bin East Coast Pinot Gris

The 2010 vintage (★★★☆) was grown in Gisborne (46 per cent), Hawke's Bay (24 per cent), Marlborough (22 per cent) and Waipara (8 per cent). It's a mouthfilling wine with ripe, peachy, gently spicy flavours, showing very good depth, and a basically dry (4.5 grams/litre of residual sugar) finish.

Vintage	11	10	09	08
WR	7	6	6	6
Drink	12-14	11-12	P	P

DRY $22 AV

Villa Maria Single Vineyard Seddon Pinot Gris ★★★★★

One of the country's top Pinot Gris, this Awatere Valley, Marlborough wine is typically sturdy, beautifully scented and intense. The 2010 vintage (★★★★★) was mostly tank-fermented and lees-aged for six months, but 10 per cent was fermented in seasoned French oak barriques. Fleshy, elegant and rich, it has concentrated, very fresh, vibrant and pure pear, lychee and spice flavours, with a dryish (7 grams/litre of residual sugar), lasting finish.

Vintage	10	09	08	07	06
WR	7	7	7	7	6
Drink	11-15	11-15	11-14	11-13	P

MED/DRY $33 AV

Volcanic Hills Marlborough Pinot Gris (★★★★)

Offering fine value, the 2010 vintage (★★★★) is a full-bodied, off-dry wine (8 grams/litre of residual sugar) with very fresh, delicate and pure flavours of pears, lychees and spices, finely balanced and long.

Vintage	10
WR	6
Drink	11-13

MED/DRY $20 V+

Waimarie Huapai Pinot Gris (★★★☆)

A single-vineyard wine, grown in West Auckland, the pale straw 2010 vintage (★★★☆) is mouthfilling, with plenty of ripe, spicy, slightly nutty and honeyed flavour, crisp and dryish (6 grams/litre of residual sugar).

MED/DRY $20 AV

Waimea Bolitho SV Pinot Gris ★★★☆

The 2009 vintage (★★★☆) was estate-grown on the Waimea Plains in Nelson and hand-picked. A gently sweet style (22 grams/litre of residual sugar), it is weighty, with generous, ripe, peachy flavours, hints of pears and spices, gentle acidity and good harmony.

Vintage	09	08	07	06	05
WR	6	NM	7	7	6
Drink	11-13	NM	11-12	P	P

MED $25 –V

Waimea Nelson Pinot Gris ★★★★

In top vintages, this is one of the best-value Pinot Gris in the country. The 2009 (★★★★★), hand-picked at 24 brix, is a powerful, Alsace style, fleshy and ripely scented, with a slightly oily texture and deep stone-fruit and spice flavours. The 2010 vintage (★★★☆) is mouthfilling and peachy, with hints of spice and apricot, slight sweetness (8 grams/litre of residual sugar) balanced by fresh acidity, and very good flavour depth, but less compelling than the 2009.

Vintage	10	09	08	07	06
WR	7	6	7	7	6
Drink	11-15	11-13	11-12	P	P

MED/DRY $23 AV

Waipara Hills Equinox Waipara Pinot Gris   ★★★★

Estate-grown in the Glasnevin Vineyard, the 2010 vintage (★★★★) is a powerful, big-bodied wine (14.5 per cent alcohol), with fresh pear, lychee and apricot flavours, a minerally streak, and a dry, spicy finish. It's still very youthful; open mid-2012+.

DRY $30 –V

Waipara Springs Waipara Pinot Gris   (★★★☆)

The floral, medium-bodied 2010 vintage (★★★☆) was partly barrel-fermented. Vibrantly fruity and finely poised, it has very good depth of peach, pear and lychee flavours, a sliver of sweetness and a refreshingly crisp finish.

MED/DRY $19 V+

Wairau River Marlborough Pinot Gris   ★★★★

Maturing well, the 2010 vintage (★★★★) was mostly handled in tanks, but 15 per cent was French oak-aged. Ripely scented, it is weighty and fleshy, with ripe peach, lemon and spice flavours, showing excellent depth, gentle acidity and a softly textured, well-rounded finish. The 2011 (★★★★) is a dryish style (5 grams/litre of residual sugar), with mouthfilling body and strong stone-fruit and spice flavours, finely textured and lingering.

Vintage	11	10	09	08
WR	6	6	6	4
Drink	12-15	11-13	11-12	P

MED/DRY $25 AV

Weeping Sands Waiheke Island Pinot Gris   ★★★☆

The debut 2010 vintage (★★★☆) was hand-picked in the Edbrooke Vineyard and made in an off-dry (5 grams/litre of residual sugar) style. Floral, with pear and spice aromas, it is mouthfilling, with very good depth of vibrant, citrusy, slightly appley and spicy flavours. The 2011 (★★★☆) is mouthfilling and youthful, with fresh, pure peach, pear and spice flavours and a dryish finish. Open mid-2012+.

Vintage	11	10
WR	6	7
Drink	11-12	11-14

MED/DRY $26 –V

West Brook Waimauku Pinot Gris   ★★★☆

The 2010 vintage (★★★★) was estate-grown in West Auckland, hand-picked and fermented in tanks (78 per cent) and seasoned barrels (22 per cent). It's a stylish wine, attractively scented, full-bodied and finely textured, in a medium-dry style with rich stone-fruit flavours that linger well.

MED/DRY $26 –V

Whitecliff Pinot Gris   (★★)

A blend of Australian and New Zealand wines, the 2009 vintage (★★) is lightly scented, with moderate depth of pear, apple and spice flavours and a smooth finish. An easy-drinking quaffer.

MED/DRY $18 –V

White Gold Single Vineyard Marlborough Pinot Gris   (★★★)

From Gibson Bridge, the 2009 vintage (★★★), hand-picked at Renwick, is the result of 'fastidious viticulture and low groping'. Faintly pink, it is full-bodied and fleshy, with a touch of hardness amid its strong, ripe, peachy, spicy flavours.

MED/DRY $15 V+

Whitehaven Marlborough Pinot Gris   ★★★☆

Mouthfilling, with fresh pear, lychee and spice flavours, gentle sweetness (7 grams/litre of residual sugar) and a slightly oily texture, the 2009 vintage (★★★☆) is a very easy-drinking style with good depth.

Vintage	09	08	07	06
WR	7	6	6	7
Drink	11-13	P	P	P

MED/DRY $20 AV

White Knight Matakana Pinot Gris   (★★★)

From Michael Ramon, the 2010 vintage (★★★) is a single-vineyard, barrel-fermented wine. Fresh and lively, it has obvious cellaring potential, but in its youth the fruit characters are overshadowed by oak. Open mid-2012+.

DRY $25 –V

Whitestone Waipara Pinot Gris   ★★☆

The slightly creamy 2009 vintage (★★) lacks a bit of freshness and vibrancy.

MED/DRY $20 –V

Wild Rock Sur Lie Otago Pinot Gris   (★★★★)

From a Craggy Range subsidiary, the instantly attractive 2009 vintage (★★★★) was grown in the Waitaki Valley and Bendigo. Mostly handled in tanks, but 5 per cent French oak-matured, it is fleshy and creamy, deliciously scented and smooth, with slight sweetness (5.2 grams/litre of residual sugar) and ripe stone-fruit flavours, showing good richness and harmony.

Vintage	09	08
WR	7	6
Drink	11-13	P

MED/DRY $20 V+

Wild South Marlborough Pinot Gris   ★★★☆

From Sacred Hill and grown in the Waihopai Valley, the 2010 vintage (★★★★) is a dry style (4 grams/litre of residual sugar). Mouthfilling, sweet-fruited and very finely balanced, with ripe peach, pear and spice flavours, it has a slightly oily texture and considerable richness. The 2011 (★★★☆), also basically dry (4 grams/litre of residual sugar), is floral and vibrantly fruity, with peachy, citrusy, spicy flavours woven with fresh, appetising acidity. A good buy.

DRY $19 V+

Wither Hills Wairau Valley Marlborough Pinot Gris   ★★★☆

Scented and mouthfilling, the 2010 vintage (★★★★) is a very finely poised wine, full-bodied, with strong, ripe pear, spice and peach flavours, a sliver of sweetness, and excellent harmony and richness.

Vintage	10
WR	6
Drink	11-13

 MED/DRY $20 AV

Wooing Tree Central Otago Pinot Gris   ★★★☆

The 2010 vintage (★★★☆) was grown in the Cromwell Basin and barrel-fermented. Still pale and youthful, it has fresh peach, apricot and spice flavours, with subtle oak adding a touch of complexity, good depth and a well-rounded finish.

 DRY $28 –V

Woollaston Nelson Pinot Gris   ★★★☆

The 2010 vintage (★★★☆), hand-picked and handled entirely in tanks, is a fresh, crisp, full-bodied wine, slightly sweet (7 grams/litre of residual sugar), with citrus-fruit, peach and spice flavours showing good delicacy, harmony and depth.

Vintage	10
WR	6
Drink	11-15

 MED/DRY $20 AV

Yealands Estate Marlborough Pinot Gris   ★★★☆

Estate-grown in the Awatere Valley, the 2010 vintage (★★★★) is mouthfilling and vibrantly fruity, with rich, citrusy, peachy flavours, a slightly oily texture and a dryish, long finish.

MED/DRY $26 –V

Riesling

Riesling isn't yet one of New Zealand's great successes in overseas markets – the 118,000 cases shipped in the year to June 2011 accounted for just 0.7 per cent of our total wine exports.

Many New Zealand wine lovers also ignore Riesling. The favourite white-wine variety of many winemakers, Riesling barely registers on the wine sales charts in supermarkets, generating about 1 per cent of the dollar turnover. In the past year, the number of Riesling bottles we purchased slumped by 14 per cent.

Perhaps the country's Riesling producers are not trying hard enough. *Decanter*, in the UK, declared in July 2011, after tasting 134 wines from both countries, that Australian Riesling is 'head and shoulders above New Zealand'. The judges complained that New Zealand Rieslings were 'too inconsistent ... disjointed and often too sweet'.

On a happier note, Lawson's Dry Hills Marlborough Riesling 2008 won the trophies for Best Aromatic Wine of Competition and Best White Table Wine of Competition at the 2011 Sydney International Wine Competition.

Around the world, Riesling has traditionally been regarded as Chardonnay's great rival in the white-wine quality stakes, well ahead of Sauvignon Blanc. So why are wine lovers here slow to appreciate Riesling's stature?

Riesling is usually made in a slightly sweet style, to balance the grape's natural high acidity, but this obvious touch of sweetness runs counter to the fashion for dry wines. And fine Riesling demands time (at the very least, a couple of years) to unfold its full potential; drunk in its infancy, as it so often is, it lacks the toasty, minerally, honeyed richness that is the real glory of Riesling.

After recently being overhauled by Pinot Gris, Riesling ranks as New Zealand's fourth most extensively planted white-wine variety. Between 2007 and 2012, its total area of bearing vines is expanding slowly, from 868 to 1009 hectares.

The great grape of Germany, Riesling is a classic cool-climate variety, particularly well suited to the cooler growing temperatures and lower humidity of the South Island. Its stronghold is Marlborough, where 45 per cent of the vines are clustered, but the grape is also extensively planted in Nelson, Canterbury and Otago.

Riesling styles vary markedly around the world. Most Marlborough wines are medium to full-bodied (12 to 13.5 per cent alcohol), with just a touch of sweetness. However, a new breed of Riesling has emerged in the past five years – lighter (only 7.5 to 10 per cent alcohol) and markedly sweeter. These refreshingly light, sweet Rieslings offer a more vivid contrast in style to New Zealand's other major white wines, and are much closer in style to the classic German model.

Abbey Cellars Hawke's Bay Riesling ★★★☆

Estate-grown and hand-picked in The Triangle, the 2009 vintage (★★★☆) is floral and medium-bodied, with limey, slightly toasty flavours showing a touch of sweetness (10 grams/litre of residual sugar). Crisp and lively, it has very good balance and depth.

MED/DRY $18 V+

Akarua Central Otago Riesling (★★★★)

Estate-grown at Bannockburn, the 2010 vintage (★★★★) was picked from first-crop vines. Medium-bodied, with very fresh, harmonious, gently sweet flavours (12 grams/litre of residual sugar), it is citrusy, appley and slightly spicy, with excellent delicacy and depth.

MED/DRY $25 AV

Allan Scott Marlborough Riesling   ★★★☆

A typically attractive wine, grown in the heart of the Wairau Valley. The 2009 vintage (★★★☆) is mouthfilling, with very good depth of citrusy, grapefruit-like flavours and a minerally streak. Made in a medium-dry style (10 grams/litre of residual sugar), it's enjoyable young.

Vintage	09
WR	6
Drink	11-19

MED/DRY $18 V+

Allan Scott Moorlands Marlborough Riesling   ★★★★☆

A basically dry style (harbouring only 4 grams/litre of residual sugar), the 2009 vintage (★★★★☆) is from vines around 30 years old, adjacent to the winery. Tank-fermented and matured for six months in old oak barrels, it is rich and finely poised, with concentrated grapefruit, spice and slight honey flavours, a very subtle seasoning of oak and good acid spine. It's a distinctive, rewarding wine; drink now or cellar.

Vintage	09
WR	6
Drink	11-13

DRY $26 AV

Amisfield Dry Riesling   ★★★★

Estate-grown in the Cromwell Basin of Central Otago, the 2010 vintage (★★★★) was hand-picked and fermented to a medium-dry style (7 grams/litre of residual sugar). It shows good intensity, with fresh, lively, citrusy, limey flavours, a minerally streak and a lingering finish.

Vintage	10	09	08	07	06
WR	7	6	6	5	5
Drink	11-18	11-17	11-12	11-12	P

MED/DRY $30 –V

Amisfield Lowburn Terrace Riesling – see Sweet White Wines

Anchorage Classic Nelson Riesling   ★★★☆

Bargain-priced, the 2010 vintage (★★★) is a gently sweet style (22 grams/litre of residual sugar). Pale and crisp, it is light (10.5 per cent alcohol) and lively, with citrusy, slightly minerally flavours.

MED $14 V+

Ant Moore Nelson Riesling   ★★★☆

The 2010 vintage (★★★☆) is ripely scented, with fresh, finely focused citrus-fruit and spice flavours, slightly sweet and strong.

MED/DRY $23 –V

Archangel Central Otago Riesling   (★★★☆)

Estate-grown at Queensberry, south of Wanaka, the 2010 vintage (★★★☆) is a pale, tight wine, full-bodied, with very youthful lemon/lime flavours, crisp, pure and zingy. A dryish wine (5 grams/litre of residual sugar), it needs time; open 2013+.

MED/DRY $24 –V

Astrolabe Experience Marlborough Riesling   (★★★★)

Estate-grown at Astrolabe Farm, Grovetown, in the lower Wairau Valley, the 2009 vintage (★★★★) was stop-fermented with 9 per cent alcohol and abundant sweetness (50 grams/litre of residual sugar). Light and lively, it has fresh, intense, lemony, appley flavours, with a hint of sherbet, appetising acidity and instant appeal. Drink now or cellar.

Vintage	09
WR	6
Drink	11-14

MED $25 AV

Astrolabe Voyage Marlborough Dry Riesling   ★★★★

The 2009 vintage (★★★★) is a single-vineyard, Waihopai Valley wine. It's a racy, medium-bodied wine, dryish (7.5 grams/litre of residual sugar), with citrusy, appley, limey flavours showing good freshness, purity and intensity.

Vintage	09	08
WR	6	6
Drink	12-13	11-13

MED/DRY $22 V+

Ataahua Waipara Riesling   (★★★★)

The scented, finely poised 2010 vintage (★★★★) is medium-bodied (12.5 per cent alcohol), with gentle sweetness (13 grams/litre of residual sugar). It has strong, vibrant, citrusy, peachy, slightly spicy flavours, showing excellent delicacy and depth.

MED/DRY $22 V+

Auburn Alexandra Riesling   (★★★★)

The 2010 vintage (★★★★) is rare – only 740 bottles were produced. A medium-sweet style (45 grams/litre of residual sugar) from Central Otago with lemon, lime and passionfruit flavours, fresh and penetrating, it has fairly low alcohol (10.5 per cent), with sweetness giving early appeal and a long, crisp finish. Best drinking 2012+.

MED $30 –V

Auburn Lowburn Riesling – see Sweet White Wines

Auburn Twilight Riesling   (★★★★☆)

From mature vines at Lowburn, in Central Otago, the 2009 vintage (★★★★☆) has a slightly honeyed bouquet and flavours. Rare – only 242 bottles were made – it is peachy and rounded, in a low-alcohol (10 per cent) style, enriched but not dominated by botrytis. Showing impressive delicacy and depth, it's already delicious.

Vintage	09
WR	6
Drink	11-14

MED $30 –V

Aurum Central Otago Riesling ★★★★

Still on sale, the 2008 vintage (★★★★ was estate-grown at Lowburn, in the Cromwell Basin. It's a mouth-wateringly crisp, cool-climate style with a lemony, slightly toasty bouquet. Lively with a distinctly minerally streak, it has good intensity of vibrant, slightly sweet (7.9 grams/litre of residual sugar) lemon/lime flavours and a tangy, lingering finish.

Vintage	08	07
WR	6	6
Drink	11-18	11-15

MED/DRY $20 V+

Babich Family Estates Cowslip Valley Marlborough Riesling (★★★★)

The debut 2011 vintage (★★★★) was estate-grown in the Waihopai Valley. Mouthfilling, it is ripe and rounded, with generous, citrusy, limey and spicy flavours, in a medium-dry style, with excellent balance and depth. It's quite forward in its appeal; drink now or cellar.

Vintage	11
WR	6
Drink	11-16

MED/DRY $25 AV

Babich Marlborough Riesling ★★★☆

Typically a well-crafted wine with good drinkability. The 2010 vintage (★★★☆) is fresh, crisp and lemony, with a basically dry feel (5.3 grams/litre of residual sugar). Still very youthful, it shows good delicacy, vigour and harmony; open 2013+.

MED/DRY $20 AV

Bald Hills Last Light Central Otago Riesling ★★★☆

Estate-grown at Bannockburn, the 2010 vintage (★★★☆) is full-bodied, with strong, ripe, citrusy, limey flavours, slightly sweet (10 grams/litre of residual sugar), fresh and crisp. Worth cellaring.

MED/DRY $25 –V

Bannock Brae Goldfields Dry Riesling ★★★

This Central Otago wine is designed to 'exhibit the characteristics of a bygone age'. The 2009 vintage (★★★★), fermented and matured in old oak barriques, is the finest yet – fresh and vibrant, with substantial body, strong lemon, lime and spice flavours, firm acid spine and a long, dryish (8 grams/litre of residual sugar) but not austere finish.

MED/DRY $24 –V

Bascand Waipara Riesling ★★☆

The easy-drinking 2009 vintage (★★☆) is light-bodied, with decent depth of lemony, appley flavours, a splash of sweetness (18 grams/litre of residual sugar) and a fresh, smooth finish.

MED $17 –V

Bird Old Schoolhouse Vineyard Marlborough Riesling   ★★★★

Estate-grown in the Omaka Valley, the 2010 vintage (★★★★) has strong, fresh, ripe lemon and slight passionfruit flavours in a juicy, medium-dry (6 grams/litre of residual sugar) style, showing excellent depth and harmony.

MED/DRY $25 AV

Black Estate Omihi Waipara Riesling   ★★★★

Hand-harvested at Waipara at 23.5 brix, but not estate-grown, the 2010 vintage (★★★★☆) is full-bodied (13.5 per cent alcohol) and impressively rich, with peachy, spicy, slightly honeyed flavours. A youthful, concentrated wine with a powerful presence, it has good acid spine and a fresh, tight, off-dry (9 grams/litre of residual sugar) finish. Best drinking 2013+.

MED/DRY $23 AV

Blackenbrook Vineyard Nelson Riesling   ★★★★☆

The youthful, tight, racy 2009 vintage (★★★★☆) was estate-grown and hand-picked. A medium style (15 grams/litre of residual sugar), it has strong peach, lemon and lime flavours, threaded with lively acidity. Vibrantly fruity, with a minerally streak, it shows excellent intensity and obvious cellaring potential.

Vintage	09	08	07
WR	7	7	7
Drink	11-13	P	P

MED $23 V+

Bladen Marlborough Riesling   ★★★☆

The 2010 vintage (★★★★) is a single-vineyard wine, made in a dryish style (7 grams/litre of residual sugar). Medium-bodied (12.5 per cent alcohol), it is fresh, lemony, slightly gingery and spicy, with a minerally streak and good intensity and harmony.

MED/DRY $21 AV

Borthwick Vineyard Paddy Borthwick Wairarapa Riesling   ★★★☆

Estate-grown at Gladstone, the 2010 vintage (★★★☆) is very youthful. Medium-bodied, it has fresh, ripe, lemony flavours, a distinct hint of passionfruit, slight sweetness (7 grams/litre of residual sugar), and very good balance and depth.

MED/DRY $22 AV

Boulders Martinborough Prosecco Style Riesling   (★★★☆)

Made by Allan Johnson, the 2009 vintage (★★★☆) has 'subtle effervescence'. Light and crisp, with low alcohol (9 per cent) and slightly sweet, green-apple and lime flavours, it's a fresh and lively, slightly *spritzig* wine, that makes a very stimulating thirst quencher.

MED/DRY $20 AV

Boulders Martinborough Riesling   (★★★)

Grown on the Martinborough Terraces, the 2009 vintage (★★★) is a medium-bodied wine with lemony, appley flavours, lively acidity and an off-dry finish, finely balanced for easy drinking.

MED/DRY $20 –V

Bouldevines Marlborough Riesling   ★★★☆

From the south side of the Wairau Valley, the 2010 vintage (★★★★) is a single-vineyard wine, fleshy and fully dry (2.5 grams/litre of residual sugar), but not at all austere. Mouthfilling, it shows good intensity of peachy, slightly citrusy flavours in a 'serious' style with excellent delicacy, ripeness and richness.

Vintage	10
WR	7
Drink	11-15

 DRY $20 AV

Brancott Estate Reserve Waipara Riesling   (★★★)

The 2010 vintage (★★★) from Pernod Ricard NZ, previously branded Montana Reserve, is a medium-dry style with lemon, apple and slight passionfruit flavours, balanced for easy drinking. It's still unfolding.

 MED $24 –V

Brightside Brightwater Riesling   ★★★

From Kaimira Estate, the 2009 vintage (★★★) is a medium style (15 grams/litre of residual sugar) with strong, citrusy flavours, balanced for easy drinking. Crisp, with a vague hint of honey, it's priced sharply.

Vintage	09	08
WR	6	5
Drink	11-14	11-12

 MED $16 V+

Brightwater Vineyards Nelson Riesling   ★★★☆

Estate-grown on the Waimea Plains, the 2011 vintage (★★★☆) is still very youthful, with fresh lemon, apple and lime flavours, slightly sweet (13 grams/litre of residual sugar) and crisp. Showing very good depth, it should blossom with cellaring.

Vintage	10	09	08	07	06
WR	5	5	5	6	6
Drink	11-15	11-12	P	P	P

 MED/DRY $20 AV

Camshorn Classic Waipara Riesling   ★★★★

The 2010 vintage (★★★★) from Pernod Ricard NZ is light-bodied (9.5 per cent alcohol) and lively, with concentrated, crisp, citrusy, limey flavours, a hint of sherbet and a gently sweet, racy, long finish.

MED $26 –V

Camshorn Waipara Dry Riesling ★★★★

Still on sale, the 2007 vintage (★★★★) from Pernod Ricard NZ is a classic dry style (4.5 grams/ litre of residual sugar), with rich, ripe grapefruit and peach flavours and a rounded finish. It's maturing very gracefully, with toasty, bottle-aged notes adding complexity.

Vintage	07	06
WR	6	6
Drink	11-12	P

 DRY $27 –V

Carrick Central Otago Dry Riesling ★★★★

Grown at Bannockburn and fermented with indigenous yeasts, the 2010 vintage (★★★★) is a scented, youthful wine, showing excellent richness, delicacy and potential. It has strong, vibrant lemon/lime flavours, a minerally streak and a finely poised, dryish (5 grams/litre of residual sugar) but not austere finish.

 MED/DRY $22 V+

Carrick Central Otago Riesling ★★★★

Consistently good value. A single-vineyard Bannockburn wine, the 2010 vintage (★★★★) is an instantly appealing, medium style (18 grams/litre of residual sugar), with strong grapefruit, peach and lime flavours, fresh and harmonious. Vivacious, it has good acid spine and excellent intensity.

Vintage	09	08	07	06
WR	6	6	6	6
Drink	11-15	11-14	11-14	11-12

 MED $22 V+

Carrick Josephine Central Otago Riesling ★★★★★

The 2010 vintage (★★★★) was grown in the Lot 8 Vineyard, on the Cairnmuir Terraces at Bannockburn, hand-picked and stop-fermented in a low-alcohol (8 per cent), sweet style (60 grams/litre of residual sugar). Showing a Mosel-like lightness and vivacity, it has crisp, strong lemon/lime flavours, with hints of spice and sherbet and racy acidity. Certified organic, the 2011 (★★★★★) is light and lovely, with intense, citrusy, sweetish flavours, a hint of sherbet, and racy acidity. It's a rich wine, with beautiful length.

 MED $26 V+

Chard Farm Central Otago Riesling ★★★★

The 2009 vintage (★★★★★) is outstanding. Hand-picked (mostly in the Viper Vineyard) at Parkburn, in the Cromwell Basin, and given extended lees contact, it is weighty and concentrated, with fresh, vibrant grapefruit/lime flavours, showing lovely richness and harmony. Already delicious, it's a medium style (16 grams/litre of residual sugar) with real presence.

Vintage	09
WR	7
Drink	11-16

MED $24 AV

Charles Wiffen Marlborough Riesling ★★★☆

The 2009 vintage (★★★☆) is slightly sweet and crisp, with apple and slight passionfruit flavours, showing good depth.

MED/DRY $19 V+

Clark Estate Single Vineyard Awatere Valley Riesling ★★★★☆

The 2010 vintage (★★★★) is a youthful, tightly structured, medium-bodied wine with a minerally streak. It has fresh lemon and apple flavours, showing good intensity, a splash of sweetness and firm acid spine.

MED $26 AV

Clayridge Wild Riesling ★★★☆

The 2009 vintage (★★★☆), a medium style (18 grams/litre of residual sugar), will be a walk on the 'wild' side for many wine lovers, but the 'wild' is simply a reference to the use of indigenous rather than cultured yeasts. Pale yellow, it's a fleshy Marlborough wine with generous, peachy, citrusy flavours, showing some toasty, bottle-aged complexity.

MED $24 –V

Clos St William Waipara Riesling (★★★☆)

The 2009 vintage (★★★☆) was estate-grown and harvested from first-crop vines. Tank-fermented, it is crisp and lively, in a medium style (15 grams/litre of residual sugar) with citrusy, appley flavours showing very good depth.

MED $20 AV

Cloudy Bay Riesling ★★★★☆

Released at over four years old, the 2006 vintage (★★★★☆) was grown in the Wairau Valley of Marlborough, fermented with indigenous yeasts and matured for six months in old French oak barrels. Still youthful in colour, it is medium to full-bodied, with penetrating grapefruit and spice flavours, minerally and toasty, a sliver of sweetness (8 grams/litre of residual sugar) and good acid spine. Showing good, bottle-aged complexity, it is likely to be long-lived.

MED/DRY $30 –V

Coney Ragtime Riesling ★★★☆

This characterful Martinborough wine is made in a medium-dry style. The 2010 vintage (★★★☆) is fleshy, with very good depth of ripe, citrusy, slightly spicy flavours, hints of honey and passionfruit, and a gently sweet (12 grams/litre of residual sugar) finish.

Vintage	10
WR	5
Drink	11-14

MED/DRY $20 AV

Coney Rallentando Riesling   ★★★☆

This Martinborough wine is a drier style than its stablemate (above). The 2009 vintage
(★★★☆) is medium-bodied, with strong, ripe lemon/lime flavours, fresh, crisp and fully dry.
Drink now or cellar.

Vintage	09
WR	5
Drink	11-16

DRY $20 AV

Coney The Ritz Martinborough Riesling   (★★★★)

Lemon-scented and racy, the 2010 vintage (★★★★) is a light-bodied (10 per cent alcohol),
distinctly medium style (34 grams/litre of residual sugar). Showing good intensity, it is citrusy
and appley, with a hint of sherbet, appetising acidity and a poised, slightly minerally finish.
Best drinking 2013+.

Vintage	10
WR	5
Drink	11-13

MED $20 V+

Coopers Creek Marlborough Riesling   ★★★

The 2009 vintage (★★★), a medium-dry style, is fresh, vibrant and youthful, with lemony,
appley flavours, showing good depth. The 2010 (★★★) is full-bodied and slightly sweet (7
grams/litre of residual sugar), with fresh, citrusy, crisp flavours, balanced for easy drinking.

Vintage	10	09	08
WR	6	6	5
Drink	12-16	11-14	11-13

MED/DRY $17 AV

Coopers Creek SV Mister Phebus Marlborough Riesling   (★★★★)

The 2009 vintage (★★★★) has a floral, slightly musky bouquet, leading into a peachy, limey
wine, full-flavoured, gently sweet (12 grams/litre of residual sugar) and spicy, with excellent
delicacy, harmony and intensity.

Vintage	09
WR	7
Drink	12-16

MED/DRY $20 V+

Corbans Homestead Waipara Riesling   (★★★)

The 2009 vintage (★★★) flowed from Pernod Ricard NZ's vineyards in North Canterbury.
Balanced for easy drinking, it has passionfruit and citrus-fruit flavours, showing good depth,
and a slightly sweet, crisp finish.

MED/DRY $17 AV

Craggy Range Fletcher Family Vineyard Riesling   ★★★☆

Past vintages have matured well. The 2010 (★★★☆), grown in Marlborough's Wairau Valley, is light and lively, with fresh, youthful lemon, apple and spice flavours, gentle sweetness (10 grams/litre of residual sugar), a minerally thread, and good depth and harmony.

Vintage	10	09	08	07	06
WR	7	7	6	6	7
Drink	11-21	11-16	11-15	11-12	11-14

 MED/DRY $23 –V

Craggy Range Te Muna Road Vineyard Riesling   ★★★☆

Hand-harvested in Martinborough, the 2009 vintage (★★☆) was fermented with indigenous yeasts and matured for four months in seasoned oak puncheons. A light, slightly spicy wine, it did not shine in my blind tasting – with Riesling, oak influence often throws the cat among the pigeons.

 MED/DRY $26 –V

Crater Rim, The, Canterbury Riesling   ★★★

The 2010 vintage (★★★) is a gently sweet (22 grams/litre of residual sugar), single-vineyard wine, grown at Waipara. Light-bodied (8.5 per cent), it is lemony and appley, with good delicacy and decent depth. It's enjoyable now.

MED $18 AV

Crater Rim, The, Dr Kohl's Waipara Riesling – see Sweet White Wines

Crater Rim, The, From The Ashes Waipara Riesling   (★★★☆)

The 2010 vintage (★★★☆) is a good buy. All lightness, delicacy and fragility, it's a low-alcohol style (8.5 per cent) with citrusy, appley flavours and plentiful sweetness (40 grams/litre of residual sugar), balanced by crisp acidity. Drink now or cellar.

 MED $18 V+

Crater Rim, The, Waipara Riesling   ★★★

The 2009 vintage (★★★★) is a medium-sweet style (45 grams/litre of residual sugar), grown on the valley floor and tank-fermented. Light (only 9.5 per cent alcohol) and vivacious, it has good intensity of lemon and apple flavours, crisp and slightly minerally, with excellent depth and harmony. The 2010 (★★☆) is light-bodied (10 per cent alcohol), with abundant sweetness (52 grams/litre of residual sugar) amid its lemony, appley flavours, but less scented and concentrated than the 2009.

Vintage	10	09	08	07
WR	6	7	6	5
Drink	11-16	11-18	11-16	11-14

 MED $21 –V

Crossroads Marlborough Medway Vineyard Riesling   ★★★☆

Offering good value, the 2009 vintage (★★★★) is a medium style (25 grams/litre of residual sugar), with rich, citrusy, spicy, limey flavours, a hint of passionfruit, and excellent freshness and depth.

Vintage	09
WR	6
Drink	11-15

MED $19 V+

Darjon North Canterbury Riesling   (★★★☆)

The 2009 (★★★☆) is Darjon's first Riesling in a medium style – past vintages were drier. Harvested at Swannanoa at 18 to 22 brix, it is fresh, floral and light in body (11 per cent alcohol), with gentle sweetness (20 grams/litre of residual sugar) and crisp, lively, lemony flavours. Well worth cellaring.

MED $20 AV

Desert Heart Central Otago Riesling   ★★★☆

The 2009 vintage (★★★☆) was hand-harvested at Bannockburn. An off-dry, minerally style, it has strong, fresh lemon, apple and lime flavours and firm acidity. It's a slightly austere wine, but shows good delicacy and length.

Vintage	09	08	07	06
WR	6	6	5	4
Drink	11-16	11-15	11-16	P

MED/DRY $24 –V

Distant Land Marlborough Riesling   ★★★★

Highly expressive in its youth, the 2010 vintage (★★★★) is a single-vineyard, Omaka Valley wine with strong lemon/lime flavours, a hint of passionfruit, and gentle sweetness (12 grams/litre of residual sugar) balanced by lively acidity. It shows excellent freshness, poise and vivacity. The 2011 (★★★★) is similar – very fresh and immaculate, with slightly sweet, lemony, appley flavours, tightly structured, delicate and lingering. It should unfold well.

MED/DRY $20 V+

Doctors', The, Marlborough Riesling   ★★★★☆

From Forrest Estate, this deliberately low-alcohol style is like biting into a fresh, crunchy Granny Smith apple. The 2010 vintage (★★★★☆) is deliciously light (8.5 per cent alcohol) and lively, with plentiful sweetness (42 grams/litre of residual sugar) and fresh, strong lemon and lime flavours, showing lovely delicacy and poise. (Most vintages break into full stride at about two years old.)

Vintage	10
WR	6
Drink	11-20

MED $22 V+

Domain Road Vineyard Central Otago Riesling   ★★★★

Grown at Bannockburn, the 2009 vintage (★★★★) is a full-bodied style with concentrated lemon/lime flavours, a gentle splash of sweetness (13.5 grams/litre of residual sugar) and racy acidity. It has citrus-fruit and slight passionfruit flavours, showing excellent intensity and vibrancy.

Vintage	09	08
WR	6	6
Drink	11-15	11-14

MED/DRY $22 V+

Domain Road Vineyard Duffer's Creek Riesling   (★★★★☆)

Grown at Bannockburn, in Central Otago, the debut 2010 vintage (★★★★☆) is full of potential. A classy wine, it is medium-bodied, with pure, delicate lemon, lime and spice flavours, slightly sweet (12.5 grams/litre of residual sugar) and minerally, and a poised, lingering finish.

Vintage	10
WR	6
Drink	11-16

MED/DRY $24 V+

Domain Road Vineyard The Water Race Dry Riesling   (★★★★)

The 2010 vintage (★★★★) was grown at Bannockburn, in Central Otago. Tightly structured, it is dryish (7 grams/litre of residual sugar), with good weight and depth of grapefruit, spice and apple flavours, balanced acidity and obvious potential.

Vintage	10
WR	6
Drink	11-16

MED/DRY $24 AV

Dry River Craighall Vineyard Riesling   ★★★★★

Founder Neil McCallum – who retired in 2011 – believes that, in quality terms, Riesling is at least the equal of Pinot Noir in Martinborough. His Craighall Riesling, one of the finest in the country, is a wine of exceptional purity, delicacy and depth, with a proven ability to flourish in the cellar for many years: 'It's not smart to drink them at less than five years old,' says McCallum. The grapes are sourced from a small block (0.8 hectare) of vines, mostly 20 to 25 years old, in the Craighall Vineyard, with yields limited to an average of 6 tonnes per hectare, and the wine is stop-fermented just short of dryness. The 2011 vintage (★★★★★) is quite approachable in its infancy. Weighty, it is highly concentrated, with fresh, pure, well-ripened grapefruit and spice flavours, showing lovely delicacy and depth, in a basically dry (5 grams/litre of residual sugar), but still very harmonious, style.

Vintage	11	10	09	08	07	06
WR	7	7	6	7	7	7
Drink	13-18	12-18	11-16	11-15	11-14	11-12

MED/DRY $45 AV

Esk Valley Marlborough Riesling ★★★★

The 2009 (★★★★) was the winery's first Marlborough Riesling – earlier vintages were grown in Hawke's Bay. The 2010 (★★★★) is a medium-dry style (7 grams/litre of residual sugar), hand-picked at two sites in the Wairau and Awatere valleys. It's a highly scented wine, tightly structured, with strong, citrusy flavours, showing excellent purity and length.

Vintage	10	MED/DRY $24 AV
WR	7	
Drink	12-18	

Fallen Angel Marlborough Riesling ★★★☆

From Stonyridge Vineyard, the 2010 (★★★☆) is a steely, tightly structured wine with a distinct splash of sweetness (18 grams/litre of residual sugar) and strong lemon/apple flavours, showing very good freshness, delicacy and depth. The 2011 vintage (★★★☆) is still a baby. Pale, with strong, citrusy, limey flavours, threaded with flinty acidity, it is a dryish style, likely to be at its best 2013+.

Vintage	10	MED $25 –V
WR	7	
Drink	11-18	

Felton Road Bannockburn Central Otago Riesling ★★★★★

Estate-grown on mature vines, this is a gently sweet wine with deep flavours cut with fresh acidity. It offers more drink-young appeal than its Dry Riesling stablemate, but invites long-term cellaring. Tank-fermented mostly with indigenous yeasts, it is bottled with 20 to 50 grams per litre of residual sugar. The 2010 vintage (★★★★★), grown in The Elms and Calvert vineyards, is scented and light (9 per cent alcohol), with lemon, lime, apple and spice flavours, a hint of sherbet, and lovely poise, intensity and immediacy.

Vintage	10	09	08	07	06	MED $26 V+
WR	7	6	6	7	6	
Drink	11-30	11-29	11-23	11-22	11-16	

Felton Road Block 1 Riesling – see Sweet White Wines

Felton Road Dry Riesling ★★★★☆

Based on low-yielding vines in schisty soils at Bannockburn, in Central Otago, this wine is hand-picked and fermented with indigenous yeasts. The 2010 vintage (★★★★), grown in The Elms and Calvert vineyards, is full-bodied (12.5 per cent alcohol) and dry, with good weight and crisp, citrusy, appley, spicy flavours, poised and minerally. It needs time to unfold; open mid-2012+.

Vintage	10	09	08	07	06	DRY $26 AV
WR	7	6	6	7	6	
Drink	12-22	11-19	11-18	11-17	11-16	

Fiddler's Green Waipara Classic Riesling ★★★★

Still on sale, the 2008 vintage (★★★★) is light-bodied and vibrantly fruity, in a distinctly medium style with lemony, appley flavours showing good intensity. The 2009 (★★★☆) is vibrant and smooth, with light body (10.5 per cent alcohol), a splash of sweetness (20 grams/litre of residual sugar), and lemony, appley flavours that linger well.

Vintage	09	08
WR	6	6
Drink	11-16	11-13

 MED $22 V+

Fiddler's Green Waipara Dry Riesling (★★★★)

Still on sale, the 2008 vintage (★★★★) has good intensity of lemon, lime and passionfruit flavours and a hint of honey. It's a basically dry style (5 grams/litre of residual sugar), finely balanced and maturing well.

Vintage	08
WR	6
Drink	11-15

 MED/DRY $25 AV

Five Flax Waipara Riesling (★★★)

The 2010 vintage (★★★) from Pernod Ricard NZ offers good value, with citrusy aromas and flavours in a medium-bodied, lively, medium-dry style.

MED/DRY $15 V+

Forrest Collection Riesling – see John Forrest Collection Riesling

Forrest Marlborough Riesling ★★★☆

John Forrest believes Riesling will one day be Marlborough's greatest wine. The 2009 vintage (★★★☆) is attractively scented, in a vibrant, gently sweet style (14 grams/litre of residual sugar) with very good depth of crisp, lemony, appley flavours, balanced for easy drinking.

Vintage	09	08	07
WR	7	6	7
Drink	11-20	11-12	11-15

 MED/DRY $20 AV

Forrest The Doctors' Riesling – see Doctors', The, Riesling

Forrest The Valleys Brancott Riesling ★★★★☆

Described by John Forrest as 'an Alsace style', the 2008 vintage (★★★★☆) is rich, with gently sweet (12 grams/litre of residual sugar), ripe citrus and peach flavours, showing impressive concentration and harmony.

Vintage	08	07
WR	7	7
Drink	11-20	11-20

MED/DRY $25 V+

Forrest The Valleys Wairau Dry Riesling ★★★★

The 2009 vintage (★★★★☆) is full-bodied (13 per cent alcohol) and minerally, with a sliver of sweetness (5 grams/litre of residual sugar) and strong, delicate lemon, apple and lime flavours, slightly spicy, tight, minerally and long. It should cellar well, but is already highly expressive.

Vintage	09	08	07
WR	6	5	6
Drink	11-20	11-20	11-20

 MED/DRY $30 –V

Framingham Classic Riesling ★★★★★

Top vintages of this Marlborough wine are strikingly aromatic, richly flavoured and zesty. The 2010 (★★★★★) has an invitingly scented bouquet leading into a gently sweet wine (18 grams/litre of residual sugar), showing lovely depth of vibrant, citrusy, peachy flavours, with hints of apricots and spices, firm acid spine, and a long, minerally finish. It's all there for cellaring, but highly approachable already.

Vintage	10	09	08	07	06
WR	6	7	6	7	7
Drink	11-17	11-16	11-15	11-13	P

 MED $25 V+

Framingham Dry Riesling ★★★★★

Still on sale, the 2005 vintage (★★★★★) has flourished with cellaring. A classic, slow-maturing dry style (5 grams/litre of residual sugar) from Marlborough, it is bright, light lemon/green, with a rich, toasty, complex bouquet. On the palate, it is citrusy and concentrated, slightly minerally and long. A very harmonious wine, starting to round out, it offers lovely drinking from now onwards.

 MED/DRY $40 AV

Framingham F Series Old Vine Riesling ★★★★☆

From estate vines planted at Renwick, in Marlborough, 30 years ago, the 2009 (★★★★☆) was hand-picked and fermented with indigenous yeasts, mostly in tanks; 20 per cent was barrel-fermented. Medium-bodied, it has concentrated grapefruit and lemon flavours, in a dryish style with excellent depth and harmony. The 2010 vintage (★★★★☆) is unusually complex. Light lemon/green, it is mouthfilling (12.5 per cent alcohol) and slightly sweet (9 grams/litre of residual sugar), with deep citrus-fruit, spice and lime flavours, finely textured and long. Open 2013+.

Vintage	10	09
WR	7	6
Drink	11-16	11-15

MED/DRY $40 –V

Fromm Riesling Dry ★★★★☆

Typically a beautifully poised Marlborough wine, citrusy and minerally. The 2009 vintage (★★★★☆) is a fully dry style (2 grams/litre of residual sugar), but finely balanced, with mouthfilling body and strong, grapefruit-like flavours, slightly spicy and minerally. Tight but not austere, it's a generous wine, with a touch of toastiness and a long finish.

Vintage	11	10	09	08	07	06	05	04
WR	6	NM	7	6	6	7	6	7
Drink	11-15	NM	11-15	11-14	11-13	11-14	P	11-12

DRY $24 V+

Gibbston Valley Central Otago Riesling ★★★★

The 2010 vintage (★★★★), estate-grown and hand-harvested at Bendigo, is lemon-scented, with lemon, lime and passionfruit flavours, fractionally sweet (8 grams/litre of residual sugar), strong and tangy.

Vintage	10
WR	7
Drink	11-20

MED/DRY $25 AV

Gibbston Valley Le Fou The Expressionist Series Riesling ★★★★☆

Estate-grown at Bendigo, in Central Otago, the 2009 vintage (★★★★) has abundant sweetness and mouth-watering acidity. Light-bodied and racy, it is finely poised, with lemony, appley flavours, showing some complexity, and is likely to be long-lived. The 2010 (★★★★) is also a medium style (25 grams/litre of residual sugar), scented and light (10 per cent alcohol), with richness through the palate and a long, lemony finish. Best 2013+.

Vintage	10	09	08	07
WR	7	6	7	7
Drink	13-23	11-20	11-20	11-18

MED $35 –V

Giesen Marlborough Riesling (★★★★)

The 2010 vintage (★★★★) is a top buy. Skilfully crafted, with some use of hand-picking and indigenous yeasts, it is medium-bodied, with impressive intensity of fresh, citrusy, appley flavours, a hint of passionfruit, and lovely balance of sweetness (32 grams/litre of residual sugar) and mouth-watering acidity. Delicious now onwards. The vivacious 2009 (★★★★) is also fine value, with slightly toasty, minerally notes now adding complexity.

MED $19 V+

Gladstone Vineyard Riesling ★★★☆

The 2010 vintage (★★★☆) is fully dry (2 grams/litre of residual sugar) – but carries the dry style well. From 24-year-old vines in the Winery Block, in the Wairarapa, it is full-bodied, with strong lemon, lime and spice flavours and firm acid spine. Fresh, tightly structured and minerally, it needs time; open mid-2012+.

DRY $24 –V

Glasnevin Classic Riesling   (★★★★☆)

From Fiddler's Green, the 2008 vintage (★★★★☆) was fermented with indigenous yeasts and lees-aged in tanks. It's a medium-sweet style (43 grams/litre of residual sugar), light (9.5 per cent alcohol) and lively, with good intensity of lemony, appley flavours, showing excellent delicacy and poise. Maturing gracefully, it's delicious now.

Vintage	08
WR	6
Drink	11-14

MED $25 V+

Goldridge Estate Marlborough Riesling   ★★☆

The 2009 vintage (★★★) is a single-vineyard wine, fresh and lively, with lemon/lime flavours woven with appetising acidity, a sliver of sweetness and good depth.

MED/DRY $16 AV

Greenhough Apple Valley Nelson Riesling   ★★★★☆

Grown in a coastal vineyard at Mapua, the 2010 vintage (★★★★☆) is light (10 per cent alcohol) and sweetish. Very fresh and lively, with strong lime and green-apple flavours, it is vivacious and racy. A lovely summer sipper, it also has obvious cellaring potential. The 2011 (★★★★) is very light (8.5 per cent alcohol), with abundant sweetness (41 grams/litre of residual sugar). Fresh, crisp and tangy, it has good intensity, in a vibrantly fruity, poised, very youthful style, best cellared to 2013+.

Vintage	11	10	09	08	07
WR	7	6	6	6	6
Drink	11-17	11-16	11-15	11-14	11-13

MED $22 V+

Greenhough Hope Vineyard Riesling   ★★★★☆

This Nelson wine is hand-picked from vines planted in 1979. The 2009 vintage (★★★★★) is very intense and racy, in a medium-dry style (14 grams/litre of residual sugar). Beautifully poised, with concentrated, citrusy, limey, slightly spicy flavours, a minerally streak and loads of personality, it should be long-lived. BioGro-certified, the 2011 vintage (★★★★☆) is a baby. Made in an off-dry style (11 grams/litre of residual sugar), it is weighty and highly concentrated, with fresh, intense, limey, spicy flavours, a minerally streak and excellent structure and length. Full of potential, it's one for the cellar.

Vintage	11	10	09	08	07	06
WR	7	7	7	7	7	6
Drink	11-17	11-16	11-15	11-13	11-14	11-13

MED/DRY $22 V+

Greystone Feather Star Waipara Valley Riesling   ★★★★

Picked early to produce a light style, the 2010 vintage (★★★★) has strong, lemony, appley, slightly spicy flavours. Low in alcohol, with abundant sweetness, it has good acid spine and excellent poise and intensity. The 2011 (★★★★☆) is light (8.5 per cent alcohol) and vivacious, with strong lemon, peach and spice, woven with fresh acidity, plentiful sweetness and instant appeal. It should mature well.

MED $27 –V

Greystone Sea Star Waipara Valley Riesling (★★★★☆)

Mouthfilling, dry (4 grams/litre of residual sugar), but not austere, the 2010 vintage (★★★★☆) is already drinking well. A full-bodied wine (13.5 per cent alcohol), it is ripely scented, with strong, citrusy, peachy flavours, very fresh and vibrant, spicy, minerally notes adding complexity, and excellent depth and harmony.

Vintage	10
WR	7
Drink	11-14

 DRY $27 AV

Greystone Waipara Dry Riesling ★★★☆

The 2009 vintage (★★★★) is an off-dry style (6 grams/litre of residual sugar), invitingly scented, with good weight and intensity of ripe peach, passionfruit and spice flavours, fresh and already drinking well.

Vintage	09
WR	6
Drink	11-16

 MED/DRY $26 –V

Greystone Waipara Riesling ★★★★☆

Greystone sees this wine as 'the truest expression of the variety for us'. Estate-grown and hand-harvested, the 2010 vintage (★★★★) is a medium style (30 grams/litre of residual sugar), tank-fermented and briefly lees-aged. Showing lovely freshness and immediacy, it is medium-bodied, with gentle sweetness and deliciously rich, pure, citrusy, limey flavours, crisp and long.

Vintage	10	09	08	07
WR	7	6	6	5
Drink	11-20	11-16	11-12	P

 MED $27 AV

Greywacke Marlborough Riesling ★★★★☆

The 2010 vintage (★★★★☆) is a single-vineyard wine, hand-picked at Fairhall. Half of the juice was fermented in barrels, the rest in tanks; then the wine was all matured for four months in old French oak barriques. A medium style (20 grams/litre of residual sugar), it is mouthfilling, very vibrant and youthful, with concentrated, ripe, peachy, slightly limey and spicy flavours, showing considerable complexity, a fine thread of acidity and excellent depth. It should be long-lived.

Vintage	10	09
WR	5	6
Drink	11-17	11-17

 MED $30 –V

Grove Mill Grand Reserve Seventeen Valley Vineyard Marlborough Riesling (★★★★★)

The debut 2009 vintage (★★★★★) is beautifully scented, with intense grapefruit and lime flavours, enlivened with fresh acidity, a slightly honeyed richness, and a long, harmonious finish. Delicious from the start.

MED/DRY $26 V+

Hans Herzog Marlborough Riesling   (★★★★)

The 2009 vintage (★★★★) was partly handled in tanks, but 50 per cent was matured for nine months in seasoned French oak puncheons. It's a mouthfilling (13.5 per cent alcohol), fleshy wine with very ripe, citrusy flavours, in a dryish style (less than 6 grams/litre of residual sugar), showing excellent harmony and richness.

Vintage	09
WR	7
Drink	11-15

 MED/DRY $44 –V

Hawkshead Central Otago Riesling   ★★★★

Grown at Bendigo, hand-picked and tank-fermented, the 2010 vintage (★★★★☆) is a medium-dry style (9 grams/litre of residual sugar). Tight and youthful, it has a scented, citrusy bouquet. Full-bodied, it shows good intensity of lemony, slightly peachy and spicy flavours, a minerally thread, and excellent vigour and length. Best 2013+.

 MED/DRY $22 V+

Hell or Highwater Central Otago Riesling   (★★★☆)

From the Highwater Vineyard, on the Tarras-Cromwell Road, the 2009 vintage (★★★☆) is crisp and vibrant, with lemony, appley, gently sweet flavours, showing good balance, depth and immediacy.

 MED/DRY $20 AV

Highfield Marlborough Riesling   ★★★★

This is a consistently rewarding wine, priced sharply. The 2010 vintage (★★★★) is light and vivacious, with lemon/lime flavours, a hint of apricots, plentiful sweetness (32 grams/litre of residual sugar) and excellent intensity. The 2011 (★★★★☆) is light-bodied (11 per cent alcohol) and gently sweet, with excellent intensity of vibrant, peachy, citrusy, spicy flavours, a hint of sherbet and good harmony.

Vintage	11	10	09	08	07	06
WR	6	6	6	5	6	6
Drink	11-14	11-14	P	P	P	P

 MED $19 V+

Hudson Wharekaka Martinborough Riesling   ★★★

The 2009 vintage (★★★) is mouthfilling (13 per cent alcohol), fleshy and dryish (7 grams/litre of residual sugar). Crisp and minerally, it's a full-flavoured wine, drinking well now.

Vintage	09
WR	6
Drink	11-15

MED/DRY $22 –V

Huia Marlborough Dry Riesling   ★★★★

The 2010 vintage (★★★★☆) is a richly scented, full-bodied wine with penetrating lemon and lime flavours. Intensely varietal, with fresh, vibrant fruit characters and a long, basically dry finish, it's a powerful wine, already approachable, but a good candidate for cellaring.

 MED/DRY $28 –V

Hunter's Marlborough Riesling ★★★★

This wine is consistently excellent – and bargain-priced. The 2010 vintage (★★★★) is a fleshy, full-bodied wine (13 per cent alcohol), with strong lemon, lime and spice flavours, a sliver of sweetness (10 grams/litre of residual sugar) and good acid spine. Fresh and concentrated, it's already enjoyable; drink now or cellar.

Vintage	10	09	08	07	06
WR	6	6	6	6	6
Drink	11-13	11-14	11-12	P	P

 MED/DRY $20 V+

Hurunui River Riesling ★★★☆

Grown north-west of Waipara, at Hawarden, in North Canterbury, the 2009 vintage (★★★) has lemony, appley flavours, slightly peachy and well-balanced, with a crisp, dryish finish.

 MED/DRY $20 AV

Isabel Marlborough Dry Riesling ★★★☆

Still on sale, the 2008 vintage (★★★★) is scented and citrusy, with good ripeness, richness and roundness. It's drinking well now.

Vintage	08	07
WR	6	6
Drink	11-17	11-14

DRY $23 –V

Jack's Canyon Waipara Classic Riesling (★★★☆)

From Waipara Springs, the 2009 vintage (★★★☆) is an attractively scented, medium-bodied wine with fresh, gently sweet, lemon/apple flavours, lively and strong.

 MED/DRY $15 V+

Johanneshof Marlborough Riesling (★★★★)

Light and lively, the 2010 vintage (★★★★) is very fresh and crisp, with good intensity of citrusy, slightly appley and spicy flavours. A medium style (20 grams/litre of residual sugar), it shows excellent delicacy and length. Best drinking 2013+.

 MED $24 AV

John Forrest Collection Riesling ★★★★★

Still on sale, the 2006 vintage (★★★★★) is very intense and refined. Grown in the Brancott and Wairau valleys, it was hand-picked from low-yielding vines and stop-fermented in a medium-dry style (12 grams/litre of residual sugar). Finely structured, with great delicacy, it has a scented, floral bouquet and pure lemon/apple flavours, slightly minerally, intense and harmonious. With bottle-age, it's drinking superbly, building great complexity and length. The 2005 vintage (★★★★★) is also in peak form, with a rich, complex bouquet and deep, citrusy, minerally flavours.

Vintage	06
WR	6
Drink	11-20

 MED/DRY $40 AV

Johner Estate Wairarapa Riesling   ★★★★

The 2011 vintage (★★★★) is instantly appealing. A medium-dry style (12 grams/litre of residual sugar), it is fresh and finely balanced, with generous passionfruit, lime and citrus-fruit flavours, gently sweet, ripe and rich.

MED/DRY $22 V+

Julicher Martinborough Riesling   ★★★★

Still on sale, the 2008 vintage (★★★☆) was grown at Te Muna and made in a medium-dry (12 grams/litre of residual sugar) style. Mouthfilling (13 per cent alcohol), it is ripe and rounded, with citrusy flavours revealing good, bottle-aged complexity.

MED/DRY $20 V+

Junction, The, Runaway Riesling   ★★★

Grown on the Takapau Plains, in Central Hawke's Bay, the 2010 vintage (★★☆) is medium-bodied, tight and citrusy. It's currently fairly restrained, but balanced for easy drinking and may well open out with bottle-age.

MED/DRY $22 –V

Kahurangi Estate Moutere Dry Riesling   (★★★★)

The tightly structured 2009 vintage (★★★★) is a Nelson wine with very good depth of citrusy, limey, slightly minerally and spicy flavour. Showing good freshness, vigour and intensity, it should be long-lived.

DRY $18 V+

Kaimira Estate Brightwater Riesling   ★★★★

This wine typically matures well. The 2010 vintage (★★★★) is youthful, with fresh lemon, lime and peach flavours showing excellent depth. A medium-dry style (7 grams/litre of residual sugar), it is crisp and slightly minerally, with obvious potential.

Vintage	10	09	08	07	06
WR	6	6	7	5	6
Drink	11-16	11-15	11-13	11-12	P

MED/DRY $22 V+

Kaimira Estate Iti Selection Brightwater Riesling   ★★★★

Made in a refreshing, low-alcohol style ('Iti' is Maori for 'Small'), the debut 2010 vintage (★★★★☆) is poised, light (10 per cent alcohol) and vivacious, with citrusy, peachy, limey flavours, gentle sweetness (25 grams/litre of residual sugar), good acid spine and excellent harmony. The 2011 (★★★☆) is still very youthful. Fresh, vibrant, lemony and appley, it is light-bodied, with a distinct splash of sweetness (28 grams/litre of residual sugar) and racy acidity. Well worth cellaring.

Vintage	11	10
WR	6	5
Drink	11-18	11-16

MED $22 V+

Kim Crawford First Pick Riesling   (★★★☆)

'First Pick' here just means the 'first pick for any occasion'. The 2010 vintage (★★★☆), not identified by region, is ripely scented, fresh and vibrantly fruity, with strong, citrusy, limey flavours, slightly sweet and crisp. Enjoyable from the start.

MED $18 V+

Kingsmill Tippet's Race Riesling   ★★★★

This single-vineyard Central Otago wine is hand-picked at Bendigo. The 2009 vintage (★★★★) is mouthfilling (13 per cent alcohol), with citrusy, appley, slightly spicy flavours, showing excellent depth and balance, a sliver of sweetness and obvious potential.

MED/DRY $25 AV

Konrad Marlborough Dry Riesling   ★★★

Estate-grown in the Waihopai Valley, the 2010 vintage (★★★) is full-bodied and drier than most (5 grams/litre of residual sugar). Fleshy and citrusy, with hints of spices and passionfruit, it's enjoyably ripe and rounded.

Vintage	10	09	08	07	06
WR	6	5	4	4	6
Drink	11-16	11-15	11-12	P	P

MED/DRY $18 AV

Lake Chalice Falcon Vineyard Marlborough Riesling   ★★★☆

Grown in the company's Falcon Vineyard at Rapaura, the 2009 vintage (★★★☆) is a medium style (27 grams/litre of residual sugar), light-bodied (10.5 per cent alcohol), with fresh, strong grapefruit, apple and lemon flavours, showing good varietal character, and a smooth finish. Enjoyable from the start.

MED $20 AV

Lawson's Dry Hills Marlborough Riesling   ★★★★

Here's a chance to buy a dry style of Riesling with some bottle development. The 2008 vintage (★★★★) is drinking well now. Pale yellow, fleshy and rounded, it has ripe grapefruit-like flavours, concentrated, slightly toasty and lingering. Good value.

Vintage	08	07	06	05	04
WR	7	6	7	6	6
Drink	11-12	P	P	P	P

MED/DRY $20 V+

Locharburn Central Otago Riesling   (★★★★)

Grown in the Cromwell Basin, the 2010 vintage (★★★★) was hand-picked and briefly lees-aged in tanks. Medium-dry (11 grams/litre of residual sugar), fresh and crisp, it has lemon, apple and slight spice flavours that build well across the palate. Racy, with good poise, delicacy and intensity, it's a stylish wine with good potential.

Vintage	10
WR	6
Drink	11-17

MED/DRY $20 AV

Loopline Riesling   (★★★★)

Grown at Opaki, near Masterton, in the northern Wairarapa, the 2009 vintage (★★★★) has a scented, lemony bouquet. Medium-bodied, it is fresh, citrusy and limey, with a touch of sweetness, appetising acidity, and excellent delicacy and length.

MED/DRY $21 V+

Maimai Creek Hawke's Bay Riesling   ★★★

The 2009 vintage (★★☆) is medium-bodied, with crisp, ripe flavours, showing some early development, and a hint of sweetness.

MED/DRY $20 –V

Main Divide Waipara Valley Riesling   ★★★★

From Pegasus Bay, this is a bargain. The 2009 vintage (★★★★) is scented, fresh and poised, with strong lemon, lime and nectarine flavours, a splash of sweetness (30 grams/litre of residual sugar) and good acid spine. Deliberately made in a slightly *spritzig* style (to accentuate freshness), it has good vigour and intensity.

Vintage	10	09	08	07
WR	7	7	7	7
Drink	11-20	11-17	11-15	11-15

MED $20 V+

Marble Point Hanmer Springs Riesling Classic   ★★★☆

Estate-grown in North Canterbury, the 2010 vintage (★★★☆) is fresh and medium-bodied (10 per cent alcohol), with good depth of lemony, gently sweet (23 grams/litre of residual sugar) flavours, ripe and rounded. Balanced for easy drinking, it's enjoyable now. (The 2009 vintage is much sweeter – see Sweet White Wines.)

Vintage	10
WR	6
Drink	11+

MED $22 AV

Marble Point Hanmer Springs Riesling Dry   ★★★★

Estate-grown in North Canterbury, the 2009 vintage (★★★★) is weighty and fleshy, with strong, lemony flavours, moderate acidity and a dryish (5 grams/litre of residual sugar), finely balanced finish. It's maturing well.

Vintage	09	08
WR	6	6
Drink	12-15	11-13

MED/DRY $22 V+

Margrain Proprietors Selection Riesling ★★★☆

Tightly structured and minerally, the 2009 vintage (★★★★), grown in Martinborough, is medium-bodied, with a splash of sweetness (12 grams/litre of residual sugar) and citrusy, slightly peachy flavours, showing good intensity. Lively, with firm acid spine, it has good aging potential.

Vintage	09	08
WR	6	6
Drink	11-16	11-17

 MED/DRY $24 –V

Margrain River's Edge Martinborough Riesling (★★★☆)

The 2009 vintage (★★★☆) is a medium style (20 grams/litre of residual sugar) with peachy, slightly spicy flavours, showing very good depth, and lively acidity. Drink now or cellar.

Vintage	09
WR	6
Drink	11-13

 MED $20 AV

Martinborough Vineyard Bruno Riesling – see Sweet White Wines

Martinborough Vineyard Jackson Block Riesling ★★★★

The 2009 vintage (★★★★), from 19-year-old vines in the Jackson Vineyard, near the winery, was hand-picked, with no botrytis influence. Daringly dry (4 grams/litre of residual sugar), it is full-bodied, with fresh, vibrant lemon and apple flavours, crisp, racy and strong. The 2010 (★★★★) is an elegant, lemon-scented wine, lean and tightly structured, crisp and dry, with excellent depth and delicacy of pure, citrusy, limey flavours, and obvious cellaring potential.

 DRY $26 –V

Martinborough Vineyard Manu Riesling ★★★★

The 2009 vintage (★★★★) was grown in the Jackson Vineyard. A medium style (27 grams/litre of residual sugar), harvested with a gentle botrytis influence, it is fresh, with ripe lemon, apple and spice flavours, finely balanced, delicate and lingering. The 2010 (★★★☆) is generous, with ripe, slightly sweet lemon, lime and spice flavours, woven with fresh acidity. It's already enjoyable, with good balance and length.

 MED $27 –V

Maude Mt Maude Family Vineyard Dry Riesling (★★★★)

Grown in the Mount Maude Vineyard, at Wanaka, the 2010 vintage (★★★★) shows obvious potential. Off-dry (7 grams/litre of residual sugar), it is fresh and full-bodied, with ripe, peachy flavours, a minerally streak and good intensity.

 MED/DRY $20 V+

Mills Reef Hawke's Bay Riesling ★★★

The 2009 vintage (★★★) is a full-bodied, dry style (4 grams/litre of residual sugar), with good depth of lemony, slightly spicy flavours and a fresh, crisp finish.

DRY $18 AV

Millton Opou Vineyard Riesling ★★★★

Typically scented, with rich, lemony, often honeyed flavours, this is the country's northernmost fine-quality Riesling. Grown in Gisborne (from vines dating back to 1981), it is gently sweet, in a softer, less racy style than the classic Marlborough wines. The grapes, grown organically in the Opou Vineyard at Manutuke, are hand-harvested over a month at three stages of ripening, usually culminating in a final pick of botrytis-affected fruit. The 2010 vintage (★★★★), certified organic, is light-bodied (9.5 per cent alcohol), with searching lemon and apple flavours, pure and delicate. A distinctly medium style (40 grams/litre of residual sugar), it's delicious in its youth, but should be at its best 2013+.

Vintage	10
WR	6
Drink	11-21

 MED $28 –V

Misha's Vineyard Limelight Riesling ★★★★☆

The classy 2010 vintage (★★★★★) is a single-vineyard wine, hand-harvested at Bendigo, in Central Otago. It was mostly handled in tanks, but 30 per cent was fermented with indigenous yeasts in old French oak casks. A gently sweet style (27 grams/litre of residual sugar), it is medium-bodied (11.5 per cent alcohol), with vibrant lemon, apple and spice flavours showing lovely delicacy, poise and concentration. Tight and finely balanced, with a long finish, it has real immediacy; drink now or cellar.

Vintage	10	09	08
WR	6	7	6
Drink	11-16	11-15	11-13

 MED $25 V+

Misha's Vineyard Lyric Riesling ★★★★☆

A basically dry style (5 grams/litre of residual sugar), the 2010 vintage (★★★★) was estate-grown at Bendigo, in Central Otago, and mostly handled in tanks; 13 per cent was fermented with indigenous yeasts in seasoned French oak casks. Lemon-scented, it is mouthfilling, with finely balanced, citrusy, limey flavours, faintly biscuity and showing good richness. Already enjoyable, it carries the dry style well.

Vintage	10	09
WR	6	7
Drink	11-15	11-16

 MED/DRY $25 V+

Mission Hawke's Bay Riesling ★★★☆

The 2010 vintage (★★★☆) is floral, fresh and lively, in a low-alcohol (10 per cent), distinctly medium style (19 grams/litre of residual sugar). Vibrantly fruity, with lemon and green-apple flavours, it shows good vigour and depth.

MED $20 AV

Momo Marlborough Riesling   ★★★☆

From Seresin, the 2009 vintage (★★★☆) was hand-picked at two sites. Medium-bodied (11 per cent alcohol), it is crisp and slightly minerally, with a sliver of sweetness (12 grams/litre of residual sugar) and citrus-fruit, lime and spice flavours showing very good delicacy and depth. Fine value.

Vintage	09	08
WR	7	5
Drink	11-14	11-13

MED/DRY $18 V+

Mondillo Central Otago Riesling   ★★★★

Estate-grown at Bendigo, the 2011 vintage (★★★★) is enticingly fragrant, with crisp, citrusy, appley flavours and impressive poise, delicacy, vibrancy and richness. It's a slightly sweet style (9 grams/litre of residual sugar), still very youthful; open mid-2012+.

Vintage	11	10	09	08	07
WR	6	NM	7	7	7
Drink	12-15	NM	12-14	12-14	12-13

MED/DRY $26 –V

Montana Reserve Waipara Riesling – see Brancott Estate Reserve Waipara Riesling

Montana Waipara Riesling   (★★★☆)

The 2010 vintage (★★★☆) is a slightly sweet style with very good depth of citrus-fruit, lime and passionfruit flavours. It's a fairly low-alcohol style (10.7 per cent), with gentle sweetness (16 grams/litre of residual sugar) and good drive and richness.

MED $18 V+

Mount Edward Central Otago Riesling   ★★★★

Delicious now, the 2008 vintage (★★★★☆) is a single-vineyard wine grown at Lowburn, on the shores of Lake Dunstan. Scented, it's medium-bodied and tangy, with gentle sweetness, strong lemon/lime flavours, minerally and toasty notes adding complexity, and lovely vibrancy and depth. The 2009 (★★★★) is poised and youthful, in a complex style with strong, citrusy, appley, spicy flavours, slight sweetness and firm acid spine. Best 2013+.

Vintage	08	07	06
WR	6	6	6
Drink	11-15	11-14	11-13

MED/DRY $25 AV

Mount Edward The Drumlin Riesling   (★★★★★)

Estate-grown at Gibbston, the 2009 vintage (★★★★★) is a Mosel-like beauty, very light (9.5 per cent alcohol) and intense. From very low-cropped vines (1 tonne/hectare), it has rich lemon, lime and peach flavours, abundant sweetness (49 grams/litre of residual sugar), racy acidity and lovely poise and length.

MED $29 V+

Mountford Waipara Pure Riesling   (★★★☆)

Lively and light (9.5 per cent alcohol), the 2010 vintage (★★★☆) was made from bought-in, freeze-concentrated grapes. It has fresh, ripe, peachy, slightly spicy flavours, showing very good depth and harmony.

 MED $35 –V

Mount Riley Marlborough Riesling   ★★★

The 2011 vintage (★★★☆) was grown in the Wairau Valley and made in a medium-dry style (8 grams/litre of residual sugar). Very fresh and tight, it has good depth and delicacy of youthful lemon, lime and slight spice flavours, threaded with lively acidity. Open mid-2012+.

 MED/DRY $18 AV

Mt Beautiful North Canterbury Riesling   ★★★★

Grown at Cheviot, north of Waipara, the 2009 vintage (★★★★) is a tight, medium-dry style (13 grams/litre of residual sugar) with lemon and passionfruit flavours, showing good weight, texture and freshness. The 2010 (★★★★) is tight and youthful, tangy and minerally, with fresh lemon, apple and spice flavours, showing excellent delicacy, harmony and depth. Best drinking mid-2012+.

Vintage	10
WR	5
Drink	11-14

 MED/DRY $22 V+

Mt Difficulty Dry Central Otago Riesling   ★★★★

Grown at Bannockburn, this is a wine for purists – steely and austere in its youth, but rewarding (almost demanding) time. The 2010 vintage (★★★★) is fresh and full-bodied (13.5 per cent alcohol), lemony, slightly minerally and spicy, with good vigour and concentration and a tight, dry finish. Open 2013+.

 DRY $26 –V

Mt Difficulty Target Gully Riesling   ★★★★

Grown in the Target Gully Vineyard at Bannockburn, in Central Otago, the 2010 vintage (★★★★) is a rich, medium style (31 grams/litre of residual sugar), with vibrant citrus-fruit and peach flavours, slightly spicy, finely balanced and instantly appealing.

 MED $26 –V

Muddy Water Dry Waipara Riesling   ★★★★☆

The 2009 vintage (★★★★★) was hand-harvested at Waipara and fermented with indigenous yeasts to near dryness. It's medium to full-bodied, with highly concentrated, citrusy, limey flavours, very tight and finely poised, and a crisp, lasting finish. The 2010 (★★★★☆) is youthful and dry (5 grams/litre of residual sugar) but not at all austere. Full-bodied (13.5 per cent alcohol), it is rich and ripe, with citrusy, spicy, slightly minerally flavours, showing good complexity. Best drinking 2013+.

Vintage	10	09	08
WR	6	7	7
Drink	11-19	11-20	11-15

MED/DRY $29 AV

Muddy Water Growers' Series James Hardwick Waipara Riesling ★★★★★

The 2009 vintage (★★★★☆) was hand-harvested and fermented with indigenous yeasts. It's a rich, medium-dry style (12 grams/litre of residual sugar) with concentrated grapefruit and spice flavours, a hint of marmalade, minerally notes, good complexity and a crisp, long finish. Well worth cellaring.

Vintage	09	08
WR	7	6
Drink	11-19	11-18

MED/DRY $25 V+

Muddy Water Unplugged Riesling– see Sweet White Wines

Muddy Water Waipara Riesling Reloaded   (★★★★☆)

The distinctive 2009 vintage (★★★★☆) was fermented and matured on its yeast lees for eight months in old French oak puncheons. An unusually dry style (2.4 grams/litre of residual sugar), it carries the dry style well, with concentrated, ripe grapefruit and slight peach flavours, showing good complexity. Tight and minerally, crisp and long, it's full of promise.

Vintage	09
WR	7
Drink	11-22

DRY $35 –V

Mud House Waipara Riesling   ★★★★

The lemon-scented 2010 vintage (★★★★) is a single-vineyard, estate-grown wine. A medium-dry style (12 grams/litre of residual sugar), it is very harmonious, with lemony, appley flavours, showing good delicacy and freshness, finely balanced acidity and a lingering finish. Good value.

MED/DRY $19 V+

Neudorf Brightwater Riesling   ★★★★

The 2009 vintage (★★★★) is still youthful, in a dryish style (10 grams/litre of residual sugar) with strong grapefruit, lemon and lime flavours, woven with firm acidity, and good freshness, delicacy and intensity. Still a baby, the 2010 (★★★☆) is poised and lively, with a fairly dry impression (9 grams/litre of residual sugar) on the palate, and restrained, citrusy, minerally flavours. It's worth cellaring; open 2013+.

Vintage	10	09	08	07	06
WR	6	7	5	6	6
Drink	11-16	11-15	11-14	11-13	11-12

MED/DRY $24 AV

Neudorf Moutere Riesling ★★★★★

A copybook cool-climate style with excellent intensity, estate-grown at Upper Moutere. The 2009 vintage (★★★★★) was hand-picked in the Beuke Block, on a hill overlooking the Home Vineyard, and mostly lees-aged in tanks; 6 per cent was fermented with indigenous yeasts in an old barrel. It is light (9.2 per cent alcohol) and vivacious, with abundant sweetness balanced by mouth-watering acidity, and lovely poise and intensity of citrusy, limey, slightly spicy flavours. The 2010 (★★★★☆), grown in the Rosedale Vineyard, is medium-sweet (45 grams/litre of residual sugar), light-bodied (10.5 per cent alcohol) and racy, with fresh lemon/lime flavours showing excellent intensity. It's still youthful; open 2013+.

Vintage	10	09	08	07	06	05
WR	6	7	6	6	7	7
Drink	11-18	11-18	11-17	11-17	11-16	11-15

 MED $30 AV

Nga Waka Martinborough Riesling ★★★★

Still on sale, the 2005 vintage (★★★★★) has youthful, light lemon/green colour. The bouquet is fresh and minerally, with bottle-aged complexity; the palate is dry and minerally, with ripe grapefruit-like flavours, balanced acidity and a rounding finish. A good 'food' wine, it should be long-lived.

Vintage	05
WR	7
Drink	11+

 DRY $25 AV

Northburn Station Central Otago Riesling ★★★☆

Grown at Northburn, on the eastern side of Lake Dunstan, the 2009 vintage (★★★★) is drinking well now. A medium-dry style, it is fleshy, with rich lemon, lime and passionfruit flavours, showing good delicacy and harmony.

Vintage	09	08	07
WR	6	5	5
Drink	11-14	11-13	11-12

MED/DRY $24 –V

Northburn Station Jeweller's Shop Central Otago Riesling (★★☆)

A sweetish style (45 grams/litre of residual sugar), the 2009 vintage (★★☆) is light (10.5 per cent alcohol), with plenty of lemony flavour, but less floral than its stablemate (above).

 MED $24 –V

Ohinemuri Estate Gisborne Riesling ★★★

Waikato winemaker Horst Hillerich usually, although not always, draws his Riesling grapes from Gisborne. Still on sale, the 2008 vintage (★★★), grown at Patutahi and briefly oak-matured, is citrusy, slightly honeyed and flavoursome, with a touch of sweetness (10 grams/litre of residual sugar) and a well-rounded finish. It's an easy-drinking style, enjoyable now.

Vintage	08
WR	5
Drink	11-14

MED/DRY $20 –V

Old Coach Road Nelson Riesling ★★★☆

From Seifried, this is a medium style, typically offering good value. The 2010 (★★★) is a crisp, medium-bodied wine with moderately concentrated lemon/lime flavours, fresh and lively. The 2011 vintage (★★★☆) is lemon-scented, with vibrant, citrusy, slightly spicy flavours, gently sweet (17 grams/litre of residual sugar), finely balanced and already enjoyable.

Vintage	11	10	09	08
WR	6	6	6	7
Drink	11-15	11-15	11-14	P

 MED $17 V+

Olssens Annieburn Riesling ★★★★☆

The debut 2009 vintage (★★★★★) is a medium style, very vibrant and light, with searching, citrusy, appley, slightly peachy flavours, threaded with mouth-wateringly crisp acidity. Finely poised, it's already highly expressive, but should also reward cellaring. The 2010 (★★★★) is light-bodied (9.5 per cent alcohol), with a distinct splash of sweetness (32 grams/litre of residual sugar). Still unfolding, it has generous lemon, apple and peach flavours, slightly spicy and crisp, with good balance and richness.

Vintage	10	09
WR	7	7
Drink	11-18	11-17

 MED $29 AV

Olssens Central Otago Riesling Dry (★★★)

The 2009 vintage (★★★) was estate-grown at Bannockburn. Hand-picked at 23.4 brix and lees-aged in tanks, it's an off-dry style (6.5 grams/litre of residual sugar), with lemony, appley aromas and flavours, fresh and crisp, but is less concentrated than its stablemate (above).

 MED/DRY $29 –V

Opihi Vineyard South Canterbury Riesling ★★★☆

Estate-grown and hand-picked, the 2009 vintage (★★★☆) is light and lively, with strong, crisp lemon, apple and lime flavours and a slightly sweet (7.5 grams/litre of residual sugar), tightly structured finish. Worth cellaring.

 MED/DRY $22 AV

Ostler Blue House Vines Waitaki Valley Riesling ★★★☆

From the Blue House Vineyard, the 2009 (★★★☆) is tightly structured, with very good depth of lemony, appley flavours, slightly minerally and spicy. One of the best vintages yet, the 2010 (★★★★) is medium-bodied (11 per cent alcohol), with concentrated, citrusy flavours, showing excellent balance (12 grams/litre of residual sugar), delicacy and drive. It's a rich, very harmonious wine, for drinking now or cellaring.

Vintage	10	09
WR	6	6
Drink	11-18	11-18

MED/DRY $28 –V

Palliser Estate Martinborough Riesling   ★★★☆

This wine typically matures well. The 2010 (★★★) is medium-bodied (12.5 per cent alcohol), fresh and crisp, with slightly sweet, lemony, spicy flavours, but lacks the richness of top past vintages.

MED/DRY $16 V+

Pasquale Waitaki Valley Riesling   (★★★★)

The 2010 vintage (★★★★) was hand-picked and made in a 'not quite dry' (9 grams/litre of residual sugar) style. Attractively scented, it has strong, fresh, citrusy, appley, slightly spicy flavours, steely acidity, and a tight, long finish. Building up well with bottle-age, it's well worth cellaring.

MED/DRY $30 –V

Pasquale Waitaki Valley Riesling 16   (★★★)

The 2010 vintage (★★★), with a near-invisible '16' on the label, was estate-grown at Kurow. It has strong, lemony, limey flavours, with a splash of sweetness (16 grams/litre of residual sugar) balanced by steely acidity.

MED $27 –V

Pegasus Bay Aria Late Harvest Riesling – see Sweet White Wines

Pegasus Bay Bel Canto Riesling Dry   ★★★★

Bel Canto means 'Beautiful Singing'. Late-harvested at Waipara from mature vines and produced with some influence from noble rot and indigenous yeasts, but not barrel-aged, the 2009 (★★★★★) is a rich, dryish (8 grams/litre of residual sugar), powerful wine (14 per cent alcohol), with notably intense, citrusy flavours. Lemon-scented, with a hint of honey, it is complex, slightly spicy and minerally, with good acid spine and a lasting, basically dry finish. It shows great individuality and poise; open 2012+.

Vintage	10	09	08	07
WR	5	7	7	7
Drink	11-17	11-14	11-12	P

MED/DRY $32 –V

Pegasus Bay Riesling   ★★★★★

Classy stuff. Estate-grown at Waipara, in North Canterbury, it is richly fragrant and thrillingly intense, with flavours of citrus fruits and honey, complex and luscious. Based on mature vines and stop-fermented in a distinctly medium style, it breaks into full stride at about three years old and most vintages keep well for a decade. The 2009 (★★★★★) is bright, light yellow/green, with a musky perfume. Mouthfilling, it has concentrated grapefruit, peach, spice and slight honey flavours, with a splash of sweetness (26 grams/litre of residual sugar), fresh, appetising acidity and lovely balance and richness. Drink now or cellar.

Vintage	09	08	07	06	05	04
WR	7	7	7	6	6	7
Drink	11-20	11-19	11-18	11-16	11-16	11-15

MED $28 V+

Peregrine Central Otago Dry Riesling   ★★★★

Still on sale, the tightly structured 2008 vintage (★★★★★), grown in the Cromwell Basin, is
unfolding well. Minerally and dryish (5.9 grams/litre of residual sugar), it has intense, lemony,
slightly spicy flavours, showing excellent vigour and richness.

MED/DRY $22 V+

Peregrine Rastasburn Riesling   ★★★★

Hand-picked in the Cromwell Basin, this Central Otago wine is made in a slightly sweet style. It
typically has a scented bouquet and excellent depth, delicacy and harmony, maturing for several
years, acquiring a complex, toasty, honeyed richness.

MED $23 AV

Peter Yealands Marlborough Riesling   ★★★

The 2011 vintage (★★☆) is light-bodied, with lemony, appley, slightly spicy flavours, fresh and
crisp. Made in a medium-dry style (13 grams/litre of residual sugar), it is balanced with steely
acidity. The 2010 (★★★) is lemon-scented, with pleasing depth of slightly sweet, very fresh and
vibrant flavours, balanced for easy drinking.

MED/DRY $20 –V

Picnic by Two Paddocks Central Otago Riesling   (★★★☆)

The 2009 vintage (★★★☆) is an enjoyable, drink-young style. Medium-bodied, it is lemony,
slightly sweet (14 grams/litre of residual sugar) and crisp, with good freshness, balance and
vivacity.

MED/DRY $22 AV

Prophet's Rock Central Otago Dry Riesling   ★★★★

The 2009 vintage (★★★★☆) was estate-grown and hand-picked at Pisa, fermented with
indigenous yeasts and lees-aged. Still very youthful, it is highly scented, with citrusy, slightly
appley and spicy flavours, gentle sweetness (9 grams/litre of residual sugar), and excellent purity,
delicacy, harmony and length.

Vintage	08	07	06
WR	6	7	6
Drink	11-13	11-14	11-12

MED/DRY $28 –V

Quail Lane Hawke's Bay Riesling   ★★★

From Abbey Cellars and still on sale, the 2007 vintage (★★★☆) is a single-vineyard, Bridge
Pa wine, tangy, slightly minerally and drinking well now. Bright, light lemon/green, with some
toasty, bottle-aged notes on the nose, it is gently sweet and crisp, with strong lemon/lime
flavours. Good value. The 2008 (★★★) is fleshy and rounded, with ripe citrus-fruit and stone-
fruit flavours, gently sweet and crisp, but less scented than the 2007.

MED/DRY $15 V+

Redoubt Hill Vineyard Nelson Riesling   ★★★★

This single-vineyard wine is grown at Motueka. The 2010 vintage (★★★★) is lemony, limey and minerally, with good intensity and excellent freshness, vigour and length.

DRY $29 –V

Ribbonwood Marlborough Riesling   ★★★

Balanced for easy drinking, the 2010 vintage (★★★) is medium-bodied, with fresh, lemony scents and a splash of sweetness (9 grams/litre of residual sugar) amid its citrusy, slightly spicy flavours. (From Framingham.)

Vintage	10
WR	5
Drink	10-13

MED/DRY $18 AV

Richmond Plains Nelson Riesling   ★★★☆

The 2009 vintage (★★★★) is fresh and vibrant, with strong, lemony, limey flavours, slightly sweet and crisp. It's a very harmonious wine, likely to age well. The 2010 (★★★☆) is also attractive. Freshly scented, it is medium-bodied, with lemon, apple and lime flavours, showing very good delicacy and depth, a touch of sweetness (12 grams/litre of residual sugar) and refreshing acidity.

Vintage	10	09
WR	5	6
Drink	11-16	11-14

MED/DRY $20 AV

Rimu Grove Nelson Riesling   (★★★★☆)

The 2009 vintage (★★★★☆) was grown on the Waimea Plains and in Moutere clay gravels, hand-picked, and tank-fermented with some use of indigenous yeasts. Rich and finely balanced, it's a medium style (25 grams/litre of residual sugar) with lemon, apple and grapefruit flavours, showing excellent poise, delicacy and depth. Minerally and slightly spicy, it was delicious from the start.

Vintage	09
WR	7
Drink	11-17

MED $29 AV

Rippon Jeunesse Young Vines Riesling   ★★★★☆

The 2010 vintage (★★★★☆) was estate-grown at Lake Wanaka, in Central Otago. Lemon-scented, it's a medium style, already drinking well, with rich, citrusy, peachy, slightly spicy flavours, an undertow of steely acidity, and excellent vigour, concentration and harmony. Drink now or cellar.

MED $25 V+

Rippon Riesling   ★★★★★

This single-vineyard, Lake Wanaka, Central Otago wine is a distinctly cool-climate style, steely, long-lived and penetratingly flavoured. Based on mature vines, the 2010 vintage (★★★★★) was fermented with indigenous yeasts and given extended lees-aging. It's an authoritative wine, weighty and intense, with ripe, peachy flavours, tight and controlled, and a minerally, lasting finish. A top vintage, it is full of potential; open 2013+.

Vintage	10	09	08	07	06
WR	7	7	7	7	6
Drink	11-19	11-18	11-17	11-17	11-16

 MED/DRY $32 AV

Riverby Estate Marlborough Riesling   ★★★

The 2009 vintage (★★★) is a dry style with fresh lemon, apple and lime flavours, crisp and minerally. A tight, youthful wine, it should reward cellaring.

DRY $20 –V

Riverby Estate Sali's Block Marlborough Riesling   ★★★☆

Designed for very easy drinking, the 2009 vintage (★★★☆) is a medium style (20 grams/litre of residual sugar) with satisfying depth of fresh, lively lemon, apple and lime flavours, crisp acidity and a hint of botrytis. Drink now or cellar.

MED $20 AV

Rockburn Central Otago Parkburn Riesling   ★★★

Estate-grown in the Cromwell Basin, the 2009 vintage (★★★) is a crisp, medium-dry style (12 grams/litre of residual sugar), finely balanced, with fresh, lively flavours, lemony and zesty.

Vintage	09	08	07	06
WR	5	5	7	6
Drink	11-20	11-15	11-15	11-13

 MED/DRY $23 –V

Rockburn Central Otago Tigermoth Riesling   (★★★★)

Launched from the 2011 vintage (★★★★), this wine was estate-grown at Parkburn and made in a low-alcohol (9 per cent), medium-sweet style (40 grams/litre of residual sugar). Enjoyable from the start, it is light, very racy and rich, with vibrant peach, apple and spice flavours, abundant sweetness balanced by fresh, zingy acidity, and excellent depth and harmony. Drink now or cellar.

Vintage	11
WR	6
Drink	11-25

MED/DRY $33 –V

Rock Ferry Central Otago Riesling   (★★★☆)

A full-bodied, medium-dry style, the 2009 vintage (★★★☆) was hand-picked at Bendigo and lees-aged for four months. Citrusy, with a vague hint of honey, it has very good balance and some bottle-aged complexity. It's drinking well now.

MED/DRY $29 –V

Ruby Bay Vineyard Nelson Riesling ★★★

The 2009 vintage (★★★) is a Nelson wine, estate-grown, hand-picked and lees-aged. It's a light-bodied style with good varietal character and depth of lemony, appley, slightly spicy flavours and a dry (4.5 grams/litre of residual sugar) finish.

Vintage	09
WR	4
Drink	11-12

DRY $24 –V

Saint Clair Marlborough Riesling ★★★☆

Typically an attractive, finely balanced wine. The 2010 vintage (★★★☆), a medium-dry style (10 grams/litre of residual sugar), was grown mostly in the Omaka and upper Wairau valleys, with some Awatere Valley fruit. Crafted for easy, satisfying drinking, it has good body and depth of citrusy, appley flavours, with gentle sweetness and lively acidity. Very fresh and vibrant, it's worth cellaring.

MED/DRY $21 AV

Saint Clair Pioneer Block 9 Big John Marlborough Riesling ★★★★

Grown in the lower Brancott Valley, the 2010 vintage (★★★★) is a single-vineyard wine with low alcohol (9 per cent) and plentiful sweetness (49 grams/litre of residual sugar). A fresh, strong, *spätlese* (late-harvested) style, it is very light and lively, with incisive lemon, apple and spice flavours, a hint of sherbet, tangy acidity and obvious potential.

MED $24 AV

Scott Base Central Otago Riesling (★★★☆)

From mature vines in the Cromwell Basin, the 2009 vintage (★★★☆) is a single-vineyard wine, handled in tanks. Medium-bodied, it shows good sugar/acid balance (13 grams/litre of residual sugar), with a crisp, minerally streak and strong, ripe, citrusy aromas and flavours. (From Allan Scott.)

Vintage	09
WR	6
Drink	11-19

MED/DRY $26 –V

Seifried Nelson Riesling ★★★☆

From a key pioneer of Riesling here, the 2010 (★★★☆) has fresh, lemony, limey flavours, appetising acidity, and good depth and harmony. The 2011 vintage (★★★★) has excellent intensity of lemony, limey, spicy flavours. Fresh and finely poised, it is slightly sweet (10 grams/litre of residual sugar), lively and long.

Vintage	11	10	09	08
WR	6	6	6	6
Drink	11-15	11-15	11-14	11-12

MED/DRY $19 V+

Seresin Memento Riesling

Harvested by hand from 18-year-old vines in the Home Vineyard at Renwick, in Marlborough, this is a medium-sweet style. The 2010 vintage (★★★★), certified organic, has strong, citrusy, limey flavours, crisp and lively. A youthful wine with good intensity and firm acid spine, it's already drinking well.

Vintage	10	09	08
WR	7	7	5
Drink	11-17	11-18	11-18

MED $28 –V

Shaky Bridge Central Otago Riesling

Estate-grown and hand-picked at Alexandra, the 2009 vintage (★★★☆) is a dryish style (5 grams/litre of residual sugar), lemony, slightly spicy and flavoursome, with fresh acidity and good harmony.

Vintage	09
WR	6
Drink	11-13

MED/DRY $20 AV

Shingle Peak Marlborough Riesling

Still very youthful, the 2011 vintage (★★★) is medium-bodied, with fresh lemon, lime and spice flavours, a hint of passionfruit and gentle sweetness balanced by lively acidity. Open mid-2012+.

MED/DRY $18 AV

Sileni The Don Hawke's Bay Riesling

The 2009 vintage (★★★☆) is almost dry (6.3 grams/litre of residual sugar), with strong, lemony, appley flavours, ripe and rounded. With bottle-age, it is developing toasty, minerally, honeyed notes and considerable complexity.

Vintage	09	08	07
WR	5	NM	7
Drink	11-16	NM	11-14

MED/DRY $25 AV

Soljans Marlborough Riesling

Drinking well now, the 2009 vintage (★★★) is a medium-dry style (13 grams/litre of residual sugar) with plenty of citrusy, peachy, slightly spicy flavour and a rounded finish.

MED/DRY $20 –V

Spinyback Nelson Riesling ★★★☆

Good value from Waimea Estate – and the 2009 vintage (★★★★) is a real bargain. Showing plenty of personality, it has a slightly toasty bouquet leading into a medium-dry palate (11 grams/litre of residual sugar), offering strong, citrusy, slightly spicy, lingering flavours. Drink now.

Vintage	09	08	07
WR	7	7	7
Drink	11-14	11-13	11-12

 MED/DRY $16 V+

Spring Creek Estate Marlborough Riesling ★★★☆

Grown at Rapaura, the 2009 vintage (★★★) is freshly scented and off-dry (6.3 grams/litre of residual sugar), with mouthfilling body and plenty of lemony, limey, slightly spicy flavour.

Vintage	09
WR	5
Drink	11-12

MED/DRY $15 V+

Spy Valley Envoy Marlborough Riesling – see Sweet White Wines

Spy Valley Marlborough Riesling ★★★★

The 2010 vintage (★★★★) is an off-dry style, hand-harvested and handled mostly in tanks, with some use of barrel fermentation. Mouthfilling (13 per cent alcohol), it has good intensity of citrusy, slightly limey and spicy flavours, crisp, tight and lingering. Drink now or cellar. The 2011 (★★★☆) is vibrantly fruity, with lemon/lime flavours, slightly sweet (9 grams/litre of residual sugar), crisp and strong.

Vintage	11	10	09	08	07	06
WR	7	6	6	6	7	6
Drink	12-16	11-14	11-14	11-12	P	P

 MED/DRY $23 AV

Staete Landt Marlborough Riesling Auslese – see Sweet White Wines

Staete Landt Marlborough Riesling Dry ★★★★

The 2010 vintage (★★★★), estate-grown and hand-picked from six rows at Rapaura, was fermented and matured for six months in old French oak puncheons. It's a 'serious' style for cellaring. The bouquet is scented and citrusy, with good intensity; the palate has strong, lemony, slightly spicy flavours, firm acid spine and a dry finish. Open 2013+.

Vintage	10	09	08
WR	7	7	7
Drink	11-18	11-17	11-14

MED/DRY $26 –V

Stafford Lane Estate Riesling ★★★

The 2009 vintage (★★) is an off-dry Nelson wine, light, crisp, lemony and appley, but it lacks flavour depth.

 MED/DRY $18 AV

Stoneleigh Marlborough Riesling   ★★★★

This is typically a refined wine from Pernod Ricard NZ with incisive flavours and a crisp, long finish. The 2009 vintage (★★★★) is fresh and elegant, with finely balanced, gently sweet lemon, apple and passionfruit flavours, showing excellent ripeness, delicacy and depth. Tasted just after bottling, the 2011 (★★★☆) is light-bodied (11 per cent alcohol), with fresh, pure lemon/lime flavours, showing good delicacy and length.

Vintage	11
WR	6
Drink	11-15

Summerhouse Marlborough Dry Riesling   ★★★★

Estate-grown and hand-harvested, the 2011 vintage (★★★★) is dryish (5 grams/litre of residual sugar), tight and very youthful. Finely poised, with citrusy, spicy flavours, delicate, crisp and long, it should blossom with cellaring.

Takutai Nelson Riesling   ★★☆

From Waimea Estates, the 2009 vintage (★★☆) is fresh, citrusy and limey, with a slightly sweet (11 grams/litre of residual sugar), crisp finish. It lacks a bit of delicacy, but the price is sharp. The 2008 (★★☆) is full-bodied, lemony and spicy, with a slightly honeyed, rounded finish. Ready.

Vintage	09	08
WR	6	5
Drink	11-13	11-12

Te Kairanga Martinborough Estate Riesling   ★★★★

A consistently good wine, priced right. Lemon-scented, the 2009 vintage (★★★★) is a medium-dry style with rich, ripe, citrusy, slightly honeyed flavours, lively acidity, a touch of botrytis and excellent concentration. The 2010 (★★★☆) is crisp and tight, with lemon/lime flavours, slight sweetness (7 grams/litre of residual sugar), good vigour and bottle-aged, toasty characters starting to emerge.

Vintage	10	09	08	07	06
WR	7	6	7	7	7
Drink	11-19	11-19	11-15	11-14	11-12

Te Mania Nelson Riesling   ★★★★

A bargain. The 2010 vintage (★★★★) is punchy and vibrant, with a floral bouquet, strong, citrusy, limey flavours and a fresh, dryish, crisp finish that lingers well.

Vintage	10	09
WR	7	6
Drink	11-15	11-14

MED/DRY $19 V+

Terrace Edge Waipara Valley Riesling   ★★★★

Fine value. The fleshy, full-bodied 2010 vintage (★★★★) was made in a medium-dry style. It has fresh, ripe passionfruit and peach flavours, with a hint of honey, good concentration and strong drink-young appeal.

MED $18 V+

Thornbury Waipara Riesling   (★★★☆)

From Villa Maria, the 2011 vintage was tasted prior to bottling (and so not rated). A blend of Waipara (87 per cent) and Marlborough (13 per cent) fruit, it's medium-dry (10 grams/litre of residual sugar) with moderate alcohol (11 per cent) and fresh, punchy, citrusy flavours, vibrant and crisp.

MED/DRY $21 AV

Three Paddles Martinborough Riesling   ★★★☆

From Nga Waka, the 2009 vintage (★★★★) is fresh and vibrant, with strong, citrusy, limey flavours, a hint of apricot, and a distinct splash of sweetness. It's a very harmonious wine, delicious young.

MED $18 V+

Tohu Raiha Reserve Marlborough Riesling   (★★★★☆)

The racy, light-bodied (10.5 per cent alcohol) 2010 vintage (★★★★☆) was estate-grown in the Awatere Valley. Very tight, vivacious and intense, it's a medium-sweet style (36 grams/litre of residual sugar), appley and slightly spicy, with appetising acidity and excellent depth and harmony.

Vintage	10
WR	6
Drink	11-14

MED $25 V+

Tohu Single Vineyard Marlborough Riesling   ★★★★

Estate-grown in the Awatere Valley, the 2011 vintage (★★★★) is a dry style (4 grams/litre of residual sugar), lemon-scented, with fresh, ripe, slightly spicy and minerally flavours, showing excellent delicacy and purity. Well worth cellaring.

Vintage	11
WR	7
Drink	11-15

DRY $20 V+

Toi Toi Marlborough Riesling   ★★★★

Still unfolding, the 2010 vintage (★★★★) is very fresh, citrusy and limey, with a gentle splash of sweetness (18 grams/litre of residual sugar), a minerally streak, firm acid spine and good intensity.

MED $22 V+

Torlesse Waipara Riesling   ★★★☆

Priced right, the 2009 vintage (★★★☆) is a good drink-young style, medium-bodied, with faintly honeyed, citrusy, slightly peachy flavours, a gentle splash of sweetness (16 grams/litre of residual sugar) and fresh acidity.

Vintage	09	08
WR	6	7
Drink	12-15	11-15

MED $18 V+

Tupari Awatere Valley Dry Riesling   (★★★★☆)

The classy 2010 vintage (★★★★☆) is a generous, dry style (4.5 grams/litre of residual sugar), weighty and finely textured, with concentrated, citrusy flavours, pear and spice notes, a minerally streak and gentle acidity. It's a very harmonious wine, already drinking well.

 DRY $26 AV

Two Rivers of Marlborough Juliet Riesling   ★★★★

Full of promise, the 2011 vintage (★★★★☆) is a single-vineyard Wairau Valley wine, packed with lemon, passionfruit, apricot and spice flavours. Slightly sweet, with fresh acidity, it shows excellent poise, delicacy and length.

 MED/DRY $22 V+

Urlar Gladstone Riesling   (★★★★)

Hand-harvested in the Wairarapa and tank-fermented, the 2010 vintage (★★★★) is a medium-dry style (7 grams/litre of residual sugar). Tight and citrusy, it is medium-bodied and very youthful, with fresh, strong, peachy, spicy flavours, a hint of apricot, a minerally streak and a lingering finish. It needs time; open mid-2012+.

 MED/DRY $22 V+

Valli Old Vine Central Otago Riesling   ★★★★★

The 2010 vintage (★★★★★) was harvested from ultra low-cropping vines planted at Black Ridge, in Alexandra, in 1980. Finely scented, it's an unusually dry style (4 grams/litre of residual sugar) with compelling depth of grapefruit, peach and spice flavours, minerally and racy, and lovely balance and length. A classic cellaring style.

Vintage	10	09	08
WR	7	7	7
Drink	12-16	11-20	11-19

DRY $28 V+

Vidal [White Series] Marlborough Riesling   ★★★★

The 2011 vintage (★★★☆) is still very youthful. A mouthfilling style with crisp, citrusy, appley aromas and flavours and a dryish finish (7 grams/litre of residual sugar), it shows very good body, freshness and depth; open mid-2012+.

Vintage	10	09	08	07	06
WR	7	7	7	7	7
Drink	11-16	11-15	11-13	11-12	P

MED/DRY $22 V+

Villa Maria Cellar Selection Marlborough Riesling   ★★★★

The 2010 vintage (★★★★☆), labelled 'Dry', was grown in the Awatere and Wairau valleys and mostly hand-picked. Still very youthful, it is a fresh, tight, concentrated wine with citrusy flavours, hints of passionfruit, limes and spices, good acid spine, and excellent delicacy and depth. The 2011, tasted prior to bottling (and so not rated), is an off-dry style (6 grams/litre of residual sugar) with fresh and strong, yet delicate lemon/lime flavours, lively and lingering.

Vintage	11	10	09
WR	6	6	7
Drink	11-17	11-16	11-17

 MED/DRY $25 AV

Villa Maria Private Bin Marlborough Dry Riesling   ★★★★

The 2010 vintage (★★★★) is a medium-dry style (8 grams/litre of residual sugar). Mouthfilling, it has rich lemon/lime flavours, showing excellent freshness, delicacy and harmony, and a hint of sweetness balanced by firm acidity, giving the impression of dryness. The 2011 (★★★★), also medium-dry (7 grams/litre of residual sugar) is highly scented, with vibrant fruit flavours, showing excellent concentration and harmony.

Vintage	11	10	09
WR	6	6	7
Drink	11-16	11-16	11-14

 MED/DRY $23 AV

Villa Maria Reserve Marlborough Riesling   ★★★★★

The 2009 (★★★★★), grown in the Awatere Valley, was hand-picked, partly barrel-fermented and lees-aged for four months. It's a highly refined wine, beautifully scented, with intense, lemony flavours, appetising acidity, and lovely balance (9 grams/litre of residual sugar) and length. The 2010 vintage (★★★★★), grown mostly (65 per cent) in the Taylors Pass Vineyard, in the Awatere Valley, is a beauty. It's a classic dry style (in reality off-dry, with 9 grams/litre of residual sugar), with lovely depth of pure, citrusy flavour, minerally, rich and long.

Vintage	10	09
WR	7	7
Drink	11-18	11-17

 MED/DRY $28 V+

Voss Estate Riesling   ★★★☆

Still on sale, the 2008 vintage (★★★) is a medium-bodied wine from Martinborough with dryish (7 grams/litre of residual sugar), lemony flavours, fresh and finely balanced. There is no 2009.

Vintage	09	08	07	06
WR	NM	6	NM	5
Drink	NM	11-16	NM	11-12

MED/DRY $20 AV

Vynfields Classic Riesling ★★★★☆

Certified organic, the 2009 vintage (★★★★★) of this Martinborough wine is a fleshy, medium style (40 grams/litre of residual sugar). Full-bodied, with rich, peachy, slightly spicy and honeyed flavours, a hint of marmalade, and powerful personality, it is notably concentrated and harmonious, and delicious from the start.

 MED $29 AV

Waimea Bolitho SV Nelson Riesling ★★★★

The 2008 vintage (★★★★) is clearly botrytis-influenced, with rich, gently honeyed flavours, ripe and peachy, showing good complexity and harmony.

Vintage	08	07	06
WR	7	7	7
Drink	11-18	11-17	11-16

 MED/DRY $22 V+

Waimea Classic Nelson Riesling ★★★★☆

This luscious wine is balanced for easy drinking, consistently impressive – and great value. The 2009 vintage (★★★★☆) is rich and vibrant, with slightly toasty, bottle-aged notes emerging, appetising acidity and generous lemon/lime flavours, dryish (14 grams/litre of residual sugar) and long.

Vintage	09	08	07	06
WR	7	7	7	7
Drink	11-17	11-16	11-17	11-13

 MED/DRY $20 V+

Waimea Dry Nelson Riesling ★★★★

Still on sale, the 2006 vintage (★★★☆) is a tightly structured wine, dry (3.7 grams/litre of residual sugar) with a minerally streak and lemony, appley flavours that linger well.

Vintage	07	06	05	04
WR	6	7	5	6
Drink	11-17	11-16	P	P

 MED/DRY $20 V+

Waipara Hills Equinox Waipara Riesling ★★★★☆

Highly scented, the 2010 vintage (★★★★☆) is a concentrated, medium style with ripe, peachy, limey, slightly gingery and honeyed flavours, rich and rounded. Already drinking well, it shows good personality and harmony.

 MED $29 AV

Waipara Hills Soul of the South Waipara Riesling (★★★★☆)

The 2009 vintage (★★★★☆), estate-grown, is highly scented, with fresh, pure lemon/lime flavours and a gentle splash of sweetness (14 grams/litre of residual sugar). It's an immaculate, punchy wine, well worth cellaring.

MED/DRY $21 V+

Waipara Springs Dry Riesling   (★★★☆)

The 2009 vintage (★★★☆) is mouthfilling and dryish (6 grams/litre of residual sugar), with a honeyed bouquet. Fleshy, with ripe, grapefruit-like flavours, it is slightly spicy, with a minerally streak and plenty of drink-young appeal.

 MED/DRY $19 V+

Waipara Springs Premo Dry Riesling   ★★★★

The 2009 vintage (★★★☆) was mostly handled in tanks, but 30 per cent was fermented in old barrels. It's a fully dry style (3.5 grams/litre of residual sugar) with a slightly honeyed bouquet, mouthfilling body (14 per cent alcohol) and lemony, spicy flavours, showing a touch of complexity and good depth.

 DRY $22 V+

Waipara Springs Premo Waipara Riesling   (★★★★☆)

Here's a good chance to buy a bottle-aged Riesling. The 2006 vintage (★★★★☆) is a medium style (29 grams/litre of residual sugar), matured for eight weeks in old oak casks. Developing good complexity, it is light and racy, with fresh acid spine and concentrated, lemony, limey, slightly toasty flavours. It should be very long-lived.

 MED $22 V+

Waipara Springs Riesling   ★★★☆

The 2009 vintage (★★★★) is scented, with fresh, intense, citrusy, limey, gently sweet flavours (28 grams/litre of residual sugar), showing considerable complexity, finely balanced acidity and good harmony.

 MED $19 V+

Waipipi Wairarapa Riesling   ★★★

A medium style with a slightly honeyed bouquet, the 2009 vintage (★★★☆) has strong lemon, apple and passionfruit flavours, with a hint of botrytis and good acid spine.

MED $25 –V

Wairau River Marlborough Riesling   ★★★☆

The 2009 (★★★☆), 10 per cent barrel-aged, is tight and crisp, with lemony, appley flavours, a splash of sweetness and a slightly spicy, lingering finish. The 2010 vintage (★★★☆) is still very youthful, with good depth of fresh lemon and spice flavours, slight sweetness (7 grams/litre of residual sugar) and a crisp, finely balanced finish.

 MED/DRY $20 AV

Vintage	10	09	08
WR	6	6	4
Drink	12-16	11-12	P

Wairau River Summer Riesling   ★★★☆

'Sup with frivolous frivolity' urges the back label of this Marlborough wine. Light (9.5 per cent alcohol) and sweetish (39 grams/litre of residual sugar), the 2011 vintage (★★★☆) has strong lemon and green-apple flavours, crisp, lively and very tangy. It's balanced for easy drinking, anytime from now onwards.

Vintage	11
WR	7
Drink	12-16

 MED $20 AV

West Brook Marlborough Riesling   ★★★★

In a vertical tasting of the 2006–2010 vintages, held in April 2011, the rich, toasty 2007 (★★★★) was the best for current enjoyment. The 2010 (★★★★) is still a baby, but shows excellent vigour and intensity of fresh, racy, lemon/lime flavours, off-dry, crisp and long.

 MED/DRY $21 V+

Whitehaven Marlborough Riesling   ★★★

Full-bodied, the 2009 vintage (★★★) has dryish (5 grams/litre of residual sugar), lemony, slightly spicy flavours, showing decent depth and good delicacy and harmony. A single-vineyard, Brancott Valley wine, it should mature well.

Vintage	10	09
WR	6	7
Drink	11-15	11-13

 MED/DRY $20 –V

Wild Earth Central Otago Riesling   ★★★★

The instantly appealing 2009 vintage (★★★★) was estate-grown at Bannockburn. Very fresh, with good intensity and harmony, it is medium-bodied, with ripe, citrusy, limey flavours, good acid spine, a gentle splash of sweetness, and excellent balance and depth.

 MED $27 –V

Wild South Marlborough Riesling   ★★★☆

Scented and poised, the 2009 vintage (★★★★) from Sacred Hill is a single-vineyard wine, grown in the Awatere Valley. Basically dry (4 grams/litre of residual sugar), it is medium-bodied, with strong lemon, lime and slight passionfruit flavours, showing good delicacy and freshness, and a long, tight but not austere finish. Fine value.

 DRY $19 V+

Wither Hills Single Vineyard Kerseley Riesling   (★★★☆)

The debut 2009 vintage (★★★☆) is a floral, finely balanced Marlborough wine with fresh citrus and stone-fruit flavours and a dryish, crisp finish.

MED/DRY $20 AV

Wither Hills Single Vineyard Rarangi Riesling   (★★★)

Grown in Marlborough, the 2009 vintage (★★★) is lemony, appley and crisp, in a dryish style with refreshing acidity.

MED/DRY $20 –V

Woollaston Mahana Nelson Riesling   (★★★★☆)

The debut 2010 vintage (★★★★☆) of this 'ultra-premium' label was hand-picked and made in a medium-sweet style (45 grams/litre of residual sugar). Rich and light (10.5 per cent alcohol), it has concentrated, citrusy, slightly honeyed flavours, with hints of apricots and spices, good complexity, fresh acidity, and loads of personality. Drink now or cellar.

Vintage	10
WR	6
Drink	11-15

MED $24 V+

Woollaston Nelson Riesling   ★★★★

The 2010 vintage (★★★★) is a delicious drink-young style. From hand-picked grapes, it is very fresh, crisp and lively, with strong lemon/lime flavours, hints of apricot and passionfruit, and gentle sweetness (26 grams/litre of residual sugar) adding an easy-drinking appeal.

Vintage	10
WR	6
Drink	11-15

MED $19 V+

Yealands Estate Single Vineyard Awatere Valley Marlborough Riesling   ★★★★

Estate-grown at Seaview, the refined 2010 vintage (★★★★) is a still-youthful, off-dry style with excellent delicacy and depth. Vibrant and tangy, it is medium-bodied, with strong, lemony, slightly appley and limey flavours, crisp and lingering. The 2011 (★★★), tasted in its infancy, is very tightly structured, with citrusy, peachy flavours and firm acid spine. It needs time; open 2013+.

MED/DRY $26 –V

Roussanne

Roussanne is a traditional ingredient in the white wines of France's northern Rhône Valley, where typically it is blended with the more widely grown Marsanne. Known for its fine acidity and 'haunting aroma', likened by some tasters to herbal tea, it is also found in the south of France, Italy and Australia, but this late-ripening variety is extremely scarce in New Zealand, with only 2 hectares bearing in 2012.

Garden of Light Roussanne

(★★★★)

The 2010 vintage (★★★★) was grown at Matakana and fermented in old French oak barrels. Pale straw, it is rich, peachy and dry, in a Chardonnay-like style, fleshy and concentrated. Slightly buttery, nutty, spicy and honeyed, with good complexity, it's a serious 'food' wine, with plenty of personality. (Note: the quality rating is very subjective, as this is only the country's second example of the variety, after the Grove Mill Winemakers Reserve 2001.)

DRY $39 –V

Sauvignon Blanc

Sauvignon Blanc is New Zealand's key calling card in the wine markets of the world. At the 2011 *Decanter* World Wine Awards, in London, the trophy for Best Sauvignon Blanc under £10 was awarded to Waimea Nelson Sauvignon Blanc 2010, and the over-£10 trophy went to Vavasour Awatere Valley Marlborough Sauvignon Blanc 2010 (the year before, both trophies were claimed by Chilean Sauvignon Blancs). In *Winestate*'s 2010 Wine of the Year Awards, judged in Australia, the top five places in the Sauvignon Blanc category all went to New Zealand wines – headed by the 2010 Vavasour.

The rise to international stardom of New Zealand Sauvignon Blanc was remarkably swift. Government Viticulturist Romeo Bragato imported the first Sauvignon Blanc vines from Italy in 1906, but it was not until 1974 that Matua Valley marketed New Zealand's first varietal Sauvignon Blanc. Montana established its first Sauvignon Blanc vines in Marlborough in 1975, allowing Sauvignon Blanc to get into full commercial swing in the early 1980s. In the year to June 2011, 84 per cent by volume of all New Zealand's wine exports were based on Sauvignon Blanc.

Sauvignon Blanc is by far New Zealand's most extensively planted variety, in 2012 comprising well over 50 per cent of the bearing national vineyard. Over 85 per cent of all vines are concentrated in Marlborough, with further significant plantings in Hawke's Bay, Nelson, Wairarapa and Waipara. Between 2005 and 2012, the area of bearing Sauvignon Blanc vines will surge from 7277 hectares to 17,297 hectares.

The flavour of New Zealand Sauvignon Blanc varies according to fruit ripeness. At the herbaceous, under-ripe end of the spectrum, vegetal and fresh-cut grass aromas hold sway; riper wines show capsicum, gooseberry and melon-like characters; very ripe fruit displays tropical-fruit flavours.

Intensely herbaceous Sauvignon Blancs are not hard to make in the viticulturally cool climate of the South Island and the lower North Island (Wairarapa). 'The challenge faced by New Zealand winemakers is to keep those herbaceous characters in check,' says Kevin Judd, of Greywacke Vineyards, formerly chief winemaker at Cloudy Bay. 'It would be foolish to suggest that these herbaceous notes detract from the wines; in fact I am sure that this fresh edge and intense varietal aroma are the reason for its recent international popularity. The better of these wines have these herbaceous characters in context and in balance with the more tropical-fruit characters associated with riper fruit.'

There are two key styles of Sauvignon Blanc produced in New Zealand. Wines handled entirely in stainless steel tanks – by far the most common – place their accent squarely on their fresh, direct fruit flavours. Alternatively, many top labels are handled principally in tanks, but 5 to 10 per cent of the blend is barrel-fermented, adding a touch of complexity without subduing the wine's fresh, punchy fruit aromas and flavours.

Another major style difference is regionally based: the crisp, incisively flavoured wines of Marlborough contrast with the softer, less pungently herbaceous Hawke's Bay style. These are wines to drink young (traditionally within 18 months of the vintage) while they are irresistibly fresh, aromatic and tangy, although the oak-matured, more complex wines sometimes found in Hawke's Bay (currently an endangered species, despite their quality) can mature well for several years.

The recent swing from corks to screw-caps has also boosted the longevity of the wines. Rather than running out of steam, many are now highly enjoyable at two years old.

¼ Acre Wines Hawke's Bay Sauvignon Blanc (★★★☆)

From Rod McDonald, the 2010 vintage (★★★☆) is ripely scented, fleshy and sweet-fruited, with very good depth of tropical-fruit flavours and a well-rounded finish.

DRY $22 AV

3 Stones Marlborough Sauvignon Blanc   ★★★☆

The 2010 vintage (★★★☆) is a fleshy, mouthfilling wine, ripe and smooth, with citrusy, limey flavours, a slightly oily texture and good concentration. The 2011 (★★★☆) is aromatic, with strong, crisp tropical-fruit and herbaceous flavours, fresh and zingy.

Vintage	11	DRY $19 V+
WR	5	
Drink	11-13	

900 Grapes Marlborough Sauvignon Blanc   (★★★)

From Matua Valley, the debut 2011 vintage (★★★) has 'sweaty armpit' aromas, leading into a fleshy, easy-drinking wine with ripe, distinctly tropical-fruit flavours, showing moderate length.

 DRY $20 –V

12,000 Miles Sauvignon Blanc   ★★★☆

From Gladstone Vineyard, the 2011 vintage (★★★☆) is a full-bodied Wairarapa wine, tank-fermented to dryness. Fresh and lively, it has crisp, ripe tropical-fruit flavours, showing good intensity.

 DRY $17 V+

Ake Ake Sauvignon Blanc   (★★☆)

Grown in Marlborough but made at the Ake Ake winery in Northland, the 2011 vintage (★★☆) was handled without oak. It's a medium-bodied wine (11.5 per cent alcohol), fresh and ripely flavoured, offering smooth, easy drinking.

 DRY $20 –V

Alana Estate Martinborough Sauvignon Blanc   ★★★☆

The 2010 vintage (★★★☆) is a single-vineyard wine, very crisp and lively, in a ripely herbaceous style with fresh, strong melon and green-capsicum flavours. Ready.

 DRY $20 AV

Alexia Wairarapa Sauvignon Blanc   ★★★☆

From Jane Cooper, winemaker at Matahiwi, the 2010 vintage (★★★★) is ripely scented and smooth, with passionfruit and lime flavours, showing excellent freshness, delicacy and depth. It's already delicious.

Vintage	10	DRY $18 V+
WR	5	
Drink	11-12	

Allan Scott Marlborough Sauvignon Blanc

The Scotts aim for a 'ripe tropical fruit' Sauvignon – a style typical of the Rapaura area of the Wairau Valley, where most of the company's vineyards are clustered. The 2010 vintage (★★★★) is freshly scented and bone-dry, with ripe sweet-fruit flavours of melons and capsicums. It's a mouthfilling wine, crisp and racy, with excellent delicacy and purity.

Vintage	10	09	08	DRY $18 V+
WR	6	6	6	
Drink	11-12	P	P	

Allan Scott Millstone Marlborough Sauvignon Blanc ★★★

From a company-owned vineyard certified as in 'conversion to organic', the 2009 vintage (★★★) is $10 cheaper than its predecessor. A medium-bodied (11 per cent alcohol), dry wine (5 per cent oak-aged), it is crisp and dry, with tight, minerally characters, showing some potential.

Vintage	09	08	DRY $20 –V
WR	6	6	
Drink	11-13	11-12	

Allan Scott Moorlands Marlborough Sauvignon Blanc ★★★★

Based on vines planted in 1980 next to the winery at Rapaura, the 2009 vintage (★★★★) was tank-fermented and matured for 10 months in old oak barrels, with regular lees-stirring. It's a crisp, bone-dry style, tightly structured and mouthfilling, with fresh, ripe tropical-fruit flavours and leesy, nutty notes adding complexity.

Vintage	10	09	08	DRY $26 –V
WR	5	6	6	
Drink	11-15	11-13	11-12	

Alpha Domus The Pilot Hawke's Bay Sauvignon Blanc ★★★

The 2010 vintage (★★★) is a typical regional style with mouthfilling body, ripe tropical-fruit flavours, showing a hint of pineapple, and a fully dry, rounded finish.

Vintage	10	09	08	DRY $20 –V
WR	6	6	6	
Drink	11-14	11-13	11-12	

Amisfield Central Otago Sauvignon Blanc ★★★★

The fresh, vibrant 2011 vintage (★★★☆), estate-grown at Lowburn, was mostly handled in tanks, but 5 per cent of the blend was fermented in old French oak barriques. It's a stylish wine, full-bodied, with an aromatic bouquet, citrus-fruit, passionfruit and lime flavours, showing a touch of complexity, moderate intensity, and a dry, rounded finish.

Vintage	11	10	09	DRY $25 AV
WR	6	6	5	
Drink	11-14	11-12	P	

Amisfield Fumé Blanc   (★★★☆)

The 2009 vintage (★★★☆) was estate-grown and hand-picked in Central Otago, barrel-fermented with indigenous yeasts, and oak-aged for 15 months. It has an assertive oak influence, but also impressive weight, ripeness and roundness, in a nutty, creamy style with considerable complexity.

 DRY $35 –V

Anchorage Nelson Sauvignon Blanc   ★★★☆

Estate-grown at Motueka, this wine offers good value. The 2010 (★★★☆) is a crisp, punchy, dry style (2.7 grams/litre of residual sugar), with vibrant tropical-fruit and herbaceous aromas and flavours, showing very good freshness and depth.

 DRY $19 V+

Anchorage Winemakers Release Nelson Sauvignon Blanc   ★★★

The 2010 vintage (★★★) is a slightly off-dry style (5.4 grams/litre of residual sugar), crisp, grassy and punchy, with good intensity of nettley, green-edged flavours. If you like a strongly herbaceous style of Sauvignon Blanc, this is for you.

 MED/DRY $19 AV

Ant Moore Marlborough Sauvignon Blanc   (★★★★)

The tightly structured 2010 vintage (★★★★) is a crisp, nettley blend of Awatere and Waihopai Valley grapes, partly barrel-fermented. It has a lifted bouquet and good intensity of citrusy, grassy, dry flavours that linger well.

 DRY $23 AV

Aotea Nelson Sauvignon Blanc   (★★★☆)

From Seifried, the 2011 vintage (★★★☆) has replaced the former Winemakers Collection label. Finely poised, it is a medium-bodied wine (12 per cent alcohol), ripely flavoured, dry and crisp, with very good freshness, delicacy and depth, but needs time; open mid-2012+.

Vintage	11	DRY $23 –V
WR	6	
Drink	11-12	

Ara Pathway Marlborough Sauvignon Blanc   ★★★☆

Estate-grown in the lower Waihopai Valley, the 2010 vintage (★★★☆) is a mouthfilling, fully dry wine, with ripe melon, lime and green-capsicum flavours. Crisp and slightly minerally, it has very good weight, balance and depth.

 DRY $19 V+

Ara Resolute Marlborough Sauvignon Blanc ★★★★

From the heart of the Waihopai Valley site, this wine is tank-fermented and given lengthy lees-aging. The 2009 vintage (★★★★) is tightly structured, with ripe sweet-fruit flavours of melons and limes, showing good vigour and intensity. Crisp, minerally and dry, it's a cellaring style.

Vintage	09	
WR	7	
Drink	11-12	

DRY $28 –V

Ara Select Blocks Marlborough Sauvignon Blanc (★★★★☆)

The 2010 vintage (★★★★☆) is quietly satisfying, mouthfilling and fleshy, with tropical-fruit flavours that build well across the palate, a minerally undercurrent and a dry, rounded, lasting finish. Great drinkability.

DRY $25 V+

Ara Single Estate Marlborough Sauvignon Blanc (★★★★)

Weighty, with tropical-fruit flavours, reminiscent of passionfruit, the 2010 vintage (★★★★) is a restrained, ripe style with fresh acidity, very good richness and harmony, and a dry, finely balanced finish.

DRY $22 V+

Artisan The Sands Block Marlborough Sauvignon Blanc ★★★★

Always good value, this single-vineyard wine is grown at the eastern (cooler) end of the Wairau Valley. The 2010 vintage (★★★★) is mouthfilling, with good intensity of tropical-fruit flavours, fresh and vibrant, a sliver of sweetness (4 grams/litre of residual sugar) and crisp acidity. Delicious, easy drinking.

DRY $19 V+

Ash Ridge Hawke's Bay Barrel Fermented Sauvignon Blanc ★★★☆

Grown in The Triangle, the 2010 vintage (★★★★) is a single-vineyard wine, fermented and lees-aged for five months in old oak barrels. It's a classic regional style, weighty, ripe and rich, with good complexity and generous tropical-fruit flavours.

Vintage	10	
WR	6	
Drink	11-14	

DRY $30 –V

Ashwell Sauvignon Blanc ★★★☆

This Martinborough wine is typically good, with mouthfilling body and ripely herbaceous flavours, fresh and strong. The 2011 vintage (★★★☆) is fresh-scented, with melon/lime flavours, showing very good vibrancy, delicacy and depth.

DRY $20 AV

Askerne Hawke's Bay Barrel Fermented Sauvignon Blanc   (★★★☆)

Mouthfilling and dry, the 2010 vintage (★★★☆) has very satisfying depth of tropical-fruit flavours, ripe and rounded. It shows good weight and texture, with some complexity, but in its youth is slightly oaky (it was fermented and aged for 10 months in French oak casks, 17 per cent new); open mid-2012+.

Vintage	10
WR	6
Drink	12-14

 DRY $20 AV

Askerne Hawke's Bay Sauvignon Blanc   ★★★

The 2011 vintage (★★☆) was mostly handled in tanks, but 2 per cent of the blend was barrel-fermented. Made in a bone-dry style, it is medium-bodied, with fresh, ripe tropical-fruit flavours and a smooth finish.

Vintage	11	10	09	08
WR	5	6	6	6
Drink	12-13	11-12	P	P

 DRY $16 V+

Astrolabe Discovery Kekerengu Coast Sauvignon Blanc   ★★★☆

From two vineyards at Kekerengu, half-way between Blenheim and Kaikoura, the 2010 vintage (★★★☆) was mostly handled in tanks, but a small portion was barrel-fermented. It's a full-bodied, herbaceous wine, showing considerable development, but also some complexity and richness.

 DRY $26 –V

Astrolabe Valleys Awatere Valley Sauvignon Blanc   (★★★★)

The 2011 vintage (★★★★), grown at two sites, is a very ripe style, fresh and full-bodied, with generous tropical-fruit flavours to the fore, a herbal undercurrent, and a rounded, fully dry finish.

DRY 25 AV

Astrolabe Vineyards Taihoa Vineyard Sauvignon Blanc   ★★★★☆

The 2010 vintage (★★★★☆), grown at Kekerengu, in south-eastern Marlborough, was fermented with indigenous yeasts in old French oak barrels. Weighty, it's a lively, non-herbaceous style, minerally, with a rich, complex bouquet and fresh pear, grapefruit and lime flavours, dry and long.

 DRY $37 –V

Astrolabe Voyage Marlborough Sauvignon Blanc   ★★★★☆

Grown at sites from the Wairau Valley to Kekerengu, the 2010 vintage (★★★★) shows some development. It's a clearly herbaceous style, fleshy, dry and strongly flavoured, drinking well now.

 DRY $21 V+

Ata Rangi Martinborough Sauvignon Blanc ★★★★☆

A consistently attractive wine, with ripe tropical-fruit rather than grassy, herbaceous flavours. The 2010 vintage (★★★★☆) was mostly handled in tanks, but 10 per cent of the blend was fermented and lees-aged in seasoned (three-year-old) oak barrels. Weighty and sweet-fruited, it is vibrantly fruity, with strong melon, passionfruit and lime flavours to the fore, a hint of oak adding richness, fresh acidity, and excellent depth, complexity and harmony.

Vintage	10	09	08
WR	7	6	7
Drink	11-13	11-12	P

 DRY $24 V+

Auntsfield Estate Marlborough Sauvignon Blanc ★★★★☆

Grown and hand-harvested on the south side of the Wairau Valley, on the property where Marlborough's first wines were made in the 1870s, the 2010 vintage (★★★★★) was 15 per cent fermented and lees-aged in seasoned French oak barriques. It's a very classy wine, highly scented, with penetrating melon and green-capsicum flavours, a very subtle seasoning of oak adding complexity, a crisp, dry finish – and loads of personality.

Vintage	10	09	08
WR	7	7	7
Drink	11-12	P	P

 DRY $23 V+

Auntsfield Reserve Marlborough Sauvignon Blanc ★★★★★

The 2009 vintage (★★★★☆) was 50 per cent barrel-fermented and fully barrel-aged, all in old oak. An unusually complex wine, it is richly and ripely scented, with a lovely array of deep melon, pear, citrus-fruit and spice flavours, a subtle seasoning of oak and a very smooth, off-dry (7.5 grams/litre of residual sugar) finish.

 MED/DRY $34 AV

Babich Black Label Marlborough Sauvignon Blanc ★★★★☆

Sold principally in restaurants, this is a consistently impressive wine. The 2011 vintage (★★★★) was mostly handled in tanks; a small part of the blend was fermented in seasoned oak casks. Delicious from the start, it has fresh, strong tropical-fruit flavours in a very non-herbaceous style, fleshy, ripe and rounded.

 DRY $25 V+

Babich Individual Vineyards Cowslip Valley Marlborough Sauvignon Blanc ★★★★☆

Estate-grown in the Waihopai Valley, the 2010 vintage (★★★★★) has real power through the palate. Weighty and fleshy, with generous tropical-fruit flavours, it is also fresh, crisp and minerally, with lovely body, vibrancy and texture and a finely poised, dry, long finish.

DRY $25 V+

Babich Individual Vineyards Headwaters Organic Block
Marlborough Sauvignon Blanc   (★★★☆)

Certified organic, the 2011 vintage (★★★☆) is a subtle, dry wine, grown in the Wairau Valley. Still a baby, it is weighty and zingy, with fresh, ripe melon/lime flavours, very delicate and pure. A quietly satisfying wine, it needs time; open mid-2012+.

DRY $25 –V

Babich Lone Tree Hawke's Bay Sauvignon Blanc   ★★☆

Grown in Hawke's Bay, the 2010 vintage (★★☆) is fresh and lively, with decent depth of ripe, citrusy, limey fruit flavours and a dry, rounded finish.

DRY $16 AV

Babich Marlborough Sauvignon Blanc   ★★★★

Joe Babich favours 'a fuller, riper, softer style of Sauvignon Blanc. It's not a jump out of the glass style, but the wines develop well.' The latest releases reflect a rising input of grapes from the company's Cowslip Valley Vineyard in the Waihopai Valley, which gives less herbaceous fruit characters than its other Marlborough vineyards. The 2011 vintage (★★★★) is ripely scented, with a distinct suggestion of 'sweaty armpit'. Full-bodied and dry, it's a very non-herbaceous style, with strong yet delicate, well-ripened flavours of passionfruit and lime, a rounded finish and great drinkability.

DRY $20 V+

Babich Winemakers Reserve Marlborough Sauvignon Blanc   ★★★★☆

A stylish example of gently oaked Sauvignon Blanc. Estate-grown in the Waihopai and Awatere valleys, it is mostly handled in tanks, but 10 per cent is fermented and lees-aged in French oak barriques. The 2011 (★★★★☆) is fleshy and finely textured, with strong, very ripe fruit flavours, a subtle seasoning of oak adding richness and complexity, and a dry, long finish. Best drinking mid-2012+.

DRY $30 –V

Baby Doll Marlborough Sauvignon Blanc   (★★☆)

From Yealands Estate, the 2010 vintage (★★☆) is mouthfilling, with grassy aromas and flavours in a strongly herbaceous style, crisp and dry.

DRY $17 –V

Barking Hedge Marlborough Sauvignon Blanc   (★★★☆)

From Crighton Estate, in the Wairau Valley, the 2009 vintage (★★★☆) is mouthfilling and crisp, with strong gooseberry/lime flavours and good acid spine. It's a fresh, lively wine, offering good value.

DRY $18 V+

Bascand Marlborough Sauvignon Blanc   (★★★☆)

A strongly herbaceous style, the 2009 vintage (★★★☆) was estate-grown at Rapaura, in the Wairau Valley. Aromatic and lively, with very good body and depth of melon and green-capsicum flavours, crisp and finely balanced, it's bargain-priced.

DRY $17 V+

Bel Echo by Clos Henri Marlborough Sauvignon Blanc   ★★★☆

This wine is grown in the more clay-based soils at Clos Henri (the top wine, sold as 'Clos Henri', is from the stoniest blocks). The 2010 vintage (★★★★) was hand-picked, tank-fermented and matured on its yeast lees for eight months. The best yet, it is weighty and fleshy, with sweet-fruit delights and strong, ripely herbaceous flavours, slightly minerally and well-rounded. It's drinking well now.

Vintage	10	09	08	07	06
WR	6	6	7	5	6
Drink	11-15	11-14	11-13	P	P

DRY $24 –V

Bellbird Spring Block Eight Waipara Sauvignon Blanc   ★★★★

The tight, minerally, complex 2010 vintage (★★★★) was hand-picked and fermented with indigenous yeasts in old oak barriques. It has slightly 'funky' aromas, with a subtle wood seasoning and good intensity of grapefruit, lime, spice and nettle flavours, lively and lingering. Open mid-2012+.

Vintage	10	09
WR	5	6
Drink	11-14	11-13

DRY $32 –V

Belmonte Marlborough Sauvignon Blanc   ★★★☆

From a company with family links to John Forrest, the 2009 vintage (★★★) is vibrantly fruity, in a medium-bodied style with good depth of smooth, ripe tropical-fruit flavours, finely balanced for easy drinking.

DRY $17 V+

Bird Old Schoolhouse Vineyard Marlborough Sauvignon Blanc   ★★★☆

Estate-grown in the Omaka Valley, the 2010 vintage (★★★☆) is crisp and ripely herbaceous, in a fresh, full-bodied style with very good depth of flavour and a dry, tangy finish.

DRY $24 –V

Black Barn Vineyards Hawke's Bay Tuki Tuki Valley Sauvignon Blanc   (★★★☆)

Handled in tanks, with some use of indigenous yeasts, the easy-drinking 2009 vintage (★★★☆) is mouthfilling and smooth, with ripe tropical-fruit flavours, showing very good delicacy and depth.

DRY $22 AV

Blackbirch Marlborough Sauvignon Blanc   (★★★)

From The New Zealand Wine Company (Grove Mill, Sanctuary), the 2010 vintage (★★★) is mouthfilling, fresh and punchy, with tropical-fruit and herbaceous flavours, crisp and lively.

DRY $17 AV

Black Cottage Marlborough Sauvignon Blanc   ★★★☆

From Two Rivers, the 2011 vintage (★★★) is a blend of fruit from the Wairau and Awatere valleys. It's an easy-drinking style, vibrantly fruity and smooth, with fresh, ripely herbaceous flavours, showing good depth.

DRY $18 V+

Blackenbrook Vineyard Nelson Sauvignon Blanc   ★★★★

Estate-grown at Tasman, harvested by hand at 23 brix and lees-aged in tanks, the 2011 vintage (★★★★) is a basically dry style (4.8 grams/litre of residual sugar). Very aromatic and zingy, it is vibrantly fruity, with pure, penetrating passionfruit and lime flavours, woven with appetising acidity.

Vintage	11	10	09	08
WR	6	7	6	6
Drink	11-12	P	P	P

DRY $22 V+

Bladen Marlborough Sauvignon Blanc   ★★★★

This label shows steadily rising form. The 2011 vintage (★★★★), grown in the Bladen and Hunter vineyards, is fleshy and rounded, with ripe tropical-fruit flavours, fresh, dry and concentrated. It's a generous, finely poised wine, enjoyable from the start.

DRY $21 V+

Blind River Marlborough Sauvignon Blanc   ★★★★☆

The 2011 vintage (★★★★☆) was estate-grown in the Awatere Valley and mostly handled in tanks; 10 per cent was fermented in seasoned oak barriques. It's an intensely aromatic wine, punchy and crisp, with gooseberry, passionfruit and lime flavours, slightly nettley and nutty, good complexity and a dry, lingering finish.

Vintage	10	09	08	07
WR	7	7	6	6
Drink	11-16	11-15	P	11-14

DRY $25 V+

Bloody Bay Marlborough Sauvignon Blanc   (★★☆)

Showing some development, the 2009 vintage is full-bodied and ripe-tasting, with decent depth and a dry, rounded finish. Ready.

DRY $17 –V

Boatshed Bay by Goldwater Marlborough Sauvignon Blanc   ★★★☆

The 2010 vintage (★★★☆) has a slightly nettley bouquet. Mouthfilling and dry, it has strong, green-edged flavours, crisp and lively. The 2011 (★★★☆) is fresh, direct and punchy, with tropical-fruit and herbaceous flavours, crisp and lively. Fine value.

DRY $18 V+

Boreham Wood Single Vineyard Marlborough Sauvignon Blanc   ★★★

Grown in the Awatere Valley, the 2011 vintage (★★★) is mouthfilling, with good depth of fresh, lively tropical-fruit flavours, a herbal undercurrent, and a smooth finish. Priced very sharply.

DRY $14 V+

Borthwick Vineyard Wairarapa Sauvignon Blanc   ★★★★

The 2009 vintage (★★★★☆) is a deliciously fresh and punchy wine from Gladstone, 25 per cent barrel-fermented (in old oak). It is weighty and concentrated, with rich, ripe sweet-fruit flavours, a herbal undercurrent and a crisp, bone-dry finish.

DRY $23 AV

Boulder Bank Road Marlborough Sauvignon Blanc   ★★★☆

From Vernon Family Estate, this wine is estate-grown at a coastal site on Vernon Station, above the Wairau Lagoons. The 2010 vintage (★★★☆) is freshly aromatic and full-bodied, with tropical-fruit and green-capsicum flavours, vibrant and strong. Fine value.

DRY $17 V+

Bouldevines Granite Garden Reserve Sauvignon Blanc   (★★★☆)

The 2009 vintage (★★★☆) is a fleshy, ripe and rounded wine, grown in a rocky seam on a small ridge on the south side of the Wairau Valley. Mouthfilling, it has tropical-fruit flavours, moderate acidity and a dry finish, with very good texture and depth.

DRY $25 –V

Bouldevines Marlborough Sauvignon Blanc   ★★★☆

The 2010 vintage (★★★☆), harvested at over 24 brix, is fleshy and bone-dry, with good depth of ripe, non-herbaceous tropical-fruit flavours, enlivened by crisp acidity.

Vintage	10
WR	6
Drink	11-13

DRY $20 AV

Boundary Vineyards Matapiro Road Sauvignon Blanc/Pinot Gris   (★★★☆)

Grown in Hawke's Bay, the debut 2011 vintage (★★★☆) is instantly appealing, with a fresh and lively marriage of peachy, spicy Pinot Gris and ripely herbaceous Sauvignon Blanc. The blend works well.

DRY $20 AV

Boundary Vineyards Rapaura Road Marlborough Sauvignon Blanc   ★★★☆

From Pernod Ricard NZ, this is typically a ripe, rounded style with distinctly tropical-fruit flavours, smooth and strong. The 2010 vintage (★★★☆) is slightly 'greener', with nettley aromas and fresh, strong tropical-fruit and herbaceous flavours that linger well.

DRY $20 AV

Brams Run Marlborough Sauvignon Blanc

The 2009 vintage (★★★☆) is crisp and gently aromatic, with vibrant tropical-fruit and herbaceous flavours, finely balanced and strong.

DRY $20 V+

Brancott Estate 'B' Brancott Marlborough Sauvignon Blanc   ★★★★★

Formerly sold under the Montana brand, this wine is promoted by Pernod Ricard NZ as 'our finest expression of Marlborough's most famous variety' – and lives up to its billing. 'Palate weight, concentration and longevity' are the goals. It has traditionally been grown in the company's sweeping Brancott Vineyard, on the south, slightly cooler side of the Wairau Valley, and a small portion is fermented and lees-aged in French oak barriques and cuves, to add 'some toast and spice as well as palate richness'. It matures well for several years, developing nutty, minerally, toasty flavours in some vintages and fresh asparagus notes in others. The 2010 (★★★★★), sourced from 'key Marlborough vineyards', is mouthfilling, sweet-fruited and highly refined, in a more complex style than most. It has fresh, searching tropical-fruit flavours, showing lovely richness, delicacy, harmony and length. The 2011 vintage, tasted prior to bottling (and so not rated), is weighty, well-rounded and concentrated, with some nettley notes, but an accent on generous, ripe tropical-fruit flavours.

DRY $35 AV

Brancott Estate Living Land Series Marlborough Sauvignon Blanc   ★★★☆

From a Wairau Valley vineyard under conversion to organic, the 2010 vintage (★★★☆) is fresh and lively, with very good depth of ripe melon/lime flavours, smooth and dry. The 2011, tasted prior to bottling (and so not rated), is ripely herbaceous, very fresh and punchy.

DRY $20 AV

Brancott Estate Reserve Marlborough Sauvignon Blanc   ★★★★

Up to and including the 2009 vintage, this wine was branded 'Montana'. It is designed to highlight the fresh, herbaceous style of Sauvignon Blanc that Pernod Ricard NZ achieves on the south side of the Wairau Valley, compared to its more tropical fruit-flavoured Stoneleigh Sauvignon Blanc, grown on the north side of the valley. The 2010 (★★★★), the first to carry the Brancott Estate brand, is crisp and dry, tightly structured and slightly minerally, with fresh, pure varietal flavours, showing good intensity. The 2011 (★★★★) 'Limited Edition Pack', released specifically for the 2011 Rugby World Cup, is an identical wine to the main commercial release. It's a classic regional style, deliciously fresh and racy, mingling tropical-fruit and herbaceous aromas and flavours, slightly nettley, crisp, dry and punchy.

Vintage	11	10	09	08	07
WR	7	7	7	6	6
Drink	11-14	11-13	11-12	P	P

DRY $24 AV

Breakers Bay Nelson Sauvignon Blanc

From Anchorage, the 2009 vintage (★★★☆) is a good buy. Fresh and nettley, it is aromatic and lively, with good varietal character and drink-young appeal.

DRY $12 V+

Brightside Nelson Sauvignon Blanc ★★☆

The 2010 vintage (★★★) from Kaimira is crisp and strongly herbaceous, with some riper tropical-fruit notes. It shows good vigour, freshness and balance, with a smooth (5 grams/litre of residual sugar) finish.

MED/DRY $16 AV

Brightwater Vineyards Lord Rutherford Sauvignon Blanc ★★★★☆

Grown in Nelson, the 2011 vintage (★★★★★) is very powerful and punchy, with ripe 'sweaty armpit' aromas and fresh, ripe, concentrated tropical-fruit flavours, crisp, dry (3 grams/litre of residual sugar) and long.

Vintage	11	10
WR	7	6
Drink	11-14	11-13

 DRY $25 V+

Brightwater Vineyards Nelson Sauvignon Blanc ★★★★

Grown on the Waimea Plains, this is a consistently enjoyable, ripely flavoured wine, fresh and punchy. The 2011 vintage (★★★★) is dry (4 grams/litre of residual sugar) and mouthfilling, with smooth, ripe tropical-fruit flavours, fresh and concentrated.

Vintage	11	10
WR	7	6
Drink	11-13	11-12

 DRY $20 V+

Brookfields Ohiti Estate Hawke's Bay Sauvignon Blanc ★★★

The 2009 vintage (★★★) is mouthfilling and smooth, with good depth of vibrant tropical-fruit flavours, and a sliver of sweetness (5 grams/litre of residual sugar) balanced by fresh, crisp acidity.

Vintage	09	08
WR	7	7
Drink	11-12	P

MED/DRY $19 AV

Burnt Spur Martinborough Sauvignon Blanc ★★★

The 2010 vintage (★★★☆) is a single-vineyard wine, lively and lingering, with fresh, ripe, citrusy, limey flavours, and hints of passionfruit and herbs. (From Martinborough Vineyard.)

DRY $18 AV

Cable Bay Marlborough Sauvignon Blanc ★★★★

This Waiheke Island-based producer wants a wine with 'restraint and textural interest, to enjoy with food'. The 2011 vintage (★★★★) was grown in the Omaka Valley and handled entirely in tanks. It's a weighty, sweet-fruited wine with punchy, ripe tropical-fruit flavours, dry and rich.

Vintage	11	10
WR	7	7
Drink	11-14	11-12

 DRY $25 AV

Cable Bay Marlborough Selection Sauvignon Blanc ★★★

(Formerly sold under the Culley brand.) The 2010 vintage (★★★☆) is fleshy, with ripe tropical-fruit flavours, showing very good depth, and a crisp, dry finish. The 2011 (★★★) is medium-bodied, with fresh, ripe melon and slight capsicum flavours, showing good vigour, and a smooth finish.

Vintage	11
WR	7
Drink	11-13

DRY $17 AV

Camshorn Waipara Sauvignon Blanc ★★★☆

From Pernod Ricard NZ, the 2010 vintage (★★★☆) is lively, with 'tomato stalk' aromas, very good depth of fresh, zingy melon/lime flavours and a crisp, dry finish.

DRY $27 –V

Carrick Central Otago Sauvignon Blanc ★★★☆

Grown at Bannockburn, this wine is mostly handled in tanks, but partly oak-aged. The 2010 vintage (★★★☆) was hand-picked and 30 per cent barrel-fermented. Punchy and crisp, it is dry (3.6 grams/litre of residual sugar) and aromatic, with slightly nettley, melon/lime flavours and a touch of complexity.

DRY $20 AV

Catalina Sounds Marlborough Sauvignon Blanc ★★★★☆

The 2010 vintage (★★★★☆) was mostly handled in tanks, with extended lees-aging, but 7 per cent of the blend was barrel-fermented. Fresh, aromatic and punchy, it is full-bodied, with a touch of complexity and fresh, dry (2.6 grams/litre of residual sugar) gooseberry, grapefruit and lime flavours, showing excellent purity, vigour and length.

DRY $24 V+

Cathedral Cove Marlborough Sauvignon Blanc (★★☆)

From One Tree Hill Vineyards, a division of Morton Estate, the 2009 vintage (★★☆) offers very good value. Medium to full-bodied, it is crisp, with decent depth of gooseberry and lime flavours.

DRY $8 V+

Charles Wiffen Marlborough Sauvignon Blanc ★★★

The 2009 vintage (★★★) is crisp, with gooseberry and lime flavours, slightly minerally and showing good depth.

DRY $20 –V

Cheeky Little Sav ★★☆

From Babich, the 2011 vintage (★★☆) is a low-priced, solid Marlborough wine, with citrusy, grassy flavours, fresh, crisp and lively.

DRY $12 V+

Church Road Cuve Series Sauvignon Blanc   (★★★★☆)

The 2009 vintage (★★★★★) is a superb Hawke's Bay wine. Fleshy and rich, it was estate-grown in the Redstone Vineyard, in The Triangle, hand-harvested, and fermented and lees-aged in French oak barriques (30 per cent new). Powerful, with highly concentrated tropical-fruit flavours and notable complexity and harmony, it's highly reminiscent of a fine white Bordeaux.

 DRY $29 AV

Church Road Hawke's Bay Sauvignon Blanc   ★★★★

Aiming for a wine that is 'more refined and softer than a typical New Zealand Sauvignon Blanc, with restrained varietal characters', the 2009 vintage (★★★★) was based mostly (87 per cent) on aromatic fruit from Pernod Ricard NZ's elevated Matapiro site (300 metres above sea level), blended with grapes from a warmer site at Havelock North. Partly barrel-fermented (13 per cent), it has slightly sweaty aromas leading into a mouthfilling wine, fresh and crisp, with sweet-fruit delights and ripe tropical-fruit flavours, dry and generous. The 2010 (★★★★), grown at Matapiro (92 per cent) and in the company's Redstone Vineyard in The Triangle, is similar, with fresh, ripe tropical-fruit flavours, showing good complexity and richness.

Vintage	10	09	08	07
WR	7	7	7	7
Drink	11-13	11-12	P	P

DRY $27 –V

Church Road Reserve Hawke's Bay Sauvignon Blanc   (★★★★★)

Fleshy, rich and complex, the deeply satisfying 2010 vintage (★★★★★) is an outstanding example of wood-aged Sauvignon Blanc, in the mould of white Bordeaux. Estate-grown, mostly in the Redstone Vineyard, in The Triangle, and fermented with indigenous yeasts in French oak barriques (30 per cent new), it's a powerful, very full-bodied wine with concentrated, ripe stone-fruit flavours, integrated oak, and a long, slightly creamy finish. Best drinking mid-2012+.

Vintage	10
WR	7
Drink	12-15

DRY $37 AV

Churton Marlborough Sauvignon Blanc   ★★★★☆

This small producer aims for a style that 'combines the renowned flavour and aromatic intensity of Marlborough fruit with the finesse and complexity of fine European wines'. The 2010 vintage (★★★★☆) was (for the first time) entirely estate-grown, on an elevated site in the Waihopai Valley, and 10 per cent of the blend was barrel-fermented (in large, seasoned French oak casks). It's a full-bodied wine with ripe tropical-fruit flavours, a touch of complexity, and gentle acidity. It shows good mouthfeel and texture, with a bone-dry, well-rounded finish.

Vintage	10	09	08	07	06
WR	7	7	6	7	6
Drink	11-18	11-17	11-15	11-13	11-13

 DRY $27 AV

Cicada Marlborough Sauvignon Blanc   (★★☆)

The 2009 vintage (★★☆), grown at Rapaura, is a medium to full-bodied wine with solid depth of ripely herbaceous flavours, crisp and dry.

DRY $18 –V

C.J. Pask Roy's Hill Sauvignon Blanc   ★★☆

Winemaker Kate Radburnd aims for 'an easy-drinking style with its emphasis on tropical-fruit flavours and a tangy lift'. Grown in Hawke's Bay, the 2009 vintage (★★☆) is medium-bodied, with smooth tropical-fruit flavours and an underlying crispness.

DRY $15 AV

Clark Estate Single Vineyard Awatere Valley Marlborough Sauvignon Blanc   ★★★

The 2010 vintage (★★★☆) is a crisp, dry style with mouthfilling body and fresh, citrusy, nettley flavours, tight, minerally and flinty. The 2011 (★★★) is fresh and full-bodied, with good vigour and ripe, slightly spicy and minerally flavours. Priced sharply.

DRY $14 V+

Clayfork Vineyard Waihopai Ridge Marlborough Sauvignon Blanc   (★★★★)

From Endeavour (owner of Catalina Sounds, Crowded House and Nanny Goat), the 2009 vintage (★★★★) is a single-vineyard wine, 15 per cent barrel-fermented. Mouthfilling, it is fresh and vibrant, with ripe melon/lime flavours in a quietly classy, minerally style with sweet-fruit characters, a subtle oak influence and tight structure.

DRY $28 –V

Claylaur Family Estate Marlborough Sauvignon Blanc   (★★★)

The 2009 vintage (★★★) was grown at two sites, in the Omaka Valley and central Wairau Valley. Lees-aged for three months, it is smooth and full-bodied, with crisp, basically dry (4.5 grams/litre of residual sugar) melon/lime flavours, balanced for easy drinking.

DRY $18 AV

Clayridge Excalibur Marlborough Sauvignon Blanc   ★★★★☆

The 2010 vintage (★★★★☆) was made from 'very ripe' grapes, fermented with indigenous yeasts, and lees-stirred in French oak barriques. A creamy-textured, ripely herbaceous style, it has fresh, strong tropical-fruit and nut flavours, showing excellent vibrancy and harmony, and a dry, long finish. It's drinking well now.

DRY $27 AV

Clayridge Marlborough Sauvignon Blanc   ★★★★

The 2010 vintage (★★★★) was grown on clay slopes in Taylors Pass and on the floor of the Wairau Valley. Made with some use of indigenous yeasts and French oak casks, it is fresh and lively, with strong tropical-fruit flavours, some herbaceous notes, a subtle seasoning of oak, and good complexity. Drink now to 2012.

DRY $21 V+

Clearview Reserve Hawke's Bay Sauvignon Blanc ★★★★

The 2009 vintage (★★★★☆) was grown at Te Awanga, hand-picked and fermented and matured for 11 months in seasoned French oak barriques. Crisp and dry, it's an impressively rich wine, with ripe tropical-fruit flavours, integrated nutty oak, and excellent poise, vigour and intensity.

Vintage	09	08	07	06
WR	7	6	7	6
Drink	11-15	11-14	P	P

 DRY $23 AV

Clifford Bay Marlborough Sauvignon Blanc ★★★☆

Bargain-priced. The 2011 vintage (★★★☆) is fleshy, with tropical-fruit flavours, slightly spicy, ripe and rounded, and good immediacy.

 DRY $18 V+

Clos Henri Marlborough Sauvignon Blanc ★★★★★

The Clos Henri Vineyard near Renwick is owned by Henri Bourgeois, a leading, family-owned producer in the Loire Valley, which feels this wine expresses 'a unique terroir … and French winemaking approach'. A sophisticated and distinctive Sauvignon Blanc, in top years it's a joy to drink. The 2010 vintage (★★★★★) was hand-picked and mostly fermented and matured for 10 months on its yeast lees in tanks; 8 per cent was barrel-fermented. Drinking well now, but still developing, it is full-bodied and sweet-fruited, with layers of stone-fruit, lime and faintly nutty flavours, slightly minerally, dry, poised and long.

Vintage	10	09	08	07
WR	7	6	7	5
Drink	11-16	11-15	11-13	P

 DRY $29 V+

Clos Marguerite Marlborough Sauvignon Blanc ★★★★☆

Estate-grown and hand-picked in the Awatere Valley, and handled entirely in tanks, the 2010 vintage (★★★★★) is an outstanding single-vineyard wine, far riper and less herbaceous than most from the sub-region. Weighty and highly concentrated, with peach, pineapple and lime flavours, it is sweet-fruited and minerally, with a crisp, bone-dry, lasting finish. Delicious now.

 DRY $26 AV

Clos Marguerite Sauvignon Blanc Aged on Lees ★★★★☆

The fleshy, finely textured 2010 vintage (★★★★★) was estate-grown in the Awatere Valley of Marlborough and matured for a year in tanks, on light yeast lees, before bottling. Richly scented, it is a very ripe, non-herbaceous style, mouthfilling and generous, with a slightly minerally streak, and excellent complexity and personality.

DRY $26 AV

Cloudy Bay Sauvignon Blanc ★★★★★

New Zealand's most internationally acclaimed wine is sought after from Sydney to New York and London. Its irresistibly aromatic and zesty style and intense flavours stem from 'the fruit characters that are in the grapes when they arrive at the winery'. It is sourced from company-owned and several long-term contract growers' vineyards in the Rapaura, Fairhall, Renwick and Brancott districts of the Wairau Valley, Marlborough. The juice is mostly cool-fermented in stainless steel tanks and aged for up to two months on its yeast lees before bottling. The 2011 vintage (★★★★★) was harvested over a month, at an average of 22.5 brix, and a small portion of the blend was fermented in old French oak barriques. A weighty, dry wine, finely textured, it has fresh, ripe passionfruit, melon, capsicum and lime flavours that build across the palate to a resounding finish. A sophisticated – rather than 'full-on', pungently herbaceous – style of Sauvignon Blanc, it has great finesse and drinkability.

Vintage	11	10	09	08
WR	7	7	7	5
Drink	11-13	11-12	P	P

DRY $30 AV

Cloudy Bay Te Koko – see the Branded and Other White Wines section

Coal Pit Central Otago Sauvignon Blanc ★★☆

Estate-grown at Gibbston, the 2010 vintage (★★) is green-edged, with crisp gooseberry and green-capsicum flavours that lack real ripeness and richness.

Vintage	10	09	08
WR	6	5	7
Drink	11-13	11-12	P

DRY $25 –V

Compassion New Zealand Sauvignon Blanc (★★★)

From Spencer Hill, based in Nelson, the 2009 vintage (★★★) is lively, with fresh, slightly grassy aromas and ripe, citrusy, limey flavours. (All winery profits are donated to an alliance of charities.)

DRY $19 AV

Coopers Creek Marlborough Sauvignon Blanc ★★★

The 2010 vintage (★★☆) is a fresh, easy-drinking wine with ripely herbaceous flavours and a dry (3.7 grams/litre of residual sugar) finish.

Vintage	10	09	08
WR	6	6	6
Drink	11-12	P	P

DRY $17 AV

Coopers Creek SV Dillons Point Marlborough Sauvignon Blanc ★★★★

From young vines at Dillons Point – between Blenheim and the Cloudy Bay coast – the easy-drinking 2010 vintage (★★★★) is generous, with fresh, ripe tropical-fruit flavours, balanced acidity and a rich, rounded (4 grams/litre of residual sugar) finish.

Vintage	10	09	08	07
WR	6	7	6	6
Drink	11-12	P	P	P

DRY $20 V+

Corazon Single Vineyard Sauvignon Blanc   ★★★☆

Grown in Marlborough, in the lower Wairau Valley, and fermented in tanks (85 per cent) and seasoned oak barrels, the 2010 vintage (★★★☆) is creamy-textured, with very good depth of ripe tropical-fruit flavours, slightly spicy notes, and a smooth, dry finish. Fine value.

Vintage	10
WR	6
Drink	11-13

 DRY $17 V+

Corbans Cottage Block Hawke's Bay Sauvignon Blanc   ★★★★

The 2009 vintage (★★★★) was grown by Pernod Ricard NZ at Matapiro, 40 kilometres inland. Fleshy and smooth, it has strong, ripe stone-fruit, lime and spice flavours, a subtle oak influence and good complexity and roundness.

 DRY $32 –V

Corbans Private Bin Hawke's Bay Sauvignon Blanc   ★★★☆

The 2010 vintage (★★★☆) is a crisp, dry, slightly minerally style with good depth of fresh melon/lime flavours and a touch of complexity.

 DRY $24 –V

Couper's Shed Hawke's Bay Sauvignon Blanc   (★★★☆)

The debut 2010 vintage (★★★☆) from Pernod Ricard NZ is attractively scented, with strong, ripely herbaceous flavours, fresh, crisp and lively.

 DRY $20 AV

Craggy Range Avery Vineyard Marlborough Sauvignon Blanc   ★★★★

Grown at a slightly cooler site in the Wairau Valley than its Old Renwick Vineyard stablemate (below), the 2010 vintage (★★★★) is weighty, with ripe stone-fruit and lime flavours, showing excellent texture and concentration. It's a bone-dry style, generous and slightly minerally, with a long finish.

Vintage	10	09	08
WR	5	6	7
Drink	11-13	11-12	P

 DRY $20 V+

Craggy Range Old Renwick Vineyard Sauvignon Blanc   ★★★★

From mature vines in the heart of the Wairau Valley, the 2010 vintage (★★★★) has a fresh, lifted, limey bouquet. Mouthfilling and crisp, with an array of apple, grapefruit and lime flavours, it is sweet-fruited and dry, with a mineral undertow and poised, tight finish. Not 'showy', it's a serious wine for drinking over the next several years.

Vintage	10	09	08
WR	7	7	7
Drink	11-13	11-12	P

DRY $20 V+

Craggy Range Te Muna Road Vineyard Martinborough Sauvignon Blanc   ★★★★

Grown a few kilometres south of Martinborough township, this wine is mostly fermented and lees-aged in tanks, but partly fermented with indigenous yeasts in seasoned French oak barrels. Drinking well from the start, the 2011 vintage (★★★★) is mouthfilling and dry, with pure, ripe gooseberry/lime flavours, slightly minerally, fresh, poised and lingering.

Vintage	10	09	08
WR	5	7	7
Drink	11-13	11-13	P

 DRY $23 AV

Crater Rim, The, Waipara Sauvignon Blanc   ★★★★

A great buy, the 2010 vintage (★★★☆) was grown in a single vineyard on the valley floor and tank-fermented. Mouthfilling (14 per cent alcohol), it has fresh, strong tropical-fruit flavours, hints of spices and herbs, and a smooth, dryish (4 grams/litre of residual sugar) finish.

 DRY $15 V+

Crater Rim, The, Woolshed Block Sauvignon Blanc   (★★★★)

A fully dry style, the 2009 vintage (★★★★) is a single-vineyard wine, mouthfilling and rich, with ripe melon/lime flavours and good weight. Slightly minerally, with a long finish, it offers excellent value.

 DRY $19 V+

Crossings, The, Awatere Valley Marlborough Sauvignon Blanc   ★★★☆

The 2010 vintage (★★★☆) is racy, with melon/lime flavours showing good delicacy and depth and a lingering finish. The 2011 (★★★☆), handled almost entirely in tanks (2 per cent barrel-fermented), is a dry wine (3 grams/litre of residual sugar), with fresh, crisp melon/lime flavours, light and lively.

Vintage	11
WR	6
Drink	11-15

 DRY $19 V+

Crossroads Marlborough Sauvignon Blanc   ★★☆

The 2009 vintage (★★☆) is a medium-bodied, dry wine with restrained, citrusy, limey flavours, pleasant and smooth. The 2011 (★★), mostly handled in tanks (12 per cent barrel-fermented), is a dry wine, medium-bodied, with crisp melon/lime flavours, firm acidity and moderate depth.

Vintage	11
WR	5
Drink	11-13

 DRY $19 –V

Crowded House Marlborough Sauvignon Blanc   ★★★☆

A good buy. The 2010 vintage (★★★☆), grown in the Wairau Valley, is punchy, with melon, lime and green-capsicum flavours, fresh and delicate, and a lingering, dry (2.9 grams/litre of residual sugar) finish.

DRY $18 V+

Darling, The, Barrel Marlborough Sauvignon Blanc   (★★★★)

Certified organic, the debut 2010 vintage (★★★★) is a single-vineyard, Wairau Valley wine, handled in old oak casks. It's a mouthfilling wine with ripe melon, lime and capsicum flavours, showing good complexity, a subtle seasoning of oak, fresh acidity, and a rounded, dry finish.

Vintage	10
WR	7
Drink	11-14

 DRY $28 –V

Darling, The, Marlborough Sauvignon Blanc   ★★★★

Certified BioGro, the 2011 vintage (★★★★) was grown at two sites in the Wairau Valley, and mostly handled in tanks; 15 per cent was fermented with indigenous yeasts in old oak casks. Mouthfilling, it has fresh, rich melon/lime flavours, slightly spicy, with good complexity and personality, and a finely poised, dry (4 grams/litre of residual sugar) finish.

Vintage	11
WR	6
Drink	11-14

 DRY $23 AV

Darling, The, Moscato Inspired Sauvignon Blanc   ★★★☆

The seductive, highly distinctive 2011 vintage (★★★★) should really be in the Sweet White Wines section of the *Buyer's Guide*, since it harbours 55 grams per litre of residual sugar. BioGro certified, it was grown at Rapaura, in Marlborough, and made in a low-alcohol style (9.5 per cent), with 'a little spritz'. Light and lively, it is very refreshing and yummy, with concentrated, ripe flavours and lovely balance of sweetness and crispness.

Vintage	11	10
WR	7	5
Drink	11-13	11-12

 SW $24 –V

Dashwood Marlborough Sauvignon Blanc   ★★★☆

Typically great value. The 2010 vintage (★★★★) is a slightly minerally, appetisingly crisp blend of Wairau Valley and Awatere Valley grapes, with good intensity of melon/lime flavours, fresh, aromatic, lively and refreshing. The 2011 (★★★) is light and crisp, with a freshly herbaceous bouquet and melon, gooseberry and lime flavours, showing good depth.

Vintage	09	08
WR	6	6
Drink	11	P

 DRY $19 V+

Day Break Gisborne Sauvignon Blanc   (★★★☆)

Unusually punchy for a Gisborne savvy, the 2009 vintage (★★★☆) was made by Nick Nobilo for Day Break Wines and on sale by May 2009. Freshly aromatic, it is crisp, tangy and ripely herbaceous, with strong passionfruit and lime flavours, balanced for early drinking.

DRY $19 V+

Delegat Marlborough Sauvignon Blanc   ★★★☆

Winemaker Michael Ivicevich aims for 'a tropical fruit-flavoured style, a bit broader and softer than some'. The 2009 vintage (★★★★) is crisp and dry, with fresh, strong melon/lime flavours, woven with racy acidity. Good value.

Vintage	09	08
WR	6	6
Drink	11-13	11-12

Delta Marlborough Sauvignon Blanc   ★★★★

Estate-grown at Dillons Point, in the lower Wairau Valley, the 2011 vintage (★★★★) of this single-vineyard wine is refined, tight and dry, with fresh, citrusy, limey, spicy flavours, slightly flinty acidity, and good poise and intensity. It should unfold well during 2012.

Vintage	11
WR	6
Drink	11-14

Discovery Point Marlborough Sauvignon Blanc   ★★★★

From wine distributor Bennett & Deller, the 2009 vintage (★★★★) was grown in the Wairau Valley and lees-aged for four months. Fully dry, it is fresh and zingy, with good intensity of ripely herbaceous flavours, substantial body and a rounded finish.

Distant Land Hawke's Bay Sauvignon Blanc   ★★★

The 2010 vintage (★★★) is an easy-drinking style, mouthfilling and smooth. Grown in the Dartmoor Valley, it is fresh and ripe, with tropical-fruit flavours and a dry (3.6 grams/litre of residual sugar) finish.

Distant Land Marlborough Sauvignon Blanc   ★★★☆

The 2010 (★★★☆) is punchy, with green-capsicum/lime aromas leading into a strongly varietal wine, vibrantly fruity, crisp and dry. The 2011 vintage (★★★☆), grown in the Wairau Valley, is mouthfilling, with fresh, crisp gooseberry/lime flavours, showing very good vigour and depth.

Doctors', The, Marlborough Sauvignon Blanc   ★★★

From Forrest, this low-alcohol style (9.5 per cent in 2011) is made for 'easy drinking at lunchtime'. Aromatic, it is typically light and lively, fresh and punchy, with gently herbaceous, limey flavours and a slightly sweet, crisp finish. The 2011 (★★★) offers vibrant gooseberry, apple and lime flavours, enjoyable young.

MED/DRY $20 –V

Dog Point Vineyard Marlborough Sauvignon Blanc ★★★★

This wine offers a clear style contrast to Section 94, the company's complex, barrel-aged Sauvignon Blanc (see the Branded and Other White Wines section). Hand-picked, it is lees-aged in tanks, with no exposure to oak. The 2010 vintage (★★★★) is mouthfilling and dry, with a slightly 'funky' bouquet and good concentration of ripe, citrusy, limey flavours, tight and long.

DRY $25 AV

Dolbel Estate Hawke's Bay Sauvignon Blanc ★★★★

A label worth discovering. Grown at Springfield Vineyard, on the banks of the Tutaekuri River, and made by Tony Prichard, formerly of Church Road, the 2008 vintage (★★★★) is a subtle, complex Bordeaux style, fully fermented (half with indigenous yeasts) in seasoned French oak barriques. Mouthfilling and dry, it has rich, ripe tropical-fruit flavours, slightly nutty and rounded.

Vintage	08	07	06
WR	6	6	6
Drink	11-12	11-12	P

DRY $22 V+

Domain Road Vineyard Central Otago Sauvignon Blanc ★★★☆

Grown at Bannockburn, the 2010 vintage (★★★) was 30 per cent barrel-fermented. Tasted in its infancy, it was very fresh, vibrant and crisp, with fractional sweetness (4 grams/litre of residual sugar) adding smoothness, mouthfilling body and some complexity.

DRY $24 –V

Drylands Marlborough Sauvignon Blanc ★★★★

From Constellation NZ, the 2010 vintage (★★★★) is powerful, with fresh, ripe tropical-fruit flavours, showing excellent depth, vigour and roundness.

DRY $22 V+

Durvillea Marlborough Sauvignon Blanc ★★★☆

From Astrolabe, the 2010 vintage (★★★☆) is named after a local seaweed. A clearly herbaceous style, grown in the Wairau, Waihopai and Awatere valleys, it is punchy, with 'tomato stalk' aromas leading into a melon and green capsicum-flavoured wine, fresh, strong and lively.

DRY $16 V+

Elephant Hill Hawke's Bay Sauvignon Blanc ★★★☆

Estate-grown at Te Awanga, the 2009 vintage (★★★☆) has limey aromas leading into a medium-bodied wine with lively acidity, pure melon and green-capsicum flavours and a crisp, slightly minerally, dry finish.

DRY $22 AV

Eradus Awatere Valley Marlborough Sauvignon Blanc ★★★★

The 2011 vintage (★★★★) is a good buy. Vibrant and racy, with punchy melon and green-capsicum flavours, it shows excellent freshness, intensity and immediacy.

Vintage	11
WR	7
Drink	11-13

DRY $18 V+

Esk Valley Marlborough Sauvignon Blanc ★★★★

The 2010 vintage (★★★★), grown in the Wairau and Awatere valleys, is an intensely aromatic wine with fresh, strong tropical-fruit and herbaceous flavours and a crisp, dry (2.8 grams/litre of residual sugar) finish. The 2011, tasted prior to bottling (and so not rated), is clearly herbaceous, fresh and punchy.

Vintage	11	10	09
WR	6	7	7
Drink	12-14	11-12	P

DRY $24 AV

Fairbourne Marlborough Sauvignon Blanc ★★★★☆

From elevated, north-facing slopes in the Wairau Valley, the 2010 vintage (★★★★☆) was hand-picked and fermented in tanks to full dryness. Full-bodied, it is very vibrant, crisp and minerally, with sweet-fruit characters, strong, ripe melon and slight spice flavours, and impressive refinement, delicacy and length.

Vintage	10	09	08
WR	6	6	5
Drink	12-13	11-12	P

DRY $35 –V

Fairhall Downs Hugo Marlborough Sauvignon Blanc ★★★★☆

The 2010 vintage (★★★★☆) is a complex style, grown in a single, elevated vineyard on the south side of the Wairau Valley, barrel-fermented with indigenous yeasts and French oak-matured for 10 months. Weighty and concentrated, it is sweet-fruited, with an array of rich, citrusy, peachy, nettley flavours, a gentle seasoning of oak, and excellent harmony and complexity. Best drinking mid-2012+.

DRY $30 –V

Fairhall Downs Single Vineyard Marlborough Sauvignon Blanc ★★★★

Grown at the head of the Brancott Valley, the 2011 vintage (★★★★) is delicious from the start. Fresh, ripely scented and mouthfilling, it is sweet-fruited and softly textured, showing good harmony and richness. Fine value.

DRY $20 V+

Fairmont Estate Gladstone Terraces Sauvignon Blanc (★★★)

The 2010 vintage (★★★), grown in the northern Wairarapa, is fresh and lively, in a briskly herbaceous style with green capsicum-like flavours that linger well.

DRY $19 AV

Fallen Angel Marlborough Sauvignon Blanc   ★★★★

From Stonyridge Vineyard, on Waiheke Island, the 2010 vintage (★★★★) is mouthfilling and lively, with ripe tropical-fruit characters, a herbal undercurrent, and loads of crisp, dry (3.9 grams/litre of residual sugar) flavour. The 2011 (★★★★) is fresh, crisp and punchy, with tropical-fruit and herbaceous flavours, rich and zingy.

Vintage	11	10
WR	7	7
Drink	11-13	11-12

 DRY $25 AV

Farmers Market Marlborough Sauvignon Blanc   ★★★☆

The 2011 vintage (★★★☆) is fresh and punchy, with tropical-fruit flavours and a herbal undercurrent. It shows very good depth, balance and length.

 DRY $20 AV

Farmgate Hawke's Bay Sauvignon Blanc   ★★★☆

From Ngatarawa, the 2010 vintage (★★★☆) was 'made with a little oak to add complexity'. It's a typical regional style, full-bodied and ripe-tasting, with good depth of lively tropical-fruit flavours, slightly spicy notes and a creamy-smooth finish.

Vintage	10	09
WR	7	7
Drink	11-14	11-13

 DRY $22 AV

Fiddler's Green Waipara Valley Sauvignon Blanc   ★★★★

A distinctly cool-climate style, typically with excellent vibrancy and depth. Estate-grown and tank-fermented, the 2010 vintage (★★★★) is very fresh and lively, with incisive, ripe melon and green-capsicum flavours and a crisp, lingering, finely balanced finish. It's drinking well now.

Vintage	10	09
WR	6	6
Drink	11-12	P

 DRY $21 V+

Fisherman's Bite Marlborough Sauvignon Blanc   (★★★)

From Vernon Family Estate, the 2010 vintage (★★★) is a great buy. Nettley aromas lead into a full-bodied, basically dry wine (4.8 grams/litre of residual sugar) with good depth of gooseberry and green-capsicum flavours, fresh and racy.

DRY $13 V+

Five Flax Sauvignon Blanc   ★★☆

From Pernod Ricard NZ, the 2010 vintage (★★☆) is clearly herbaceous, in a medium-bodied style with distinctly 'green', nettley flavours, and a smooth finish.

 DRY $15 AV

Five Flax Sauvignon Blanc/Pinot Gris   (★★☆)

The 2011 vintage (★★☆) from Pernod Ricard NZ is light and smooth, with fresh pear and lime flavours in a fruity, easy-drinking style.

MED/DRY $15 AV

Forrest Marlborough Sauvignon Blanc   ★★★☆

This aromatic, vibrantly fruity wine has recently become noticeably drier, while retaining good drinkability. The 2010 vintage (★★★★), grown in the central Wairau Valley, is a classic sub-regional style, with mouthfilling body and well-ripened, citrusy, herbal flavours, crisp, dry and strong. It shows excellent freshness, harmony and length.

Vintage	10	09	08
WR	6	6	5
Drink	11-16	11-15	11-15

DRY $22 AV

Forrest The Valleys Awatere Marlborough Sauvignon Blanc   ★★★★☆

The 2010 vintage (★★★★☆) is a classic Awatere style – racy, with intense 'tomato stalk' aromas leading into a full-bodied palate with incisive, ripely herbaceous flavours, crisp, dryish (6 grams/litre of residual sugar), tangy and lingering.

Vintage	10
WR	6
Drink	P

MED/DRY $22 V+

Forrest The Valleys Wairau Sauvignon Blanc   ★★★★☆

(Previously labelled as James Randall.) The 2009 vintage (★★★★☆) is weighty, fleshy, finely textured and rich, with very ripe passionfruit/lime flavours, showing excellent delicacy and depth. Softer and drier (3 grams/litre of residual sugar) than its Awatere Valley stablemate (above), it's tightly structured, with good potential.

Vintage	09
WR	6
Drink	11-15

DRY $35 –V

Framingham F Series Marlborough Sauvignon Blanc   ★★★★☆

The powerful 2008 vintage (★★★★★) was hand-picked, fermented with indigenous yeasts in a 2:1 mix of old oak barrels and stainless steel 'barrels', and 50 per cent of the blend went through a softening malolactic fermentation. Rich, ripe and rounded, with barrel-ferment complexity and some slightly 'funky' notes, it's a non-herbaceous style, concentrated and complex, with gentle acidity and a bone-dry, finely textured finish. The 2010 (★★★★) is a mouthfilling (14.5 per cent alcohol), subtle wine with youthful colour, ripely herbaceous flavours, slightly nutty and creamy, and a dry (3 grams/litre of residual sugar), finely textured finish.

Vintage	09	08
WR	6	6
Drink	11-13	11-12

DRY $35 –V

Framingham Marlborough Sauvignon Blanc ★★★★☆

Consistently impressive and fine value. Grown at eight sites around the Wairau Valley, the 2011 vintage (★★★★☆) was mostly handled in tanks, but a small portion of the blend was hand-picked and barrel-fermented. The bouquet is lifted, with ripe, slightly 'sweaty' aromas and a hint of passionfruit; the palate is dry (3.5 grams/litre of residual sugar), poised and slightly minerally, with penetrating, limey, faintly nutty flavours, showing good drive and complexity, and a long finish.

Vintage	11	10
WR	6	6
Drink	11-13	11-12

 DRY $22 V+

Frizzell Sauvignon Blanc ★★★☆

The label on the 2010 vintage (★★★☆) warns: 'Please Note: May Contain Traces of Summer.' Grown in the Wairau Valley, Marlborough, and lees-aged over winter, it is a punchy, herbaceous style with strong lime and green-capsicum flavours, leesy, yeasty notes adding a touch of complexity and a crisp, tight, dry (2 grams/litre of residual sugar) finish.

 DRY $22 AV

Fromm La Strada Marlborough Sauvignon Blanc ★★★★

After 16 vintages, the Fromm winery, renowned for Pinot Noir, finally made its first Sauvignon Blanc in 2008. The excellent 2010 vintage (★★★★☆) was partly handled in tanks, but 60 per cent of the blend was fermented and matured for nine months in old French oak barrels. Made in a bone-dry style, it's a 'serious' but delicious wine, weighty, with ripe tropical-fruit flavours, a touch of nutty oak adding complexity, impressive delicacy and depth, and a finely balanced, lingering finish. Full-bodied and rich, it's a wine with strong personality.

Vintage	10	09	08
WR	7	6	6
Drink	11-15	11-14	11-12

 DRY $24 AV

Full Circle Marlborough Sauvignon Blanc ★★☆

From Yealands, the 2010 vintage (★★☆), packaged in a plastic bottle, is recommended for consumption 'before 07/09/12'. Grown in the Awatere and Wairau valleys, it has fresh, very grassy aromas, leading into a medium-bodied, strongly herbaceous wine, with lots of youthful impact.

 DRY $17 –V

Gem Marlborough Sauvignon Blanc ★★★☆

The 2008 vintage (★★★☆), currently on sale, was grown at Rapaura, in the Wairau Valley, tank-fermented to dryness, and lees-aged for a year before bottling. Still youthful in colour, it shows some development, with gooseberry and lime flavours, strong and smooth. Drink now.

Vintage	08	07
WR	6	6
Drink	11-17	11-16

DRY $27 –V

Georges Michel Golden Mile Marlborough Sauvignon Blanc ★★★

Grown in the Rapaura ('golden mile') district of the Wairau Valley, the easy-drinking 2009 vintage (★★★) is mouthfilling, ripe and rounded, with tropical-fruit flavours, gentle acidity and a smooth, dryish (5.5 grams/litre of residual sugar) finish.

MED/DRY $18 AV

Georges Michel La Reserve Marlborough Sauvignon Blanc ★★★☆

The 2009 vintage (★★★☆) is a tightly structured wine, hand-harvested and fermented and matured for eight months in seasoned French oak barrels. Ripely scented, with subtle oak, it is medium to full-bodied, with very good depth of tropical-fruit flavours, crisp and bone-dry.

Vintage	10	09
WR	6	6
Drink	11-15	11-15

DRY $22 AV

Gibbston Highgate Estate Summer Breeze Sauvignon Blanc (★★★)

A single-vineyard wine, grown at Gibbston, in Central Otago, and tank-fermented, the 2010 vintage (★★★) is medium-bodied, fresh and lively, with citrusy, appley flavours showing some leesy complexity, appetising acidity and good length.

DRY $18 AV

Giesen Marlborough Sauvignon Blanc ★★★

The largest-volume wine from Giesen has a low profile in New Zealand, but enjoys major export success. It is typically light and lively, with tangy acidity and good depth of fresh melon, capsicum and lime flavours. The 2011 vintage (★★★) is a multi-site, Wairau Valley blend. Fresh and medium-bodied, it has ripe, citrusy, slightly limey and spicy flavours, balanced for easy drinking.

DRY $19 AV

Giesen Marlborough Sauvignon Blanc The August ★★★★★

This striking wine is named after the Giesen brothers' grandfather, August (pronounced 'ow-goost') Giesen. The 2010 vintage (★★★★★) was hand-picked in the Wairau Valley, fermented with indigenous yeasts in French oak casks (8 per cent new), and oak-aged on its yeast lees for 10 months. Full of personality, with lovely richness and complexity, it is mouthfilling and youthful, with layers of tropical-fruit and nut flavours and a dry, highly sustained finish. Best drinking mid-2012+.

DRY $37 AV

Giesen Marlborough Sauvignon Blanc The Brothers ★★★★☆

The 2010 vintage (★★★★☆) was grown mostly at Rapaura, in the Wairau Valley, and tank-fermented; 5 per cent of the blend was matured in old French oak barriques. A punchy wine with lifted, 'sweaty armpit' aromas, it has an intense palate, with rich gooseberry and lime flavours, very fresh, crisp and long.

DRY $25 V+

Gladstone Vineyard Reserve Sophie's Choice Sauvignon Blanc ★★★★

From estate-grown, 25-year-old vines in the northern Wairarapa, the 2010 vintage (★★★☆) was hand-picked, French oak-fermented and barrel-aged for 11 months. The bouquet is creamy and toasty; the palate is rich and slightly buttery, in a Chardonnay-like style that shows considerable development. Ready.

 DRY $36 –V

Gladstone Vineyard Sauvignon Blanc ★★★☆

The 2011 vintage (★★★) was grown in the northern Wairarapa. Tasted in October 2011, it showed mouthfilling body and crisp, bone-dry flavours of passionfruit and lime, but was still settling down.

 DRY $25 –V

Glazebrook Regional Reserve Marlborough Sauvignon Blanc ★★★☆

The 2010 vintage (★★★★) is one of the best yet. A fleshy, sweet-fruited, Wairau Valley style, it has strong, ripe passionfruit/lime flavours, deliciously fresh, vibrant and crisp.

Vintage	10	09
WR	7	6
Drink	11-13	11-12

 DRY $20 AV

Golden Hills Estate Nelson Sauvignon Blanc (★★★★)

The tightly structured, single-vineyard 2009 vintage (★★★★) was partly barrel-fermented. Weighty, it is ripely flavoured, with a subtle seasoning of oak, strong tropical-fruit flavours and good acid spine.

 DRY $20 V+

Goldridge Marlborough Sauvignon Blanc ★★☆

The 2009 vintage (★★☆) was grown in the Wairau and Awatere valleys. It's clearly herbaceous, with crisp gooseberry and green-capsicum flavours, a sliver of sweetness (7.2 grams/litre of residual sugar) and solid depth.

 MED/DRY $16 AV

Goldridge Premium Reserve Marlborough Sauvignon Blanc ★★★

The 2009 vintage (★★★☆) is crisp, with strong melon, lime and green-capsicum flavours and a dry (3.4 grams/litre of residual sugar) finish. Grown in the Wairau and Awatere valleys, it shows some richness.

DRY $19 AV

Goldwater Wairau Valley Sauvignon Blanc   ★★★★

The 2010 vintage (★★★★★) is a beauty. Mouthfilling, it is tight, dry and rich, with generous tropical-fruit flavours, showing lovely ripeness and delicacy, and firm acid spine. The 2011 (★★★★) is a typical Wairau Valley style, with ripe 'sweaty armpit' aromas and a fleshy palate, offering fresh, strong tropical-fruit flavours, rich and rounded.

Vintage	11	10	09
WR	7	6	6
Drink	11-13	11-12	11-12

DRY $22 V+

Greenhough Nelson Sauvignon Blanc   ★★★★★

Andrew Greenhough aims for a 'rich Sauvignon Blanc style with ripe, creamy mouthfeel' – and hits the target with ease. It is mostly handled in tanks, but part of the blend (5 per cent in 2011) is fermented with indigenous yeasts in new French oak casks. The 2010 vintage (★★★★★) has slightly 'sweaty' aromas, leading into a classy, authoritative wine. Very mouthfilling, it is sweet-fruited, with ripe tropical-fruit flavours, showing lovely delicacy and richness, finely balanced acidity, and a long, slightly spicy, dry finish. The 2011 (★★★★) is fresh, punchy and dry (3.5 grams/litre of residual sugar), with vibrant melon/lime flavours, crisp and strong.

Vintage	11	10	09	08	07	06
WR	6	7	7	7	7	6
Drink	12-15	11-14	11-12	11-12	P	P

DRY $22 V+

Greystone Waipara Sauvignon Blanc   ★★★★

The outstanding 2010 vintage (★★★★★) was fermented in a 2:1 mix of tanks and French oak barrels. Intense, tight and racy, it is concentrated, with an array of grapefruit, melon and lime flavours, showing excellent vigour, and a dry, long finish. The 2011 (★★★☆) is more restrained. Partly barrel-fermented (20 per cent), it is still very youthful, with fresh, citrusy, limey, slightly spicy flavours, dry and minerally, and a poised, lengthy finish. Open mid-2012+.

Vintage	11	10
WR	6	6
Drink	11-13	11-13

DRY $23 AV

Greywacke Marlborough Sauvignon Blanc   ★★★★★

The 2010 vintage (★★★★★) was grown at sites in the central Wairau Valley and its southern offshoots, and partly barrel-fermented. An authoritative, finely crafted wine from Kevin Judd, it has very rich grapefruit/lime flavours, subtle oak adding complexity, and a finely textured, dry finish. The 2011 vintage (★★★★★) was 10 per cent barrel-fermented (French, old). Fleshy and rounded, with great drinkability, it is aromatic, sweet-fruited and layered, in a subtle, very satisfying style, delicious from the start.

Vintage	11	10	09
WR	6	6	6
Drink	12-17	11-16	11-15

DRY $27 V+

Greywacke Wild Sauvignon   (★★★★★)

Lovely now, the 2009 vintage (★★★★★) was grown at sites in the Brancott Valley and on the central Wairau Plains, barrel-fermented with indigenous yeasts, and aged for a year in French oak barriques (10 per cent new). Two-thirds of the blend also went through a softening malolactic fermentation. Still youthful, it is highly scented, weighty and dry, with a smooth 'entry' (initial impression), concentrated, ripe passionfruit and lime flavours and a very harmonious, rounded finish.

Vintage	09
WR	6
Drink	11-16

Grove Mill Grand Reserve Seventeen Valley Vineyard
Marlborough Sauvignon Blanc   (★★★★☆)

The tightly structured, elegant 2009 vintage (★★★★☆) is a partly barrel-fermented style with concentrated, ripe melon/lime flavours, a subtle twist of oak and a lingering, crisp, dry finish.

Growers Mark Marlborough Sauvignon Blanc   ★★★☆

The 2011 vintage (★★★☆) is freshly aromatic and lively, with good body, tropical-fruit flavours and a rounded finish. (From Farmers Market Wine Company.)

Gunn Estate Sauvignon Blanc   (★★☆)

From 'East Coast' regions, the 2009 vintage (★★☆) is vibrantly fruity, with a sliver of sweetness (5.9 grams/litre of residual sugar) and fresh, tangy acidity. It's a solid wine with tropical-fruit and apple flavours, balanced for easy drinking.

Hans Herzog Marlborough Sauvignon Blanc Sur Lie   ★★★★☆

Far outside the mainstream regional style, the 2009 vintage (★★★★★) was estate-grown on the north side of the Wairau Valley, hand-picked at 23.5 to 24.4 brix, fermented with indigenous yeasts in French oak puncheons and barriques, oak-matured for a year, and given a full, softening malolactic fermentation. A lovely example of fully oak-aged Sauvignon Blanc, it is weighty, very ripe, creamy-textured and dry, with highly concentrated tropical-fruit flavours gently seasoned with oak, and a rich, rounded finish.

Vintage	09	08
WR	7	7
Drink	11-18	11-17

DRY $44 –V

Harwood Hall Marlborough Sauvignon Blanc   ★★★☆

The 2010 vintage (★★★☆) is enjoyable now. Mouthfilling and smooth, it has tropical-fruit flavours, with a herbal undercurrent, and very good freshness, harmony and depth.

Vintage	10	09
WR	6	5
Drink	12-13	11-12

Heart of Stone Marlborough Sauvignon Blanc   ★★★☆

From Forrest Estate, the 2009 vintage (★★★☆) is punchy, with melon, capsicum and slight 'tomato stalk' characters, showing good vigour, delicacy and depth. Fine value.

Highfield Lone Gum Marlborough Sauvignon Blanc   (★★★★)

The 2010 vintage (★★★★) is the winery's first single-vineyard Sauvignon Blanc. Grown in the Omaka Valley, it is intensely aromatic, in a medium-bodied style with strong, citrusy, limey flavours, ripe, minerally and tight. A quietly classy wine, it should reward cellaring.

DRY $26 –V

Highfield Marlborough Sauvignon Blanc   ★★★★★

Typically an impressive wine – scented and harmonious, with rich limey fruit flavours and excellent depth. The 2010 (★★★★★) is classy, with deep, very pure and delicate flavours of melons and limes, slightly nettley, crisp, minerally and long. The 2011 vintage (★★★★) is ripely scented and medium-bodied, with strong melon/lime flavours, racy acidity, and lees-aging notes adding complexity.

Vintage	11	10	09
WR	6	7	6
Drink	11-13	11-12	P

Hole in the Water Marlborough Sauvignon Blanc   (★★★)

From Konrad, the 2011 vintage (★★★) is a sharply priced wine, grown in the Waihopai and Wairau valleys (and 6 per cent French oak-aged). Fresh and lively, it has plenty of crisp, smooth (4.9 grams/litre of residual sugar), ripely herbaceous flavour. A good drink-young style.

Vintage	11
WR	6
Drink	12-14

Homer Marlborough Sauvignon Blanc   ★★☆

From Odyssey, the 2010 vintage (★★☆) was estate-grown in the Brancott Valley. It's a drink-young style, offering decent depth of fresh melon and lime flavours, balanced for easy drinking. Priced right.

DRY $15 AV

Hudson Mokopuna Martinborough Sauvignon Blanc   ★★★

The 2010 vintage (★★★) is a single-vineyard wine, fleshy and rounded, with good depth of ripe passionfruit/lime flavours and a basically dry (4 grams/litre of residual sugar) finish.

Vintage	10
WR	6
Drink	11-13

Huia Marlborough Sauvignon Blanc ★★★☆

Grown at several sites in the Wairau Valley, the 2010 vintage (★★★☆) has some 'sweaty armpit' notes on the nose and fresh, moderately concentrated, ripe tropical-fruit flavours, dry and lively.

DRY $22 AV

Hunky Dory Marlborough Sauvignon Blanc (★★★☆)

From Huia, the 2010 vintage (★★★☆) is a good, everyday-drinking style with punchy, ripe tropical-fruit flavours, crisp and dry. Fresh and lively, it's priced sharply.

DRY $16 V+

Huntaway Reserve Marlborough Sauvignon Blanc ★★★★

Grown on heavy clay soils in the lower Wairau Valley, the 2010 vintage (★★★★) is fleshy, concentrated and rounded, with mouthfilling body and fresh, very ripe flavours, slightly spicy and rich.

DRY $24 AV

Hunter's Kaho Roa Marlborough Sauvignon Blanc ★★★★

Based on the ripest, least-herbaceous grapes, this wine is grown in stony vineyards along Rapaura Road, on the relatively warm, north side of the Wairau Valley. Part of the blend is handled entirely in stainless steel tanks; another is tank-fermented but barrel-aged; and the third is fermented and lees-aged for eight to nine months in new French oak barriques. It typically matures well for up to five years. The 2010 vintage (★★★★) is fleshy, ripe and rounded, with a rich, creamy-textured palate, showing considerable complexity, slightly nutty notes, and good potential. Best drinking mid-2012+.

Vintage	10
WR	5
Drink	11-14

DRY $22 V+

Hunter's Marlborough Sauvignon Blanc ★★★★

Hunter's fame rests on this fully dry wine, which has the intense aromas of cool-climate grapes, uncluttered by oak handling. The goal is 'a strong expression of Marlborough fruit – a bell-clear wine with a mix of tropical and searing gooseberry characters'. The grapes are sourced from numerous sites in the Wairau Valley, and to retain their fresh, vibrant characters, they are processed very quickly, with protective anaerobic techniques and minimal handling. The wine is usually at its best between one and two years old. The 2010 vintage (★★★★) is crisp, strong and bone-dry (1.4 grams/litre of residual sugar), in a finely balanced style with melon, citrus-fruit and lime flavours, pure, zingy and lingering.

Vintage	10	09	08
WR	5	6	5
Drink	11-12	11-13	11-12

DRY $19 V+

Hurunui River Sauvignon Blanc ★★☆

Grown in North Canterbury, the 2009 vintage (★★☆) is a mouthfilling wine, fleshy and slightly creamy-textured, with crisp pear and spice flavours.

 DRY $20 –V

Invivo Marlborough Sauvignon Blanc ★★★★★

From an Auckland-based company, the 2010 vintage (★★★★★) is a punchy, dry style from the Awatere Valley (mostly the late-ripening Westhaven Vineyard, at Dashwood), lees-aged and stirred for three months. Pungently aromatic, it is incisive, ripely herbaceous, crisp and minerally, with a long finish. The 2011 vintage (★★★★★) is also rich and refined, with finely balanced, slightly nettley flavours, minerally and tight, and impressive intensity, delicacy, harmony and length. A label to watch.

Vintage	10
WR	5
Drink	11-12

 DRY $20 V+

Isabel Marlborough Sauvignon Blanc ★★★☆

Grown at three sites, on the Wairau Valley floor and elevated, the 2010 vintage (★★★★) is a full-bodied wine with ripe tropical-fruit flavours, fresh, crisp and strong. Dry (4 grams/litre of residual sugar) and slightly minerally, it's drinking well now.

 DRY $22 AV

Jack's Canyon Waipara Sauvignon Blanc (★★★)

Enjoyable young, the 2010 vintage (★★★) is a fresh, crisply herbaceous style with melon and lime flavours, lively and smooth. (From Waipara Springs.)

DRY $17 AV

Jackson Estate Grey Ghost Sauvignon Blanc ★★★★☆

Far outside the commercial mainstream, the 2009 vintage (★★★★★) was hand-harvested in Marlborough and fermented in tanks and seasoned French oak barriques. Delicious now, it is very weighty and concentrated, with beautifully ripe melon, lime and passionfruit flavours, a slightly nutty, spicy complexity and a dry, lasting finish.

Vintage	10	09	08	07	06
WR	7	7	5	7	6
Drink	11-20	11-20	11-14	11-15	P

 DRY $33 –V

Jackson Estate Stich Marlborough Sauvignon Blanc ★★★★★

Grown at a dozen sites in the Wairau Valley and its southern off-shoots, this is typically a lush, ripe and rounded wine with concentration and huge drinkability. It has excellent aging ability, and the latest vintages are consistently outstanding. The 2010 (★★★★★) is another winner. A sophisticated wine, it is mouthfilling, rich, vibrant and sweet-fruited, with grapefruit, lime and slight spice flavours, woven with fresh acidity, and lovely harmony and length.

Vintage	11	10	09
WR	6	6	7
Drink	11-15	11-15	11-12

 DRY $23 V+

Johanneshof Marlborough Sauvignon Blanc   ★★★☆

The 2010 vintage (★★★) from this small producer has an obvious splash of sweetness (12 grams/litre of residual sugar) – unusual in Sauvignon Blanc. Partly oak-fermented, it is fleshy, with clearly herbaceous flavours, fresh, lively, crisp and strong.

MED/DRY $23 –V

Johner Estate Gladstone Sur Lie Sauvignon Blanc   ★★★☆

The 2010 vintage (★★★) is an easy-drinking style, full-bodied, with soft, ripe, slightly herbaceous flavours, rounded and ready.

DRY $22 AV

Johner Estate Single Vineyard Gladstone Sauvignon Blanc   (★★★☆)

The 2011 vintage (★★★☆) is youthful, with strong tropical-fruit flavours, ripe and fresh, and a finely balanced, smooth finish.

DRY $22 AV

Johner Estate Wairarapa Sauvignon Blanc   ★★★

The 2010 vintage (★★★★) is full-bodied, with racy tropical-fruit and herbaceous flavours, crisp and concentrated. The 2011 (★★☆) is a pleasant, easy-drinking wine, with moderate depth of pear and spice flavours, ripe and rounded.

DRY $18 AV

John Forrest Collection Marlborough Sauvignon Blanc   (★★★★☆)

The quietly classy 2009 vintage (★★★★☆) was harvested from mature (over 20 years old), low-cropped vines, grown in stony soils, and mostly handled in tanks; 10 per cent of the blend was fermented and lees-aged for 10 months in old oak barrels. It's a weighty, subtle wine, ripe, citrusy and limey, with leesy notes adding complexity and a finely textured finish.

DRY $33 –V

Jules Taylor Marlborough Sauvignon Blanc   ★★★★☆

Grown in the Awatere and Wairau valleys, the 2010 vintage (★★★★☆) is fresh, punchy and vibrantly fruity, with pure, penetrating tropical-fruit and herbaceous flavours, showing excellent delicacy and length.

Vintage	10	09
WR	7	6
Drink	11-13	11-12

DRY $22 V+

Julicher Martinborough Sauvignon Blanc   ★★★☆

The 2010 vintage (★★★) was estate-grown at Te Muna, hand-picked and handled mostly in tanks; 5 per cent of the blend was barrel-fermented. It's a fresh, medium-bodied wine, with citrusy, slightly nettley flavours, showing good varietal character, and a crisp, dry finish.

DRY $19 V+

Jumper, The, Marlborough Sauvignon Blanc   ★★★

Priced sharply, the 2009 vintage (★★★), grown in the Wairau Valley, is a crisp, clearly varietal wine with pineapple, melon and green-capsicum flavours, showing good depth.

 DRY $16 V+

Junction Free Run Sauvignon Blanc   ★★★★

There's 'nothing subtle about it' states the back label of this Central Hawke's Bay wine, grown at Takapau. Very fresh and green-edged, the 2010 vintage (★★★★) has penetrating, lively, herbaceous flavours, crisp and intensely varietal. Drink now. The 2009 (★★★★) is similar – fresh, incisive, pure and racy.

 DRY $20 V+

Kaimira Estate Brightwater Sauvignon Blanc   ★★★

The estate-grown 2010 vintage (★★★) is a full-bodied wine with good vigour, fresh, ripe melon/lime flavours and a refreshingly crisp, dry (2 grams/litre of residual sugar) finish.

 DRY $19 AV

Karikari Estate Calypso Marlborough Sauvignon Blanc   (★★★☆)

Full-bodied, fresh and lively, the 2011 vintage (★★★☆) is finely balanced, showing very good delicacy and depth of ripe melon/lime flavours, a hint of passionfruit, and faint sweetness (4 grams/litre of residual sugar) balanced by appetising acidity.

 DRY $22 AV

Kate Radburnd Bud Burst Marlborough Sauvignon Blanc   (★★★)

From C.J. Pask, the 2010 vintage (★★★) is a strongly herbaceous style, mouthfilling, with fresh, nettley aromas, some riper tropical-fruit notes on the palate and a crisp, dry finish.

 DRY $19 AV

Kennedy Point Marlborough Sauvignon Blanc   ★★★

The 2009 vintage (★★★) from this Waiheke Island producer was grown in the Wairau Valley. It's a mouthfilling, fleshy, ripe tropical fruit-flavoured wine with a hint of pineapples and a dry, rounded finish. Ready.

 DRY $19 AV

Kerner Estate Marlborough Sauvignon Blanc   (★★☆)

The 2009 vintage (★★☆) is mouthfilling and dry, with tight, minerally, citrusy flavours, showing a touch of complexity. It's a 'non-commercial' style, not aromatic or obviously varietal, but a decent 'food' wine.

DRY $25 –V

Kerr Farm Vineyard Kumeu Sauvignon Blanc   ★★☆

Estate-grown in West Auckland, the 2009 vintage (★★★) is a good example of the northern style. Full-bodied and dry, it has ripe tropical-fruit flavours, fresh and lively, showing good depth.

 DRY $20 –V

Kim Crawford Marlborough Sauvignon Blanc   ★★★★

This is typically a very fresh and punchy style from Constellation NZ. The 2010 vintage (★★★★★) ticks all the right boxes, with excellent balance of tropical-fruit and herbaceous flavours, concentration, acidity, drive and length. Very lively and intense, it's highly impressive, especially for such a large-volume label.

DRY $23 AV

Kim Crawford SP Spitfire Marlborough Sauvignon Blanc   ★★★★☆

The 2010 vintage (★★★★), from two sites, is a classic Wairau Valley style – full-bodied and ripe, with strong tropical-fruit flavours, a herbal undercurrent and good concentration. Why is it called 'Spitfire'? The grapes were grown principally on the site of an old airbase.

DRY $33 –V

Kina Beach Estuary Block Nelson Sauvignon Blanc   ★★★★

Estate-grown at a coastal site, the 2010 (★★★★) is delicious from the start. Freshly scented, poised and punchy, it is lively, with melon/lime flavours showing very good delicacy and depth, and a well-rounded finish. The 2011 vintage (★★★★) is similar – fleshy, with strong, fresh and lively ripe-fruit flavours, a touch of complexity, good texture and a smooth, lingering finish.

Vintage	11	10	09	08
WR	6	6	7	6
Drink	11-13	11-12	P	P

MED/DRY $20 V+

Kina Cliffs Nelson Sauvignon Blanc   ★★★☆

From a vineyard overlooking Tasman Bay, the 2010 vintage (★★★☆) has slightly nettley aromas and flavours. Crisp and lively, it is very fresh, with a lingering finish.

Vintage	10	09
WR	5	6
Drink	11-12	P

DRY $20 AV

Konrad Marlborough Sauvignon Blanc   ★★★☆

The 2010 vintage (★★★☆), estate-grown in the Wairau and Waihopai valleys, was mostly handled in tanks; 3 per cent of the blend was barrel-fermented. Crisp and punchy, it has fresh, ripe flavours of melons, limes and spices, showing a touch of complexity, and a dry finish.

DRY $18 V+

Koura Bay Awatere Valley Sauvignon Blanc   ★★★☆

The 2009 vintage (★★★☆), estate-grown, is aromatic and punchy, with strong, clearly herbaceous flavours of gooseberries and capsicums, fresh and crisp.

Vintage	09	08
WR	7	5
Drink	11-12	P

DRY $19 V+

Kumeu River Sauvignon Blanc ★★★★

The 2009 vintage (★★★★), grown in Marlborough, is mouthfilling, with a slightly 'funky' bouquet, reflecting the use of indigenous yeasts. It offers ripe tropical-fruit rather than herbaceous flavours, good weight and concentration, and a crisp, fully dry finish.

Kumeu River Village Sauvignon Blanc ★★★

Grown in Marlborough, the 2009 vintage (★★★) has 'funky', indigenous yeast aromas, leading into a lively, dry and flavoursome wine with ripe citrus-fruit, lime and spice characters, showing good individuality.

Lake Chalice Marlborough Sauvignon Blanc ★★★

The 2010 vintage (★★☆), grown at three sites in the lower Wairau Valley, is medium-bodied, with fresh, ripely herbaceous flavours, dry (2.7 grams/litre of residual sugar), crisp and lively, and moderate depth.

Lake Chalice The Raptor Marlborough Sauvignon Blanc ★★★☆

Less than 2 per cent of the winery's Sauvignon Blanc grapes go into this top label. The 2010 vintage (★★★), grown at two sites in the lower Wairau Valley, is crisp and dry, with pear, lime and spice flavours, showing good but not great depth.

Lawson's Dry Hills Marlborough Sauvignon Blanc ★★★★★

One of the region's best, widely available Sauvignon Blancs, this stylish wine is vibrantly fruity, intense and finely structured. The grapes are grown at several sites (seven in 2011) in the Wairau (mostly) and Waihopai valleys. To add a subtle extra dimension, 4 to 8 per cent of the blend is fermented in seasoned French oak barriques. The wine typically has great impact in its youth, but also has a proven ability to age, acquiring toasty, minerally complexities. The 2011 vintage (★★★★☆) is dry (4 grams/litre of residual sugar), richly flavoured and racy, with a lifted bouquet, showing some 'sweaty armpit' notes, and fresh, concentrated flavours of ripe citrus-fruit, passionfruit and lime, with the restrained oak influence adding complexity. Drink now to 2013.

Lawson's Dry Hills The Pioneer Marlborough Sauvignon Blanc (★★★★★)

The 2009 vintage (★★★★★) was grown in two vineyards near the winery, in the lower Wairau Valley, and mostly handled in tanks, with a small portion of barrel fermentation. The bouquet is very fresh and lifted, with ripe-fruit aromas and hints of 'sweaty armpit' and oak; the palate is crisp, concentrated and dry, with passionfruit, capsicum and spice flavours, showing excellent intensity and vigour.

Lil Rippa Marlborough Awatere Sauvignon Blanc   (★★★★)

From Shoestring Wines, the 2010 vintage (★★★★) has 'tomato stalk' aromas, leading into a green-edged wine with fresh, strong melon, lime and green-capsicum flavours, showing excellent purity and harmony, and a minerally, lively finish. Fine value. Drink now.

`DRY $17 V+`

Lil Rippa Marlborough Sauvignon Blanc   (★★★☆)

The 2010 vintage (★★★☆) is apparently the 'same wine' as the second, 'Awatere' bottling (above), but fractionally drier.

`DRY $17 V+`

Lime Rock Central Hawke's Bay Sauvignon Blanc   ★★★

Grown at altitude, the 2010 vintage (★★★) is a single-vineyard wine, tank-fermented and lees-aged. Green-edged and slightly nettley, it is now soft and approachable, with some developed, 'canned peas' characters on the nose, but good depth and harmony.

`DRY $19 AV`

Little Black Shag Sauvignon Blanc   (★★☆)

From Anchorage, in Nelson, the 2009 vintage (★★☆) is a pleasant, easy-drinking wine with ripe, citrusy, limey flavours, showing decent depth. Priced sharply.

`DRY $12 V+`

Locharburn Central Otago Sauvignon Blanc   (★★★☆)

The 2010 vintage (★★★☆) was hand-harvested at 24 brix and mostly handled in tanks; 20 per cent of the blend was barrel-fermented, but not oak-aged. A full-bodied wine, woven with fresh acidity, it is vibrant and ripely flavoured, with good mouthfeel and texture and a touch of complexity.

Vintage	10
WR	6
Drink	11-17

`DRY $25 –V`

Longridge Hawke's Bay Sauvignon Blanc   ★★★

From Pernod Ricard NZ, the 2010 (★★★) is fresh, with punchy passionfruit and herb flavours, ripe and rounded. It's drinking well now.

`DRY $18 AV`

Loopline Sauvignon Blanc   (★★★☆)

Grown at Opaki, in the northern Wairarapa, the 2009 vintage (★★★☆) has tropical-fruit flavours, a slightly creamy texture and a finely balanced, dry finish.

`DRY $21 AV`

Lumina Marlborough Sauvignon Blanc

From Matua Valley, the 2010 vintage (★★☆) is a low-alcohol style (9 per cent), light and smooth, with fresh melon/lime flavours. It slips down very easily.

DRY $15 AV

Lynfer Estate Wairarapa Sauvignon Blanc

Grown at Gladstone, this single-vineyard wine offers good value. The 2010 vintage (★★★☆) is full-bodied and dry, with ripe passionfruit and lime flavours, cut with lively acidity.

DRY $17 V+

MacKenzies Pardon Waipara Sauvignon Blanc

The 2010 vintage (★★☆) of this single-vineyard wine is a herbaceous style with fresh, simple flavours, showing decent depth, and a crisp, grassy finish.

DRY $21 –V

Mahi Ballot Block Marlborough Sauvignon Blanc

From a slightly elevated, relatively cool site in the Brancott Valley, the distinctive 2010 vintage (★★★★☆) was hand-picked, barrel-fermented with indigenous yeasts and oak-aged for 10 months. A 'serious' style of Sauvignon Blanc with concentrated, slightly nettley and spicy flavours, seasoned with toasty oak, good complexity and a crisp, bone-dry finish, it should be at its best 2012+.

Vintage	10	09	08
WR	6	6	6
Drink	11-16	11-15	11-14

DRY $27 AV

Mahi Boundary Farm Sauvignon Blanc

Grown on the lower slopes of the Wither Hills, at an early-ripening site, the 2010 vintage (★★★★☆) was hand-picked, fermented with indigenous yeasts and lees-aged for 10 months in French oak barriques. It's a robust wine (14.5 per cent alcohol), with a very complex, slightly nettley and nutty bouquet. The palate is weighty, with rich stone-fruit, capsicum and nut flavours, and a long, dry finish. An age-worthy wine, it's full of personality.

Vintage	10	09	08	07
WR	6	6	6	6
Drink	11-16	11-14	11-12	11-12

DRY $27 AV

Mahi Marlborough Sauvignon Blanc ★★★★

The 2010 vintage (★★★★) was grown at several sites and mostly handled in tanks; 8 per cent of the final blend (the ripest, hand-picked fruit) was barrel-fermented. A tight, elegant wine, it has good weight and texture, with fresh melon, lime and capsicum flavours, a hint of nutty oak, and a crisp, fully dry finish. Priced sharply.

Vintage	10	09	08	07
WR	7	6	6	6
Drink	11-14	11-13	P	P

DRY $20 V+

Maimai Creek Hawke's Bay Sauvignon Blanc   ★★★

A good buy. The 2009 vintage (★★★) is fruity and flavoursome, in a ripe style with fresh, lively acidity and a smooth finish.

DRY $15 V+

Main Divide Sauvignon Blanc   ★★★☆

From Pegasus Bay. The 2009 vintage (★★★☆), not identified on the label by region, was grown in Marlborough. It's a mouthfilling wine, fleshy and sweet-fruited, with very good flavour depth and a smooth, dry finish. (The 2010 was grown at Waipara.)

DRY $20 AV

Maker, The, Fleur de Lis Marlborough Sauvignon Blanc   (★★★)

Showing good vigour and depth, the 2010 vintage (★★★) is a strongly herbaceous style, offering citrus-fruit and green-capsicum flavours, crisp and dry. (From Farmers Market Wine Company.)

DRY $18 AV

Man O'War Gravestone Waiheke Island Sauvignon Blanc/Sémillon   ★★★★

Estate-grown at the eastern end of the island, the 2010 vintage (★★★★) is a blend of 70 per cent Sauvignon Blanc, tank-fermented with indigenous yeasts, and 30 per cent Sémillon, harvested at 26 brix and barrel-aged. It's a fleshy, ripe, concentrated wine with tropical-fruit flavours, showing excellent richness and harmony, and a slightly off-dry finish (5 grams/litre of residual sugar). Worth cellaring.

Vintage	10
WR	6
Drink	11-15

MED/DRY $35 –V

Man O'War Waiheke Island Sauvignon Blanc   ★★★☆

Grown at the eastern end of the island, the 2010 vintage (★★★☆) was handled entirely in tanks. It's an aromatic, fleshy and steely wine with strong ripe-fruit flavours, appetising acidity, a herbal undercurrent and a crisp, off-dry (6 grams/litre of residual sugar) finish. The 2011 (★★★), which includes a 'touch' of Sémillon, is medium-bodied, with fresh, grassy aromas, melon/herb flavours, showing good vigour and depth, and a dryish (5 grams/litre of residual sugar), crisp finish.

Vintage	11
WR	5
Drink	11-13

MED/DRY $25 –V

Manu Marlborough Sauvignon Blanc   ★★★

From Steve Bird, the 2009 vintage (★★★) is a full-bodied, dry wine, grown in the Wairau Valley. Fresh, with good balance and depth of ripe passionfruit and lime flavours, it's priced sharply.

DRY $15 V+

Map Maker Marlborough Sauvignon Blanc ★★★☆

The 2010 vintage (★★★☆) was estate-grown by Staete Landt at Rapaura and made with a small portion of barrel fermentation. It's a fresh, crisp and lively wine with tropical-fruit flavours, showing very good depth, and a touch of complexity.

DRY $19 V+

Marble Point Hanmer Springs Sauvignon Blanc (★★★★)

Grown in North Canterbury, the 2009 vintage (★★★★) was handled without oak. Vibrant, crisp and dry, it shows good intensity of fresh, ripe melon and lime flavours, a minerally streak and a long, slightly flinty finish. It's a 'serious' style of Sauvignon Blanc, not pungently varietal, but full of interest.

DRY $22 V+

Margrain Martinborough Sauvignon Blanc ★★★☆

A pungently herbaceous style, the 2010 vintage (★★★☆) has fresh-cut grass aromas and green capsicum-like flavours. Slightly sweet (7 grams/litre of residual sugar), it has moderate intensity, good freshness and vigour.

MED/DRY $24 –V

Marisco The King's Favour Marlborough Sauvignon Blanc (★★★★☆)

The classy 2009 vintage (★★★★☆) was estate-grown in the Waihopai Valley. Weighty and dry (2.7 grams/litre of residual sugar), it is vibrant and sweet-fruited, with incisive melon, capsicum and lime flavours, finely poised, crisp, slightly minerally and long.

DRY $23 V+

Marsden Marlborough Sauvignon Blanc ★★★

The 2009 vintage (★★★) from this Northland-based producer is a herbaceous style with punchy gooseberry and green-capsicum flavours. Ready.

DRY $25 –V

Martinborough Vineyard Sauvignon Blanc ★★★★

The 2010 vintage (★★★☆) was hand-harvested in Martinborough and mostly handled in tanks; 20 per cent of the blend was barrel-fermented. Mouthfilling, it is fleshy and finely textured, with moderately concentrated, ripe tropical-fruit flavours, good complexity and a smooth finish.

Vintage	10	09	08	07	06
WR	7	7	7	7	7
Drink	11-13	11-12	P	P	P

DRY $26 –V

Martinborough Vineyard Te Tera Sauvignon Blanc ★★★

The 2010 vintage (★★★) was hand-picked and lees-aged for four months in tanks. Fresh, fruity and smooth, it has mouthfilling body, with very ripe passionfruit-like flavours and a well-rounded finish.

Vintage	10	09	08
WR	6	6	6
Drink	11-13	11-12	P

DRY $22 –V

Massey Dacta Marlborough Sauvignon Blanc ★★★

From Glover Family Vineyards, the 2009 vintage (★★★☆) offers fine value. Fresh and finely balanced, it has vibrant tropical-fruit and gentle herbaceous flavours, moderately concentrated, ripe and smooth.

 DRY $15 V+

Matahiwi Estate Holly Wairarapa Sauvignon Blanc ★★★☆

The 2009 vintage (★★★☆) was grown at Opaki, near Masterton, and mostly fermented with indigenous yeasts in seasoned oak barrels. Crisp and dry, it is mouthfilling, with fresh, ripe tropical-fruit flavours, a seasoning of nutty oak, and good depth. Maturing well.

Vintage	09	08
WR	5	5
Drink	11-12	P

 DRY $26 –V

Matahiwi Estate Wairarapa Sauvignon Blanc ★★★☆

The 2010 vintage (★★★★) is a zingy, very lively wine, partly estate-grown near Masterton, with other fruit drawn from Martinborough. Partly barrel-fermented (5 per cent), it is ripely scented, mouthfilling and crisp, with sweet-fruit delights and peachy, limey flavours, very fresh, vibrant and strong.

Vintage	10	09	08
WR	5	5	7
Drink	P	P	P

 DRY $19 V+

Matakana Estate Marlborough Sauvignon Blanc ★★★☆

The 2009 vintage (★★★☆) was mostly handled in tanks, but a small portion (10 per cent) of barrel fermentation and lees-aging adds a touch of complexity. Fresh, crisp and dry, it has strong, lively melon and green-capsicum flavours.

 DRY $22 AV

Matawhero Gisborne Sauvignon Blanc (★★★)

The historic Matawhero brand has been revived by the Searle family, owners of Brunton Road. The 2009 vintage (★★★) was grown at Makaraka, near Matawhero. A medium-bodied wine (11.5 per cent alcohol), it is smooth (4.8 grams/litre of residual sugar), with ripe citrus and tropical-fruit flavours and an appetisingly crisp finish.

DRY $30 –V

Matua Valley First Frost Marlborough Sauvignon Blanc (★★☆)

The debut 2010 vintage (★★☆) is made to be 'lighter in alcohol and calories'. Only 9 per cent alcohol, it's a fruity, strongly herbaceous style, with a distinct splash of sweetness (8.9 grams/litre of residual sugar) balanced by firm acidity.

 MED/DRY $20 –V

Matua Valley Hawke's Bay Sauvignon Blanc ★★★

Consistently good and bargain-priced. The 2009 vintage (★★★) is fresh, ripe and rounded, with satisfying depth of tropical-fruit flavours and a dry, finely balanced finish.

DRY $17 AV

Matua Valley Marlborough Sauvignon Blanc ★★★

Balanced for easy drinking, the 2010 vintage (★★★) is mouthfilling, ripe and smooth, with good depth of fresh tropical-fruit flavours, some distinctly herbaceous notes, and lively acidity. The 2011 (★★★) is enjoyably light and lively, with some 'tomato stalk' aromas and fresh, vibrant melon, capsicum and lime flavours.

DRY $17 AV

Matua Valley Paretai Marlborough Sauvignon Blanc ★★★★☆

The winery's flagship Sauvignon Blanc is sometimes but not always sourced from the company-controlled Northbank Vineyard, an inland site on the north bank of the Wairau River. The 2009 vintage (★★★★★) was grown in the Awatere Valley, tank-fermented and lees-aged. Punchy and dry (2 grams/litre of residual sugar), it has excellent weight and richness of ripe gooseberry/lime flavours, in a fleshy, concentrated style with a minerally streak and a lasting finish.

DRY $25 V+

Matua Valley Reserve Release Marlborough Sauvignon Blanc ★★★☆

The 2010 vintage (★★★☆) is full-bodied, dry and crisp, with punchy tropical-fruit and herbaceous flavours, showing very good depth and vigour. The 2011 (★★★★) has punchy, 'sweaty armpit' aromas, leading into a high-impact wine with strong, ripe passionfruit and lime flavours, fresh, crisp and tight. It's already delicious.

DRY $20 AV

Maude Marlborough Sauvignon Blanc ★★★☆

Grown in the Wairau Valley, the 2009 vintage (★★★☆) is mouthfilling and fleshy, with good depth of tropical-fruit and herbaceous flavours, a sliver of sweetness (5 grams/litre of residual sugar) and lively acidity.

MED/DRY $18 V+

Maui New Zealand Sauvignon Blanc (★★★☆)

From Tiki Wines, the 2011 vintage (★★★☆) was estate-grown in the upper Wairau Valley, Marlborough. It's a fresh, mouthfilling, vibrantly fruity wine with strong, ripe pineapple/lime flavours and a splash of sweetness (6.2 grams/litre of residual sugar) adding an easy-drinking appeal.

MED/DRY $17 V+

Maven Marlborough Sauvignon Blanc ★★★☆

The 2009 vintage (★★★☆) was estate-grown on the northern side of the Wairau Valley. Crisp, with a touch of complexity from some use of seasoned French oak casks, it has moderately concentrated passionfruit and lime flavours, showing good freshness and vigour.

DRY $18 V+

McNaught & Walker White Ash Bluff Marlborough Sauvignon Blanc   ★★★★☆

This rare wine is grown in the heart of the Awatere Valley, 'before it rises into the frost barrier', where the vines are tended by Richard Bowling, the valley's most experienced viticulturist. The 2010 vintage (★★★★★) is superb. A strikingly rich, ripe wine, without any of the 'tomato stalk' characters usually associated with the valley, it is mouthfilling and sweet-fruited, with concentrated tropical-fruit flavours and a minerally undercurrent. It builds across the palate to a finely textured, lasting finish. Ready.

DRY $24 V+

Metis Hawke's Bay Sauvignon Blanc   ★★★★

From a joint venture between Trinity Hill and Loire producer Pascal Jolivet, this wine has set out to pioneer a new style of Hawke's Bay Sauvignon Blanc – tight, long-lived and unoaked. Weighty and dry, sweet-fruited, minerally and concentrated, the 2009 vintage (★★★★☆) is a very age-worthy wine, with ripe, rounded flavours, finely textured and lingering.

DRY $30 –V

Michelle Richardson Marlborough Sauvignon Blanc   ★★★★

The 2010 vintage (★★★★☆) was grown at Renwick, in the Wairau Valley, and partly (20 per cent) fermented with indigenous yeasts in old oak casks. Mouthfilling, full-flavoured and zingy, it has strong, ripe melon/lime characters, crisp and dry, a touch of complexity, and excellent vibrancy and length.

DRY $23 AV

Mills Reef Marlborough Sauvignon Blanc   ★★★

The lower-tier Sauvignon Blanc from Mills Reef used to be a Hawke's Bay regional wine, evolved into a blend of Hawke's Bay and Marlborough – and is now almost entirely from Marlborough (a small amount of Hawke's Bay wine was blended into the 2011 to add 'depth'). The 2011 vintage (★★★) has a freshly herbaceous bouquet, leading into a mouthfilling, smooth wine with good depth of ripe passionfruit/lime flavours and a slightly off-dry (5 grams/litre of residual sugar) finish.

Vintage	11
WR	6
Drink	11-13

MED/DRY $17 AV

Mills Reef Reserve Hawke's Bay Sauvignon Blanc   ★★★☆

The 2011 vintage (★★★), grown at Meeanee, was harvested at 19.8 brix, tank-fermented to dryness, briefly lees-aged and bottled by June. It's a medium-bodied wine with fresh, dry flavours, crisp and punchy.

Vintage	11
WR	7
Drink	11-13

DRY $21 AV

Misha's Vineyard The Starlet Sauvignon Blanc ★★★☆

Grown at Bendigo, in Central Otago, the 2010 vintage (★★★★) was hand-picked at 24 brix and mostly handled in tanks; 16 per cent of the blend was fermented with indigenous yeasts in seasoned oak barrels. Full-bodied, it is very vibrant and tangy, with strong, ripe grapefruit and lime flavours, showing a touch of complexity, a sliver of sweetness (5 grams/litre of residual sugar), and a tight, racy finish.

Vintage	10	09
WR	6	7
Drink	11-14	11-13

 MED/DRY $25 –V

Mission Hawke's Bay Sauvignon Blanc ★★★

The 2011 (★★★) was the first wine I tasted from that vintage – in May! Medium-bodied, it has fresh, ripe tropical-fruit flavours of pineapples and limes, with a crisp, dry (3 grams/litre of residual sugar) finish.

 DRY $20 –V

Mission Reserve Sauvignon Blanc ★★★★

The 2010 vintage (★★★★) was grown at Mangatahi, and fermented and lees-aged for eight months in French oak barriques (20 per cent new). It's a weighty, complex wine, rich, sweet-fruited and slightly minerally, with a fine thread of acidity, a subtle seasoning of oak and a finely balanced, bone-dry finish. It should mature well.

Vintage	10	09	08	07
WR	4	5	4	6
Drink	11-15	11-15	11-12	P

 DRY $28 –V

Mission Vineyard Selection Sauvignon Blanc ★★★★

The 2011 vintage (★★★★) is delicious already. Grown at Maraekakaho, it is mouthfilling, dry and ripely scented, with melon, lime and pineapple flavours, showing some lees-aging complexity, and a fresh, strong finish.

 DRY $22 V+

Moana Park Small Batch Sauvignon Blanc (★★★★)

The fleshy, complex 2010 vintage (★★★★) is a Hawke's Bay wine, hand-picked and given full barrel fermentation and malolactic fermentation. Concentrated, it has ripe tropical-fruit flavours, seasoned with nutty oak, and excellent texture, richness and roundness. Open 2012+.

 DRY $25 AV

Moana Park Vineyard Selection Cover Point Sauvignon Blanc ★★★

Grown in the Dartmoor Valley, Hawke's Bay, the 2009 vintage (★★☆) is full-bodied, dry and rounded, with tropical-fruit flavours, showing decent depth.

DRY $20 –V

Mobius Marlborough Sauvignon Blanc ★★★

From Grove Mill, the 2009 vintage (★★★) offers top value at $10. Illustrating 'the actual carbon footprint of the product', via the use of carbon-reduction labelling, it's a medium-bodied, ripely herbaceous wine, crisp and lively. Ready.

DRY $10 V+

Mojo Marlborough Sauvignon Blanc (★★★☆)

From Rockbare, the 2010 vintage (★★★☆) is fleshy, with very good depth of fresh, ripe, distinctly tropical-fruit flavours, threaded with fresh acidity, and a smooth finish.

DRY $20 AV

Momo Marlborough Sauvignon Blanc ★★★☆

From Seresin, the 2010 vintage (★★★☆) is a BioGro-certified wine, estate-grown and hand-picked at three sites. Fleshy, ripe and smooth, it has very good depth of gooseberry/lime flavours, slightly minerally and spicy, indigenous yeast notes adding complexity, and a crisp, dry finish.

DRY $20 AV

Moncellier Marlborough Sauvignon Blanc ★★★★☆

The 2010 vintage (★★★★☆) was grown mostly in the Wairau Valley, with a small portion of Awatere Valley fruit. Weighty and dry, it shows excellent substance, ripeness and roundness, in a tightly structured, age-worthy style. The 2011 (★★★★) is aromatic, punchy and crisp, with melon, green-capsicum and lime flavours, slightly minerally, dry and lingering.

Vintage	09
WR	5
Drink	11-12

DRY $20 V+

Monkey Bay Hawke's Bay Sauvignon Blanc/Pinot Gris (★★☆)

The debut 2010 vintage (★★☆) is a lively blend of Sauvignon Blanc (80 per cent) and Pinot Gris (20 per cent). Fresh, citrusy and limey, with hints of passionfruit and spices, it's an off-dry style, offering very easy drinking.

MED/DRY $16 AV

Monkey Bay Marlborough Sauvignon Blanc ★★★

From Constellation NZ, this wine is a roaring success in the US (reflecting its effective promotion, style and modest price). It is typically gently sweet, fresh and vibrant, with medium body, ripe-fruit flavours of melons and limes, and lots of drink-young charm.

MED/DRY $15 V+

Monowai Crownthorpe Sauvignon Blanc ★★★★

Estate-grown at a cool, elevated, inland site in Hawke's Bay, the 2011 vintage (★★★☆) was lees-aged in tanks. Medium-bodied, it has strong melon, passionfruit and lime flavours, fresh, crisp and lively, and a basically dry (4.5 grams/litre of residual sugar) finish. Priced sharply.

Vintage	11
WR	7
Drink	11-14

DRY $18 V+

Montana Hawke's Bay Sauvignon Blanc/Pinot Gris (★★☆)

The 2010 vintage (★★☆) is fresh and lively, with ripely herbaceous flavours, hints of pears and spices, and drink-young appeal. (Under $9 in supermarkets.)

DRY $19 –V

Montana Festival Block Marlborough Sauvignon Blanc (★★★☆)

This label is designed for 'on-premise' (meaning restaurant and bar) sales. The 2010 vintage (★★★☆) is good – aromatic, with strong, ripely herbaceous flavours, finely balanced, fresh and zingy.

DRY $? V?

Montana Marlborough Sauvignon Blanc ★★★☆

Now sold only in New Zealand, this famous, bargain-priced label from Pernod Ricard NZ rests its case on the flavour explosion of Marlborough fruit – a breathtaking style which this wine, more than any other, for 30 years introduced to wine lovers around the world. Production is now running at about one million cases per year, but since 2010 the wine has all been exported under the Brancott Estate, rather than Montana, brand. It is grown mostly in the Wairau Valley, but since 2008 the inclusion of Awatere Valley fruit has given 'a more herbal note, vibrancy and aromatic lift'. Punchy and fresh, with good vigour and depth, it's typically highly enjoyable in its youth. The 2010 vintage (★★★☆) is medium-bodied and ripely scented, with very good vibrancy and depth of melon, lime and capsicum flavours, fresh and finely balanced (3.9 grams/litre of residual sugar) for early drinking.

Vintage	11	10	09
WR	7	7	7
Drink	11-12	P	P

DRY $18 V+

Morton Estate Black Label Awatere Sauvignon Blanc (★★★★)

The classy 2009 vintage (★★★★) was estate-grown in the upper Awatere Valley and mostly handled in tanks; 30 per cent of the blend was oak-aged for several months. Full-bodied, it is rich and lively, with citrusy, grassy, slightly nutty flavours, a minerally streak, and a dry finish.

Vintage	09
WR	7
Drink	11-14

DRY $26 –V

Morton Estate Black Label Marlborough Sauvignon Blanc   (★★★☆)

Estate-grown in the upper Awatere Valley, the 2009 vintage (★★★☆) is a strongly herbaceous style with some riper passionfruit and lime characters. Full-bodied and rounded, it's ready now.

DRY $26 –V

Morton Estate Private Reserve Marlborough Sauvignon Blanc   (★★★☆)

Estate-grown in the upper Awatere Valley, the 2009 vintage (★★★☆) is punchy, with tropical-fruit and herbaceous flavours, crisp and lively, and a smooth finish.

Vintage	09
WR	7
Drink	11-12

DRY $21 AV

Morton Estate Stone Creek Marlborough Sauvignon Blanc   ★★★☆

The 2011 vintage (★★★☆) is mouthfilling, with very good depth of fresh, ripe melon, capsicum and spice flavours, finely balanced and enjoyable from the start.

DRY $20 AV

Morton Estate White Label Hawke's Bay Sauvignon Blanc   ★★★☆

The 2009 vintage (★★★) is an easy-drinking style, ripely scented, with satisfying depth of tropical-fruit flavours, crisp and lively, and a well-rounded finish.

Vintage	09	08
WR	6	5
Drink	P	P

MED/DRY $16 V+

Morton Estate White Label Marlborough Sauvignon Blanc   ★★★

If you like strongly herbaceous Sauvignon Blanc, try the 2010 vintage (★★★☆). Grown in the upper Awatere and lower Wairau valleys, it has 'tomato stalk' aromas, fresh and strong, and punchy, green capsicum-like flavours, woven with appetising acidity.

Vintage	10	09
WR	6	7
Drink	11-12	P

DRY $18 AV

Mountain Road Taranaki Sauvignon Blanc   ★★★

Grown north of New Plymouth, the 2010 vintage (★★★) is from vines planted in 2004. Made with some use of barrel fermentation and lees-stirring, it's a fresh, well-made wine with passionfruit, citrus-fruit and lime flavours, some toasty complexity, and a smooth finish. Ready.

DRY $22 –V

Mount Brown Waipara Valley Sauvignon Blanc   (★★☆)

Showing some development, the 2010 vintage (★★☆) is full-bodied, with herbaceous flavours, some tropical-fruit notes, lively acidity and a green-edged finish.

 DRY $16 AV

Mount Fishtail Marlborough Sauvignon Blanc ★★★

From Konrad and Co, the 2010 vintage (★★★☆), grown in the Wairau and Waihopai valleys, is lively, with an attractive combination of tropical-fruit and herbaceous flavours, slightly off-dry (4.6 grams/litre of residual sugar), fresh and crisp. Fine value.

Vintage	10
WR	6
Drink	11-12

Mount Nelson Marlborough Sauvignon Blanc ★★★☆

Mount Nelson is owned by Tenuta Di Biserno, itself controlled by members of the famous Tuscan wine family, Antinori. The company owns a vineyard on the south side of the Wairau Valley, from which most of the grapes are drawn. The aim is to make 'a classic Marlborough Sauvignon Blanc, with stronger emphasis on texture and length'. This is typically a full-bodied wine with very good depth of melon/lime flavours and a slightly minerally, lingering finish. The 2010 vintage (★★★☆) offers melon and green-capsicum flavours, fresh, crisp and dry, with very good depth.

Mount Riley Limited Release Marlborough Sauvignon Blanc ★★★★

The 2010 (★★★★) is Mount Riley's 'best effort' from the vintage. Mouthfilling, it is fresh and aromatic, with rich, dry passionfruit, capsicum and lime flavours, punchy, tangy and long.

Mount Riley Marlborough Sauvignon Blanc ★★★★

Fine value. The 2010 vintage (★★★★) is fleshy, sweet-fruited and harmonious, with good intensity of fresh, ripe tropical-fruit flavours and a dry, rounded, lingering finish.

Mount Riley Seventeen Valley Sauvignon Blanc ★★★★

Built to last, the 2009 vintage (★★★★) is a fleshy, single-vineyard wine, hand-picked in the Wairau Valley and fermented with indigenous yeasts in seasoned French oak barrels. Fresh, full-bodied and finely textured, it is slightly creamy and toasty, with sweet-fruit delights, tropical-fruit flavours, gentle acidity, and excellent complexity and richness.

Vintage	09
WR	6
Drink	11-12

Mount Vernon Marlborough Sauvignon Blanc ★★★☆

From Lawson's Dry Hills, the 2010 vintage (★★★★) is a great buy. A very easy-drinking style, with slightly 'sweaty', ripe-fruit aromas, it is rich and rounded, with tropical-fruit flavours showing excellent depth and fresh acidity keeping things lively.

DRY $17 V+

MSB Marlborough Sauvignon Blanc   (★★★)

From Waimarie, the 2010 vintage (★★★) was tank-fermented with indigenous yeasts and made in a slightly off-dry (6 grams/litre of residual sugar) style. It's a full-bodied wine with ripely herbaceous flavours, still fresh and lively, appetising acidity and a rounded finish. Ready.

MED/DRY $19 V

Mt Beautiful Cheviot Hills North Canterbury Sauvignon Blanc   ★★★☆

From a new sub-region, north of Waipara, the 2010 vintage (★★★) has slightly developed, toasty aromas leading into a fruity palate with good depth of ripe passionfruit-like flavours and a slightly creamy texture.

DRY $20 AV

Mt Campbell Nelson Sauvignon Blanc   ★★★

From Anchorage, the 2009 vintage (★★★☆) is priced sharply. It is full-bodied and finely balanced, with ripely herbaceous flavours, showing good vigour and length.

DRY $15 V+

Mt Difficulty Central Otago Sauvignon Blanc   ★★★☆

Grown at Bannockburn, the 2009 vintage (★★★★) was hand-picked, tank-fermented and matured for four months on its yeast lees, with weekly stirring. Weighty and fully dry, but not austere, it has crisp, ripe tropical-fruit flavours to the fore and a touch of lees-aged complexity. Showing excellent body, vigour and richness, it's one of the best Central Otago Sauvignon Blancs I've tasted.

Vintage	09	08
WR	7	6
Drink	11-13	11-12

DRY $25 –V

Mt Hector Wairarapa Sauvignon Blanc   ★★☆

From Matahiwi, the 2010 vintage (★★☆) is fresh, crisp, ripe and smooth, with tropical-fruit flavours and decent depth. Priced sharply.

Vintage	10
WR	5
Drink	11-12

DRY $13 V+

Mud House Marlborough Sauvignon Blanc   ★★★★

This is typically a strongly herbaceous style, offering a style contrast to its riper-tasting stablemate under the Waipara Hills Marlborough Sauvignon Blanc label. The 2010 vintage (★★★★☆), grown in the Wairau, Awatere and Ure valleys, is very stylish for such a large-volume wine. Garden-fresh, nettley aromas lead into a crisp, vibrantly fruity, finely poised palate with incisive but not aggressive flavours, a herbal undercurrent and a dry (3.5 grams/litre of residual sugar), lingering finish.

Vintage	10
WR	7
Drink	11-12

DRY $20 V+

Mud House The Woolshed Vineyard Marlborough Sauvignon Blanc   (★★★★☆)

The refined, sweet-fruited 2010 vintage (★★★★☆) was estate-grown on hillside blocks in the upper Wairau Valley and tank-fermented. Fully dry, with a minerally streak and good intensity of melon, lime and green-capsicum flavours, it shows excellent delicacy and length.

DRY $25 V+

Muddy Water Growers' Series Waipara Sauvignon Blanc   ★★★★

Hand-picked at three sites at Waipara, the 2011 vintage (★★★☆) was fermented in tanks (75 per cent) and French oak barrels (25 per cent). It is mouthfilling, with fresh, ripe stone-fruit, pear and slight spice flavours, lively acidity, and good balance for early drinking.

Vintage	11
WR	6
Drink	11-13

DRY $22 V+

Murdoch James Martinborough Blue Rock Sauvignon Blanc   ★★★☆

Drinking well now, the 2010 vintage (★★★☆) is fleshy and rounded, with very good depth of grapefruit and lime flavours, slightly spicy, dryish (6 grams/litre of residual sugar) and lingering.

MED/DRY $20 AV

Murray's Barn Marlborough Sauvignon Blanc   ★★★

From Terrace Heights, the 2011 vintage (★★★☆) is fine value. Mouthfilling and fleshy, it has ripe tropical-fruit flavours, showing very good delicacy and depth, and a dry (4 grams/litre of residual sugar) finish.

Vintage	11
WR	5
Drink	11-13

DRY $15 V+

Murrays Road Marlborough Sauvignon Blanc   ★★★★

The 2010 vintage (★★★★) is a single-vineyard wine, grown at Spring Creek, in the lower Wairau Valley. Mouthfilling and very finely balanced, it has a freshly aromatic bouquet, with ripely herbaceous flavours, slightly leesy and showing good intensity.

DRY $25 AV

Naked Vine Organic Marlborough Sauvignon Blanc   (★★★☆)

Certified BioGro, the 2010 vintage (★★☆) is a fresh, medium-bodied, single-vineyard Awatere Valley wine, with limey, citrusy, slightly spicy flavours, showing good delicacy. Crisp and dry, it's not a showy style, but quietly satisfying, with a touch of complexity and good length.

DRY $22 AV

Nautilus Marlborough Sauvignon Blanc   ★★★★☆

Released a year after the harvest, this is typically a richly fragrant wine with mouthfilling body and a surge of ripe passionfruit and lime-like flavours, enlivened by fresh acidity. Oak plays no part in the recipe, but it is briefly matured on its yeast lees. The 2010 vintage (★★★★) was grown at several sites, some estate-owned, in the Wairau and Awatere valleys. Opening up well, it is a zingy wine with freshly herbaceous aromas and strong melon, lime and green-capsicum flavours, crisp and dry (2 grams/litre of residual sugar).

Vintage	10	09	08	07	06
WR	7	7	6	7	6
Drink	11-13	11-12	P	P	P

DRY $25 V+

Navrina Cove Marlborough Sauvignon Blanc (★★★☆)

From Two Rivers, the 2009 vintage (★★★☆) is slightly minerally, with very good delicacy and depth of gooseberry, 'tomato stalk' and lime flavours.

DRY $20 AV

Ned, The, Waihopai River Marlborough Sauvignon Blanc ★★★☆

The 2011 vintage (★★★☆) is a single-vineyard wine, full-bodied, with slightly 'sweaty' aromas and fresh, ripe tropical-fruit flavours, with a herbal undercurrent. It's a finely balanced wine, showing good depth and immediacy.

DRY $19 V+

Neudorf Nelson Sauvignon Blanc ★★★★☆

Looking for a Sauvignon Blanc 'with texture, that is complex and satisfying', Neudorf grew the grapes for the 2010 vintage (★★★★) at Brightwater, on the Waimea Plains. Partly (9 per cent) fermented in old oak barrels, and bottle-aged prior to its release, it is a fully dry style (2 grams/litre of residual sugar), with fresh, strong, slightly nettley flavours, a touch of complexity, a minerally thread, and excellent vigour and length.

Vintage	10	09	08	07	06	05
WR	6	6	5	6	6	5
Drink	11-13	11-12	P	11-12	P	P

DRY $23 V+

Ngatarawa Stables Reserve Marlborough Sauvignon Blanc (★★★☆)

The 2010 vintage (★★★☆) is drinking well now. Full-bodied, it has ripely herbaceous flavours, fresh and strong, and a dry finish.

Vintage	10
WR	7
Drink	11-13

DRY $22 AV

Ngatarawa Stables Sauvignon Blanc ★★★

Grown in Hawke's Bay and Marlborough, the 2011 vintage (★★★) is enjoyable young. It's a medium-bodied wine, with fresh melon/lime flavours, crisp and lively, and good balance, vigour and depth.

Vintage	11
WR	6
Drink	11-14

DRY $18 AV

Nga Waka Martinborough Sauvignon Blanc ★★★★

Substantial in body, with concentrated, ripe, bone-dry flavours, this is a cool-climate style of Sauvignon Blanc, highly aromatic and zingy. The vinification, 'very straightforward', with no use of oak, yields a wine that typically peaks at four to six years old, when it is rich, toasty, minerally and complex. The 2010 (★★★☆) is less striking than some past vintages. It has fresh, herbaceous aromas, leading into a crisp, dry wine, strongly flavoured, but also showing some asparagus and 'canned peas' notes, suggesting relatively early development.

Vintage	10	DRY $25 AV
WR	7	
Drink	11+	

Nikau Point Hawke's Bay Sauvignon Blanc ★★☆

From One Tree Hill Vineyards (owned by Morton Estate), the 2009 vintage (★★☆) is a crisp, medium-bodied wine with melon/lime flavours, light and lively.

Vintage	09	DRY $15 AV
WR	6	
Drink	P	

Nikau Point Marlborough Reserve Sauvignon Blanc ★★★☆

This is Morton Estate's 'most minerally, acidic and grassy' Sauvignon Blanc. The 2009 vintage (★★★☆) is fresh and punchy, with vibrant melon and green-capsicum flavours, showing good balance and depth.

Vintage	09	DRY $18 V+
WR	7	
Drink	P	

Nikau Point Marlborough Sauvignon Blanc (★★☆)

The 2009 vintage (★★☆) from Morton Estate is a medium-bodied wine, freshly herbaceous, with gooseberry and lime flavours, showing solid depth.

Vintage	09	DRY $15 AV
WR	6	
Drink	P	

Nobilo Icon Marlborough Sauvignon Blanc ★★★★☆

A consistently impressive wine from Constellation NZ. The 2010 vintage (★★★★★) is a high-impact, Awatere Valley style with strong, herbaceous aromas leading into a weighty wine with crisp, vibrant melon and green-capsicum flavours, highly concentrated, minerally and long.

DRY $24 V+

Nobilo Regional Collection Marlborough Sauvignon Blanc   ★★★

A riper style from Constellation NZ than its more herbaceous stablemate under the Selaks Premium Selection label, this wine tops the Sauvignon Blanc sales charts in the US. It typically has fresh gooseberry/lime flavours and a crisp, slightly off-dry finish. Balanced for easy drinking, the lightly scented 2009 vintage (★★★) is a medium-bodied wine with lively, citrusy, limey flavours, a hint of grassiness, and a crisp, smooth (5 grams/litre of residual sugar) finish.

 MED/DRY $17 AV

Odyssey Marlborough Sauvignon Blanc   ★★★☆

Estate-grown in the Brancott Valley, the 2011 vintage (★★★) is fresh, crisp and dry (2.5 grams/litre of residual sugar), with melon/lime flavours, a hint of passionfruit, and moderate concentration.

 DRY $19 V+

Ohau Gravels Sauvignon Blanc   ★★★☆

Grown in Horowhenua, the 2010 vintage (★★★) was hand-picked from second-crop vines and mostly handled in tanks; 5 per cent of the blend was fermented with indigenous yeasts in old oak barrels. Medium-bodied, it is smooth, with faint sweetness (4.5 grams/litre of residual sugar), a touch of complexity, and good depth.

 DRY $21 AV

Ohinemuri Estate Wairau Valley Marlborough Sauvignon Blanc   ★★★

The 2010 vintage (★★★☆) was mostly handled in tanks, but 27 per cent of the blend was barrel-fermented. The bouquet is herbaceous; the palate is mouthfilling, generous and dry, with fresh, vibrant ripe-fruit flavours, showing considerable complexity.

		DRY $24 –V
Vintage	10	
WR	5	
Drink	11-13	

Old Coach Road Nelson Sauvignon Blanc   ★★★

Seifried Estate's lower-tier Sauvignon. The 2011 vintage (★★★) is crisp and lively, with fresh, rounded passionfruit/lime flavours, showing good immediacy.

 DRY $17 AV

Omaha Bay Vineyard Marlborough Sauvignon Blanc   (★★★)

The 2010 vintage (★★★) is mouthfilling and fleshy, with ripe tropical-fruit flavours, a herbal undercurrent, firm acidity and some development showing. Ready.

		DRY $22 –V
Vintage	10	
WR	6	
Drink	11-12	

Omaka Springs Marlborough Sauvignon Blanc ★★☆

This wine has fresh, grassy aromas in a traditional style of Marlborough Sauvignon, zesty and strongly herbaceous. The 2011 vintage (★★☆) is crisp and dryish (5 grams/litre of residual sugar), with fresh melon and green-capsicum flavours, light and lively.

Vintage	11	10	09
WR	7	6	6
Drink	11-14	11-13	11-12

 MED/DRY $16 AV

Omihi Road Waipara Sauvignon Blanc ★★★★

Barrel-fermented and lees-aged, the 2009 vintage (★★★★) from Torlesse has good body, sweet-fruit delights and excellent depth of ripe melon, lime and pear flavours. It has a subtle oak influence adding complexity and a well-rounded finish.

Vintage	09
WR	6
Drink	12-15

 DRY $20 V+

Opawa Marlborough Sauvignon Blanc ★★★★

From Nautilus, the 2010 vintage (★★★★) was handled principally in tanks, with a touch of barrel fermentation (5 per cent). Delicious from the start, it is mouthfilling and vibrant, with fresh, ripe passionfruit and lime flavours, a touch of complexity, and a finely textured, smooth finish.

 DRY $22 V+

Open House Smooth Marlborough Sauvignon Blanc ★★★

Created 'especially with women in mind', the 2009 vintage (★★★) was produced at Wither Hills. Offering good value, it is medium-bodied, fresh and crisp, with tropical-fruit and herbaceous flavours, balanced for easy drinking.

 MED/DRY $15 V+

Oyster Bay Marlborough Sauvignon Blanc ★★★★

Oyster Bay is a Delegat's brand, reserved principally for Marlborough wines and enjoying huge success in international markets. Handled entirely in stainless steel tanks, this wine is grown at dozens of sites around the Wairau and Awatere valleys and made in a dry style with tropical-fruit and herbaceous flavours, crisp and punchy. It is typically weighty and intense, with fresh, dry melon, lime, passionfruit and green-capsicum flavours.

 DRY $20 V+

Palliser Estate Martinborough Sauvignon Blanc ★★★★★

At its best, this is a wholly seductive wine, one of the best Sauvignons in the country. A distinctly cool-climate style, it offers an exquisite harmony of crisp acidity, mouthfilling body and fresh, penetrating fruit characters. The grapes are mostly estate-grown, but are also purchased from growers on the Martinborough Terrace and a few kilometres away, at Te Muna. The fruit gives the intensity of flavour – there's no blending with Sémillon, no barrel fermentation, no oak-aging. The 2010 vintage (★★★★★) is highly aromatic, with fresh passionfruit and lime flavours, crisp and punchy, a minerally thread and a long finish. Great value.

DRY $22 V+

Pass, The, Marlborough Sauvignon Blanc (★★★★)

From Vavasour, the 2010 vintage (★★★★) is a fleshy, smooth blend of Wairau and Awatere Valley fruit, with ripe sweet-fruit delights, balanced acidity and good harmony. It's a slightly 'sweaty' wine, very fruity and well-rounded.

DRY $18 V+

Passage Rock Waiheke Island Sauvignon Blanc ★★★

The 2009 (★★★), estate-grown at Te Matuku Bay, is a fleshy, mouthfilling, well-rounded wine, sweet-fruited and creamy-textured, in a typical northern style. The 2010 vintage (★★★) is similar – fresh, ripe and rounded, with some richness.

DRY $25 –V

Paua Marlborough Sauvignon Blanc ★★★☆

From Highfield, the 2010 vintage (★★★) is a typical Wairau Valley style – full-bodied and sweet-fruited, with good depth of tropical-fruit flavours and balanced acidity. The 2011 (★★★☆) is very fresh and lively, with a minerally streak and melon/capsicum flavours, showing very good delicacy and depth.

DRY $19 V+

Pebble Row Marlborough Sauvignon Blanc (★★★☆)

From Vavasour, the punchy 2010 vintage (★★★☆) has slightly nettley aromas leading into a mouthfilling wine with fresh, vibrant melon/lime flavours, showing very good vigour and depth. Fine value.

DRY $18 V+

Pegasus Bay Sauvignon/Sémillon ★★★★☆

At its best, this Waipara, North Canterbury wine is lush, concentrated and complex, with loads of personality. The 2008 vintage (★★★★☆) is a slightly minerally and nutty blend of Sauvignon Blanc (70 per cent) and Sémillon (30 per cent), fermented with indigenous yeasts and lees-aged for nine months in a mix of stainless steel tanks, large oak vats and old barriques. Weighty and sweet-fruited, it has ripe flavours of citrus fruits, gooseberries and lime, appetising acidity and impressive vigour, complexity and length.

Vintage	09	08	07
WR	6	7	6
Drink	11-20	11-15	11-13

DRY $28 AV

Pencarrow Martinborough Sauvignon Blanc   ★★★☆

Pencarrow is the second-tier label of Palliser Estate, but this is typically a satisfying wine in its own right, bargain-priced. The 2010 vintage (★★★☆) is full-bodied, fresh and lively, with melon/lime flavours, a hint of passionfruit, and very good depth.

DRY $15 V+

Penny Lane Marlborough Sauvignon Blanc   ★★☆

From Morton Estate, the 2009 vintage (★★★) has a freshly herbaceous bouquet and lively, nettley flavours, strong and smooth. Priced sharply.

Vintage	09
WR	6
Drink	P

MED/DRY $15 AV

People's, The, Marlborough Sauvignon Blanc   (★★★☆)

Within weeks of its launch by Constellation NZ at $23, the 2010 vintage (★★★☆) could be bought for closer to $15. Grown in the Awatere Valley, it has grassy aromas and strong, herbaceous flavours, in a very upfront style with lots of youthful impact.

DRY $23 –V

People's, The, Marlborough Sauvignon Blanc/Pinot Gris   (★★★☆)

The 2010 vintage (★★★☆) is a blend of Sauvignon Blanc (80 per cent) and Pinot Gris (20 per cent). Mouthfilling, it is very fruity, with clearly herbaceous flavours, distinct hints of pears and spices, and a tangy, finely balanced finish.

DRY $23 –V

Peregrine Central Otago Sauvignon Blanc   ★★★☆

The aromatic, clearly herbaceous 2009 vintage (★★★★) was grown at Gibbston and Cromwell. It has excellent vigour, impact and length of citrusy, limey, minerally flavours.

DRY $22 AV

Peter Yealands Marlborough Sauvignon Blanc   ★★★☆

The 2010 vintage (★★★★) has punchy, nettley aromas, suggestive of the Awatere Valley, in a full-flavoured style with excellent weight and harmony. The 2011 (★★★☆) has a fresh, grassy bouquet and green-edged flavours, very fresh and lively, in an intensely varietal style.

DRY $20 AV

Petit Clos by Clos Henri Marlborough Sauvignon Blanc   ★★★☆

From young, estate-grown vines, the 2010 vintage (★★★☆) was harvested in the Wairau Valley and lees-aged for six months. It is fresh, with very good depth of ripe tropical-fruit and herb flavours, finely textured and bone-dry.

Vintage	10
WR	6
Drink	11-14

DRY $20 AV

Pruner's Reward, The, Waipara Sauvignon Blanc   ★★★☆

From Bellbird Spring, the 2011 vintage (★★★★) was estate-grown and handled without oak. It has fresh, lifted aromas, leading into a medium-bodied wine with good intensity of tropical-fruit and green capsicum-like flavours, enlivened by tangy acidity.

DRY $21 AV

Ra Nui Marlborough Wairau Valley Sauvignon Blanc   ★★★☆

This wine is cool-fermented in tanks, with a small percentage of barrel fermentation. The 2011 vintage (★★★☆) is a typical Wairau Valley style – mouthfilling, with generous, ripe tropical-fruit flavours and a rounded finish.

DRY $21 AV

Rapaura Springs Marlborough Sauvignon Blanc   ★★☆

The 2011 vintage (★★☆) is an easy-drinking wine, with moderate depth of ripe tropical-fruit flavours, a slightly creamy texture and a soft, dry (3 grams/litre of residual sugar) finish. Priced right.

DRY $15 AV

Rapaura Springs Marlborough Sauvignon Blanc Limited Release   ★★★☆

The rich, soft 2009 vintage (★★★★) was fermented and matured for 18 months in seasoned French oak casks. The bouquet is creamy and toasty; the palate is fleshy, rich and rounded, in a very ripe-tasting style, showing impressive complexity and concentration. Ready.

DRY $33 –V

Rapaura Springs Vineyard Reserve Marlborough Sauvignon Blanc   ★★★☆

The 2011 vintage (★★★☆) was mostly handled in tanks, but 20 per cent of the blend was oak-aged. Crisp and dry, it offers fresh, ripe tropical-fruit flavours, with slightly spicy and nutty notes adding a touch of complexity, and good length.

DRY $23 –V

Rata Marlborough Sauvignon Blanc   (★★)

The non-vintage wine (★★) on sale in 2011 is a low-alcohol style (8.5 per cent). From Marlborough Wine Ltd (Toi Toi), it is light and crisp, with citrusy, gently herbaceous flavours, fresh acidity and a short finish.

DRY $16 –V

Redoubt Hill Vineyard Nelson Sauvignon Blanc   ★★★☆

From 'probably the steepest vineyard in Nelson', the 2010 vintage (★★★☆) was grown at Motueka, hand-picked and handled entirely in tanks. A crisp, medium-bodied wine, it is tight, with ripe melon, herb and slight spice flavours, minerally and lingering. Worth cellaring.

DRY $23 –V

Redwood Pass Marlborough Sauvignon Blanc   ★★★☆

The 2010 vintage (★★★☆) is fresh, crisp and lively, with good depth of gooseberry and lime flavours and a dry finish. The 2011 (★★★☆) also has good immediacy, with fresh, youthful, green-edged flavours, crisp and strong. A good buy.

DRY $17 V+

Renato Nelson Sauvignon Blanc   ★★★☆

The 2010 vintage (★★★★) was 15 per cent barrel-aged. Instantly appealing, it's a generous wine with vibrant passionfruit and lime flavours, woven with racy acidity. The 2011 (★★★☆) is mouthfilling, with very good depth of ripe passionfruit/lime flavours, fresh and lively, and a finely balanced, dry finish (3 grams/litre of residual sugar).

Vintage	11	10	09	08	07
WR	6	7	7	5	6
Drink	12-14	11-14	11-13	11-12	P

DRY $19 V+

Ribbonwood Marlborough Sauvignon Blanc   ★★★

From Framingham, the 2011 vintage (★★☆) is mouthfilling, with fresh, citrusy, appley, slightly spicy flavours, dry (4 grams/litre of residual sugar), crisp and light.

Vintage	11
WR	6
Drink	11-12

DRY $19 AV

Richmond Plains Nelson Sauvignon Blanc   ★★★☆

Certified by BioGro, the 2010 (★★★★) has good weight and intensity, with crisp, ripe tropical-fruit flavours, some herbal notes adding interest, and a finely balanced, basically dry (4 grams/litre of residual sugar) finish. The 2011 vintage (★★★☆) is mouthfilling and ripely scented, with crisp acidity and fresh melon, lime and capsicum flavours, showing very good vigour and depth.

DRY $20 AV

Richmond Plains Whakatu Sauvignon Blanc   ★★★★

The 2009 vintage (★★★★), certified organic, has strong, herbaceous aromas leading into a concentrated, lively wine with crisp, dry, lasting flavours.

DRY $20 V+

Ripponvale Marlborough Sauvignon Blanc   ★★☆

From a Rapaura-based company, the 2009 vintage (★★☆) is a crisp, green-edged style with dry, herbaceous flavours, still fresh and lively.

DRY $17 −V

Riverby Estate Marlborough Sauvignon Blanc ★★★☆

A single-vineyard wine, from the heart of the Wairau Valley, the 2010 vintage (★★★☆) is ripely scented and full-bodied, with melon/lime flavours and crisp acidity. Tangy and sweet-fruited, it shows good depth.

 DRY $19 V+

River Farm Ben Morven Marlborough Sauvignon Blanc ★★★☆

The 2010 vintage (★★★★) was grown in the Ben Morven Vineyard, on the south side of the Wairau Valley, and 19 per cent of the blend was barrel-fermented with indigenous yeasts. Mouthfilling, it's a tightly structured wine with tropical-fruit flavours to the fore, showing good concentration, a subtle overlay of oak adding complexity, and a crisp, dry, lingering finish.

Vintage	10	DRY $20 AV
WR	6	
Drink	11-13	

Rochfort Rees Marlborough Sauvignon Blanc ★★★★☆

From an Auckland-based company, the 2010 vintage (★★★★★) offers great value. A blend of Awatere Valley and Wairau Valley grapes, with slightly nettley aromas, it is very vibrant and punchy, with concentrated tropical-fruit and herbaceous flavours, showing excellent freshness, richness and harmony.

 DRY $19 V+

Rockburn Central Otago Sauvignon Blanc ★★★

The 2010 vintage (★★★) was grown in the Cromwell Basin and at Gibbston, and 45 per cent barrel-fermented. It's a distinctive, slightly developed wine, with good palate weight, a touch of complexity and a crisp, dry finish.

 DRY $22 –V

Rockburn Three Barrels Central Otago Sauvignon Blanc ★★★★

Only 60 cases were made of the 2009 vintage (★★★★). Estate-grown at Parkburn, in the Cromwell Basin, it was barrel-fermented and lees-aged for 16 months in oak. Showing strong personality, it's a weighty, complex wine, limey, grassy, nutty and minerally, with excellent vigour and depth. Ready.

 DRY $35 –V

Rock Ferry Marlborough Sauvignon Blanc ★★★★

Certified BioGro, the 2010 vintage (★★★★) was hand-picked in The Corners Vineyard, in the Wairau Valley, and 70 per cent of the blend was fermented in large oak cuves with indigenous yeasts; the rest was handled in tanks. Creamy and complex, it has fresh, ripe grapefruit and lime flavours, bone-dry and slightly nutty, showing excellent depth and personality.

Vintage	10	DRY $25 AV
WR	6	
Drink	11-16	

Rock Ferry Rapaura Sauvignon Blanc

Offering great value, the 2010 vintage (★★★★) is a BioGro-certified wine, estate-grown in The Corners Vineyard, in the Wairau Valley. Compared to its higher-priced stablemate (above), it is less oak-influenced (10 per cent) and fractionally sweeter (3.5 grams/litre of residual sugar). Fleshy and rich, it has good complexity and drive, with pure melon, lime and slight nut flavours, a herbal undercurrent, and a finely poised finish. It's delicious now.

Vintage	10	DRY $18 V+
WR	6	
Drink	11-13	

Rongopai Marlborough Sauvignon Blanc ★★★

From Babich, the 2010 vintage (★★★) was grown in the Wairau and Awatere valleys. It has clearly herbaceous, 'tomato stalk' aromas, in a crisp and lively style, balanced for easy drinking. The 2011 (★★★) is medium-bodied, with tropical-fruit and herbaceous flavours, fresh, crisp and showing good balance and depth. Fine value.

 DRY $15 V+

Ruby Bay Vineyard Sauvignon Blanc ★★★

The 2009 vintage (★★★) is a single-vineyard Nelson wine. It's a medium-bodied style (11.5 per cent alcohol), with ripe gooseberry and lime flavours, appetisingly crisp and dry.

Vintage	09	DRY $20 –V
WR	5	
Drink	11-12	

Sacred Hill Halo Awatere Marlborough Sauvignon Blanc

The 2011 vintage (★★★★) is fleshy, pure and punchy, with generous, fresh, ripe gooseberry and green-capsicum flavours and a dry (2.5 grams/litre of residual sugar), well-rounded finish.

 DRY $26 –V

Sacred Hill Halo Marlborough Sauvignon Blanc ★★★★

Richly aromatic, the 2010 vintage (★★★★☆) is a bone-dry Wairau Valley wine with strong tropical-fruit flavours, highly concentrated and zingy. Full-bodied, ripe, punchy and minerally, it has a long, harmonious finish.

 DRY $26 –V

Sacred Hill Marlborough Sauvignon Blanc ★★★☆

The 2011 vintage (★★★☆) is fresh and crisp, with racy melon, lime and green-capsicum flavours, dry and lingering.

 DRY $21 AV

Sacred Hill Sauvage Sauvignon Blanc ★★★★

One of the country's most expensive Sauvignon Blancs, at its best this is an impressively rich, complex example of the widely underrated, barrel-matured Hawke's Bay Sauvignon Blanc style. The 2008 (★★★★) was hand-picked in the Dartmoor Valley, barrel-fermented with indigenous yeasts and French oak-aged for 10 months. Weighty and tightly structured, it's a fully dry (3 grams/litre of residual sugar), mouth-wateringly crisp wine with strong, pineappley, slightly nutty flavours, woven with tense acidity, and obvious cellaring potential.

DRY $33 –V

Saint Clair Marlborough Sauvignon Blanc   ★★★★☆

This label has shown fine form lately and is a top buy. Grown in the Wairau Valley, it is handled entirely in tanks. The 2010 (★★★★☆) is pungently aromatic, with passionfruit, lime and green-capsicum flavours, crisp, lively and concentrated. It's a high-impact style, delicious from the start. The 2011 vintage (★★★★) is highly scented, with slightly 'sweaty' aromas. An instantly likeable wine, it has distinct tropical-fruit flavours, strong, ripe and rounded.

Vintage	11	10	09
WR	6	7	7
Drink	11-13	11-12	P

 DRY $21 V+

Saint Clair Pioneer Block 1 Foundation Marlborough Sauvignon Blanc   ★★★★☆

This single-vineyard Marlborough wine is grown east of Blenheim, in the lower Wairau Valley, at a site formerly the source of the Wairau Reserve Sauvignon Blanc. The 2009 vintage (★★★★★) is finely scented and weighty, with tropical-fruit and gently herbaceous flavours, strikingly pure, intense and racy.

Vintage	09
WR	7
Drink	P

DRY $25 V+

Saint Clair Pioneer Block 2 Swamp Block Marlborough Sauvignon Blanc

★★★★

Sourced from a vineyard with a 'cooler climate', close to the coast at Dillons Point, in the lower Wairau Valley of Marlborough, the 2010 vintage (★★★★) is mouthfilling and vibrantly fruity, with good intensity of fresh, pure melon, lime and passionfruit flavours, crisp and long.

Vintage	10	09
WR	7	7
Drink	P	P

 DRY $25 AV

Saint Clair Pioneer Block 3 43 Degrees Marlborough Sauvignon Blanc   ★★★★☆

This Marlborough wine is grown in the lower Wairau Valley, at a site with rows 'running at an unusual angle of 43 degrees north-east to south-west', which gives 'a slightly more herbaceous Sauvignon Blanc'. The 2010 vintage (★★★★☆) is mouthfilling and sweet-fruited, with vibrant gooseberry and lime flavours, slightly spicy, very rich and harmonious.

Vintage	10	09
WR	7	7
Drink	P	P

DRY $25 V+

Saint Clair Pioneer Block 6 Oh! Block Marlborough Sauvignon Blanc ★★★★☆

Grown in fertile, silty soils in the lower Rapaura district of Marlborough's Wairau Valley, the 2009 vintage (★★★★) has lifted, herbaceous aromas and vibrant flavours of melons, capsicums and limes, crisp and strong. If you like a 'full-on' style of Sauvignon Blanc, try this.

Vintage	09
WR	7
Drink	P

DRY $25 V+

Saint Clair Pioneer Block 11 Cell Block Marlborough Sauvignon Blanc ★★★★☆

From a relatively cool site at Dillons Point, east of Blenheim, the 2010 vintage (★★★★☆) is full-bodied and vibrant, with deep, delicate passionfruit, pear and lime flavours, showing excellent texture and length.

Vintage	10
WR	7
Drink	P

DRY $25 V+

Saint Clair Pioneer Block 18 Snap Block Marlborough Sauvignon Blanc ★★★☆

Grown east of Blenheim, in the lower Wairau Valley, the 2010 (★★★☆) is an easy-drinking style, full-bodied, ripe and rounded, with strong, citrusy, limey flavours. The 2011 vintage (★★★☆) is mouthfilling, with slightly 'sweaty' aromas, fresh, ripe flavours of melons, lychees and limes, and a finely textured, dry (3 grams/litre of residual sugar) finish.

Vintage	10	09
WR	7	7
Drink	P	P

DRY $25 –V

Saint Clair Pioneer Block 19 Bird Block Marlborough Sauvignon Blanc ★★★★

Grown north of Blenheim, in the lower Rapaura district of the Wairau Valley, the 2010 vintage (★★★★) is full-bodied, ripe and rounded, with fresh melon, capsicum and lime flavours, showing excellent delicacy and length.

Vintage	10	09
WR	7	7
Drink	P	P

DRY $25 AV

Saint Clair Pioneer Block 20 Cash Block Marlborough Sauvignon Blanc (★★★★)

Grown close to the sea, at a relatively cool site east of Blenheim, the 2009 vintage (★★★★) is a 'full-on' style, with a blast of herbaceous aromas and penetrating gooseberry and green-capsicum flavours, crisp and long.

Vintage	09
WR	7
Drink	P

DRY $25 AV

Saint Clair Pioneer Block 21 Bell Block Marlborough Sauvignon Blanc ★★★★

Grown east of Blenheim, close to the sea in the lower Wairau Valley, the 2010 (★★★★) is a briskly herbaceous style, with nettley aromas and flavours. Fresh and racy, it shows good intensity, with a crisp, dry finish. The 2011 vintage (★★★☆) is a mouthfilling wine, ripely herbaceous and smooth, with fresh melon and green-capsicum flavours, showing very good harmony and depth.

 DRY $25 AV

Saint Clair Vicar's Choice Marlborough Sauvignon Blanc ★★★☆

Vicars, like many of us, will gladly worship a bargain – and this easy-drinking wine delivers the goods. The 2010 vintage (★★★☆) is smooth, with very good depth of vibrant passionfruit/lime flavours, a herbal undercurrent and instant appeal.

 DRY $19 V+

Saint Clair Wairau Reserve Marlborough Sauvignon Blanc ★★★★★

The 2001 and subsequent vintages have been exceptional, in a super-charged, deliciously ripe and concentrated style, lush and rounded, that has enjoyed glowing success on the show circuit, here and overseas. The vineyards vary from vintage to vintage, but all are at the cooler, lower end of the Wairau Valley. The wine is handled entirely in stainless steel tanks and drinks best in its first couple of years, while still fresh, zingy and exuberantly fruity. The 2010 vintage (★★★★★) has ripe 'sweaty armpit' aromas. Mouthfilling, with vibrant melon, passionfruit and lime flavours, possessing an almost oily richness, it has lovely purity, delicacy and flow, fresh acidity and a long, finely poised finish. It's not the region's most complex Sauvignon Blanc, but in terms of sheer pungency, it's a star.

Vintage	10	09
WR	7	7
Drink	P	P

 DRY $33 AV

Saints Hawke's Bay Sauvignon Blanc (★★★☆)

Tasted prior to bottling (and so not rated), the 2010 vintage has ripe-fruit aromas and lively tropical-fruit flavours, fresh, crisp and dry.

DRY $20 AV

Satellite Marlborough Sauvignon Blanc ★★★

From Spy Valley, the 2011 vintage (★★★) is already enjoyable, with fresh, lively melon/capsicum flavours, green-edged, crisp and strong.

DRY $17 AV

Sea Level Awatere Marlborough Sauvignon Blanc ★★★☆

The 2011 vintage (★★★★) offers very good value. It has fresh, nettley aromas, leading into a mouthfilling, rounded wine, with generous gooseberry and lime flavours, finely balanced, dry (2.5 grams/litre of residual sugar) and lingering.

Vintage	11
WR	6
Drink	11-14

 DRY $19 V+

Sears Road Hawke's Bay Sauvignon Blanc   ★★☆

'Best enjoyed barefoot on a sunny deck', the 2009 vintage (★★☆) is a pleasant quaffer, light, crisp and smooth. A bargain.

Secret Stone Marlborough Sauvignon Blanc   ★★★★

From Matua Valley, the 2009 vintage (★★★★) was 'passionately created'. Full-bodied, it shows good intensity, with crisp, vibrant passionfruit and lime flavours, finely balanced and dry.

Seifried Nelson Sauvignon Blanc   ★★★★

Typically a good buy. The 2010 vintage (★★★☆) is mouthfilling and smooth, with very good depth of ripe tropical-fruit flavours and a crisp, fully dry finish. The 2011 (★★★☆) is medium-bodied, with melon, lime and green-capsicum flavours, fresh, crisp and racy.

Vintage	11	10	09
WR	5	6	6
Drink	11-12	11-12	P

Seifried Winemakers Collection Nelson Sauvignon Blanc   ★★★★☆

The 2010 vintage (★★★★★) has 'sweaty armpit' aromas, fresh and lifted. Very rich and racy, it is crisp, dry and slightly minerally, with ripe sweet-fruit characters and searching passionfruit and green-capsicum flavours, showing excellent vigour and length. (The 2011 vintage is branded 'Aotea' – see that wine.)

Vintage	10	09
WR	6	6
Drink	11-12	11

Selaks Heritage Reserve Marlborough Sauvignon Blanc   (★★★★)

The debut 2011 vintage (★★★★) from Constellation NZ is a high-impact style, offering good value. It has fresh, punchy, herbaceous aromas, leading into a crisp, lively, nettley wine with excellent depth and vigour, and a tangy, lingering finish.

Selaks Heritage Reserve Marlborough Sauvignon Blanc/Pinot Gris   (★★★)

Offering easy drinking, the 2010 vintage (★★★) has fresh, nettley flavours, typical of Sauvignon Blanc, and some peachy notes from Pinot Gris; the Sauvignon Blanc predominates. It's a flavoursome, smooth wine, ready to roll.

DRY $22 –V

Selaks Premium Selection Hawke's Bay Sauvignon Blanc/Pinot Gris   (★★★)

The 2010 vintage (★★★) is not a Sauvignon Gris – a variety in its own right – but a blend of two grapes, Sauvignon Blanc and Pinot Gris. Sauvignon Blanc (70 per cent) has the upper hand here, in a mouthfilling dry wine with fresh acidity and good depth of ripe tropical-fruit flavours.

DRY $17 AV

Selaks Premium Selection Marlborough Sauvignon Blanc   ★★★

The 2009 vintage (★★★) from Constellation NZ is freshly herbaceous, in a traditional style with lively green capsicum-like flavours and a smooth finish.

DRY $17 AV

Selaks Winemaker's Favourite Marlborough Sauvignon Blanc   ★★★☆

From Constellation NZ, the 2010 vintage (★★★☆) is a fresh, lively wine, grown in the Awatere Valley. It has moderately concentrated, ripe tropical-fruit characters mingled with greener, more herbaceous notes, and a smooth finish.

DRY $21 AV

Seresin Marama Sauvignon Blanc   ★★★★★

This complex style of Sauvignon Blanc is hand-picked from the oldest vines in the estate vineyard at Renwick, in Marlborough, fermented with indigenous yeasts in French oak barriques (25 per cent new in 2008), and wood-matured for well over a year. BioGro-certified, the 2008 vintage (★★★★★) is notably rich and complex, with loads of personality. Mouthfilling (14.5 per cent alcohol), it is lush, with very ripe tropical-fruit flavours, deep, dry and lasting.

DRY $45 AV

Vintage	08	07
WR	6	7
Drink	11-14	11-15

Seresin Marlborough Sauvignon Blanc   ★★★★★

This is one of the region's most sophisticated, subtle and satisfying Sauvignons. It's also one of the most important, given its widespread international distribution and certified BioGro status. The grapes are grown in the original estate vineyard near Renwick, and in the company's two younger vineyards – Tatou, further inland, and Raupo Creek, on an elevated slope in the Omaka Valley. The wine (which includes 5 to 9 per cent Sémillon) is mostly fermented in tanks (84 per cent with indigenous yeasts in 2010), but about 15 per cent of the blend is fermented and lees-aged in seasoned French oak casks. The 2010 vintage (★★★★) is still very fresh, tight and youthful. It shows good complexity, with strong, vibrant melon and lime flavours, minerally, slightly nutty, crisp and dry.

DRY $28 V+

Vintage	10	09	08	07
WR	7	7	6	7
Drink	11-14	11-15	11-15	11-12

Seresin Reserve Marlborough Sauvignon Blanc ★★★★★

Put simply, the 2009 vintage (★★★★★) is a great wine. From the oldest vines in the Home Vineyard – low-cropped to produce the ripest fruit – and partly barrel-fermented, it is authoritative, mouthfilling, concentrated and dry, with deep melon/lime flavours, a hint of nuts, and lovely vibrancy, complexity and length. The 2010 (★★★★☆), certified by BioGro, was 40 per cent barrel-fermented (French barriques, seasoned, for five months). Still very youthful, it needs, almost demands, time. Very mouthfilling (14.5 per cent alcohol), it is crisp and gently oaked, with strong, very vibrant melon, lime and nut flavours, minerally, complex and dry. Best drinking 2013+.

Vintage	10	DRY $55 AV
WR	7	
Drink	11-16	

Shepherds Ridge Vineyard Marlborough Sauvignon Blanc ★★★☆

From Wither Hills, the 2009 vintage (★★★☆) is a medium to full-bodied wine with crisp, lively gooseberry and lime flavours, showing very good delicacy and depth.

Vintage	09	DRY $20 AV
WR	6	
Drink	P	

Shingle Peak Marlborough Sauvignon Blanc ★★★☆

From Matua Valley, the 2010 (★★★☆) has strong, vibrant tropical-fruit and herbaceous flavours, crisp and dry. As usual, it's a good buy. The fresh, crisp 2011 vintage (★★★☆) is enjoyable from the start, with tropical-fruit flavours, a herbal undercurrent, and very good depth.

 DRY $16 V+

Shingle Peak Reserve Release Marlborough Sauvignon Blanc ★★★★

The 2010 vintage (★★★★) is weighty and sweet-fruited, with excellent depth of fresh, pure passionfruit and lime flavours, good acid spine, and a lingering finish. The 2011 (★★★★) has 'sweaty armpit' aromas. Mouthfilling (14 per cent alcohol), it has rich passionfruit and lime flavours, woven with fresh acidity, and should unfold well during 2012.

 DRY $20 V+

Sileni Benchmark Block Trinity Vines Marlborough Sauvignon Blanc (★★★☆)

A single-vineyard, Awatere Valley wine, grown at Blind River, the 2009 vintage (★★★☆) is medium-bodied, with tight melon, lime and green-capsicum flavours, showing fresh acidity and very good depth.

Vintage	09	DRY $25 –V
WR	5	
Drink	11-12	

Sileni Benchmark Block Woolshed Marlborough Sauvignon Blanc   (★★★★☆)

Harvested from first-crop vines on Benmorven Station, the 2009 vintage (★★★★☆) has a pungent, lifted, ripely herbaceous bouquet. Mouthfilling, it is fresh and vibrant, with pure passionfruit and lime flavours, rich, dry and rounded.

		DRY $25 V+
Vintage	09	
WR	4	
Drink	11-12	

Sileni Cellar Selection Marlborough Sauvignon Blanc   ★★★☆

Showing lots of drink-young charm, the 2010 vintage (★★★☆) has fresh, strong passionfruit and lime flavours and a crisp, dry, finely balanced finish.

			DRY $20 AV
Vintage	10	09	
WR	6	6	
Drink	P	P	

Sileni The Cape Hawke's Bay Sauvignon Blanc   ★★★★

The 2009 vintage (★★★★) is mouthfilling, with strong tropical-fruit flavours, hints of pears and spices, lively acidity, and good freshness and length. It's a top example of the regional style.

		DRY $25 AV
Vintage	09	
WR	6	
Drink	11-12	

Sileni The Straits Marlborough Sauvignon Blanc   ★★★★☆

The 2009 vintage (★★★★☆) is very aromatic, crisp and punchy, with excellent weight and intensity of fresh gooseberry, lime and capsicum flavours.

		DRY $25 V+
Vintage	09	
WR	7	
Drink	P	

Sisters Ridge North Canterbury Sauvignon Blanc   (★★★☆)

From Mt Beautiful, in the Cheviot Hills, the 2010 vintage (★★★☆) is a high-alcohol style (14.5 per cent), ripely scented, with generous tropical-fruit flavours, dry and rounded. Good value.

DRY $15 V+

Sisters, The, Awatere Valley Marlborough Sauvignon Blanc   ★★★★

From Blind River. The 2010 (★★★★) is crisp and lively, with a highly aromatic, grassy bouquet, melon/lime flavours, a slightly nettley streak, and good length. The 2011 vintage (★★★★) is medium-bodied, with good intensity of vibrant melon, lime and capsicum flavours, dry and lingering.

DRY $17 V+

Soho Stella Marlborough Sauvignon Blanc ★★★★

From an Auckland-based company, the 2011 vintage (★★★★) is mouthfilling and ripe, with fresh, strong tropical-fruit flavours, showing a touch of complexity, and a dry, lingering finish.

 DRY $23 AV

Soho White Collection Marlborough Sauvignon Blanc ★★★

The 2011 vintage (★★★) is full-bodied, with fresh, ripe melon/lime flavours that build to a finely balanced, zingy finish.

 DRY $18 AV

Soljans Marlborough Sauvignon Blanc ★★☆

Drinking well now, the 2010 vintage (★★★) is one of the best. A single-vineyard wine, it is mouthfilling, with pleasing depth of ripe tropical-fruit flavours, dry and rounded.

DRY $20 –V

Soulo Marlborough Sauvignon Blanc (★★★)

Packaged in a single-serve, 175 ml plastic glass, the non-vintage wine (★★★) released in 2011 is from a Clevedon, South Auckland-based company. 'Best before 22 February 2012', it has fresh grapefruit and lime aromas, leading into a full-bodied, fresh wine, flavoursome and zingy. It's very sound and lively.

 DRY $5 AV

Southbank Estate Marlborough Sauvignon Blanc ★★☆

The 2010 vintage (★★), grown in the Wairau Valley, is citrusy, appley and limey, with green-edged flavours and fresh acidity. Solid but plain.

 DRY $20 –V

Southern Cross Marlborough Sauvignon Blanc ★★☆

From One Tree Hill Vineyards, a division of Morton Estate, the 2010 vintage (★★★☆) is fresh, crisp and lively, in a herbaceous, nettley style with decent depth. Priced right.

Vintage	10
WR	6
Drink	11-12

DRY $15 AV

Southern Lighthouse Nelson Sauvignon Blanc ★★★

From Anchorage, the 2010 vintage (★★★) is herbaceous, with fresh-cut grass and green-capsicum aromas leading into a medium-bodied wine, strongly varietal, very crisp and lively.

 DRY $17 AV

Spinyback Nelson Sauvignon Blanc ★★★★

From Waimea Estates, this is a great buy. The 2010 vintage (★★★★) is nettley, with fresh, crisp, clearly herbaceous flavours, lively and punchy, dry (3.4 grams/litre of residual sugar) and long.

Vintage	10	09
WR	7	6
Drink	P	P

DRY $16 V+

Sprig Marlborough Sauvignon Blanc ★★★

From Bouldevines, the 2010 vintage (★★★) is good value. It's a generous, smooth wine with plenty of ripely herbaceous flavour, fresh and forward.

Vintage	10
WR	6
Drink	11-12

DRY $15 V+

Spring Creek Estate Marlborough Sauvignon Blanc ★★★

Priced sharply, the 2011 vintage (★★★☆) was grown at Rapaura, in the Wairau Valley. Already enjoyable, it's a full-bodied, ripely herbaceous wine with tropical-fruit flavours to the fore, a herbal undercurrent, and good freshness and depth.

Vintage	11
WR	5
Drink	11-13

DRY $14 V+

Spring Creek Estate Seismic Marlborough Sauvignon Blanc (★★★☆)

The 2009 vintage (★★★☆) is a fleshy, ripe, gently herbaceous style with slightly 'sweaty' aromas and very good depth of passionfruit and lime flavours.

DRY $20 AV

Spy Valley Envoy Marlborough Sauvignon Blanc (★★★★)

Estate-grown in the Waihopai Valley, the 2010 vintage (★★★★☆) was hand-picked from the oldest vines, and fermented and lees-aged for a year in French oak barrels. Drinking well now, but still developing, it is fragrant, rich and creamy, with an obvious oak influence, coupled with concentrated, ripe tropical-fruit flavours. A wine of real substance, it is complex and well worth cellaring; open mid-2012+.

Vintage	10	09
WR	6	6
Drink	11-16	11-15

DRY $30 –V

Spy Valley Marlborough Sauvignon Blanc   ★★★★

Always a good buy. The 2011 vintage (★★★★), tank-fermented, is mouthfilling, with slightly 'sweaty' aromas. It has strong, ripe tropical-fruit flavours to the fore, with a herbal undercurrent, and excellent vigour, freshness and intensity.

Vintage	11	10	09
WR	7	6	6
Drink	11-13	11-12	P

 DRY $20 V+

Squawking Magpie Reserve Marlborough Sauvignon Blanc   ★★☆

The 2010 vintage (★★☆) is mouthfilling and dry, but plain, with crisp melon, lime and capsicum flavours that lack richness.

 DRY $20 –V

Squealing Pig Marlborough Sauvignon Blanc   ★★★☆

From Matua Valley, the 2011 vintage (★★★☆) was grown in the Awatere Valley. It's a fleshier, riper-tasting style than most of the valley's wines, with passionfruit/lime flavours, ripe and rounded, and drink-young appeal.

 DRY $19 V+

Staete Landt Annabel Marlborough Sauvignon Blanc   (★★★★★)

The 2010 vintage (★★★★★) is a classic ripe, non-herbaceous style from the Rapaura district. Estate-grown in a single vineyard and partly barrel-fermented, it is fleshy and rich, with deep, passionfruit-like flavours, tight and dry, a vague hint of oak, minerally notes and excellent complexity.

 DRY $24 V+

Staete Landt Marlborough Sauvignon Blanc   ★★★★★

Ripely scented, rich and zingy, this single-vineyard wine is grown at Rapaura and mostly handled in tanks, with some fermentation and lees-aging in seasoned French oak casks (20 per cent in 2009). The 2009 vintage (★★★★★) is very subtle and satisfying. Bone-dry, it is fleshy, with rich, ripe tropical-fruit flavours, crisp and lively, and excellent drive, immediacy and punch.

Vintage	09	08	07	06
WR	6	7	6	6
Drink	11-17	11-13	11-12	P

 DRY $23 V+

Stanley Estates Marlborough Sauvignon Blanc   ★★★★

The 2010 vintage (★★★★☆) is a single-vineyard, Awatere Valley wine. It has a pungent, clearly herbaceous bouquet and a concentrated, finely balanced palate with good acid spine and fresh gooseberry, lime and capsicum flavours, deliciously vibrant and minerally.

Vintage	10	09
WR	6	5
Drink	11-12	P

DRY $23 AV

Starborough Marlborough Sauvignon Blanc ★★★★

The 2010 vintage (★★★★) is based on estate-grown grapes, from the Awatere Valley (60 per cent) and Wairau Valley (40 per cent), and was mostly handled in tanks; 7 per cent of the blend was barrel-fermented. Freshly herbaceous and highly aromatic, it has a clear, pure Awatere Valley influence, but also shows some riper, Wairau Valley notes. Very fresh and vibrant, it's a finely balanced wine with a dry (4 grams/litre of residual sugar) finish. The 2011 (★★★☆) is fresh, sweet-fruited and finely poised, with ripe stone-fruit, spice and herb flavours, showing very good delicacy and length.

Vintage	10
WR	5
Drink	11-12

 DRY $21 V+

Stoneburn Marlborough Sauvignon Blanc ★★★

From Hunter's, the 2010 vintage (★★★) is a Rapaura wine, mouthfilling and dry, with ripe tropical-fruit flavours. It's drinking well now. A top buy.

 DRY $12 V+

Stonecroft Sauvignon Blanc ★★★

This Hawke's Bay winery sources grapes from Te Mata Estate's Woodthorpe vineyard, in the Dartmoor Valley. The 2010 vintage (★★★) is an easy-drinking wine, with tropical-fruit flavours, ripe and rounded.

DRY $20 –V

Stoneleigh Latitude Marlborough Sauvignon Blanc (★★★★)

From 'vineyards on the Golden Mile' (Rapaura Road), the debut 2011 vintage (★★★★) is a tightly structured, vigorous wine with crisp, punchy tropical-fruit flavours, showing good freshness and concentration.

 DRY $27 –V

Stoneleigh Marlborough Sauvignon Blanc ★★★☆

From Pernod Ricard NZ, this consistently good wine flows from the stony and relatively warm Rapaura district of the Wairau Valley, which produces a ripe style of Sauvignon Blanc, yet retains good acidity and vigour. Over 300,000 cases are produced. The 2011 vintage (★★★☆) has a slightly 'sweaty' bouquet, leading into a mouthfilling, dry wine with ripe melon/lime flavours, showing very good delicacy and depth, and a rounded finish.

Vintage	11	10	09
WR	6	7	7
Drink	11-12	P	P

 DRY $22 AV

Stoneleigh Vineyards Rapaura Series Marlborough Sauvignon Blanc   ★★★★☆

This richly flavoured wine is grown in the warm, shingly soils of the Rapaura district and lees-aged for two months, with regular stirring. The 2010 vintage (★★★★☆) was on the market by July 2010. Richly scented, it is a medium-bodied wine, sweet-fruited, with intense, ripe non-herbaceous flavours, slightly minerally, dry, rounded and long.

Vintage	10	09
WR	7	7
Drink	P	P

DRY $27 AV

Stonewall Marlborough Sauvignon Blanc   ★★☆

The 2009 vintage (★★☆) is a solid, no-fuss wine from Forrest, medium-bodied, with citrusy, appley, limey flavours, crisp and dry.

DRY $17 –V

Sugar Loaf Marlborough Sauvignon Blanc   ★★★★

Good value. The 2010 vintage (★★★★) is a mouthfilling, 50:50 blend of Wairau Valley and Awatere Valley grapes, showing good intensity of crisp, lively gooseberry/lime flavours. It's a ripely herbaceous wine, with plenty of drive and depth.

DRY $17 V+

Summerhouse Marlborough Sauvignon Blanc   ★★★★☆

This single-vineyard, Wairau Valley wine is consistently impressive, and the especially intense 2010 vintage (★★★★★) is outstanding. Richly scented, it is mouthfilling and sweet-fruited, with concentrated, ripe passionfruit/lime flavours, very fresh and vibrant, and a racy, bone-dry, long finish. The 2011 (★★★★) is generous, ripe and finely balanced, in a sweet-fruited, dry style with tropical-fruit flavours, showing good purity and concentration.

DRY $22 V+

Takutai Sauvignon Blanc   ★★☆

From Waimea Estates, in Nelson, the 2009 vintage (★★☆) is a crisp, medium-bodied wine with strong, green-edged flavours, still lively. Ready.

Vintage	09
WR	5
Drink	11

DRY $13 V+

Te Awa Hawke's Bay Sauvignon/Sémillon   ★★★★☆

'A wine for the table, not the bar' is the winery description, which sums up well the 2009 vintage (★★★★☆), labelled as a straight Sauvignon Blanc. The 2010 (★★★★☆) is a blend of estate-grown Sauvignon Blanc (61 per cent) and bought-in Sémillon (39 per cent). Partly barrel-fermented, it is poised and very youthful, but already approachable, with excellent intensity of ripe, fully dry, delicate melon/lime flavours, a subtle seasoning of oak, and obvious potential. A label worth following.

DRY $27 AV

Te Awa Left Field Sauvignon Blanc   (★★★☆)

Crisp and bone-dry, the 2010 vintage (★★★☆) is a very lively Hawke's Bay wine. Medium-bodied, it has ripe pineapple and lime-evoking flavours, showing good intensity, and a mouth-wateringly crisp finish.

Te Henga The Westie Premium Marlborough Sauvignon Blanc   ★★★☆

From Babich, the 2010 vintage (★★★☆) is a bargain. Full-bodied, fresh and punchy, it has vibrant melon, lime and green-capsicum flavours, showing very good balance and depth.

Te Henga The Westie Sauvignon Blanc   ★★☆

From Babich, the 2010 vintage (★★☆) is a North Island blend. Medium-bodied, it has fresh, ripe grapefruit and lime flavours, offering smooth, easy drinking.

Te Kairanga Martinborough Estate Sauvignon Blanc   ★★★☆

The 2010 vintage (★★★) was grown at two sites, and 10 per cent of the blend was barrel-fermented and oak-matured for a year. It's a fleshy, herbaceous, slightly developed wine, with a rounded finish.

Vintage	10	09
WR	7	7
Drink	11-13	11-13

Te Mania Nelson Sauvignon Blanc   ★★★☆

Typically a good wine – full-flavoured, with tropical-fruit characters, nettley notes and fresh, lively acidity. The 2011 vintage (★★★☆), BioGro certified, has crisp, strong flavours of melon, lime and passionfruit, already quite open and expressive.

Vintage	10	09
WR	7	6
Drink	11-12	P

Te Mata Cape Crest Sauvignon Blanc   ★★★★★

This oak-aged Hawke's Bay label is impressive for its ripely herbal, complex, sustained flavours. Most of the grapes are hand-picked in the company's relatively warm Bullnose Vineyard, inland from Hastings (the rest is grown at Woodthorpe, in the Dartmoor Valley), and the blend includes small proportions of Sémillon (to add longevity) and Sauvignon Gris (which contributes weight and mouthfeel). The wine is fully fermented and lees-aged for eight months in French oak barriques (33 per cent new). In a vertical tasting, the two to four-year-old wines look best – still fresh, but very harmonious. The 2010 (★★★★★) is a blend of Sauvignon Blanc (85 per cent), Sémillon (11 per cent) and Sauvignon Gris (4 per cent). The bouquet is beautifully rich, ripe and fragrant; the palate is fleshy and tightly structured, with concentrated tropical-fruit flavours, oak-derived complexity and richness, and obvious potential.

Vintage	10	09	08	07	06	05	04
WR	7	7	7	7	7	7	7
Drink	11-15	11-14	11-12	11-12	P	P	P

Te Mata Estate Woodthorpe Vineyard Sauvignon Blanc   ★★★★

Estate-grown at an inland site in the Dartmoor Valley, Hawke's Bay, and handled without oak, this is typically one of the region's liveliest Sauvignon Blancs. The 2010 (★★★★) is mouthfilling and tight, with fresh, zingy melon/lime flavours, crisp, dry and lingering. The 2011 vintage (★★★☆) is full-bodied and ripe-tasting, with pineapple and lime flavours, dry, crisp and zesty.

 DRY $20 V+

Terrace Heights Estate Marlborough Sauvignon Blanc   ★★★☆

The 2010 vintage (★★★☆) is full-bodied and fresh, with very good depth of ripe melon, passionfruit, herb and spice flavours, and a dry, finely balanced finish. The 2011 (★★★☆) is similar – fresh, punchy and harmonious.

Vintage	11	10
WR	6	5
Drink	11-13	11-12

 DRY $19 V+

Terrain Marlborough Sauvignon Blanc   ★★☆

Sold in supermarkets, the 2009 vintage (★★☆) is a distinctly ripe style with hints of pineapples and a dry finish. Smooth, easy, no-fuss drinking.

 DRY $12 V+

Terravin Marlborough Sauvignon Blanc   ★★★★

The 2009 vintage (★★★★) was mostly handled in tanks; 9 per cent of the blend was barrel-fermented. Weighty and vibrantly fruity, it has rich tropical-fruit flavours, sweet-fruited and crisp, with a touch of complexity and a finely balanced, dry finish.

 DRY $24 AV

Terravin Single Vineyard Marlborough Sauvignon Blanc   (★★★★☆)

Hand-harvested on the south side of the Wairau Valley, the 2009 vintage (★★★★☆) is a classy wine, mostly handled in tanks; one-third of the blend was fermented and matured for five months in seasoned French oak. Weighty and tightly structured, it is ripely scented and flavoured, with excellent intensity, a very subtle seasoning of nutty oak and a rich, dry finish.

DRY $29 AV

Thornbury Marlborough Sauvignon Blanc   ★★★★☆

The 2010 vintage (★★★★★) from Villa Maria is striking. Grown in the Awatere and Wairau valleys, it is intensely aromatic, weighty, sweet-fruited and dry, with a lovely array of fresh, pure fruit flavours – passionfruit, lime and grapefruit – and a sustained, slightly minerally, racy finish. A top buy. The 2011 (★★★★☆) has vibrant, ripely herbaceous flavours, very pure and punchy, a touch of minerality, and a dry (3.5 grams/litre of residual sugar), refreshingly crisp finish.

Vintage	11	10	09
WR	6	7	7
Drink	11-12	P	P

 DRY $22 V+

Three Stones Marlborough Sauvignon Blanc –
see 3 Stones Marlborough Sauvignon Blanc (at the start of this section)

Three Paddles Martinborough Sauvignon Blanc   ★★★

From Nga Waka, the 2010 vintage (★★☆) is freshly herbaceous, with melon and green-capsicum flavours, showing decent depth. The 2011 (★★★) is a very easy-drinking style, sweet-fruited and smooth, with ripe tropical-fruit flavours and a dry finish.

Vintage	11	10	09
WR	6	7	7
Drink	11+	11+	P

DRY $18 AV

Tiki Single Vineyard Marlborough Sauvignon Blanc   (★★★★)

Grown in the Wairau Valley, the 2009 vintage (★★★★) is a finely textured wine from McKean Estates, fresh and full-bodied, with excellent delicacy and depth of ripe gooseberry and lime flavours and a well-rounded finish.

DRY $25 AV

Tiki Single Vineyard Waipara Sauvignon Blanc   (★★★★)

A high-impact style, the 2010 vintage (★★★★) has slightly 'sweaty' aromas and crisp, penetrating passionfruit and lime flavours, very fresh and racy.

DRY $28 –V

Tiki Single Vineyard Wairau Alpine Valley Sauvignon Blanc   (★★★★★)

The intense, immaculate 2010 vintage (★★★★★) is notably aromatic, vibrant and punchy, with ripe tropical-fruit flavours, a herbal undercurrent and a long, minerally, dry (3.6 grams/litre of residual sugar) finish. Mouth-wateringly fresh, crisp and intense, it's delicious from the start.

DRY $28 V+

Tiki Wairau Alpine Valley Marlborough Sauvignon Blanc   ★★★☆

(This is the 'standard' label.) The 2010 vintage (★★★☆) is mouthfilling, with fresh, ripe tropical-fruit flavours, showing very good depth, and a smooth (5 grams/litre of residual sugar), rounded finish. The 2011 (★★★★), grown at three sites, is very open and expressive in its youth. Vibrantly fruity, it has strong melon, grapefruit and lime flavours, dryish (5.8 grams/litre of residual sugar), appetisingly crisp, and skilfully balanced for easy drinking.

MED/DRY $20 AV

Tinpot Hut Marlborough Sauvignon Blanc   ★★★★

Mostly estate-grown at Blind River, in the Awatere Valley, the 2009 vintage (★★★★★) is a richly scented wine with 'tomato stalk' aromas and concentrated tropical-fruit and herbal flavours. Crisp, lively and finely poised, with a minerally streak, it shows real intensity through the palate. The 2010 (★★★★) is fleshy, with good body, fresh, ripe tropical-fruit flavours, herbal notes, good intensity, and a finely balanced, lingering finish.

DRY $21 V+

Ti Point Marlborough Sauvignon Blanc ★★★★

The lively, finely balanced 2010 vintage (★★★★) has a punchy, aromatic bouquet, leading into a vibrantly fruity wine with strong tropical-fruit flavours, a herbal undercurrent, and good vigour and length. The 2011 (★★★☆), tank-fermented, is a fresh, lively, medium-bodied wine, with ripely herbaceous flavours, showing good delicacy, a sliver of sweetness (4 grams/litre of residual sugar) and good length.

Vintage	11
WR	6
Drink	11-14

DRY $20 V+

Tohu Marlborough Sauvignon Blanc ★★★★

This is a consistently excellent, single-vineyard wine, grown in the Awatere Valley. It typically has strong, ripe passionfruit-like flavours to the fore, some of the herbaceous, 'tomato stalk' notes typical of the valley, excellent concentration and a crisp, dry (3 grams/litre of residual sugar), racy finish. The 2011 (★★★★) is weighty, with strong, fresh melon, lime and green-capsicum flavours, appetising acidity and good vivacity and richness.

DRY $20 V+

Tohu Mugwi Marlborough Sauvignon Blanc ★★★★

The 2010 vintage (★★★★☆) was estate-grown in the Awatere Valley and fermented with indigenous yeasts in seasoned French oak barriques. It has a fragrant, slightly nettley and nutty bouquet, leading into a mouthfilling, rich wine with layers of flavour and excellent vigour and complexity. The green-edged notes detract slightly, suggesting the oak-aged style is better suited to the slightly warmer Wairau Valley, but this wine has an almost honeyed richness and is full of personality.

Vintage	10
WR	6
Drink	11-14

DRY $23 AV

Tohu Single Vineyard Nelson Sauvignon Blanc (★★★)

Grown at Brightwater, on the Waimea Plains, the 2011 vintage (★★★) is fleshy, with fresh, moderately concentrated, ripely herbaceous flavours, vibrant, crisp and dry (3.5 grams/litre of residual sugar).

DRY $20 –V

Toi Toi Marlborough Reserve Sauvignon Blanc ★★★☆

The 2010 vintage (★★★☆) is a weighty, tightly structured blend of Wairau Valley and Awatere Valley grapes. Crisp and dry, it has mouthfilling body and strong, vibrant gooseberry, passionfruit and lime flavours.

DRY $22 AV

Toi Toi Marlborough Sauvignon Blanc   ★★☆

The 2011 vintage (★★☆) has fresh, limey aromas leading into a mouthfilling, smooth wine with decent depth of lively, citrusy, limey flavours and a smooth (5.3 grams/litre of residual sugar) finish.

 MED/DRY $17 –V

Torea Marlborough Sauvignon Blanc   ★★★☆

From Fairhall Downs, the 2011 vintage (★★★☆) is fleshy and forward, mouthfilling and dry, with ripe grapefruit and peach flavours in a non-herbaceous, well-rounded style, offering good drinking.

 DRY $19 V+

Torlesse Waipara Sauvignon Blanc   ★★★☆

The 2009 vintage (★★★☆) is sweet-fruited, with lively gooseberryish flavours showing very good depth, and a smooth (5 grams/litre of residual sugar) finish. Still fresh, it's drinking well now.

Vintage	10	09
WR	6	5
Drink	11-12	11-15

 MED/DRY $18 V+

Torrent Bay Nelson Sauvignon Blanc   ★★★

From Anchorage Wines, at Motueka, the 2009 vintage (★★★) is citrusy and limey, with a sliver of sweetness amid its fresh, tangy flavours, which show good depth. The 2010 (★★☆) is fresh, crisp and dry (2.7 grams/litre of residual sugar), with brisk, herbaceous flavours, showing decent depth.

 DRY $16 V+

Totara Marlborough Sauvignon Blanc   (★★☆)

The 2010 vintage (★★☆) is an easy-drinking wine with smooth, ripe tropical-fruit flavours, showing moderate depth.

DRY $18 –V

Tranquillity Bay Nelson Sauvignon Blanc   (★★☆)

From Anchorage, the sharply priced 2009 vintage (★★☆) is an easy-drinking style, medium-bodied, with fresh, citrusy, ripely herbaceous flavours and a smooth finish.

 DRY $12 V+

Trinity Hill Hawke's Bay Sauvignon Blanc   ★★★★

This 'Sancerre-like' wine is consistently one of the region's finest, mid-priced Sauvignon Blancs. Grown in several vineyards, coastal and inland, it is tank-fermented to dryness (4 grams/litre of residual sugar in 2011). The 2011 vintage (★★★☆) is freshly scented, with lime and green-melon aromas, showing good intensity. Light and lively on the palate, it has tropical-fruit flavours and a finely balanced, rounded finish.

 DRY $19 V+

Triplebank Awatere Valley Marlborough Sauvignon Blanc   ★★★★

From Pernod Ricard NZ, the 2010 vintage (★★★★) is weighty, with an attractive mingling of tropical-fruit and herbaceous notes, crisp, slightly minerally and long. The 2011 (★★★★) is very aromatic, pure and punchy, with finely balanced, ripely herbaceous flavours, slightly nettley, crisp and lingering.

Vintage	10	09
WR	7	7
Drink	11-12	P

Tupari Awatere Valley Marlborough Sauvignon Blanc   ★★★★★

Grown in the upper Awatere Valley, this single-vineyard wine is made by Glenn Thomas, formerly of Vavasour. Handled in tanks and matured on its yeast lees for six or seven months, with weekly stirring (to give 'creaminess on the palate'), it is typically mouthfilling, rich and ripe, yet also minerally and racy, with concentrated passionfruit and lime flavours that build to a zingy, dry, lasting finish. The 2010 vintage (★★★★★) is an authoritative wine, richly scented, sweet-fruited and minerally, with gooseberry/lime flavours that show lovely drive, delicacy and depth. Classy stuff.

Tussock Nelson Sauvignon Blanc   ★★★

From Woollaston, the 2010 vintage (★★★) is a crisp, medium-bodied wine with strongly varietal melon, lime and herb flavours, slightly nettley and dry. The 2011 (★★☆) is light and crisp, with lively melon, citrus-fruit and lime flavours, showing only moderate depth.

Twin Islands Marlborough Sauvignon Blanc   ★★★

Negociants' wine offers easy drinking and is priced right. The 2010 vintage (★★★☆) has fresh, ripe melon and lime flavours, showing good depth, delicacy and liveliness, and a smooth finish. The 2011 (★★★) is crisp and lively, with melon, capsicum and lime flavours, not concentrated, but showing good purity and freshness.

Vintage	10
WR	7
Drink	11-13

Two Rivers of Marlborough Convergence Sauvignon Blanc   ★★★★★

From vineyards in the Awatere Valley and Wairau Valley, this classy wine is made with a small portion of barrel fermentation. The 2010 vintage (★★★★★), lees-aged for four months, is mouthfilling, beautifully vibrant, poised and concentrated, with sweet-fruit delights, a touch of complexity and deep passionfruit, gooseberry and lime flavours. Classy, tight-knit and intense, the 2011 (★★★★★) is another winner. Ripely scented, it is a weighty wine with strong tropical-fruit flavours, a herbal undercurrent, lovely delicacy and depth, and a long, zingy finish. Layered and slightly minerally, it shows excellent vivacity and richness.

Two Tails Marlborough Sauvignon Blanc

★★★☆

From Fairbourne, the 2010 vintage (★★★☆) was grown in the Wairau Valley. Fresh and vibrant, it is sweet-fruited and slightly minerally, with melon/lime flavours showing very good delicacy and depth.

DRY $18 V+

Two Tracks Marlborough Sauvignon Blanc

★★★

From Wither Hills, the 2010 vintage (★★★☆) is fresh and crisp, with ripe tropical-fruit flavours and hints of citrus fruit and spices. It's a vibrant, refreshing wine, with good length.

DRY $17 AV

Unison Hawke's Bay Sauvignon Blanc

(★★★☆)

The 2010 vintage (★★★☆) was hand-picked and fermented in a mix of tanks and barrels. Mouthfilling and dry, it's a ripely flavoured wine with tropical-fruit characters, hints of spice and toasty oak adding complexity, and a crisp finish.

DRY $20 AV

Urlar Gladstone Sauvignon Blanc

★★★★

Certified by BioGro, the 2010 vintage (★★★★) was partly (10 per cent) barrel-fermented. It has 'sweaty armpit' aromas leading into a fleshy, well-rounded, dry wine (3 grams/litre of residual sugar), with ripe nectarine and passionfruit flavours, a hint of herbs, and excellent concentration.

DRY $22 V+

Vavasour Awatere Valley Sauvignon Blanc

★★★★★

Consistently classy. The 2010 (★★★★★) is a classic sub-regional style, weighty, vibrant and racy. Intensely aromatic, it has pure melon and green-capsicum flavours, slightly nettley, with a dry, lasting finish. The youthful 2011 vintage (★★★★☆) is mouthfilling and creamy-textured, ripe and rounded, with a slightly oily texture and deep, ripely herbaceous flavours.

Vintage	11	10	09
WR	7	7	6
Drink	11-13	11-12	P

DRY $24 V+

Vidal Reserve Series Marlborough Sauvignon Blanc

(★★★☆)

The 2010 vintage (★★★☆) is a blend of Awatere Valley (72 per cent) and Wairau Valley (28 per cent) grapes, tank-fermented to dryness (2 grams/litre of residual sugar). It's a fresh, appetisingly crisp wine, with herbaceous, nettley aromas and flavours, showing very good vibrancy and immediacy.

Vintage	10
WR	7
Drink	11-12

DRY $24 –V

Vidal Reserve Series Organic Hawke's Bay Sauvignon Blanc   (★★★☆)

BioGro certified, the 2010 vintage (★★★☆) was mostly handled in tanks; 15 per cent of the blend was fermented and lees-aged in old French oak casks. Very fresh and limey, it shows a good balance between tropical-fruit and herbaceous flavours, appetisingly crisp and dry.

Vintage	10		DRY $24 –V
WR	6		
Drink	11-14		

Vidal White Series Marlborough Sauvignon Blanc   ★★★☆

The 2011 vintage (★★★) is the first to be labelled as 'White Series'. Grown in the Wairau and Awatere valleys, and tank-fermented, it is an easy-drinking wine, ripely herbaceous, fresh, smooth and dry (3 grams/litre of residual sugar).

Vintage	11	10	09	DRY $22 AV
WR	6	7	7	
Drink	11-13	11-12	P	

Villa Maria Cellar Selection Marlborough Sauvignon Blanc   ★★★★☆

An intensely flavoured wine, typically of a very high standard. Grown in the Wairau and Awatere valleys and tank-fermented, the 2010 vintage (★★★★☆), matured on its yeast lees for several months, is weighty, with concentrated, ripe tropical-fruit flavours, deliciously crisp and dry. The 2011 (★★★★☆) was grown in both valleys, tank-fermented to dryness (2.9 grams/litre of residual sugar), and lees-aged for several months. It's a fleshy, finely balanced wine, with fresh, rich tropical-fruit flavours and a long, well-rounded finish.

Vintage	11	10	09	DRY $25 V+
WR	7	7	7	
Drink	11-13	11-12	P	

Villa Maria Private Bin Marlborough Sauvignon Blanc   ★★★★

This large-volume label offers impressive quality and consistently great value. The 2010 vintage (★★★★) was grown in the Wairau and Awatere valleys, and made in a dry style (3.5 grams/litre of residual sugar). Offering wonderful value at its average price on special of $11.99, it is fleshy, ripe and finely textured, yet also fresh and zingy, with sweet-fruit delights and rich melon, lime and capsicum flavours, crisp and lingering. The 2011 (★★★★) is another winner. It has a lifted, ripely herbaceous bouquet, mouthfilling body, and fresh melon and green-capsicum flavours, showing excellent purity, harmony and depth. Target price: under $15.

Vintage	11	10	09	DRY $22 V+
WR	6	6	7	
Drink	11-13	11-12	P	

Villa Maria Reserve Clifford Bay Sauvignon Blanc   ★★★★★

Grown in the Awatere Valley (although the label refers only to 'Clifford Bay', into which the Awatere River empties), this is an exceptional Marlborough wine. Seddon Vineyards and the Taylors Pass Vineyard – both managed but not owned by Villa Maria – are the key sources of fruit. Handled entirely in stainless steel tanks and aged on its light yeast lees for two months, the wine typically exhibits the leap-out-of-the-glass fragrance and zingy, explosive flavour of Marlborough Sauvignon Blanc at its inimitable best. The 2010 (★★★★★) is a lovely wine – weighty, rich and zingy, with intense, pure gooseberry/lime flavours and a long, dry (2.5 grams/litre of residual sugar) finish. The 2011 vintage (★★★★★) has a fresh, aromatic, nettley bouquet, leading into an intense wine with strong yet delicate flavours, finely textured, very vibrant, minerally and long.

Vintage	11	10	09
WR	7	7	7
Drink	11-13	11-12	P

DRY $28 V+

Villa Maria Reserve Wairau Valley Sauvignon Blanc   ★★★★★

An authoritative wine, it is typically ripe and zingy, with impressive weight and length of flavour, and tends to be fuller in body, less herbaceous and rounder than its Clifford Bay stablemate (above). The contributing vineyards vary from vintage to vintage, but Peter and Deborah Jackson's warm, stony vineyard in the heart of the valley has long been a key source of grapes, and sometimes a small part of the blend is barrel-fermented, to enhance its complexity and texture. The 2010 (★★★★★) is mouthfilling, deliciously rich and rounded, with concentrated, ripe tropical-fruit flavours, a hint of 'sweaty armpit' and a finely textured, long, dry finish. The 2011 (★★★★★), lees-aged for three to four months, is fleshy and highly concentrated, with fresh, rich, racy tropical-fruit flavours, dry (2.6 grams/litre of residual sugar) and lingering.

Vintage	11	10	09
WR	7	7	7
Drink	11-13	11-12	P

DRY $28 V+

Villa Maria Single Vineyard Graham Marlborough Sauvignon Blanc   ★★★★☆

Grown in the Awatere Valley, near the coast, this wine has strong 'tomato stalk' aromas and flavours, crisp, zingy and incisive. The 2011 vintage (★★★★☆) is herbaceous, in a weighty style with concentrated gooseberry and lime flavours, minerally, dry (2 grams/litre of residual sugar) and long.

Vintage	11	10	09
WR	7	7	7
Drink	11-13	11-12	P

DRY $28 AV

Villa Maria Single Vineyard Southern Clays Marlborough Sauvignon Blanc   ★★★★☆

Grown in the foothills on the south side of the Wairau Valley, this wine is ripely scented and zingy, with incisive passionfruit and lime flavours, and a deliciously long and dry finish. The 2010 vintage (★★★★★) is a powerful style, pungently scented, with a hint of 'sweaty armpit'. It shows lovely freshness and intensity, with crisp, vibrant gooseberry, lime and passionfruit flavours, ripe, dry and very long.

Vintage	11	10
WR	7	7
Drink	11-13	11-12

DRY $28 AV

Villa Maria Single Vineyard Taylors Pass Marlborough Sauvignon Blanc   ★★★★★

Taylors Pass Vineyard lies 100 metres above sea level in the Awatere Valley. This wine is typically a classic example of the sub-regional style – vibrant, punchy, minerally and herbal, with intense capsicum and 'tomato stalk' aromas and a long, dry, racy finish. Tasted prior to bottling (and so not rated), the 2011 vintage looked great – rich, finely poised and punchy, with vibrant, minerally, herbaceous and tropical-fruit flavours, searching and scented.

Vintage	11	10	09
WR	7	7	7
Drink	11-13	11-12	P

 DRY $28 V+

Volcanic Hills Marlborough Sauvignon Blanc   ★★★★

From Green Rocket, an Auckland-based producer, the 2011 vintage (★★★★) is fine value. Crisp and vibrant, it has an array of pear, melon, lime and capsicum flavours, showing good intensity, delicacy, poise and length.

Vintage	11
WR	6
Drink	11-13

 DRY $20 V+

Waimea Barrel Fermented Nelson Sauvignon Blanc   (★★★★)

The full-bodied 2008 vintage (★★★★) was grown on the Waimea Plains and fermented and matured for four months in seasoned oak barrels. A fleshy, ripely flavoured wine, nutty, dry, slightly creamy and rounded, it's maturing well.

Vintage	08
WR	6
Drink	11-13

 DRY $23 AV

Waimea Nelson Sauvignon Blanc   ★★★★

Always a good buy. The 2011 vintage (★★★★), estate-grown on the Waimea Plains, is very punchy and crisp, with good acid spine and strong melon, lime and slight spice flavours, vibrantly fruity, tangy and long.

Vintage	11	10	09
WR	7	7	6
Drink	11-13	11-12	11-12

 DRY $20 V+

Waimea Sauvignon Blanc Naturally Low Alcohol   (★★★)

Launched from the 2011 vintage (★★★), this wine contains '30 per cent less calories and alcohol' than Waimea's standard Sauvignon Blanc (above). Grown in Nelson, it's a good example of the style, light-bodied (8 per cent alcohol) and slightly sweet (9 grams/litre of residual sugar), with lively, citrusy, slightly limey flavours, fresh, juicy and enjoyable young.

Vintage	11
WR	7
Drink	11-12

MED/DRY $20 –V

Waipara Hills Soul of the South Marlborough Sauvignon Blanc   (★★★★★)

A wine of strong presence, the 2009 vintage (★★★★★) was grown in the Awatere and Wairau valleys. Weighty and rich, it is generous and very finely balanced, with strong, ripe tropical-fruit flavours, good acid spine, and a lingering finish.

DRY $21 V+

Waipara Springs Waipara Sauvignon Blanc   ★★★☆

The 2009 vintage (★★★) is mouthfilling, with fresh, ripe grapefruit and lime flavours and a fully dry finish.

DRY $19 V+

Waipara Springs Waipara Sauvignon/Gris   (★★★)

The very user-friendly 2010 vintage (★★★) was produced not from the Sauvignon Gris variety, but rather a 2:1 blend of Sauvignon Blanc and Pinot Gris. It's a fruity, off-dry style, with plenty of ripely herbaceous, slightly peachy and spicy flavour.

MED/DRY $19 AV

Waipipi Wairarapa Sauvignon Blanc   ★★☆

The 2009 vintage (★★☆) was grown near Masterton and made with some use of indigenous yeasts and barrel-fermentation. It's a solid, moderately varietal wine with fresh, crisp pear and lime flavours.

Vintage	09	
WR	5	
Drink	P	

DRY $25 –V

Wairau River Marlborough Sauvignon Blanc   ★★★☆

The 2010 vintage (★★★☆) is freshly herbaceous and dry (4 grams/litre of residual sugar), with vibrant, pure melon and green-capsicum flavours, showing good depth. The 2011 (★★★☆) is fresh and forward, mouthfilling and rounded, with ripe passionfruit/lime flavours, offering good drinkability.

Vintage	11
WR	6
Drink	12-14

DRY $20 AV

Wairau River Reserve Marlborough Sauvignon Blanc   ★★★★

The 2010 vintage (★★★★) is fresh and dry (2.7 grams/litre of residual sugar), weighty and punchy, with concentrated pineapple/lime flavours, a herbal undercurrent, and a finely textured, long finish. The 2011 (★★★★) is weighty and vibrant, with fresh, concentrated tropical-fruit flavours, balanced acidity and a rich, smooth, lingering finish.

Vintage	11
WR	7
Drink	12-15

DRY $30 –V

Walnut Block Collectables Marlborough Sauvignon Blanc ★★★☆

The 2010 vintage (★★★☆) is good value. Fresh and clearly herbaceous, with strong gooseberry and lime flavours, crisp and direct, it's a dry wine (3 grams/litre of residual sugar), drinking well now.

Walnut Block Marlborough Sauvignon Blanc ★★★★

The 2010 vintage (★★★★) is a single-vineyard, hand-picked Wairau Valley wine. Tightly structured, full-bodied, sweet-fruited and dry, with concentrated, ripe melon/lime flavours, it has a clear indigenous yeast influence (29 per cent) adding a touch of complexity and personality.

West Brook Marlborough Sauvignon Blanc ★★★☆

The 2010 vintage (★★★☆) is a strong tropical fruit-flavoured wine, partly (6 per cent) barrel-fermented, with good acid spine, purity, vigour and freshness.

Whitehaven Greg Marlborough Sauvignon Blanc ★★★★★

Dedicated to the memory of founder Greg White, the 2010 vintage (★★★★★) was grown in the Awatere and Ure valleys. Mouthfilling and smooth, it shows lovely balance, delicacy and depth of tropical-fruit and herbaceous flavours, in a highly concentrated style with a basically dry (4.5 grams/litre of residual sugar) finish, balanced by racy acidity. The 2011 (★★★★) was grown in the lower Wairau and Waihopai valleys. It's a medium-bodied wine, still very youthful, with fresh melon, capsicum and lime flavours, dry (3 grams/litre of residual sugar), poised, tight and lingering.

Vintage	11	10	09
WR	6	7	7
Drink	11-13	11-12	P

Whitehaven Marlborough Sauvignon Blanc ★★★★★

This consistently impressive wine is a huge seller in the US, where it is distributed by one of its shareholders, global wine giant E & J Gallo. The grapes are grown at dozens of sites in the Wairau and Awatere valleys, and the wine is handled entirely in tanks. At its best within two years, it offers beautifully fresh, deep and delicate flavours of passionfruit and limes, pure and smooth. The 2011 vintage (★★★★★) is a great buy. Mouthfilling, punchy, crisp and dry (3 grams/litre of residual sugar), it is a classic regional style, with youthful tropical-fruit and herbaceous flavours, showing excellent purity, delicacy and length. A finely textured wine, already very expressive, it floats smoothly across the palate, building to a long finish. At under $20, it's a steal.

Vintage	11	10	09
WR	6	7	7
Drink	11-13	11-12	P

Whitestone Waipara Sauvignon Blanc ★★★☆

The 2009 vintage (★★★☆), a single-vineyard wine, is an attractively ripe and rounded style with good flavour depth and harmony. It's balanced for fresh, easy drinking.

DRY $20 AV

Wild Rock Elevation Marlborough Sauvignon Blanc ★★★☆

Full-bodied, crisp and dry, this wine is designed to accentuate 'floral' and 'stone-fruit' characters, by blending Sauvignon Blanc with small portions of Riesling and Viognier. Delicious from the start, the 2010 vintage (★★★★) is weighty, with an array of tropical-fruit, peach and spice flavours, fresh and vibrant, excellent mouthfeel, and a finely textured, dry (2.5 grams/litre of residual sugar) finish.

Vintage	10	09
WR	7	6
Drink	11-13	P

DRY $19 V+

Wild Rock The Infamous Goose Marlborough Sauvignon Blanc ★★★

From Wild Rock, a division of Craggy Range, the 2010 vintage (★★★☆) is punchy and vibrant, with crisp, dry melon and lime flavours, showing good freshness, vigour and depth.

Vintage	10	09
WR	7	6
Drink	11-13	P

DRY $19 AV

Wild South Marlborough Sauvignon Blanc ★★★☆

From Sacred Hill, the 2010 vintage (★★★☆) is fresh, lively and appetisingly crisp, with citrusy, limey flavours, good acid spine and a bone-dry finish. The 2011 (★★★☆) is a fresh, lively, medium-bodied wine with pure melon, lime and capsicum flavours, a minerally streak and a basically dry (4 grams/litre of residual sugar), lively finish.

DRY $20 AV

Wingspan Nelson Sauvignon Blanc ★★☆

From Woollaston, the 2011 vintage (★★☆) is a dryish wine, light and lively, with appley, limey flavours, fresh and crisp. Priced sharply.

MED/DRY $11 V+

Wither Hills Single Vineyard Rarangi Sauvignon Blanc ★★★★★

Grown at Rarangi, on the Wairau Valley coast, this can be a striking wine. The 2010 vintage (★★★★☆) is tight and youthful, with refined, gently herbaceous aromas and flavours that build well across the palate. Limey and minerally, with excellent delicacy and length, it has definite aging potential.

Vintage	10
WR	7
Drink	11-14

DRY $25 V+

Wither Hills Wairau Valley Marlborough Sauvignon Blanc   ★★★☆

This huge-selling, bargain-priced wine is grown mostly in company-owned vineyards, planted since 1993 in the Wairau Valley. Oak plays no part in the recipe: 'The vines are old enough to offer weight, texture and length,' says winemaker Ben Glover, who matures part of the final blend on yeast lees to add palate weight, but avoids lees-stirring. The 2010 vintage (★★★★) has a fresh, slightly herbaceous bouquet, leading into a punchy, tropical fruit-flavoured wine, finely balanced for easy drinking (4.5 grams/litre of residual sugar). It shows excellent richness, harmony, vigour and length.

Vintage	10	09
WR	6	5
Drink	11-12	P

DRY $20 AV

Woollaston Nelson Sauvignon Blanc   ★★★

The 2010 vintage (★★★☆) is punchy, vibrantly fruity and crisp, with fresh, tight, ripely herbaceous flavours and good, youthful impact. The 2011 (★★☆) is crisp and dry, with a minerally streak and ripe tropical-fruit flavours.

DRY $18 AV

Woven Stone Ohau Sauvignon Blanc   ★★★☆

The 2010 vintage (★★★) is from young vines at Ohau, north of the Kapiti Coast, in Horowhenua. It's a dry wine (2.8 grams/litre of residual sugar), medium-bodied, with a nettley bouquet, fresh, vibrant tropical-fruit and herbaceous flavours, showing good depth, and a smooth finish.

DRY $17 V+

Yealands Estate Marlborough Sauvignon Blanc   ★★★★

Estate-grown at Seaview, in the lower Awatere Valley, the 2011 vintage (★★★★☆) has a scented bouquet, showing 'tomato stalk' notes, and a mouthfilling palate with fresh, strong melon/lime flavours, pure, finely textured and lingering.

DRY $26 –V

Sauvignon Gris

Pernod Ricard NZ launched New Zealand's first commercial bottlings of an old French variety, Sauvignon Gris, from the 2009 vintage. Also known as Sauvignon Rosé – due to its pink skin – Sauvignon Gris typically produces less aromatic, but more substantial, wines than Sauvignon Blanc.

Sauvignon Gris is not a blend of Sauvignon Blanc and Pinot Gris (watch out for the confusing, recently released 'Sauvignon Blanc/Pinot Gris' under several brands); nor is it a new vine, bred by crossing those grapes. Sauvignon Gris is a variety in its own right.

In Bordeaux, Sauvignon Gris is commonly used as a minority partner in dry white blends dominated by Sauvignon Blanc, but in Chile – like New Zealand – producers are bottling and exporting Sauvignon Gris as a varietal wine. In Marlborough, where the majority of the vines are planted, Sauvignon Gris has proved to be fairly disease-resistant, ripening in the middle of the Sauvignon Blanc harvest.

Brancott Estate 'R' Renwick Marlborough Sauvignon Gris (★★★★☆)

Estate-grown at Brancott Estate (mostly) but also at Renwick, and handled entirely in tanks, the 2010 vintage (★★★★☆) is a mouthfilling, ripely herbal wine with rich grapefruit and lime flavours, lively acidity and a long, tight, dry (3.8 grams/litre of residual sugar) finish. Pure and punchy, with a minerally streak, it shows excellent delicacy and freshness.

DRY $35 –V

Clearview Reserve Hawke's Bay Sauvignon Gris (★★★★)

The region's first Sauvignon Gris, the 2010 vintage (★★★★) was estate-grown at Te Awanga and barrel-fermented. Crisp and weighty, with good freshness and vigour, it is dry (2 grams/litre of residual sugar), with peachy, slightly limey, spicy and nutty flavours, showing good complexity, and a tight finish. Worth cellaring.

DRY $28 –V

Montana Reserve Marlborough Sauvignon Gris (★★★★)

The 2009 vintage (★★★★) was grown in the Wairau and Awatere valleys and handled without oak. It shows good weight (nearly 14 per cent alcohol), with richness from lees-aging and crisp, dryish (5.2 grams/litre of residual sugar) flavours of citrus fruits, limes and nectarines, lively and lingering.

MED/DRY $24 AV

Montana Showcase Series Marlborough Sauvignon Gris (★★★★)

The 2009 vintage (★★★★) smells and tastes like a ripe Sauvignon Blanc, or even Sémillon. Weighty and smooth, with peach/melon flavours and hints of herbs, spices and limes, it has a touch of complexity and an off-dry (5 grams/litre of residual sugar), lengthy finish.

MED/DRY $24 AV

Sémillon

You'd never guess it from the tiny selection of labels on the shelves, but Sémillon is New Zealand's seventh most widely planted white-wine variety – just behind Viognier. The few winemakers who 20 years ago played around with Sémillon could hardly give it away, so aggressively stemmy and spiky was its flavour. Now, there is a new breed of riper, richer, rounder Sémillons on the market – and they are ten times more enjoyable to drink.

The Sémillon variety is beset by a similar problem to Chenin Blanc. Despite being the foundation of outstanding white wines in Bordeaux and Australia, Sémillon is out of fashion in the rest of the world, and in New Zealand its potential is still largely untapped. The area of bearing Sémillon vines has contracted markedly between 2007 and 2012, from 230 to 182 hectares.

Sémillon is highly prized in Bordeaux, where as one of the two key varieties both in dry wines, most notably white Graves, and the inimitable sweet Sauternes, its high levels of alcohol and extract are perfect foils for Sauvignon Blanc's verdant aroma and tartness. With its propensity to rot 'nobly', Sémillon forms about 80 per cent of a classic Sauternes.

Cooler climates like those of New Zealand's South Island, however, bring out a grassy-green character in Sémillon which, coupled with its higher acidity in these regions, can give the variety strikingly Sauvignon-like characteristics.

Grown principally in Marlborough (44 per cent of the country's plantings), Gisborne (32 per cent) and Hawke's Bay (21 per cent), Sémillon is mostly used in New Zealand not as a varietal wine, but as a minor (and anonymous) partner in wines labelled Sauvignon Blanc, contributing complexity and aging potential. By curbing the variety's natural tendency to grow vigorously and crop bountifully, winemakers are now overcoming the aggressive cut-grass characters that in the past plagued the majority of New Zealand's unblended Sémillons. The spread of clones capable of giving riper fruit characters (notably BVRC-14 from the Barossa Valley) has also contributed to quality advances.

However, very few wineries in New Zealand are exploring Sémillon's potential to produce complex, long-lived dry whites.

Askerne Hawke's Bay Sémillon   ★★★

Estate-grown near Havelock North, the 2010 vintage (★★★) was matured in French oak casks (33 per cent). It's a mouthfilling, fully dry wine with ripe tropical-fruit flavours seasoned with nutty oak, a slightly creamy texture and good depth. Worth cellaring.

Vintage	10	09	DRY $20 –V
WR	6	6	
Drink	12-15	11-12	

Clearview Hawke's Bay Sémillon   ★★★★

The 'gloriously oaky' 2009 vintage (★★★☆) was hand-picked at Te Awanga and fermented with indigenous yeasts in new American and one-year-old French oak barriques. An easy-drinking style with some complexity, it is mouthfilling, with good depth of fresh, ripe tropical-fruit flavours, strongly seasoned with toasty oak, and an off-dry (6 grams/litre of residual sugar) finish. Well worth cellaring.

Vintage	09	08	MED/DRY $25 AV
WR	7	6	
Drink	11-20	11-18	

Kaimira Estate Brightwater Sémillon   ★★★

Grown in Nelson, the 2009 vintage (★★★) is a medium to full-bodied, fully dry wine with fresh, smooth, citrusy, slightly spicy and herbal flavours, showing a touch of complexity. Worth cellaring.

Vintage	09	08	07
WR	6	6	5
Drink	11-16	11-15	11-12

 DRY $20 –V

Poverty Bay Riverpoint Sémillon   (★★★☆)

Grown in the Manutuke district of Gisborne, the 2010 vintage (★★★☆) was fermented in old French oak barriques. Made in a bone-dry style, it is medium-bodied, crisp and lively, with ripely herbal flavours, hints of nettles and hay, good acid spine, and a fresh, strong finish. It should build up good complexity with age.

 DRY $20 AV

Sileni Estate The Circle Hawke's Bay Sémillon   (★★★)

The easy-drinking 2010 vintage (★★★) is a fruit-driven style with citrusy, slightly appley and limey flavours, fresh and rounded.

DRY $25 –V

Verdelho

Verdelho, a Portuguese variety traditionally grown on the island of Madeira, preserves its acidity well in hot regions, yielding enjoyably full-bodied, lively, lemony table wines in Australia. It is still extremely rare in New Zealand, with only 2 hectares of bearing Verdelho vines in 2012, mostly in Hawke's Bay.

Esk Valley Hawke's Bay Verdelho   ★★★★

The 2010 vintage (★★★★) is a pale, summery wine with fresh, inviting scents and a vague hint of nuts. Mouthfilling, it has strong, youthful flavours of quinces and lychees and a dryish, mouth-wateringly crisp finish. The 2011 (tasted before bottling, and so not rated), was hand-picked in the company's Omahu Gravels and Joseph Soler vineyards, and 35 per cent of the blend was barrel-fermented with indigenous yeasts; the rest was handled in tanks. It's an off-dry style (7 grams/litre of residual sugar), fragrant and fleshy, with vibrant, distinctly tropical-fruit flavours and a smooth finish.

Vintage	11	10	09	08	07
WR	6	6	7	7	7
Drink	12-14	11-12	P	P	P

MED/DRY $24 AV

TW PT's Verdelho   (★★★★☆)

The 2010 vintage (★★★★☆) was grown in Gisborne, hand-harvested at 24.5 brix and made in a dry, barrel-fermented style. Scented and weighty (14.5 per cent alcohol), it is creamy-textured, with rich, ripe tropical-fruit flavours and a musky perfume. An excellent debut, it's already delicious.

 DRY $25 V+

Villa Maria Single Vineyard Ihumatao Vineyard Auckland Verdelho   ★★★★☆

Estate-grown at Mangere, in South Auckland, the 2010 vintage (★★★★☆) was mostly (65 per cent) fermented with indigenous yeasts in seasoned French oak barriques; the rest was handled in tanks. Fleshy and rich, it's a powerful wine with concentrated, very ripe tropical-fruit flavours, fresh acidity and a finely balanced, dry (2.5 grams/litre of residual sugar) finish.

Vintage	11	10
WR	6	6
Drink	12-15	11-14

DRY $28 AV

Viognier

Viognier is a classic grape of the Rhône Valley, in France, where it is renowned for its exotically perfumed, substantial, peach and apricot-flavoured dry whites. A delicious alternative to Chardonnay, Viognier (pronounced *Vee-yon-yay*) is an internationally modish variety, popping up with increasing frequency in shops and restaurants here.

Viognier accounts for only 0.6 per cent of the national vineyard, but the area of bearing vines is expanding steadily, from 15 hectares in 2002 to 204 hectares in 2012. Over 70 per cent of the vines are clustered in Gisborne and Hawke's Bay, with further significant plantings in Marlborough (15 per cent) and Auckland (5 per cent).

As in the Rhône, Viognier's flowering and fruit set have been highly variable here. The deeply coloured grapes go through bud-burst, flowering and *veraison* (the start of the final stage of ripening) slightly behind Chardonnay and are harvested about the same time as Pinot Noir.

The wine is often fermented in seasoned oak barrels, yielding scented, substantial, richly alcoholic wines with gentle acidity and subtle flavours. If you enjoy mouthfilling, softly textured, dry or dryish white wines, but feel like a change from Chardonnay and Pinot Gris, try Viognier. You won't be disappointed.

Alpha Domus The Wingwalker Hawke's Bay Viognier ★★★★

The 2010 vintage (★★★★), fermented and aged for 11 months in French and European oak casks (25 per cent new), is a smooth, basically dry style (4 grams/litre of residual sugar). Full-bodied, it is skilfully balanced and harmonious, with a creamy texture and strong, ripe, peachy, slightly biscuity flavours.

Vintage	10	09
WR	7	6
Drink	12-16	11-14

 DRY $25 AV

Anchorage Nelson Viognier ★★☆

The 2009 vintage (★★☆) is a light, easy-drinking style with lemony, appley flavours, some creamy notes and a dry (4.4 grams/litre of residual sugar) finish.

DRY $19 –V

Ascension The Vestal Virgin Matakana Viognier (★★★)

The 2010 vintage (★★★), hand-picked and handled entirely in tanks, is aromatic and vibrantly fruity, with citrusy, appley, slightly spicy flavours, fresh and lively.

MED/DRY $29 –V

Askerne Hawke's Bay Viognier ★★★☆

The 2010 vintage (★★★☆) is dry and full-bodied (14.5 per cent alcohol), with pear, lemon and spice flavours, showing good ripeness and complexity, some creamy notes and a well-rounded finish. Slightly lighter, the 2011 (★★★), hand-picked and fermented in French oak casks (50 per cent new), has peachy, slightly limey and toasty flavours, fresh acidity and a fully dry finish.

Vintage	11	10
WR	5	5
Drink	12-14	11-12

 DRY $20 AV

Babich Family Estates Individual Vineyard Fernhill Viognier   (★★★☆)

The 2010 vintage (★★★☆) is a dry, full-bodied Hawke's Bay wine, sweet-fruited, with fresh, vibrant peach and apricot flavours, balanced acidity, a slightly creamy texture, and very good focus and depth.

 DRY $25 –V

Brookfields Milestone Viognier   ★★★☆

Grown in Hawke's Bay and fermented in a 50:50 split of tanks and barrels, the 2010 vintage (★★★☆) is full-bodied (14.5 per cent alcohol) and creamy-textured, with melon, grapefruit and spice flavours, showing some leesy complexity, and a soft, dry finish.

Vintage	10
WR	7
Drink	12-16

 DRY $20 AV

Brunton Road Gisborne Viognier   (★★★)

The 2009 vintage (★★★), mostly barrel-fermented, is a full-bodied, dry style, nutty and rounded, with a strong, creamy 'malo' influence.

 DRY $22 –V

Bushmere Estate Gisborne Viognier   ★★★☆

The 2010 vintage (★★★☆) was hand-picked at nearly 26 brix, and fermented and lees-aged in seasoned French oak barriques. Sturdy, with a floral, delicate bouquet, it is very full-bodied (15 per cent alcohol), with good depth of pear and spice flavours, a touch of barrel-ferment complexity and a smooth (4 grams/litre of residual sugar) finish.

 DRY $22 AV

Butterfish Bay Northland Viognier   (★★★★)

Grown in the Far North on Paewhenua Island – a small peninsula reaching into Mangonui Harbour – the 2009 vintage (★★★★) is an impressive debut. Robust (14.5 per cent alcohol), it is fresh and vibrant, with a deliciously soft, slightly oily texture, ripe citrus-fruit, pear and spice flavours, and a rounded, fully dry finish.

Vintage	09
WR	6
Drink	P

 DRY $28 –V

Cable Bay Waiheke Island Viognier   ★★★★☆

The 2010 vintage (★★★★☆) was hand-picked and mostly barrel-fermented. It's a sturdy, bold, powerful wine, fresh and vibrant, with rich, ripe stone-fruit and spice flavours, savoury and complex. Well worth cellaring.

Vintage	10	09
WR	7	7
Drink	11-15	11-14

DRY $35 –V

Church Road Reserve Hawke's Bay Viognier ★★★★☆

Hand-picked in Pernod Ricard NZ's Redstone Vineyard and fermented in seasoned French oak barriques, the 2009 vintage (★★★★☆) is fleshy and concentrated, with mouthfilling body, an oily texture and concentrated, ripe fruit flavours, deliciously peachy, creamy and rounded. Already drinking well, the 2010 (★★★★☆) is rich, lush and very soft, with concentrated stone-fruit flavours, slightly spicy, honeyed and buttery, gentle acidity and a dry, rich, rounded finish.

DRY $37 –V

Churton Marlborough Viognier (★★★★)

The debut 2010 vintage (★★★★) was estate-grown and hand-picked in the Waihopai Valley, and fermented and lees-aged in French oak casks. An off-dry style (10 grams/litre of residual sugar), it is sturdy (over 14.5 per cent alcohol), complex and creamy, with vibrant, youthful, peachy, citrusy flavours, showing good concentration, and a rounded finish.

Vintage	10
WR	6
Drink	11-17

MED/DRY $37 –V

C.J. Pask Gimblett Road Hawke's Bay Viognier (★★★★)

The 2010 vintage (★★★★) is a top buy. A mouthfilling wine, made in an unoaked style to celebrate its rich peach, apricot and spice aromas and flavours, it is very fresh and finely balanced, with a persistent finish.

DRY $20 V+

Clayridge Marlborough Viognier ★★★

The 2009 vintage (★★☆) was grown in the Escaroth Vineyard, in Taylors Pass. It's a fleshy, peachy wine with some richness, but the finish is a bit hard and austere. There's some complexity here, but also a lack of charm.

MED/DRY $24 –V

Clos de Ste Anne Viognier Les Arbres ★★★★★

This organically certified Gisborne wine from Millton has arresting richness and complexity. The 2009 vintage (★★★★★) is delectable now. Hill-grown, hand-harvested and fermented with indigenous yeasts in large, 600-litre barrels, it has a beautifully scented, peachy, floral bouquet. A powerful, sweet-fruited, fully dry wine, it is rich and rounded, with concentrated peach and nectarine flavours and a seductively soft finish. A real treat.

Vintage	09
WR	6
Drink	11-21

DRY $55 AV

Coopers Creek Gisborne Viognier   ★★★☆

Good value, the 2009 vintage (★★★☆) is sturdy (14 per cent alcohol) and dry (3.9 grams/litre of residual sugar), with a slightly creamy texture and ripe, peachy, slightly spicy and nutty flavours. The very easy-drinking 2010 (★★★★) is a generous wine with rich, ripe fruit flavours, a slightly nutty, buttery complexity, and a soft finish. At well under $20, it's arguably the best-value Viognier on the market.

Vintage	10	09	08	07
WR	7	5	5	6
Drink	11-13	11-12	P	P

DRY $17 V+

Coopers Creek SV Chalk Ridge Hawke's Bay Viognier   ★★★★

Mouthfilling, dry and vibrantly fruity, the 2009 vintage (★★★★) is a barrel-fermented style with concentrated, peachy, slightly spicy flavours, a subtle oak influence, and a rich, dry (3 grams/litre of residual sugar) finish.

Vintage	09	08	07
WR	6	6	5
Drink	11-12	P	P

DRY $20 V+

Craggy Range Gimblett Gravels Vineyard Viognier   ★★★★★

The softly seductive 2009 vintage (★★★★★) is a dry wine, hand-picked at 24 brix and fermented and matured for six months in seasoned French oak barriques. It's a very generous, sturdy and enticingly floral wine, with the subtle oak influence adding complexity without overpowering its concentrated, ripe peach, pear and spice varietal flavours.

Vintage	09	08
WR	6	6
Drink	11-13	11-12

DRY $38 AV

Cypress Terraces Hawke's Bay Viognier   ★★★★

From a sloping site overlooking the Gimblett Gravels, the 2010 vintage (★★★★) is a powerful (14.5 per cent alcohol) dry wine, fermented in French oak casks (40 per cent new). Mouthfilling and fleshy, it is peachy, slightly toasty and biscuity, with good concentration and complexity, a slightly creamy texture, and a rounded finish.

Vintage	10
WR	7
Drink	12-14

DRY $31 –V

Dry River Estate Martinborough Viognier   ★★★★☆

Already delicious, the 2011 vintage (★★★★☆) has a late-harvest feel. Handled without oak, it is gently sweet (20 grams/litre of residual sugar), fleshy and forward, with very fresh and vibrant, concentrated stone-fruit and spice flavours, gentle acidity and a soft finish.

Vintage	11	10	09	08
WR	7	7	7	7
Drink	12-16	11-15	11-14	11-13

MED $45 –V

Elephant Hill Hawke's Bay Viognier   ★★★★

Estate-grown and hand-picked at Te Awanga, the 2010 vintage (★★★★) is mouthfilling, vibrantly fruity and dry, with ripe peach and apricot flavours and a well-rounded finish. It's a generous wine, drinking well from the start.

DRY $28 –V

Framingham F Series Marlborough Viognier   ★★★★

From estate-grown vines, the 2010 vintage (★★★★) was handled without oak. It's a robust wine (14.5 per cent alcohol), fleshy and rich, with strong, vibrant flavours of stone-fruit and spices and a dryish (5 grams/litre of residual sugar) finish. Worth cellaring.

Vintage	10	09
WR	6	6
Drink	12-13	11-12

MED/DRY $35 –V

Georges Michel La Reserve Marlborough Viognier   ★★★☆

The fleshy, flavoursome 2010 vintage (★★★☆) was fermented and matured for eight months in barrels (new and seasoned). Sturdy, it has citrusy, peachy, slightly buttery flavours, some 'funky' notes, considerable complexity and a fully dry, well-rounded finish.

Vintage	10	09
WR	6	6
Drink	11-17	11-15

DRY $26 –V

Gladstone Vineyard Viognier   ★★★★☆

The 2010 vintage (★★★★☆) was hand-picked in the northern Wairarapa and mostly handled in tanks; 20 per cent was matured in seasoned French oak barrels. A highly refined wine, it is poised and youthful, mouthfilling and vibrantly fruity, with rich stone-fruit flavours to the fore, subtle oak and lees-aging notes adding complexity, good acid spine, and obvious cellaring potential.

DRY $24 V+

Glazebrook Regional Reserve Hawke's Bay Viognier   ★★★

From Ngatarawa, the 2010 vintage (★★★☆) is full-bodied, with generous, peachy, slightly honeyed and toasty flavours. It's a creamy-textured wine, drinking well now.

Vintage	10
WR	7
Drink	11-12

DRY $27 –V

Hans Herzog Marlborough Viognier   ★★★★☆

The 2009 vintage (★★★★☆) was hand-picked from mature vines and fermented and lees-aged for a year in French oak puncheons. Full-bodied and rounded, with peachy, spicy aromas and flavours, showing good complexity and harmony, it is fragrant, sweet-fruited, dry and rich.

Vintage	09	08
WR	7	7
Drink	11-15	11-14

DRY $44 –V

Harwood Hall Marlborough Viognier   (★★★☆)

The 2009 vintage (★★★☆) was fermented with indigenous yeasts and lees-aged for eight months in barriques. Scented and smooth, it's a fruit-driven style with slight sweetness (7 grams/litre of residual sugar) and very good body and depth of vibrant, peachy flavour.

Vintage	09
WR	6
Drink	11-15

MED/DRY $24 –V

Matawhero Gisborne Viognier   (★★★)

The debut 2009 vintage (★★★) is a medium-bodied wine, grown at Patutahi. A slightly sweet style (8 grams/litre of residual sugar), with drink-young appeal, it has a gently floral bouquet and decent depth of citrus-fruit, apple and pear flavours.

MED/DRY $30 –V

Mills Reef Reserve Gimblett Gravels Hawke's Bay Viognier   ★★★☆

The 2010 vintage (★★★★) – not labelled as 'Gimblett Gravels' but grown there – is full-bodied and vibrantly fruity, with strong, ripe stone-fruit flavours, a touch of oak-derived complexity, and excellent texture, varietal character and depth. The 2011 (★★★), fermented and matured for 10 weeks in seasoned oak barrels, is fresh and moderately concentrated, with citrusy, peachy flavours and a dryish (5.8 grams/litre of residual sugar) finish.

Vintage	11
WR	7
Drink	11-13

MED/DRY $24 –V

Millton Clos de Ste Anne Viognier Les Arbres – see Clos de Ste Anne Viognier Les Arbres

Millton Riverpoint Vineyard Gisborne Viognier   ★★★★☆

The 2010 vintage (★★★★☆), certified organic, was hand-picked and fermented in a mix of tanks and French oak hogsheads. Full-bodied, it is freshly scented, with rich, citrusy, slightly spicy flavours, lively acidity and a dryish (5 grams/litre of residual sugar), slightly creamy, lingering finish. Best drinking mid-2012+.

Vintage	10	09	08	07
WR	7	7	6	7
Drink	11-12	P	P	P

MED/DRY $28 AV

Mission Reserve Hawke's Bay Viognier   ★★★☆

The 2009 vintage (★★★★), grown in the Dartmoor Valley, was fermented and matured for six months in French oak barriques. Rich and rounded, it's a dry style with stone-fruit and spice flavours, a subtle seasoning of oak, and a creamy, finely textured finish. Delicious drinking now onwards.

DRY $28 –V

Moana Park Hawke's Bay Viognier   (★★★☆)

An enjoyable, drink-young style, the 2010 vintage (★★★☆) was blended from grapes grown at Gimblett Road, Te Awanga and in the Dartmoor Valley. Fleshy and forward, it has very good depth of ripe, peachy flavour, softly textured and harmonious.

 DRY $19 V+

Moana Park Vineyard Tribute Viognier   ★★★☆

Grown in the Gimblett Gravels of Hawke's Bay, hand-picked at 24.6 brix and matured in seasoned French oak barriques, the 2009 vintage (★★★☆) is fleshy and creamy, with a slightly oily texture, strong, citrusy flavours and a dry finish.

 DRY $26 –V

Morton Estate White Label Hawke's Bay Viognier   ★★★☆

The 2009 vintage (★★★☆) is a full-bodied (14 per cent alcohol), fruity wine with ripe stone-fruit and spice flavours, showing good depth, and a soft, well-rounded finish.

Vintage	09
WR	7
Drink	11-12

 DRY $19 V+

Morton Estate White Label Private Reserve Hawke's Bay Viognier   ★★★☆

The 2009 vintage (★★★) is aromatic, with hints of apricots, mouthfilling body, good depth of ripe, peachy flavours and a rounded finish.

Vintage	09
WR	7
Drink	11-12

 DRY $23 –V

Mudbrick Vineyard Reserve Viognier   (★★★★)

Grown on Waiheke Island and fermented in a 50:50 split of tanks and oak barrels, the 2009 vintage (★★★★) is a weighty, fruit-driven style with a subtle oak influence and fresh, strong citrus and stone-fruit flavours.

DRY $36 –V

Obsidian Waiheke Island Viognier   ★★★★

Grown on the 'north face' of the estate vineyard at Onetangi, the 2010 vintage (★★★★☆) was fermented in seasoned French oak casks. Generous, soft and dry, with peachy, slightly buttery and toasty aromas and flavours, it is very concentrated and harmonious, with excellent texture and richness. Best drinking mid-2012+.

Vintage	10	09	08	07
WR	7	6	7	6
Drink	11-13	11-15	P	P

 DRY $43 –V

Passage Rock Viognier   ★★★★☆

Grown and barrel-fermented on Waiheke Island, the 2010 vintage (★★★★★) is the best yet. A complex style, fleshy and layered, it has concentrated, well-ripened stone-fruit and oak flavours, slightly creamy and nutty. Rich and tightly structured, with hints of apricots and spices, it should unfold well.

DRY $35 –V

Selaks Winemaker's Favourite Hawke's Bay Viognier   ★★★★

The 2009 vintage (★★★★) from Constellation NZ is a seductively soft, strapping wine (15 per cent alcohol), grown at Haumoana and handled without oak. It has fresh stone-fruit and spice flavours, very ripe-tasting, with a slightly oily richness and dry finish.

DRY $21 V+

Seresin Marlborough Viognier   ★★★★

Weighty and dry, the 2009 vintage (★★★★☆) has excellent body, concentration and complexity. It is fleshy, sweet-fruited and rounded, with peachy, mealy flavours, hints of melons and spices, and a finely textured, rich, harmonious finish. Estate-grown in the Omaka Valley and fermented and matured for eight months in French oak puncheons (50 per cent new), the 2010 (★★★★) is an organically certified wine, still very youthful. Full-bodied, with strong, peachy, slightly spicy and nutty flavours, it shows good complexity, but needs more time; open mid-2012+.

Vintage	10
WR	7
Drink	11-15

DRY $55 –V

Staete Landt Marlborough Viognier   ★★★★☆

Estate-grown at Rapaura, the 2010 vintage (★★★★☆) is one of the region's finest Viogniers yet. Hand-harvested and fermented and lees-aged for eight months in old French oak puncheons, it has rich, ripe stone-fruit flavours to the fore, with subtle oak and lees-aging characters adding complexity. Mouthfilling, very fresh and vibrant, it has obvious cellaring potential.

Vintage	09	08	07
WR	6	6	5
Drink	11-15	11-13	11-12

MED/DRY $48 –V

Stone Bridge Gisborne Viognier   ★★★☆

The 2009 vintage (★★★★) was estate-grown and matured in seasoned French oak casks. Richly scented and vibrantly fruity, with good concentration of ripe peach and apricot flavours, it is fresh and fully dry.

DRY $22 AV

Te Mata Zara Viognier   ★★★★☆

This estate-grown wine is from Woodthorpe Terraces, on the south side of the Dartmoor Valley in Hawke's Bay. Hand-picked, it is mostly (80 per cent in 2009) fermented and lees-aged for eight months in seasoned French oak barriques. The 2009 vintage (★★★★★) is fragrant, with aromas of pears, cream and nuts. Full-bodied, rich and seductively soft, it is drinking well from the start, with peach and slight apricot flavours, a creamy texture, and lovely ripeness and concentration.

Vintage	10	09	08	07	06
WR	7	7	7	7	7
Drink	11-14	11-13	11-12	11-12	P

DRY $28 AV

Terrace Heights Estate Marlborough Viognier ★★★

The 2010 vintage (★★★), handled without oak, is full-bodied, fresh and smooth, with a sliver of sweetness (7 grams/litre of residual sugar) and lively peach, lemon and slight apricot flavours.

Vintage	10
WR	6
Drink	11-14

MED/DRY $24 –V

Ti Point Gisborne Viognier (★★★☆)

The 2009 vintage (★★★☆) is a fruit-driven style, harvested at 24 brix and 20 per cent barrel-fermented. It's a mouthfilling wine with peachy, citrusy, slightly spicy flavours, a touch of oak and a fresh, crisp, bone-dry finish.

Vintage	09
WR	5
Drink	11-16

DRY $21 AV

Trinity Hill Gimblett Gravels Hawke's Bay Viognier ★★★★★

The 2010 vintage (★★★★) was hand-picked and fermented in a 50:50 split of tanks and seasoned French oak barrels. A fleshy, softly textured wine, it is peachy and slightly biscuity, with good complexity and richness and a dry finish. Worth cellaring.

Vintage	10
WR	6
Drink	12-14

DRY $35 AV

Turanga Creek New Zealand Viognier (★★★)

Estate-grown at Whitford, in South Auckland, the 2009 vintage (★★★) is weighty (14.5 per cent alcohol), ripe and soft, with good depth of stone-fruit and spice flavours and a hint of honey. Ready.

Vintage	09
WR	6
Drink	11-13

DRY $26 –V

TW Gisborne Viognier

Some vintages, for instance 2007 (★★★★★), have been outstanding, but others, such as 2008 (★★☆) have disappointed. The fleshy, partly barrel-fermented 2009 (★★★☆) offers ripe stone-fruit flavours, a touch of complexity and a fully dry finish. Fleshy and creamy, it's drinking well now.

DRY $22 AV

Vidal East Coast Viognier ★★★★

A good, well-priced introduction to Viognier. The 2009 vintage (★★★☆) is a blend of Gisborne (59 per cent), Hawke's Bay and Marlborough grapes, partly handled in tanks, but 60 per cent of the blend was fermented and lees-aged for four months in seasoned French oak barriques. A bone-dry style, it's full-bodied (14.5 per cent alcohol), with gentle acidity, a touch of complexity and good depth of pear and spice flavours, fresh and well-rounded. There is no 2010.

Vintage	10	09	08	07
WR	NM	6	7	7
Drink	NM	P	P	P

DRY $20 V+

Villa Maria Cellar Selection Hawke's Bay Viognier

The 2010 vintage (★★★★★) was hand-picked and partly handled in tanks, but 85 per cent of the blend was fermented in French oak barriques (15 per cent new). It's a fleshy (14.5 per cent alcohol), rich wine with a fresh, fragrant bouquet of peaches and apricots. Creamy-textured, with concentrated stone-fruit flavours, a hint of spices and a fully dry (1.6 grams/litre of residual sugar) finish, it is blossoming with bottle-age and offers great value.

Vintage	10	09
WR	7	7
Drink	11-14	11-14

DRY $24 V+

Villa Maria Private Bin East Coast Viognier ★★★☆

The 2010 vintage (★★★★) was mostly handled in tanks; 20 per cent of the blend was fermented in seasoned oak barrels. Full-bodied (14.5 per cent alcohol), it is floral and finely textured, with strong, vibrantly fruity, peachy, slightly spicy flavours and a dry (2 grams/litre of residual sugar), well-rounded finish. Fine value.

Vintage	10	09	08
WR	7	6	6
Drink	11-13	11-12	P

DRY $21 AV

Villa Maria Single Vineyard Omahu Gravels Vineyard Hawke's Bay Viognier ★★★★★

The powerful, lush, very rich and rounded 2010 vintage (★★★★★) was fermented and lees-aged for 10 months in French oak barriques (43 per cent new). Showing excellent complexity, it has deep, layered stone-fruit and nut flavours, with a bone-dry, lasting finish.

Vintage	10	09	08	07	06
WR	7	7	7	7	6
Drink	11-15	11-14	11-14	11-12	11-12

DRY $33 AV

Waimea Nelson Viognier ★★★★

A consistently good buy. The 2010 vintage (★★★★) is mouthfilling, slightly nutty and spicy, with rich, very fresh and vibrant stone-fruit flavours to the fore, lively acidity, a sliver of sweetness (8 grams/litre of residual sugar), and excellent harmony and personality.

Vintage	10	09	08	07	06
WR	7	7	7	6	5
Drink	11-13	11-13	11-12	P	P

 MED/DRY $22 V+

Wairau River Reserve Marlborough Viognier (★★★★)

The 2010 vintage (★★★★) was estate-grown on the banks of the Wairau River and mostly handled in tanks; 10 per cent was matured in seasoned French oak barriques. Floral, full-bodied, fresh and lively, it is finely textured, with peachy, slightly spicy flavours, hints of pears, oranges and honey, and a smooth (7.8 grams/litre of residual sugar) finish. Delicious from the start.

 MED/DRY $30 –V

Waitapu Estate Reef Point Viognier/Chardonnay (★★★☆)

Grown at Ahipara, in Northland, the 2009 vintage (★★★☆) is a mouthfilling, creamy-smooth blend of Viognier (75 per cent) and oak-aged Chardonnay (25 per cent). It shows good concentration of ripe tropical-fruit flavours, slightly buttery, nutty and honeyed.

DRY $22 AV

Wrights Gisborne Viognier (★★)

The 2010 vintage (★★) was grown in the Ormond Valley and matured for six months in French oak casks. Medium-bodied, it has dry, citrusy flavours, showing a hint of oak, and moderate depth.

DRY $25 –V

Yealands Estate Awatere Valley Marlborough Viognier ★★★

The 2010 vintage (★★★☆) is the best yet. A fleshy, fruit-driven style, it has vibrant stone-fruit and spice flavours, a creamy texture and a dry, rounded finish.

 DRY $25 –V

Würzer

A German crossing of Gewürztraminer and Müller-Thurgau, Würzer is extremely rare in New Zealand, with 1 hectare of bearing vines in 2012. Seifried has 'a few rows' at its Redwood Valley Vineyard, in Nelson.

Seifried Nelson Würzer   ★★★★

The 2010 vintage (★★★★) is a fleshy, medium style (16 grams/litre of residual sugar), floral and weighty (14.5 per cent alcohol), with strong pear, apricot and well-spiced flavours.

Vintage	10	09	08
WR	6	6	6
Drink	11-12	P	P

MED $20 V+

Sweet White Wines

New Zealand's sweet white wines (often called dessert wines) are hardly taking the world by storm, with only about 4000 cases exported in the year to mid-2011. Yet around the country, winemakers work hard to produce some ravishingly beautiful, honey-sweet white wines that are worth discovering and can certainly hold their own internationally. In *Winestate*'s 2010 Wine of the Year Awards, judged in Australia, the trophy for Sweet Whites was given to John Forrest Collection Marlborough Noble Riesling 2006.

New Zealand's most luscious, concentrated and honeyish sweet whites are made from grapes which have been shrivelled and dehydrated on the vines by 'noble rot', the dry form of the *Botrytis cinerea* mould. Misty mornings, followed by clear, fine days with light winds and low humidity, are ideal conditions for the spread of noble rot, but in New Zealand this favourable interplay of weather factors occurs irregularly.

Some enjoyable but rarely exciting dessert wines are made by the 'freeze-concentration' method, whereby a proportion of the natural water content in the grape juice is frozen out, leaving a sweet, concentrated juice to be fermented.

Marlborough has so far yielded a majority of the finest sweet whites. Most of the other wine regions, however, can also point to the successful production of botrytised sweet whites in favourable vintages.

Riesling has been the foundation of the majority of New Zealand's most opulent sweet whites, but Sauvignon Blanc, Sémillon, Gewürztraminer, Pinot Gris, Müller-Thurgau, Chenin Blanc, Viognier and Chardonnay have all yielded fine dessert styles. With their high levels of extract and firm acidity, most of these wines mature well for two to three years, although few are very long-lived.

Abbey Cellars Mary Noble Riesling (★★★)

Estate-grown in The Triangle district of Hawke's Bay, the 2009 vintage (★★★) was hand-picked at 30.5 brix and matured for six months in seasoned French oak casks. Mouthfilling, it is citrusy, slightly appley and spicy, with moderate sweetness (59 grams/litre of residual sugar), lively acidity and good drink-young appeal.

SW $23 (375ML) –V

Allan Scott Late Harvest Marlborough Sauvignon Blanc (★★★★☆)

The golden, fleshy 2008 vintage (★★★★☆) is a rich, complex, Sauternes style, hand-picked and fermented and matured for six months in old French oak barriques. Mouthfilling (although only 9 per cent alcohol), with a fragrant, honeyed bouquet, it has an oily texture and lovely depth of sweet (230 grams/litre of residual sugar), very ripe, apricot-like flavours, enriched by noble rot.

SW $29 (375ML) V+

Alluviale Anobli (★★★★★)

The light gold, Sauternes-style 2008 vintage (★★★★★) was made from botrytised Sauvignon Blanc grapes, harvested at Mangatahi, in Hawke's Bay, at 52 brix. French oak-aged, with a beautiful, richly honeyed fragrance, it is a flawless wine, concentrated and sweet (270 grams/litre of residual sugar), with an oily texture and lovely ripeness, richness and roundness.

SW $40 (375ML) AV

Alluviale Mangatahi Hawke's Bay Tardif (★★★☆)

Ensconced in a full-sized bottle, the 2010 vintage (★★★☆) was picked at Mangatahi, in Hawke's Bay, in early June. Made from late-harvested (35 brix), raisined but not botrytised grapes, it's ripely scented, mouthfilling, sweet (65 grams/litre of residual sugar) and soft, with fresh, gentle peach, pear and spice flavours. Enjoyable from the start, it's recommended by the producer as an apéritif.

 SW $27 (750ML) V+

Alpha Domus AD Noble Selection ★★★★★

The golden 2009 vintage (★★★★★) is a richly botrytised blend of Sémillon and Sauvignon Blanc, fermented and matured for eight months in French oak barrels (60 per cent new). It's a gloriously lush, decadent wine, very honeyed, sweet, concentrated and oily, while retaining good freshness and harmony. The 2011 (★★★★★), based entirely on botrytised Sémillon, was fermented and matured for three months in new French oak barriques. Golden and honey-sweet (220 grams/litre of residual sugar), with an oily richness, it has hugely concentrated flavours of apricots and honey, threaded with tense, racy acidity. Best drinking 2013+.

Vintage	11	10	09
WR	7	NM	6
Drink	12+	NM	11-15

 SW $42 (375ML) AV

Alpha Domus The Pilot Leonarda Late Harvest Sémillon ★★★☆

Delicious young, the pale gold 2010 vintage (★★★☆) is honeyed, sweet (90 grams/litre of residual sugar) and soft, with good complexity. Fermented in one-year-old French oak barrels, it's a gentle Sauternes style from Hawke's Bay.

Vintage	10	09	08	07
WR	6	6	6	6
Drink	11-15	11-14	P	P

 SW $20 (375ML) AV

Amisfield Lowburn Terrace Central Otago Riesling ★★★★☆

Estate-grown in the Cromwell Basin, the classy 2009 vintage (★★★★★) was harvested early (at 21 brix) and stop-fermented with low alcohol (8.8 per cent) and plentiful sweetness (51 grams/litre of residual sugar), balanced by racy acidity. The bouquet is complex; the palate is light, delicate and very refined, with intense lemon, apple, spice and slight sherbet flavours, crisp, minerally and lasting. It should be long-lived. The 2010 (★★★★), 'low in alcohol and high in extract', has just 7.9 per cent alcohol and is fractionally less sweet (47 grams/litre of residual sugar). Mosel-like, with green-apple aromas, showing good intensity, it is very lively, with citrusy, appley flavours, fresh, minerally, light and lovely. Drink now or cellar.

Vintage	10
WR	7
Drink	11-18

SW $35 (750ML) V+

Anchorage Noble Nelson Chardonnay   (★★★★)

Pale gold, the 2009 vintage (★★★★) is delicious young. The bouquet is fresh and honeyed; the palate is concentrated, with flavours of peaches, nectarines and apricots, enriched by botrytis, and a sweet (165 grams/litre of residual sugar), smooth finish.

 SW $26 (375ML) AV

Aotea Sweet Agnes Nelson Riesling   ★★★★

(Previously labelled as Seifried Winemakers Collection Sweet Agnes Riesling.) The 2011 vintage (★★★☆) is a freeze-concentrated wine with fresh, strong, citrusy flavours, sweet (204 grams/litre of residual sugar) and slightly spicy, with a hint of sherbet and lively acidity. It's still a baby; open mid-2012+.

Vintage	11
WR	7
Drink	11-18

 SW $22 (375ML) V+

Askerne Late Harvest Sémillon   ★★☆

The 2009 vintage (★★★) was estate-grown in Hawke's Bay, hand-picked and fermented in old oak barrels. Amber-hued, it's a very rich and raisiny, unabashedly sweet wine (168 grams/litre of residual sugar) with concentrated apricot, honey and nut flavours. Only a slight loss of freshness and vibrancy holds it back from a higher rating.

Vintage	09
WR	5
Drink	12-14

 SW $20 (375ML) –V

Askerne Noble Sémillon   ★★★★

At its best, this is a ravishing Hawke's Bay beauty in the mould of classic Sauternes. The 2008 vintage (★★★★) was fermented in French oak barrels (25 per cent new). Amber/green, with a bouquet of apricots and honey, it is oily and sweet (200 grams/litre of residual sugar), with concentrated honey, tea and apricot flavours, very rich and treacly. Ready.

Vintage	08	07	06	05	04
WR	6	5	6	6	7
Drink	12-16	11-14	11-12	P	P

 SW $30 (375ML) –V

Ata Rangi Kahu Botrytis Riesling   ★★★★

Grown in the Kahu Vineyard, neighbouring the Ata Rangi winery in Martinborough, the 2009 vintage (★★★★) is a late-harvest style with a gentle botrytis influence. It's delicious young, with fresh acidity and rich, sweet, citrusy, slightly spicy and honeyed flavours.

Vintage	09	08
WR	6	6
Drink	11-13	11-12

SW $32 (375 ML) –V

Auburn Central Otago Aura Riesling (★★★★★)

Late-picked in June at Bendigo, the Mosel-like 2010 vintage (★★★★★) is rare (277 bottles), with low alcohol (8.5 per cent) and abundant sweetness (104 grams/litre of residual sugar). Finely scented, with a hint of sherbet, it's already lovely, with vibrant, citrusy, appley, slightly honeyed flavours, poised, minerally and rich. A 'complete' wine.

SW $30 (750ML) V+

Auburn Central Otago Lowburn Riesling (★★★★☆)

Sweet but not super-sweet (64 grams/litre of residual sugar), the 2010 vintage (★★★★☆) shows lovely harmony. Scented and rich, it has ripe, citrusy, slightly spicy flavours, a hint of passionfruit and strong drink-young appeal.

SW $30 (750ML) V+

Aurum Pinot Gris 18 Carat (★★★★)

Estate-grown at Lowburn, in Central Otago, the 2009 vintage (★★★★) was made only from bunches with at least a 50 per cent 'noble rot' infection and not oak-aged. Delicious young, it has good weight, abundant sweetness (170 grams/litre of residual sugar) and strong, pure pear and spice flavours, faintly honeyed, very smooth and harmonious.

Vintage	09
WR	6
Drink	11-20

SW $32 (375ML) –V

Aurum Port Molyneux (★★★☆)

For something different, try this Central Otago 'white grape blend, fortified with brandy distilled from Pinot Noir lees'. Pale, with a slightly spirity bouquet, it is full-bodied (17 per cent alcohol) but not heavy, with very fresh, vibrant, gently sweet pear and spice flavours, and a hint of oranges.

SW $25 (375ML) –V

Beach House Noble Sauvignon Blanc (★★★★)

The 2009 vintage (★★★★) was harvested in Hawke's Bay at 28 to 40 brix, with a 70 per cent botrytis infection. The fragrant, strongly honeyed bouquet leads into a concentrated, luscious, finely textured wine, although not highly complex, with rich, sweet, marmalade-like flavours and a rounded finish.

SW $28 (375ML) AV

Bladen Marlborough Botrytised Riesling (★★★★)

Instantly appealing, the 2011 vintage (★★★★) was estate-grown, hand-picked in late May and made in a low-alcohol (9.5 per cent alcohol), sweet style (180 grams/litre of residual sugar). Light yellow, it is fresh and concentrated, citrusy and finely balanced, with a slightly spicy, rounded finish.

SW $25 (375ML) AV

Brancott Estate 'B' Marlborough Late Harvest Sauvignon Blanc   (★★★★☆)

The debut 2011 vintage (★★★★☆) was estate-grown in the Brancott Vineyard, near Renwick, hand-picked in late May at 43.5 brix and handled entirely in tanks, without oak. Golden, with an enticingly honeyed bouquet, it is already delicious, with concentrated peach and apricot flavours, plentiful sweetness (232 grams/litre of residual sugar), an oily texture and lovely richness and harmony.

 SW $37 (375ML) –V

Charles Wiffen Late Harvest Marlborough Riesling   ★★★★

From grapes picked five to six weeks after the main harvest, the 2009 vintage (★★★★★) is an enticingly scented wine with youthful colour, very fresh, pure, citrusy flavours, a hint of apricots, and lovely elegance and richness.

SW $32 (500ML) V+

Church Road Reserve Noble Viognier   ★★★★★

The 2008 vintage (★★★★★) is classy. Hand-picked from 'raisined and botrytised' grapes in the company's Redstone Vineyard, in Hawke's Bay, it's a beautifully scented, deliciously soft wine with a subtle oak influence and lush, ripe stone-fruit, pear and spice flavours, slightly oily, concentrated, sweet and complex. The 2009 (★★★★★) is another winner. Impossible to resist, it is very rich and soft, with sweet stone-fruit, spice and honey flavours, showing lovely depth, complexity and harmony.

 SW $36 (375 ML) AV

Cloudy Bay Late Harvest Riesling   ★★★★★

Cloudy Bay only makes this Marlborough wine about every second year, on average, but it's usually worth waiting for. The 2005 vintage (★★★★★) was matured for six months in old oak barrels. Pale gold, it is highly scented, poised and rich, with citrusy, peachy, slightly spicy and honeyed flavours, considerable sweetness (128 grams/litre of residual sugar), a minerally streak and good, bottle-aged complexity. Full of personality, it's lovely now.

Vintage	05	04	03	02
WR	6	6	NM	6
Drink	P	P	NM	P

SW $35 (375ML) AV

Coopers Creek Reserve Marlborough Late Harvest Riesling   ★★★★

The 2009 vintage (★★★★) was made from heavily botrytised grapes, grown at the mouth of the Omaka Valley. It's a youthful, finely poised wine, light (8.5 per cent alcohol), with rich, ripe, lemony, honeyed flavours, a hint of sherbet, plentiful sweetness (200 grams/litre of residual sugar) and good potential. Priced sharply.

Vintage	09
WR	7
Drink	11-16

 SW $23 (375ML) V+

Corazon Single Vineyard Little Sweet One (★★☆)

The 2010 vintage (★★☆) was late-harvested at 28 brix at Kumeu, West Auckland. A blend of Sauvignon Blanc (95 per cent) and Sémillon (5 per cent), fermented in tanks and barrels, it is light-bodied (10 per cent alcohol), with peachy, slightly toasty flavours, gently sweet (120 grams/litre of residual sugar) and smooth.

Vintage	10
WR	6
Drink	11-15

SW $22 (375ML) –V

Crater Rim, The, Dr Kohl's Waipara Riesling ★★★★

The stylish 2008 vintage (★★★★) is a light (8.5 per cent alcohol), sweet wine (90 grams/litre of residual sugar), fermented with indigenous yeasts and matured on its yeast lees for 14 months. Pale lemon/green, it is rich and soft, with vibrant, lemony flavours, showing good delicacy, concentration and harmony. It's maturing very gracefully.

Vintage	08
WR	6
Drink	11-20

SW $28 (750ML) V+

Dry River Bunch Selection Martinborough Gewürztraminer (★★★★★)

Estate-grown in the Lovat Vineyard, the 2009 vintage (★★★★★) was picked at over 30 brix. Delicious from the start, it is full-bodied (although 10 per cent alcohol), citrusy, peachy, spicy and slightly honeyed, with notable richness and harmony. Showing advanced ripeness, it's a lovely late-harvest style.

SW $60 (750ML) AV

Dry River Late Harvest Riesling ★★★★★

Dry River produces beautiful, botrytised sweet wines in Martinborough – sometimes very light and fragile, sometimes high in alcohol and powerful – from a range of varieties, but Riesling is viewed as the 'queen' of dessert wines. Grown in the Craighall Vineyard, a few hundred metres from the winery, the grapes are usually hand-selected over a one-month period, extending into late May. However, the 2010 vintage (★★★★★), labelled 'Amaranth' (especially recommended for cellaring), was harvested at 22.5 brix, without botrytis, on 10 May, and made in a 'rich *spätlese* style'. Finely scented, it is very light (9.5 per cent alcohol) and delicate, with lovely, finely poised pear, apple, peach and slight orange flavours, gently sweet (60 grams/litre of residual sugar) and very youthful. Highly refined, it should be at its best 2015+.

Vintage	10
WR	7
Drink	12-16

SW $56 (750ML) AV

Elephant Hill Hawke's Bay Rania   (★★★★★)

Deep gold, the 2009 vintage (★★★★★) was made from unspecified grape varieties, harvested at 47 to 53 brix at Te Awanga, in Hawke's Bay, and fermented in French oak barriques (40 per cent new). Showing a powerful botrytis influence, it is low in alcohol (7 per cent) and unabashedly sweet (366 grams/litre of residual sugar), very lush and oily, with fresh, vibrant, splendidly concentrated apricot and honey flavours. A decadent mouthful, it's hard to resist.

SW $45 (375ML) AV

Fallen Angel Sweet FA   ★★★☆

The 2009 vintage (★★★☆) from Stonyridge is a sweet (104 grams/litre of residual sugar), late-harvest Riesling from Marlborough. Fresh and light, it has vibrant pear, lemon and apple flavours, gentle acidity, and very good delicacy and depth.

Vintage	09
WR	7
Drink	P

SW $35 (375ML) –V

Felton Road Block 1 Central Otago Riesling   ★★★★★

Estate-grown in The Elms Vineyard, on a 'steeper slope' which yields 'riper fruit' without noble rot, this Bannockburn wine is made in a style 'similar to a late-harvest, Mosel *spätlese*'. The 2010 vintage (★★★★★) is light (10 per cent alcohol) and lovely, with intense citrus-fruit and slight sherbet flavours, appetising acidity and a sweet, harmonious finish.

Vintage	10	09	08	07	06
WR	7	7	6	7	6
Drink	11-30	11-29	11-28	11-27	11-26

SW $40 (750 ML) AV

Forrest Estate Botrytised Riesling   ★★★★★

Since 2001, this Marlborough beauty has been outstanding. The 2009 vintage (★★★★★) is golden and richly scented, with mouthfilling body, sweet (180 grams/litre of residual sugar) flavours of apricots and honey, an oily richness, good acid spine, and lovely poise and length.

Vintage	09	08	07	06	05	04
WR	5	6	6	6	4	6
Drink	11-15	11-20	11-12	11-12	P	P

SW $35 (375ML) AV

Framingham F Series Gewürztraminer VT   (★★★★★)

The 2009 vintage (★★★★★) was made from dehydrated Marlborough grapes, harvested at 34 brix with just a touch of botrytis (5 per cent). Fermented with indigenous yeasts in old oak barrels, it's a low-alcohol style (8.5 per cent), golden, with a gingery fragrance and lovely richness of sweet (180 grams/litre of residual sugar), citrusy, spicy flavours, layered, complex and well-rounded.

Vintage	09
WR	7
Drink	11-12

SW $40 (500 ML) V+

Framingham F Series Riesling Auslese (★★★★☆)

The 2009 vintage (★★★★☆) was harvested early at 19 brix, with a 30–40 per cent botrytis infection, to protect the rest of the crop during a spell of bad weather. The grapes were initially discarded on the ground, but then salvaged and made into wine. Fermented in an even split of tanks and old oak casks, it's light (7.5 per cent alcohol) and sweet (140 grams/litre of residual sugar), with a honeyed bouquet, firm acid spine, and intense, lemony, slightly honeyed flavours, showing a hint of sherbet. Drink now or cellar.

Vintage	09
WR	7
Drink	11-12

SW $40 (500ML) AV

Framingham Noble Riesling ★★★★★

From two blocks of vines around 30 years old on the estate in Marlborough, the 2009 vintage (★★★★★) is delicious now. Finely scented, it is ripe, citrusy and gently honeyed, with low alcohol (7.5 per cent), an oily texture, advanced sweetness, and lovely harmony and richness. The 2011 (★★★★★) is another winner. Bright yellow/green, it is rich and sweet (180 grams/litre of residual sugar), citrusy and gently honeyed, with hints of apricot and sherbet, and lovely vibrancy, concentration and harmony. Drink now or cellar.

Vintage	09	08	07	06	05
WR	7	6	6	7	6
Drink	11-14	11-13	11-12	11	P

SW $40 (375ML) AV

Framingham Select Riesling ★★★★☆

The 2010 vintage (★★★★☆), estate-grown in Marlborough and late-picked, was inspired by the German *spätlese* style. Light (8 per cent alcohol), it is pale and youthful, with lemony, appley, minerally aromas. The palate is finely poised, fresh and intense, with citrusy, appley, slightly spicy flavours, gentle sweetness (70 grams/litre of residual sugar) and racy acidity. It's still a baby; open 2013+.

Vintage	10	09	08	07	06
WR	6	7	6	7	6
Drink	11-18	11-17	11-17	11-14	11-12

SW $31 (750ML) V+

Fromm Gewürztraminer Late Harvest ★★★★

The 2009 vintage (★★★★), grown in Marlborough, is intensely varietal, soft and rich, with moderate sweetness (60 grams/litre of residual sugar) and concentrated, peachy, spicy, slightly gingery flavours.

Vintage	10	09	08	07	06
WR	6	6	6	6	6
Drink	11-16	11-15	11-14	11-13	11-12

SW $24 (375ML) V+

Fromm Riesling Spätlese   ★★★★☆

This vivacious Marlborough wine is made from the ripest, hand-picked grapes with no botrytis infection, in an intense, low-alcohol style with plentiful sweetness and incisive, lemony, limey, minerally flavours. The 2010 vintage (★★★★☆) is an absorbing wine, finely poised and youthful, with strong, citrusy, appley, slightly minerally flavours, showing excellent freshness, delicacy, purity and poise. Drink now or cellar.

Vintage	11	10	09	08	07	06
WR	6	7	7	5	6	7
Drink	11-21	11-20	11-19	11-14	11-15	11-16

 SW $30 (750ML) V+

Gibbston Valley Late Harvest   ★★★★

The 2010 (★★★★), labelled 'Late Harvest Riesling', was grown at Bendigo, in Central Otago. Light and lovely, with soft, ripe flavours, it is lemony, appley and slightly spicy, with excellent concentration. The 2011 vintage (★★★★) is a blend of Riesling (66 per cent) and Pinot Blanc (34 per cent). Pale gold, it is rich and honeyed, with light body (10.5 per cent alcohol), fresh acidity, and deep peach, spice and lime flavours, with a hint of marmalade. It's highly enjoyable already; drink now or cellar.

Vintage	11
WR	7
Drink	11-25

 SW $30 (375ML) –V

Gibson Bridge Marlborough Sweet 16   (★★★★)

The gently botrytised 2009 vintage (★★★★) was late-harvested from 16 rows of Pinot Gris vines in mid-July. It has a scented bouquet of stone-fruit and honey, leading into a soft, sweet palate with peach, spice, apricot and honey flavours, rich and rounded.

 SW $35 (375ML) –V

Glazebrook Regional Reserve Noble Harvest Riesling   ★★★★★

From Ngatarawa, this Hawke's Bay wine is typically richly botrytised and honey-sweet, concentrated and treacly, in top vintages dripping with honey, apricot and raisin flavours. The luscious 2009 (★★★★) is golden, with concentrated lemon/lime flavours and a strong botrytis influence, adding apricot and honey notes.

Vintage	09
WR	7
Drink	11-14

SW $32 (375ML) V+

Greystone Basket Star Waipara Riesling   ★★★★☆

Estate-grown, the pale gold 2010 vintage (★★★★☆) is light (10 per cent alcohol) and very sweet (216 grams/litre of residual sugar), with a honeyed bouquet, oily texture and deep, rich grapefruit and apricot flavours, showing a strong botrytis influence.

Vintage	10
WR	6
Drink	11-15

 SW $40 (375ML) –V

Greywacke Marlborough Late Harvest Gewürztraminer   (★★★★☆)

The debut 2009 vintage (★★★★☆) is a single-vineyard wine, hand-picked in the Brancott Valley, tank-fermented and lees-aged for four months in old barrels. Bright, light lemon/green, it is youthful, sweet (90 grams/litre of residual sugar) and rich, with concentrated, ripe peach, lychee and spice flavours, showing lovely vibrancy, delicacy and harmony. Worth cellaring.

Vintage	09
WR	5
Drink	11-15

SW $38 (375ML) –V

Hudson Late Harvest Martinborough Riesling   (★★★★)

The gently botrytised 2009 vintage (★★★★), ensconced in a full bottle, has citrusy, moderately sweet (95 grams/litre of residual sugar) and honeyed flavours, showing good acid spine and intensity.

Vintage	09
WR	7
Drink	11-17

SW $45 (750ML) AV

Huia Marlborough Botrytised Riesling   (★★★★)

Showing considerable complexity, the 2009 vintage (★★★★) is a single-vineyard wine, full-bodied, with sweet, citrusy flavours, hints of apricots, spices and honey, and a rich, rounded finish. It's drinking well now.

SW $28 (375ML) AV

Hunter's Hukapapa Riesling Dessert Wine   ★★★

Freeze-concentrated, the 2009 vintage (★★☆) is a medium-bodied Marlborough wine, with lemon, apple and pear flavours, gently sweet (101 grams/litre of residual sugar) and smooth.

Vintage	09
WR	4
Drink	11-12

SW $24 (375ML) –V

Johanneshof Gewürztraminer Vendange Tardive   (★★★★☆)

The 2009 vintage (★★★★☆), grown in Marlborough, is rich and ripe, sweet but not super-sweet, with concentrated lychee and spice flavours, slightly gingery and honeyed, and impressive freshness and concentration. It should be long-lived.

Vintage	09
WR	6
Drink	11-15

SW $29 (375ML) V+

Johanneshof Noble Late Harvest Riesling   ★★★★☆

Lovely now, but likely to be long-lived, the 2008 vintage (★★★★★) is a fresh, honey-sweet (198 grams/litre of residual sugar) Marlborough wine, fermented in tanks and French oak barrels. Light gold, with a nectareous bouquet and flavours, it has very rich peach and apricot flavours, enlivened by racy acidity, and a finely poised, lasting finish.

Vintage	08	07	06
WR	6	6	6
Drink	11-17	11-16	11-15

SW $36 (375ML) –V

Johner Estate Wairarapa Noble Pinot Noir   ★★★

Estate-grown at Gladstone, the 2009 vintage (★★★☆) is a distinctive dessert wine, straw-coloured, with a hint of amber. Rich and oily, with apricot and honey flavours, sweet and crisp, it's drinking well now.

SW $22 (375ML) –V

Johner Estate Wairarapa Noble Sauvignon Blanc   (★★★☆)

Estate-grown at Gladstone, the 2009 vintage (★★★☆) is vibrant, sweet and peachy, with firm acidity and a hint of honey.

SW $22 (375ML) AV

John Forrest Collection Noble Riesling   ★★★★★

The lovely 2006 vintage (★★★★★) was grown in the Brancott Valley, Marlborough. Golden, rich and sweet (220 grams/litre of residual sugar), it has a richly honeyed, complex bouquet and concentrated stone-fruit and marmalade flavours. Still available, the 2005 (★★★★★) is drinking superbly now – golden, gloriously rich, honeyed and long.

Vintage	06	05
WR	6	6
Drink	11-15	11-15

SW $50 (375ML) AV

Konrad Bunch Selection Marlborough Riesling   ★★★★

The 2009 vintage (★★★★) was estate-grown in the Waihopai Valley and stop-fermented with low alcohol (8.5 per cent) and gentle sweetness (57 grams/litre of residual sugar). Tightly structured, with good acid spine, it is citrusy, tense and minerally, with excellent intensity, vivacity and length.

Vintage	09	08
WR	6	5
Drink	11-18	11-19

SW $25 (750ML) V+

Konrad Sigrun Noble Two   ★★★★

Showing a Sauternes-style richness, the 2008 vintage (★★★★☆) of this estate-grown, Waihopai Valley beauty is a blend of 58 per cent tank-fermented Riesling and 42 per cent barrel-fermented Sauvignon Blanc, hand-picked between early May and mid-June at an average of 45 brix. Pale gold, it is weighty and luscious, with impressively concentrated, honey-sweet flavours (168 grams/litre of residual sugar), showing lovely harmony and depth. Ready.

Vintage	09	08	07
WR	6	6	5
Drink	11-19	11-18	11-17

SW $25 (375ML) AV

La Collina Viognier Tardi   (★★★★★)

From Bilancia, the 2010 (★★★★★) was estate-grown on la collina ('the hill'), overlooking the Gimblett Gravels of Hawke's Bay, and fermented in old oak barrels. Weighty (13 per cent alcohol) and complex, it is sweet and poised, with highly concentrated peach and apricot flavours, and obvious cellaring potential.

Vintage	10
WR	6
Drink	11-14

SW $35 (375ML) AV

Lincoln Ice Wine   ★★★

The 2009 vintage (★★★) is a freeze-concentrated Riesling, light (10 per cent alcohol) and lively, with ripe, citrusy, limey, spicy flavours, sweet, crisp and already drinking well.

SW $20 (375ML) –V

Main Divide Pokiri Reserve Late Picked Waipara Valley Pinot Gris   (★★★★★)

From Pegasus Bay, the 2009 vintage (★★★★★) was harvested at 28 brix, 'long after the leaves had gone', when the grapes had dehydrated and shrivelled. Sweet but not super-sweet (70 grams/litre of residual sugar), it is fragrant, beautifully ripe and rounded, with concentrated stone-fruit and spice flavours, hints of ginger and honey, and great poise and personality. Great value.

Vintage	09
WR	7
Drink	11-17

SW $25 (750 ML) V+

Man O' War Exiled Ponui Island Pinot Gris   (★★★★☆)

The 2010 vintage (★★★★☆), ensconced in a full-sized bottle, was hand-harvested at 25.8 brix on Ponui Island, off the eastern end of Waiheke Island, and handled without oak. It's a sweet but not super-sweet style (60 grams/litre of residual sugar), vibrant, pure, peachy and citrusy, with lively acidity and lovely richness.

Vintage	10
WR	7
Drink	11-15

SW $35 (750ML) V+

Marble Point Hanmer Springs Riesling Classic   ★★★☆

'A low-alcohol style, for the mother-in-law', the 2009 vintage (★★★☆) was harvested at 19.4 brix in North Canterbury. Light (8.5 per cent alcohol) and lively, it is crisp, lemony and appley, with gentle sweetness (80 grams/litre of residual sugar) and very good flavour depth. Worth cellaring. (The 2010 is a medium style.)

Vintage	09
WR	6
Drink	12-15

 SW $22 (750ML) V+

Martinborough Vineyard Bruno Riesling   ★★★★

Hand-picked from mature vines in the Jackson Block, the 2009 vintage (★★★★) is a sweet but not super-sweet wine, fresh, lemony and limey, with appetising acidity. It's delicious from the start. The 2010 (★★★★) is also a lively, low-alcohol, Mosel style, limey and gently sweet (54 grams/litre of residual sugar), with a hint of sherbet, and excellent vigour and intensity.

 SW $27 (750ML) V+

Maude Mt Maude Vineyard East Block Riesling   (★★★★)

Grown at Wanaka, in Central Otago, the 2010 vintage (★★★★) is light-bodied (9 per cent alcohol), with vibrant, citrusy, appley flavours, gently sweet (65 grams/litre of residual sugar) and mouth-wateringly crisp. Finely balanced, very fresh and racy, it should flourish with cellaring.

 SW $20 (750ML) V+

Millton Clos Samuel Viognier Special Berry Selection   (★★★★★)

The pale gold 2010 vintage (★★★★★), grown in Gisborne, was hand-harvested from 'a lower river terrace at the east end of the Te Arai Vineyard'. Decadently rich and soft, with lush, peachy, spicy, honeyed flavours, an oily texture and abundant sweetness (180 grams/litre of residual sugar), it's very hard to resist.

Vintage	07
WR	7
Drink	10-15

 SW $36 (375ML) AV

Mission Late Harvest Hawke's Bay Sémillon   (★★☆)

From 30-year-old vines at Taradale, in Hawke's Bay, the 2009 vintage (★★☆) is peachy, slightly honeyed and strongly flavoured, with plentiful sweetness (90 grams/litre of residual sugar) and a hint of apricots, but it also shows a slight lack of freshness and vibrancy. Ready.

 SW $22 (750ML) –V

Mondillo Nina   (★★★★)

A late-harvest Riesling, grown at Bendigo, in Central Otago, the 2011 vintage (★★★★) has a very inviting, ripely scented bouquet. It has good balance of acidity and sweetness (93 grams/litre of residual sugar), with a hint of sherbet amid its fresh, concentrated, citrusy, limey flavours.

SW $28 (375ML) AV

Muddy Water Waipara Unplugged Riesling   ★★★★

The 2009 vintage (★★★★☆), estate-grown, was made from hand-picked, botrytis-infected bunches. Rich and honeyed, it is full-bodied (13.5 per cent alcohol), sweet (77 grams/litre of residual sugar) and crisp, with slight apricot and marmalade notes, a minerally streak and good complexity.

Vintage	09	08
WR	7	6
Drink	11-19	11-17

 SW $29 (750ML) V+

Ngatarawa Alwyn Winemaker's Reserve Noble Harvest Riesling   ★★★★★

'Botrytis plays a huge part in this wine,' says Hawke's Bay winemaker Alwyn Corban. The 2006 vintage (★★★★★) was hand-harvested at 44 brix and fermented and matured for five months in French oak barriques (one and two years old). A golden, abundantly sweet wine (220 grams/litre of residual sugar), with beautifully ripe pear, spice and honey flavours, enriched but not overwhelmed by botrytis, it's the most finely balanced, exquisite wine yet under this label. There is no 2007 or 2008.

Vintage	08	07	06	05
WR	NM	NM	7	NM
Drink	NM	NM	P	NM

 SW $60 (375ML) –V

Ngatarawa Glazebrook Noble Harvest Riesling –
see Glazebrook Regional Reserve Noble Harvest Riesling

Ngatarawa Stables Late Harvest   ★★★☆

This Hawke's Bay wine is called 'a fruit style' by winemaker Alwyn Corban, meaning it doesn't possess the qualities of a fully botrytised wine. The 2010 vintage (★★★☆), a blend of Viognier (70 per cent), Riesling (26 per cent) and Gewürztraminer (4 per cent), is mouthfilling, with very good depth of peach, pear and spice flavours, slightly honeyed, sweet (78 grams/litre of residual sugar) and soft. Enjoyable young.

Vintage	10	09
WR	6	6
Drink	11-15	11-14

 SW $17 (375ML) V+

Olssens Liquid Gold Late Harvest   (★★★★★)

Exotically perfumed, the 2010 vintage (★★★★★) is a Central Otago Gewürztraminer, late-harvested in mid-June. Rich, sweet (129 grams/litre of residual sugar) and soft, with lovely delicacy and depth, it is very harmonious and seductive.

SW $45 (375ML) AV

Omaha Bay Vineyard Late Harvest Matakana Flora/Viognier   (★★★)

Pale straw, the 2010 vintage (★★★) is a fleshy wine, soft and sweet (140 grams/litre of residual sugar), with generous peach, apricot and spice flavours. It's already drinking well.

Vintage	10
WR	6
Drink	12-20

SW $25 (375ML) –V

Paulownia Noble Sauvignon Blanc   (★★★☆)

The 2009 vintage (★★★☆), grown at Gladstone, in the northern Wairarapa, has honeyed aromas and flavours, with sweet, vibrantly fruity, pear-like flavours woven with fresh acidity.

SW $18 (375ML) V+

Pegasus Bay Aria Late Harvest Riesling   ★★★★★

Still on sale, the 2008 vintage (★★★★★) is a classy, very elegant Waipara wine, made from ripe bunches in which at least a third of the berries were nobly rotten. It has a floral, gently honeyed bouquet and fresh, pure late-harvest fruit flavours, showing excellent richness. Finely focused, with a luscious sweetness (100 grams/litre of residual sugar) coupled with mouth-watering acidity, it's a beauty.

Vintage	09	08	07	06	05	04
WR	7	7	7	7	NM	6
Drink	11-21	11-20	11-18	11-15	NM	11-14

SW $37 (750ML) V+

Pegasus Bay Encore Noble Riesling   ★★★★☆

Still on sale, the 2008 vintage (★★★★★) is a Waipara beauty, made from botrytised bunches, late-harvested at 32 brix. It is fresh, sweet (124 grams/litre of residual sugar), concentrated and citrusy, with a gentle overlay of honey, an oily richness and lovely poise and length.

Vintage	08	07
WR	6	5
Drink	11-20	11-19

SW $37 (375ML) –V

Pyramid Valley Vineyards Growers Collection Late Harvest
Rose Vineyard Marlborough Riesling   (★★★★★)

Pale gold, the compelling 2008 vintage (★★★★★) was hand-picked in the Wairau Valley from low-cropping (4.3 tonnes/hectare) vines at an average of 39 brix, when 85 per cent of the berries were infected with 'noble rot' and the rest were shrivelled. Highly individual, it is a strapping wine (14.7 per cent alcohol), with notably concentrated, citrusy, limey flavours, tightly structured and sweet (110 grams/litre of residual sugar). Drink now or cellar.

SW $60 (750ML) AV

Riverby Estate Marlborough Noble Riesling   ★★★★☆

From 'totally botrytised' grapes, harvested in Marlborough, the 2009 vintage (★★★★) is a low-alcohol style (9 per cent), with fresh passionfruit, spice and citrus flavours, sweet (230 grams/litre of residual sugar), rounded and luscious.

Vintage	09	08
WR	7	7
Drink	11-13	11-12

SW $26 (375 ML) V+

Rock Ferry Marlborough Late Harvest Riesling   (★★★★★)

BioGro certified, the finely poised 2009 vintage (★★★★★) is a late-harvest style, grown in the Corners Vineyard, in the Wairau Valley, and fermented with indigenous yeasts in seasoned oak barrels. Highly scented, with a citrusy bouquet, it is light (9.5 per cent alcohol) and rich, with a hint of sherbet, lovely freshness and depth of lemon and apricot flavours, abundant sweetness (143 grams/litre of residual sugar), good acid spine, and real complexity. It should be long-lived.

Vintage	09
WR	5
Drink	11-12

SW $29 (375ML) V+

Rose Tree Cottage Noble Riesling   ★★★★

From Constellation NZ, the 2007 vintage (★★★★) was grown at the Matador Estate in Marlborough. Golden, it's an elegant wine with citrusy, slightly honeyed flavours, sweet (150 grams/litre of residual sugar) and rich.

SW $24 (375 ML) V+

Saints Gisborne Noble Sémillon   ★★★★

The 2009 vintage (★★★★) is a Sauternes style with a clear botrytis influence. Pale gold, with mouthfilling body and concentrated tropical-fruit flavours, it is sweet, gently honeyed and smooth, with good harmony and loads of drink-young appeal.

SW $20 (375ML) V+

Seifried Winemakers Collection Sweet Agnes Riesling   ★★★★

This freeze-concentrated Nelson wine is priced sharply. Sweet and mouth-wateringly crisp, it typically offers strong, lemony, limey, spicy flavours, fresh, pure, lively and long. The 2010 vintage (★★★★☆) is sweet (195 grams/litre of residual sugar), with rich lemon and apricot flavours, hints of sherbet and spices, and lovely concentration and poise. (The 2011 is labelled as Aotea Sweet Agnes Riesling – see above.)

Vintage	10	09
WR	7	7
Drink	10-18	10-17

SW $19 (375ML) V+

Selaks Heritage Reserve Gisborne/Waipara Gewürztraminer/Riesling   (★★★★)

Delicious in its youth, the 2011 vintage (★★★★) is a blend of almost equal portions of Gisborne Gewürztraminer and Waipara Riesling. Bright yellow/green, with a gingery, spicy, slightly honeyed fragrance, it has strongly spicy flavours, suggestive of Gewürztraminer, but also Riesling's citrusy notes. Soft and sweet (120 grams/litre of residual sugar), with excellent harmony and richness, it's ready to roll.

SW $20 (375ML) V+

Seresin Noble Riesling   (★★★★★)

Certified organic, the memorable 2008 vintage (★★★★★) was made from hand-picked, botrytised bunches, estate-grown in Marlborough, crushed by foot and fermented with indigenous yeasts 'for more than a year'. Gorgeous now, it is light gold, with moderate alcohol (9 per cent) and wonderful depth of peach, spice, apricot and honey flavours, oily, sweet (198 grams/litre of residual sugar), very rich and harmonious. A triumph.

Vintage	08
WR	6
Drink	11-20

SW $35 (375ML) AV

Sileni Estate Selection Late Harvest Sémillon   ★★★☆

The 2009 (★★★★) is a top vintage. A gently sweet style (96 grams/litre of residual sugar) from Hawke's Bay, it is full-bodied, with concentrated, ripe citrus-fruit, pear and spice flavours. Handled entirely in tanks, it shows good richness and cellaring potential.

SW $21 (375 ML) AV

Sileni Exceptional Vintage Pourriture Noble   ★★★★☆

The light gold 2009 vintage (★★★★☆) is a full-bodied, honeyed wine made from Chardonnay grapes harvested in Hawke's Bay at 38 brix. Rich, oily and finely balanced, it has ripe peach, apricot and honey flavours, sweet (105 grams/litre of residual sugar) and concentrated, with a botrytis-derived, marmalade-like richness.

SW $32 (375ML) AV

Sileni Late Harvest Hawke's Bay Sémillon   ★★★

An easy-drinking style with a distinct late-harvest feel, the 2010 vintage (★★★) is light-bodied, with gentle sweetness (76 grams/litre of residual sugar) and smooth, ripe pear, spice and pineapple flavours, which show good harmony.

SW $20 (375ML) –V

Soljans Estate Late Harvest Marlborough Riesling   (★★★)

Light and lemony, the 2009 vintage (★★★) is fresh, citrusy and gently spicy, with abundant sweetness (85 grams/litre of residual sugar) and a smooth finish. It's a very easy-drinking style, for enjoying now or cellaring.

Vintage	09
WR	6
Drink	11-20

SW $20 (375ML) –V

Spy Valley Envoy Marlborough Riesling ★★★★☆

The 2008 (★★★★★) was hand-picked and partly barrel-fermented. Beautifully scented, it is light (9 per cent alcohol) and gently sweet (79 grams/litre of residual sugar). Finely poised, in a very Germanic style, it shows lovely delicacy and intensity of lemony, limey flavours, a minerally streak, fresh acidity and great harmony, complexity and length. The 2010 vintage (★★★★☆) is bright, light lemon/green, with a richly botrytised bouquet. It's an elegant sweet wine with citrusy, honeyed flavours, a hint of marmalade, and strong, drink-young appeal.

 SW $30 (375ML) AV

Spy Valley Marlborough Noble Chardonnay ★★★★

The 2009 vintage (★★★☆) was late-harvested at 31 brix and barrel-fermented. Sweet (120 grams/litre of residual sugar), ripe and smooth, it is peachy, slightly spicy and honeyed, with a touch of complexity and drink-young charm.

Vintage	09
WR	6
Drink	11-13

 SW $23 (375ML) V+

Spy Valley Marlborough Noble Sauvignon Blanc ★★★☆

The 2009 vintage (★★★☆) was late-harvested at 31 brix, and fermented and matured for three months in old French oak barrels. Balanced for easy drinking, it's a medium-bodied, sweet wine (120 grams/litre of residual sugar), with ripe tropical-fruit flavours, slightly spicy and well-rounded.

Vintage	09
WR	7
Drink	11-13

 SW $23 (375ML) AV

Staete Landt Marlborough Riesling Auslese ★★★★

Estate-grown and hand-picked from three rows at Rapaura, the 2009 vintage (★★★★★) is a lovely, light wine, beautifully scented and harmonious, fermented and matured in old oak puncheons. Gently sweet (74 grams/litre of residual sugar), it has strong, lemony flavours, showing excellent delicacy and purity, hints of apricots and spices, and some bottle-aged complexity.

Vintage	09	08	07
WR	7	7	5
Drink	11-16	11-15	11-15

 SW $32 (750ML) V+

Stonecroft Late Harvest Gimblett Gravels Gewürztraminer ★★★★

Estate-grown in Hawke's Bay and handled entirely in tanks, the 2011 vintage (★★★★) is full-bodied, with a spicy, perfumed bouquet. Concentrated, citrusy, gingery and well-spiced, with a hint of oranges, it's a sweet (100 grams/litre of residual sugar), intensely varietal wine with excellent ripeness and richness.

Vintage	11
WR	6
Drink	12-22

 SW $30 (375ML) –V

Te Awa Noble Chardonnay (★★★★)

The 2009 vintage (★★★★) was harvested at 42.3 brix in Hawke's Bay. Pale gold, it's a honey-sweet beauty, very fresh and lively, with rich, ripe, citrusy flavours, a gentle botrytis influence, and excellent balance of sweetness (250 grams/litre of residual sugar) and acidity.

SW $30 (375ML) –V

Te Mania Nelson Koha Ice Wine ★★★★

From hand-picked Riesling grapes, freeze-concentrated in tanks, the 2009 (★★★★) is a low-alcohol style (8.5 per cent), lemony and sweet (120 grams/litre of residual sugar), with good sugar/acid balance and lovely lightness, delicacy and harmony. The 2010 vintage (★★★★) is equally attractive. Showing excellent freshness, depth and poise, it is light and lively, sweet and pure, with a long finish.

SW $22 (375ML) V+

Terravin Late Harvest Pinot Gris (★★★★☆)

A distinctive Marlborough wine, the 2011 vintage (★★★★☆) is pale pink, with mouthfilling body and rich, sweet (70 grams/litre of residual sugar) flavours of strawberries and apricots. Very fresh and vibrant, with good complexity, it's a distinctive wine, priced sharply.

SW $27 (750ML) V+

Trinity Hill Gimblett Gravels Hawke's Bay Noble Viognier ★★★★☆

The 2009 vintage (★★★★) was handled in tanks and old French oak barrels. Unabashedly sweet (200 grams/litre of residual sugar), it has concentrated peach and apricot flavours, an oily texture, and good complexity and richness.

Vintage	09	08	07	06	05
WR	5	6	6	4	6
Drink	11-17	11-17	11-15	P	11-12

SW $35 (375ML) –V

Turanga Creek New Zealand Late Harvest Viognier ★★★

Grown at Whitford, in South Auckland, the 2010 vintage (★★★) is mouthfilling and fresh, with pear, lychee and spice flavours, ripe and soft. It's a sweet but not super-sweet wine (95 grams/litre of residual sugar), enjoyable now.

Vintage	10
WR	6
Drink	11-16

SW $30 (375ML) –V

Urlar Noble Riesling (★★★★)

Grown at Gladstone, in the northern Wairarapa, the 2009 vintage (★★★★) has concentrated flavours of citrus fruits, spices, marmalade and honey, and a sweet, lingering finish.

SW $28 (375ML) AV

Valli Dolce Vita Late Harvest Riesling   (★★★★★)

The 2010 vintage (★★★★★) only exists, says winemaker Grant Taylor, 'because of the almost two weeks of warmish rains we had beginning Anzac weekend 2010'. Very fresh and sweet (150 grams/litre of residual sugar), it is highly concentrated, with peach, apricot and honey flavours, showing lovely vibrancy, depth and richness. Drink now or cellar.

Vintage	10
WR	7
Drink	12-16

 SW $45 (375ML) AV

Villa Maria Reserve Noble Riesling   ★★★★★

One of New Zealand's top sweet wines on the show circuit. It is typically stunningly perfumed, weighty and oily, with intense, very sweet honey/citrus flavours and a lush, long finish. The grapes are grown mainly in the Fletcher Vineyard, in the centre of Marlborough's Wairau Plains, where trees create a 'humidity crib' around the vines and sprinklers along the vines' fruit zone create ideal conditions for the spread of noble rot. The 2007 vintage (★★★★★) is outstanding. Deep yellow, with a richly honeyed bouquet, it is very refined and youthful, with concentrated, citrusy, honeyed flavours, enriched but not overpowered by botrytis, and lovely balance of sweetness and acidity. (The 2009 is in the wings.)

Vintage	07
WR	7
Drink	11-18

 SW $50 (375ML) AV

Wairau River Botrytised Reserve Riesling   (★★★★)

Light gold, the 2010 vintage (★★★★) is a finely balanced, rich Marlborough wine with ripe peach, apricot and honey flavours, abundant sweetness (215 grams/litre of residual sugar) and good acid spine. Oily-textured, with impressive depth, it's a drink-now or cellaring proposition.

Vintage	10
WR	6
Drink	12-14

 SW $36 (375ML) –V

Wooing Tree Tickled Pink   ★★★☆

The 2011 vintage (★★★) was made from Pinot Noir, late-harvested on 28 April in the Cromwell Basin, Central Otago. The fermentation, in tanks, was arrested when the wine had reached 9.5 per cent alcohol and 100 grams per litre of residual sugar. Bright pink, with strawberryish scents, it is light, lively and smooth, with fresh, simple, berryish flavours, offering lots of drink-young charm.

SW $35 (375ML) –V

Sparkling Wines

Fizz, bubbly, *méthode traditionnelle*, sparkling – whatever name you call it by (the word Champagne is reserved for the wines of that most famous of all wine regions), wine with bubbles in it is universally adored.

How good are Kiwi bubblies? Good enough for the industry to export 141,000 cases in the year to June 2011. In the past year, sparkling wine accounted for 0.8 per cent of New Zealand's overseas wine shipments.

Nautilus Cuvée Marlborough NV won the trophy for champion sparkling wine at the 2011 Sydney International Wine Show. *Winestate* gave its 2010 Wine of the Year sparkling trophy to La Michelle 2007, from the Margrain winery in Martinborough, ahead of four other finalists from Australia.

The selection of New Zealand bubblies is not wide but has lately been boosted by an influx of low-priced sparkling Sauvignon Blancs, sparkling Pinot Gris and the like (no doubt reflecting the current oversupply of wine). Most small wineries find the production of bottle-fermented sparkling wine too time-consuming and costly, and the domestic demand for premium bubbly is limited. The vast majority of purchases are under $15.

New Zealand's sparkling wines can be divided into two key classes. The bottom end of the market is dominated by extremely sweet, simple wines which acquire their bubbles by simply having carbon dioxide pumped into them. Upon pouring, the bubbles race out of the glass.

At the middle and top end of the market are the much drier, bottle-fermented, *méthode traditionnelle* (formerly *méthode Champenoise*, until the French got upset) labels, in which the wine undergoes its secondary, bubble-creating fermentation not in a tank but in the bottle, as in Champagne itself. Ultimately, the quality of any fine sparkling wine is a reflection both of the standard of its base wine and of its later period of maturation in the bottle in contact with its yeast lees. Only bottle-fermented sparkling wines possess the additional flavour richness and complexity derived from extended lees-aging.

Pinot Noir and Chardonnay, both varieties of key importance in Champagne, are also the foundation of New Zealand's top sparkling wines. Pinot Meunier, also extensively planted in Champagne, is still rare here, with 19 hectares planted.

Marlborough, with its cool nights preserving the grapes' fresh natural acidity, has emerged as the country's premier region for bottle-fermented sparkling wines (8 per cent of the region's Pinot Noir is cultivated specifically for sparkling – rather than red – wine).

The vast majority of sparkling wines are ready to drink when marketed, and need no extra maturation. A short spell in the cellar, however, can benefit the very best bottle-fermented sparklings.

---

3 Stones Sparkling Pinot Gris (★★★)

The non-vintage (★★★) wine on sale in 2011 is a very easy-drinking regional blend with fresh, peachy, slightly spicy flavours and an off-dry, creamy-smooth finish. (From Ager Sectus.)

MED/DRY $23 –V

Allan Scott Blanc de Blancs Marlborough Brut NV ★★★★

This refreshing bubbly is based entirely on Chardonnay and matured for two years on its yeast lees. The batch on sale in 2011 (★★★★☆) has a rich, toasty, yeasty fragrance. Crisp, lively and concentrated, it has fresh, citrusy, yeasty, complex flavours and a finely balanced, dryish, lengthy finish.

MED/DRY $29 AV

Allan Scott Cecilia Marlborough Brut NV   ★★★★

The batch on sale in 2011 (★★★★) is a fresh, crisp, lively blend of Pinot Noir and Chardonnay, disgorged after 18 months' maturation on its yeast lees. It has citrusy, appley, moderately yeasty flavours and a tight-knit, lingering finish.

MED/DRY $26 AV

Allan Scott Les Joues Rouges Reserve Brut NV   ★★★★

Based entirely on Pinot Noir, grown in Marlborough, the batch on sale in 2011 (★★★★) has a pale pink/onion skin hue. Fresh and crisp, with moderately yeasty flavours, it has hints of oranges and strawberries and a long, fairly dry finish.

MED/DRY $26 AV

Allan Scott Marlborough Sparkling Sauvignon Blanc NV   (★★★☆)

The non-vintage batch I tasted in late 2010 (★★★☆) was made mostly from that year's grapes, with some older material included. Fresh, crisp and dry, with tropical-fruit flavours, it is gently yeasty, with good vigour and depth.

DRY $20 AV

Aurum Blanc de Blancs NV   ★★★☆

This fresh, lively Central Otago wine is based on estate-grown, hand-picked Chardonnay, and disgorged after two years on its yeast lees. It's a gently yeasty, moderately complex style showing very good vivacity, delicacy and depth.

MED/DRY $35 –V

Bernadino Spumante   ★★★

Great value! Pernod Ricard NZ's popular Asti-style wine is an uncomplicated style, based on Muscat (75 per cent) and Müller-Thurgau (25 per cent) grapes, grown in Gisborne. A slightly higher-alcohol wine (9.5 per cent) than most true Asti Spumantes (which average around 7.5 per cent) and less ravishingly perfumed, it's still delicious, with grapey flavours and distinct sweetness (75 grams/litre of residual sugar).

SW $8 V+

Brancott Estate Reserve Brut Cuvée   ★★★☆

This non-vintage wine is a blend of Chardonnay (mostly) and Pinot Noir, grown in East Coast vineyards. The wine I tasted in August 2011 (★★★☆) was crisp and lively, with gently yeasty, citrusy, slightly creamy flavours, a hint of cashews, and good harmony and length.

MED/DRY $22 AV

Brancott Estate Reserve Sparkling Pinot Gris   (★★★)

Grown at Waipara, the non-vintage (★★★) wine I tasted in August 2011 was freshly scented and gently sweet, with lively pear and lychee flavours, slightly yeasty and smooth. It's a very easy-drinking style.

MED/DRY $23 –V

Brancott Estate Reserve Sparkling Pinot Noir ★★★☆

Grown in Waipara (mostly) and Marlborough, the non-vintage wine (★★★☆) on sale in mid to late 2011 is deeply coloured, buoyantly fruity and smooth, with an inviting, floral bouquet and fresh raspberry and plum flavours, showing very good depth and vivacity.

MED/DRY $23 AV

Brancott Estate Reserve Sparkling Sauvignon Blanc ★★★☆

The non-vintage wine (★★★☆) I tasted in August 2011 was grown in Marlborough's Wairau Valley. It is not bottle-fermented, but still very fresh, lively and crisp, in a medium-dry style (13 grams/litre of residual sugar), with strong, ripe melon and lime flavours and instant appeal. It tastes exactly what it is – Sauvignon Blanc with bubbles.

MED/DRY $23 AV

Clayridge Sauvignon Blanc de Blancs ★★★★

Showing greater richness and complexity than most, the 2010 vintage (★★★★) is an elegant wine, grown in Marlborough and partly (14 per cent) barrel-fermented. Scented and lively, it is fruity and moderately yeasty, with finely balanced, limey flavours, very crisp and refreshing.

MED/DRY $21 V+

Clayridge Sparkling Pinot Rosé Brut ★★★☆

The 2010 vintage (★★★☆) is a floral, fresh blend of Pinot Noir (60 per cent), Pinot Gris (30 per cent) and Pinot Blanc (10 per cent), all barrel-fermented. Bright pink, with lively, plummy flavours, it's a moderately complex, slightly confectionery style, widely appealing.

MED/DRY $24 AV

Cuvée No. 1 ★★★★

This is a non-vintage *blanc de blancs*, based entirely on Marlborough Chardonnay. Made by Daniel Le Brun (in his family company) and matured for two years on its yeast lees, it is typically a stylish wine, fresh-scented, with tight-knit, delicate flavours, citrusy, yeasty and biscuity, and a crisp, dryish finish.

MED/DRY $35 –V

Cuvée No. 1 Rosé (★★★★)

This non-vintage sparkling rosé is made from Marlborough Pinot Noir. Made in a drier style than most, it typically has strawberryish, yeasty flavours, showing good delicacy, freshness, crispness and length.

MED/DRY $47 –V

Cuvée Number Eight ★★★

Designed as an 'apéritif style' from Daniel Le Brun's family company, this is a non-vintage blend of Marlborough Pinot Noir and Chardonnay. Typically disgorged after two years on its yeast lees, it has shown some batch variation in the past, but at its best is highly fragrant, with rich flavours, crisp, gently yeasty, tight and long.

MED/DRY $30 –V

Cuvée Remy   (★★★★☆)

The 2007 vintage (★★★★☆) from No. 1 Family Estate is a tribute to Daniel and Adele Le Brun's son, Remy. Made from Marlborough Pinot Noir (80 per cent) and Chardonnay (20 per cent), disgorged after two years on its yeast lees, it is pale straw, with generous, citrusy, biscuity flavours, showing good freshness, yeasty, bready notes, and excellent vigour, complexity and length.

Daniel Le Brun Brut NV   ★★★★

The Daniel Le Brun brand is now owned by the beer giant, Lion – which also owns Wither Hills. The non-vintage wine (★★★★) on the market in 2011 has no producer on the label, just the name of its distributor, Lion-owned Distinguished Beverages. A blend of Pinot Noir and Chardonnay, disgorged after at least two years on its yeast lees, it is pale, with an aromatic, pungently yeasty bouquet. The palate is crisp and vivacious, with tight, lemony, appley flavours, showing a pronounced yeast autolysis influence.

Deutz Marlborough Cuvée Blanc de Blancs   ★★★★★

New Zealand's most awarded bubbly on the show circuit. This Chardonnay-predominant blend is hand-harvested on the south side of the Wairau Valley, at Renwick Estate and in the Brancott Vineyard, and matured for up to three years on its yeast lees. It is typically a very classy wine with delicate, piercing, lemony, appley flavours, well-integrated yeastiness and a slightly creamy finish. The 2007 vintage (★★★★★) has a lemony, biscuity fragrance. It has citrus-fruit, yeast and cashew nut flavours, showing lovely freshness, depth, delicacy and harmony, which float effortlessly across the palate to a crisp, racy finish. The 2008 (★★★★★) is very refined and vivacious, with rich, citrusy, slightly biscuity flavours, racy and long.

Deutz Marlborough Cuvée Brut NV   ★★★★★

The marriage of Pernod Ricard NZ's fruit at Marlborough with the Champagne house of Deutz's 150 years of experience created an instant winner. Bottled-fermented and matured on its yeast lees for two to three years, this non-vintage wine has evolved over the past decade into a less overtly fruity, more delicate and flinty style. The Pinot Noir grapes are drawn principally from Kaituna Estate, on the north side of the Wairau Valley; the Chardonnay comes mostly from Renwick Estate, in the middle of the valley. Before being bottled, the base wine is lees-aged for up to three months and given a full malolactic fermentation. Reserve wines, a year or two older than the rest, are added to each batch, contributing consistency and complexity to the final blend. The wine I tasted in August 2011 (★★★★★) was highly impressive – notably fragrant and rich, with generous, complex, Pinot Noir-ish flavours, yeasty and long. (The average retail price in supermarkets is currently $22.50.)

Deutz Marlborough Cuvée Rosé   ★★★★☆

The 2006 vintage (★★★★☆), made predominantly from Pinot Noir, is pale pink, very fresh and finely balanced, with smooth strawberry and spice flavours, showing yeast-derived complexity and lovely lightness and vivacity.

MED/DRY $37 –V

Deutz Prestige Marlborough Cuvée   ★★★★★

Launched from 2005 (★★★★★), this is a very classy, Chardonnay-predominant style, blended with Pinot Noir, disgorged after long (three and a half years) maturation on its yeast lees. The 2006 (★★★★★) is highly distinguished – weighty, with a powerful surge of rich, citrusy, yeasty flavours, showing excellent freshness, complexity and roundness. The 2007 (★★★★★) is also a standout, with citrusy, yeasty flavours, showing lovely complexity, vigour and richness.

MED/DRY $37 AV

Dolbel Estate Méthode Traditionnelle   (★★★★)

Full of personality, the 2006 vintage (★★★★) is a rich, ripe style from Hawke's Bay, made from equal portions of Chardonnay and Pinot Noir, fermented in old French barriques and disgorged after two years on its yeast lees. Straw-hued, it has strong, peachy, very toasty and nutty flavours and a long, dry, yeasty finish.

MED/DRY $30 –V

Elstree Marlborough Cuvée Brut   ★★★★

The 2006 vintage (★★★★☆) from Highfield is a blend of hand-picked Pinot Noir and Chardonnay, partly barrel-fermented and disgorged after three years on its yeast lees. Pale yellow, with a very yeasty, rich fragrance, it is tight and elegant, with strong, crisp, lemony, toasty flavours, showing excellent vigour, complexity and richness.

Vintage	07	06	05	04
WR	6	6	6	5
Drink	11-13	11-12	P	P

MED/DRY $38 –V

Fallen Angel Marlborough Méthode Traditionnelle NV Brut   ★★★☆

From Stonyridge, the non-vintage wine on sale in 2011 (★★★☆) is crisp and lively, with citrusy, slightly nutty and bready flavours, showing considerable complexity.

MED/DRY $40 –V

Frizzell Méthode Traditionnelle Brut NV   (★★★★)

This non-vintage Hawke's Bay wine (★★★★) is crisp, with lemony, limey flavours, yeasty and toasty, and excellent complexity, vigour and length. (Tasted mid to late 2010.)

MED/DRY $32 –V

Fusion Sparkling Muscat – see Soljans Fusion Sparkling Muscat

Georges Michel Marlborough Méthode Traditionnelle NV   (★★★)

This *blanc de blancs* is a crisp, lively blend of Sémillon (90 per cent) and Sauvignon Blanc (10 per cent), disgorged after four months on its yeast lees. Lemony, appley and slightly grassy, it has moderate complexity, good delicacy and freshness.

 MED/DRY $25 –V

Huia Blanc de Blancs   ★★★★

The 2005 vintage (★★★★★) is a refined, youthful Marlborough sparkling, Chardonnay-based, with a fragrant, citrusy, yeasty bouquet, showing excellent freshness and complexity. The palate is very vivacious, crisp, elegant and citrusy, with lovely intensity and delicacy and a lingering, dryish, yeasty, nutty finish. The 2004 (★★★☆) is pale gold, with mature, toasty, peachy and slightly buttery flavours.

 MED/DRY $34 –V

Hunter's Miru Miru NV   ★★★☆

'Miru Miru' means 'Bubbles'. This wine is disgorged earlier than its Reserve stablemate (below), has a lower Pinot Noir content and a crisper finish. A blend of Chardonnay, Pinot Noir and Pinot Meunier, the wine on sale in 2011 (★★★☆) is pale yellow, with plenty of crisp, yeasty, toasty flavour and a dryish finish (6 grams/litre of residual sugar).

 MED/DRY $27 –V

Hunter's Miru Miru Reserve   ★★★★

This has long been one of Marlborough's finest sparklings, full and lively, with loads of citrusy, yeasty, nutty flavour and a creamy, long finish. It is matured on its yeast lees for an average of three and a half years. The 2008 vintage (★★★★) is a blend of Pinot Noir (59 per cent), Chardonnay (39 per cent) and Pinot Meunier (2 per cent). Pale straw, it is rich and yeasty, with a slightly creamy texture and excellent delicacy, complexity and roundness.

 MED/DRY $34 –V

Johanneshof Cellars Blanc de Noirs   (★★★★)

The vivacious non-vintage wine (★★★★) on sale in 2011 was made from barrel-aged Marlborough Pinot Noir and disgorged after three years on its yeast lees. Pale straw, it has an invitingly scented, slightly biscuity bouquet. Crisp and lively, citrusy, nutty and yeasty, it shows excellent freshness and complexity, with an almost bone-dry, but finely balanced, smooth, long finish.

 DRY $38 –V

Johner Chardonnay Méthode Traditionnelle   (★★☆)

The 2009 vintage (★★☆), grown in the Wairarapa, was based entirely on Chardonnay, given extended lees contact. It's a lemony, appley, crisp wine, but when tasted in late 2011 lacked real complexity and richness.

MED/DRY $40 –V

Joseph Ryan Méthode Traditionnelle (★★☆)

Grown in the northern Wairarapa, the 2008 vintage (★★☆) is straw-hued, with crisp, strawberryish, toasty flavours, showing some complexity and richness, but lacks fragrance.

MED/DRY $36 –V

Kaimira June (★★★☆)

The 2007 vintage (★★★☆), a bone-dry style, was grown in Nelson and bottle-fermented. Pale, smooth and crisp, it is moderately yeasty, with citrusy, slightly limey and biscuity flavours, showing good delicacy and lively acidity.

DRY $29 –V

Kiki Marlborough Sparkling Sauvignon Blanc (★★★☆)

From Ant Moore, the 2009 vintage (★★★☆) is 'ready to escape from the bottle and make your world a better place'. It's a crisp, off-dry style with strong tropical-fruit flavours, slightly toasty, very fresh and lively.

MED/DRY $19 V+

Kim Crawford First Pick Sparkling Sauvignon Blanc (★★★)

The easy-drinking, non-vintage wine (★★★) currently on sale is fresh and lively, with ripe tropical-fruit flavours, slightly sweet and smooth.

MED/DRY $18 AV

La Michelle ★★★★

From Margrain, the classy 2008 vintage (★★★★) is a lean, lively, bottle-fermented bubbly, blended from Pinot Noir (66 per cent) and Chardonnay (34 per cent), grown in Martinborough and made in an unusually dry style (4 grams/litre of residual sugar). Pale straw, with a scented, yeasty bouquet, showing good complexity, it is vivacious, with strawberry and spice flavours, nutty and yeasty, and a tight, lingering finish.

MED/DRY $38 –V

Lindauer Brut NV ★★★☆

Given its very good quality, ultra-low price (the current average in supermarkets is $10) and huge volumes (batch variation is inevitable), this non-vintage bubbly is a miracle of modern winemaking. It is blended from Pinot Noir and Chardonnay, grown in Gisborne and Hawke's Bay, and matured for a year on its yeast lees. Fractionally sweet (12 grams/litre of residual sugar), it generally shows good vigour and depth in a refined style, crisp and finely balanced, with lively, lemony, slightly nutty and yeasty flavours. The wine I tasted in September 2011 (★★★☆) was pale straw, with a steady 'bead' and peachy, slightly toasty and creamy flavours, crisp and gently sweet. For the price, it offered plenty of personality. (In 2010, the Lindauer brand was sold by Pernod Ricard NZ to a joint venture by brewer Lion and Indevin, New Zealand's largest independent contract winemaker.)

MED/DRY $16 V+

Lindauer Sauvignon   ★★★

The only Lindauer-branded bubbly that is not bottle-fermented, this is a *spritzig* (gently sparkling) blend of Marlborough Sauvignon Blanc (85 per cent), Chardonnay (14 per cent) and Pinot Noir (1 per cent). It's an easy summer sipper – refreshing, with lively, limey flavours and a slightly sweet (16 grams/litre of residual sugar), appetisingly crisp finish. It tastes just like a sparkling Sauvignon Blanc – light, crisp, simple and herbaceous, with good freshness and vivacity.

MED $15 AV

Lindauer Special Reserve Blanc de Blancs   ★★★☆

This non-vintage wine, based entirely on Chardonnay grown in Gisborne (mostly) and Hawke's Bay, is disgorged after two years on its yeast lees. It's a deliciously well-balanced wine, lemony and nutty, with gentle yeast autolysis characters and a slightly creamy, dryish (12 grams/litre of residual sugar) finish.

MED/DRY $21 AV

Lindauer Special Reserve Brut Cuvée   ★★★☆

This immensely drinkable bubbly is a non-vintage blend of Pinot Noir (60 per cent) and Chardonnay (40 per cent), grown in Gisborne and Hawke's Bay, and matured on its yeast lees for two years. It is typically pale pink, with strawberryish, yeasty aromas and flavours, very crisp, dryish (12 grams/litre of residual sugar) and lively. (The average price in supermarkets is $12.80.)

MED/DRY $20 AV

Lumina Vintage Marlborough Sauvignon Blanc   (★★★)

From Matua Valley, the 2010 vintage (★★★) is 'lighter in alcohol' (9 per cent), fresh and lively, with tropical-fruit flavours, crisp and dryish.

MED/DRY $20 –V

Matua Valley Sparkling Chardonnay   (★★☆)

Launched in late 2010, this non-vintage wine (★★☆) was grown in Gisborne. Crisp and lively, with fresh, lemony, appley flavours, it is light and simple, slightly sweet and frothy, with easy-drinking appeal.

MED $15 –V

Matua Valley Sparkling Pinot Gris   (★★☆)

The non-vintage wine launched in late 2010 (★★☆) was grown in Gisborne. Fresh and lively, it's a simple but enjoyable wine, lemony, slightly sweet and crisp.

MED $15 –V

Matua Valley Sparkling Sauvignon Blanc   (★★★)

Easy to enjoy, the wine launched in late 2010 (★★★) is bouncy and cheerful, with fresh pineapple and lime flavours, crisp, off-dry, lively and zesty.

MED/DRY $15 AV

Mimi ★★★☆

From Morton Estate, the non-vintage wine on the market in 2011 (★★★☆) is a medium style, very lively and harmonious, with citrusy, peachy flavours, slightly biscuity and smooth. It's a very easy-drinking wine with good personality.

MED $15 V+

Monkey Bay Sparkling Sauvignon Blanc/Pinot Gris (★★☆)

From Constellation NZ, the non-vintage wine (★★☆) released in late 2010 is a Hawke's Bay blend of the 'fresh crisp fruit' of Sauvignon Blanc (77 per cent) with the 'rich texture' of Pinot Gris (23 per cent). Fresh, crisp and smooth, it's a gently sweet wine with an easy-drinking appeal.

MED/DRY $17 –V

Morton Blanc de Blancs ★★★★

Still on sale, the 2002 vintage (★★★★) was made solely from Chardonnay, grown in Hawke's Bay and Marlborough, and disgorged after seven years on its yeast lees. The colour is a youthful, bright, light lemon/green; the palate is rich, with mature but lively, citrusy, slightly nutty and buttery flavours, crisp, dryish and lingering.

MED/DRY $29 AV

Morton Blanc de Noirs (★★★★)

Pale straw, the 2005 vintage (★★★★) is a blend of Pinot Noir and Pinot Meunier, disgorged after more than five years on its yeast lees. Fresh and lively, it has rich, ripe, peachy, yeasty, nutty flavours, showing excellent vigour and depth.

MED/DRY $29 AV

Morton Premium Brut ★★★☆

This has long been popular as an easy-drinking, creamy-smooth, bottle-fermented bubbly. Blended from Pinot Noir, Chardonnay and Pinot Meunier, grown in Marlborough and Hawke's Bay, and given a full, softening malolactic fermentation, it is disgorged on demand after a minimum of 18 months on its yeast lees, and includes base wine from earlier vintages. It typically shows some elegance and lovely harmony, with crisp, citrusy, appley flavours, very fresh, delicate and lively, and a moderately yeasty finish.

MED/DRY $21 AV

Morton Sparkling Rosé (★★★☆)

The non-vintage wine (★★★☆) on sale in 2011 was made from Pinot Noir and disgorged after four years on its yeast lees. Brick red (rather than the 'pink' stated on the label), it is smooth and obviously mature, with strawberryish, yeasty flavours, showing some complexity, a hint of oranges, and a slightly sweet finish. Ready.

MED/DRY $22 AV

Mount Riley Savée Sparkling Sauvignon Blanc ★★★☆

The first of its breed (launched in 2000), this Marlborough sparkling Sauvignon Blanc is bottle-fermented, but made to retain its fresh, tangy varietal characters. The 2009 vintage (★★★☆) is crisp, with tropical-fruit flavours to the fore, some yeasty, creamy notes, and an easy, slightly sweet finish.

Nautilus Cuvée Marlborough ★★★★★

Recent releases of this non-vintage, bottle-fermented sparkling have generally revealed an intensity and refinement that positions the label among the finest in the country. A blend of Pinot Noir (75 per cent) and Chardonnay (25 per cent), it is blended with older, reserve stocks held in old oak barriques and disgorged after a minimum of three years aging on its yeast lees. Lean and crisp, piercing and long, it's a beautifully tight, vivacious and refined wine, its Marlborough fruit characters enriched with intense, bready aromas and flavours. The wine I tasted in mid to late 2011 (★★★★★) was pale straw, with a highly fragrant, complex, slightly nutty bouquet. Rich and lively, with nutty, yeasty flavours, showing excellent depth, poise and complexity, it's right on form.

Omaha Bay Vineyard FAB Flora Avec Bulles Matakana Sparkling Flora (★★☆)

An enjoyable summer sipper, the pale 2010 vintage (★★☆) is slightly sweet, with fresh, appley flavours, crisp and lively.

One Estate Marlborough Sauvignon Brut (★★★☆)

From Winegrowers of Ara, the non-vintage wine (★★★☆) on the market in mid to late 2011 is fresh and buoyantly fruity, with very good depth of crisp, ripe tropical-fruit flavours, finely balanced, dryish and zesty.

Palliser Estate Martinborough Méthode Traditionnelle ★★★★

This is Martinborough's finest sparkling (although few have been produced). The 2006 vintage (★★★★), made from Pinot Noir and Chardonnay, has a fragrant, complex bouquet, yeasty and biscuity. Richly flavoured, it is fresh, citrusy and toasty, with excellent liveliness and length.

Pelorus ★★★★★

Cloudy Bay's bottle-fermented sparkling is typically a powerful wine, creamy, nutty and full-flavoured. A blend of Pinot Noir and Chardonnay – with always a higher proportion of Pinot Noir – it is given its primary alcoholic fermentation (partly with indigenous yeasts) in a mixture of stainless steel tanks, large oak vats and French oak barriques, followed by malolactic fermentation and lengthy lees-aging of the base wines prior to blending, and once bottled it is matured for three years on its yeast lees before it is disgorged. The pale straw 2006 vintage

(★★★★★) is rich, nutty, lively and dry, in a slightly more elegant, less bold and buttery style than some past releases. It's still notably rich, but shows greater delicacy and finesse, with a yeasty, crisp, long finish.

MED/DRY $45 AV

Pelorus NV ★★★★☆

Cloudy Bay's non-vintage Marlborough bubbly is a Chardonnay-dominant style, with 20 per cent Pinot Noir, matured for at least two years on its yeast lees (a year less than for the vintage). It is made in a more fruit-driven style than the vintage, but still refined. The batch on sale in 2011 (★★★★☆) is pale straw, with a very fresh and inviting, citrusy, yeasty bouquet. Vivacious, with incisive, lemony, biscuity, gently yeasty flavours, it is crisp, elegant and refreshing.

MED/DRY $33 AV

Poderi Crisci Ombra (★★★)

In the Veneto, 'ombra' means 'shade' and 'the first glass of wine'. The non-vintage wine on sale in 2011 (★★★) is a sparkling rosé, blended from Waiheke Island Cabernet Franc and Merlot. Very pale pink, it is full-bodied, crisp and lively, with gently sweet citrus-fruit, orange and spice flavours.

MED/DRY $35 –V

Quartz Reef Méthode Traditionnelle NV ★★★★☆

This increasingly Champagne-like, non-vintage bubbly is from a Central Otago company. The batches vary in varietal composition, but the latest release (★★★★) in 2011 is a blend of Pinot Noir (61 per cent) and Chardonnay (39 per cent), grown at Bendigo. Faintly pink, with fine, tiny bubbles, it is vivacious and smooth, tight and youthful, with crisp, yeasty, slightly nutty flavours that linger well.

MED/DRY $30 AV

Quartz Reef Méthode Traditionnelle Rosé ★★★★

The non-vintage wine (★★★★☆) on sale in 2011 is based entirely on Pinot Noir, grown at Bendigo, in Central Otago. An inviting pale pink, it is very fresh and lively, with strong strawberry and spice flavours, gently yeasty and smooth. Dryish, it's an instantly appealing wine, with excellent harmony and length.

MED/DRY $35 –V

Quartz Reef Méthode Traditionnelle [Vintage] ★★★★★

The 2000–2002 vintages were all outstanding, showing great vigour and complexity in a distinctly Champagne-like style, intense and highly refined. The 2007 vintage (★★★★☆) is a blend of Chardonnay (80 per cent) and Pinot Noir (20 per cent), grown at Bendigo, in Central Otago, disgorged after maturing for four years on its yeast lees. Pale, with a scented, lemony, slightly nutty bouquet, it is very vibrant, with lemony, limey flavours, creamy and yeasty, that float smoothly across the palate, and a tight, unusually dry (5 grams/litre of residual sugar) finish.

MED/DRY $40 AV

Rock Ferry Marlborough Blanc de Blancs ★★★☆

Chardonnay-based, fermented in tanks and barrels, then barrel-aged for six months, the 2007 vintage (★★★★) has tight-knit, citrusy, yeasty flavours, showing excellent delicacy and freshness. Disgorged after two and a half years on its yeast lees, it is scented, very lively and lemony, with good intensity and a dry (4 grams/litre of residual sugar), harmonious finish.

Vintage	07	
WR	5	DRY $39 –V
Drink	11-15	

Saint Clair Vicar's Choice Marlborough Sauvignon Blanc Bubbles (★★★★)

The 2010 vintage (★★★★) is an easy-drinking style, crisp and lively, with a lifted, limey bouquet. It has strong, ripe, fruity flavours, showing excellent freshness, vivacity and drive, a sliver of sweetness (8 grams/litre of residual sugar), and a lingering finish.

 MED/DRY $20 V+

Shingle Peak Marlborough Sparkling Sauvignon Blanc ★★★

From Matua Valley, the 2010 vintage (★★★☆) has tropical-fruit aromas and flavours, fresh and strong. It's an instantly appealing wine, slightly sweet, crisp and punchy.

 MED/DRY $20 –V

Shooting Star Marlborough Méthode Traditionnelle Sauvignon Blanc (★★★☆)

From No. 1 Family Estate, the non-vintage wine (★★★☆) on the market in 2011 was bottle-fermented. It's a very good example of the breed – crisp and lively, with fresh, citrusy, limey flavours, slightly yeasty and dryish.

 MED/DRY $24 AV

Sileni Cellar Selection Sparkling Brut (★★★)

Light and lively, the non-vintage wine (★★★) released in 2010 is made from Hawke's Bay Chardonnay. Fermented in tanks, it was matured briefly on its yeast lees, then bottled, without secondary bottle fermentation. It offers fresh lemon/apple flavours, crisp and refreshing, with a touch of nutty, yeasty complexity.

 MED/DRY $20 –V

Sileni Cellar Selection Sparkling Pinot Gris (★★☆)

Faintly pink, the non-vintage wine (★★☆) on sale in 2011 is a fruity, tank-fermented wine, slightly sweet (10 grams/litre of residual sugar), peachy and smooth.

 MED/DRY $20 –V

Sileni Cellar Selection Sparkling Rosé (★★★)

The non-vintage wine (★★★) on sale in 2011 is a crisp and lively, Merlot-based bubbly from Hawke's Bay with fruity, berryish aromas and flavours. Slightly sweet, it's not complex, but offers enjoyable, easy drinking.

 MED/DRY $20 –V

Sileni Cellar Selection Sparkling Sauvignon Blanc   (★★★)

This non-vintage bubbly (★★★) is made from Hawke's Bay grapes, cool-fermented in tanks and bottled young. Slightly sweet and appetisingly crisp, with fresh, ripe fruit flavours, it's an uncomplicated but lively, enjoyable style that makes a stimulating apéritif.

MED/DRY $20 –V

Soljans Fusion Sparkling Muscat   ★★★★

Soljans produces this delicious bubbly from Muscat grapes grown in Gisborne. It is fresh and vivacious, perfumed and sweetly seductive (80 grams/litre of residual sugar), with low alcohol (8 per cent), a steady stream of bubbles and rich, lemony, appley flavours, ripe and smooth. An excellent Asti Spumante copy, it's full of easy-drinking charm and bargain-priced.

SW $16 V+

Soljans Fusion Sparkling Rosé   (★★★☆)

The non-vintage wine on sale in 2011 (★★★) is a Gisborne blend of Pinotage (75 per cent) and Muscat (25 per cent). Pink and lively, with berryish aromas and flavours, it is gently sweet, crisp and vibrantly fruity.

SW $19 V+

Soljans Legacy Méthode Traditionnelle   ★★★★

The 2006 vintage (★★★★) is a blend of Pinot Noir and Chardonnay, grown in Marlborough. It's a stylish wine, rich, lively and mouth-wateringly crisp, with peachy, nutty notes and good, yeast-derived complexity.

Vintage	06
WR	7
Drink	11-15

MED/DRY $32 –V

Spy Valley Echelon Marlborough Méthode Traditionnelle   ★★★★

The 2008 vintage (★★★★) is a blend of Pinot Noir (53 per cent) and Chardonnay (47 per cent). The base wine was fermented and aged for a year in old oak casks, and after its secondary fermentation in the bottle, the wine matured for 18 months on its yeast lees, prior to disgorging. Crisp and bone-dry (2 grams/litre of residual sugar), lively and yeasty, it's an elegant wine with citrusy, nutty flavours, showing excellent delicacy and complexity.

Vintage	08
WR	6
Drink	11-15

DRY $32 –V

Squawking Magpie SQM Blanc de Blancs Brut NV   (★★★★)

The stylish non-vintage wine (★★★★) on the market in 2011 is a bottle-fermented Hawke's Bay sparkling, based entirely on Chardonnay. It has a citrusy, slightly toasty bouquet, leading into a vivacious palate with crisp lemon and toasty flavours and a tightly structured, lingering finish.

MED/DRY $50 –V

Summerhouse Marlborough Blanc de Blancs   ★★★★

From estate-grown Chardonnay, lees-aged for two years, the non-vintage wine (★★★★☆) on sale in 2011 is very elegant, with citrusy flavours, a hint of cashew nuts, a slightly creamy texture and excellent freshness, richness and complexity.

MED/DRY $32 –V

Te Hana Sparkling Reserve Cuvée   (★★★☆)

The non-vintage wine (★★★☆) launched in 2010 is a blend of Chardonnay and Pinot Noir, grown in Marlborough. Pale, with lemony, appley aromas and flavours, it is crisp and dryish, with a gentle yeast influence adding some bready, nutty complexity, and good freshness and vigour. (From Wither Hills.)

MED/DRY $18 V+

Tohu Rewa Blanc de Blancs Méthode Traditionnelle   (★★★★)

Elegant and tight-knit, the 2009 vintage (★★★★) is a Chardonnay-based wine from a single vineyard in Marlborough. Mouthfilling and very lively, with strong, citrusy, slightly limey and nutty flavours, it shows good, yeast-derived complexity and a crisp, dry finish.

Vintage	09
WR	6
Drink	11-13

MED/DRY $28 AV

Toi Toi Marlborough Sparkling Rosé   (★★★)

The non-vintage wine (★★★) on sale in 2011 is a very easy-drinking style (30 grams/litre of residual sugar), pale pink, with red-berry and strawberry flavours, crisp, gently sweet and smooth.

MED $17 AV

Toi Toi Marlborough Sparkling Sauvignon Blanc   (★★★)

Fresh and frisky, with citrusy, limey flavours, slightly sweet, refreshing and balanced for easy drinking, the non-vintage wine (★★★) on sale in 2011 is fruity and uncomplicated, but a good, lively example of the style.

MED $17 AV

Toi Toi Prosecco   (★★☆)

Made to 'broadly reflect the origins and style of the Italian wine', the non-vintage wine (★★☆) on sale in 2011 is a blend of Riesling, Müller-Thurgau and Pinot Gris, 'primarily' from Marlborough. It's a gently sweet, lemony, simple wine, fresh, fruity and frothy.

MED $19 –V

Trinity Hill 'H' Blanc de Blancs NV   ★★★☆

This elegant, non-vintage wine is made from Hawke's Bay Chardonnay. The batch on sale in 2011 (★★★☆) is attractively scented, light and lively, with subtle 'fresh baked bread' aromas, moderate complexity and very good freshness, delicacy and harmony.

MED/DRY $29 –V

Twin Islands Chardonnay/Pinot Noir Brut NV ★★★★

'A great bottle to be seen with in some of the classiest bars and restaurants', Nautilus's lower-priced bubbly sold for $17 a few years ago, vanished for a while, then reappeared in late 2009. The price is now $25, but it's worth it. The batch I tasted in September 2011 (★★★★) is pale straw, scented and tight, with slightly creamy and toasty flavours, showing good richness and harmony.

MED/DRY $25 AV

Villa Maria Méthode Traditionnelle NV (★★★★)

Launched in 2009, this is a rich, mature style, based on 68 per cent Pinot Noir (grown in Hawke's Bay and Auckland) and 32 per cent Chardonnay (Marlborough), with base wines dating back to 2003. Disgorged after three years on its yeast lees (and closed with a crown seal, rather than a cork), it's pale yellow, citrusy, yeasty and nutty, with a crisp, almost bone-dry finish (3.5 grams/litre of residual sugar), and excellent complexity and harmony.

DRY $38 –V

Villa Maria Private Bin Lightly Sparkling Marlborough Sauvignon Blanc (★★★☆)

Mouthfilling, punchy and crisp, the *frizzante* (lightly sparkling) 2010 vintage (★★★☆) has slightly sweet, citrusy, appley, limey flavours, showing good freshness and impact.

MED/DRY $20 AV

Violet Marlborough Sparkling Sauvignon Blanc (★★☆)

From Yealands, the non-vintage wine (★★☆) on sale in 2011 is distinctly herbaceous, with plenty of fresh, crisp flavour.

MED/DRY $17 –V

Rosé Wines

The number of rosé labels on the market has exploded recently, as drinkers discover that rosé is not an inherently inferior lolly water, but a worthwhile and delicious wine style in its own right. New Zealand rosé is even finding offshore markets (69,111 cases shipped in the year to June 2011, a steep rise from 905 cases in 2003) and collecting overseas awards.

In Europe many pink or copper-coloured wines, such as the rosés of Provence, Anjou and Tavel, are produced from red-wine varieties. (Dark-skinned grapes are even used to make white wines: Champagne, heavily based on Pinot Meunier and Pinot Noir, is a classic case.) To make a rosé, after the grapes are crushed, the time the juice spends in contact with its skins is crucial; the longer the contact, the greater the diffusion of colour, tannin and flavour from the skins into the juice.

'Saignée' (bled) is a French term that is seen occasionally on rosé labels. A technique designed to produce a pink wine or a more concentrated red wine – or both – it involves running off or 'bleeding' free-run juice from crushed, dark-skinned grapes after a brief, pre-ferment maceration on skins. An alternative is to commence the fermentation as for a red wine, then after 12 or 24 hours, when its colour starts to deepen, drain part of the juice for rosé production and vinify the rest as a red wine.

Pinot Noir and Merlot are the grape varieties most commonly used in New Zealand to produce rosé wines. Regional differences are emerging. South Island and Wairarapa rosés, usually made from Pinot Noir, are typically fresh, slightly sweet and crisp, while those from the middle and upper North Island – Hawke's Bay, Gisborne and Auckland – tend to be Merlot-based, fuller-bodied and drier.

These are typically charming, 'now-or-never' wines, peaking in their first six to 18 months with seductive strawberry/raspberry-like fruit flavours. Freshness is the essence of the wines' appeal.

Abbey Cellars Blushing Monk Hawke's Bay Rosé (★★★)

The fresh, smooth 2011 vintage (★★★) is a single-vineyard wine, made from hand-picked Merlot (50 per cent) and Malbec (50 per cent). Bright pink/pale red, it has raspberryish scents and vibrant red-berry and spice flavours, finely balanced for easy drinking.

MED/DRY $18 AV

Akarua Central Otago Pinot Rosé ★★★★

Estate-grown at Bannockburn, the 2010 vintage (★★★★) has an inviting deep pink/light red colour and fresh, raspberryish scents. It shows lovely vibrancy, with strong red-berry and spice flavours and a gentle splash of sweetness (9 grams/litre of residual sugar). Good drinking for the summer of 2011–12.

MED/DRY $23 AV

Ake Ake Vineyard Rosé (★★★★)

A good buy. Grown at Kerikeri, in Northland, the 2010 vintage (★★★★) was made mostly from Chambourcin, with some Merlot and Cabernet Franc. Bright, light red in hue, it is mouthfilling (14.5 per cent alcohol), ripe and rounded, with fresh cherry, red-berry and spice flavours, showing excellent delicacy, vibrancy and richness, and a bone-dry but balanced finish.

Vintage	10
WR	6
Drink	P

DRY $18 V+

Alpha Domus The Pilot Hawke's Bay Rosé ★★★

Pale pink, the 2011 vintage (★★★) is a mouthfilling, bone-dry wine, obviously made for the table, rather than casual sipping. It offers strawberryish, slightly spicy flavours, with hints of oranges and peaches, and good depth.

DRY $20 –V

Amisfield Saignée Rosé ★★★★

From Pinot Noir, estate-grown in the Cromwell Basin and tank-fermented, the classy 2010 vintage (★★★★☆) of this Central Otago wine is bright pink and invitingly scented, with very fresh and delicate strawberry/spice flavours, finely textured and harmonious, and a fractionally off-dry finish. The 2011 (★★★☆) is bright pink and mouthfilling, with fresh strawberry and spice flavours, finely balanced and well-rounded (5.8 grams/litre of residual sugar).

Vintage	11	10	09	08
WR	6	6	5	6
Drink	11-13	11-12	P	11-12

MED/DRY $25 AV

Anchorage Winemakers Release Nelson Pinot Rosé (★★★)

The back label of the buoyantly fruity 2010 vintage (★★★) promises a lot in a single bottle – the aromas and flavours of confectionery, strawberries, marshmallows, wild rose, honey, raspberries, pears, spice, liquorice and fresh meringue. What you get is a pink, thoroughly pleasant wine with fresh strawberry and spice flavours, gentle sweetness and good freshness and depth.

MED/DRY $19 AV

Aravin Central Otago Rosé (★★★☆)

Bright pink, the 2010 vintage (★★★☆) is attractively scented, with red-berry and spice flavours, still very fresh and lively.

MED/DRY $19 V+

Artisan Oratia Rosé (★★☆)

Grown in West Auckland, the 2009 vintage (★★☆) was made mostly from Syrah, with a small portion of Gamay Noir. Showing some development, it's a dry style (4 grams/litre of residual sugar), with slightly herbal strawberry and spice flavours. Ready.

DRY $19 –V

Askerne Hawke's Bay Rosé ★★★

The 2011 vintage (★★★) is a full-bodied wine, bright pink, made in a drier style than most (3 grams/litre of residual sugar). It has lively, berryish flavours, fresh and crisp, and lots of drink-young appeal.

Vintage	11	10	09
WR	6	6	6
Drink	12-13	P	P

DRY $16 V+

Ataahua Waipara Rosé   (★★★☆)

Estate-grown, tank-fermented and briefly oak-aged, the 2011 vintage (★★★☆) has a very inviting, pale pink hue. Mouthfilling (13.5 per cent alcohol), it is a slightly sweet style (12 grams/litre of residual sugar), with fresh strawberry and spice flavours, hints of peaches and oranges, and very good depth and roundness.

MED/DRY $22 AV

Ata Rangi Summer Rosé   ★★★★

The 2010 vintage (★★★★☆) is a blend of Merlot, Cabernet Franc and Cabernet Sauvignon, grown in Martinborough. Floral and weighty (13.5 per cent alcohol), smooth and dry, it offers strong, vibrant berry, plum and slight spice flavours, with balanced acidity and excellent freshness and immediacy.

DRY $18 V+

Bald Hills Friends and Lovers Rosé   ★★★★

From Pinot Noir vines managed specifically for rosé, the 2010 vintage (★★★★) was estate-grown at Bannockburn, in Central Otago, and mostly handled in tanks; 20 per cent of the blend was barrel-fermented. Pink/pale red, with berryish aromas, it is fresh and lively, berryish and spicy, with strong, refreshing flavours and a crisp, dryish (5 grams/litre of residual sugar) finish.

MED/DRY $22 V+

Bannock Brae Cathy's Rosé   ★★★☆

Named after the partnership's 'better-looking half', the 2010 vintage (★★★★) was produced from estate-grown, Central Otago Pinot Noir. Bright pink, it is mouthfilling (14 per cent alcohol) and buoyantly fruity, with fresh strawberry and spice flavours, lively acidity and a slightly sweet (7 grams/litre of residual sugar), finely balanced finish.

MED/DRY $24 –V

Black Cottage Marlborough Rosé   (★★★★)

Pale pink, the 2011 vintage (★★★★) is a drink-young charmer, blended from Pinot Gris (95 per cent) and Pinot Noir (5 per cent). A slightly sweet style with balanced acidity, it has strawberry, spice and peach flavours, showing excellent depth.

MED/DRY $18 V+

Blackenbrook Vineyard Nelson Pinot Noir Rosé   (★★★)

Estate-grown and hand-picked, the very easy-drinking 2011 vintage (★★★) is pale pink, with slightly earthy aromas. The palate is strawberryish, with good delicacy and freshness, and a well-rounded (6 grams/litre of residual sugar) finish.

Vintage	11
WR	6
Drink	11-13

MED/DRY $21 –V

Bracken's Order Blanc de Pinot Noir   ★★★

The 2010 vintage (★★☆) was hand-picked at Gibbston, in Central Otago. It has slightly developed, light red/orange colour, with crisp, slightly herbal flavours. Ready.

MED/DRY $16 V+

Brodie Estate Summer Blush (★★★)

Grown in Martinborough, the 2009 vintage (★★★) was blended from Sauvignon Blanc (50 per cent), Pinot Noir (25 per cent) and Pinot Gris (25 per cent). Deep pink, it has fresh, crisp strawberry and spice flavours, hints of oranges and peaches, and an unusually dry finish. A 'serious' style, best enjoyed with food.

DRY $25 –V

Cable Bay Waiheke Island Rosé ★★★★

Waiheke Island is producing excellent rosés, such as the 2010 vintage (★★★★). Made from Merlot and Malbec grapes, grown at Church Bay, it is full-bodied, with smooth raspberry and spice flavours, showing very good depth and texture. A 'serious' style of rosé, it is designed to accompany food. The 2011 (★★★☆) is pale pink and light-bodied (11.5 per cent alcohol), with ripe strawberry, spice and peach flavours, slightly sweet (6 grams/litre of residual sugar), crisp and lively.

Vintage	11	10
WR	7	7
Drink	11-13	11-12

MED/DRY $25 AV

Coal Pit Pinot Rosé ★★★

Estate-grown at Gibbston, in Central Otago, the 2010 vintage (★★★) was made from Pinot Noir. Pale red, it has mouthfilling body and berryish, spicy, slightly herbal flavours, woven with fresh acidity.

MED/ DRY $19 AV

Coopers Creek Huapai Rosé ★★★☆

Enjoyable from the start, the 2010 vintage (★★★☆) is an estate-grown blend of Malbec and Merlot. Pink/pale red, it is full-bodied, fresh, berryish, plummy and smooth, in a dryish style (5 grams/litre of residual sugar) with lots of drink-young charm.

MED/DRY $17 V+

Domain Road Vineyard Pinot Noir Rosé ★★★★

The 2010 vintage (★★★★), estate-grown at Bannockburn, in Central Otago, and partly barrel-fermented, has an inviting, bright pink hue and a floral, scented bouquet. Mouthfilling, it offers fresh, delicate strawberry and spice flavours, a hint of peaches and a dry (3 grams/litre of residual sugar) finish.

DRY $24 AV

Drumsara Central Otago Pinot Rosé ★★★☆

Grown at Alexandra, the 2010 vintage (★★★☆) is bright pink/pale red, with strawberry and spice flavours, still very fresh and lively. It's a fully dry style, crisp and appetising.

Vintage	10
WR	7
Drink	11-12

DRY $28 –V

Elephant Hill Rosé ★★★☆

Made from Central Otago Pinot Noir, the 2010 vintage (★★★★) is bright pink, floral and vibrantly fruity, with good body and depth of peach and strawberry flavours, hints of oranges and apricots, and a smooth finish. Full of drink-young charm.

MED/DRY $20 AV

Esk Valley Merlot/Malbec Rosé ★★★★★

This has been clearly New Zealand's best rosé over the past decade, with several trophies to prove it. The 2010 vintage (★★★★) is a Hawke's Bay blend of Merlot (94 per cent) and Malbec (6 per cent). Handled without oak, it's a mouthfilling, dry wine (4 grams/litre of residual sugar) with attractive, bright pink colour and fresh, ripe, berryish scents. Fleshy and generous, it has smooth, berryish, plummy, slightly spicy flavours, lively and refreshing. The 2011 (★★★★), blended from Merlot (91 per cent) and Malbec (9 per cent), is vibrantly fruity, with fresh, strong flavours of plums and spices and a dryish (5 grams/litre of residual sugar) finish.

Vintage	11	10	09	08	07
WR	7	7	NM	6	6
Drink	12-13	11-12	NM	P	P

MED/DRY $24 V+

Framingham F-Series Montepulciano Rosato ★★★★

The instantly attractive 2010 vintage (★★★★) was made from Montepulciano grapes, grown in Marlborough. It's a vivacious wine, off-dry (5 grams/litre of residual sugar), with vibrant, delicate flavours of raspberries and strawberries, showing lovely freshness and harmony. The 2011 vintage (★★★★) is very similar, with an enticing, bright pink/pale red colour, mouthfilling body and vibrant, berryish flavours, showing excellent delicacy, freshness, poise and depth.

Vintage	11	10
WR	6	6
Drink	11-13	11-12

MED/DRY $25 AV

Georges Michel Summer Folly Marlborough Pinot Noir Rosé (★★☆)

The 2010 vintage (★★☆) is pale pink, with gentle strawberry and spice flavours, fresh and smooth. Pleasant, light, easy drinking.

MED/DRY $16 AV

Gibbston Valley Blanc de Pinot Noir ★★★☆

This Central Otago wine 'is dark enough to stain your shirt, fun enough for you not to care'. The 2011 vintage (★★★) is bright pink/pale red, with fresh strawberry and spice aromas and flavours. Fleshy and smooth, it's ready to roll.

MED/DRY $25 –V

Gibson Bridge Marlborough Pinot Gris Rosé ★★★

Pale pink/orange, the 2010 vintage (★★★☆) is made from Pinot Gris, rather than Pinot Noir. Full-bodied, peachy and spicy, with a touch of barrel-ferment complexity, good depth and a dryish finish, it's a good 'food' wine, with plenty of personality.

DRY $22 –V

Gillman Matakana Clairet (★★★★)

Maturing well, the very distinctive 2009 vintage (★★★★) is closer to a light red than a rosé. Made from Cabernet Franc and Merlot, it was matured for a year in oak casks (50 per cent new). Pale red in hue, it is weighty, berryish, spicy, dry and smooth, with considerable complexity, gentle tannins, and an enjoyable mellowness. Drink now.

Vintage	09
WR	6
Drink	12-19

 DRY $30 –V

Gladstone Vineyard Rosé ★★★

The 2011 vintage (★★★) is a blend of Cabernet Franc, Merlot and Malbec, grown in the northern Wairarapa and made in an unusually dry style (2.8 grams/litre of residual sugar). Bright pink, it is mouthfilling, with good depth of strawberry and spice flavours, and a hint of oranges. It's already drinking well.

 DRY $25 –V

Greystone Waipara Valley Pinot Noir Rosé ★★★☆

'Designed to be plonked on a long table under big trees on days when time is not important', the 2010 vintage (★★★☆) has floral, berryish scents. Refreshing, with buoyant, fruity, slightly spicy flavours, lively acidity and a well-rounded finish, it has lots of drink-young appeal.

 MED/DRY $21 AV

Hay Paddock, The, Silk Rosé (★★★)

Estate-grown at Onetangi, on Waiheke Island, the 2011 vintage (★★★) was made from Syrah grapes, harvested at 21 brix. Bright pink/pale red, it's a lively, medium-bodied wine with fresh, crisp berry and spice flavours and a bone-dry finish.

 DRY $28 –V

Hitchen Road Rosé ★★★

Estate-grown at Pokeno, in North Waikato, the 2011 vintage (★★☆) was produced from hand-picked Pinotage. It's a solid but plain wine with dry, berryish, spicy, slightly herbal flavours that lack the freshness and vibrancy of a good year. Ready.

Vintage	11	10	09
WR	6	7	7
Drink	11-12	11-12	11-12

DRY $15 V+

Huia Marlborough Rosé ★★★

Grown principally in the Brancott Valley, the 2010 vintage (★★★☆) is a blend of Merlot (90 per cent), Malbec (8 per cent) and Pinot Noir (2 per cent), matured briefly in old oak casks. Pale red, it's a basically dry style (4.7 grams/litre of residual sugar), mouthfilling, with strawberryish, spicy flavours, earthy, savoury notes adding a touch of complexity, and very satisfying depth.

 DRY $21 –V

Hunter's Marlborough Rosé ★★★☆

Top summer sipping, the 2011 vintage (★★★★) is bright pink and mouthfilling (14 per cent alcohol), with instantly appealing flavours of plums, strawberries and spices, strong, fresh, dryish and lively. A great buy.

MED/DRY $15 V+

Johner Estate Wairarapa Pinot Noir Rosé ★★★☆

The 2010 vintage (★★★☆) is pale pink, crisp and dryish, with strawberry and spice flavours, very fresh and lively.

MED/DRY $18 V+

Judge Rock Central Otago Rosé (★★★★)

The delicious 2010 vintage (★★★★) was made from Pinot Noir, grown at Alexandra and fermented in seasoned oak barriques. Bright, pale pink, it is mouthfilling and vivacious, with strawberry and spice flavours, showing greater complexity than most rosés, a sliver of sweetness (5 grams/litre of residual sugar), and excellent freshness and harmony.

MED/DRY $20 V+

Jules Taylor Gisborne Rosé ★★★☆

The 2010 vintage (★★★☆) is bright pink/pale red, floral, fresh and smooth, with vibrant raspberry, strawberry and spice flavours, offering very easy drinking.

Vintage	10	09
WR	7	5
Drink	11-13	11-12

MED/DRY $22 AV

Kina Beach Vineyard Nelson Merlot Rosé ★★★

The 2010 vintage (★★★) includes 15 per cent Cabernet Franc. Bright pink, it's a medium-bodied, smooth wine with plum, spice and slight herb flavours, showing good depth, and a rounded (8 grams/litre of residual sugar) finish.

Vintage	10	09	08
WR	6	6	6
Drink	11-12	P	P

MED/DRY $20 –V

Kurow Village Penny Rose Pinot Noir Rosé (★★★☆)

The 2010 vintage (★★★☆) was made from Pinot Noir grown in the Hakataramea Valley, South Canterbury. An inviting bright pink, it is fresh and vibrant, with crisp strawberry and spice flavours, very fruity and lively, and good personality.

DRY $24 –V

Lake Road Gisborne Merlot Rosé (★★☆)

Crisp and dry, the 2010 vintage (★★☆) is a single-vineyard wine, pale red/orange, with berry and spice flavours, a hint of herbs, and decent depth.

DRY $18 –V

Lawson's Dry Hills Pinot Rosé   ★★★

Floral, with bright pink/pale red colour, the 2010 vintage (★★★) of this Marlborough wine is very lively and fruity, with ripe strawberry and plum flavours, crisp and dryish. The 2011 (★★★) is bright pink, with fresh strawberry and spice flavours, slightly sweet (7 grams/litre of residual sugar), crisp and lively.

 MED/DRY $19 AV

Lime Rock Pinot Rosé   (★★★☆)

Grown in Central Hawke's Bay, the 2010 vintage (★★★☆) is bright pink, very fresh and smooth, with slightly sweet (10 grams/litre of residual sugar) strawberry and red-berry flavours, showing very good depth.

 MED/DRY $19 V+

Mahurangi River Pretty in Pink Merlot Rosé   (★★★)

Launched from the 2010 vintage (★★★), this is a medium style (20 grams/litre of residual sugar). From Merlot grapes, estate-grown at Matakana, it is bright pink, with plenty of fresh, crisp, berryish, spicy, slightly peachy flavour and an easy-drinking charm.

Vintage	10
WR	7
Drink	11-12

 MED $24 –V

Maori Point Central Otago Pinot Noir Rosé   ★★★☆

Grown at Tarras, the 2010 vintage (★★★☆) is a pink/pale orange wine, barrel-fermented. It offers strong, ripe strawberry, plum and spice flavours, fresh and lively, and good harmony.

 DRY $19 V+

Marsden Bay of Islands Rosé   ★★★

Grown in Northland, the 2011 vintage (★★★) is pink/pale red, with fresh, crisp strawberry and spice flavours, slightly sweet (7 grams/litre of residual sugar) and lively. A good, summertime sipper.

Vintage	11
WR	6
Drink	11-12

 MED/DRY $18 AV

Michelle Richardson Central Otago Pinot Noir Rosé   (★★★☆)

Delicious now, the 2010 vintage (★★★☆), grown in the Cromwell Basin, was designed as 'an "almost" red wine'. Pink/pale red, it is mouthfilling, with lively cherry, plum and spice flavours, finely balanced and smooth (9 grams/litre of residual sugar).

MED/DRY $20 AV

Mission Hawke's Bay Rosé   ★★★

The 2011 vintage (★★★) is bright pink/pale red, with lively red-berry and spice flavours, a hint of herbs, and good freshness and crispness. Drink this summer.

 DRY $20 –V

Muddy Water Waipara Rosé ★★★☆

The 2011 vintage (★★★☆), made from Pinot Noir, was tank-fermented with indigenous yeasts to full dryness. Very pale pink, it is mouthfilling (14 per cent alcohol), with peach, orange and spice flavours, a touch of complexity and a smooth, well-rounded finish.

DRY $19 V+

Northburn Station Central Otago Rosé (★★★)

Made from Pinot Noir grown in the Cromwell Basin, the 2010 vintage (★★★) has bright red colour, deep for a rosé. Fresh, berryish aromas lead into a crisp, plummy, berryish wine with plenty of flavour and an off-dry, crisp finish.

MED/DRY $23 –V

Odyssey Marlborough Rosé ★★★☆

Made from estate-grown, hand-picked Pinot Noir, the 2010 vintage (★★★) is pink, fresh and crisp, with lively, off-dry flavours of strawberries and spices. Drink this summer.

MED/DRY $19 V+

Old Coach Road Pinot Noir Rosé (★★☆)

From Seifried, the 2011 vintage (★★☆) is an easy-drinking Nelson wine, bright pink, fresh and lively, with light strawberry and spice flavours, slightly peachy, crisp and dryish.

MED/DRY $17 –V

Olssens Summer Dreaming Pinot Noir Rosé ★★★☆

Estate-grown at Bannockburn, in Central Otago, the vibrant 2010 vintage (★★★☆) was hand-picked at 23.5 brix and partly barrel-fermented. Bright pink, it is fresh-scented, with lively strawberry and spice flavours, a hint of herbs, and a slightly sweet (8.6 grams/litre of residual sugar), refreshingly crisp finish.

MED/DRY $25 –V

Omaha Bay Vineyard Matakana Rosé ★★★★

Made from Syrah, the 2010 vintage (★★★★) is pink, with strong berry and spice flavours, lively and slightly sweet. Woven with fresh acidity, it is immediately appealing, with excellent depth for a rosé.

Vintage	10	09
WR	6	6
Drink	11-12	11-12

MED/DRY $22 V+

Peacock Sky Rosé ★★★

The 2010 vintage (★★★☆) is a Waiheke Island blend of estate-grown Cabernet Franc (mostly) and Cabernet Sauvignon. Full-bodied, it is dry (3 grams/litre of residual sugar), with fresh, ripe strawberry, peach and spice flavours and a well-rounded finish.

Vintage	11
WR	5
Drink	11-13

DRY $26 –V

Poverty Bay Riverpoint Rosé ★★★★☆

The 2010 vintage (★★★★) was grown at Bridge Estate Vineyard, in Gisborne. A blend of Merlot (70 per cent) and Malbec (30 per cent), it is pink/pale red and invitingly scented, mouthfilling and smooth, with strong, ripe strawberry and spice flavours, fresh acidity, and a bone-dry, finely balanced finish.

DRY $20 V+

Richmond Plains Nelson Monarch Rosé ★★★☆

Pale pink, with a hint of orange, the 2010 vintage (★★★☆) has an attractive bouquet of strawberries and dried herbs. It's a basically dry style (4.5 grams/litre of residual sugar) with mouthfilling body (14 per cent alcohol), vibrant berry, spice and slight apricot flavours, and a seductively smooth finish.

DRY $20 AV

Rockburn Stolen Kiss ★★★☆

The 2010 vintage (★★★) showcases 'the sweetly frivolous and fruity side of Central Otago Pinot Noir'. Bright, light pink, with gentle strawberry, peach and spice flavours, it offers smooth, easy drinking, with a slightly sweet, appetisingly crisp finish. The 2011 (★★☆) is pale pink, with strawberry, spice and peach flavours, fresh acidity and moderate length.

MED/DRY $20 AV

Saint Clair Marlborough Pinot Gris Rosé ★★★

The 2010 vintage (★★★☆) is a blend of Pinot Gris and Pinot Noir. Bright pink, it is mouthfilling and smooth, with fresh, lively strawberry, peach and spice flavours and a dry (4 grams/litre of residual sugar) finish.

DRY $21 –V

Shaky Bridge Pinot Noir Rosé ★★★

The 2010 vintage (★★☆), grown in Central Otago, is described on the back label as 'low alcohol' – but it's 12.5 per cent. Made in an off-dry (6 grams/litre of residual sugar) style, it has fresh raspberry, spice and herb flavours, balanced for easy drinking.

MED/DRY $20 –V

Sileni Cellar Selection Hawke's Bay Cabernet Franc Rosé ★★★☆

The 2010 vintage (★★★☆) is bright pink/pale red, with a floral bouquet and fresh raspberry/spice flavours, buoyantly fruity and smooth. A dryish style with very good balance and depth, it offers fine value.

MED/DRY $16 V+

Soho Westwood Waiheke Island Rosé ★★★☆

The 2010 vintage (★★★★) is pink/pale red, with mouthfilling body, sweet-fruit delights and very good depth of fresh, ripe berry and plum flavours. It's a buoyantly fruity wine, delicious young. The 2011 (★★★) is a bright pink blend of Merlot (87 per cent) and Malbec. Fresh, vibrantly fruity and smooth, it has ripe, berryish flavours, lively acidity and satisfying depth.

MED/DRY $25 –V

Soljans Gisborne Rosé Wine Two Daughters   (★★)

The 2010 vintage (★★) is an off-dry (14 grams/litre of residual sugar) blend of Pinotage and Muscat. Pink, with slightly developed colour, it has light strawberry and spice flavours and a smooth finish. Ready.

MED/DRY $18 –V

Spy Valley Pinot Noir Rosé   ★★★★

'Guaranteed to enhance a romantic evening for two', the 2011 vintage (★★★★) is a pale pink Marlborough wine, delicious from the start. It has strong, vibrant strawberry and spice flavours, with a hint of apricot, slight sweetness (6 grams/litre of residual sugar), and excellent freshness, delicacy and harmony.

Vintage	11
WR	7
Drink	11-13

MED/DRY $23 AV

Stonecroft Hawke's Bay Rosé   (★★★☆)

The debut 2010 vintage (★★★☆) is a blend of Cabernet Sauvignon and Syrah. Bright pink, it's a good food wine, fully dry, with ripe red-berry and spice flavours, a hint of peaches, and good freshness and vivacity.

DRY $21 AV

Stoneleigh Marlborough Pinot Noir Rosé   ★★★

The 2010 vintage (★★★) is a fresh, off-dry style, pink and light, with red-berry, strawberry and spice flavours, showing an easy-drinking charm.

MED/DRY $21 –V

Takatu Poppies Rosé   ★★★☆

Grown at Matakana, the 2011 vintage (★★★☆) is a single-vineyard blend of Merlot and Cabernet Franc. Matured in seasoned French oak casks, it's a bone-dry style, faintly pink and medium-bodied (12 per cent alcohol), with strawberry, peach and apricot flavours, dry and refreshing.

Vintage	11	10	09
WR	6	7	7
Drink	11-14	11-13	11-12

DRY $25 –V

Tatty Bogler Otago Pinot Noir Rosé   (★★★★)

The 2010 vintage (★★★★) from Forrest has raspberryish scents and an inviting, pink/red hue. It's a deliciously fresh wine with vibrant red-berry and plum flavours, showing good immediacy, and a smooth (7 grams/litre of residual sugar) finish.

Vintage	10
WR	7
Drink	P

MED/DRY $25 AV

Te Henga The Westie Rosé   ★★☆

From Babich, the 2010 (★★☆) is sturdy (14 per cent alcohol), with slightly developed colour. Berryish, slightly spicy and smooth, it's ready for drinking. The 2011 vintage (★★☆) is pink, fruity and smooth, with gentle strawberry and spice flavours and a rounded finish. Drink this summer.

DRY $13 V+

Te Mania Nelson Pinot Noir Rosé   ★★★

The 2010 vintage (★★★) is a full-bodied style with good depth of strawberry and spice flavours, fresh and lingering.

MED/DRY $19 AV

Te Whau Rosé of Merlot   ★★★★

Estate-grown on Waiheke Island, this is a rare wine – only 290 bottles were produced of the 2011 vintage (★★★☆). Barrel-fermented with indigenous yeasts, it is pink/orange, with soft apricot and orange flavours, showing good complexity, in a forward, very individual style.

DRY $35 –V

Tiki Estate Marlborough Pinot Noir Rosé   (★★★☆)

The pink/pale red 2011 vintage (★★★☆) is full-bodied, with fresh raspberry and spice flavours, slightly sweet and lively. Showing good depth and vivacity, it's already delicious. (Note: the back label calls it 'Tiki Estate Wairau Alpine Valley Pinot Noir Rosé'.)

MED/DRY $19 V+

Ti Point Matakana Coast Rosé   (★★★☆)

Estate-grown at Leigh, near Matakana, the 2010 vintage (★★★☆) was made from early-picked Merlot grapes. Bright pink, it's a 'serious', food-friendly style, unusually dry (2.3 grams/litre of residual sugar) for a rosé, with very good depth of berryish, slightly spicy flavour, fresh and lively.

Vintage	10
WR	5
Drink	P

DRY $21 AV

Tohu Single Vineyard Nelson Pinot Rosé   (★★★★)

Estate-grown at Upper Moutere, the 2011 vintage (★★★★) is a bright pink, fleshy wine (14.5 per cent alcohol), with strong, berryish, plummy flavours, slightly sweet (12 grams/litre of residual sugar) and rich.

MED/DRY $22 V+

Torlesse Rosé NV   ★★★

The label doesn't mention its region of origin or vintage, but the bright pink wine I tasted in August 2011 (★★★) was made from Sauvignon Blanc and Cabernet Sauvignon. It has a fresh, floral bouquet in an easy-drinking, slightly sweet style, berryish and buoyantly fruity.

MED/DRY $15 V+

Trinity Hill Hawke's Bay Rosé   ★★★

The 2011 vintage (★★★) was made mostly from Cabernet Franc, plus Merlot, Cabernet Sauvignon and Syrah. Bright pink, it is vibrantly fruity, berryish and smooth, with enough acidity to keep things lively.

DRY $19 AV

Tussock Nelson Pinot Noir Rosé   ★★☆

From Woollaston, the 2011 vintage (★★★) is certified organic. Pale pink, with strawberry and spice flavours, a hint of apricot and a crisp, lively finish, it's a fresh, dry wine (3.8 grams/litre of residual sugar) with drink-young appeal.

DRY $17 –V

Unison Hawke's Bay Rosé   ★★★★

This is a 'serious', dry style. The 2010 vintage (★★★★), pink/pale red, is a medium-bodied wine, slightly earthy and savoury, with dry flavours of raspberries, strawberries and spices. A good 'food' wine.

DRY $20 V+

Villa Maria Private Bin East Coast Rosé   ★★★☆

A pale pink blend of Hawke's Bay, Gisborne and Marlborough grapes, the 2010 vintage (★★★☆) is crisp and dry, with refreshing strawberry, spice and slight peach flavours, showing very good depth. The 2011 (★★★☆), also dry (4.8 grams/litre of residual sugar), is bright pink, with strawberry and spice flavours, a creamy-soft texture and instant appeal.

Vintage	11	10
WR	6	5
Drink	11-13	P

DRY $22 AV

Waimea Pinot Rosé   ★★★☆

The lively 2011 vintage (★★★), made from Nelson Pinot Noir, was partly (15 per cent) fermented in American oak barrels, 'adding nuances of vanilla cream'; the rest was handled in tanks. Bright pink/pale red, it is fresh, berryish and slightly spicy, with a splash of sweetness (7.5 grams/litre of residual sugar) finely balanced by refreshing acidity.

Vintage	11	10	09	08
WR	7	7	7	6
Drink	11-12	P	P	P

MED/DRY $20 AV

Waipara Springs Waipara Sauvignon Rouge   (★★☆)

Effectively a rosé, the 2010 vintage (★★☆) is based on Sauvignon Blanc (95 per cent), blended with a small amount of Pinot Noir. Pale pink, it's a fresh, medium-bodied wine with herbaceous, Sauvignon Blanc flavours holding sway, and a hint of Pinot Noir's strawberry and spice. Light summer sipping.

MED/DRY $16 AV

Wairau River Marlborough Rosé   (★★★)

Slightly sweeter than most rosés (17.6 grams/litre of residual sugar), the 2011 vintage (★★★) is bright pink, fresh and smooth, with cherry, spice and apricot flavours, offering very easy drinking.

Vintage	11
WR	5
Drink	12-14

MED $20 –V

Weeping Sands Waiheke Island Rosé   ★★★☆

From Obsidian, the 2011 vintage (★★★) was made from Merlot, estate-grown and hand-picked at Onetangi. Pink-hued, it is dry, with satisfying depth of fresh red-berry and spice flavours and a rounded finish.

Vintage	11
WR	6
Drink	11-12

DRY $24 –V

Wooing Tree Rosé   ★★★★

The 2010 vintage (★★★★), from estate-grown Pinot Noir, was hand-picked in the Cromwell Basin, Central Otago, and 20 per cent was fermented in seasoned French oak casks. Pale pink, it is mouthfilling, with strong strawberry, spice and peach flavours and a slightly creamy texture. The 2011 (★★★★) is pale pink, with fresh strawberry, peach and slight apricot flavours, smooth, slightly sweet and rich.

MED/DRY $25 AV

Yealands Estate Marlborough Pinot Noir Rosé   (★★★)

The pink, fresh-scented 2011 vintage (★★★) is a very easy-drinking style, with vibrant flavours of strawberries and spices, a hint of apricots and a slightly sweet, smooth finish.

MED/DRY $19 AV

Red Wines

Branded and Other Red Wines

Most New Zealand red wines carry a varietal label, such as Pinot Noir, Syrah, Merlot or Cabernet Sauvignon (or blends of the last two). Those not labelled prominently by their principal grape varieties – often prestigious wines such as Church Road Tom, Esk Valley The Terraces or Unison Selection – can be found here.

Although not varietally labelled, these wines are mostly of high quality and sometimes of outstanding quality.

Abbey Cellars Prophet (★★★)

Deeply coloured, the 2009 vintage (★★★) is a Cabernet Sauvignon-based red (54 per cent), blended with Cabernet Franc (22 per cent), Malbec (15 per cent) and Merlot (9 per cent). French and American oak-aged for nine months, it has herbal, brambly, slightly nutty flavours, slightly rustic but showing good concentration.

DRY $20 –V

Abbey Cellars Rapture (★★★★)

Blended from Merlot (85 per cent) and equal portions of Cabernet Franc and Malbec, the 2009 vintage (★★★★) was hand-picked in Hawke's Bay and French and American oak-aged for 10 months. Deeply coloured, it has rich blackcurrant and plum flavours, hints of spices and nuts, and gentle tannins. A generous, early-drinking style, it shows some concentration and class.

DRY $21 V+

Abbey Cellars Testament (★★★☆)

Fleshy and dark, the 2008 vintage (★★★☆) is a blend of Cabernet Franc (50 per cent), Cabernet Sauvignon, Merlot and Malbec, French and American oak-aged. Full-bodied, it has very satisfying depth of blackcurrant, herb and spice flavours and a well-rounded finish.

DRY $25 –V

Alluviale ★★★★★

A great buy. The 2009 vintage (★★★★★), blended from Merlot (63 per cent), Cabernet Franc (23 per cent) and Cabernet Sauvignon (14 per cent), was grown at two sites in the heart of the Gimblett Gravels, Hawke's Bay, and matured for 16 months in French oak barriques (40 per cent new). Boldly coloured, it is ripely scented and mouthfilling, with fresh, rich flavours showing lovely concentration of pure blackcurrant, plum, spice and nut flavours, hints of herbs and dark chocolate, and buried, fine-grained tannins. A sexy, savoury, Merlot-dominant style, it's a steal at $33.

Vintage	09	08
WR	7	6
Drink	11-18	11-17

DRY $33 V+

Alpha Domus AD The Aviator ★★★★☆

The 2007 (★★★★☆), estate-grown in The Triangle, is a blend of Cabernet Sauvignon (36 per cent), Cabernet Franc (27 per cent), Merlot (23 per cent) and Malbec (14 per cent), matured for 17 months in French oak barriques (75 per cent new). Deeply coloured, it is scented and supple, with rich blackcurrant and nut flavours, hints of dark chocolate and herbs, and impressive complexity. The very classy, finely textured 2009 vintage (★★★★★) is full-coloured and weighty, with highly concentrated, blackcurrant-like flavours to the fore, herb and nut characters, and ripe, supple tannins. It's already approachable, but should mature gracefully for a decade.

Vintage	09	08	07
WR	7	NM	6
Drink	11+	11-20	11-20

DRY $52 –V

Alpha Domus AD The Navigator   ★★★☆

The 2007 vintage (★★★☆) is a blend of Merlot, Cabernet Sauvignon, Cabernet Franc and Malbec, estate-grown at Maraekakaho, in Hawke's Bay, and matured for 20 months in French (85 per cent) and American oak barriques (30 per cent new). Full-coloured, it shows very good depth of spicy, slightly herbal and nutty flavours, with a fairly firm finish.

Vintage	07
WR	6
Drink	11+

DRY $27 –V

Ata Rangi Célèbre   ★★★★☆

Pronounced *say-lebr*, this is a blend of grape varieties and in some years a regional blend too. Robust and vibrantly fruity, it typically has impressive weight and depth of plummy, spicy flavour in a complex style that matures well. The 2008 vintage (★★★★☆), sourced entirely from Martinborough, is a blend of Merlot (35 per cent), Syrah (35 per cent), and the two Cabernets (Sauvignon and Franc). Deep and bright in colour, it is mouthfilling, with strong, ripe plum, spice and nut flavours, complex and savoury, and a well-rounded finish.

Vintage	08	07	06	05	04
WR	7	7	7	7	6
Drink	11-20	11-19	11-18	P	P

DRY $32 AV

Babich The Patriarch   ★★★★★

This is Babich's best red, regardless of the variety or vineyard, but all vintages have been grown in the company's shingly vineyards in Gimblett Road, Hawke's Bay. It is typically a dark, ripe and complex, deliciously rich red, matured in mostly French oak barriques (30 to 35 per cent new). The 2009 vintage (★★★★★) is a very powerful blend of Cabernet Sauvignon (50 per cent), Malbec (25 per cent) and Cabernet Franc (25 per cent). Highly fragrant, with coffee and spice aromas, mouthfilling body and fresh, concentrated blackcurrant, dark chocolate and plum flavours, showing the boldness and rich spiciness of Malbec, it is finely balanced, complex and savoury. The 2010 (★★★★☆) is a blend of Merlot (44 per cent), Cabernet Sauvignon (36 per cent) and Malbec (20 per cent). Deeply coloured, it's very youthful, with a strong surge of vibrant blackcurrant, plum and spice flavours and ripe, supple tannins. It's a very harmonious, finely structured wine, full of potential; open 2014+.

Vintage	10	09	08
WR	7	7	5
Drink	13-22	12-21	11-18

DRY $60 AV

Brick Bay Martello Rock   (★★★)

Estate-grown at Matakana, the 2006 vintage (★★★) is a medium-bodied blend of Malbec (44 per cent), Cabernet Sauvignon (25 per cent), Merlot (25 per cent) and Petit Verdot (6 per cent). Matured for a year in French oak casks, it is fullish in colour, with berry, herb and plum flavours, showing some spicy, nutty complexity, and a smooth finish. Drink now.

Vintage	06
WR	6
Drink	11-14

 DRY $24 –V

Brick Bay Pharos   ★★★★

Brick Bay's top red (pronounced *fair-ross*) is named after the famous lighthouse off the coast of Alexandria. A blend of Malbec (30 per cent), Cabernet Franc (23 per cent), Cabernet Sauvignon (21.5 per cent), Merlot (21.5 per cent) and Petit Verdot (4 per cent), the 2006 vintage (★★★☆) was grown at Sandspit, near Matakana, and matured in new French oak barriques. Full but not dense in colour, it is mouthfilling and smooth, with moderately concentrated plum, spice and slight herb flavours, showing some savoury complexity.

Vintage	06	05	04
WR	6	7	7
Drink	11-16	11-13	11-12

 DRY $32 –V

Bushmere Estate Gisborne The Italians   (★★★)

The poised, youthful 2010 vintage (★★★) is a middleweight red, blended from Sangiovese (71 per cent) and Montepulciano (29 per cent), hand-picked at 23.7 to 24.7 brix and matured for 10 months in seasoned American oak barriques. Fullish in colour, with cherry and almond flavours, woven with fresh acidity, it has some aging potential.

 DRY $23 –V

Cheeky Little Red   ★★☆

The 2010 vintage (★★☆) is a decent varietal and regional blend that reminded me of Merlot. Medium-bodied, it is fruity and plummy, with slightly earthy notes and balanced tannins. From Babich, it offers good value.

 DRY $12 V+

Clearview Enigma   ★★★★★

This consistently distinguished Hawke's Bay red is a Merlot-based blend. Typically dark and flavour-crammed, it matures well and is matured for about 18 months in French oak barriques (predominantly new). The 2008 vintage (★★★★☆) is a powerful, concentrated blend of Merlot (75 per cent), Malbec (11 per cent) and Cabernet Franc (14 per cent). Dark and sturdy, with ripe plum and spice flavours, slight coffee notes, and excellent complexity and density, it's still youthful.

Vintage	08	07	06	05	04
WR	7	7	6	7	7
Drink	11-18	11-18	11-15	11-14	11-15

DRY $45 AV

Clearview Old Olive Block ★★★★★

This Hawke's Bay red, based on Cabernet Sauvignon and Cabernet Franc, is grown in the estate vineyard at Te Awanga, which has a very old olive tree in the centre, and in the Gimblett Gravels. The rich 2008 vintage (★★★★★) is a dark, complex blend of 59 per cent Cabernets (Sauvignon and Franc), supplemented by Merlot (38 per cent) and Malbec (3 per cent). Matured for 17 months in predominantly new French oak barriques, it is bold and youthful in colour, with deep, blackcurrant-like flavours, ripe and supple, a hint of coffee and good complexity. Dense and savoury, it's very age-worthy.

Vintage	08	07	06	05	04
WR	6	7	6	7	7
Drink	11-17	11-17	11-14	11-14	P

DRY $40 AV

Clearview The Basket Press ★★★★★

The rare, high-priced 2007 vintage (★★★★★) is a Cabernet Sauvignon-based blend (75 per cent), with minor portions of Merlot, Cabernet Franc and Malbec. Matured for 30 months in new French oak barriques, it's a powerful Hawke's Bay red, dark and fleshy, with highly concentrated blackcurrant, plum, spice and nut flavours and ripe, supple tannins. Still youthful, it's a notably stylish, complex and harmonious wine, likely to mature gracefully for a decade or longer.

Vintage	07
WR	6
Drink	11-18

DRY $145 –V

Clearview Two Pinnacles ★★★★

Estate-grown at Te Awanga, in Hawke's Bay, the 2008 vintage (★★★★) is a blend of Malbec (85 per cent) and the two Cabernets (Sauvignon and Franc), matured for 17 months in mostly French oak barriques. Deliciously rich and smooth, it's fleshy, dark and purple-flushed, with mouthfilling body and strong plum, spice, coffee and sweet oak flavours, showing good complexity.

DRY $28 AV

Coopers Creek Four Daughters ★★★☆

The 2007 vintage (★★★☆) currently on sale is a Hawke's Bay blend of Cabernet Franc, Malbec, Merlot and Syrah, grown in The Triangle, the Gimblett Gravels and at Havelock North. Bright and fullish in colour, it is medium to full-bodied, firm and savoury, with slightly leathery, herbal, nutty characters and good complexity. Fine value.

Vintage	07	06	05
WR	5	6	6
Drink	11-13	11-12	P

DRY $17 V+

Craggy Range Aroha ★★★★★

The silky-textured 2009 vintage (★★★★☆) is a single-vineyard Pinot Noir from Te Muna Road, on the edge of Martinborough, hand-harvested at over 24 brix and matured for more than a year in French oak casks (35 per cent new). Ruby-hued, mouthfilling and supple, with cherry, plum and spice flavours, ripe and savoury, it is delicious in its youth, showing notable 'completeness' and harmony.

Vintage	09	08	07
WR	6	7	7
Drink	11-20	11-21	11-18

 DRY $100 –V

Craggy Range Le Sol ★★★★★

This super-charged Syrah has pushed the boundaries in terms of its enormous scale – and succeeded brilliantly. Grown in the Gimblett Gravels district of Hawke's Bay, it is hand-harvested when the grapes are 'supremely ripe', in several 'passes' through the vineyard, and bottled without fining or filtering. The 2009 vintage (★★★★★), matured for 20 months in French oak barriques (39 per cent new), is deeply coloured and already highly approachable. It has a fragrant, spicy, slightly nutty bouquet. Dense and smooth, with highly concentrated cassis, plum and black-pepper flavours, braced by ripe, supple tannins, it should unfold well over the next decade.

Vintage	09	08	07	06	05	04
WR	7	7	7	6	7	7
Drink	11-26	11-23	11-22	11-20	11-15	11-13

DRY $100 AV

Craggy Range Sophia ★★★★★

Deliciously rich and smooth in its youth, the 2009 vintage (★★★★★) is a Gimblett Gravels, Hawke's Bay blend of Merlot (65 per cent) and Cabernet Sauvignon (25 per cent), with splashes of Cabernet Franc (7 per cent) and Petit Verdot (3 per cent). Matured for 18 months in French oak barriques (45 per cent new), it is deeply coloured, full-bodied, sweet-fruited and supple, with highly concentrated, ripe cassis, plum and spice flavours. Drink now or cellar.

Vintage	09	08	07	06	05	04
WR	7	7	7	7	7	6
Drink	11-26	11-23	11-27	11-26	11-20	11-15

DRY $70 AV

Craggy Range Te Kahu ★★★★☆

The 2009 vintage (★★★★) is a Hawke's Bay red, Merlot-based (80 per cent), with smaller portions of Cabernet Franc, Cabernet Sauvignon and Malbec. Matured for 15 months in French oak barriques (22 per cent new), it is a delicious, drink-young style, deeply coloured, with concentrated blackcurrant, plum and spice flavours, a hint of coffee, and good warmth, stuffing and structure.

Vintage	09	08	07	06
WR	6	6	7	6
Drink	11-18	11-15	11-22	11-20

DRY $27 V+

Craggy Range The Quarry

Powerful but not heavy, the 2009 vintage (★★★★★) of this Gimblett Gravels, Hawke's Bay red was based entirely on Cabernet Sauvignon. Matured for 20 months in French oak barriques (50 per cent new), it is deeply coloured and rich, with highly concentrated, blackcurrant-like flavours, hints of plums and spices, and fine, supple tannins. A very elegant, pure expression of Cabernet Sauvignon, it should mature well.

Vintage	09	08	07	06	05	04
WR	7	7	7	7	7	6
Drink	11-26	11-23	11-27	11-26	11-17	11-14

DRY $60 AV

Crazy by Nature Cosmo Red   (★★★☆)

The 2009 vintage (★★★☆) is a medium-bodied, buoyantly fruity Gisborne red from Millton, blended from Malbec, Merlot, Syrah and Viognier. Full-coloured, with a spicy fragrance, it is fresh, berryish and lively, with some savoury complexity and ripe, supple tannins.

DRY $20 AV

Crossroads Hawke's Bay Talisman   ★★★★

A blend of several red varieties whose identities the winery delights in concealing (I see Malbec as a prime suspect), Talisman has long been estate-grown in the Origin Vineyard at Fernhill, in Hawke's Bay, but now also includes fruit from the Gimblett Gravels. The youthful 2009 vintage (★★★★) was matured for over a year in French (85 per cent) and American oak barriques (all new). Weighty and rich, it is very dark, with dense, ripe plum, spice and nut flavours, showing excellent complexity.

Vintage	09	08	07	06	05
WR	6	6	7	NM	6
Drink	11-20	11-14	11-13	NM	P

DRY $40 –V

Dada   (★★★★★)

From Alluviale, the inky 2009 vintage (★★★★★) was estate-grown in the Gimblett Gravels of Hawke's Bay. A blend of Merlot, Syrah and Cabernet Franc, it is the first red wine made in New Zealand without sulphur dioxide. Densely coloured, it is still very youthful, with concentrated blackcurrant, plum and spice flavours, a hint of liquorice, and firm underlying tannins. Muscular yet flowing, it's a very ripe and powerful red; open 2014+.

Vintage	09	08	07
WR	7	7	6
Drink	11-21	11-20	11-18

DRY $70 AV

Destiny Bay Destinae   ★★★★☆

Estate-grown on Waiheke Island, the 2007 (★★★★) is a blend of Cabernet Sauvignon (35 per cent), Merlot (33 per cent), Cabernet Franc (21 per cent) and Malbec (11 per cent). Berryish, plummy, ripe and silky, but slightly less concentrated than the 2006 (★★★★★), it's already enjoyable. The 2008 vintage (★★★★☆) is a blend of Cabernet Sauvignon (39 per cent), Merlot (29 per cent), Malbec (16 per cent), Cabernet Franc (15 per cent) and Petit Verdot (1 per cent). Matured in a 50:50 split of French and American oak casks (half new), it is deeply coloured, with a fragrant bouquet of blackcurrants, herbs and nuts. Mouthfilling, it is vibrantly fruity, with rich, sweetly oaked flavours, the drink-young appeal of Malbec and American oak, and good tannin grip. ($45 to Patron Club members.)

Vintage	08	07	06
WR	7	6	6
Drink	12-18	12-16	11-16

 DRY $75 –V

Destiny Bay Magna Praemia   ★★★★★

The 2007 vintage (★★★★★) of this Waiheke Island producer's flagship red is a Cabernet Sauvignon-based blend (69 per cent). Invitingly fragrant, it has substantial body, sweet-fruit delights and deep blackcurrant and nut flavours, complex, savoury and supple. The classy and distinctive 2008 (★★★★★) is a blend of Cabernet Sauvignon (71 per cent) and Merlot (14 per cent), with minor portions of Cabernet Franc, Malbec and Petit Verdot. French and American oak-aged, it is dark, with a welcoming bouquet of blackcurrants, spice and nuts, leading into a rich, generous palate, with concentrated cassis, plum, spice and nut flavours. It's a very harmonious and supple wine, for drinking now onwards. ($165 to Patron Club members.)

Vintage	08	07	06	05
WR	7	7	7	7
Drink	12-22	12-20	12-16	11-15

 DRY $275 –V

Destiny Bay Mystae   ★★★★☆

The 2007 vintage (★★★★☆) of this Waiheke Island red is Cabernet Sauvignon-based (55 per cent), with Merlot (26 per cent), Cabernet Franc (11 per cent), Malbec (6 per cent) and Petit Verdot (2 per cent). Very finely textured, it has impressive depth of plum, berry, spice and herb flavours, seasoned with nutty oak, and good complexity. The 2008 (★★★★★) is a blend of Cabernet Sauvignon (61 per cent), Merlot (23 per cent) and Cabernet Franc (9 per cent), with smaller portions of Malbec and Petit Verdot. Matured in French (60 per cent) and American oak casks, it is dark, concentrated and flowing, with Cabernet Sauvignon clearly to the fore, beautifully ripe cassis, plum, spice and nut flavours, and good supporting tannins. A sophisticated, Bordeaux-like red, it's already highly enjoyable. ($70 to Patron Club members.)

Vintage	08	07	06
WR	7	6	6
Drink	12-20	12-18	11-16

 DRY $115 –V

Esk Valley The Terraces   ★★★★★

Grown on the steep, terraced, north-facing hillside flanking the winery at Bay View, in Hawke's Bay, this is a strikingly bold, dark wine with bottomless depth of blackcurrant, plum and strongly spicy flavour. Malbec (43 per cent of the vines) and Merlot (35 per cent) are typically the major ingredients, supplemented by Cabernet Franc; the Malbec gives 'perfume, spice, tannin and brilliant colour'. Yields in the 1-hectare vineyard are very low, and the wine is matured for 17 to 22 months in all-new French oak barriques. *En primeur* (payment at a reduced price of $99, in advance of delivery) has been the best way to buy. It typically matures well, developing a beautiful fragrance and spicy, Rhône-like complexity. At a vertical tasting in 2011 of the six vintages produced between 1991 and 2000, the stars were the powerful, strikingly rich and complex 1998 and the dense, savoury, leathery 1995. The 2009 (★★★★★) is notably elegant and supple, with deep colour and lovely concentration and ripeness of blackcurrant, plum and spice flavours. Very silky and savoury, it's already approachable; open 2014+.

Vintage	09	08	07	06	05	04	03	02
WR	7	NM	NM	7	NM	7	NM	7
Drink	12-20	NM	NM	12-20	NM	12-18	NM	12-20

DRY $125 AV

Gibson Bridge Trésor Rouge   (★★★☆)

The rare (300 bottles only) 2009 vintage (★★★☆) is a Marlborough blend of Syrah, Merlot, Pinot Noir and Malbec. Full but not dense in colour, with fresh plum and spice flavours, it's a middleweight style with some complexity and very good depth.

DRY $65 –V

Gillman   ★★★★☆

This rare Matakana red is blended from Cabernet Franc, Merlot and Malbec, and matured for two years in French oak barriques (most recently 60 per cent new). The star wine to date is the finely scented, deeply coloured 2004 vintage (★★★★★), which shows lovely concentration and complexity. Drinking well now, the 2005 (★★★★) is very savoury and leathery; the 2006 (★★★★) has cassis, plum, herb and spice flavours, showing good complexity. Still youthful, the 2007 (★★★★☆) is deeply coloured, rich, spicy, nutty and firm, with obvious potential. The 2008 vintage (★★★★★) is the finest since 2004 – dark and generous, in a bold, muscular style, fleshy, complex and likely to be long-lived. The 2009 (★★★★) is also dark and youthful, with strong blackcurrant/herb flavours, firm backbone and the power to age. (Tasted prior to bottling, and so not rated, the 2010 looked outstanding – densely coloured, with a powerful surge of lush, savoury, nutty flavour, deliciously ripe and rich.) These are classy wines, worth discovering.

Vintage	10	09	08	07	06
WR	7	6	7	6	6
Drink	15-30	14-21	14-24	13-19	12-18

DRY $70 –V

Gladstone Auld Alliance   ★★★☆

The 'premier Bordeaux-style' from this Wairarapa winery struggles to match the quality of those from Hawke's Bay. The 2008 vintage (★★★) is a blend of Cabernet Franc (54 per cent), Merlot (27 per cent), Malbec (10 per cent) and Cabernet Sauvignon (9 per cent), barrel-aged for over a year. The colour is fullish, with a hint of development; the palate is fresh and smooth, with some savoury notes, but lacks real warmth and stuffing.

Vintage	08
WR	5
Drink	11-15

DRY $45 –V

Hay Paddock, The   ★★★★☆

The 2008 vintage (★★★★★) of this Waiheke Island red is an Onetangi blend of Syrah (88 per cent) and Petit Verdot (12 per cent), which makes it a 'slightly bigger wine'. Matured in French (76 per cent) and American oak barriques, it is very bold, rich and complex, with warm spice, liquorice and nut flavours, slightly earthy and showing real power through the palate.

Vintage	08	07	06	DRY $75 –V
WR	7	6	5	
Drink	11-17	11-15	11-13	

Karikari Estate Hell Hole   (★★★)

The 2008 vintage (★★★) is a full-flavoured, estate-grown Northland red, blended from Cabernet Franc, Cabernet Sauvignon, Tannat, Merlot and Pinotage. It has coffee and spice characters, with a herbal thread and some spicy complexity.

DRY $22 –V

Karikari Estate Toa   (★★★☆)

The 2007 vintage (★★★☆), grown at Muriwhenua, in Northland, is a blend of Cabernet Franc, Malbec and Pinotage. Barrel-aged for 15 months, it is brambly and nutty, with slightly earthy, herbal, leathery notes adding complexity, good concentration and a firm finish.

Vintage	07	DRY $40 –V
WR	6	
Drink	11-16	

Karikari Estate Toa Iti   ★★★☆

Estate-grown on the Karikari Peninsula, in the Far North, the 2008 vintage (★★★☆) is a Malbec-based red (74 per cent), with Cabernet Franc (20 per cent) and a splash of Merlot. Matured for 15 months in mostly American oak barriques (20 per cent new), it has deep, youthful colour, sweet oak aromas, good muscle and very satisfying depth of blackcurrant and plum flavours, ripe and smooth.

DRY $25 –V

Kidnapper Cliffs Ariki   ★★★★★

The 2009 vintage (★★★★★) from Te Awa is an estate-grown blend of Merlot, Cabernet Franc and Cabernet Sauvignon, grown in the Gimblett Gravels district of Hawke's Bay. Dark and youthful in colour, it has lovely richness and flow, with deep blackcurrant, plum and spice flavours, very fresh, savoury, supple and youthful. Best drinking 2013+.

DRY $55 AV

Man O' War Ironclad   ★★★★☆

The powerful, sturdy but finely textured 2009 vintage (★★★★☆), grown at the eastern end of Waiheke Island, is a classy blend of Cabernet Franc (34 per cent), Merlot (31 per cent) and Malbec (22 per cent), with smaller portions of Petit Verdot and Cabernet Sauvignon. Hand-harvested at 24.5 to 26 brix, it was matured in seasoned French (75 per cent) and new American (25 per cent new) oak casks. Densely coloured, it is rich and supple, with deep blackcurrant, plum, spice and nut flavours, a hint of mint and very fine-grained tannins. Drink now or cellar.

Vintage	09	08	07
WR	7	6	6
Drink	12-19	11-18	11-12

 DRY $50 –V

Marsden Bay of Islands Cavalli ★★☆

The 2008 vintage (★★☆), grown at Kerikeri, is a blend of Chambourcin (50 per cent), Pinotage and Merlot. Full-coloured, it is plummy and slightly herbal, with some rustic notes.

DRY $22 –V

Matariki Quintology ★★★★☆

This Gimblett Gravels, Hawke's Bay red is a marriage of five varieties, in 2007 (★★★★☆) Merlot (38 per cent), Syrah (23 per cent), Cabernet Sauvignon (17 per cent), Cabernet Franc (14 per cent) and Malbec (8 per cent). Matured for 20 months in oak casks (30 per cent new), it is distinctive, weighty and rich, with deep colour and a brambly, spicy, sweetly oaked bouquet. It has fresh blackcurrant, plum and spice flavours, showing excellent concentration and complexity, and a rich, savoury, rounded finish.

Vintage	07	06	05	04	03	02
WR	7	NM	7	7	NM	7
Drink	11-17	NM	11-15	11-14	NM	11-14

 DRY $80 –V

Messenger Le Ménage A Trois ★★★★★

Estate-grown by Duck Creek at Stillwater, north of Auckland city, the 2009 vintage (★★★★★) is a blend of Merlot (39 per cent), Cabernet Franc (38 per cent) and Malbec (23 per cent), matured for two years in French oak barrels. Bold and youthful in colour, it is a strikingly rich wine with dense blackcurrant, plum, olive and spice flavours, lush, supple and very harmonious. After the lovely debut 2008 (★★★★★), Messenger is established as one of Auckland's greatest reds. (One retailer advertised it in late 2011 at just under $50.)

DRY $105 –V

Morton Estate White Label The Mercure ★★★

The 2009 vintage (★★★) is a Hawke's Bay blend of Merlot, Cabernet Sauvignon, Cabernet Franc and Malbec. Fullish in colour, it has good depth of blackcurrant, herb and red-berry flavours, slightly nutty and smooth.

 DRY $18 AV

Mud Brick Vineyard Velvet (★★★★★)

The debut 2008 vintage (★★★★★) is a sumptuous, beautifully fragrant Waiheke Island red made from unidentified grapes – but it smells and tastes of Cabernet Sauvignon and Merlot. Sturdy and rich, with blackcurrant and plum flavours, hints of spice, liquorice and coffee, and notable concentration and complexity, it's already delicious, but should mature gracefully for many years. There is no 2009.

 DRY $105 –V

Muddy Water Deliverance Red Table Wine ★★★☆

The 2009 vintage (★★★☆) is a blend of Pinotage and Syrah, grown at Waipara, which did not meet the winery's standards for varietal wines. Full-coloured, with a spicy, slightly rustic bouquet, it is mouthfilling and firmly structured, with plum, spice and dark chocolate flavours, showing very good depth.

Vintage	09	08
WR	6	6
Drink	11-16	11-14

 DRY $15 V+

Newton Forrest Estate Cornerstone ★★★★★

Grown in the Cornerstone Vineyard, on the corner of Gimblett Road and State Highway 50 – where the first vines were planted in 1989 – this is a distinguished Hawke's Bay blend, matured in French (principally) and American oak barriques. The 2007 vintage (★★★★★) is deliciously rich and rounded. Dark and still purple-flushed, it's an upfront, almost hedonistic wine with a compelling depth of ripe blackcurrant, plum and spice flavours, hints of liquorice and coffee, and a smooth, sustained finish. Still very youthful, the 2009 (★★★★☆) is a blend of Cabernet Sauvignon (65 per cent), Malbec (25 per cent) and Merlot (10 per cent). Boldly coloured, with a fragrant bouquet of blackcurrants, coffee and spices, it is full-bodied and vibrantly fruity, with fresh, strong flavours, a slightly sweet oak influence and excellent ripeness and density.

Vintage	07	06	05	04
WR	6	6	7	5
Drink	11-20	11-20	15-25	11-12

 DRY $50 AV

Obsidian ★★★★★

The Obsidian Vineyard at Onetangi produces one of the most stylish Waiheke Island reds. Looking set for a decade, but already enjoyable, the 2008 vintage (★★★★★) is notably dark and rich, with dense, ripe flavours of blackcurrant, plums, spices and dark chocolate. The 2009 (★★★★☆) is a blend of Cabernet Sauvignon (35 per cent), Merlot (31 per cent), Cabernet Franc (15 per cent), Petit Verdot (13 per cent) and Malbec (6 per cent), matured for a year in French oak barriques. Deeply coloured, it is youthful, concentrated and savoury, with strong blackcurrant, spice and nut flavours, firm and lingering. Open 2013+.

Vintage	09	08	07	06	05	04	03	02
WR	6	7	5	NM	7	6	NM	7
Drink	11-20	11-20	11-19	NM	11-15	11-14	NM	11-12

 DRY $54 AV

Olssens Robert the Bruce ★★★☆

The 2010 vintage (★★★☆) is a Central Otago blend of Pinotage, Syrah and Cabernet Sauvignon, estate-grown at Bannockburn and matured in French and American oak barriques. A distinctive wine, it is fruity and supple, with ripe tannins and concentrated, spicy flavours.

DRY $29 –V

Paritua 21.12   ★★★★★

Grown at 2112 (hence the name) Maraekakaho Road, in Hawke's Bay, the 2008 vintage (★★★★☆) is a Cabernet Sauvignon-based (54 per cent) blend, with substantial amounts of Merlot (28 per cent) and Cabernet Franc (18 per cent), matured in French oak barriques (60 per cent new). Dark, sturdy and savoury, it offers layers of blackcurrant, herb and nutty oak flavours, impressively complex and concentrated.

 DRY $43 AV

Paritua Red   ★★★★

Grown in The Triangle, Hawke's Bay, the 2008 vintage (★★★★) is a fleshy, full-flavoured blend of Merlot (40 per cent), Cabernet Sauvignon (29 per cent), Cabernet Franc (29 per cent), and a splash of Malbec. Dark, with a slightly herbal, nutty bouquet, it is a bold style with generous blackcurrant, plum, herb and spice flavours, a strong oak influence (French barriques, 60 per cent new), and good complexity. Drink now or cellar.

 DRY $31 –V

Passage Rock Sisters   ★★★☆

The Waiheke Island winery's early-drinking red from 2009 (★★★☆) is a blend of Merlot (55 per cent), Cabernet Sauvignon (15 per cent), Cabernet Franc (15 per cent) and Syrah (15 per cent). Floral and vibrantly fruity, it is medium-bodied, with ripe, blackcurrant-like flavours to the fore, spicy, savoury notes adding complexity and good tannin backbone. The 2010 vintage (★★★★) is the finest yet. Made from Cabernet Sauvignon (37 per cent), Merlot (33 per cent), Syrah (17 per cent) and Malbec (13 per cent), matured for a year in oak barriques (30 per cent new), it is rich and ripe, with fresh, strong, plummy, spicy flavours, showing good complexity. Drink now or cellar.

 DRY $25 –V

Pegasus Bay Maestro   ★★★★

The 2006 vintage (★★★★☆) is an estate-grown Waipara blend of Merlot (predominantly) and Malbec, matured for two years in French oak barriques. Dark and still youthful in colour, it is rich and silky-textured, with substantial body (14.5 per cent alcohol) and generous blackcurrant, herb, plum and spice flavours, showing excellent ripeness, complexity and roundness. The 2007 (★★★★) is dark, with blackcurrant, plum, spice and coffee flavours, rich and rounded. A complex, savoury, nutty wine, it's drinking well now.

Vintage	07	06	05
WR	6	6	7
Drink	11-21	11-18	11-16

 DRY $47 –V

Poderi Crisci Viburno   ★★★★

Grown on Waiheke Island, the 2008 vintage (★★★★) is a blend of Merlot (70 per cent) and Cabernet Franc (30 per cent). Drinking well now, it's a weighty wine with strong, ripe, plummy, spicy and nutty flavours, with bottle-age acquiring a leathery, savoury complexity. The 2009 (★★★★) is deeply coloured, with concentrated blackcurrant, herb and spice flavours, leathery, nutty notes adding complexity and a soft, well-rounded finish. Drink now or cellar.

DRY $39 –V

Providence – see Providence Private Reserve Merlot/Cabernet Franc/Malbec in the Merlot section

---

Pukeora Estate Ruahine Range The Benches Red   ★★★☆

(Previously San Hill The Benches Red.) Grown at 240 metres above sea level in Central Hawke's Bay, the 2009 vintage (★★★★) is the best yet. A blend of Merlot (77 per cent), Cabernet Sauvignon (9 per cent), Malbec (9 per cent) and Syrah (5 per cent), matured for 20 months in French and American oak barriques, it is dark, with slightly 'coconutty' oak aromas. Very full-bodied (14.9 per cent alcohol), with strong blackcurrant, plum, spice and olive flavours, seasoned with sweet oak, it is powerful and concentrated, with good tannin backbone. Open 2013+.

Vintage	09
WR	6
Drink	12-15

 DRY $25 –V

Puriri Hills Estate   ★★★★☆

Estate-grown at Clevedon, in South Auckland, this is a stylish, Merlot-based blend. The 2006 vintage (★★★☆) has full, slightly developed colour and a fragrant, nutty, slightly herbal bouquet. A sturdy, concentrated wine with a touch of rusticity, it was available in 2011 at the reduced price of $24. The refined, elegant 2007 vintage (★★★★☆) – from a season which did not yield the Reserve label – is a blend of Merlot (56 per cent), Cabernet Franc (24 per cent), and Carmenère (20 per cent), matured for three years in French oak casks (60 per cent new). Deeply coloured, fragrant, mouthfilling and supple, it's still opening out, with strong blackcurrant, plum, herb and spice flavours, unfolding a leathery, savoury complexity. The 2008 (★★★★☆), made from Merlot (53 per cent), Cabernet Sauvignon (25 per cent), Malbec (16 per cent) and Carmenère (6 per cent), was matured for two years in French oak barriques (40 per cent new). Deep and youthful in colour, it is full-bodied, with a spicy bouquet and an array of blackcurrant, plum, herb, spice and nut flavours, showing excellent depth and complexity. Fresh, vibrant and firm, it should be long-lived; open 2013+.

Vintage	08	07	06	05	04	03	02
WR	7	6	4	7	7	6	6
Drink	12-25	12-20	11-15	11-20	11-15	P	P

DRY $40 –V

Puriri Hills Pope   (★★★★★)

The very classy debut 2005 vintage (★★★★★) was named after Ivan Pope, who planted and tended the vines at this Clevedon, South Auckland vineyard. Blended from Merlot (47 per cent), Carmenère (33 per cent), Cabernet Franc (10 per cent) and Malbec (10 per cent), it has dark colour and a brambly, slightly toasty bouquet. Rich, ripe and highly concentrated, it has hints of coffee and spices, and notable power, complexity and density. The 2008 (★★★★★), made from Cabernet Franc (52 per cent), Merlot (32 per cent) and Carmenère (16 per cent), was matured for two years in French oak barriques (80 per cent new). Deeply coloured, it is mouthfilling, fresh and supple, with substantial body and deep, lush blackcurrant, herb, spice and nut flavours, framed by fine, silky tannins. Showing lovely richness and texture, it's already approachable; drink now or cellar.

Vintage	08	07	06	05
WR	7	NM	NM	7
Drink	13-25	NM	NM	11-20

 DRY $120 –V

Puriri Hills Reserve ★★★★★

A regional classic. Grown at Clevedon, in South Auckland, the 2006 (★★★★★), a blend of Merlot (53 per cent), Carmenère (33 per cent) and Cabernet Franc (14 per cent), was matured in French oak barrels (60 per cent new), and bottled unfined and unfiltered. Dark, fragrant, rich and supple, it is lush and finely textured, with blackcurrant, spice, herb and plum flavours, showing lovely richness, complexity and roundness. It's drinking superbly now. There is no 2007. The 2008 vintage (★★★★★) is a deeply coloured blend of Merlot (51 per cent), Cabernet Franc (20 per cent), Carmenère (13 per cent), Cabernet Sauvignon (9 per cent) and Malbec (7 per cent), matured for two years in French oak barriques (60 per cent new). Invitingly fragrant, with strong, beautifully ripe blackcurrant, plum, herb and spice flavours, seasoned with nutty oak, it is a complex, very fresh and youthful wine with a seductively silky texture. It should flourish with bottle-age; open 2013+.

Vintage	08	07	06	05	04
WR	7	NM	6	7	7
Drink	12-25	NM	11-20	11-20	11-20

DRY $70 AV

Ransom Dark Summit ★★★☆

The 2007 vintage (★★★), grown at Mahurangi, is a blend of Cabernet Sauvignon (47 per cent), Carmenère (19 per cent), Malbec (19 per cent), Cabernet Franc (8 per cent) and Merlot (7 per cent). Matured for nearly two years in French and American oak puncheons and barriques, it is spicy, herbal and leathery, in a moderately ripe style with some leafy notes, but also good complexity and depth. Drink now.

DRY $38 –V

Redd Gravels ★★★★★

The 2006 vintage (★★★★★) is the third release of the top label from Blake Family Vineyard, which was sold a few years ago (the 2007 vintage was the last). Grown in Gimblett Road, Hawke's Bay, it was fermented with indigenous yeasts, and matured for 18 months in French oak barriques (92 per cent new). A blend of Merlot (84 per cent) and Cabernet Franc (16 per cent), like its predecessors it is notably generous and refined. Deep and youthful in colour, with a fragrant, ripe, spicy bouquet, it is concentrated and silky-textured, with an array of blackcurrant, plum, coffee and dark chocolate flavours, complex and deliciously rich and smooth. Drink now or cellar.

DRY $80 AV

Red Wire ★★★☆

From Mount George, owned by Paritua, the 2008 vintage (★★★) is a Hawke's Bay blend of Merlot, Malbec, Cabernet Franc and Cabernet Sauvignon, partly barrel-aged. It's a full-coloured wine, fresh and vibrantly fruity, with plenty of plummy, berryish flavour and gentle tannins, in an easy-drinking style.

Vintage	08
WR	6
Drink	11-13

DRY $15 V+

Richmond Plains Nelson Admiral (★★★)

The deeply coloured, purple-flushed 2010 vintage (★★★) is a blend of Merlot, Malbec and Cabernet Franc, French oak-aged and certified organic. Vibrantly fruity, it has smooth blackcurrant, plum and spice flavours and drink-young charm.

Vintage	10
WR	6
Drink	11-15

 DRY $20 –V

Runner Duck Red ★★★☆

The 2009 (★★★☆) is a distinctive, estate-grown Matakana blend of Cabernet Franc (46 per cent), Pinotage, Malbec and Merlot, barrel-aged for 18 months. Full-coloured, it has vibrant blackcurrant, plum and spice flavours, tinged with sweet oak, fresh, lively acidity and very good depth. The 2007 vintage (★★★☆), made from the same varieties, is full-coloured, with plum, red-berry and spice flavours, showing some savoury complexity, lively acidity and good texture. It reminded me of some Italian reds.

 DRY $35 –V

Sacred Hill Brokenstone ★★★★★

(Formerly labelled Brokenstone Merlot.) This is a typically outstanding Hawke's Bay red from the Gimblett Gravels (mostly the company's joint-venture Deerstalkers Vineyard). The wine spends its first year in mostly new French oak barriques, then another several months in new and older barrels. The 2009 vintage (★★★★★) is a blend of Merlot, Cabernet Sauvignon and Syrah. Dense and youthful in colour, it is bold, with highly concentrated blackcurrant, plum, spice and nut flavours, showing excellent ripeness and complexity. Still a baby, it is rich and flowing; open 2014+.

Vintage	09	08	07
WR	7	6	7
Drink	11-18	11-15	11-15

DRY $80 AV

San Hill The Benches Red – see Pukeora Estate Ruahine Range The Benches Red

San Hill The Benches Red Reserve (★★★☆)

Maturing well, the 2007 vintage (★★★☆) of this Central Hawke's Bay red from Pukeora Estate is a deeply coloured, Merlot-predominant blend (58 per cent) with smaller portions of Cabernet Sauvignon, Syrah and Malbec. Matured for 20 months in French and American oak barriques (half new), it has a fragrant, berryish, spicy bouquet, tinged with sweet oak. Mouthfilling and vibrantly fruity, it is plummy, spicy and oaky, with some savoury complexity and very good depth.

Vintage	07
WR	6
Drink	11-13

DRY $25 –V

Seifried Sylvia   ★★☆

Named after Agnes Seifried's late mother, this Nelson red is made from an Austrian variety, Zweigelt, which the Seifrieds have pioneered here. Grown at Brightwater and French oak-aged, the 2008 vintage (★★☆) is a full-bodied, easy-drinking quaffer, slightly raisiny, simple and smooth.

Vintage	08
WR	5
Drink	11-14

 DRY $19 –V

Soho Revolver   ★★★★

The 2008 vintage (★★★★) is a Waiheke Island blend of Merlot (46 per cent), Malbec (31 per cent), Cabernet Sauvignon (17 per cent) and Cabernet Franc (6 per cent), matured in French oak casks (20 per cent new). It's a full-coloured wine, fragrant and ripe, with strong, plummy, spicy flavours, showing good concentration and complexity.

Vintage	09
WR	7
Drink	10-16

 DRY $38 –V

Stone Paddock Scarlet   ★★★☆

Estate-grown by Paritua in The Triangle district of Hawke's Bay, the 2008 vintage (★★★) is a blend of Bordeaux varieties with a splash of Syrah. Mouthfilling, with blackcurrant, herb and spice flavours and fresh acidity, it shows a bit more complexity than you'd expect at this price.

 DRY $16 V+

Stonyridge Airfield   ★★★★

Sold as 'the little brother of our flagship wine, Larose', the 2010 vintage (★★★★) is a blend of Cabernet Sauvignon (43 per cent), Malbec (31 per cent) and Merlot (26 per cent), grown at Onetangi, on Waiheke Island, and matured in French oak casks. Showing deep, purple-flushed colour, it is youthful and sweet-fruited, with concentrated red-berry and plum flavours, and a good backbone of tannin. It should be long-lived; open 2014+.

Vintage	10	09
WR	7	7
Drink	12-20	11-15

 DRY $45 –V

Stonyridge Faithful   ★★★☆

From a neighbouring vineyard, managed by Stonyridge, the 2010 (★★★☆) is a Waiheke Island blend of Merlot (88 per cent) and Cabernet Franc (12 per cent), matured in French (75 per cent) and American oak casks. Full-coloured, it is sweet-fruited, plummy and spicy, with some leathery notes adding complexity and a firm finish. Like a minor Bordeaux.

Vintage	10	09
WR	7	5
Drink	12-20	11-14

DRY $30 –V

Stonyridge Larose ★★★★★

Typically a stunning Waiheke wine. Dark and seductively perfumed, with smashing fruit flavours, at its best it is a magnificently concentrated red that matures superbly for a decade or longer, acquiring great complexity. The vines – Cabernet Sauvignon, Merlot, Cabernet Franc, Malbec and Petit Verdot, ranging up to 29 years old – are grown in free-draining clay soils on a north-facing slope, a kilometre from the sea at Onetangi, and are very low-yielding (4 tonnes/hectare). The wine is matured for a year in French (80 to 90 per cent) and American oak barriques (half new, half one year old), and is sold largely on an *en primeur* basis, whereby the customers, in return for paying for their wine about nine months in advance of its delivery, secure a substantial price reduction. The 2009 (★★★★★) is a blend of Cabernet Sauvignon (52 per cent), Malbec (18 per cent), Petit Verdot (15 per cent), Merlot (10 per cent) and Cabernet Franc (5 per cent). Highly Bordeaux-like, it has dark, youthful colour, fresh, dense, brambly, spicy flavours, with hints of leather and dark chocolate, and ripe, supple tannins. The 2010 vintage (★★★★★) is boldly coloured, powerful but not heavy, with sweet-fruit delights, concentrated red-berry, plum and spice flavours and a firm backbone of tannin. Densely structured and complex, it should be a 20-year wine.

Vintage	10	09	08	07	06	05	04	03	02
WR	7°	7	7	7	7	7	7	7	7
Drink	15-30	11-21	14-25	11-17	11-17	11-22	11-17	11-14	11-15

Te Awa Boundary ★★★★★

This stylish Hawke's Bay red is an estate-grown, Merlot-based blend from low-yielding, mature vines in the Gimblett Gravels, matured in French oak barriques. It is typically more savoury than most of the region's reds and the 2006 vintage (★★★★★), not released until 2010, is drinking beautifully now. A densely coloured blend of Merlot (74 per cent) and Cabernet Sauvignon (21 per cent), with splashes of Cabernet Franc and Malbec, it is powerful and highly concentrated, with dense blackcurrant, spice, dark chocolate and nut flavours, substantial body and impressive complexity. A distinctly Bordeaux-like red, it should be very long-lived.

Vintage	06	05	04	03	02	01	00
WR	7	NM	7	NM	7	6	7
Drink	11-16	NM	11-14	NM	11-12	P	P

Te Henga The Westie Vintara Red ★★☆

From Babich, the 2009 vintage (★★☆) is a North Island blend, medium-bodied, fruity, ripe and smooth, with fresh, berryish, plummy flavours, showing decent depth. The 2010 (★★☆) is ruby-hued, fresh and fruity, in a medium-bodied style with decent depth of plum and spice flavours, well balanced for easy drinking.

Te Mata Coleraine ★★★★★

Breed, rather than brute power, is the hallmark of Coleraine, which since its first vintage in 1982 has carved out an illustrious reputation among New Zealand's claret-style reds. Since the 2005 vintage, it is no longer labelled as a Cabernet/Merlot, but simply as Coleraine (and in some recent vintages has contained more Merlot than Cabernet Sauvignon). At its best, it is a magical Hawke's Bay wine, with a depth, complexity and subtlety on the level of a top-class Bordeaux. The grapes are grown in the Havelock North hills, in the company's warm, north-facing Buck and 1892 vineyards, and the wine is matured for 18 to 20 months in French oak barriques, predominantly new. Cabernet Sauvignon in 2009 accounted for 52 per cent of the blend, Merlot 43 per cent and Cabernet Franc 5 per cent (Malbec is definitely not in the recipe). Sturdy (14 per cent alcohol) and dense, it has highly concentrated, ripe blackcurrant, spice, plum and nut flavours, very elegant, lithe and finely poised, in a style that reminds me of a fine Margaux. Yet to really unfold, it should be at its best for drinking around 2020.

Vintage	09	08	07	06	05	04	03	02
WR	7	7	7	7	7	7	7	7
Drink	15-21	14-20	11-27	11-26	11-25	11-16	11-18	11-15

DRY $75 AV

Te Whau The Point ★★★★☆

This classy Waiheke Island red flows from a steeply sloping vineyard at Putiki Bay. The distinguished 2008 vintage (★★★★★) is a Cabernet Sauvignon-based blend (57 per cent), with Merlot (30 per cent), Cabernet Franc (10 per cent) and Malbec (3 per cent). Fermented with indigenous yeasts and matured for 18 months in French oak barriques (one-third new), it is deeply coloured, mouthfilling and sweet-fruited, with concentrated plum, spice, dark chocolate and nut flavours and good tannin backbone. Very generous and highly complex, with a long life ahead, it's a wine of great depth, structure and personality. (In a vertical tasting of the 1999–2009 vintages, held in late 2010, the 2005 was also a star – dark and powerful, with very generous, ripe blackcurrant and nut flavours, still unfolding.) The 2009 vintage (★★★★☆), slightly less powerful than the 2008, is a blend of Cabernet Sauvignon (55 per cent), Merlot (31 per cent), Cabernet Franc (11 per cent) and Malbec (3 per cent), barrel-aged for 18 months. Full and youthful in colour, it is full-bodied, complex and savoury, with blackcurrant, plum, spice and herb flavours, seasoned with quality oak, and ripe, supple tannins. Best drinking 2013+.

Vintage	09	08	07	06	05	04	03	02
WR	6	7	7	6	7	6	5	7
Drink	13-20	13-25	12-22	11-15	11-20	11-15	P	10-15

DRY $70 –V

Tom ★★★★★

Pernod Ricard NZ's top Hawke's Bay claret-style red honours pioneer winemaker Tom McDonald, the driving force behind New Zealand's first prestige red, McWilliam's Cabernet Sauvignon. The early vintages in the mid-1990s were Cabernet Sauvignon-predominant, but since 1998 Merlot has emerged as an equally crucial part of the recipe. Made at the Church Road winery, it is typically not a blockbuster but a wine of great finesse; it is savoury, complex and more akin to a quality Bordeaux than other New World reds. I have not tasted the 2005 vintage, released in 2009 at $95 – down from $135 for the 2002 (★★★★★). The 2007 (★★★★★) is a wine of great richness, subtlety and refinement. Dense and youthful in colour, it is finely scented, with highly concentrated blackcurrant, plum, spice and slight nut flavours, beautifully ripe, deep and smooth. Elegant and finely poised, a wine of real beauty, it should flourish for 15–20 years.

Vintage	07	06	05	04	03	02	01	00	99	98
WR	7	NM	7	NM	NM	7	NM	6	NM	7
Drink	11-20	NM	11-15	NM	NM	11-12	NM	P	NM	11-15

DRY $95 AV

Trinity Hill The Gimblett ★★★★★

A great buy, from one vintage to the next. The classy 2009 (★★★★★), hand-harvested at three sites in the Gimblett Gravels, Hawke's Bay, is a blend of Merlot (38 per cent), Cabernet Sauvignon (37 per cent), Cabernet Franc (15 per cent), Petit Verdot (8 per cent) and Malbec (2 per cent), matured for 18 months in predominantly French oak barriques (35 per cent new). Mouthfilling, fragrant and boldly coloured, it has deep, beautifully ripe blackcurrant, plum, slight herb and spice flavours, a hint of coffee, tight-knit tannins and a long finish.

Vintage	09	08	07	06	05
WR	6	5	6	6	6
Drink	12-18	12-18	13-18	12-18	11-14

 DRY $35 V+

Trinity Hill The Trinity ★★★★

Grown in the Gimblett Gravels, Hawke's Bay, the 2009 vintage (★★★★) is a top-value blend of Cabernet Sauvignon (57 per cent), Merlot (28 per cent) and Cabernet Franc (15 per cent), deeply coloured, concentrated, fleshy and supple. The 2010 vintage (★★★★), matured for a year in seasoned oak barrels, is still very youthful. Dark, with excellent depth of blackcurrant, plum and herb flavours, it is a finely balanced wine, rich and flowing, with a rounded finish. Best drinking 2013+.

Vintage	10
WR	6
Drink	12-15

 DRY $22 V+

TW M 'n M (★★★)

The 2008 vintage (★★★) is a Gisborne blend of Merlot (70 per cent) and Malbec (30 per cent), hand-picked and matured for 15 months in French and American oak barriques. Full but not dense in colour, with sweet-oak aromas, it's an easy-drinking style, ripe, plummy and spicy, with some savoury complexity. Ready.

 DRY $20 –V

Two Gates Hawke's Bay Omahu (★★★★★)

The 2007 vintage (★★★★★) is an outstanding debut. Certified organic, it is a single-vineyard, Hawke's Bay blend of Merlot (62 per cent), Cabernet Franc (29 per cent) and Cabernet Sauvignon (9 per cent), hand-picked at over 24 brix and matured for 18 months in French oak barriques (45 per cent new). Deep and bright in colour, with a beautifully scented bouquet, it is highly concentrated and silky-textured, with rich, ripe blackcurrant, plum, coffee and nut flavours, very refined and harmonious. Best drinking 2012+.

 DRY $55 AV

Unison Classic Blend ★★★★☆

Based on a block of mature, densely planted vines in the Gimblett Gravels, Hawke's Bay, this blend of Merlot, Cabernet Sauvignon and Syrah is typically dark, concentrated and tightly structured. The 2008 vintage (★★★★), barrel-matured for 20 months, is full and youthful in colour, with strong berry, spice and nut flavours, fresh and firm, and good complexity.

Vintage	08	07	06	05	04	03	02
WR	6	7	6	6	7	NM	7
Drink	11-15	11-16	11-15	11-14	11-14	NM	11-12

DRY $35 AV

Unison Selection ★★★★★

Designed for cellaring and oak-matured longer than the above wine, this is a consistently outstanding Hawke's Bay red. The vines, densely planted in the Gimblett Gravels in the early 1990s, are cropped lightly. A vineyard (rather than barrel) selection of Merlot, Cabernet Sauvignon and Syrah, it is matured initially in French and American oak barriques, then (for 'harmonising') for a further year in a large Italian cask of French and Slavonian oak. The 2007 vintage (★★★★★) is promisingly dark and youthful in colour. The bouquet is fragrant, with blackcurrant and spice aromas; the palate rich and flowing, with highly concentrated cassis, plum and spice flavours, hints of herbs and nuts, and ripe, supple tannins. It's still unfolding, but already delicious.

Vintage	07	06	05	04	03	02	01	00
WR	7	6	6	7	NM	7	6	7
Drink	11-20	11-17	11-16	11-16	NM	11-15	11-13	11-13

Waimea Trev's Red (★★★☆)

'Round up your mates and enjoy', suggests the back label on this deeply coloured Nelson blend of Cabernet Franc (63 per cent) and Syrah (32 per cent), which has a splash of Malbec. American oak-aged, the 2010 vintage (★★★☆) has fresh, berryish aromas leading into a full-flavoured, youthful wine, vibrantly fruity, spicy and slightly savoury, with some complexity.

DRY $24 AV

Cabernet Franc

New Zealand's fifth most widely planted red-wine variety – just ahead of Malbec – Cabernet Franc is probably a mutation of Cabernet Sauvignon, the much higher-profile variety with which it is so often blended. Jancis Robinson's phrase, 'a sort of claret Beaujolais', aptly sums up the nature of this versatile and underrated red-wine grape.

As a minority ingredient in the recipe of many of New Zealand's top reds, Cabernet Franc lends a delicious softness and concentrated fruitiness to its blends with Cabernet Sauvignon and Merlot. However, admirers of Château Cheval Blanc, the illustrious St Émilion (which is two-thirds planted in Cabernet Franc), have long appreciated that Cabernet Franc need not always be Cabernet Sauvignon's bridesmaid, but can yield fine red wines in its own right. The supple, fruity wines of Chinon and Bourgueil, in the Loire Valley, have also proved Cabernet Franc's ability to produce highly attractive, soft light reds.

According to the latest national vineyard survey, the bearing area of Cabernet Franc will be 162 hectares in 2012 – well below the 213 hectares in 2004. Two-thirds of the vines are clustered in Hawke's Bay. As a varietal red, Cabernet Franc is lower in tannin and acid than Cabernet Sauvignon; or as Michael Brajkovich, of Kumeu River, has put it: 'more approachable and easy'.

Ake Ake Northland Cabernet Franc (★★★☆)

Hand-picked at Kerikeri and handled mostly in tanks (20 per cent in seasoned American barriques), the 2009 vintage (★★★☆) is full-coloured and mouthfilling, with generous, ripe blackcurrant, plum and spice flavours, seasoned with sweet oak. Drink now or cellar.

Vintage	09	DRY $20 AV
WR	5	
Drink	11-14	

Ake Ake Northland Cabernet/Merlot (★★★☆)

'Cabernet', here, means Cabernet Franc. Grown at Kerikeri, the 2010 vintage (★★★☆), a nearly 50:50 blend of Cabernet Franc and Merlot, was matured for 10 months in tanks and seasoned American oak barriques. Full-coloured, it is mouthfilling, vibrantly fruity and supple, with generous, plummy, slightly spicy flavours, a restrained oak influence and lots of drink-young appeal.

Vintage	10	DRY $20 AV
WR	4	
Drink	12-15	

Askerne Hawke's Bay Cabernet Franc (★★★)

The 2009 vintage (★★★) was estate-grown, hand-picked and matured in French oak casks (33 per cent new). It's a fleshy wine with brambly, herbal flavours, and hints of chocolates and nuts. Ready.

Vintage	09	DRY $20 –V
WR	6	
Drink	12-15	

Clearview Reserve Hawke's Bay Cabernet Franc ★★★★☆

The 2009 vintage (★★★★★) includes a splash of Merlot (9 per cent) and was matured in French oak barriques (mostly new). It's a classic, claret-style red with excellent muscle and concentration. Deep and youthful in colour, with mouthfilling body and blackcurrant, plum and spice flavours, fresh and strong, it is very rich and savoury, with ripe, supple tannins. (Based principally on 23-year-old vines at Te Awanga.)

DRY $50 –V

Crossroads Vineyard Selection Mere Road
Vineyard Gimblett Gravels Cabernet Franc

The powerful 2009 vintage (★★★★☆) is still unfolding. A blend of Cabernet Franc (85 per cent) and Cabernet Sauvignon (15 per cent), it was hand-picked and matured for over a year in French oak barriques (58 per cent new). Dark, mouthfilling and silky-textured, with concentrated blackcurrant, red-berry and spice flavours to the fore, and hints of coffee and nuts adding complexity, it is a deliciously rich, savoury and smooth red, likely to be long-lived.

DRY $45 –V

Jurassic Ridge Cabernet Franc ★★★★

Grown at Church Bay, on Waiheke Island, and French oak-aged, the 2008 vintage (★★★★) is deeply coloured, sturdy and rich, with good density of blackcurrant, plum and spice flavours, warm and savoury, a hint of dark chocolate, and substantial tannins.

Vintage	08
WR	7
Drink	11-14

DRY $29 AV

Kidnapper Cliffs Hawke's Bay Cabernet Franc

From Te Awa, the 2009 vintage (★★★★★) is hugely charming in its youth. Deep and purple-flushed in colour, it is fruit-packed, ripe and supple, with lovely plum, spice, blackcurrant and dark chocolate flavours, and very fine-grained tannins. Showing the power to age, it's a beautifully textured wine, for drinking now and over the next decade.

DRY $45 AV

Matakana Estate Hawke's Bay Cabernet Franc/Merlot ★★★

Deeply coloured, the 2008 vintage (★★★☆) has a bouquet of blackcurrants and herbs. Full-flavoured, it is cedary, spicy and savoury, with some development showing.

DRY $27 –V

Omaha Bay Vineyard Matakana Cabernet Franc/Merlot/Malbec   ★★★☆

The 2009 vintage (★★★☆) was matured for 10 months in French oak casks (25 per cent new). Fullish in colour, it is sturdy, with fresh, strong blackcurrant and spice flavours, showing good complexity, and firm tannins. Worth cellaring.

Vintage	09	08
WR	5	6
Drink	11-15	11-15

 DRY $27 –V

Pyramid Valley Vineyards Growers Collection
Howell Family Vineyard Hawke's Bay Cabernet Franc   (★★★★★)

Powerful and densely coloured, the 2007 vintage (★★★★★) was hand-picked in The Triangle from low-cropped vines (2 tonnes/hectare), fermented with indigenous yeasts, and matured for 20 months in French oak barriques (35 per cent new). It's a highly concentrated red with ripe blackcurrant, herb and plum flavours showing excellent density, structure and cellaring potential. Still on sale, it's drinking superbly now.

 DRY $66 AV

Sileni The Pacemaker Hawke's Bay Cabernet Franc   ★★★★

The stylish, youthful 2009 vintage (★★★★) is a single-vineyard red, grown at Bridge Pa. Matured for over a year in French (85 per cent) and American oak barriques, it is full-coloured, with fresh, strong blackcurrant, plum and spice flavours, a hint of coffee and obvious potential.

 DRY $32 –V

Waimarie Muriwai Valley Cabernet Franc/Merlot   (★★☆)

The fairly mature 2008 vintage (★★☆) was estate-grown in West Auckland and matured for 18 months in French oak casks. It's a medium-bodied wine, showing moderate depth of colour and plummy, spicy flavour.

DRY $24 –V

Cabernet Sauvignon and Cabernet-predominant blends

Cabernet Sauvignon has proved a tough nut to crack in New Zealand. Mid-priced models were – until recently – usually of lower quality than a comparable offering from Australia, where the relative warmth suits the late-ripening Cabernet Sauvignon variety. Yet a top New Zealand Cabernet-based red from a favourable vintage can hold its own in illustrious company – Mission Jewelstone Cabernet/Merlot 2009 ($39) headed off three legendary Bordeaux (2008 Margaux, Lafite-Rothschild and Latour, around $1000 each) in a June 2011 tasting in Hong Kong. And the overall standard of today's middle-tier, $20 to $25 bottlings is far higher than many wine lovers realise – which makes for some great bargains.

Cabernet Sauvignon was widely planted here in the nineteenth century. The modern resurgence of interest in the great Bordeaux variety was led by Tom McDonald, the legendary Hawke's Bay winemaker, whose string of elegant (though, by today's standards, light) Cabernet Sauvignons under the McWilliam's label, from the much-acclaimed 1965 vintage to the gold medal-winning 1975, proved beyond all doubt that fine-quality red wines could be produced in New Zealand.

During the 1970s and 1980s, Cabernet Sauvignon ruled the red-wine roost in New Zealand. Since then, as winemakers – especially in the South Island, but also Hawke's Bay – searched for red-wine varieties that would ripen more fully and consistently in our relatively cool grape-growing climate than Cabernet Sauvignon, it has been pushed out of the limelight by Merlot, Pinot Noir and Syrah. According to the latest national vineyard survey, between 2003 and 2012 the country's total area of bearing Cabernet Sauvignon vines will contract from 741 to 521 hectares. Growers with suitably warm sites have often retained faith in Cabernet Sauvignon, but others have moved on to less challenging varieties.

Three-quarters of the country's Cabernet Sauvignon vines are clustered in Hawke's Bay, and Auckland also has significant plantings. In the South Island, where only 7 per cent of the vines are planted, Cabernet-based reds have typically lacked warmth and richness. This magnificent but late-ripening variety's future in New Zealand clearly lies in the warmer vineyard sites of the north.

What is the flavour of Cabernet Sauvignon? When newly fermented a herbal character is common, intertwined with blackcurrant-like fruit aromas. New oak flavours, firm acidity and taut tannins are other hallmarks of young, fine Cabernet Sauvignon. With maturity the flavour loses its aggression and the wine develops roundness and complexity, with assorted cigar-box, minty and floral scents emerging. It is infanticide to broach a Cabernet Sauvignon-based red with any pretensions to quality at less than two years old; at about four years old the rewards of cellaring really start to flow.

Ake Ake Northland Cabernet/Merlot – see the Cabernet Franc section

Ash Ridge Vineyard Cabernet/Merlot ★★★

The easy-drinking 2008 vintage (★★★) is rare – only 50 cases were produced. Grown in Hawke's Bay and matured in a 50:50 split of French and American oak casks, it is plummy and spicy, with some savoury complexity.

DRY $25 –V

Vintage	09	08
WR	6	5
Drink	13-17	12-16

Ashwell Martinborough Cabernet Sauvignon ★★★

The 2009 (★★★☆) is deeply coloured, fruity and smooth, with ripe blackcurrant, herb and nut flavours, gentle tannins and some savoury complexity. The 2010 vintage (★★☆), matured in French oak casks (one-third new), has fresh, moderately ripe, plummy, herbal flavours. A vibrantly fruity wine, it has drink-young appeal, but also shows a slight lack of warmth and richness.

Vintage	10	09	08
WR	6	6	5
Drink	11-18	11-16	11-14

DRY $28 –V

Babich Irongate Cabernet/Merlot/Franc ★★★★★

Grown in the Irongate Vineyard in Gimblett Road, Hawke's Bay and matured in French oak barriques (30 per cent new), this elegant, complex, firmly structured red is designed for cellaring. The 2009 vintage (★★★★★) is a sturdy, rich and flowing blend of Cabernet Sauvignon (67 per cent), Merlot (25 per cent) and Cabernet Franc (8 per cent). A very stylish wine in the Bordeaux mould, it has deep blackcurrant, plum and spice flavours, finely integrated French oak and ripe, supple tannins. The 2010 (★★★★☆) is fragrant and full-coloured, with good concentration of youthful blackcurrant, herb, plum and spice flavours, hints of coffee and dark chocolate, ripe tannins and the structure to age well; open 2013 onwards. These are not blockbuster reds, but quietly classy and very satisfying.

Vintage	10	09	08
WR	7	7	5
Drink	13-22	12-21	11-17

DRY $35 V+

Babich The Patriarch – see the Branded and Other Red Wines section

Bridge Estate Matawhero Cabernet/Merlot (★★★★)

From a Gisborne vineyard established in 1985 – since partly replanted – the 2009 vintage (★★★★) is a blend of Cabernet Sauvignon, Cabernet Franc, Merlot and Malbec. Fullish but not dense in colour, it is quite Bordeaux-like, with generous blackcurrant, spice and herb flavours, already quite nutty, leathery and savoury, good complexity, and supple tannins. It's drinking well now.

DRY $48 –V

Brookfields Ohiti Estate Cabernet Sauvignon ★★★☆

Hawke's Bay winemaker Peter Robertson believes that the warm, shingly Ohiti Estate, inland from Fernhill, produces 'sound Cabernet Sauvignon year after year – which is a major challenge to any vineyard'. The 2009 vintage (★★★☆), matured for 18 months in French and American oak casks, is full-coloured and sturdy, with strong flavours of blackcurrants, plums, spices and herbs, braced by firm tannins. A good, gutsy red, it's priced right.

Vintage	09
WR	7
Drink	13-18

DRY $20 AV

Brookfields Reserve Vintage Cabernet/Merlot ★★★★★

Brookfields' top red is one of the most powerful and long-lived reds in Hawke's Bay. At its best, it is a thrilling wine – robust, tannin-laden and overflowing with very rich cassis, plum and mint flavours. The grapes are sourced from the Lyons family's sloping, north-facing vineyard at Bridge Pa, and the wine is matured for 15 to 18 months in French oak barriques (95 to 100 per cent new). The 2009 vintage (★★★★☆) is deeply coloured, fleshy and sweet-fruited, with a youthful array of rich cassis, plum, herb, spice and nut flavours, showing notable concentration and complexity. Still unfolding, it should mature well; drink 2014+.

Vintage	09	08	07	06	05	04	03	02
WR	7	NM	7	7	NM	7	NM	7
Drink	14-20	NM	11-19	11-16	NM	11-12	NM	P

DRY $57 AV

Church Road Cabernet/Merlot – see Church Road Merlot/Cabernet

Church Road Cuve Series Hawke's Bay Cabernet Sauvignon (★★★★★)

The 2007 vintage (★★★★★) was grown at two sites – Pernod Ricard NZ's Redstone Vineyard in The Triangle and in the Gimblett Gravels – and matured for 22 months in French oak barriques (50 per cent new). A classic claret style, with deep colour and deliciously concentrated blackcurrant and spice flavours, it shows lovely fruit sweetness and varietal purity, with firm, fine-grained tannins. A top buy.

DRY $26 V+

Church Road Reserve Hawke's Bay Cabernet/Merlot ★★★★★

The dark, flavour-drenched 2007 vintage (★★★★★) shows just what Hawke's Bay can do in a favourable season with Cabernet Sauvignon-predominant reds. Hand-picked and matured for 21 months in French oak barriques, it is dense and boldly coloured, with concentrated blackcurrant, herb and nut flavours, showing good, savoury complexity, and a firm underlay of tannin. The 2009 (★★★★★) was grown in the company's Redstone Vineyard – in The Triangle – and in the Gimblett Gravels. French oak-aged for 21 months, it has a real 'Wow!' factor. Dark and fleshy, it is powerful (14.5 per cent alcohol) and strikingly concentrated, with dense cassis, plum and spice flavours, braced by firm tannins. It should flourish for at least a decade.

Vintage	07
WR	7
Drink	11-15

DRY $36 V+

C.J. Pask Declaration Cabernet/Merlot/Malbec ★★★★

The 2007 vintage (★★★★) is a Gimblett Gravels blend of Cabernet Sauvignon (45 per cent), Merlot (35 per cent) and Malbec (20 per cent), matured for 18 months in French and American oak casks (100 per cent new). A big, structured wine, it is fleshy, savoury and firm, with concentrated blackcurrant, spice, herb and nut flavours, good complexity and tight tannins. Worth cellaring.

DRY $49 –V

C.J. Pask Gimblett Road Cabernet/Merlot/Malbec   ★★★☆

The 2007 vintage (★★★☆), barrel-aged for 16 to 18 months, has concentrated plum and spice flavours, the leafy notes typical of Cabernet Sauvignon, and good structure and complexity. The 2008 (★★★) has deep, slightly developed colour. A blend of Cabernet Sauvignon (45 per cent), Merlot (35 per cent) and Malbec (20 per cent), it is full-bodied, with herbal, nutty flavours and some savoury, leathery notes adding complexity.

 DRY $20 AV

Clearview Cape Kidnappers Cabernet/Merlot   ★★★☆

Grown in Hawke's Bay and matured for a year in French and American oak casks (mostly seasoned), this is typically a sturdy red with sweet-fruit characters and plenty of savoury, spicy flavour. The 2009 vintage (★★★★) is a dark, generous blend of Gimblett Gravels Cabernet Sauvignon and estate-grown, Te Awanga Merlot. It offers fresh, strong blackcurrant, plum and spice flavours, gently seasoned with sweet oak, and a rich, rounded finish.

 DRY $26 –V

Coopers Creek SV Gimblett Gravels Cabernet Sauvignon   (★★★)

The 2007 vintage (★★★) is a 'straight' Cabernet Sauvignon, barrel-aged for a year. Dark, it is concentrated and tannic, with ripe blackcurrant and cedar notes, showing some complexity and length, but also a slight lack of charm.

Vintage	07
WR	7
Drink	11-13

 DRY $28 –V

Coopers Creek SV Gimblett Gravels Hawke's Bay Cabernet/Merlot   ★★★★

The 2007 vintage (★★★★) is dark, with blackcurrant and spice flavours, hints of herbs and coffee, and a firm finish. A tightly structured blend (65 per cent Cabernet Sauvignon, 35 per cent Merlot), barrel-aged for a year, it shows good concentration and length.

Vintage	07
WR	7
Drink	11-13

 DRY $28 AV

Corbans Cottage Block Hawke's Bay Cabernet/Merlot   (★★★★★)

The 2007 vintage (★★★★★) is a majestic red. Matured for two years in French oak barriques (new and one year old), and bottled without fining or filtration, it is deeply coloured, with layers of blackcurrant, plum and spice flavours, complex and concentrated, and ripe, supple tannins. Dense and savoury, it should flourish for a decade; open 2012+.

DRY $35 V+

Corbans Homestead Hawke's Bay Cabernet Sauvignon/Merlot   ★★★

The 2008 vintage (★★★) is deeply coloured, with good body, satisfying depth of blackcurrant and herb flavours and a smooth finish.

 DRY $17 AV

Cornerstone Cabernet/Merlot/Malbec – see Newton Forrest Estate Cornerstone Cabernet/ Merlot/Malbec in the Branded and Other Red Wine Wines section

Delegat Hawke's Bay Cabernet/Merlot   ★★★☆

The 2007 vintage (★★★☆) is dark, with generous blackcurrant, plum and spice flavours. Fruity and supple, with a gentle seasoning of oak, it shows very good ripeness, balance and depth. The 2008 (★★★) is medium-bodied, with fresh blackcurrant and herb flavours in a fruit-driven style with a touch of complexity.

Vintage	08	07	06	05
WR	7	6	6	6
Drink	11-14	11-13	11-12	11-12

DRY $17 V+

Delegat Reserve Hawke's Bay Cabernet Sauvignon/Merlot   ★★★★

Top vintages offer great value. The 2007 (★★★★) is a 50:50 blend of Cabernet Sauvignon and Merlot, grown in the Gimblett Gravels and barrel-aged for a year. Dark, with cedary, spicy oak seasoning blackberry and green-olive flavours, it shows good richness and complexity.

Vintage	07	06
WR	6	5
Drink	11-13	11-13

DRY $20 V+

Distant Land [Reserve] Hawke's Bay Cabernet/Merlot   (★★★★)

(Note: the word 'Reserve' appears only on the back label.) The 2009 vintage (★★★★) is a full-coloured blend of Cabernet Sauvignon (principally) and Merlot, matured for a year in French and American oak casks. Fleshy, with good substance, it has generous, youthful blackcurrant, plum, herb and spice flavours, a hint of coffee, and ripe, supple tannins. Drink mid-2012+.

DRY $32 –V

Dunleavy Cabernet/Merlot   ★★★☆

The second-tier red from Waiheke Vineyards, best known for Te Motu Cabernet/Merlot. It is typically like a minor Bordeaux – medium-bodied, with blackcurrant, plum and spice flavours, slightly leafy and showing some savoury complexity.

DRY $45 –V

Frizzell Ka Mate Hawke's Bay Cabernet Sauvignon/Merlot/Cabernet Franc   (★★★★☆)

Launched in early 2011, the 2007 vintage (★★★★☆), matured in French oak barriques, has bold, dark, still youthful colour. Mouthfilling, it is rich and silky, with concentrated blackcurrant, herb and spice flavours. A finely textured wine, it's highly approachable now but also worth cellaring.

DRY $30 AV

Hyperion The Titan Cabernet Sauvignon   ★★★☆

This Matakana red is very good, but not as gigantic as the term 'titan' suggests. The 2007 vintage (★★★☆), matured in European and American oak casks, is full-coloured, with perfumed, sweet-oak aromas. Mouthfilling and smooth, with blackcurrant, herb, olive and spice flavours tinged with sweet oak, it is savoury and complex, and drinking well now.

Vintage	07	06	05	04
WR	6	6	4	6
Drink	11-20	11-16	11-14	11-14

DRY $42 –V

Isola Estate Cabernet/Merlot   (★★★★)

Grown on Waiheke Island, the 2008 vintage (★★★★) is an impressive blend of Cabernet Sauvignon (52 per cent), Merlot (42 per cent), Cabernet Franc (5 per cent) and Malbec (1 per cent). Deeply coloured, it offers fresh, generous berry and plum flavours, showing excellent concentration. Drink 2011+.

DRY $37 –V

John Forrest Collection Cabernet Sauvignon   ★★★★★

A star label on the rise. The authoritative 2005 vintage (★★★★★) is based on mature, low-cropped (4 to 5.6 tonnes/hectare) vines in the Gimblett Gravels district of Hawke's Bay, and matured in French oak barriques (one-third new). Notably concentrated, complex and well-structured, with bold colour, it is dense, warm, spicy, nutty and layered, with firm, ripe tannins and great potential. The more forward 2006 vintage (★★★★☆) is already delicious. Dark, with rich, ripe blackcurrant, plum, spice and nut flavours, it shows impressive complexity and density, with a well-rounded finish.

Vintage	06	05
WR	6	6
Drink	12-20	12-20

DRY $60 AV

Johner Estate Lyndor Wairarapa Cabernet & Merlot   ★★★★

Full of personality, the 2009 vintage (★★★★) is deeply coloured, with hints of coffee and spices on the nose. Fresh, sweet-fruited and rich, it has strong blackcurrant, plum, herb and spice flavours, seasoned with nutty oak, and fairly firm tannins. Well worth cellaring.

Vintage	09	08
WR	6	6
Drink	11-20	11-17

DRY $50 –V

Johner Estate Wairarapa Cabernet/Merlot/Malbec   ★★★☆

The deeply coloured 2009 vintage (★★★☆) has concentrated plum, nut, herb and spice flavours. A mouthfilling wine, it's enjoyable now, but with bottle-age, a distinct leafy streak is emerging.

Vintage	10	09	08	07
WR	6	5	6	5
Drink	11-25	13-16	12-17	11

DRY $39 –V

Kennedy Point Reserve Cabernet Sauvignon   ★★★★

The 2005 vintage (★★★★☆) was grown on Waiheke Island, in Auckland, and blended with
Merlot (12 per cent) and Cabernet Franc (3 per cent). Deeply coloured, with rich, ripe flavours
of blackcurrants, herbs and spices, it's drinking beautifully now.

Vintage	05	04
WR	7	6
Drink	11-17	11-15

 DRY $49 –V

Kidnapper Cliffs Hawke's Bay Cabernet Sauvignon   (★★★★★)

Dense and inky in colour, the distinctly classy 2009 vintage (★★★★★) was estate-grown at
Te Awa, in the Gimblett Gravels. Highly concentrated, yet supple, it has very fresh and ripe
blackcurrant, plum, mint and spice flavours, seasoned with quality French oak, in a beautifully
rich, but not at all tough, style. It should be long-lived.

 DRY $55 AV

Matariki Hawke's Bay Cabernet Sauvignon/Merlot   (★★★★)

The sturdy, rich 2007 vintage (★★★★) is a blend of Cabernet Sauvignon (57 per cent), Merlot
(28 per cent), Cabernet Franc (10 per cent) and Syrah (5 per cent), grown in the Gimblett Gravels,
Hawke's Bay, and matured for 21 months in French oak barriques (20 per cent new). Boldly coloured,
with deep blackcurrant, plum, mint and spice flavours, vibrant and supple, it's worth cellaring.

Vintage	07
WR	6
Drink	11-14

DRY $27 AV

Matariki Reserve Cabernet Sauvignon   (★★★★★)

Showing power and elegance, the outstanding 2007 vintage (★★★★★) is a hand-picked blend
of Cabernet Sauvignon (90 per cent), Merlot (5 per cent) and Cabernet Franc (5 per cent),
grown in the Gimblett Gravels, Hawke's Bay, and matured for 22 months in oak casks (58 per
cent new). Deeply coloured, it is fleshy and ripe, with concentrated blackcurrant, plum and
spice flavours, a hint of mint, and fine-grained tannins giving a lovely texture.

Vintage	07
WR	7
Drink	11-15

DRY $40 AV

Mills Reef Elspeth Cabernet/Merlot   ★★★★★

Grown at the company's close-planted Mere Road site in the Gimblett Gravels, this is a
consistently impressive Hawke's Bay red. The 2009 vintage (★★★★☆), harvested at 24 brix, is
a blend of Cabernet Sauvignon (52 per cent) and Merlot (48 per cent) matured for 16 months
in French oak hogsheads (32 per cent new). Deeply coloured, it is fleshy and generous, with
dense, ripe red-berry, plum and spice flavours, power through the palate and a strongly spicy
finish. It's built to last; open 2013+.

Vintage	09	08	07	06	05	04
WR	7	NM	7	7	7	7
Drink	11-18	NM	11-17	11-16	11-15	11-15

DRY $44 AV

Mills Reef Elspeth Cabernet Sauvignon ★★★★★

The 2009 vintage (★★★★☆) was hand-harvested at 22.3 brix in the company's Mere Road Vineyard, in the Gimblett Gravels of Hawke's Bay, and matured for 16 months in French oak hogsheads (27 per cent new). Deep and youthful in colour, it is mouthfilling and silky-textured, with concentrated blackcurrant, red-berry, spice and nut flavours and a smooth finish. Drink now or cellar.

Vintage	09	08	07	06	05	04
WR	7	NM	7	7	7	7
Drink	11-18	NM	11-18	11-17	11-16	11-15

Mills Reef Elspeth Trust Vineyard Cabernet Sauvignon ★★★★☆

The elegant 2007 vintage (★★★★☆) is a blend of Cabernet Sauvignon (85 per cent) and Cabernet Franc (15 per cent), harvested at 24.2 brix in Mere Road, in the Gimblett Gravels of Hawke's Bay, and matured for over a year in French oak casks (60 per cent new). Fragrant and boldly coloured, with a distinct but attractive herbal element, it has rich blackcurrant, green-olive and nut flavours, and fine, supple tannins.

Vintage	09	08	07	06
WR	7	NM	7	6
Drink	11-18	NM	11-17	11-16

Mills Reef Reserve Gimblett Gravels Hawke's Bay Cabernet/Merlot ★★★★

The latest releases of this Hawke's Bay red have delivered fine value. The 2009 vintage (★★★★), a blend of Cabernet Sauvignon (64 per cent) and Merlot (36 per cent), was matured for 15 months in French (60 per cent) and American (40 per cent) oak hogsheads (less than 20 per cent new). Deeply coloured, it is fresh, vibrantly fruity and supple, with blackcurrant, plum and spice flavours, ripe and strong. Showing good substance and potential, it's still youthful; open mid-2012+.

Vintage	09	08	07	06	05	04
WR	7	NM	7	7	7	7
Drink	11-14	NM	11-12	P	P	P

Miro Cabernet/Merlot/Franc/Malbec (★★★★)

The highly attractive 2008 vintage (★★★★) is a Waiheke Island blend of Cabernet Sauvignon (52 per cent), Merlot (30 per cent), Cabernet Franc (17 per cent) and Malbec (1 per cent). An elegant, still youthful red, it is deeply coloured, with concentrated, plummy, spicy flavours, ripe, savoury and complex.

DRY $55 –V

Mission Hawke's Bay Cabernet/Merlot ★★★☆

The 2009 vintage (★★★☆) is a 'lightly oaked' blend with a 'predominance of Cabernet Sauvignon'. Deep and youthful in colour, it is mouthfilling, with strong blackcurrant, plum and spice flavours, a herbal thread, a subtle seasoning of oak and very smooth tannins. Drink now or cellar.

Mission Hawke's Bay Cabernet Sauvignon ★★★☆

In favourable vintages, this red offers good value. The 2009 (★★★☆) is described on the back label as 'a robust Cabernet with pure fruit aromas' – and rightly so. Deep and bright in colour, it is fresh and full-bodied, with very good depth of blackcurrant, herb, spice and nut flavours. Drink now onwards.

DRY $20 AV

Mission Jewelstone Hawke's Bay Cabernet/Merlot ★★★★☆

The splendid 2009 vintage (★★★★★) is a blend of Cabernet Sauvignon (54 per cent), Merlot (39 per cent) and Cabernet Franc (7 per cent), grown in the Gimblett Gravels and matured in French oak casks (half new). Dark and powerful, with layers of blackcurrant, plum, spice and nut flavours, it shows wonderful ripeness and richness, with good tannin support. It should flourish for at least a decade; open 2013+. A great buy.

Vintage	09
WR	7
Drink	12-22

DRY $39 AV

Mission Reserve Hawke's Bay Cabernet/Merlot ★★★★

Deeply coloured, the 2009 vintage (★★★★) is a Gimblett Gravels (86 per cent) blend of Cabernet Sauvignon (45 per cent), Merlot (41 per cent) and Cabernet Franc (14 per cent), matured for 15 months in French oak casks (10 per cent new). Savoury, with firm but fine tannins, it has plum, herb and spice flavours, showing excellent complexity and density.

Vintage	09
WR	7
Drink	12-20

DRY $25 AV

Mission Reserve Hawke's Bay Cabernet Sauvignon ★★★★

The 2009 vintage (★★★★☆) was grown in the Gimblett Gravels (66 per cent) and at Bridge Pa, in The Triangle (34 per cent), and matured for 15 months in French oak casks (12 per cent new). A blend of Cabernet Sauvignon (85 per cent), Merlot (10 per cent) and Cabernet Franc (5 per cent), it is powerful (14.5 per cent alcohol), densely coloured and unusually rich for its price category, with dense, firm blackcurrant, plum and spice flavours in a classic claret style. Best drinking 2014+.

Vintage	09	08
WR	7	7
Drink	12-20	11-20

DRY $25 AV

Mudbrick Vineyard Cabernet Sauvignon/Merlot (★★★★)

Grown at Church Bay and Onetangi, on Waiheke Island, the 2008 vintage (★★★★) is deeply coloured and sturdy (14.2 per cent alcohol), with fresh, strong cassis, plum and spice flavours and ripe, supple tannins.

DRY $29 AV

Newton Forrest Estate Cornerstone Cabernet/Merlot/Malbec –
see Newton Forrest Cornerstone in the Branded and Other Red WInes section

---

Ngatarawa Stables Cabernet/Merlot ★★★

Typically a sturdy Hawke's Bay red with drink-young appeal. The 2010 vintage (★★☆) is full-coloured, with a leafy bouquet and fresh, smooth flavours of blackcurrants and herbs.

Vintage	10	09	08	07	
WR	6	7	6	6	DRY $17 AV
Drink	11-15	11-14	11-13	11-12	

Passage Rock Reserve Waiheke Island Cabernet Sauvignon ★★★★

The 2009 vintage (★★★☆) is a deeply coloured, full-bodied red with strong plum, spice and slight herb flavours, fresh acidity and a firm, tightly structured finish. It's still unfolding; open 2013+.

DRY $35 –V

Peacock Sky Cabernet Sauvignon (★★★☆)

The 2009 vintage (★★★☆) is a Waiheke Island red, blended from Cabernet Sauvignon (90 per cent) and Cabernet Franc (10 per cent). Matured for a year in new barrels, French and American, it is sweetly oaked, with blackcurrant and plum flavours in a smooth, easy-drinking style.

Vintage	10	09	
WR	6	5	DRY $34 –V
Drink	12-21	11-20	

Quail Lane Hawke's Bay Cabernet Sauvignon (★★★)

From Abbey Cellars, the 2008 vintage (★★★) is a single-vineyard wine from The Triangle, blended from Cabernet Sauvignon (85 per cent) and minor portions of Merlot, Cabernet Franc and Malbec. Matured in French oak barrels, it is deeply coloured, fleshy, plummy and slightly spicy, in a smooth, easy-drinking style, enjoyable now.

DRY $17 AV

Sacred Hill Helmsman Cabernet/Merlot ★★★★★

The classy 2009 vintage (★★★★★) of this distinguished, single-vineyard Gimblett Gravels red is based on Cabernet Sauvignon (47 per cent), Cabernet Franc and Merlot. Hand-picked and matured for 18 months in French oak casks, it is a powerful wine with dark, purple-flushed colour and a complex bouquet of cassis, plum, spice, coffee and nuts. Superbly concentrated, with real density, it is also finely textured, with ripe, harmonious tannins and a lasting finish. Combining power and elegance, it shows excellent vigour and potential longevity, and should be a 20-year wine.

Vintage	09	08	07	06
WR	7	NM	7	7
Drink	11-20	NM	11-25	11-23

DRY $85 AV

Saints Hawke's Bay Cabernet/Merlot ★★★☆

The easy-drinking 2007 vintage (★★★☆) was partly matured in French and American oak casks. Deeply coloured, it has very good depth. The 2008 (★★★☆) is dark, with strong blackcurrant and plum flavours, showing some savoury complexity, and a smooth finish.

Vintage	08	07	06
WR	5	6	5
Drink	11-12	P	P

DRY $20 AV

Seifried Nelson Cabernet/Merlot ★★☆

Typically a medium-bodied red with lightish colour and berryish, leafy flavours, offering easy drinking. The 2009 vintage (★★★) was matured for a year in French oak barriques. Fullish in colour, it is gutsy (14.5 per cent alcohol), with strong berry, plum and spice flavours.

Vintage	09
WR	5
Drink	11-16

DRY $19 –V

Stonecroft Gimblett Gravels Cabernet Sauvignon (★★★★)

The 2009 vintage (★★★★) of this Hawke's Bay red includes a minor portion of Merlot (12.5 per cent) and was matured for 18 months in seasoned French oak casks. Deeply coloured, with a spicy bouquet, it is mouthfilling and supple, with generous, youthful blackcurrant, plum and spice flavours, ripe and savoury, and gentle tannins.

Vintage	09
WR	7
Drink	13-20

DRY $35 –V

Te Awa Cabernet/Merlot ★★★★☆

Estate-grown in the Gimblett Gravels, Hawke's Bay, the 2009 vintage (★★★★☆) is a blend of Cabernet Sauvignon (44 per cent), Merlot (40 per cent), Cabernet Franc (14 per cent) and Malbec (2 per cent). Matured for 20 months in French oak barrels, it is dark and rich, with strong, fresh blackcurrant, plum and slight herb flavours, well-integrated oak and fine, supple tannins. Best drinking 2013+.

DRY $36 AV

Te Mata Awatea Cabernets/Merlot ★★★★★

Positioned below its Coleraine stablemate in Te Mata's hierarchy of Hawke's Bay, claret-style reds, since 1995 Awatea has been grown at Havelock North and in the Bullnose Vineyard, inland from Hastings. A blend of Cabernet Sauvignon, Merlot and Cabernet Franc – with a splash of Petit Verdot in most years since 2001 – it is hand-harvested and matured for about 18 months in French oak barriques (partly new). Compared to Coleraine, in its youth Awatea is more seductive, more perfumed, and tastes more of sweet, ripe fruit, but is more forward and slightly less concentrated. The wine can mature gracefully for many years, but is also typically delicious in its youth. The 2009 vintage (★★★★★) is a blend of Cabernet Sauvignon (45 per cent), Merlot (40 per cent) and Cabernet Franc (15 per cent). Highly fragrant, with deep, bright colour, it is sweet-fruited, with fresh blackcurrant, plum, red-berry and spice flavours, revealing lovely ripeness, complexity and richness. Already approachable, yet with the power and structure to mature well, it could be the finest Awatea yet (that's certainly Te Mata's view).

Vintage	09	08	07	06	05	04	03	02	DRY $34 V+
WR	7	7	7	7	7	7	6	7	
Drink	11-17	11-16	11-20	11-16	11-15	11-12	P	P	

Te Mata Coleraine – see the Branded and Other Red Wines section

Te Mata Woodthorpe Cabernet/Merlot – see Te Mata Woodthorpe Vineyard Merlot/Cabernets in the Merlot section

Te Motu Cabernet/Merlot ★★★★☆

This Waiheke Island red is grown at Onetangi – over the fence from Stonyridge – and matured for three winters (about 28 months) in French (mostly), American and Hungarian barrels. Compared to its neighbour, it has typically been less opulent than Stonyridge Larose, in a more earthy, leafy and savoury style. The latest vintages are the best. The 2005 (★★★★☆) is fragrant and full-coloured, with rich, complex, spicy flavours, hints of herbs and leather, and a good foundation of tannin. Maturing well, the 2006 (★★★★☆) is full-bodied and savoury, with blackcurrant and spice flavours, showing excellent complexity, and silky, ripe tannins. (Note: the price varies slightly from vintage to vintage.)

DRY $99 –V

Terravin J Cabernet/Merlot/Malbec – see Terravin J Merlot/Malbec/Cabernet in the Merlot section

Toi Toi Organic Reserve Hawke's Bay Cabernet Sauvignon (★★★☆)

Certified organic, the 2010 vintage (★★★☆) is a single-vineyard red, grown at Mangatahi and French oak-matured for nine months. Bold and youthful in colour, it is a fruit-packed style with strong blackcurrant, plum and mint flavours, a hint of oak and firm, underlying tannins.

DRY $35 –V

Villa Maria Reserve Hawke's Bay Cabernet Sauvignon/Merlot   ★★★★★

The dark 2009 vintage (★★★★★) is a blend of Cabernet Sauvignon (75 per cent) and Merlot (25 per cent), grown in the Gimblett Gravels and matured for 20 months in French oak barriques (40 per cent new). Finely fragrant, with excellent density of blackcurrant, plum, olive and nut flavours and lovely texture, it is very savoury and complex, with the 'brooding' quality that suggests great longevity.

Vintage	09	08	07	06	05	04
WR	6	6	7	7	6	7
Drink	12-22	12-18	11-22	11-19	11-20	11-14

 DRY $51 AV

Waimarie Waimauku Cabernet/Merlot   (★★★)

The 2010 vintage (★★★), barrel-aged for a year, is full and youthful in colour, with fresh blackcurrant, spice, plum and olive flavours, a distinct herbal streak and gentle tannins. A good buy.

 DRY $12 V+

Weeping Sands Waiheke Cabernet/Merlot   ★★★★

The second label of Obsidian is grown at Onetangi ('Weeping Sands'). The 2008 vintage (★★★★) is a blend of Cabernet Sauvignon (54 per cent), Merlot (40 per cent), Petit Verdot (5 per cent) and Malbec (1 per cent). Matured in new French (20 per cent) and seasoned French and American oak casks, it is a generous, deeply coloured red, offering top value by the island's standards. Full-bodied and smooth, it has strong, ripe blackcurrant, plum and spice flavours and a hint of sweet oak. Drink now or cellar.

Vintage	08	07	06	05	04
WR	7	5	6	6	6
Drink	11-18	11-15	11-14	11-14	P

DRY $26 AV

Carmenère

Ransom, at Matakana, in 2007 released New Zealand's first Carmenère. Now virtually extinct in France, Carmenère was once widely grown in Bordeaux and still is in Chile, where, until the 1990s, it was often mistaken for Merlot. In Italy it was long thought to be Cabernet Franc. In 1988, viticulturist Alan Clarke imported Cabernet Franc cuttings here from Italy. Planted by Robin Ransom in 1997, the grapes ripened about the same time as the rest of his Cabernet Franc, but the look of the fruit and the taste of the wine were 'totally different'. So Ransom arranged DNA testing at the University of Adelaide. The result? His Cabernet Franc vines are in fact Carmenère.

The latest national vineyard survey records just 1 hectare of Carmenère in New Zealand.

Ransom Carmenère   ★★★

The 2008 vintage (★★★☆) is a full-coloured Matakana red, estate-grown and matured for nearly two years in French oak puncheons. A medium to full-bodied wine, it's drinking well now, with very good depth of red-berry, plum and spice flavours, leathery and savoury notes adding complexity, and fresh acidity.

DRY $32 –V

Chambourcin

Chambourcin is one of the more highly rated French hybrids, well known in Muscadet for its good disease-resistance and bold, crimson hue. Rare in New Zealand (with only 4 hectares planted), it is most often found as a varietal red in Northland.

Ake Ake Chambourcin ★★★★

New Zealand's best Chambourcin. Grown near Kerikeri, in the Bay of Islands, the 2010 vintage (★★★★) is another fine example of the variety. Harvested at 25 brix and matured for a year in seasoned American and French barrels, it is boldly coloured, robust and sweet-fruited, with dense plum and blackcurrant flavours in a fresh, exuberantly fruity style with plenty of muscle. If you enjoy Malbec, try this.

Vintage	10	09	08
WR	6	6	5
Drink	11-15	11-13	11-12

 DRY $24 AV

Marsden Bay of Islands Chambourcin ★★★☆

The 2010 vintage (★★★★) is a generous Northland red, barrel-matured for 16 months. Bold and youthful in colour, with a fragrant, sweetly oaked bouquet, it's a real fruit bomb, with substantial body and loads of flavour, very fresh, vibrant, plummy and smooth.

Vintage	10
WR	7
Drink	12-16

 DRY $28 –V

Pukeko Vineyard Bay of Islands Sticky Beak Chambourcin (★★★)

The 2010 vintage (★★★) is a deeply coloured Northland red, oak-aged for eight months. Made in a simple, fruit-packed style, fresh, vibrant and plummy, it's very gluggable.

DRY $22 –V

Dolcetto

Grown in the north of Italy, where it produces purple-flushed, fruity, supple reds, usually enjoyed young, Dolcetto is extremely rare in New Zealand, with 2 hectares of bearing vines in 2012.

Hitchen Road Dolcetto ★★★☆

Grown at Pokeno, in North Waikato, the 2010 vintage (★★★) was barrel-matured for 10 months. Ruby-hued, it is medium to full-bodied, vibrantly fruity and supple, with cherry and plum flavours, fresh acidity and decent depth. It shows a slight lack of optimal warmth and roundness, but is a skilfully crafted wine, priced sharply.

Vintage	10	09
WR	6	6
Drink	11-13	11-13

 DRY $15 V+

Waimea Nelson Dolcetto ★★★

The 2009 vintage (★★★☆) is a single-vineyard red, aged for eight months in new French (28 per cent) and older barrels. Full-coloured, mouthfilling, vibrantly fruity and supple, it has very good depth of plum and cherry flavours, seasoned with sweet oak. A powerful, sturdy wine (14.5 per cent alcohol), with underlying tannins, it's worth cellaring.

Vintage	08
WR	6
Drink	11-12

DRY $23 –V

Gamay Noir

Gamay Noir is single-handedly responsible for the seductively scented and soft red wines of Beaujolais. The grape is still rare in New Zealand, although the area of bearing vines will rise between 2005 and 2012 from 9 to 12 hectares. In the Omaka Springs Vineyard in Marlborough, Gamay ripened later than Cabernet Sauvignon (itself an end-of-season ripener), with higher levels of acidity than in Beaujolais, but at Te Mata's Woodthorpe Terraces Vineyard in Hawke's Bay, the crop is harvested as early as mid-March.

Te Mata Estate Woodthorpe Vineyard Gamay Noir ★★★★

The 2011 vintage (★★★) is a single-vineyard Hawke's Bay red, whole bunch-fermented (in the traditional Beaujolais manner) and matured for three months in seasoned French oak casks. Pink/red, with floral, berryish scents, it is light and smooth, with raspberry, plum and spice flavours, fresh and vibrant, but lacks the richness of such top years as 2009.

Vintage	11	10	09	08
WR	4	7	7	7
Drink	11-12	11-12	P	P

DRY $20 V+

Grenache

Grenache, one of the world's most extensively planted grape varieties, thrives in the hot, dry vineyards of Spain and southern France. It is also yielding exciting wines in Australia, especially from old, unirrigated, bush-pruned vines, but is exceedingly rare in New Zealand, with a total producing area in 2012 of 1 hectare.

Villa Maria Reserve Hawke's Bay Grenache (★★★★)

The 2007 vintage (★★★★) is a full-coloured and fleshy, juicy, very easy-drinking blend of Grenache (86 per cent), Syrah and Malbec. Hand-harvested from 14-year-old vines in the company's Ngakirikiri Vineyard, in the Gimblett Gravels, and matured for 15 months in French oak barriques (35 per cent new), it has generous cherry, red-berry and subtle spice flavours, with balanced acidity and a rounded finish.

Vintage	07
WR	7
Drink	11-15

DRY $60 –V

Malbec

With a leap from 25 hectares of bearing vines in 1998 to 161 hectares in 2012, this old Bordeaux variety is starting to make its presence felt in New Zealand, where two-thirds of all plantings are clustered in Hawke's Bay. It is often used as a blending variety, adding brilliant colour and rich, sweet fruit flavours to its blends with Merlot, Cabernet Sauvignon and Cabernet Franc. Numerous unblended Malbecs have also been released recently, possessing loads of flavour and often the slight rusticity typical of the variety.

Abbey Cellars Temptation Malbec (★★★☆)

The generous 2009 vintage (★★★☆) was estate-grown and hand-picked in The Triangle district of Hawke's Bay and French oak-matured for nine months. A 'fruit bomb' style, it has bold, purple-flushed colour and loads of plummy, smooth flavour, not complex, but enjoyably soft, fresh and strong.

DRY $31 –V

Aotea Vineyard South Kaipara Norman Malbec (★★★★)

Fewer than 25 cases were made of the 2008 vintage (★★★★). Grown at Shelly Beach and matured in 'a seasoned American oak barrique', it is deeply coloured, with coconutty, sweet oak aromas. Concentrated, with plum, blackcurrant and red-berry flavours, still very fresh, it is sweet-fruited and likely to be long-lived.

DRY $50 –V

Awa Valley Malbec (★★☆)

Grown in West Auckland and oak-matured for a year, the 2009 vintage (★★☆) is full-coloured and fruity, in a medium-bodied style with vibrant berry and plum flavours that show a slight lack of warmth and roundness.

DRY $19 –V

Brookfields Hawke's Bay Sun Dried Malbec ★★★★

Labelled as 'Malbec on steroids!' the bold, flavour-crammed 2010 vintage (★★★★☆) was made from sun-dried grapes, which concentrates their sugars and flavours. Very dark and youthful in colour, it is a powerful, bold wine (14.5 per cent alcohol), with blackcurrant, plum and spice flavours, fresh and dense. The perfect barbecue red.

Vintage	10	09
WR	7	7
Drink	13-20	11-20

DRY $24 V+

Coopers Creek SV Gisborne Malbec The Exile (★★★★☆)

Boldly coloured, the skilfully crafted 2010 vintage (★★★★☆) has coconutty aromas (suggestive of American oak) leading into a fresh, full-bodied wine with rich, vibrant plum and coffee flavours, concentrated, spicy and nutty.

Vintage	10
WR	7
Drink	11-13

DRY $28 V+

Coopers Creek SV Hawke's Bay Saint John Malbec   (★★★★★)

Deep and youthful in colour, with sweet-oak aromas, the 2010 vintage (★★★★★) is a 'serious' yet delicious red with layers of blackcurrant, plum, spice and coffee flavours. Combining power and elegance, it's a stylish wine, dense and age-worthy, with obvious potential; open mid-2012+.

Vintage	10
WR	6
Drink	11-13

 DRY $28 V+

Coopers Creek SV Huapai Malbec The Clays   ★★★★

The boldly coloured 2008 vintage (★★★★) was estate-grown in West Auckland and matured for over a year in French oak casks (50 per cent new). Fleshy and vibrantly fruity, with concentrated plum and pepper flavours, it's a more elegant wine than many Malbecs, with fine-grained tannins and some aging potential.

Vintage	08	07	06
WR	6	NM	6
Drink	11-13	NM	11-12

DRY $28 AV

Fromm Malbec Fromm Vineyard   ★★★★☆

Estate-grown in Marlborough and matured for 16–18 months in French oak casks (up to 30 per cent new), this wine is recommended by winemaker Hätsch Kalberer for drinking with 'a large piece of wild venison'. The 2007–2008 vintages, only available in magnums, will be released in 2012, when the winery is 20 years old. The youthful 2009 (★★★★★) is densely coloured, powerful and concentrated, with finely poised, ripe blackcurrant and nut flavours, warm and savoury, and good tannin support. Drink 2013+.

Vintage	09	08	07	06	05	04
WR	6	6	7	6	6	6
Drink	13-21	13-23	12-22	11-18	11-17	11-16

 DRY $49 –V

Growers Mark Gisborne Malbec   (★★★)

Deeply coloured, the 2010 vintage (★★★) from the Tietjen Vineyard is lively, with plum and spice flavours in an attractive, drink-young style.

DRY $25 –V

Kennedy Point Reserve Waiheke Island Malbec   (★★)

Likely to stir a bit of controversy, the 2008 vintage (★★) was matured for 15 months in French oak casks. Bold and youthful in colour, it has highly concentrated plum and spice flavours, but also a very distinct whiff of volatile acidity. Disappointing.

DRY $45 –V

Kidnapper Cliffs Hawke's Bay Malbec   (★★★★☆)

Deeply coloured and exuberantly fruity, the finely poised 2009 vintage (★★★★☆) is rich, sweet-fruited and supple, with vibrant blackcurrant, plum and spice flavours, hints of nuts and dark chocolate, and excellent harmony. Drink now or cellar.

DRY $45 –V

Kirkpatrick Estate Winery Patutahi Reserve Malbec   (★★★★)

The impressive 2009 vintage (★★★★) was estate-grown in Gisborne and barrel-aged for a year (with 30 per cent new oak). Dark and purple-flushed, it is fresh and vibrant, with blackcurrant, plum and spice flavours, showing excellent complexity and density. It's still very youthful; open 2012+.

Vintage	09
WR	7
Drink	11-15

DRY $35 –V

Mission Reserve Gimblett Gravels Malbec   (★★★★★)

The 2009 vintage (★★★★★) was matured for 15 months in French oak casks. A strapping Hawke's Bay wine (15 per cent alcohol), it has inky colour and fresh, very youthful and vibrant blackcurrant, plum and spice flavours, which avoid the rusticity that Malbec often shows. Dense and sweet-fruited, with hints of chocolate and liquorice, good tannin backbone and a long, spicy finish, it's an age-worthy wine, perfect for those who like power-packed reds.

DRY $28 V+

Omaha Bay Vineyard Malbec   (★★★★)

Grown at Matakana, the powerful 2010 vintage (★★★★) was matured for a year in French oak casks (40 per cent new). Bold and deeply coloured, it has strong plum and spice flavours, fresh acidity and good density. Best drinking 2013+.

Vintage	10
WR	6
Drink	12-20

DRY $38 –V

Stonyridge Luna Negra Waiheke Island Hillside Malbec   ★★★★★

This consistently bold and classy red is estate-grown in the Vina del Mar Vineyard at Onetangi and matured for a year in American oak barriques (50 per cent new). The 2010 vintage (★★★★★), bottled without filtering, should flourish for a decade. Densely coloured, it is a powerful wine with blackcurrant, plum and spice flavours, youthful, sweet-fruited and highly concentrated, braced with slightly chewy tannins. Best drinking 2014+.

Vintage	10	09	08	07	06
WR	7	7	7	7	7
Drink	12-20	11-15	11-15	11-13	11-12

DRY $60 AV

Turanga Creek L'Autre Terroir Malbec   (★★★☆)

The 2009 vintage (★★★☆), grown at Whitford, in South Auckland, was matured for 14 months in French oak casks. Full-coloured, with a sweet oak influence, it is generous, with very good depth of berryish, spicy flavours and a well-rounded finish.

Vintage	09
WR	7
Drink	12-16

DRY $30 –V

Villa Maria Reserve Hawke's Bay Gimblett Gravels Malbec   (★★★★★)

The densely coloured, almost black 2009 vintage (★★★★★) was grown in the Gimblett Gravels and matured for 20 months in French oak barriques (65 per cent new). It possesses notable richness of blackcurrant, plum, liquorice and peppery flavours, in a multi-layered, smoothly flowing style with well-tamed tannins and a sustained finish. It's a sophisticated, 'serious' yet highly approachable wine.

Vintage	09
WR	7
Drink	12-22

DRY $60 AV

Marzemino

Once famous, but today rare, Marzemino is cultivated in northern Italy, where it typically yields light, plummy reds. Not recorded separately in the latest national vineyard survey, it was first planted in New Zealand in 1995. Pernod Ricard NZ made the country's first commercial Marzemino under the Church Road brand in 2005.

Church Road Cuve Series Hawke's Bay Marzemino   ★★★☆

The 2007 vintage (★★★☆) is densely coloured and gutsy, with bold blackcurrant and plum flavours and a rustic streak. The 2008 (★★★☆) is very well crafted, but suggests that Marzemino is not a classy variety. Dense and inky in colour, it is weighty and fruit-packed, but simple, with moderate length.

DRY $30 –V

Merlot

Pinot Noir is New Zealand's red-wine calling card on the world stage, but our Merlots are also proving competitive. In the year to June 2011, New Zealand exported 260,777 cases of Merlot – a steep rise from only 24,194 cases in 2003. In *Winestate's* Wine of the Year Awards for 2010, judged in Australia, the Merlot trophy was scooped by Kim Crawford SP Corner 50 Vineyard Hawke's Bay Merlot 2008; the top five also included Villa Maria Reserve Gimblett Gravels Hawke's Bay Merlot 2008 and Thornbury Hawke's Bay Merlot 2008.

Interest in this most extensively cultivated red-wine grape in Bordeaux is especially strong in Hawke's Bay (although Syrah has recently become the region's hottest red-wine variety). Everywhere in Bordeaux – the world's greatest red-wine region – except in the Médoc and Graves districts, the internationally higher-profile Cabernet Sauvignon variety plays second fiddle to Merlot. The elegant, fleshy wines of Pomerol and St Émilion bear delicious testimony to Merlot's capacity to produce great, yet relatively early-maturing, reds.

In New Zealand, after initial preoccupation with the more austere and slowly evolving Cabernet Sauvignon, the rich, rounded flavours and (more practically) earlier-ripening ability of Merlot are now fully appreciated. Poor set can be a major drawback with the older clones, reducing yields, but Merlot ripens ahead of Cabernet Sauvignon, a major asset in cooler wine regions, especially in vineyards with colder clay soils. Merlot grapes are typically lower in tannin and higher in sugar than Cabernet Sauvignon's; its wines are thus silkier and a shade stronger in alcohol.

Hawke's Bay has almost three-quarters of New Zealand's Merlot vines; the rest are clustered in Marlborough, Auckland and Gisborne. The country's fifth most widely planted variety, Merlot covers nearly three times the area of Cabernet Sauvignon. Between 2003 and 2012, the total area of bearing Merlot vines is expanding at a very moderate pace, from 1249 to 1403 hectares, but in top vintages, such as 2007, the wines offer terrific value.

Merlot's key role in New Zealand was traditionally that of a minority blending variety, bringing a soft, mouthfilling richness and floral, plummy fruitiness to its marriages with the predominant Cabernet Sauvignon. Now, with a host of straight Merlots and Merlot-predominant blends on the market, this aristocratic grape is fully recognised as a top-flight wine in its own right.

¼ Acre Wines Merlot/Malbec   (★★★★)

From winemaker Rod McDonald, the 2009 vintage (★★★★) is a hugely drinkable Hawke's Bay red. French oak-aged, it is deeply coloured, with fresh, concentrated blackcurrant and spice flavours and ripe, supple tannins. Drink now or cellar.

DRY $28 AV

3 Stones Hawke's Bay Merlot/Cabernet   (★★☆)

A solid quaffer, the 2008 vintage (★★☆) was matured for a year in oak barriques (12 per cent new). It has lightish, slightly developed colour, with plum, spice and herb flavours, slightly earthy and showing moderate depth. Ready.

Vintage	08
WR	4
Drink	11-12

DRY $19 –V

Ake Ake Northland Merlot (★★★)

Grown at Kerikeri, the 2009 vintage (★★★) was matured in tanks and seasoned American oak barriques. Perfumed, sweet oak aromas lead into a vibrant wine with ripe, plummy flavours, seasoned with sweet, coconut-like oak, and some savoury complexity.

Vintage	09
WR	5
Drink	11-13

 DRY $20 –V

Alexander Martinborough Merlot ★★★

The 2009 vintage (★★★☆) is a single-vineyard red, matured in American and French oak barrels. Full and bright in colour, it is mouthfilling and vibrantly fruity, with generous, plummy flavours, tinged with sweet oak, and ripe, supple tannins. It's enjoyable young.

 DRY $25 –V

Alexia Hawke's Bay Merlot ★★☆

The 2009 vintage (★★☆) is a lightly oaked, fruit-driven style. Full-coloured, fresh and lively, it is plummy and spicy, with gentle tannins. Fruity, undemanding drinking.

 DRY $18 –V

Alpha Domus The Pilot Hawke's Bay Merlot (★★★)

Matured for nearly a year in seasoned French oak casks, the 2008 vintage (★★★) is full-coloured, with good depth of cassis, plum, herb and spice flavours, a touch of savoury complexity and a firm finish. It's drinking well now, but the 2008 Merlot/Cabernet (below) has the edge.

Vintage	08
WR	6
Drink	11-12

 DRY $20 –V

Alpha Domus The Pilot Hawke's Bay Merlot/Cabernet ★★★☆

Enjoyable now, the full-coloured 2008 vintage (★★★☆) is a blend of Merlot, Cabernet Sauvignon, Cabernet Franc and Malbec, matured for 15 months in seasoned French (80 per cent) and American oak barriques. It's a generous wine with very good depth of blackcurrant, plum, herb and nut flavours, finely balanced and smooth. Priced right.

Vintage	08	07
WR	6	6
Drink	11-13	11-15

 DRY $20 AV

Ascension the Benediction Reserve Matakana Merlot (★★☆)

The 2008 vintage (★★☆), a blend of Merlot (90 per cent) and Cabernet Franc (10 per cent), was matured in French (mostly) and American oak casks. Plummy, spicy and slightly leafy, it has moderate depth of colour and flavour, showing some savoury complexity, but lacks a touch of ripeness and richness.

DRY $39 –V

Askerne Hawke's Bay Merlot/Franc/Malbec ★★☆

The 2008 vintage (★★☆) was estate-grown and hand-picked, but shows a slight lack of ripeness. Fullish and slightly developed in colour, it is distinctly leafy, with plummy, spicy flavours, showing some complexity, and satisfying depth.

Vintage	08	07	06	05
WR	5	6	5	6
Drink	11-12	12-15	P	P

DRY $20 –V

Askerne Reserve Hawke's Bay Merlot ★★★

The 2007 vintage (★★★) was estate-grown near Havelock North and matured for a year in French oak casks (62 per cent new). It is fleshy, with generous blackcurrant, spice and plum flavours, seasoned with quality oak, but with bottle-age, distinctly leafy notes are emerging.

Vintage	07	06
WR	5	6
Drink	13-17	11-12

DRY $30 –V

Ataahua Waipara Merlot ★★★☆

Estate-grown at Waipara and matured for over a year in seasoned oak casks, the 2009 vintage (★★★☆) is mouthfilling and smooth, with generous, plummy, moderately complex flavours. Vibrantly fruity and supple, it's enjoyable from the start. The 2010 (★★★) is full-coloured, full-bodied and fruity, with good density of plum and herb flavours, slightly leafy and rounded.

DRY $26 –V

Awa Valley James Reserve Single Vineyard Merlot/Malbec (★★★★)

Offering great value, the 2009 vintage (★★★★) is an estate-grown, Kumeu blend of Merlot and Malbec, hand-picked and barrel-aged for a year. It's a powerful, full-coloured wine, sweet-fruited, with concentrated plum, spice, liquorice and nut flavours, firm underlying tannins and the structure to age.

DRY $20 V+

Awa Valley Merlot (★★★☆)

A good buy, the 2009 vintage (★★★☆) was grown in West Auckland, and oak-aged for a year. Medium to full-bodied, it's a slightly Bordeaux-like red, full-coloured, with smooth plum and spice flavours, a hint of dark chocolate, and some savoury notes adding complexity.

DRY $19 V+

Awa Valley Merlot/Cabernet Franc ★★☆

Grown at Kumeu, in West Auckland, the 2009 vintage (★★☆) was oak-aged for a year. Medium-bodied, it is fullish in colour, with fresh berry and plum flavours that show a slight lack of ripeness and richness. Priced right.

DRY $15 AV

Babich Family Estates Individual Vineyard Gimblett Gravels Merlot   (★★☆)

The 2009 vintage (★★☆) is a full-bodied Hawke's Bay red with moderately ripe plum and herb flavours, showing decent depth, and a smooth finish. Verging on three stars.

Babich Lone Tree Hawke's Bay Merlot/Cabernet   ★★☆

The 2009 vintage (★★☆) is full-bodied, with a leafy bouquet and satisfying depth of plummy, green-edged flavours.

DRY $16 AV

Babich Winemakers Reserve Hawke's Bay Merlot   ★★★☆

Estate-grown in the Gimblett Gravels and matured in French oak casks, the 2010 vintage (★★★☆) is a full-coloured wine with good density of plummy, spicy flavour, finely integrated oak and some savoury, nutty complexity. Worth cellaring.

Vintage	10
WR	6
Drink	11-16

Bell Bird Bay Hawke's Bay Merlot   ★★★☆

A great buy. Made at Alpha Domus, the 2008 vintage (★★★☆) is fleshy and deeply coloured, with strong, plummy, slightly herbal flavours and some oak-derived complexity.

Bensen Block Merlot   ★★★

From Pernod Ricard NZ, the 2008 vintage (★★★☆) makes no claims about region of origin. It's a spicy red with good depth of ripe-fruit flavours and some savoury complexity.

DRY $17 AV

Black Barn Hawke's Bay Merlot/Cabernet Franc/Malbec   ★★★

The slightly rustic 2007 vintage (★★★) is a full-coloured blend of Merlot (42 per cent), Cabernet Franc (32 per cent), Malbec (20 per cent) and Cabernet Sauvignon (6 per cent), with plenty of blackcurrant and spice flavour and some toasty oak complexity. Ready.

DRY $28 –V

Bladen Marlborough Merlot/Malbec   ★★★

The fresh, easy-drinking 2010 vintage (★★★) is a blend of Merlot (mostly) and Malbec, estate-grown, hand-harvested and matured for 18 months in French oak casks. Boldly coloured, it is a medium to full-bodied wine, vibrantly fruity, with plum/spice flavours and a smooth finish. The 2009 (★★★☆) is dark and mouthfilling, with generous, plummy, spicy flavours and a well-rounded finish.

DRY $32 –V

Brancott Estate Reserve Hawke's Bay Merlot   (★★★☆)

Deeply coloured, the 2009 vintage (★★★☆) is a fruit-driven style with fresh, smooth blackcurrant/plum flavours, hints of herbs and dark chocolate, and good density. Drink mid-2012+.

DRY $26 –V

Brookfields Burnfoot Merlot   ★★★☆

The 2009 vintage (★★★★), the best yet, is dark and full-bodied, with concentrated plum and spice flavours, seasoned with toasty oak, and a firm backbone of tannin. The 2010 (★★★☆) is full-coloured, mouthfilling, fruity and smooth, with very good depth of plum, spice and herb flavours, and drink-young appeal.

Vintage	10	09	08	07
WR	7	7	7	7
Drink	13-18	11-19	11-16	11-14

DRY $20 AV

Brunton Road Gisborne Merlot   ★★★☆

The 2009 vintage (★★★☆) was estate-grown at Patutahi and matured in old French and American oak barrels. Mouthfilling and full-coloured, it has very good depth of berry, spice and slight herb flavours, showing good balance and some savoury complexity.

Vintage	09	08	07
WR	6	5	6
Drink	11-12	P	P

DRY $22 AV

Bushmere Estate Gisborne Merlot   (★★★)

The mouthfilling, smooth 2009 vintage (★★★) is berryish and slightly spicy, with fullish colour and some savoury complexity from maturation for nine months in seasoned French oak barriques. It's an easy-drinking style, enjoyable now.

DRY $23 –V

Cable Bay Vineyards Five Hills Merlot/Malbec/Cabernet   ★★★★☆

Grown at several sites on Waiheke Island, the 2008 vintage (★★★★☆) is one of the finest yet. A blend of Merlot (46 per cent), Malbec (31 per cent), Cabernet Sauvignon (17 per cent) and Cabernet Franc (6 per cent), French oak-aged for a year, it is deeply coloured, with a fragrant, spicy bouquet. Refined and concentrated, it has blackcurrant, red-berry and spice flavours, showing excellent ripeness and density. The 2007 (★★★★☆), sold only at the winery, is also classy, with pure, blackcurrant-like flavours, finely poised and lingering.

Vintage	08	07	06	05	04
WR	7	6	6	7	6
Drink	11-16	11-15	11-13	P	P

DRY $35 AV

Church Road Cuve Hawke's Bay Merlot ★★★★★

The great-value 2008 vintage (★★★★☆) was grown in the Gimblett Gravels and matured for nearly two years in French oak barriques (43 per cent new). Deeply coloured, it is very generous and sweet-fruited, with concentrated plum and spice flavours, spicy oak and buried tannins. A complex wine with slight coffee and dark chocolate notes, it should be long-lived.

 DRY $27 V+

Church Road Hawke's Bay Merlot/Cabernet Sauvignon ★★★★☆

This full-flavoured, complex, Bordeaux-like red from Pernod Ricard NZ offers terrific value. The 2009 vintage (★★★★☆), a blend of Merlot (50 per cent), Cabernet Sauvignon (40 per cent), Malbec (8 per cent) and Syrah (2 per cent), was bottled without filtering. Grown in the company's Redstone Vineyard, in The Triangle (52 per cent), the Gimblett Gravels (23 per cent) and at Havelock North (25 per cent), it was matured for a year in French and Hungarian oak barriques (30 per cent new). Densely coloured, it has concentrated, ripe blackcurrant, plum and spice flavours, with hints of coffee and dark chocolate, finely integrated oak and supple tannins. It's likely to be long-lived (and on special at around $15, it's a great buy).

Vintage	09	08	07	06
WR	7	6	7	6
Drink	11-16	11-14	11-14	P

 DRY $26 V+

Church Road Reserve Hawke's Bay Merlot/Cabernet Sauvignon ★★★★★

The dark, authoritative 2008 vintage (★★★★★) was hand-harvested in the Gimblett Gravels, matured for 20 months in French oak barriques (53 per cent new), and bottled unfined and unfiltered. A fleshy, rich blend, Merlot-dominated (86 per cent), with a splash of Cabernet Sauvignon (12 per cent) and Petit Verdot (2 per cent), it is powerful but not heavy, with a fragrant, spicy bouquet and very dense, youthful palate, packed with blackcurrant, plum, spice and nut flavours. A finely textured red, it's delicious now, but still unfolding.

 DRY $36 V+

C.J. Pask Declaration Merlot ★★★★

Estate-grown in the Gimblett Gravels and matured for 18 months in new oak barriques, the 2007 vintage (★★★★) is deeply coloured, firm, savoury and nutty, with good concentration and the structure to age well. Open 2012+.

DRY $49 –V

C.J. Pask Gimblett Road Merlot ★★★

The 2008 vintage (★★★) was grown in Hawke's Bay and matured in French and American oak casks. Full and slightly developed in colour, it has plummy, slightly spicy and nutty flavours, leafy characters, some savoury complexity and a firm finish. Ready.

 DRY $20 –V

Clearview Cape Kidnappers Merlot/Malbec ★★★☆

The 2009 vintage (★★★☆) is a Hawke's Bay blend of Merlot (65 per cent), estate-grown Malbec (31 per cent) and Cabernet Sauvignon (4 per cent), matured for over a year in French and American oak casks. A characterful quaffer, it is dark and packed with berryish, spicy, slightly earthy flavours. Sturdy, ripe and smooth, it has upfront appeal.

Vintage	09	08	07
WR	7	6	7
Drink	11-14	11-13	11-13

DRY $21 AV

Cliff Edge Awhitu Merlot/Cabernet Franc ★★★★

From a vineyard planted in 1996 and originally called Garden of Dreams, on the Awhitu Peninsula of South Auckland, the 2010 vintage (★★★★☆) is a blend of Merlot (70 per cent) and Cabernet Franc (30 per cent), matured for a year in French and American oak casks. It's a classy wine, finely scented, mouthfilling and rich, with lovely colour, strong, ripe blackcurrant, plum and spice flavours, and silky tannins. Drink now or cellar.

DRY $28 AV

Coopers Creek Hawke's Bay Merlot ★★★☆

Coopers Creek's most popular red is typically great value. The 2009 vintage (★★★☆), grown mostly in The Triangle, was blended with Malbec (7 per cent) and oak-aged for 10 months. Full-coloured, it has good substance, with strong, vibrant plum, spice and dark chocolate flavours, a hint of sweet oak, and a firm finish.

Vintage	09	NM
WR	7	NM
Drink	11-13	NM

DRY $17 V+

Corazon Single Vineyard Merlot ★★★☆

The 2010 vintage (★★★☆), grown in Hawke's Bay, was matured in American and French oak casks. A sturdy (14.5 per cent alcohol), generous wine, it is deeply coloured, with a sweet-oak influence, strong, ripe plum and spice flavours, with hints of herbs and coffee, and supple tannins.

Vintage	10
WR	6
Drink	11-16

DRY $22 AV

Couper's Shed Hawke's Bay Merlot/Cabernet ★★★★

A great buy from Pernod Ricard NZ. The 2009 vintage (★★★★) is deeply coloured, with strong plum, herb and dark chocolate flavours, fresh, vibrant and generous. Fruity and supple, it's a very finely textured, harmonious wine, with drink-young appeal.

DRY $24 V+

Craggy Range Gimblett Gravels Merlot ★★★★★

This is a top buy – superior to many higher-priced Hawke's Bay reds. The 2009 vintage (★★★★☆), harvested at 23.6 brix, includes Cabernet Franc (8 per cent), Cabernet Sauvignon (4 per cent) and Malbec (2 per cent), and was matured for 16 months in French oak barriques (35 per cent new). Elegant and concentrated, it is deeply coloured, fresh, vibrant and supple, with an array of cassis, plum, dark chocolate and nut flavours that build across the palate to a rich, savoury finish. Drink now or cellar.

Vintage	09	08	07	06	05	04
WR	7	6	7	6	6	6
Drink	11-18	11-15	11-22	11-18	11-13	11-12

DRY $32 V+

Crawford Farm New Zealand Merlot ★★★☆

From Constellation NZ, the 2009 vintage (★★★) is a full-coloured Hawke's Bay red. It is mouthfilling, fresh and vibrant, with plum, spice and slight herb flavours, showing some savoury, earthy touches, satisfying depth and a smooth finish.

DRY $21 AV

Crossroads Hawke's Bay Merlot ★★☆

The 2010 vintage (★★☆) was matured for a year in French and American oak casks (23 per cent new). Full and slightly developed in colour, it is gutsy (14.5 per cent alcohol), slightly rustic and herbal, with firm tannins.

Vintage	10
WR	4
Drink	11-16

DRY $19 –V

Crossroads Vineyard Selection Kereru Road Vineyard Merlot/Cabernet (★★★★★)

The 2009 vintage (★★★★★) is a strapping (15 per cent alcohol) Hawke's Bay blend of Merlot (70 per cent) and Cabernet Sauvignon (30 per cent), estate-grown at Maraekakaho and matured for 14 months in French oak barriques (58 per cent new). Muscular but not heavy, it has dense, ripe blackcurrant, plum and spice flavours, French oak complexity and buried tannins. Powerful, fleshy, very rich and supple, it's a youthful, super-charged style, deliciously lush and smooth.

DRY $45 AV

Cypress Hawke's Bay Merlot ★★★★

Densely coloured, the 2010 vintage (★★★★) has a bouquet of coffee and spice, leading into a fresh, power-packed wine with strong cassis, plum and spice flavours, skilfully balanced for early drinking. Fine value.

Vintage	09	08	07
WR	7	6	6
Drink	11-12	P	P

DRY $21 V+

Dartmoor Road Hawke's Bay Merlot/Cabernets   ★★★☆

Estate-grown in the Dartmoor Valley, the 2009 vintage (★★★★) is the best yet. A blend of Merlot (69 per cent), Cabernet Franc (18 per cent) and Cabernet Sauvignon (13 per cent), matured for over two years in French oak casks (28 per cent new), it is full-coloured, fresh and supple, with mouthfilling body (14.4 per cent alcohol) and good concentration of ripe blackcurrant, plum and spice flavours. Still on sale, the 2008 (★★★☆) and 2007 (★★★☆) vintages, labelled 'Merlot/Cabernet Franc', are savoury, nutty and slightly herbal – and priced lower ($28).

 DRY $35 –V

Distant Land Hawke's Bay Merlot/Malbec   ★★★☆

The 2010 vintage (★★★) was matured for a year in French oak casks. Fullish in colour, it is fresh, fruity and smooth, with plum, red-berry, herb and spice flavours, showing drink-young appeal.

DRY $20 AV

Dolbel Estate Hawke's Bay Merlot/Cabernet   (★★★★)

The elegant, savoury 2007 vintage (★★★★) is a blend of Merlot (70 per cent), estate-grown inland at the Springfield Vineyard, and Cabernet Sauvignon from the Gimblett Gravels. Hand-picked and matured in French oak casks (60 per cent new), it is dark, with a highly fragrant, spicy, nutty bouquet, rich blackcurrant, herb and plum flavours, and fine-grained tannins. It shows excellent texture, complexity and length.

Vintage	07
WR	6
Drink	11-15

 DRY $30 –V

Drylands Marlborough Merlot   ★★☆

The 2009 vintage (★★☆), not barrel-matured, is full-coloured, with strong plum, spice and green-leaf flavours, showing moderate complexity, and a smooth finish.

DRY $22 –V

Elephant Hill Hawke's Bay Merlot   (★★★☆)

Grown at Te Awanga, the 2009 vintage (★★★☆) is deeply coloured, with strong, vibrant cassis and plum flavours, ripe, firm and tightly structured.

DRY $24 AV

Esk Valley Gimblett Gravels Merlot/Cabernet Sauvignon/Malbec   ★★★★

The generous 2009 vintage (★★★★) is a blend of Merlot (41 per cent), Cabernet Sauvignon (38 per cent) and Malbec (21 per cent), grown in the Gimblett Gravels and matured for a year in French oak barriques. Deeply coloured, it is mouthfilling, fresh and flowing, with strong blackcurrant and plum flavours, hints of coffee and oak, and gentle tannins. It should mature well.

Vintage	10	09	08	07	06	05
WR	7	7	6	6	7	6
Drink	12-18	11-15	11-12	11-12	11-12	P

 DRY $24 V+

Esk Valley Winemakers Reserve Merlot/Malbec/Cabernet Sauvignon   ★★★★★

This powerful, classy red was labelled 'Reserve', rather than 'Winemakers Reserve', up to and including the 2006 vintage (★★★★★). Dark, vibrantly fruity and bursting with ripe, sweet-tasting blackcurrant, plum and French oak flavours, it is one of Hawke's Bay's greatest wines. Grown in the company-owned Ngakirikiri Vineyard and the Cornerstone Vineyard, both in the Gimblett Gravels, it is matured for up to 20 months in French oak barriques (70 per cent new in 2007). The 2009 vintage (★★★★★) is notably dark, rich and dense, with power right through the palate and beautifully ripe, silky tannins. Open 2013+.

Vintage	09	08	07	06	05	04
WR	7	NM	7	7	7	7
Drink	12-20	NM	12-22	12-16	12-15	12-15

Farmers Market Hawke's Bay Merlot   ★★★

The sturdy, deeply coloured 2009 vintage (★★★☆) was grown at Te Awanga. It's a fruit-driven style with very good depth of ripe blackcurrant and plum flavours, a hint of sweet oak and gentle tannins. The 2010 (★★☆) is ruby-hued, with decent depth of plum and herb flavours, fresh and smooth.

Five Flax East Coast Merlot/Cabernet   ★★☆

From Pernod Ricard NZ, the 2010 vintage (★★) is an easy-drinking style with light, green-edged flavours.

Frizzell Hawke's Bay Merlot   (★★★★)

The 2007 vintage (★★★★) is boldly coloured, mouthfilling and vibrantly fruity, with strong plum and spice flavours, and hints of coffee and liquorice. Sweet-fruited, with good concentration, it's still fairly youthful.

Vintage	07
WR	7
Drink	10-15

Frizzell Merlot/Malbec   (★★★★)

The 2007 vintage (★★★★) is a single-vineyard Hawke's Bay red, with some Cabernet Franc in the blend, matured for 18 months in French and American oak barrels. Deeply coloured, with sweet-oak aromas, it's a fruity, moderately complex wine with hints of coffee and spices, and very good ripeness and concentration. Fine value.

DRY $22 V+

Frizzell Reserve Hawke's Bay Merlot/Cabernet   (★★★★☆)

The super-charged, still youthful 2007 vintage (★★★★☆) is a single-vineyard wine, hand-picked and matured for 18 months in French oak barriques. Densely coloured, it is muscular (14.8 per cent alcohol), with highly concentrated blackcurrant, plum, spice and dark chocolate flavours. If you like big reds, this is for you.

 DRY $44.95 –V

Full Circle Hawke's Bay Merlot   (★★☆)

From Yealands, the 2008 vintage (★★☆) was grown in Hawke's Bay, oak-aged for six months and packaged in a light, recyclable plastic bottle. Deeply coloured, with blackcurrant, plum and spice flavours, it's a decent quaffer, gutsy and firm.

 DRY $17 –V

Giesen Giesen Merlot   (★★★)

The firm, gutsy 2010 vintage (★★★), lightly oak-aged, has strong blackcurrant, plum and spice flavours and a hint of dark chocolate. It's a full-coloured wine, fresh and fruity, with drink-young appeal.

DRY $19 AV

Glazebrook Regional Reserve Hawke's Bay Merlot   ★★★☆

The 2009 vintage (★★★☆) is deeply coloured, vibrantly fruity and smooth, with strong plummy, gently oaked flavours, showing moderate complexity, and gentle tannins.

Vintage	09	08	97
WR	7	6	6
Drink	11-15	11-13	11-13

 DRY $20 AV

Glazebrook Regional Reserve Hawke's Bay Merlot/Cabernet   ★★★★☆

The 2009 vintage (★★★★★) from Ngatarawa winery is a top buy. A 50:50 blend of Merlot and Cabernet Sauvignon, it has lovely blackcurrant, plum and spice flavours, very fresh and vibrant, hints of herbs and dark chocolate, and a nutty, savoury complexity. Youthful and finely poised, with excellent ripeness and richness, it's a 'complete' wine, well worth cellaring.

Vintage	09	08	07	06	05	04
WR	7	NM	7	6	6	6
Drink	11-16	NM	11-16	11-15	11-12	P

DRY $27 V+

Goldridge Estate Hawke's Bay Merlot   ★★☆

The full-coloured 2009 vintage (★★★) was matured for a year in barriques, mostly French. An ideal quaffer, it is a fresh, fruit-driven style with vibrant plum, spice and slight coffee flavours, showing good ripeness and depth.

 DRY $16 AV

Goldridge Estate Premium Reserve Hawke's Bay Merlot   ★★★☆

Priced sharply, the 2008 vintage (★★★★) is a single-vineyard red, grown in The Triangle. A blend of Merlot (89 per cent), Cabernet Franc (6 per cent) and Malbec (5 per cent), it was matured in mostly French oak barriques (25 per cent new). It is concentrated and deeply coloured, with vibrant plum and spice flavours and firm tannins.

DRY $19 V+

Grass Cove Marlborough Merlot   (★★☆)

From an Auckland-based company, the 2008 vintage (★★☆) is brightly coloured and full-bodied, with plum, herb and spice flavours showing a slight lack of ripeness, but fresh and fruity. A solid quaffer.

DRY $24 –V

Greyrock Hawke's Bay Merlot   (★★★)

From Sileni, the 2008 vintage (★★★) is full-coloured and mouthfilling, with plenty of ripe, plummy, slightly earthy and spicy flavour. A fruit-driven style, it's enjoyable early.

DRY $17 AV

Hans Herzog Spirit of Marlborough Merlot/Cabernet Sauvignon   ★★★★★

Who says you can't make outstanding claret-style reds in the South Island? Grown on the banks of the Wairau River, matured for two years in new and one-year-old French oak barriques, and then bottle-aged for several years, this is typically a densely coloured wine with a classy fragrance, substantial body and notably concentrated blackcurrant, plum, herb and spice flavours. It is blended from Merlot (principally), with smaller amounts of Cabernet Sauvignon, Cabernet Franc and Malbec, and bottled without fining or filtration. The 2002 vintage (★★★★★) is deep, with some colour development showing. It's a very harmonious, Bordeaux-like wine, savoury and complex, with cassis, herb, spice and leather notes, like a good St Estèphe. Drink now onwards.

Vintage	02	01
WR	7	7
Drink	11-21	11-20

DRY $39 V+

Hunter's Marlborough Merlot   (★★☆)

Grown in the Wairau Valley and matured for 20 months in French oak casks, the 2009 vintage (★★☆) is a ruby-hued, medium-bodied wine with blackcurrant, plum and spice flavours. It's fresh and smooth, but lacks real warmth and richness.

Vintage	09
WR	4
Drink	11-13

DRY $24 –V

Hyperion Zeus Matakana Merlot/Cabernet ★★☆

Estate-grown, the 2008 vintage (★★☆) was matured for a year in French and American oak casks. It's a pleasant, fruity, full-coloured red with blackcurrant, plum and herb flavours and a very smooth finish.

Vintage	08	07	06	05
WR	5	5	7	6
Drink	11-15	11-13	11-12	P

 DRY $22 –V

Kennedy Point Waiheke Island Merlot ★★★★☆

The 2007 vintage (★★★★), which includes splashes of Cabernet Sauvignon (5 per cent) and Cabernet Franc (5 per cent), was matured for 18 months in French oak casks. Full and fairly youthful in colour, it is weighty, rich and supple, with strong plum and spice flavours, slight herbal notes, and good freshness and complexity.

 DRY $39 AV

Kennedy Point Waiheke Island Reserve Merlot (★★★★★)

Proving the benefits of cellaring, the 2005 vintage (★★★★★), now on sale, is deeply coloured and highly fragrant, with blackcurrant and spice characters, showing good complexity. From mature vines in the home vineyard, it's a highly Bordeaux-like wine, very leathery and savoury, with blackcurrant, plum, spice and nut flavours, showing excellent depth and harmony. Lovely drinking now onwards.

 DRY $45 AV

Kim Crawford Regional Reserve Hawke's Bay Merlot ★★★

Grown mostly in The Triangle, the 2009 vintage (★★★☆) is a medium-bodied red, vibrantly fruity, with very good depth of fresh plum and spice flavours, moderate complexity and gentle tannins. The 2010 (★★★) is a generous, drink-young style with plenty of berryish, slightly herbal and spicy flavour, subtle oak and a smooth finish.

 DRY $22 –V

Kim Crawford SP Corner 50 Vineyard Hawke's Bay Merlot (★★★★☆)

The sturdy, generous 2008 vintage (★★★★☆) was hand-picked and matured for 16 months in French and American oak casks. Deeply coloured, it has brambly, plummy flavours, showing excellent concentration, hints of coffee and sweet oak, good complexity, and the power to age.

 DRY $33 AV

Kirkpatrick Estate Merlot ★★★☆

Grown at Patutahi, in Gisborne, the 2009 vintage (★★★) was matured for nearly a year in American oak barrels (30 per cent new). Full-coloured, with fresh plum and slight herb flavours, showing a touch of complexity, and a smooth finish, it's enjoyable young.

Vintage	09
WR	5
Drink	11-15

DRY $22 AV

Lake Road Gisborne Merlot   (★★★)

The 2010 vintage (★★★) is an easy-drinking style, generous and sweet-fruited, with ripe, plummy flavours, a hint of herbs and moderate complexity.

 DRY $18 AV

Lime Rock Central Hawke's Bay Merlot   ★★★

The 2008 vintage (★★☆), hand-harvested and French oak-matured, is slightly leafy and developed, but also shows some freshness and complexity. The 2009 (★★★☆) is a step up – more generous, savoury and spicy, with very good depth and a firm finish.

 DRY $18 AV

Longridge Hawke's Bay Merlot/Cabernet Sauvignon   ★★★

The 2009 vintage (★★★) is full-coloured, vibrantly fruity, berryish, plummy and smooth, with hints of spices and dark chocolate, and gentle tannins. It's a flavoursome, easy-drinking red.

 DRY $18 AV

Mahurangi River Winery Mostly Merlot
Merlot/Cabernet Sauvignon/Malbec   (★★★☆)

The 2009 vintage (★★★☆) was estate-grown, hand-picked, fermented with indigenous yeasts and matured in French and American oak casks (25 per cent new). It shows good personality, with full colour and spicy, nutty flavours, showing some leathery, savoury complexity. Drink now or cellar.

Vintage	09
WR	6
Drink	11-15

 DRY $35 –V

Maimai Creek Hawke's Bay Merlot   ★★☆

The full-coloured 2009 vintage (★★★) is mouthfilling, with sweet, coconutty oak aromas and good depth of plummy, slightly spicy flavours in a very upfront style.

DRY $23 –V

Main Divide Marlborough Merlot/Cabernet   ★★★☆

The 2008 vintage (★★★☆) from Pegasus Bay was matured for two years in French oak barriques. A blend of Merlot (85 per cent), Cabernet Sauvignon (10 per cent) and Malbec (5 per cent), it is full-coloured and mouthfilling, with good depth of plum and slight herb flavours, showing some savoury complexity, and a smooth finish. Drink now onwards.

Vintage	09	08	07	06
WR	6	5	5	6
Drink	11-17	11-14	11-13	11-13

 DRY $20 AV

Maker, The, Kings Key Gisborne Merlot   (★★★)

From Farmers Market, the 2010 vintage (★★★) is a Merlot-based red, 'complemented by the fragrant and approachable nature of Viognier'. Medium-bodied, fresh and supple, it has berry, plum and spice flavours, very smooth and easy, with drink-young appeal.

DRY $20 –V

Man O' War Waiheke Island Merlot/Cabernet   ★★★★

Grown at the eastern end of the island, the 2009 vintage (★★★★) was matured in seasoned French and American oak casks. A blend of Merlot (42 per cent), Cabernet Franc (38 per cent), Malbec (11 per cent), Cabernet Sauvignon (7 per cent) and a splash of Petit Verdot, it is full-coloured and savoury, with ripe sweet-fruit characters of blackcurrants, plums and dark chocolate, a dash of herbs and good complexity. Fragrant and supple, it's already drinking well.

Vintage	09	08
WR	6	6
Drink	11-16	11-15

DRY $28 AV

Marsden Bay of Islands The Winemaker's Daughter Merlot   (★★★☆)

From an 'exceptional' year at Kerikeri, grapes usually earmarked for rosé were made into a red. Barrel-matured for 16 months and bottled without fining or filtering, it is deeply coloured, with fresh, ripe flavours of plums and red berries, seasoned with sweet oak, and very good depth. Best mid-2012+.

Vintage	10
WR	7
Drink	12-18

DRY $38 –V

Matahiwi Estate Hawke's Bay Merlot   ★★☆

The 2010 vintage (★★☆), not barrel-aged, is vibrantly fruity, with fresh plum and spice flavours and a smooth finish. Easy, no-fuss drinking.

Vintage	10
WR	5
Drink	11-13

DRY $19 –V

Matakana Estate Elingamite Limited Edition Merlot/Cabernet Franc   (★★★★☆)

The powerful, deeply coloured 2007 vintage (★★★★☆) is a Hawke's Bay blend of Merlot (60 per cent) and Cabernet Franc (40 per cent), with vibrant blackcurrant, plum and spice flavours, well seasoned with quality oak (mostly French, all new). It's a highly concentrated, ripe-tasting wine with good complexity, a firm foundation of tannin and obvious cellaring potential.

DRY $59 –V

Matakana Estate Hawke's Bay Merlot/Cabernet Franc ★★★★

The 2009 vintage (★★★★) was matured for a year in French oak barriques. Fleshy, with blackcurrant, plum and slight herb aromas and flavours, nutty and savoury, it is complex, with sensitive use of oak and hints of tobacco and leather giving a distinctly Bordeaux style.

 DRY $32 –V

Matawhero Gisborne Merlot (★★★☆)

The full-coloured 2009 vintage (★★★☆) was grown at Patutahi and barrel-aged. Medium to full-bodied, it has very good depth of berry and spice flavours, showing a hint of dark chocolate, and some savoury complexity.

 DRY $25 –V

Matua Valley Hawke's Bay Merlot ★★★

The 2010 vintage (★★★) is a good, honest red, priced right. Designed for early enjoyment, it is full-coloured, fresh and fruity, with mouthfilling body, satisfying depth of plummy, slightly herbal flavours and a smooth finish.

DRY $17 AV

Matua Valley Hawke's Bay Merlot/Cabernet ★★★

The 2010 vintage (★★★) is full-coloured, mouthfilling, fresh and vibrant, with plum, spice and herb flavours, showing good depth, and a smooth finish. Priced right, it's enjoyable young.

DRY $17 AV

Matua Valley Reserve Release Hawke's Bay Merlot/Cabernet ★★★☆

The 2009 vintage (★★★) is dark and sturdy, with generous blackcurrant and plum flavours, hints of herbs and liquorice, and a well-rounded finish.

 DRY $20 AV

Matua Valley Single Vineyard Matheson Hawke's Bay Merlot (★★★★☆)

The 'full-on' 2009 vintage (★★★★☆) was harvested from mature vines in the Matheson Vineyard, in The Triangle. Inky-hued, it is a bold style, densely packed with plummy, spicy flavour, and a foundation of ripe, supple tannins. For lovers of big reds, it needs more time; open 2013+.

 DRY $65 –V

Mills Reef Elspeth Merlot ★★★☆

The 2007 vintage (★★★☆) was estate-grown in Mere Road, in the Gimblett Gravels of Hawke's Bay, and matured for 13 months in French oak barriques (34 per cent new). It is a powerful, firmly structured red with full colour and generous, spicy, plummy, nutty flavours, showing considerable complexity. However, my three tasting notes suggest there is some bottle variation.

Vintage	09	08	07	06	05	04
WR	7	NM	7	7	7	7
Drink	11-18	NM	11-18	11-17	11-15	11-15

 DRY $40 –V

Mills Reef Hawke's Bay Merlot/Cabernet ★★★

The 2010 vintage (★★★) is a 60:40 blend of Merlot and Cabernet Sauvignon, barrel-aged for 10 months. Deeply coloured, it is full-flavoured, with blackcurrant, plum, herb and coffee notes, supple tannins and a well-rounded finish. Priced right.

Mills Reef Reserve Gimblett Gravels Hawke's Bay Merlot ★★★★

The 2009 vintage (★★★★) was grown in the company's Mere Road Vineyard, harvested at over 25 brix, and matured for 15 months in French (78 per cent) and American (22 per cent) oak casks. A splash of Cabernet Franc was included 'for enhanced aromatic lift'. Deeply coloured, it is rich and flowing, with lots of upfront appeal. Robust (14.5 per cent alcohol), with strong blackcurrant, plum and spice flavours, and a slightly sweet oak influence, it's a drink-now or cellaring proposition.

Vintage	09	08	07	06	05
WR	7	6	7	7	7
Drink	11-14	11-12	11-12	P	P

Mills Reef Reserve Gimblett Gravels Hawke's Bay Merlot/Malbec ★★★★

The 2009 vintage (★★★★), a blend of Merlot (79 per cent) and Malbec (21 per cent), was grown in the company's Mere Road and Plateau vineyards, and matured for 15 months in French (66 per cent) and American (34 per cent) oak casks. Dark, with a fragrant bouquet of coffee and spices, it is mouthfilling and fresh, with deep blackcurrant, plum and spice flavours and an ultra-smooth, fractionally off-dry finish. It's delicious now.

Vintage	09	08	07	06	05
WR	7	6	7	6	7
Drink	11-14	11-12	11-12	11-12	P

Mission Hawke's Bay Merlot ★★★

The 2010 vintage (★★★☆) is full-coloured, with blackcurrant, plum and herb flavours, showing some nutty, cedary, savoury complexity. It's a softly textured, medium-bodied style with drink-young appeal.

Mission Reserve Gimblett Gravels Merlot ★★★★

The 2009 vintage (★★★★) was grown in Mere Road, Hawke's Bay, harvested at over 24 brix and matured for a year in French oak casks (25 per cent new). It's a dark, powerful red (14.5 per cent alcohol), with strong, ripe blackcurrant, plum and spice flavours, a hint of dark chocolate and firm tannins. Still youthful, it's developing well and offers fine value.

Vintage	10	09	08	07
WR	5	6	5	7
Drink	12-16	11-17	11-15	11-15

Mission Vineyard Selection Hawke's Bay Merlot   ★★★☆

The 2010 vintage (★★★★) is a single-vineyard wine, matured in French oak barrels. Deeply coloured, it is sturdy, with fresh, concentrated blackcurrant, plum and spice flavours, ripe and savoury, and well-integrated oak. Showing good muscle, depth and complexity, it's an attractive, finely textured red; drink now or cellar.

DRY $20 AV

Moana Park Hawke's Bay Merlot/Malbec   (★★★☆)

An excellent quaffer, the 2010 vintage (★★★☆) was grown in the Gimblett Gravels, fermented with indigenous yeasts, French oak-aged, and bottled unfined and unfiltered. Full-coloured, with loads of brambly, spicy flavour and a hint of liquorice, it is sweet-fruited and firm, with some complexity.

DRY $19 V+

Moana Park Limited Edition Merlot   (★★★☆)

The 2009 vintage (★★★☆) is a sturdy Gimblett Gravels, Hawke's Bay red, matured for 18 months in French oak casks (30 per cent new). Mouthfilling, brambly and spicy, with good, savoury complexity, it has plenty of personality.

DRY $29 –V

Monowai Hawke's Bay Merlot   (★★★☆)

Still very youthful, the 2010 vintage (★★★☆) was matured for 10 months in French (80 per cent) and American (20 per cent) oak casks. Deeply coloured, it has fresh, strong blackcurrant, plum and spice flavours, showing some leathery, nutty complexity, and the structure to age; open mid-2012+.

Vintage	10
WR	5
Drink	11-16

DRY $20 AV

Montana Festival Block Hawke's Bay Merlot/Cabernet   (★★★)

The 2010 vintage (★★★) is full-coloured, with good depth of fresh blackcurrant, plum and herb flavours, and a smooth finish.

DRY $18 AV

Morton Estate Black Label Hawke's Bay Merlot/Cabernet   ★★★☆

The 2007 vintage (★★★★) is the best since 1998. Deep and fairly youthful in colour, it is powerful, with concentrated blackcurrant, plum, red-berry and spice flavours, seasoned with nutty oak. It's still developing; open 2013+.

DRY $34 –V

Morton Estate Cellar Aged Hawke's Bay Merlot   (★★★)

The youthful 2009 vintage (★★★) is full-bodied, with fresh, ripe red-berry and plum flavours, a gentle seasoning of oak and balanced tannins. Drink now or cellar.

DRY $22 –V

Morton Estate Cellar Aged Hawke's Bay Merlot/Malbec   (★★★☆)

The 2007 vintage (★★★☆) has full, slightly developed colour. Mouthfilling, with coffee and spice flavours, it is savoury and nutty, with considerable complexity and very good depth. It's probably at its peak.

DRY $22 AV

Morton Estate White Label Hawke's Bay Merlot   ★★☆

The 2007 vintage (★★☆) is fullish in colour, with smooth berry and spice flavours, slightly leafy and rustic. Ready.

Vintage	07
WR	6
Drink	11-12

DRY $18 –V

Mount Riley Marlborough Merlot/Malbec   ★★★

Densely coloured, vibrantly fruity and supple, the 2009 vintage (★★★☆) has plummy, berryish flavours, showing good concentration.

DRY $18 AV

Mudbrick Vineyard Merlot/Cabernet Sauvignon   ★★★★

Grown on Waiheke Island, the 2009 vintage (★★★★) was blended mostly from Merlot and Cabernet Sauvignon, supplemented by Malbec (10 per cent) and Cabernet Franc (10 per cent). Drinking well, it's a savoury, medium-bodied red, with strong plum and spice flavours, showing good complexity.

DRY $30 –V

Mudbrick Vineyard Reserve Merlot/Cabernet Sauvignon   ★★★★

The 2008 vintage (★★★★☆) is a Waiheke Island blend, matured in French and American oak barriques (30 per cent new). Dark, powerful and highly concentrated, with perfumed oak aromas, it has dense blackcurrant, plum, spice, nut and coffee flavours, chewy and firm.

Vintage	08
WR	7
Drink	11-18

DRY $50 –V

Newton Forrest Estate Gimblett Gravels Hawke's Bay Merlot   ★★★★☆

The 2007 vintage (★★★★☆) was grown in the Cornerstone Vineyard and matured in a 4:1 mix of French and American oak casks. Deeply coloured, with a spicy, nutty fragrance, it is sturdy (14.3 per cent alcohol), with strong, vibrant cassis, plum and spice flavours, finely integrated oak, firm underlying tannins, and the power and structure to age well.

Vintage	07
WR	6
Drink	11-15

DRY $30 AV

Ngatarawa Alwyn Merlot/Cabernet   ★★★★★

Grown in Hawke's Bay, the highly impressive 2009 vintage (★★★★★) is a blend of Merlot (76 per cent) and Cabernet Sauvignon (24 per cent), grown in The Triangle (60 per cent) and the Gimblett Gravels (40 per cent), and matured in French oak barriques (37 per cent new). Dark and youthful in colour, it is lush and finely poised, with dense blackcurrant and plum flavours, hints of herbs and nuts, and firm tannins beneath. Best cellared until 2014+.

Vintage	09	08	07	06	05
WR	7	NM	7	6	7
Drink	11-18	NM	11-16	11-15	11-14

 DRY $55 AV

Ngatarawa Stables Hawke's Bay Merlot   ★★★

The 2010 vintage (★★★☆) includes a splash of Malbec (5 per cent). Deeply coloured, it is fruity and smooth, with mouthfilling body and very good depth of blackcurrant, plum and slight herb flavours. A drink-young charmer, it offers fine value.

Vintage	10	09	08	07
WR	6	7	6	7
Drink	11-15	11-14	11-13	11-12

 DRY $17 AV

Ngatarawa Stables Reserve Merlot   (★★★★)

The fleshy, tightly structured 2009 vintage (★★★★) is a fruit-driven style from Hawke's Bay with deep, bright colour and concentrated flavours of plums and spices, with a hint of coffee. Rich and smooth, it's drinking well now, but age-worthy too.

Vintage	09
WR	7
Drink	11-15

 DRY $22 V+

Nikau Point Hawke's Bay Merlot/Malbec   ★★☆

From One Tree Hill Vineyards (a division of Morton Estate), the 2008 vintage (★★☆) is a solid quaffer – plummy, spicy and earthy, with a rustic streak and decent flavour depth.

Vintage	08
WR	5
Drink	11-12

 DRY $17 –V

Nikau Point Reserve Hawke's Bay Merlot/Cabernet Franc   ★★☆

From Morton Estate, the 2008 vintage (★★★) is full but not dense in colour, with plum and spice flavours, showing some nutty complexity, and a smooth finish.

Vintage	08
WR	5
Drink	11-14

DRY $18 –V

Ohinemuri Estate Taniwha Merlot/Malbec/Cabernet   (★★★★)

The 2009 vintage (★★★★) is a blend of Merlot (40 per cent), Malbec (30 per cent), Cabernet Sauvignon (26 per cent) and Cabernet Franc (4 per cent), matured for 14 months in French oak barriques. Deeply coloured, it is mouthfilling, with generous plum and spice flavours, showing excellent ripeness and complexity, and power through the palate. It should mature well.

Vintage	09	DRY $27 AV
WR	6	
Drink	11-15	

Omaka Springs Marlborough Merlot   ★★

The 2009 vintage (★★), American oak-aged for 10 months, is light and green-edged, lacking any real ripeness and stuffing.

Vintage	09	08	DRY $17 –V
WR	5	6	
Drink	11-13	11-12	

Oyster Bay Hawke's Bay Merlot   ★★★☆

From Delegat's, this red accounts for a big slice of New Zealand's exports of 'Bordeaux-style' wines (Merlot or Cabernet Sauvignon). Winemaker Michael Ivicevich aims for a wine with 'sweet fruit and silky tannins. The trick is – not too much oak.' It is typically fragrant and mouthfilling, with strong blackcurrant, herb and dark chocolate flavours, supple tannins, and plenty of drink-young appeal.

DRY $20 AV

Passage Rock Reserve Waiheke Island Merlot   ★★★★

The estate-grown 2008 vintage (★★★★) is a densely coloured red with highly concentrated, plummy, spicy flavours, chocolatey, nutty notes, and powerful tannins. It shows obvious cellaring potential.

DRY $30 –V

Peacock Sky Merlot/Malbec   (★★★)

Estate-grown on Waiheke Island, the 2009 vintage (★★★) is a blend of Merlot (49 per cent), Malbec (41 per cent) and Cabernet Franc (10 per cent), matured for nearly a year in French and American oak casks. An easy-drinking, smooth, middleweight red with satisfying depth of ripe plum and spice flavours, it's enjoyable now.

Vintage	10	09	DRY $32 –V
WR	6	5	
Drink	12-18	11-17	

Pegasus Bay Merlot/Cabernet ★★★★

The 2006 vintage (★★★★) is a Waipara blend of Merlot, Cabernet Sauvignon, Malbec and Cabernet Franc, matured for two years in French oak casks. Deeply coloured, with a hint of development, it is mouthfilling, rich and complex, with blackcurrant, spice and herb flavours, dense and savoury, and a firm finish. Showing good muscle and tannin structure, it's a drink-now or cellaring proposition.

Vintage	06	05	04
WR	6	7	6
Drink	11-15	11-15	11-14

DRY $29 AV

People's, The, Hawke's Bay Merlot (★★☆)

The 2010 vintage (★★☆) from Constellation NZ is full-coloured and mouthfilling, with fresh, fruity plum and herb flavours and a smooth finish. It lacks complexity, but offers very easy drinking. Verging on three stars.

DRY $20 –V

Peter Yealands Marlborough Merlot (★★☆)

The deeply coloured 2010 vintage (★★☆) is a full-bodied, vibrant red with cassis, plum and herb flavours offering smooth, easy drinking.

DRY $20 –V

Peter Yealands Premium Selection Hawke's Bay Merlot (★★★)

The youthful, harmonious 2010 vintage (★★★) is already enjoyable. It offers fresh, strong plum, red-berry and spice flavours, with a hint of dark chocolate, savoury notes adding complexity, and a well-rounded finish.

DRY $18 AV

Poderi Crisci Waiheke Merlot Reserva (★★★★☆)

The impressive 2009 vintage (★★★★☆) was estate-grown, hand-harvested, fermented with indigenous yeasts and matured for 18 months in French oak barriques (30 per cent new). Promisingly dark, with spicy oak aromas, it has deep blackcurrant, plum, spice and nut flavours, showing good, savoury complexity, and slightly chewy tannins. It should be long-lived; open 2013+.

DRY $45 –V

Poverty Bay Matawhero Merlot/Cabernets (★★★★)

From 'the oldest vines in the Gisborne region', the 2008 vintage (★★★★) was grown at the Bridge Estate Vineyard, planted by Matawhero in 1985. A blend of Merlot (64 per cent) with smaller portions of Cabernet Sauvignon (22 per cent), Cabernet Franc and Malbec, it was matured in French oak barriques (partly new). It's a wine of strong personality – full-coloured, ripe, brambly and spicy, with good concentration and hints of leather and chocolate.

DRY $24 V+

Providence Private Reserve Merlot/Cabernet Franc/Malbec ★★★★★

Past vintages of this Matakana red were priced around $180, including the full-coloured and fragrant, very elegant and silky-textured 2002 (★★★★★). The 2005 (★★★★★) is a top vintage, beautifully perfumed, with rich, blackcurrant-like flavours, complex and harmonious. If you are a Bordeaux fan with deep pockets, it's well worth trying.

DRY $120 –V

Pukeora Estate Merlot   (★★★☆)

Grown at altitude in Central Hawke's Bay, the 2010 vintage (★★★) is a blend of Merlot (86 per cent) and Malbec (14 per cent), partly barrel-aged. It's a sturdy wine (14.5 per cent alcohol), full-coloured, with vibrant blackcurrant and plum flavours, seasoned with sweet oak, and good depth. Open mid-2012+. Fine value.

Vintage	10
WR	5
Drink	11-15

DRY $15 V+

Quail Lane Hawke's Bay Merlot   (★★☆)

From Abbey Cellars, the 2008 vintage (★★☆) is Merlot-based (86 per cent), with minor portions of Cabernet Franc, Malbec and Cabernet Sauvignon. Hand-harvested and French oak-aged, it's a deeply coloured, distinctly earthy red, berryish, spicy and herbal, with a rustic streak.

DRY $17 –V

Rapaura Springs Hawke's Bay Merlot   (★★★)

Enjoyable young but showing some potential for aging, the 2010 vintage (★★★) has full, bright colour and substantial body. Mostly barrel-aged, it is vibrantly fruity, with plummy, spicy flavours, showing good depth, and ripe, supple tannins.

DRY $18 AV

Redmetal Vineyards Hawke's Bay Merlot/Cabernet Franc   ★★★☆

The 2009 vintage (★★★☆) is a good buy. Full-coloured, it's a substantial, savoury wine with ripe, spicy, plummy flavours, showing considerable complexity, and good tannin backbone. Drink now or cellar.

DRY $17 V+

Remarkables Winemakers Mark Marlborough Merlot   (★★)

The 2009 vintage (★★) is fading, with developed colour and spicy, green-edged flavours.

DRY $17 –V

Renato Nelson Merlot (★★☆)

Hand-picked from 10-year-old vines at Kina, on the coast, the 2009 vintage (★★☆) was matured for a year in seasoned French oak casks. Fullish in colour, it is medium-bodied, fruity and berryish, with green-edged flavours showing some savoury complexity, but also a slight lack of ripeness and roundness.

Vintage	09
WR	6
Drink	11-13

 DRY $24 –V

River Farm Godfrey Road Marlborough Merlot ★★★★

Dark and dense, the 2010 vintage (★★★★) was estate-grown, hand-harvested, fermented with indigenous yeasts and matured for nearly a year in French oak barriques. It's a powerful (14.5 per cent alcohol), rich wine with blackcurrant, herb and plum flavours, fresh and supple, in a distinctly cool-climate style with notable concentration.

Vintage	10	09
WR	6	6
Drink	11-21	11-20

 DRY $29 AV

Rongopai Hawke's Bay Merlot/Cabernet ★★☆

From Babich, the 2009 vintage (★★☆) is a solid quaffer, full-coloured, with fresh berry, herb and plum flavours, gentle tannins and a smooth finish. It's an easy-drinking, 'fruit-driven' style, priced right.

 DRY $15 AV

Sacred Hill Brokenstone Merlot – see Sacred Hill Brokenstone in the Branded and Other Red Wines section

Sacred Hill Halo Hawke's Bay Merlot/Cabernet ★★★★☆

The dense, rich 2009 vintage (★★★★★) is a great buy. Estate-grown and hand-picked in the Gimblett Gravels, and matured for a year in French oak casks, it is a blend of Merlot (90 per cent), Cabernet Sauvignon (7 per cent) and Cabernet Franc (3 per cent). Still purple-flushed, it's a floral, tight-knit, finely structured wine with a strong surge of fresh, ripe plum, spice and nut flavours and a lovely silky texture.

Vintage	09
WR	6
Drink	11-15

DRY $26 V+

Sacred Hill Hawke's Bay Merlot/Cabernet ★★★☆

The 2010 vintage (★★★☆) is a blend of Merlot (96 per cent) and Cabernet Sauvignon (4 per cent). Fresh and vibrantly fruity, it is full-coloured, with berryish, plummy flavours showing very good depth and fine, supple tannins.

 DRY $21 AV

Saint Clair Marlborough Merlot ★★★

Grown in the relatively warm Rapaura district and American oak-aged, the 2010 vintage (★★★☆) is deeply coloured, fruity and smooth, with generous blackcurrant, herb and plum flavours, showing moderate complexity, and lots of drink-young charm. It's ready to roll.

DRY $21 –V

Saint Clair Rapaura Reserve Marlborough Merlot ★★★★

The 2009 vintage (★★★★) is deeply coloured, with a strong surge of blackcurrant and spice flavours, strongly seasoned with nutty oak (American and French, 57 per cent new), a hint of olives, gentle acidity and ripe, supple tannins.

DRY $27 AV

Saints Vineyards Selection Gisborne/Hawke's Bay Merlot/Cabernet (★★★☆)

Offering satisfying depth, the 2009 vintage (★★★☆) is full-coloured, with some savoury complexity and smooth, generous plum, spice and slight coffee flavours.

DRY $20 AV

Sears Road Merlot/Malbec (★★★)

Grown in Hawke's Bay, the 2008 vintage (★★★) is a good quaffer, priced sharply. Fruity and berryish, fresh, ripe and smooth, it's a lightly oaked style, gutsy and flavoursome.

DRY $14 V+

Selaks Heritage Reserve Hawke's Bay Merlot/Cabernet (★★☆)

The debut 2010 vintage (★★☆) from Constellation NZ is a full-coloured, vibrantly fruity red with decent depth of plum and herb flavours, fresh and smooth.

DRY $22 –V

Selaks Premium Selection Hawke's Bay Merlot/Cabernet ★★★

The 2009 vintage (★★★) is a blend of Merlot (57 per cent), Cabernet Sauvignon (40 per cent) and Malbec (3 per cent). Matured in tanks (mostly) and barrels, it is youthful, with mouthfilling body and vibrant, plummy, slightly herbal flavours, fresh and smooth.

DRY $18 AV

Selaks Winemaker's Favourite Hawke's Bay Merlot/Cabernet ★★★☆

The 2009 vintage (★★★☆) is a blend of Merlot (77 per cent) and Cabernet Sauvignon (23 per cent), grown in Constellation NZ's Corner 50 Vineyard, and matured in French and American oak barriques (15 per cent new). Full-coloured, it is slightly leafy, but shows very good depth and some spicy, savoury complexity.

DRY $21 AV

Shingle Peak New Zealand Merlot (★★☆)

Ruby-hued, the 2010 vintage (★★☆) is a regional blend, made in an easy-drinking style with plummy, slightly herbal, spicy and nutty flavours, showing decent depth.

DRY $18 –V

Sileni Cellar Selection Hawke's Bay Merlot ★★★☆

The 2010 vintage (★★★) is a youthful, full-coloured red with plummy, spicy, gently oaked flavours, showing good depth. It's a floral, vibrantly fruity wine, with a well-rounded finish.

DRY $20 AV

Sileni Exceptional Vintage Hawke's Bay Merlot (★★★★☆)

The densely coloured 2008 vintage (★★★★☆) was matured for 15 to 16 months in French oak barriques. Sturdy (14.5 per cent alcohol), it's a powerful, highly concentrated red, rich, ripe, plummy and savoury, with a fragrant, complex bouquet of coffee and spices. It's a finely balanced wine, well worth cellaring.

Vintage	08	07
WR	6	5
Drink	12-16	11-15

DRY $60 –V

Sileni The Plains Merlot/Cabernet Franc ★★★☆

The 2008 vintage (★★★★) is a single-vineyard blend of Merlot (72 per cent) and Cabernet Franc (28 per cent), grown in The Triangle. Full-coloured, with concentrated, plummy, spicy flavours, it has good complexity and ripe, supple tannins. The 2009 (★★★) is a 3:1 blend, matured in French (85 per cent) and American (15 per cent) oak casks. A full-bodied red, it has red-berry, spice and herb flavours, showing some hints of early development and good depth.

DRY $32 –V

Sileni The Triangle Hawke's Bay Merlot ★★★☆

The elegant 2009 vintage (★★★☆) is a generous, full-bodied red with blackcurrant, plum and slight herb flavours. Matured for over a year in French (85 per cent) and American (15 per cent) oak casks, it has smooth, ripe tannins, giving good drinkability.

DRY $25 –V

Soljans Hawke's Bay Merlot/Cabernet/Malbec ★★★

The 2010 vintage (★★☆) is a blend of Merlot, Cabernet Sauvignon and Malbec, barrel-aged for nine months. A medium-bodied style, it is fresh, fruity and smooth, with plum and herb flavours, decent depth and drink-young appeal.

Vintage	10
WR	6
Drink	11-16

DRY $20 –V

Soljans Tribute Hawke's Bay Merlot/Malbec ★★★☆

Still youthful, the 2009 vintage (★★★☆) is a blend of Merlot (76 per cent) and Malbec (24 per cent), matured for 18 months in French oak barriques, new and seasoned. It's a fresh, vibrantly fruity wine with concentrated plum, spice and nut flavours, a hint of coffee and mouthfilling body. Open 2013+.

Vintage	09
WR	7
Drink	11-16

DRY $39 –V

Soulo Merlot   (★★☆)

Packaged in a plastic glass with a tear-off tab, the non-vintage wine (★★☆) on sale in early 2011 was a 'Hawke's Bay Merlot Gimblett Road', with a use-by date of 8 March 2012. Full-coloured, it is a gutsy quaffer, with fresh, fruity, plummy, spicy flavours, slightly rustic but showing good depth.

DRY $5 (175ML) –V

Southern Cross Hawke's Bay Merlot/Cabernet Franc   (★★☆)

The 2007 vintage (★★☆) is from One Tree Hill Vineyards, a division of Morton Estate. A blend of Merlot (44 per cent) and Cabernet Franc (42 per cent), with minor portions of Cabernet Sauvignon and Malbec, it has fullish, slightly developed colour, and slightly leafy, nutty flavours, with a softening finish.

DRY $17 –V

Spinyback Nelson Merlot/Cabernet Franc   (★★☆)

From Waimea Estates, the 2009 vintage (★★☆) includes some Malbec and was barrel-aged for a year. Fullish in colour, it is moderately ripe, with plum, spice and herb flavours, showing some savoury complexity and decent depth. Verging on three stars.

Vintage	09
WR	6
Drink	11-14

DRY $18 –V

Spy Valley Marlborough Merlot/Malbec   ★★★☆

The 2009 vintage (★★★☆) was hand-harvested at 23.8 to 25.5 brix, fermented with indigenous yeasts and matured for 17 months in French oak barrels (40 per cent new). A blend of Merlot (73 per cent), Malbec (17 per cent) and Cabernet Sauvignon (10 per cent), it is a sturdy, full-coloured and supple red with vibrant plum, coffee and spice flavours, which show very good depth and considerable complexity.

Vintage	09	08	07	06	05	04
WR	6	5	7	5	6	5
Drink	11-13	11-12	11-12	P	P	P

DRY $21 AV

Squawking Magpie The Chatterer Merlot/Syrah/Malbec   ★★★★

The 2007 vintage (★★★★) is a Gimblett Gravels, Hawke's Bay blend, matured in French oak barriques. Boldly coloured, it is packed with plum and spice flavours, fresh and ripe, with a hint of chocolate, and finely balanced oak and tannins.

DRY $25 AV

Stonecroft Ruhanui Merlot/Cabernet Sauvignon ★★★★

Grown in the Gimblett Gravels, the 2008 vintage (★★★★) is a blend of Merlot (74 per cent) and Cabernet Sauvignon (26 per cent), matured for over 18 months in French oak casks. Full but not dense in colour, with a fragrant, spicy bouquet, it has plummy, spicy flavours, showing good complexity. A savoury, firmly structured red, it should be at its best 2012+.

Vintage	08	07
WR	5	6
Drink	12-17	12-20

DRY $35 –V

Stoneleigh Marlborough Merlot ★★★

The 2009 vintage (★★★☆) from Pernod Ricard NZ was grown in the Wairau Valley and matured in French oak casks. It's a sturdy, deeply coloured red with plum, herb, spice and slight coffee flavours, showing very good depth, and fairly firm tannins. The 2010 (★★★) is mouthfilling, fruity and supple, with plummy, spicy flavours showing some savoury complexity.

DRY $22 –V

Takatu Matakana Merlot/Cabernet Franc ★★★★☆

The 2008 vintage (★★★★☆), matured in French oak barrels (20 per cent new), is the first since the debut 2005 (the 2006 and 2007 were sold under the second-tier Kawau Bay and Takatu Kawau Bay labels). Deep and youthful in colour, it is powerful, with generous, brambly, plummy, herbal, spicy flavours, seasoned with fine-quality oak, and a good foundation of tannin. Open 2013+.

Vintage	08
WR	6
Drink	11-15

DRY $39 AV

Tama Matakana Merlot/Cabernet Sauvignon/Malbec (★★★)

From the property formerly known as The Antipodean, the 2008 vintage (★★★) is a blend of Merlot (46 per cent), Cabernet Sauvignon (41 per cent) and Malbec (13 per cent), matured for 15 months in French oak barrels (half new). Fullish in colour, it's a gentle Bordeaux style, not concentrated, but berryish and slightly herbal, with some savoury complexity and a smooth finish. Ready.

Vintage	08
WR	6
Drink	11-13

DRY $26 –V

Te Awa Left Field Hawke's Bay Merlot/Malbec ★★★★

The 2009 vintage (★★★★) is bold, with fresh, concentrated blackcurrant and spice flavours, a hint of liquorice, a subtle seasoning of oak, and loads of body and flavour.

DRY $25 AV

Te Henga The Westie Premium Hawke's Bay Merlot/Cabernet

From Babich, the 2009 vintage (★★☆) is full-coloured, vibrantly fruity and smooth, with plummy, slightly spicy flavours, ripe and rounded. It's enjoyable now.

DRY $15 AV

Te Mania Three Brothers Nelson Merlot/Malbec/Cabernet Franc   ★★☆

The 2009 vintage (★★☆), matured for 10 months in French and American oak casks, is fullish in colour, berryish and smooth, in a lightish, fruity, easy-drinking style.

DRY $20 –V

Te Mata Woodthorpe Vineyard Merlot/Cabernets   ★★★★

This bargain-priced red is Te Mata's biggest seller – and deservedly so. The 2008 vintage (★★★★), estate-grown in Hawke's Bay, is a blend of Merlot (44 per cent), Cabernet Franc (27 per cent), Cabernet Sauvignon (16 per cent) and Petit Verdot (13 per cent), matured for 17 months in French oak casks. Full-coloured, with a fragrant, slightly spicy bouquet, it is fresh and vibrant, with generous blackcurrant and spice flavours, slightly herbal and nutty. It's finely balanced for early drinking or moderate cellaring.

Vintage	08	07	06	05
WR	7	7	7	7
Drink	11-14	11-15	11-14	11-13

DRY $20 V+

Terravin J Merlot/Malbec/Cabernet   ★★★★☆

Can Marlborough produce a classy, Bordeaux-style red? Matured for well over a year in French oak casks (50 per cent new), the 2009 vintage (★★★★☆) is a blend of Merlot (80 per cent), Malbec (12 per cent) and Cabernet Sauvignon (8 per cent), harvested at 24.5 to 25 brix, and bottled unfined and unfiltered. Deep and youthful in colour, it is very rich, with concentrated plum, nut and liquorice flavours, showing good complexity, and the structure to age. The 2010 (★★★★★) is even better, with dense colour and exceptional concentration of blackcurrant, plum, spice and nut flavours. Notably rich and sweet-fruited, with layers of flavour, it should flourish for a decade.

DRY $60 –V

Thornbury Hawke's Bay Merlot   ★★★★☆

From Villa Maria, the 2010 vintage (★★★★) was grown principally in the Gimblett Gravels. Floral, with deep, purple-flushed colour, it has rich, ripe blackcurrant, plum and spice flavours, seasoned with French (75 per cent) and American oak (10 per cent new), and fine-grained tannins. A classy wine, it's worth cellaring.

Vintage	10	09	08
WR	6	6	6
Drink	11-15	11-15	11-15

DRY $22 V+

Ti Point Matakana Coast Merlot/Cabernet Franc   (★★★★)

The 2010 vintage (★★★★) is a blend of Merlot (90 per cent) and Cabernet Franc, estate-grown and hand-picked at Leigh. Matured for nine months in seasoned French oak casks, it is full-coloured and sturdy, with generous, well-ripened plum/spice flavours showing a nutty, savoury complexity. Refined and elegant, it should unfold well; open mid-2012 onwards.

Vintage	10
WR	6
Drink	11-20

DRY $21 V+

Ti Point One Merlot/Cabernet Franc   (★★★★☆)

Estate-grown at Leigh, near Matakana, north of Auckland, the 2010 vintage (★★★★☆) was matured in one and two-year-old French oak casks. Already approachable, but with the structure to age well, it is full-coloured, concentrated and ripe, with deep blackcurrant, plum and spice flavours, balanced tannins and excellent harmony. A lovely, highly Bordeaux-like wine, it's worth cellaring.

Vintage	10
WR	7
Drink	12-25

DRY $39 AV

Tohu Gisborne Merlot   (★★)

The 2009 vintage (★★) is plain, with fullish colour and green-edged flavours, lacking real ripeness and richness.

DRY $20 –V

Trinity Hill Hawke's Bay Merlot   (★★★★)

A delicious drink-young style, the 2010 vintage (★★★★) is a blend of Merlot (86 per cent), with minor portions of Cabernet Sauvignon, Cabernet Franc and Malbec, matured for a year in seasoned oak casks. Dark, lush and crammed with blackcurrant, plum and spice flavours, it is exuberantly fruity and supple, with good concentration and fine-grained tannins. Fine value.

Vintage	10
WR	6
Drink	12-15

DRY $20 V+

Turanga Creek Down to Earth Merlot/Cabernet Franc   (★★☆)

Estate-grown at Whitford, in South Auckland, the 2009 vintage (★★☆) is 'a simple and honest expression of our land'. French oak-aged, it is fullish in colour, with plummy, smooth flavours, offering easy, no-fuss drinking.

Vintage	09
WR	5
Drink	11-13

DRY $18 –V

Turanga Creek Notre Terroir Merlot/Malbec/Cabernet Franc (★★★☆)

The 2009 vintage (★★★☆) was grown at Whitford, in South Auckland, and French oak-aged for over a year. Full-coloured, it is mouthfilling, with strong blackcurrant, plum and spice flavours, showing considerable complexity, and a ripe, rounded finish.

Vintage	09	
WR	6	
Drink	12-15	

 DRY $28 –V

Unison Reserve Hawke's Bay Merlot ★★★☆

Estate-grown in the Gimblett Gravels and barrel-matured for 20 months, the 2008 vintage (★★★★) is full-coloured, with a savoury, spicy bouquet. Plummy and spicy, with hints of earth and dark chocolate, good complexity, and a long finish, it's well worth cellaring.

 DRY $25 –V

Vidal Reserve Hawke's Bay Merlot/Cabernet Sauvignon ★★★★★

The 2007 vintage (★★★★) is a blend of Merlot (46 per cent) and Cabernet Sauvignon (46 per cent), with a splash of Malbec, matured for 20 months in French oak barriques (64 per cent new). Boldly coloured, with a strong seasoning of toasty oak, it has concentrated, plummy, berryish, slightly chocolatey flavours, showing good complexity and richness. There is no 2008. (Future vintages will be labelled 'Legacy Series.')

Vintage	08	07
WR	NM	7
Drink	NM	11-17

 DRY $30 V+

Vidal Reserve Series Hawke's Bay Merlot/Cabernet Sauvignon · (★★★★☆)

This is the new, middle-tier range (not to be confused with the former, top-tier 'Reserve' range, now called 'Legacy Series'). Maturing well, the 2008 vintage (★★★★☆) is a blend of Merlot (55 per cent), Cabernet Sauvignon (35 per cent) and Malbec (10 per cent), matured for 16 months in French oak barriques (25 per cent new). Deep and still youthful in colour, it is full-bodied and fruity, with strong, ripe plum and herb flavours, finely integrated oak and supple tannins. Fleshy, rich, savoury and soft, it's lovely now.

Vintage	08
WR	6
Drink	11-14

DRY $24 V+

Vidal White Series Hawke's Bay Merlot/Cabernet Sauvignon ★★★★☆

A great buy, labelled 'White Series' since the 2010 vintage. The 2009 (★★★★☆) is a blend of Merlot (68 per cent), Cabernet Sauvignon (17 per cent), Malbec (9 per cent) and Cabernet Franc (6 per cent), 60 per cent barrel-aged (in seasoned French and American oak). A strong, vibrantly fruity red, it is full-coloured and silky-textured, with blackcurrant, spice and olive flavours, showing excellent concentration, and a perfumed bouquet. The 2010 vintage (★★★★) is dark and fleshy, with fine-grained tannins and loads of fresh, plummy, spicy flavour.

Vintage	10	09
WR	6	7
Drink	11-14	11-14

 DRY $22 V+

Villa Maria Cellar Selection Hawke's Bay Merlot [Organic]   (★★★★)

BioGro certified, the 2009 vintage (★★★★) is a blend of Merlot (90 per cent) and Malbec (10 per cent), grown in the company's Joseph Soler Vineyard, on the edge of the Gimblett Gravels, and matured in tanks and French oak barriques (15 per cent new). Floral and supple, it is a full-coloured, very graceful red with strong, ripe, plummy flavours that flow to a finely textured finish. Possessing good tannin backbone, it's well worth cellaring to 2012+.

Vintage	09
WR	6
Drink	11-15

Villa Maria Cellar Selection Hawke's Bay Merlot/Cabernet Sauvignon   ★★★★★

The 2000 (★★★★★) and 2002 (★★★★★) vintages offered exceptional value, winning Best Buy of the Year awards in the *Buyer's Guide*. The 2009 vintage (★★★★☆) is a blend of Merlot (56 per cent), Cabernet Sauvignon (42 per cent) and Malbec (2 per cent), grown mostly in the Gimblett Gravels and matured in French, American and Hungarian oak barriques (40 per cent new). A bold style, it's still very youthful, with deep, bright colour and concentrated blackcurrant, plum, spice and mint flavours. Finely balanced, with coffee and liquorice notes and a firm foundation of tannin, it is dark and dense, with good complexity.

Vintage	09	08	07	06
WR	7	7	7	6
Drink	11-16	11-15	11-15	11-14

Villa Maria Private Bin Hawke's Bay Merlot   ★★★☆

The easy-drinking 2010 vintage (★★★☆) is a blend of Merlot (95 per cent) with small amounts of Cabernet Franc and Malbec, grown principally in the Gimblett Gravels and matured for nine months in tanks in contact with lightly toasted French oak staves. A fresh, fruit-driven style with plum and spice flavours and finely balanced tannins, it's a fragrant, medium-bodied red with a subtle oak influence and very satisfying flavour depth.

Vintage	10	09	08
WR	6	6	6
Drink	11-15	11-13	11-12

DRY $22 AV

Villa Maria Private Bin Hawke's Bay Merlot/Cabernet Sauvignon   ★★★☆

The 2009 vintage (★★★★) is a blend of Merlot (58 per cent), Cabernet Sauvignon (28 per cent), Cabernet Franc (10 per cent) and Malbec (4 per cent). Matured in tanks and seasoned French and American oak barrels, it is fragrant and full-coloured, with strong, plummy, spicy flavours, showing good ripeness, hints of dark chocolate and coconut, and some complexity. The 2010 (★★★☆), partly barrel-aged, is mouthfilling and finely balanced, with youthful plum, spice and herb flavours, fresh and strong.

Vintage	09	08	07	06
WR	6	6	6	6
Drink	11-13	11-12	11-12	P

Villa Maria Private Bin Organic Hawke's Bay Merlot   ★★★☆

Certified BioGro, the 2010 vintage (★★★☆) was grown in the company's Joseph Soler Vineyard, on the boundary of the Gimblett Gravels, and matured in tanks and seasoned French and American oak barriques. Deeply coloured, it is vibrantly fruity, cherryish and plummy, with some savoury complexity, very good depth and a seductively smooth finish.

Vintage	10	09
WR	6	6
Drink	11-15	11-13

 DRY $22 AV

Villa Maria Reserve Hawke's Bay Merlot   ★★★★★

This consistently outstanding wine is grown at company-owned vineyards in the Gimblett Gravels – Ngakirikiri, Omahu Gravels and Twyford Gravels – and matured for 18 to 20 months in French oak barriques (38 per cent new in 2009). The 2009 vintage (★★★★★), which includes 10 per cent Malbec, is a highly concentrated, deeply coloured red with an array of plum, spice, coffee, liquorice and nut flavours, complex and youthful, a good foundation of tannin and a lasting finish. A classy, dense, tight-knit wine, it should flourish with cellaring.

Vintage	09	08	07	06	05	04
WR	6	6	7	7	7	6
Drink	12-18	12-16	11-19	11-18	11-17	11-16

 DRY $51 AV

Waimarie Waimauku Merlot/Cabernet   ★★★

Grown in West Auckland, the 2009 vintage (★★☆) is a blend of Merlot (70 per cent), Cabernet Franc (10 per cent), Cabernet Sauvignon (15 per cent) and Malbec (5 per cent), matured for 14 months in French oak casks (new and one year old). Fullish and slightly developed in colour, it is smooth and leafy, with fresh acidity and moderate depth of flavour. It's an easy-drinking wine, but lacks a bit of ripeness and stuffing.

 DRY $20 –V

Waimea Bolitho SV Merlot   ★★★☆

Grown in Nelson, the 2008 vintage (★★★☆) is a single-vineyard red, grown on the Waimea Plains, matured in French oak casks (partly new), and bottled unfined and unfiltered. A tightly structured, deeply coloured red, it is vibrantly fruity, with strong plum and spice flavours, some herbal notes and a fresh, crisp finish.

Vintage	08
WR	7
Drink	11-13

 DRY $27 –V

Waimea Nelson Merlot/Malbec   ★★☆

The 2008 vintage (★★☆) is a blend of Merlot (72 per cent) and Malbec (28 per cent), grown on the coast at Kina, and on the Waimea Plains. Matured in American and French oak casks, it is medium-bodied, with plum and herb flavours that lack real ripeness and roundness.

Vintage	08
WR	6
Drink	11-14

DRY $23 –V

Weeping Sands Waiheke Island Merlot   (★★★★)

Still youthful, the 2009 vintage (★★★★) from Obsidian is an estate-grown red, matured in French oak casks (15 per cent new). Mouthfilling and full-coloured, with fresh, deep plum and spice flavours, a hint of coffee and oak complexity, it's a concentrated, ripe and savoury red, with good cellar potential.

Vintage	09
WR	6
Drink	11-18

DRY $31 –V

Wild Rock Gravel Pit Red Merlot/Malbec   ★★★★

From Wild Rock Wine Company (a subsidiary of Craggy Range), the 2009 vintage (★★★☆) was grown in the Gimblett Gravels, Hawke's Bay, and matured for 18 months in French oak casks (18 per cent new). A blend of Merlot (73 per cent), Malbec (23 per cent) and splashes of Cabernet Franc and Cabernet Sauvignon, it is full-coloured, fruity and smooth, with very satisfying depth of blackcurrant, plum and spice flavour and ripe, rounded tannins. A softly textured wine, it's already drinking well.

Vintage	09	08	07
WR	7	7	7
Drink	11-16	11-15	11-14

DRY $22 V+

Montepulciano

Montepulciano is widely planted across central Italy, yielding deeply coloured, ripe wines with good levels of alcohol, extract and flavour. In the Abruzzi, it is the foundation of the often superb-value Montepulciano d'Abruzzo, and in the Marches it is the key ingredient in the noble Rosso Conero.

In New Zealand, Montepulciano is a rarity and there has been confusion between the Montepulciano and Sangiovese varieties. Some wines may have been incorrectly labelled. According to the latest national vineyard survey, between 2005 and 2012 New Zealand's area of bearing Montepulciano vines will expand slightly from 6 to 10 hectares (mostly in Auckland, Hawke's Bay and Marlborough).

Black Barn Hawke's Bay Montepulciano ★★★★

The 2009 vintage (★★★★★) is a lovely marriage of power and approachability. Estate-grown at Havelock North, it is floral and rich, with substantial body (14.5 per cent alcohol) and an invitingly scented bouquet. Packed with plum, cherry, spice and chocolate flavours, it shows notable ripeness and density, with a silky texture and power right through the palate. One of New Zealand's best-ever Montepulcianos.

DRY $48 –V

Blackenbrook Vineyard Nelson Montepulciano ★★★☆

The 2010 vintage (★★★★) is the best yet. Matured for a year in French oak barriques, it's a powerful (14.5 per cent alcohol), boldly coloured red, sweet-fruited and crammed with fresh plum, red-berry and liquorice flavours. Vibrantly fruity, with a subtle seasoning of oak and good tannin backbone, it's well worth cellaring.

Vintage	10
WR	7
Drink	11-15

DRY $27 –V

Coopers Creek SV Guido In Velvet Pants Huapai Montepulciano (★★★★)

Estate-grown at Huapai, in West Auckland, the 2010 vintage (★★★★) is deeply coloured, rich, plummy and spicy. Fleshy and supple, with fresh, ripe, concentrated flavours seasoned with sweet oak, it's already enjoyable, but should mature well.

Vintage	10
WR	6
Drink	11-13

DRY $28 AV

Framingham Marlborough Montepulciano ★★★☆

The 2009 vintage (★★★☆) is deeply coloured, with strong flavours of red berries, plums and spices. Woven with fresh acidity, it shows a slight lack of ripeness and roundness, but good concentration.

Vintage	09	08	07	06
WR	6	5	6	6
Drink	11-17	11-14	11-15	P

DRY $35 –V

Hans Herzog Marlborough Montepulciano   ★★★★★

Typically a giant of a red, overflowing with sweet, ripe-fruit flavours. The 2008 vintage (★★★★☆) was fermented with indigenous yeasts, matured for two years in French oak barriques (10 per cent new). Powerful yet supple, it is boldly coloured, with dense blackcurrant, plum and spice flavours, fresh, nutty and savoury. Well worth cellaring.

Vintage	08	07	06	05
WR	7	7	7	7
Drink	11-20	11-19	11-20	11-20

DRY $64 AV

Jurassic Ridge Montepulciano   (★★★★☆)

An excellent debut, the 2008 vintage (★★★★☆) is a strapping red (14.8 per cent alcohol), estate-grown at Church Bay, on Waiheke Island, and hand-picked at 25 brix from first-crop vines. Matured in French oak casks (30 per cent new), it is deeply coloured, rich and sweet-fruited, with concentrated plum, cassis and spice flavours, slightly earthy notes adding complexity, buried tannins, and a rounded finish.

Vintage	08
WR	6
Drink	11-15

DRY $35 AV

Kahurangi Estate Nelson Montepulciano   (★★★)

A fruit-driven style with deep, purple-flushed colour, the 2010 vintage (★★★) is fresh, vibrant and smooth, with generous, plummy, slightly spicy flavours and a hint of sweet oak. An enjoyable drink-young style.

DRY $21 –V

Omaha Bay Vineyard Matakana Montepulciano   ★★★☆

Sturdy and savoury, the 2009 vintage (★★★★) was estate-grown at Matakana and matured for a year in French oak casks (one-third new). Promisingly deep and youthful in colour, it is mouthfilling and rich, with an array of blackcurrant, plum, herb and nut flavours, earthy, savoury notes adding real complexity, and a rounded finish. It's drinking well now.

Vintage	09
WR	6
Drink	11-19

DRY $40 –V

Stafford Lane Estate Nelson Montepulciano   (★★)

Estate-grown and hand-harvested at 22.5 brix at Appleby, the 2008 vintage (★★) was matured for 10 months in French oak barriques (30 per cent new). Light ruby, it's a light, simple red, berryish, slightly spicy and plummy, but lacks real richness and roundness.

DRY $25 –V

Trinity Hill Hawke's Bay Montepulciano ★★★☆

Winery founder John Hancock doesn't believe Montepulciano has a wonderful future in Hawke's Bay – but still wins high accolades in favourable seasons. The 2010 vintage (★★★★), grown in the Gimblett Gravels, is a full-coloured, purple-flushed red, vibrantly fruity and smooth. It has strong, fresh berry, plum and spice flavours, showing some savoury notes, gentle tannins and loads of drink-young charm. The 2011 (★★★), not oak-aged, has a Beaujolais-like appeal. Medium-bodied, fruity and smooth, it is floral, plummy and slightly spicy, in a lighter style than usual, offering pleasant summer drinking for 2011–12.

DRY $20 AV

Weeping Sands Waiheke Island Montepulciano ★★★★★

An emerging star. The strapping 2010 vintage (★★★★★), grown in the Obsidian Vineyard at Onetangi, was matured for 10 months in new French (25 per cent new) and older French and American (75 per cent) oak casks. Robust (15 per cent alcohol) and opaque, it is deliciously rich, flowing and soft, with great depth of blackcurrant, plum and spice flavours. Dense, harmonious and silky-textured, it's already hard to resist.

Vintage	10
WR	6
Drink	11-16

DRY $35 V+

Pinotage

Pinotage is overshadowed by more glamorous varieties in New Zealand, with 68 hectares of bearing vines in 2012. Pinotage now ranks as the country's seventh most extensively planted red-wine variety, well behind Malbec, ranked sixth, and fifth-placed Cabernet Franc.

Pinotage is a cross of the great Burgundian grape Pinot Noir and Cinsaut, a heavy-cropping variety popular in the south of France. Cinsaut's typically 'meaty, chunky sort of flavour' (in Jancis Robinson's words) is also characteristic of Pinotage. Valued for its reasonably early-ripening and disease-resistant qualities, and good yields, its plantings are predominantly in the North Island – notably Hawke's Bay and Gisborne – with other significant pockets in Marlborough and Auckland.

A well-made Pinotage displays a slightly gamey bouquet and a smooth, berryish, peppery palate that can be reminiscent of a southern Rhône. It matures swiftly and usually peaks within two or three years of the vintage.

Ascension The Bell Ringer Matakana Pinotage ★★★

The 2010 vintage (★★★★) is one of the best yet. Matured in a 50:50 split of French and American oak casks, it is deep and youthful in colour, with strong, ripe plum/spice flavours, rich and smooth.

DRY $27 –V

Hitchen Road Pinotage ★★★

The 2010 vintage (★★★☆) was estate-grown at Pokeno, in North Waikato, and harvested at nearly 24 brix. Oak-matured for 10 months, it has full, youthful colour. Mouthfilling and firm, it's an age-worthy wine with very good depth of plum, spice and nut flavours, an earthy streak and a slightly chewy finish. A great buy.

Vintage	10
WR	6
Drink	11-13

DRY $15 V+

Karikari Estate Pinotage ★★★★

Estate-grown on the Karikari Peninsula, in the Far North, the 2008 (★★★★) is a generous, brambly, nutty, slightly herbal and leathery red, drinking well now. The 2010 vintage (★★★★☆) was hand-harvested, fermented with indigenous yeasts, and matured in a mix of new French and seasoned American oak casks. Dark and youthful in colour, it is sweet-fruited, mouthfilling (14.3 per cent alcohol) and smooth, with dense, fresh plum, spice and nut flavours, and fine-grained tannins. Best drinking mid-2012+.

Vintage	10
WR	7
Drink	13-16

DRY $29 –V

Kerr Farm Vineyard Kumeu Pinotage ★★☆

Kerr Farm's wine is to be enjoyed 'with friends on the verandah for a cruisy afternoon'. Estate-grown in West Auckland and matured in American and French oak barriques, it is an honest country red, at its best fresh, berryish, slightly spicy and earthy, with gentle tannins.

DRY $21 –V

Kidnapper Cliffs Hawke's Bay Pinotage   (★★★★★)

From Te Awa (a winery with a strong track record with Pinotage), the debut 2009 vintage
(★★★★★) could easily be mistaken for Syrah. Bold and bright in colour, it is vibrantly fruity,
with lovely ripeness and density of plum/pepper flavours and earthy, savoury notes adding
complexity. Notably rich and supple, it avoids the rusticity typical of Pinotage and is a wine of
real finesse.

Kowhai Point Auckland Pinotage   (★★★☆)

Grown in the foothills of the Waitakere Ranges, West Auckland, the vibrantly fruity 2010
vintage (★★★☆) was barrel-matured for nine months. Deep and youthful in colour, it is a
medium-bodied wine with strong plum and red-berry flavours, woven with fresh acidity, and
the depth and structure to age.

Marsden Bay of Islands Reserve Pinotage   (★★★★☆)

The 2010 vintage (★★★★☆) was harvested at over 25 brix and barrel-aged for 16 months.
Deeply coloured, it is fleshy and soft, ripe and concentrated, with deep, berryish flavours,
hints of liquorice and raisins, and the earthy notes typical of Pinotage. Very sweet-fruited and
generous, it's already delicious.

Vintage	10
WR	7
Drink	12-16

Muddy Water Waipara Pinotage   ★★★★

'Not for the faint-hearted', this is a robust red, full of personality. The 2009 (★★★★☆) is a top
vintage. Harvested at 26 brix and matured for over a year in French oak casks (20 per cent new),
it's like a Côtes-du-Rhône, combining power and charm. Full-coloured, mouthfilling (15.5 per
cent alcohol) and supple, with sweet-fruit flavours of cherries and plums, and a hint of liquorice,
it is deliciously fruity and smooth, in a graceful style with excellent complexity and depth. The
2010 vintage (★★★★) is deeply coloured, powerful and sweet-fruited, with a cool-climate feel
and concentrated blackcurrant, plum, spice and herb flavours, supple and rich.

Vintage	10	09
WR	6	7
Drink	11-18	11-19

Okahu Pinotage   ★★★☆

The 2008 vintage (★★★☆) is a Northland red, estate-grown, hand-picked and matured in a
50:50 split of French and American oak (partly new). It's a dark, vibrantly fruity wine, medium-
bodied (12.5 per cent alcohol), fresh, plummy and supple, with plenty of flavour.

DRY $30 –V

Soljans Gisborne Pinotage   ★★★☆

This small West Auckland winery has a strong reputation for Pinotage. The 2010 vintage (★★★☆), barrel-aged for six months, is full-coloured, fresh and fruity, with very good depth of ripe plum and spice flavours, smooth and generous. Drink now onwards.

DRY $18 V+

Vintage	10
WR	6
Drink	11-16

Pinot Noir

New Zealand Pinot Noir enjoyed strong overseas demand in the year to June 2011, with over a million cases shipped – a steep rise from the 139,188 cases exported in 2003. There are now almost countless Pinot Noir labels, as producers cater for cash-strapped consumers by introducing second and third-tier labels (and others under brands you and I have never heard of).

The wines are enjoying notable success in international competitions, but you need to be aware that most of the world's elite Pinot Noir producers, especially in Burgundy, do not enter. At *Winestate*'s Wine of the Year Awards 2010, judged in Australia, the top five Pinot Noirs were all from New Zealand. Black Estate Omihi Waipara Pinot Noir 2007 won the trophy for Best Pinot Noir at the 2010 International Wine and Spirit Competition in London.

The 2011 vintage yielded 31,156 tonnes of Pinot Noir grapes, far ahead of Merlot with 9092 tonnes and Cabernet Sauvignon with 1667 tonnes. Between 2000 and 2012, New Zealand's area of bearing Pinot Noir vines is expanding from 1126 hectares to 4828 hectares.

Pinot Noir is the princely grape variety of red Burgundy. Cheaper wines typically display light, raspberry-evoking flavours, but great Pinot Noir has substance, suppleness and a gorgeous spread of flavours: cherries, fruit cake, spice and plums.

Pinot Noir is now New Zealand's most internationally acclaimed red-wine style. The vine is the second most commonly planted variety overall, ahead of Chardonnay and behind only Sauvignon Blanc. Over 40 per cent of the country's total Pinot Noir plantings are in Marlborough (where 8 per cent of the vines are grown for bottle-fermented sparkling wine), and the variety is also well established in Central Otago, Canterbury, the Wairarapa, Hawke's Bay, Gisborne and Nelson.

Yet Pinot Noir is a frustrating variety to grow. Because it buds early, it is vulnerable to spring frosts; its compact bunches are also very prone to rot. One crucial advantage is that it ripens early, well ahead of Cabernet Sauvignon. Low cropping and the selection of superior clones are essential aspects of the production of fine wine.

Martinborough (initially) and Central Otago have enjoyed the highest profile for Pinot Noir over the past 20 years. As their output of Pinot Noir has expanded, average prices have fallen, reflecting the arrival of a tidal wave of 'entry-level' (drink-young) wines.

Of the other small regions, Nelson and Waipara, in Canterbury, are also enjoying success. Marlborough's potential for the production of outstanding – but all too often underrated – Pinot Noir, in sufficient volumes to supply the burgeoning international demand, has also been tapped.

3 Stones Marlborough Pinot Noir (★★)

Slightly past its best, the 2008 vintage (★★) was matured in a mix of tanks (42 per cent) and French oak barriques (18 per cent new). Fairly developed in colour, it is spicy and green-edged, with some savoury, nutty complexity.

Vintage	08
WR	4
Drink	11-12

DRY $19 –V

3 Terraces Wairarapa Pinot Noir ★★☆

The 2009 vintage (★★) has lightish, slightly developed colour. Fruity and plummy, with crisp acidity, it lacks ripeness and richness.

DRY $20 –V

25 Steps Central Otago Pinot Noir   ★★★☆

From a terraced site at Lowburn, the 2008 vintage (★★★) is ruby-hued, with fresh acidity, good but not great depth of cherry and plum flavours, a touch of complexity and gentle tannins.

DRY $35 –V

36 Bottles Central Otago Pinot Noir   ★★★☆

The 2009 (★★★☆) is generous and silky, with cherry/plum flavours, showing some savoury complexity, and good harmony. The 2010 vintage (★★★★) is the best yet. Hand-picked at Bendigo and matured for 10 months in French oak barriques, it is deeply coloured, fresh and vibrant, with strong cherry, plum and spice flavours, seasoned with quality oak. Showing good richness and complexity, it's well worth cellaring.

Vintage	10	09	08
WR	6	5	6
Drink	11-16	11-16	11-14

DRY $33 –V

1769 Central Otago Pinot Noir   ★★★☆

From Wild Earth, the 2009 vintage (★★★☆) is enjoyable from the start. Full-coloured, it is sweet-fruited and harmonious, with fresh cherry, plum and spice flavours, showing very good depth, supple tannins and considerable complexity.

DRY $25 AV

1912 by Lindis River Central Otago Pinot Noir   (★★★)

Enjoyable young, the 2008 vintage (★★★) is ruby-hued and supple, with ripe, moderately concentrated cherry, herb and spice flavours, showing a touch of complexity.

DRY $25 –V

12,000 Miles Pinot Noir   ★★★

From the Gladstone winery, in the northern Wairarapa, the easy-drinking 2010 vintage (★★★☆) was partly barrel-aged. Ruby-hued, it is floral and supple, with fresh cherry, strawberry and plum flavours to the fore, gentle oak and tannins and a silky-smooth texture. It's already drinking well.

DRY $26 –V

Akarua Central Otago Pinot Noir   ★★★★★

In the past called 'The Gullies', this is an early-drinking style, compared to its Reserve stablemate (below), but top vintages are still outstanding. Estate-grown at Bannockburn and matured in French oak barriques (30 per cent new), the 2010 (★★★★★) is a lovely, fruit-crammed red with bold, bright colour, deep cherry, plum and spice flavours and finely balanced oak. It shows very impressive elegance, structure and complexity.

Vintage	10	09
WR	7	7
Drink	12-18	12-18

DRY $40 V+

Akarua Reserve Central Otago Pinot Noir ★★★★★

(Formerly labelled as 'Cadence'.) Estate-grown at Bannockburn, the 2009 vintage (★★★★★) was picked at 25 brix from 13-year-old vines, matured in French oak barriques (36 per cent new), and bottled unfined and unfiltered. Deeply coloured, it is fleshy, generous and savoury, in a notably ripe style, highly fragrant, with substantial body and highly concentrated cherry, plum and spice flavours. Powerful and very sweet-fruited, it should blossom with cellaring.

Vintage	09	08
WR	6	NM
Drink	12-18	NM

DRY $55 AV

Akarua Rua Central Otago Pinot Noir ★★★★

For a third-tier label, the 2010 vintage (★★★★★) of this Bannockburn red is remarkably good. Matured for 10 months in French oak casks (15 per cent new), it is powerful and concentrated, with deliciously dense, ripe cherry/plum flavours, hints of chocolate and coffee, and gentle tannins. A great buy.

Vintage	10	09
WR	6	6
Drink	11-15	11-14

DRY $25 V+

Alana Estate Rapture Martinborough Pinot Noir (★★★☆)

The 2010 vintage (★★★☆) is a single-vineyard red, designed for early drinking. Mouthfilling and smooth, with a touch of complexity and generous cherry, plum and spice flavours, ripe and rounded, it's priced right.

DRY $24 V+

Alexander Dusty Road Martinborough Pinot Noir ★★★☆

The 2009 vintage (★★★☆) is a good-value, single-vineyard red, partly barrel-aged, with drink-young appeal. Mouthfilling and supple, it has very good depth of cherry and plum flavours, fresh, ripe and rounded.

Vintage	09	08	07	06
WR	6	5	NM	6
Drink	11-12	P	NM	P

DRY $24 V+

Alexander Martinborough Pinot Noir ★★★★

The 2008 vintage (★★★★) is a floral, supple, mid-weight style, showing good complexity and highly enjoyable young. It's an elegant wine with ripe cherry, plum and spice flavours, finely integrated French oak (22 per cent new) and silky tannins.

Vintage	08	07	06	05
WR	6	NM	6	7
Drink	11-13	NM	P	P

DRY $35 AV

Alexandra Wine Company alex.gold Central Otago Pinot Noir   ★★★★

The 2009 vintage (★★★★) is a ruby-hued, savoury red, matured in French oak casks (30 per cent new). Well worth cellaring, it has fresh, lively acidity and cherry and nut flavours showing excellent concentration and complexity.

 DRY $30 AV

Alexia Wairarapa Pinot Noir   ★★★☆

The 2009 vintage (★★★☆) is a lightly oaked style, ruby-hued, mouthfilling and vibrantly fruity, with ripe plum and spice flavours, showing some savoury complexity, and good tannin backbone. Drink now or cellar.

Vintage	09	08
WR	6	6
Drink	11-14	11-13

 DRY $24 V+

Allan Scott Hounds Marlborough Pinot Noir   ★★★★

Allan Scott's top red label. A single-vineyard wine, fermented with indigenous yeasts and matured for over a year in French oak casks (mainly new), the 2009 vintage (★★★★☆) is mouthfilling, sweet-fruited, rich and supple. Deeply coloured, with concentrated cherry and plum flavours, seasoned with fine-quality oak, it is elegant and finely poised, offering excellent drinking from now onwards.

Vintage	10	09	08
WR	4	6	6
Drink	14-18	11-15	11-14

 DRY $35 AV

Allan Scott Marlborough Pinot Noir   ★★★☆

The 2009 vintage (★★★☆) is ruby-hued, floral, fruity and supple. Fermented with indigenous yeasts, it was matured for 10 months in French oak puncheons (25 per cent new). Cherryish, plummy and slightly spicy, with some savoury complexity, it's a very enjoyable, drink-young style.

Vintage	09	08
WR	6	6
Drink	11-14	11-12

 DRY $26 AV

Amisfield Central Otago Pinot Noir   ★★★★★

Estate-grown at Lowburn, in the Cromwell Basin, and matured in French oak barriques (30 per cent new), the 2009 vintage (★★★★) is dark and vibrantly fruity, with generous plum, cherry, spice, herb and nut flavours, woven with fresh acidity. A big, youthful, fairly firm wine, it has the power to age; open mid-2012+.

Vintage	09	08	07	06	05
WR	6	7	7	6	5
Drink	12-20	11-19	11-18	11-15	11-12

 DRY $40 V+

Amisfield Rocky Knoll Pinot Noir (★★★★★)

Still on sale, the debut 2006 vintage (★★★★★) was grown at Rocky Knoll, a stony terrace within the Amisfield Vineyard at Lowburn, in Central Otago. Picked at over 26 brix, it was matured for 15 months in French oak barriques (44 per cent new). Deep ruby, it's a strikingly rich, complex and harmonious wine, notably concentrated, sweet-fruited and savoury, with supple, silky tannins giving instant appeal. (Originally released in early 2008 at $110.)

Vintage	07	06
WR	7	6
Drink	12-20	12-20

 DRY $95 –V

Anchorage Nelson Pinot Noir ★★☆

Grown at Motueka, the 2009 vintage (★★) is light and developed, with spicy, herbal flavours that lack richness. The 2010 (★★★) is a drink-young charmer, ruby-hued, with decent depth of strawberry, plum and spice flavours, fresh, ripe and well-rounded.

DRY $21 –V

Ant Moore Central Otago Pinot Noir (★★★☆)

The sturdy, savoury 2009 vintage (★★★☆) is a blend of Cromwell Basin and Alexandra grapes, French oak-aged for a year. Full-coloured, with good complexity, it has strong, cherryish, slightly spicy, herbal and nutty flavours.

 DRY $32 –V

Ant Moore Reserve Black Label Central Otago Pinot Noir (★★★☆)

The deeply coloured 2009 vintage (★★★☆) is a blend of Alexandra and Gibbston grapes. Fleshy, it has strong herb and spice aromas and flavours, showing good complexity.

 DRY $42 –V

Aotea Nelson Pinot Noir (★★★☆)

(This label replaces Seifried's former Winemakers Collection label.) The 2010 vintage (★★★☆), matured for nine months in new and one-year-old French oak barriques, is fullish in colour, mouthfilling and savoury, in a complex, firmly structured style, spicy and nutty. Open mid-2012+.

Vintage	10
WR	5
Drink	11-16

 DRY $35 –V

Ara Composite Marlborough Pinot Noir ★★★☆

From the Winegrowers of Ara Vineyard, at the entrance to the Waihopai Valley, the 2009 vintage (★★★★) was matured for 10 months in French oak casks (25 per cent new). Ruby-hued, it is strongly varietal, with cherry, plum and spice flavours, ripe and supple, good complexity, and the structure to age.

Vintage	09	08
WR	6	6
Drink	11-15	11-14

 DRY $26 AV

Ara Marlborough Pinot Noir ★★★

This label is aimed at the restaurant trade. The 2009 vintage (★★★) was made from young vines and partly oak-aged. Light ruby, it is a medium-bodied red with cherry, plum and spice flavours, showing good freshness and immediacy. An enjoyable, drink-young style.

DRY $20 AV

Ara Pathway Marlborough Pinot Noir ★★★

A drink-young style, the 2009 vintage (★★★) was partly handled in tanks; 40 per cent of the blend was matured for six months in French oak casks (10 per cent new). Ruby-hued and vibrantly fruity, it has cherryish, plummy flavours, a hint of herbs, some savoury complexity and gentle tannins.

DRY $21 AV

Ara Select Blocks Marlborough Pinot Noir (★★★)

The debut 2008 vintage (★★★) was French oak-aged for 10 months. Ruby-hued, with some development showing, it is savoury, spicy and moderately concentrated, with considerable complexity. Ready.

DRY $30 –V

Ara Single Estate Marlborough Pinot Noir (★★★)

The 2009 vintage (★★★), partly oak-aged, is ruby-hued, with cherry, herb and nut flavours, showing good harmony. It's drinking well now.

DRY $25 –V

Aravin Central Otago Pinot Noir (★★★★☆)

Grown at Alexandra, the 2009 vintage (★★★★☆) is full-coloured and fragrant, with excellent depth of ripe cherry, plum, herb and nut flavours. Full of personality, it is sweet-fruited and generous, with good complexity and a long, spicy finish. Well worth cellaring.

DRY $32 V+

Archangel Central Otago Pinot Noir ★★★★

The 2009 vintage (★★★★) is a single-vineyard red from Queensberry, halfway between Cromwell and Wanaka, and matured for 10 months in French oak barriques. Full-coloured, it is mouthfilling, sweet-fruited and vibrantly fruity, with concentrated cherry, plum, herb and spice flavours, and a subtle seasoning of oak. Potentially the best yet, the 2010 (★★★★) is deeply coloured, with good density of cherry, plum and spice flavours, showing good complexity and suppleness.

DRY $39 AV

Vintage	09	08
WR	6	5
Drink	12-15	11-14

Arrow Junction Central Otago Pinot Noir   (★★★)

The 2008 vintage (★★★) is a moderately concentrated, ruby-hued red with ripe cherry, plum and herb flavours and a very smooth finish. Ready.

Artisan The Best Paddock Marlborough Pinot Noir   ★★☆

The 2008 vintage (★★☆) was grown in the lower Wairau Valley. It's a pleasant light style, berryish and smooth, with a touch of spicy, nutty complexity.

Ashwell Martinborough Pinot Noir   ★★★☆

Grown on the Martinborough Terraces, the 2010 vintage (★★★☆) was matured in French oak casks (one-third new). A floral, ruby-hued wine, it is medium-bodied and supple, with good depth of cherry and slight herb flavours, gentle tannins and some savoury complexity. It's a very harmonious wine, with drink-young appeal.

Vintage	10	09	08
WR	6	6	6
Drink	11-18	11-15	11-14

Ashwell Martinborough Reserve Pinot Noir   ★★★★

The 2009 vintage (★★★★) was matured in French oak casks (30 per cent new). Full-coloured, it is fragrant, sturdy and firm, with ripe plum, cherry and herb flavours, showing very good depth and complexity. It's drinking well now.

Vintage	09
WR	6
Drink	11-16

Ashwell The Quails Martinborough Pinot Noir   ★★

The 2010 vintage (★★) was matured in French oak barriques (33 per cent new). Ruby-hued, it's a drink-young quaffer, lacking fragrance and finesse.

Vintage	10
WR	6
Drink	11-16

Askerne Hawke's Bay Pinot Noir   ★★★

Estate-grown near Havelock North, the 2009 vintage (★★★) was matured in French oak barriques (29 per cent new). Full and bright in colour, it is sturdy (14.5 per cent alcohol), with strong spice, herb and green-olive flavours, showing some savoury complexity.

Vintage	09
WR	6
Drink	12-15

DRY $20 AV

Astrolabe Voyage Marlborough Pinot Noir   ★★★★

The 2008 vintage (★★★★) was hand-picked, fermented partly with indigenous yeasts and oak-aged for 10 months. A generous, sweet-fruited red, it is full-coloured, with cherry, plum, spice and nut flavours, showing excellent ripeness, youthful tannins and good complexity.

Vintage	08	07	06	
WR	6	6	5	
Drink	11-12	11-14	P	

Ata Rangi Crimson Pinot Noir   ★★★★

This second-tier label, based on 'younger' vines grown at Martinborough, is designed for early drinking – within three years of the harvest. The 2009 vintage (★★★★) was hand-picked at 23 to 25.5 brix, fermented with indigenous yeasts and matured for nine months in French oak casks (20 per cent new). Ruby-hued, it is scented and supple, with fresh, ripe cherry and spice flavours, a hint of dark chocolate, good, savoury complexity and excellent depth and immediacy.

Vintage	09	08	07	
WR	7	7	6	
Drink	11-13	11-12	P	

Ata Rangi Pinot Noir   ★★★★★

One of the greatest of all New Zealand wines, this Martinborough red is powerfully built and concentrated, yet seductively fragrant and supple. 'Intense, opulent fruit with power beneath' is winemaker Clive Paton's goal. 'Complexity comes with time.' The grapes are drawn from numerous sites, including the estate vineyard, planted in 1980, and the vines, ranging up to 31 years old, have an average yield of only 4.5 tonnes of grapes per hectare. The wine is fermented with indigenous yeasts and maturation is for 11 months in French oak barriques, 25 to 30 per cent new. The 2009 vintage (★★★★★) is mouthfilling and very ripe-tasting. A 'serious', very youthful wine from a warm growing season, it is dense and notably savoury, with an array of cherry, plum, spice and nut flavours, finely textured and showing great harmony. Built to last, it's a highly complex wine, best opened 2013+.

Vintage	09	08	DRY $75 AV
WR	7	7	
Drink	11-21	11-20	

Ataahua Waipara Pinot Noir   ★★★☆

The charming 2009 vintage (★★★★) is a single-vineyard red, matured for a year in seasoned French oak barrels. Delicious young, it is ruby-hued, mouthfilling and vibrantly fruity, with sweet-fruit delights and strong cherry, plum and spice flavours, gently seasoned with oak. A finely textured wine, showing good complexity, it's a drink-now or cellaring proposition.

Vintage	09	DRY $34 –V
WR	6	
Drink	11-13	

Auntsfield Estate Marlborough Pinot Noir   ★★★★☆

Grown on north-facing slopes at Auntsfield, on the south side of the Wairau Valley, the 2009 vintage (★★★★☆) was matured for 10 months in French oak barriques (30 per cent new). Deeply coloured, it is finely scented, weighty, sweet-fruited and supple, with cherry and plum flavours, softly textured, complex and rich. The 2010 (★★★★☆) is very youthful, with deep colour, a floral bouquet and strong cherry, plum, spice and nut flavours. It shows good muscle and complexity, suggesting a long future.

Vintage	08	07	06	05
WR	6	7	6	7
Drink	11-16	11-15	11-14	11-15

DRY $40 AV

Auntsfield Heritage Pinot Noir   ★★★★☆

The 2007 vintage (★★★★☆) was estate-grown on the south side of the Wairau Valley, in Marlborough, and matured in French oak barriques (65 per cent new). Boldly coloured, with a fragrant, toasty bouquet, it is very powerful and sweet-fruited, with lush plum and spice flavours, strongly seasoned with oak, and earthy notes adding complexity. A big, ripe style, it's built for cellaring.

Vintage	07	06	05
WR	7	NM	7
Drink	11-21	NM	11-20

DRY $75 –V

Aurora Vineyard, The, Bendigo Pinot Noir   ★★★★☆

The 2009 vintage (★★★★) is a richly coloured, firmly structured Central Otago red with good concentration and complexity. Fragrant, with cherry, spice and chocolate flavours, and a strong seasoning of nutty oak, it shows good potential. The 2010 (★★★★☆), matured for nine months in French oak barriques (33 per cent new), is deeply coloured, with rich, vibrant plum/spice flavours, concentrated and complex, and a backbone of firm, ripe tannins. Still youthful, it's a cellaring style; open 2013+.

DRY $39 V+

Aurora Vineyard, The, Partners Central Otago Pinot Noir   (★★★★)

Only 41 cases were made of the 2008 vintage (★★★★) of this single-vineyard red, barrel-aged for 18 months. Still very fresh and brightly coloured, it has strong, ripe cherry, plum and spice flavours, showing good complexity.

DRY $60 –V

Aurum Central Otago Pinot Noir   ★★★★

Estate-grown at Lowburn, in the Cromwell Basin, and matured for 11 months in French oak casks, the 2009 vintage (★★★★☆) is a scented and supple, very elegant red with fresh, vibrant fruit flavours, a spicy, savoury complexity and serious depth. Already delicious, it's a classic regional style, well worth cellaring.

Vintage	09	08	07
WR	6	5	6
Drink	11-16	11-15	11-12

DRY $32 AV

Aurum Madeleine Central Otago Pinot Noir

Named after the winemaker's daughter, the 2009 vintage (★★★★★) is a four-barrel selection, estate-grown at Lowburn and French oak-aged for 20 months. Deep and bright in colour, it is finely scented, showing lovely fruit sweetness. Built for the long haul, it has strong cherry, plum and spice flavours, with hints of coffee and nuts, and fine-grained tannins, in a very complex, savoury style. Best drinking 2013+.

Vintage	09	08	07
WR	7	NM	7
Drink	11-20	NM	11-20

DRY $85 AV

Aurum Mathilde Reserve Central Otago Pinot Noir

Estate-grown in the Te Wairere Vineyard at Lowburn, in the Cromwell Basin, the 2009 vintage (★★★★★) was matured for 15 months in French oak barriques. A powerful wine with a long future, it is full-coloured, substantial, very ripe and rounded, with dense, sweet-fruit flavours, a hint of liquorice, fresh acidity and notable complexity.

Vintage	09
WR	7
Drink	11-16

DRY $45 –V

Babich Marlborough Pinot Noir

The 2009 vintage (★★★) is a light-bodied style, berryish, spicy and slightly leafy, with some complexity and length.

DRY $20 –V

Babich Winemakers' Reserve Marlborough Pinot Noir

The 2009 (★★★☆) was grown in the Waihopai Valley and French oak-matured. Ruby-hued, it is supple and moderately concentrated, with cherry, herb and spice flavours, and some aging potential. The 2010 (★★★★☆) is a top vintage. Deeply coloured and ripely scented, it is mouthfilling, sweet-fruited and flowing, with concentrated, cherryish, plummy flavours, a subtle seasoning of oak, and excellent texture and complexity.

Vintage	10	09	08	07	06
WR	7	7	7	7	7
Drink	11-16	11-15	11-14	11-13	11-12

DRY $30 AV

Bald Hills 3 Acres Bannockburn Central Otago Pinot Noir ★★★★

The 2009 (★★★★☆) is a delicious drink-young style, but also age-worthy. It has a savoury bouquet, showing good complexity; the palate is very silky and harmonious, with ripe cherry, spice and nut flavours, threaded with fresh acidity. The 2010 vintage (★★★★), matured for 11 months in French oak casks (22 per cent new), is ruby-hued, mouthfilling, vibrantly fruity and supple, with a core of sweet fruit and ripe cherry, plum and spice flavours, showing considerable complexity. Best drinking mid-2012+.

Vintage	10	09	08
WR	7	6	5
Drink	11-20	11-19	11-18

DRY $30 AV

Bald Hills Single Vineyard Central Otago Pinot Noir ★★★★☆

Estate-grown at Bannockburn, hand-harvested at over 25 brix, and matured in French oak barriques (40 per cent new), the 2009 (★★★★☆) is a concentrated, tightly structured red, showing long-term cellaring potential. It has fresh, deep cherry, plum, spice and nut flavours, savoury, complex, and underpinned by firm tannins. The 2010 vintage (★★★★★) was matured for 11 months in French oak casks (50 per cent new). Deeply coloured, it is very youthful and fruit-packed, with concentrated cherry, plum and spice flavours that have lapped up the new oak. A muscular, firm wine with lovely ripeness and richness, it should be at its best 2013+.

Vintage	10	09	08	07	06	
WR	7	7	6	6	6	DRY $44 AV
Drink	11-15	11-14	11-13	11-12	P	

Bannock Brae Estate Barrel Selection Pinot Noir ★★★★★

Top vintages of this single-vineyard Bannockburn, Central Otago red are outstanding. Showing great potential, the 2009 (★★★★★) was matured for 11 months in French oak casks, and bottled unfined and unfiltered. A powerful wine (14.3 per cent), it is richly coloured, very savoury and complex, with deep, ripe cherry and spice flavours, a hint of dark chocolate, and good tannin support. Open 2013+.

Vintage	09	08	07	06	05	
WR	7	5	6	5	6	DRY $60 AV
Drink	12-17	11-15	11-14	P	P	

Bannock Brae Estate Goldfields Pinot Noir ★★★★☆

A great buy. Estate-grown at Bannockburn, in Central Otago, this is a 'feminine', very graceful, supple wine. The 2009 vintage (★★★★☆), harvested at 24.8 brix, matured for 10 months in French oak barriques (20 per cent new), and bottled unfined and unfiltered, is one of the best. Mouthfilling and concentrated, it is youthful, with vibrant plum, cherry and spice flavours and finely integrated oak. Exuberantly fruity, yet showing good complexity, it's a drink-now or cellaring proposition.

Vintage	09	08	07	06	
WR	7	5	6	5	DRY $30 V+
Drink	12-17	11-14	11-13	P	

Bascand Marlborough Pinot Noir ★★☆

Hand-picked in the Rapaura district and matured for a year in French oak barriques, the 2009 vintage (★★☆) is light-bodied, with smooth cherry, spice and herb flavours, offering easy drinking.

DRY $20 –V

Bascand Waipara Pinot Noir (★★★☆)

The 2009 vintage (★★★☆) is a great buy. Hand-picked and matured for a year in French oak barriques (30 per cent new), it is ruby-hued, with a fragrant, spicy bouquet. Generous and sweet-fruited, it has fresh, strong plum and spice flavours, with a hint of olives, and finely balanced tannins. Open mid-2011+.

 DRY $19 V+

Bel Echo by Clos Henri Terroir Portrait Marlborough Pinot Noir   ★★★☆

The 2009 vintage (★★★★) was grown on the stonier, less clay-bound soils at Clos Henri. Matured in tanks (63 per cent) and French oak barrels (37 per cent, mostly seasoned), it's the best yet, in a fruit-driven style with concentrated cherry and plum flavours, supple and rich. The 2008 (★★★☆) is ruby-hued, with mouthfilling body and ripe cherry, plum and spice flavours, showing some savoury complexity and very good depth.

Vintage	09	08
WR	6	6
Drink	11-15	11-14

 DRY $32 –V

Bellbird Spring Block Eight Waipara Pinot Noir   ★★★☆

Developing well, the 2009 vintage (★★★★) was hand-harvested at Waipara and matured in seasoned French oak barriques. Deeply coloured, it is buoyantly fruity, with generous, ripe plum and spice flavours, showing some savoury complexity, and good roundness and richness. The 2010 (★★☆) is lighter and green-edged.

Vintage	10	09
WR	4	6
Drink	11-15	11-17

 DRY $36 –V

Bellbird Spring River Terrace Pinot Noir   (★★★★)

Grown at three sites at Waipara and barrel-aged for a year, the 2010 vintage (★★★★) is rich and silky-textured. Full-coloured and sweet-fruited, with strong cherry, spice and nut flavours, it is sturdy, youthful and well worth cellaring.

Vintage	10
WR	5
Drink	11-15

 DRY $36 AV

Bell Hill Pinot Noir   ★★★★★

From a 1-hectare plot of vines on a limestone slope at Waikari, inland from Waipara, in North Canterbury, this is a rare, highly distinguished red. It is typically a generous wine, powerful yet silky, with sweet cherry, plum and spice flavours, complex, very harmonious and graceful. The 2007 vintage (★★★★★) was matured in French oak barrels (70 per cent new). Very deeply coloured, it is gorgeously scented, with dense cherry and plum flavours, hints of herbs and spices, and a very refined, long finish. A wine with great presence, it's years away from maturity.

 DRY $95 –V

Big Sky Martinborough Pinot Noir   ★★★★

Grown in Te Muna Road and matured in French oak barriques, the 2008 vintage (★★★★) is generous, sweet-fruited, savoury and supple, with ripe plum and spice flavours, gentle tannins, good complexity, and lots of drink-young appeal.

 DRY $39 AV

Bilancia Central Otago Pinot Noir   (★★★☆)

The 2008 vintage (★★★☆) from this Hawke's Bay producer was matured in French oak casks (10 per cent new). Full and youthful in colour, it is vibrantly fruity and supple, with ripe cherry, plum and spice flavours, showing very good depth. It's an elegant wine, delicious young.

DRY $28 AV

Bird Marlborough The Old Schoolhouse Vineyard Pinot Noir   ★★★☆

Estate-grown in the Omaka Valley, and fermented and matured in 900-litre barrels, the 2009 vintage (★★★☆) is a full-bodied, moderately rich red with ripe cherry, plum and slight herb flavours, a gentle oak influence, and plenty of drink-young appeal.

Vintage	09	08
WR	6	5
Drink	11-13	11-12

DRY $39 –V

Bishop's Head Waipara Valley Pinot Noir   ★★☆

The 2008 vintage (★★) is a sub-regional blend, matured for a year in French oak barrels (20 per cent new). Like the 2009 (★★☆), it is light and green-edged, lacking real ripeness and stuffing.

DRY $30 –V

Black Barn Vineyards Hawke's Bay Pinot Noir   (★★★☆)

Grown inland at Crownthorpe, the 2008 vintage (★★★☆) is full-bodied and supple, with strong cherry, plum and spice flavours, showing good complexity and aging potential.

DRY $32 –V

Black Cottage Central Otago Pinot Noir 2009   (★★★☆)

From Two Rivers, based in Marlborough, the 2009 vintage (★★★☆) is deep ruby, with strong cherry, plum and spice flavours, ripe and firm. Fresh and vibrant, with some savoury complexity, it has good aging potential.

DRY $27 AV

Blackenbrook Vineyard Nelson Reserve Pinot Noir   ★★★★

The 2009 vintage (★★★★) was estate-grown, hand-picked at 25 brix and matured for a year in French oak barriques. Full-coloured, it is very ripely scented, fleshy, vibrant and youthful, with strong cherry, plum and spice flavours, gentle tannins, and good, savoury complexity. It's a muscular wine (14.5 per cent alcohol), yet already highly approachable.

Vintage	10	09
WR	7	7
Drink	11-15	11-13

DRY $31 AV

Black Estate Omihi Waipara Pinot Noir   ★★★★

This single-vineyard, North Canterbury red is from vines planted in 1994. The 2009 vintage (★★★★☆), hand-picked at 24.6 brix and fermented with indigenous yeasts, was matured for 15 months in French oak barrels (only 6 per cent new). Enticingly floral and supple, it is intensely varietal. Ruby-hued, with rich, ripe cherry, plum and herb flavours, a gentle seasoning of oak and a silky texture, it shows impressive complexity and harmony.

DRY $41 –V

Black Quail Estate Central Otago Pinot Noir

Grown at Bannockburn, the 2009 vintage (★★★★★) is the finest yet. It's a classic regional style, finely scented, with concentrated plum/spice flavours, showing excellent ripeness, complexity and harmony. Drink now or cellar.

DRY $44 –V

Bladen Marlborough Pinot Noir

The 2009 vintage (★★★☆) is a single-vineyard, Wairau Valley red, hand-harvested and matured for 18 months in French oak barriques. Deeply coloured, it is fleshy, with very good depth of cherryish, plummy flavour, ripe and rounded. The youthful 2010 (★★★) is ruby-hued, mouthfilling and vibrantly fruity, with cherry/plum flavours showing some savoury complexity.

DRY $32 –V

Blairpatrick Estate Pinot Noir (★★☆)

Grown in the northern Wairarapa, the 2008 vintage (★★☆) is mouthfilling, with some confectionery notes and ripe, smooth flavours in a very easy-drinking style.

DRY $20 –V

Blind River Marlborough Pinot Noir

Estate-grown in the Awatere Valley, the 2009 vintage (★★★) was hand-picked at 24 brix and matured for 10 months in French oak casks (35 per cent new). Ruby-hued, vibrant and supple, it has fresh, plummy, cherryish flavours showing moderate complexity. The 2010 (★★★☆) is full-coloured, with fresh cherry and plum flavours, hints of herbs and spices, a subtle oak influence and very good depth.

Vintage	10	09	08	07
WR	6	6	4	7
Drink	11-17	11-16	11-12	11-16

DRY $36 –V

Bloody Bay Marlborough Pinot Noir (★★☆)

From wine distributor Federal Geo, the 2009 vintage (★★☆) is a light red with gentle strawberry and spice flavours. It lacks richness, but offers pleasant, early drinking.

DRY $17 AV

Boatshed Bay by Goldwater Marlborough Pinot Noir (★★☆)

The ruby-hued 2008 vintage (★★☆) is medium-bodied, with berryish aromas and fresh raspberry and spice flavours. Tight, with a hint of toasty oak, it shows a slight lack of ripeness and roundness.

Vintage	08
WR	7
Drink	11-12

DRY $21 –V

Borthwick Vineyard Wairarapa Pinot Noir

Grown at Gladstone, near Masterton, and matured in French oak casks (40 per cent new), the 2008 vintage (★★★★☆) is a deeply coloured, attractively perfumed red with vibrant cherry and plum flavours, showing excellent depth, ripeness and suppleness. Showing good, savoury complexity and plenty of muscle, it should mature well. (I have also tasted a 2009 vintage 'Borthwick Pinot Noir', a ruby-hued, fairly light but supple and charming red, good value at $15.)

Vintage	09	08	07	06
WR	5	6	5	6
Drink	11-21	11-21	11-14	11-17

DRY $35 AV

Bouldevines Marlborough Pinot Noir

A big style of Pinot Noir, the 2009 vintage (★★★★) is powerful and deeply coloured, with concentrated cherry, plum, herb and spice flavours. The 2010 (★★★☆) was matured for 10 months in French oak casks (20 per cent new). Ruby-hued, it is fresh, vibrantly fruity and supple, with mouthfilling body and ripe, plummy, moderately complex flavours. A finely textured wine, it's already drinking well.

Vintage	10
WR	6
Drink	11-15

DRY $30 –V

Boundary Vineyards Kings Road Waipara Pinot Noir

The 2010 vintage (★★★) from Pernod Ricard NZ is full-coloured, with plum, spice, herb and olive flavours, showing some savoury complexity and good depth.

DRY $23 AV

Bracken's Order Ava Central Otago Pinot Noir

The 2008 vintage (★★★★☆) is beautifully floral and supple, with sweet-fruit delights and cherry and plum flavours showing a subtle oak influence, gentle tannins, and excellent delicacy and charm.

Vintage	08
WR	7
Drink	12-17

DRY $40 AV

Bracken's Order Central Otago Pinot Noir

A single-vineyard red, grown at Gibbston and matured in French oak casks (75 per cent new), the 2009 vintage (★★★★) is full-coloured, rich and supple, with cherry, plum and herb flavours. It's a softly textured, slightly leafy wine with a distinctly cool-climate feel, generous and harmonious. Drink now onwards.

Vintage	09
WR	7
Drink	12-17

DRY $30 AV

Brams Run Marlborough Pinot Noir   (★★★☆)

From Invivo, the 2008 vintage (★★★☆) is a ruby-hued, tightly structured wine with good depth of vibrant cherry, herb and spice flavours, showing some complexity. Hand-picked in the Brancott Valley and French oak-aged for 11 months, it's priced right.

Brancott Estate Living Land Series Marlborough Pinot Noir   ★★★★

From vines in conversion to organic, the 2010 vintage (★★★★) is scented, savoury and supple, with strong cherry and plum flavours, showing good complexity. Drink now or cellar.

Brancott Estate Reserve South Island Pinot Noir   (★★★)

The 2009 vintage (★★★) has full, slightly developed colour, mouthfilling body (14 per cent alcohol), and satisfying depth of cherry, plum, herb and spice flavours, showing some nutty, savoury complexity.

Brancott Estate 'T' Terraces Marlborough Pinot Noir   ★★★★☆

(Formerly labelled Montana.) The 2008 vintage (★★★★☆), the first branded as Brancott Estate, is finely scented and mouthfilling, with good density. Ruby-hued, it is savoury, with ripe cherry, plum and spice flavours, showing excellent complexity, and a silky texture. The 2010 (★★★★☆), grown in 'key Marlborough vineyards', is very youthful, with generous cherry and plum flavours, showing good complexity, and ripe, supple tannins.

Brennan Gibbston Pinot Noir   ★★★★

The 2008 vintage (★★★★) was grown at Gibbston, in Central Otago. A single-vineyard red, matured in French oak barriques (55 per cent new), it is ruby-hued, with ripe cherry and spice flavours, showing good complexity. Rich, ripe, savoury and harmonious, it's drinking well now, but also worth cellaring.

DRY $42 –V

Brightside Nelson Pinot Noir   ★★★

From Kaimira, the 2010 vintage (★★★) is an attractive, drink-young style. Ruby-hued, it is fresh and supple, with vibrant plum, herb and spice flavours, showing a touch of oak-derived complexity. Fine value.

Brightwater Vineyards Lord Rutherford Nelson Pinot Noir   ★★★★

The 2009 vintage (★★★★) was estate-grown and matured for a year in French oak barriques (20 per cent new). Full-coloured, it is mouthfilling and sweet-fruited, with generous plum and spice flavours, showing good complexity, and ripe, silky tannins.

Vintage	09	08	07
WR	5	5	6
Drink	12-16	11-14	P

DRY $40 –V

Brightwater Vineyards Nelson Pinot Noir   ★★★☆

Deeply coloured, the 2010 vintage (★★★☆) was matured for 10 months in French oak barrels (15 per cent new). Already enjoyable, it is fresh and vibrantly fruity, with ripe cherry and plum flavours, slightly nutty and smooth, and very good depth.

Vintage	10
WR	6
Drink	11-15

DRY $25 AV

Brodie Estate Pinot Noir   ★★★★

The 2009 vintage (★★★★), estate-grown and hand-picked in Martinborough, was matured for 11 months in French oak barrels (25 per cent new). Rich and smooth-flowing, it is full-coloured and invitingly fragrant. Already delicious, it offers good concentration of very ripe cherry/plum flavours, with hints of liquorice and spices, and finely integrated oak.

Vintage	10	09	08
WR	7	6	6
Drink	12-17	11-16	11-14

DRY $39 AV

Bronte by Rimu Grove Nelson Pinot Noir   ★★★☆

Estate-grown and hand-picked, the 2009 (★★★) was matured for 11 months in French oak barriques. Ruby-hued, it is quite forward, with fresh cherry, herb and nut flavours, showing some savoury complexity. The 2010 vintage (★★★☆) is full-coloured and freshly scented, mouthfilling and supple. Already drinking well, it has ripe, sweet-fruit characters of cherries, plums and spices, showing good, savoury complexity.

Vintage	10	09	08	07
WR	7	6	6	6
Drink	12-18	11-17	11-16	11-15

DRY $28 AV

Burn Cottage Central Otago Pinot Noir   (★★★★☆)

The 2009 vintage (★★★★☆), estate-grown in the Cromwell Basin, was matured in French oak barriques (38 per cent new). Fleshy, vibrantly fruity and supple, it is a very elegant wine, full-coloured, with sweet-fruit delights and fresh, concentrated cherry and plum flavours. Rich and rounded, it is already delicious, but should mature well.

Vintage	10	09
WR	6	6
Drink	11-17	11-16

DRY $58 –V

Burnt Spur Martinborough Pinot Noir ★★★★

This single-vineyard red is grown south of the town, on heavier soils than those found on the Martinborough Terrace. The 2009 vintage (★★★☆), French oak-aged for 10 months, is sturdy and savoury, with strong plum, spice, herb and olive flavours, considerable complexity and finely balanced tannins. Drink now or cellar.

DRY $44 –V

Cable Bay Central Otago Pinot Noir ★★★☆

The debut 2009 vintage (★★★☆) was hand-picked in the Cromwell Basin and matured in French oak barriques. Ruby-hued, it is floral, vibrantly fruity and supple, with fresh, ripe, moderately concentrated, cherryish flavours, finely textured and offering lots of drink-young appeal. The powerful, concentrated 2010 (★★★★) was transported to Waiheke Island for vinification. Full-coloured, it is mouthfilling, with strong, ripe cherry, plum and spice flavours, fresh and complex, a firm foundation of tannin, and obvious cellaring potential.

Vintage	10	09
WR	7	6
Drink	11-16	11-15

DRY $39 –V

Cable Bay Marlborough Selection Pinot Noir ★★★

The 2010 vintage (★★★), oak-aged for eight months, is a medium-bodied wine, fresh and supple, with vibrant, ripe cherry and plum flavours, showing a touch of savoury complexity.

Vintage	10
WR	5
Drink	11-15

DRY $29 –V

Camshorn Waipara Pinot Noir ★★★

From Pernod Ricard NZ, the 2007 vintage (★★★) is deeply coloured, with spice and green-olive notes on the nose and palate, lively acidity and plenty of flavour. It shows good richness and complexity, but leafy notes detract. The 2008 (★★☆) is full-bodied and savoury, but past its best.

DRY $37 –V

Carrick Central Otago Pinot Noir ★★★★★

This Bannockburn label is a regional classic. The 2009 vintage (★★★★☆) was matured for a year in French oak barriques (30 per cent new). Scented, mouthfilling, sweet-fruited and supple, it has cherry, plum and spice flavours, and gentler tannins than in some past vintages. Showing good, savoury complexity, it's an elegant wine, well worth cellaring.

Vintage	09	08	07	06	05	04
WR	7	NM	7	6	7	5
Drink	12-17	NM	11-15	11-14	11-14	11-12

DRY $45 AV

Carrick Crown & Cross Central Otago Pinot Noir   (★★★★)

The fleshy, supple 2008 vintage (★★★★) was grown at Bannockburn, hand-picked, fermented with indigenous yeasts, and bottled unfined and unfiltered. A softly mouthfilling red (14.5 per cent alcohol), it is ruby-hued, with strong, ripe sweet-fruit flavours of cherries and plums, and finely integrated oak.

DRY $33 AV

Carrick Excelsior Central Otago Pinot Noir   ★★★★★

From mature, estate-grown vines at Bannockburn, the 2007 vintage (★★★★★) was matured for 18 months in French oak barriques (30 per cent new). A serious yet sensuous red, it is richly coloured, bold and fruity, with dense plum, herb, spice and liquorice flavours, showing lovely fruit sweetness and concentration. It should be very long-lived; open 2012+.

DRY $85 AV

Carrick Unravelled Central Otago Pinot Noir   ★★★☆

Designed to be 'easy-drinking, laidback', the 2009 vintage (★★★☆) does not claim to be estate-grown at Bannockburn. Matured for a year in French oak barriques (20 per cent new), it's a freshly scented, ruby-hued wine with good depth of smooth cherry, plum and spice flavours. A drink-young style – with style.

DRY $25 AV

Catalina Sounds Pinot Noir   ★★★

The 2008 vintage (★★★) was grown in Marlborough and matured in French oak casks (20 per cent new). Ruby-hued, with a hint of development, it is medium to full-bodied, with cherry and herb flavours, showing some savoury complexity. Ready.

DRY $28 –V

Central Schist Central Otago Pinot Noir   ★★

The 2010 vintage (★★) is a very light style of Pinot Noir, ruby-hued, with pleasant cherry and plum flavours, simple and smooth.

DRY $22 –V

Charcoal Gully Sally's Pinch Pinot Noir   ★★★

Grown at Pisa, in Central Otago, the ruby-hued 2008 vintage (★★★☆) has ripe, sweet-fruit characters, good depth of cherry and spice flavours, light tannins and some savoury complexity.

DRY $29 –V

Chard Farm Mata-Au Central Otago Pinot Noir   (★★★★)

The debut 2009 vintage (★★★★) was grown at Lowburn and Parkburn, in the Cromwell Basin, on terraces formed by the Mata-Au (Clutha) River. Ruby-hued, it is savoury and supple, with sweet-fruit delights and finely textured, cherryish, plummy flavours that linger well. Delicious young, it should mature well.

DRY $44 –V

Chard Farm River Run Pinot Noir ★★★☆

This is an attractive, fruit-driven style. The 2009 vintage (★★★☆) was grown and hand-picked, mostly at Lowburn, in the Cromwell Basin, but includes some Gibbston fruit. Ruby-hued, it is mouthfilling and sweet-fruited, with ripe cherry, plum and spice flavours, gentle tannins and a floral bouquet.

Vintage	09
WR	7
Drink	11-14

DRY $31 –V

Charles Wiffen Marlborough Pinot Noir ★★★☆

The 2009 vintage (★★★★☆) is the best yet, with deep, youthful colour and an enticingly fragrant bouquet of plums, spices and olives. It's a concentrated, elegant red, savoury and complex, with excellent ripeness, texture and richness.

DRY $27 AV

Church Road Central Otago Pinot Noir (★★★★)

Pernod Ricard NZ's decision to extend the Church Road brand – indivisibly associated with Hawke's Bay – to Central Otago, is a surprise, but in the past, Marlborough has sometimes made a key contribution to the Sauvignon Blanc. The debut 2009 vintage (★★★★) was grown mostly at Bendigo and matured for nine months in French oak casks (27 per cent new). Ruby-hued, mouthfilling and supple, it is savoury and complex, with cherry, plum, spice and nut flavours, finely textured and harmonious. It's already drinking well.

DRY $27 V+

Churton Marlborough Pinot Noir ★★★★☆

Winemaker Sam Weaver wants a 'delicate, refined' style of Pinot Noir. Estate-grown at the elevated (200 metres above sea level) Waihopai Slopes site, hand-picked at 24 brix, fermented with indigenous yeasts, and matured for over a year in French oak barriques (20 per cent new), the 2009 vintage (★★★★☆) is highly scented, rich and supple, with cherry, plum and herb flavours in a very silky, savoury and complex style. It's already delicious.

Vintage	09	08	07	06	05
WR	7	6	6	5	6
Drink	11-20	11-18	11-18	11-15	11-16

DRY $44 AV

Churton The Abyss Marlborough Pinot Noir ★★★★★

The 2008 vintage (★★★★★) was estate-grown on a steep, north-east clay slope, 200 metres above sea level in the Waihopai Valley. Hand-picked from the oldest vines, fermented with indigenous yeasts, matured in French oak casks (50 per cent new) and bottled unfiltered, it is deeply coloured, with lovely richness and harmony. It offers great depth of plum, spice, herb and liquorice flavours, in a very rich, 'complete' style, more silky and graceful than its stablemate (above).

Vintage	08
WR	7
Drink	11-20

DRY $75 AV

Clayridge Crusader Marlborough Pinot Noir   (★★★★☆)

Retasted in 2011, the 2007 vintage (★★★★☆) was estate-grown and matured in new French oak casks. Deep and slightly developed in colour, it is sturdy (14.5 per cent alcohol), sweet-fruited and supple, with dense plummy, spicy flavours and hints of herbs and raisins, in a powerful, savoury and generous style. It's probably at its peak now.

DRY $67 –V

Clayridge Excalibur Marlborough Pinot Noir   ★★★

The 2007 vintage (★★★) was estate-grown in the upper reaches of the Omaka Valley and matured in French oak casks (45 per cent new). It's a powerful, savoury wine, but green-edged, with plenty of body and spicy, slightly leafy flavour.

DRY $38 –V

Clayridge Marlborough Pinot Noir   ★★★

The 2009 vintage (★★★☆) was estate-grown and French oak-aged for a year. Ruby-hued, it is mouthfilling and supple, with cherry, plum, herb and nut flavours, gentle tannins and drink-young appeal.

DRY $29 –V

Clearview Pinot Noir Des Trois   ★★★★☆

From a Hawke's Bay winery, the 2008 vintage (★★★★) is a fleshy, rich, regional blend of Central Otago, Wairarapa and Waipara grapes, barrel-aged for 15 months. Ruby-hued, it has substantial body, ripe, cherryish, spicy flavours, hints of herbs and liquorice, and a fairly firm finish. Drink now or cellar.

DRY $40 AV

Clevedon Hills Pinot Noir   ★★★☆

The 2010 vintage (★★★☆) was estate-grown at Clevedon, in South Auckland. It shows plenty of personality, with mouthfilling body and greater depth of flavour than its lightish colour suggests. Savoury, earthy, spicy and firm, with northern warmth, it has good complexity. Drink mid-2012+.

DRY $40 –V

Clifford Bay Marlborough Pinot Noir   (★★★)

Showing lots of drink-young appeal, the 2010 vintage (★★★) is a ruby-hued red, floral and sweet-fruited, with satisfying depth of ripe plum and red-berry flavours, slightly spicy and smooth.

DRY $20 AV

Clos de Ste Anne Naboth's Vineyard Pinot Noir   ★★★★

This Gisborne red from Millton is the country's northernmost quality Pinot Noir. Grown at the hillside Clos de Ste Anne site at Manutuke, the 2009 vintage (★★★★☆) was hand-harvested from vines up to 20 years old, fermented with indigenous yeasts, barrique-aged for

11 months, and bottled without fining or filtering. Ruby-hued, it is mouthfilling and supple, with cherry, spice and herb flavours. Deliciously sweet-fruited and savoury, it reveals impressive concentration and complexity, with the structure to age well.

Vintage	09	08	07	06	05
WR	6	6	7	5	6
Drink	11-18	11-13	11-13	11-12	11-12

DRY $52 –V

Clos Henri Marlborough Pinot Noir ★★★★

From Henri Bourgeois, a top Loire Valley producer with a site near Renwick, the 2009 vintage (★★★★☆) was matured for over a year in French oak barriques (25 per cent new). Deeply coloured, it is very fragrant and sweet-fruited, rich and supple, with lush cherry, plum, spice and nut flavours. The best yet.

Vintage	09	08	07
WR	6	6	6
Drink	12-17	11-16	11-15

 DRY $42 –V

Clos Marguerite Marlborough Pinot Noir ★★★☆

This single-vineyard Awatere Valley red is hand-picked and matured for a year in French oak barriques (10 to 15 per cent new in 2008). The 2008 vintage (★★★☆) is a ruby-hued, mid-weight style, with ripe cherry, plum and herb flavours, showing very good depth and complexity.

DRY $33 –V

Cloudy Bay Pinot Noir ★★★★☆

This is a consistently elegant, richly varietal red. Grown on the south side of the Wairau Valley and in the Omaka Valley, the 2008 (★★★★☆) was hand-picked at an average of 24.5 brix from low-yielding vines (6.4 tonnes/hectare), and was matured for a year in French oak barriques (50 per cent new). Softly mouthfilling, with strong cherry, plum and spice flavours, finely integrated nutty oak and ripe, supple tannins, it is enticingly scented, with a hint of herbs, good, savoury complexity and lovely flow across the palate. The 2009 vintage (★★★★☆) is savoury, ruby-hued, very graceful and harmonious. Mouthfilling, with ripe cherry, plum, spice and nut flavours, showing excellent complexity, and a rounded, lingering finish, it's a youthful wine, well worth cellaring.

Vintage	09	08	07	06	05
WR	6	5	7	6	7
Drink	11-15	11-14	11-14	11-13	11-12

 DRY $45 –V

Coal Pit Tiwha Central Otago Pinot Noir ★★★★

This single-vineyard red is grown at Gibbston. The 2009 vintage (★★★★☆), matured in French oak casks (40 per cent new), is very seductive and generous, floral and deeply coloured, with notably concentrated plum, herb and olive flavours, gentle tannins and a deliciously rich, smooth finish.

Vintage	09	08	07	06
WR	7	4	5	7
Drink	11-14	11-12	P	P

 DRY $42 –V

Coney Pizzicato Pinot Noir ★★★☆

The 2009 vintage (★★★) of this Martinborough red was matured in French oak casks (30 per cent new). It's a drink-young style, fruity and supple, with some fruit sweetness and depth, and good varietal character, but also fairly light and forward.

Vintage	09	08
WR	5	5
Drink	11-14	11-13

 DRY $30 –V

Coopers Creek Marlborough Pinot Noir ★★★

A very easy-drinking style. The 2009 vintage (★★★) is ruby-hued, floral and supple, with cherry, plum, spice and slight herb flavours, fresh, ripe and smooth. The 2010 (★★★☆), briefly oak-aged, is ruby-hued, fruity and supple, with moderately concentrated cherry and plum flavours, a hint of herbs, gentle tannins and a floral bouquet.

Vintage	10	09	08	07	06
WR	6	5	6	5	6
Drink	11-13	11-12	P	P	P

 DRY $19 AV

Coopers Creek SV Gibsons Run Marlborough Pinot Noir ★★★★

The 2009 vintage (★★★☆), French oak-aged for a year, is ruby-hued and supple, with mouthfilling body, cherryish, spicy flavours, slightly herbal and toasty, and good complexity and depth. Drink now or cellar.

Vintage	09	08	07	06
WR	6	6	NM	6
Drink	11-13	11-12	NM	P

 DRY $28 V+

Coopers Creek SV Razorback Central Otago Pinot Noir ★★★

Floral, vibrantly fruity and supple, the 2008 vintage (★★★☆) was hand-picked and matured for a year in French oak casks (33 per cent new). It's a charming, moderately concentrated wine, with ripe, sweet-fruit flavours, a subtle seasoning of oak and good harmony. The 2009 (★★☆) is ruby-hued, with firm, green-edged flavours that lack a bit of ripeness and stuffing.

Vintage	09	08
WR	6	6
Drink	11-13	11-12

DRY $28 –V

Couper's Shed Waipara Pinot Noir (★★★☆)

From Pernod Ricard NZ, the 2009 vintage (★★★☆) is a full-coloured North Canterbury red with a spicy bouquet and fresh plum, cherry, herb and spice flavours, showing very good depth. A medium to full-bodied style with some savoury complexity and a fairly firm finish, it's still very youthful; open mid-2012+.

 DRY $25 AV

Craggy Range Bannockburn Sluicings Vineyard Central Otago Pinot Noir   ★★★★☆

The 2009 vintage (★★★★★) is the best yet. Hand-harvested from a vineyard on the northern side of Felton Road, it was matured for 10 months in French oak barriques (35 per cent new). Bright ruby, it is beautifully floral and supple, with rich, sweet-fruit flavours of plums, spices and dark chocolate, very fine-grained tannins and impressive complexity. Built to last.

Vintage	09	08	07
WR	7	6	6
Drink	11-18	11-16	11-14

DRY $50 –V

Craggy Range Calvert Vineyard Bannockburn Pinot Noir   ★★★★☆

Grown in the biodynamically managed Calvert Vineyard in Felton Road, and matured for 10 months in French oak barriques (35 per cent new), the 2009 vintage (★★★★☆) is floral, mouthfilling and vibrantly fruity, with deliciously ripe sweet-fruit flavours, savoury and complex, and gentle tannins.

Vintage	09	08	07
WR	6	7	6
Drink	11-18	11-16	11-16

DRY $60 –V

Craggy Range Te Muna Road Vineyard Pinot Noir   ★★★★★

The classy 2010 vintage (★★★★★) of this Martinborough red was hand-harvested, fermented with indigenous yeasts and matured for over a year in French oak barriques. Deeply coloured, with a fragrant, spicy, smoky bouquet, it is sturdy, rich, savoury and complex, with densely packed cherry, plum, spice and nut flavours, ripe and finely textured. Still very youthful, it should be long-lived; open 2013+.

Vintage	10	09	08	07	06	05	04
WR	7	6	7	7	7	7	6
Drink	12-16	11-15	11-16	11-16	11-13	11-12	P

DRY $43 V+

Craggy Range Waitaki Valley Otago Station Vineyard Pinot Noir   ★★★★

Grown in North Otago and matured for 10 months in French oak barriques (33 per cent new), the 2009 vintage (★★★★☆) is a classy red. Deeply coloured, it is finely scented, very graceful and supple, with rich cherry and plum flavours, complex and youthful, and lovely texture and harmony.

Vintage	09	08
WR	7	7
Drink	11-18	11-16

DRY $45 –V

Craggy Range Zebra Vineyard Central Otago Pinot Noir ★★★★

The 2008 vintage (★★★★) was grown at Bendigo, hand-picked at 24.6 brix, fermented with indigenous yeasts and matured for 10 months in French oak barriques (40 per cent new). Full-coloured, it is mouthfilling, with concentrated, very ripe cherry and plum flavours, seasoned with spicy oak, and supple tannins.

Vintage	08	07
WR	6	6
Drink	11-16	11-14

 DRY $40 –V

Crater Rim, The, Bendigo Terrace Central Otago Pinot Noir ★★★☆

Ready now, the 2009 vintage (★★★☆) is a single-vineyard red, matured in seasoned French oak casks. Deeply coloured, it has moderately concentrated cherry, spice and herb flavours, showing some complexity, and a rounded finish.

 DRY $24 V+

Crater Rim, The, Black Friday Waipara Pinot Noir (★★★★)

A single-vineyard red, the 2009 vintage (★★★★) was matured in seasoned French oak casks. Full-coloured, it is mouthfilling, sweet-fruited and firm, with good weight and concentration of fresh cherry, plum and spice flavours that linger well.

 DRY $44 –V

Crater Rim, The, Canterbury Pinot Noir ★★★☆

Offering good value, the 2010 vintage (★★★☆) was fermented with indigenous yeasts and matured for 10 months in seasoned French oak barriques. Full-coloured, with a savoury, spicy bouquet, it has plum, spice and green-olive flavours, showing very good depth and complexity, and a well-rounded finish.

 DRY $22 V+

Crater Rim, The, From the Ashes Waipara Pinot Noir ★★★☆

On Friday, 13 November 2009, the Crater Rim winery burnt to the ground. The 2010 vintage (★★★☆), matured in seasoned French oak casks, is full-coloured, mouthfilling, vibrantly fruity and supple, with fresh, strong plum and spice flavours, showing good complexity. Worth cellaring.

 DRY $25 AV

Crater Rim, The, Gibbston Valley Pinot Noir (★★★★)

Instantly appealing, the 2010 vintage (★★★★) is a single-vineyard red, matured in French oak barriques (one and two years old). Ruby-hued, it is very elegant, fresh and supple, with cherry and plum flavours, silky-textured, and showing excellent delicacy and harmony. Drink now or cellar.

DRY $28 V+

Crater Rim, The, Lot Seven Waipara Pinot Noir

The 2009 vintage (★★★☆) could prove controversial. A single-vineyard red, matured in one and two-year-old French oak casks, it lacks real fragrance, but it is deeply coloured and bold, with densely packed flavours.

Vintage	09
WR	6
Drink	11-16

DRY $52 –V

Crater Rim, The, Omihi Rise Pinot Noir ★★★★★

Rich and silky, the 2009 vintage (★★★★☆) is a single-vineyard red, grown in the Omihi Valley and matured in one and two-year-old French oak casks. Deeply coloured, it has lovely mouthfeel, with very ripe cherry, plum and spice flavours, a hint of liquorice, and good, savoury complexity. Still youthful, it should be at its best from 2013+.

Vintage	09	08	07	06
WR	6	NM	6	5
Drink	11-18	NM	11-18	11-16

DRY $55 AV

Crater Rim, The, Waipara Pinot Noir ★★★★

Maturing very gracefully, the 2009 vintage (★★★★) is a multi-site blend, fermented with indigenous yeasts and barrel-aged. Deep and youthful in colour, it is fragrant, with generous cherry, plum and spice flavours, a subtle seasoning of oak, and excellent richness, complexity and harmony.

DRY $37 AV

Crawford Farm New Zealand Pinot Noir ★★☆

From Constellation NZ, the 2008 vintage (★★☆) is a blend of Marlborough, Gisborne and Hawke's Bay grapes. Light ruby, it has pleasant strawberry and spice flavours, with a hint of toasty oak, moderate depth and a fairly firm finish.

DRY $21 –V

Crayfish Marlborough Pinot Noir (★☆)

The 2008 vintage (★☆) is light, green-edged and fading.

DRY $19 –V

Croft Vineyard Martinborough Pinot Noir ★★★★

Matured in French oak casks (30 per cent new), the floral, finely balanced 2008 vintage (★★★★) is ruby-hued and supple, with strong, ripe cherry, plum and spice flavours that flow well to a long, rounded finish.

DRY $35 AV

Croney Two Ton Marlborough Pinot Noir   (★★★☆)

The sturdy, good-value 2008 (★★★☆) was hand-harvested from low-cropped vines (5 tonnes/hectare), and matured in French oak barriques (30 per cent new). It shows good concentration, with firm, ripe plum, spice and cherry flavours.

DRY $20 V+

Crossings, The, Awatere Valley Marlborough Pinot Noir   ★★★

The 2009 vintage (★★☆) spent nine months in French oak barriques (26 per cent new). Showing early development, it is light in colour, with crisp, berryish, slightly herbal flavours, lacking real ripeness and richness.

Vintage	09	08
WR	4	6
Drink	11-12	11-12

DRY $24 AV

Crossroads Marlborough Pinot Noir   ★★☆

Matured for nine months in French oak barriques (35 per cent new), the 2010 vintage (★★☆) is deeply coloured, with mouthfilling body and strong plum, herb and spice flavours. It's a sturdy, full-flavoured wine, but lacks real finesse.

Vintage	10
WR	6
Drink	11-18

DRY $19 –V

Crowded House Marlborough/Nelson/Central Otago Pinot Noir   ★★★☆

An attractive drink-young style, the 2010 vintage (★★★☆) was blended from three South Island regions: Nelson (40 per cent), Marlborough (30 per cent) and Central Otago (30 per cent). Vibrantly fruity, with cherry, plum and spice flavours to the fore, it has some savoury notes adding complexity, fresh acidity and a well-rounded finish.

DRY $21 V+

Curio Bendigo Vineyard Central Otago Pinot Noir   (★★★)

From Mud House, the stylishly packaged, debut 2008 vintage (★★★) was harvested at 24.5 brix and matured in tanks (50 per cent) and French oak barriques. Ruby-hued, it's an off-dry style (5 grams/litre of residual sugar), with fresh acidity and good depth of berryish, slightly spicy flavours.

MED/DRY $30 –V

Darling, The, Marlborough Pinot Noir   ★★★☆

Grown on the south side of the Wairau Valley, the 2010 vintage (★★★☆) was matured in one-year-old French oak casks. Light ruby, it is mouthfilling, sweet-fruited and supple, with moderately concentrated cherry and plum flavours, a touch of complexity, and drink-young charm.

Vintage	10	09
WR	6	6
Drink	11-16	11-15

DRY $32 –V

Deep Cove Central Otago Pinot Noir ★★★☆

From Wild Earth, the 2009 vintage (★★★★) is a deeply coloured red, grown at Lowburn and Gibbston. The bouquet is fresh-scented and youthful; the palate is concentrated, with buoyant plum and spice flavours, showing very good ripeness, complexity and depth.

 DRY $32 –V

Delegat Reserve Marlborough Pinot Noir ★★★★

Grown in the Awatere Valley, the charming 2009 vintage (★★★★) is ruby-hued and supple, with a finely scented bouquet and vibrant cherry/plum flavours, showing good richness and length.

 DRY $28 V+

Delta Hatters Hill Marlborough Pinot Noir ★★★★

The top label from the vineyard – six kilometres inland from Renwick, at the mouth of the Waihopai Valley – the 2008 vintage (★★★★) was 90 per cent oak-aged (barriques, 40 per cent new). Rich and full-coloured, with sweet-fruit characters, it has cherry, plum and spice flavours, woven with fresh acidity. Still firm and youthful, it offers best drinking mid-2012+.

Vintage	08	07
WR	6	7
Drink	11-16	11-13

 DRY $32 AV

Delta Marlborough Pinot Noir ★★★☆

The 2009 vintage (★★★☆) is a single-vineyard wine, partly barrel-aged. Ruby-hued, it is floral, sweet-fruited and supple, with ripe cherry, strawberry and spice flavours, slightly nutty and savoury. A very good, drink-young style.

Vintage	10	09	08
WR	7	6	6
Drink	12-19	11-16	11-13

 DRY $22 V+

Desert Heart Mackenzies Run Pinot Noir ★★★☆

Estate-grown at Bannockburn, in Central Otago, and matured in French oak casks (one-third new), the 2009 vintage (★★★★) is the best yet – deeply coloured and fragrant, with concentrated plum, spice and slight herb flavours, savoury and complex. A firmly structured wine, it shows good potential.

DRY $42 –V

Desert Heart Spencer Block Pinot Noir (★★★)

Estate-grown at Bannockburn, in Central Otago, the 2009 vintage (★★★) was matured in French oak casks (one-third new). A gutsy, full-flavoured wine with earthy, rustic notes and firm tannins, it lacks finesse but shows good concentration.

 DRY $42 –V

Devil's Staircase Central Otago Pinot Noir   ★★★☆

From Rockburn, the ruby-hued 2010 vintage (★★★☆) is an attractive, drink-young style. Fleshy, with fresh, strong cherry/plum flavours and supple tannins, it's generous and smooth, with instant appeal.

DRY $25 AV

Distant Land Central Otago Pinot Noir   (★★☆)

The 2010 vintage (★★☆) is a single-vineyard red, grown at Gibbston. French oak-aged for a year, it is ruby-hued, mouthfilling and supple, with light cherry and plum flavours, lacking real structure and depth.

DRY $25 –V

Dog Point Vineyard Marlborough Pinot Noir   ★★★★★

The typically classy 2009 vintage (★★★★★) was hand-harvested, fermented with indigenous yeasts and matured for 17 months in French oak barriques (50 per cent new). Full ruby, with a fragrant, spicy, savoury bouquet, it is mouthfilling, ripe and supple, with lovely cherry, plum and spice flavours, slightly nutty and complex. Finely poised, it offers delicious drinking from now onwards.

Vintage	09	08	07	06	05	04
WR	6	6	6	5	6	5
Drink	11-15	11-14	11-14	11-12	11-13	P

DRY $42 V+

Domain Road Vineyard Central Otago Pinot Noir   ★★★★☆

This single-vineyard, Bannockburn red is an emerging star. The 2009 vintage (★★★★★) was fermented with indigenous yeasts and barrel-aged for 10 months. Perfumed and deeply coloured, it has lush, beautifully ripe cherry, plum and spice flavours, showing excellent concentration and complexity. A powerful, densely packed wine, it has obvious cellar potential.

Vintage	09	08	07
WR	7	6	7
Drink	11-17	11-16	11-15

DRY $39 V+

Drumsara Central Otago Ventifacts Block Pinot Noir   ★★★★☆

Grown at Alexandra, in the Ventifacts Block (ventifacts are wind-shaped boulders), the 2009 vintage (★★★★) was matured for nine months in French oak casks. Full-coloured, it is highly fragrant, with spice and herb aromas leading into a youthful, supple, savoury wine, showing excellent depth and complexity. Best drinking 2013+.

Vintage	09	08	07
WR	6	7	7
Drink	11-14	11-13	11-12

DRY $45 –V

Dry Gully Central Otago Pinot Noir   ★★★☆

Grown in the Alexandra sub-region, but no longer a single-vineyard red, the 2008 vintage (★★★☆) was matured in French oak casks (25 per cent new). Ruby-hued, it is supple, with ripe, moderately concentrated flavours of plums and spices, some savoury complexity and gentle tannins.

Vintage	08	07	06	05
WR	5	5	6	5
Drink	11-15	11-12	11-13	P

 DRY $30 –V

Drylands Marlborough Pinot Noir   ★★☆

The 2009 vintage (★★☆) from Constellation NZ was matured in a 50:50 split of tanks and French oak casks. Light ruby, it is fresh and slightly herbal, in an easy-drinking, fruit-driven style.

 DRY $22 –V

Dry River Pinot Noir   ★★★★★

Dark and densely flavoured, this Martinborough red ranks among New Zealand's greatest Pinot Noirs. It is grown in three company-owned vineyards – Dry River Estate, Craighall and Lovat – on the Martinborough Terrace, and 90 per cent of the vines are over 20 years old. Matured for a year in French oak hogsheads (20 to 30 per cent new), it is a slower developing wine than other New Zealand Pinot Noirs, but matures superbly. Still a baby, the 2009 vintage (★★★★★) is enticingly floral, with full, youthful colour. Very generous and supple, it is beautifully ripe and harmonious, with concentrated berry, plum and spice flavours, youthful and built for the long haul. Open 2014+.

Vintage	09	08	07	06	05	04	03	02
WR	7	7	7	7	7	6	7	6
Drink	12-23	11-17	11-16	11-14	11-17	11-12	11-16	P

 DRY $84 AV

Drystack Central Otago Pinot Noir   (★★)

The 2009 vintage (★★) was grown at a site between Clyde and Alexandra. Light and developed in colour, it is green-edged, simple and short.

DRY $28 –V

Durvillea Marlborough Pinot Noir   (★★★☆)

From Astrolabe, the 2009 vintage (★★★☆) is fleshy, with lots of plummy, spicy flavour, slightly rustic, but strong and smooth.

DRY $20 V+

Earth's End Central Otago Pinot Noir   ★★★☆

From Mount Edward, the 2009 vintage (★★★★) is more complex and savoury than most second-tier labels. Bright ruby, with strong cherry, plum, spice and nut flavours, it's delicious now. The 2008 (★★★☆) is less concentrated, but also shows very good complexity.

 DRY $29 AV

Elder, The, Martinborough Pinot Noir   (★★★★)

The 2010 vintage (★★★★) was grown in the Hanson Vineyard, at Te Muna, and matured for 10 months in seasoned French oak casks. Deep and youthful in colour, it is fragrant, with generous plum and cherry flavours, hints of herbs and spices, and good tannin support. It's a finely balanced, age-worthy wine; drink mid-2012+.

 DRY $56 –V

Elephant Hill Central Otago Pinot Noir   ★★★☆

The 2009 vintage (★★★) from this Hawke's Bay producer was grown at Alexandra, hand-picked and matured in French oak casks (40 per cent new). It's a full-bodied red with good depth of cherryish, herbal, nutty flavours.

 DRY $29 AV

Eliot Brothers Marlborough Pinot Noir   ★★☆

From an Auckland-based company, the 2009 vintage (★★) is light and developed, with green-edged flavours.

 DRY $20 –V

Ellero Pisa Terrace Central Otago Pinot Noir   (★★★)

The 2008 vintage (★★★), matured in French oak casks (25 per cent new), is cherryish and spicy, in an earthy, slightly rustic style with firm tannins.

 DRY $36 –V

Eradus Marlborough Pinot Noir   (★★★☆)

Hand-picked in the Awatere Valley and matured in seasoned French oak barriques, the 2010 vintage (★★★☆) is ruby-hued, with a floral bouquet of cherries, herbs and spices. Supple and sweet-fruited, it has some complexity and plenty of drink-young charm.

Vintage	10
WR	7
Drink	11-16

 DRY $24 V+

Escarpment Kiwa by Escarpment Martinborough Pinot Noir   ★★★★☆

From vines planted in 1989, the 2009 vintage (★★★★☆) is 'the biggest expression' of Pinot Noir in his range of single-vineyard reds, says winemaker Larry McKenna. Grown in the Cleland Vineyard, in Cambridge Road, and matured in French oak barriques, it is deliciously savoury, dense, plummy and herbal, in a finely textured style, drinking well now.

DRY $65 –V

Escarpment Kupe by Escarpment Pinot Noir   ★★★★★

This flagship, estate-grown red, based on closely planted vines at Te Muna, in Martinborough, is fermented in French cuves and matured in French oak barriques (50 per cent new). The 2009 vintage (★★★★★) is a powerful, masculine wine, with deep, notably concentrated flavours of plums and spices. Crying out for more time, it should flourish for many years; open 2013+.

 DRY $85 AV

Escarpment Martinborough Pinot Noir   ★★★★☆

This is the third-tier label, after the single-vineyard wines and Kupe, but the 2009 vintage (★★★★★) is highly impressive. Mostly (70 per cent) estate-grown in Te Muna Road, and matured in French oak barriques (30 per cent new), it is ruby-hued and enticingly scented, with a lovely spread of plum, spice and nut flavours, showing excellent ripeness, complexity and harmony.

Vintage	09	08	07	06	05	04	03
WR	7	7	6	7	6	5	7
Drink	11-18	11-16	11-15	11-15	11-12	P	P

 DRY $45 –V

Escarpment Pahi by Escarpment Pinot Noir   ★★★★☆

Based on vines approaching 30 years old in the McCreanor Vineyard, in Princess Street, Martinborough, the 2009 vintage (★★★★☆) is a single-clone (10/5) wine, matured for a year in French oak casks (30 per cent new). A silky, softly textured wine, it is lovely now, with an array of cherry, spice and slight herb flavours, showing excellent complexity and substance.

 DRY $65 –V

Escarpment Te Rehua by Escarpment Pinot Noir   ★★★★★

Grown in the Barton Vineyard in Huangarua Road, Martinborough, where the Pinot Noir vines (of many clones) are well over 20 years old, the powerful 2009 vintage (★★★★★) was matured for a year in French oak barriques (30 per cent new). Deeply coloured, it is a very bold wine, crammed with ripe cherry, plum, spice and liquorice flavours, in an upfront style, with loads of personality.

 DRY $65 AV

Esk Valley Marlborough Pinot Noir   (★★★★)

The debut 2008 vintage (★★★★) was hand-picked in the Wairau and Awatere valleys and barrique-aged for a year. It's a sweet-fruited wine with fresh, ripe cherry and plum flavours, supple and strong. The 2010 (tasted prior to bottling, and so not rated) is rich and sweet-fruited, with fresh, generous cherry, plum and spice flavours and a well-rounded finish.

Vintage	10	09	08
WR	7	7	6
Drink	12-18	11-15	P

DRY $30 AV

Eve Central Otago Pinot Noir   (★★★)

From Wild Earth, the 2008 vintage (★★★) was estate-grown at Bannockburn and Pisa. Full-flavoured, it has deep ruby colour, with funky, barnyard notes adding complexity and a leafy streak.

 DRY $24 AV

Explorer Central Otago Pinot Noir (★★★☆)

From Surveyor Thomson, the 2009 vintage (★★★☆) was estate-grown at Lowburn. Ruby-hued, it is fruity and supple, with very satisfying depth of ripe, cherryish, spicy, slightly nutty flavours, showing some savoury complexity. Sturdy and characterful, it's a more 'serious' style than most sub-$25 Pinot Noirs.

DRY $24 V+

Fairhall Downs Single Vineyard Marlborough Pinot Noir ★★★★

Grown in the Brancott Valley, hand-harvested and matured for 11 months in French oak barriques, the 2009 (★★★☆) is lightish in colour, with plum, herb and spice flavours and a fairly firm finish. It shows a slight lack of richness, compared to other recent vintages, but also good, savoury complexity.

DRY $35 AV

Fairmont Estate Admiral Hill Block Pinot Noir (★★★★)

Grown at Gladstone, in the northern Wairarapa, the 2009 vintage (★★★★) is a full-coloured, sturdy red (14.5 per cent alcohol), sweet-fruited, with generous berry and spice flavours, softly textured and very harmonious. It's drinking well now.

DRY $26 V+

Fairmont Estate Block One Pinot Noir ★★★★

Deeply coloured, the 2008 vintage (★★★★☆) of this Gladstone, Wairarapa red has a savoury, slightly earthy bouquet, leading into a big, generous wine with concentrated, well-ripened flavours of cherries, plums and spices, good complexity and fine-grained tannins. It's drinking well now.

DRY $30 AV

Fairmont Estate Gladstone Terraces Pinot Noir (★★★★)

The fine-value 2009 vintage (★★★★), grown in the northern Wairarapa, is full-bodied (14.5 per cent alcohol) and ripe-tasting, with excellent depth of cherryish, spicy flavour, showing good complexity, and a well-rounded finish. Ready; no rush.

DRY $24 V+

Fallen Angel Central Otago Pinot Noir ★★★★

The 2008 vintage (★★★★) from Stonyridge Vineyard – far better known for Waiheke Island claret-style reds – was blended from three sub-regions of Central Otago. Floral and supple, it is ruby-hued, with mouthfilling body and strong, ripe cherry, plum, herb and spice flavours, well seasoned with toasty oak. It shows good complexity and potential.

DRY $59 –V

Fancrest Estate Waipara Di's Pinot Noir   ★★★

The 2010 vintage (★★★★) is deeply coloured and sturdy, with strong, plummy, slightly spicy and earthy flavours, showing good complexity. It's still very fresh and youthful. The 2009 (★★★) is medium-bodied, with plum, herb and spice flavours, slightly earthy and nutty. The 2008 (★★☆), not labelled as 'Di's', is lighter and greener (but cheaper at $25). The 2007 vintage (★★★☆), also still on sale, is drinking well now, showing very good body and depth of plummy, spicy, slightly herbal flavours, and bottle-aged complexity.

Vintage	10	09	08	07
WR	7	6	6	6
Drink	12-20	12-18	11-15	11-17

DRY $39 –V

Farmers Market Petite Pinot   (★★★)

'Petite Pinot' is an odd name for a Beaujolais-style red, blended from Pinot Noir, grown in Marlborough, and Gisborne Merlot. Still, the blend works. Ruby-hued, the 2009 vintage (★★★) is full-bodied, fruity and supple, with smooth, cherryish, slightly spicy flavours, a hint of herbs, and gentle tannins. Drink now.

DRY $20 AV

Felton Road Bannockburn Central Otago Pinot Noir   ★★★★★

The Bannockburn winery's 'standard' Pinot Noir is a distinguished wine in its own right, blended from its three vineyards at Bannockburn – The Elms, Cornish Point and Calvert. Matured for 11 months in French oak casks (30 per cent new), it is bottled without fining or filtering. The 2009 (★★★★★) is beautifully floral and supple, with vibrant, concentrated cherry, plum and spice flavours that build to a long finish. The 2010 vintage (★★★★☆) is deeply coloured, with a complex, savoury bouquet. Rich and sweet-fruited, with deep cherry, plum and spice flavours, good complexity and gentle tannins, it's already delicious, but well worth cellaring.

Vintage	10	09	08	07	06	05	04	03	02
WR	7	7	7	7	6	7	7	6	7
Drink	12-22	11-21	11-20	11-18	11-17	11-15	P	P	P

DRY $60 AV

Felton Road Block 3 Central Otago Pinot Noir   ★★★★★

Grown at Bannockburn, on a north-facing slope 270 metres above sea level, this is a majestic Central Otago wine, among the finest Pinot Noirs in the country. The mature vines are cultivated just in front of the winery, in a section of the vineyard where the clay content is relatively high, giving 'dried herbs and ripe fruit characters'. The wine is matured for 11 to 14 months in Burgundy oak barrels (30 per cent new in 2010), and bottled without fining or filtration. The 2010 vintage (★★★★★) is a very 'complete' wine, dense and youthful in colour, with notably rich cherry, plum, spice and nut flavours. A powerful, finely textured red, already delicious, it's benchmark stuff and a prime candidate for cellaring.

Vintage	10	09	08	07	06	05	04	03	02
WR	7	7	7	7	6	7	7	6	7
Drink	12-22	11-21	11-20	11-18	11-17	11-18	11-12	P	P

DRY $90 AV

Felton Road Block 5 Pinot Noir ★★★★★

This is winemaker Blair Walter's favourite Felton Road red. Grown in a 'special' block of The Elms Vineyard at Bannockburn, in Central Otago, it matures for a year in French oak barriques (30 per cent new), and is then held for several more months in seasoned oak casks. The 2009 vintage (★★★★★) is deeply coloured, with a fragrant, spicy, complex bouquet. The palate is powerful, savoury and firmly structured, with deep, cherryish, spicy, nutty flavours, a firm foundation of tannin, and lovely concentration and complexity. Best drinking 2013+.

Vintage	09	08	07	06	05	04	03
WR	7	7	7	6	7	7	7
Drink	12-18	11-17	11-18	11-17	11-18	P	P

Felton Road Calvert Pinot Noir ★★★★★

Gown in the Calvert Vineyard at Bannockburn – which neighbours and is managed by Felton Road – and matured for 13 months in French oak barriques (30 per cent new), the 2010 vintage (★★★★★) is a powerful Central Otago red. Densely coloured, with a complex, savoury bouquet, it is very concentrated and sweet-fruited, with dense cherry and spice flavours, a hint of liquorice, and ripe, supple tannins. A highly complex, youthful wine, it should flourish with cellaring. The 2009 (★★★★★) is rich and flowing, with lovely depth of cherry, plum, spice and nut flavours, and a finely poised, long finish. Best drinking 2013+.

Vintage	10	09	08	07	06
WR	7	7	7	7	6
Drink	12-22	11-21	11-20	11-18	11-17

Felton Road Cornish Point Pinot Noir ★★★★★

From the company-owned Cornish Point Vineyard at the eastern end of Bannockburn, six kilometres from the winery, this is always one of my favourite Felton Road reds. The 2010 vintage (★★★★★) was matured for more than a year in French oak barriques (30 per cent new). Deeply coloured, it is spicy and complex, with dense, cherryish, plummy, slightly herbal flavours, woven with fresh acidity. It's still very vibrant and youthful; open 2013+. The 2009 (★★★★★) is also full of personality, with notable density of plum, spice and herb flavours, supple and floral.

Vintage	10
WR	7
Drink	12-22

Fiddler's Green Waipara Pinot Noir ★★★☆

Matured for a year in French oak barriques (20 per cent new), the 2008 vintage (★★★☆) is ruby-hued, vibrantly fruity and supple, with very good depth of cherry, plum and nut flavours, showing some savoury complexity.

Vintage	08
WR	6
Drink	11-14

Fiddler's Green Waipara Reserve Pinot Noir   (★★★☆)

The 2008 vintage (★★★☆) was matured for 16 months in French oak barriques (40 per cent new). Ruby-hued and supple, it is moderately concentrated, with fresh, vibrant plum, herb and spice flavours, seasoned with spicy oak.

Vintage 08
WR 6
Drink 11-16

 DRY $30 –V

Folding Hill Bendigo Central Otago Pinot Noir   ★★★★

The 2009 vintage (★★★★☆) was hand-picked from low-yielding vines (3–4 tonnes/hectare), matured in French oak barriques (30 per cent new), and bottled unfined and unfiltered. A powerful, 'masculine' style of Pinot Noir, concentrated and firmly structured, it is dark and sweet-fruited, with deep cherry and plum flavours, savoury and tightly structured. Very age-worthy. Best 2013+.

 DRY $38 AV

Forrest Marlborough Pinot Noir   ★★★☆

This easy-drinking wine rests its case on charm rather than power. The 2009 vintage (★★★☆) was grown at Renwick, Northbank and in the Brancott Valley. Attractively scented, mouthfilling and supple, with cherry, plum and slight herb flavours and gentle tannins, it's a ruby-hued wine with good 'pinosity' and drink-young appeal.

Vintage 09 08 07
WR 5 5 6
Drink 11-15 11-14 11-15

 DRY $25 AV

Forrest The Valleys Brancott Marlborough Pinot Noir   (★★★☆)

The 2007 vintage (★★★☆) was hand-harvested from 25-year-old vines and matured in French oak casks (40 per cent new). A medium to full-bodied style, it is cherryish and slightly herbal, with gentle tannins, some savoury, earthy complexity and very good depth and harmony.

Vintage 07
WR 6
Drink 11-20

 DRY $40 –V

Fox Junior Marlborough Pinot Noir   (★★★★)

The debut 2008 vintage (★★★★) was hand-picked at 24 brix and matured for 10 months in French oak casks (10 per cent new). It's a generous wine with sweet-fruit delights, strong plum and cherry flavours, some savoury notes and a long, silky finish.

Vintage 08
WR 6
Drink 11-12

DRY $29 V+

Framingham F Series Marlborough Pinot Noir

The 2008 vintage (★★★★☆) was grown in clay soils at Fareham Lane, at the foot of the Waihopai Valley, and matured for 15 months in French oak casks (32 per cent new). A much more 'masculine' style than its stablemate (below), it is sturdy and rich, with full colour and a fragrant, plummy, spicy bouquet. The 2009 (★★★★☆) is deeply coloured and weighty (14.5 per cent alcohol), with deep plum, spice and herb flavours, finely poised, complex and youthful.

Vintage	09	08	DRY $40 AV
WR	6	6	
Drink	11-15	11-14	

Framingham Marlborough Pinot Noir

This wine is 'feminine', says winemaker Andrew Hedley, meaning it is elegant, rather than powerful. The 2010 vintage (★★★★), matured in French oak casks, is ruby-hued, floral and supple, with rich cherry, plum and spice flavours, slightly nutty and savoury, and good complexity. A generous, very harmonious wine, it's already drinking well.

Vintage	10	09	08	07	06	05	DRY $35 AV
WR	6	6	6	7	6	7	
Drink	11-14	11-13	11-13	P	P	P	

Frizzell Pinot Noir   (★★★)

From a Hawke's Bay company, the 2009 vintage (★★★) was grown in Central Otago. Fresh-scented, it is very fruity and smooth, with generous plum and spice flavours, woven with lively acidity, and strong drink-young appeal.

Vintage	09	DRY $24 AV
WR	6	
Drink	11-15	

Fromm Brancott Valley Marlborough Pinot Noir

The finely textured 2008 vintage (★★★★★) was grown in clay soils and matured for 14 to 16 months in French oak casks (only 10 per cent new). A top example of the winery style, it is deeply coloured, rich and rounded, with highly concentrated, ripe cherry, plum, spice and nut flavours. Mouthfilling and generous, with gentle acidity and good tannin support, it's a drink-now or cellaring proposition.

Vintage	08	07	06	05	DRY $45 –V
WR	6	7	6	6	
Drink	11-16	11-17	11-14	11-13	

Fromm Clayvin Vineyard Pinot Noir

This acclaimed Marlborough red is estate-grown at the hillside Clayvin Vineyard in the Brancott Valley, matured in French oak barriques (10–20 per cent new), and bottled without fining or filtering. It tends to be more floral and charming than its Fromm Vineyard stablemate.

The 2008 (★★★★★) is a lovely wine. Silky-textured, it is deeply coloured and very sweet-fruited, with dense plum, cherry and spice flavours, a hint of liquorice, notable complexity, ripe, supple tannins and a savoury, rounded finish. It's already delicious, but the best is yet to come.

Vintage	09	08	07	06	05	04	03	02	DRY $65 AV
WR	7	6	7	7	7	5	5	6	
Drink	12-19	11-16	11-17	11-14	11-15	11-12	P	11-12	

Fromm Fromm Vineyard Pinot Noir ★★★★☆

Winemaker Hätsch Kalberer describes this Marlborough red as 'not a typical New World style, but the truest expression of terroir you could find'. In the Fromm Vineyard near Renwick, in the heart of the Wairau Valley, many clones of Pinot Noir are close-planted on a flat site with alluvial topsoils overlying layers of clay and free-draining gravels. The wine is fermented with indigenous yeasts and matured in Burgundy oak barrels (up to 10 per cent new). It needs at least four or five years to unleash its full class. The 2009 vintage (★★★★★) is the finest since 2005 (★★★★★). Sturdy, mouthfilling, sweet-fruited and concentrated, it has deep plum, cherry, spice and nut flavours, structured and complex. Powerful and 'masculine', but not tough, it's well worth cellaring.

Vintage	09	08	07	06	05	04	03	02	DRY $65 –V
WR	7	NM	7	6	7	5	5	6	
Drink	11-21	NM	11-19	11-16	11-17	11-12	P	11-12	

Fromm La Strada Marlborough Pinot Noir ★★★★☆

This wine is designed to be ready for drinking upon release, by selecting suitable sites and clones, and 'steering the fermentation towards more fruit expression and moderate tannins and structure'. The 2009 (★★★★☆) was matured for over a year in French oak barriques (10–20 per cent new). Ruby-hued, it is a 'serious', yet highly approachable, wine, mouthfilling, with rich flavours of cherries, spices and nuts, good concentration and complexity, and a well-rounded finish. The 2008 vintage (★★★★☆) is equally appealing, in a smoothly flowing, yet rich and complex, style, delicious now.

Vintage	09	08	07	06	05	04	DRY $36 V+
WR	7	7	7	7	6	6	
Drink	12-16	11-15	11-14	11-13	P	P	

Gem Martinborough Pinot Noir (★★★☆)

The 2009 vintage (★★★☆) is a single-vineyard red, fermented with indigenous yeasts and matured for a year in French oak barriques (20 per cent new). Enjoyable now, it is cherryish, plummy and spicy, with a hint of herbs, good, savoury complexity and a rounded finish.

Vintage	09	DRY $39 –V
WR	7	
Drink	12-18	

Georges Michel Golden Mile Pinot Noir ★★☆

The easy-drinking 2008 vintage (★★☆), grown at Rapaura, in Marlborough, was oak-aged for nine months. Light ruby, it's a supple, mid-weight style with ripe plum and red-berry flavours, not concentrated, but enjoyable young.

Vintage	09	08	07
WR	6	5	6
Drink	11-16	11-12	11-12

 DRY $26 –V

Georges Michel La Reserve Marlborough Pinot Noir ★★☆

Hand-picked in the Rapaura district and matured for over a year in French oak barriques, the 2007 vintage (★★) is lightish in colour, with a hint of development. Medium-bodied, with cherry, spice and nut flavours, it's a slightly rustic wine, lacking real richness and roundness.

Vintage	08	07	06	05	04
WR	6	5	6	6	6
Drink	11-16	11-15	11-13	11-12	P

 DRY $33 –V

Georges Michel Legend Marlborough Pinot Noir ★★★☆

Grown on stony soils at Rapaura, on the north side of the Wairau Valley, and matured for over a year in new French oak casks, the 2009 vintage (★★★☆) is ruby-hued, with a hint of development. Mouthfilling and sweet-fruited, with good depth of cherry and spice flavours, it's a savoury, complex style with firm tannins. Drink now or cellar.

Vintage	09
WR	6
Drink	11-17

 DRY $45 –V

Georgetown Vineyard Central Otago Pinot Noir ★★★★☆

The supple, richly varietal 2009 vintage (★★★★☆) was grown at the Cromwell end of the Kawarau Gorge, barrel-matured for 11 months, and bottled without fining or filtering. Ruby-hued, it is invitingly scented, with spice and herb aromas. Very finely textured, with strong cherry, spice, herb and olive flavours, it shows excellent complexity, fruit sweetness and length. Drink now onwards.

 DRY $44 AV

Gibbston Highgate Estate Soultaker Pinot Noir ★★★☆

The supple, charming 2009 vintage (★★★☆), grown at Gibbston, in Central Otago, was matured in French oak barriques (25 per cent new), and bottled without filtering. Floral, it is vibrantly fruity, with very good depth of cherry, plum and spice flavours, showing moderate complexity, and lots of youthful vigour. The 2010 (★★★★) is full-coloured, scented and finely poised, with rich cherry, plum and spice flavours. A very elegant, savoury and harmonious wine, it should mature well. (In a vertical tasting of the 2004–2010 vintages, held in mid-2011, the highlights were the sturdy, moderately mature 2006 (★★★★), which shows good complexity; the 2007 (★★★★☆), fragrant and highly concentrated; and the 2010.)

Vintage	10	09
WR	7	6
Drink	12-18	11-15

DRY $30 –V

Gibbston Valley Central Otago Pinot Noir ★★★★☆

The 2009 vintage (★★★★☆) was estate-grown at Bendigo and matured for 11 months in French oak barriques (35 per cent new). It is full-coloured, finely scented and generous, with mouthfilling body and concentrated cherry, plum, spice and nut flavours. Rich and ripe, complex and savoury, it's already delicious, but well worth cellaring. The 2010 (★★★★☆), given less new oak (15 per cent), is full-coloured and vibrantly fruity, with highly concentrated cherry, plum and spice flavours, fresh, rich and supple. Well worth cellaring.

Vintage	10	09	08	07	06	05	04
WR	7	7	7	7	7	6	6
Drink	12-18	11-17	11-14	11-14	11-14	11-13	11-12

DRY $42 AV

Gibbston Valley China Terrace Central Otago Pinot Noir ★★★★★

Estate-grown in Chinaman's Terrace Vineyard, at Bendigo, the 2010 vintage (★★★★★) was matured for 10 months in French oak casks (45 per cent new). From a high-altitude site (350 metres above sea level), it is very finely scented, with lovely red-fruit flavours, woven with fresh acidity, and a nutty, savoury complexity. A notably elegant, sweet-fruited wine, it combines richness and finesse.

Vintage	10	09
WR	7	6
Drink	12-20	11-17

DRY $55 AV

Gibbston Valley Gold River Pinot Noir ★★★☆

This is the Central Otago winery's 'lighter' red, made for 'immediate enjoyment'. The 2010 vintage (★★★☆), a regional blend, barrel-aged for eight months, has loads of fresh, vibrant cherry and plum flavour. Buoyantly fruity, with a subtle seasoning of oak, some substance and gentle tannins, it should be at its best 2012+.

DRY $30 –V

Gibbston Valley Le Maitre Gibbston Pinot Noir ★★★★★

The 2009 vintage (★★★★★) was grown in the home block at Gibbston, where the majority of the vines are over 25 years old. The bouquet is very fragrant, with plum, spice and herb aromas, savoury and complex; the palate is multi-faceted, with sweet-fruit delights and a lovely array of cherry, mushroom and spice flavours, nutty, savoury, supple and long. It's a wine of great individuality.

DRY $75 AV

Gibbston Valley Le Mineur d'Orient The Expressionist Series Pinot Noir ★★★★☆

The 2008 vintage (★★★★☆), estate-grown at Chinaman's Terrace Vineyard, at Bendigo, was matured for 11 months in French oak barriques (100 per cent new). Ruby-hued, it is mouthfilling, with ripe cherry and plum flavours, very harmonious, complex and savoury. The 2009 (★★★★) is fullish in colour, with a hint of development. Mouthfilling, it is savoury, spicy and complex, with hints of herbs and liquorice in a forward style, already delicious.

DRY $50 –V

Gibbston Valley Reserve Pinot Noir ★★★★★

At its best, this Central Otago red is mouthfilling and savoury, with superb concentration of sweet-tasting, plummy fruit and lovely harmony. The grapes have been drawn from various sub-regions and vineyards over the years and yields have been very low (under 5 tonnes/hectare). The wine is typically matured in French oak barriques (50 to 70 per cent new). Grown in the School House Vineyard at Bendigo, and matured for 11 months in French oak barriques (60 per cent new), the 2008 vintage (★★★★☆) is full-coloured, scented and supple, with vibrant cherry, plum and spice flavours, ripe, savoury and concentrated. The 2009 (★★★★★) is bold and youthful in colour, with lush cherry and plum flavours. Finely textured, with advanced fruit sweetness and finely integrated oak, it's a very rich and harmonious, beautiful young wine, with a long future.

Vintage	09	08	07	06
WR	7	7	NM	7
Drink	12-20	12-20	NM	11-16

 DRY $100 –V

Gibbston Valley School House Central Otago Pinot Noir (★★★★☆)

A 'feminine' style, the debut 2009 vintage (★★★★☆) was estate-grown in the late-ripening School House Vineyard, at Bendigo, an extremely elevated site (up to 400 metres above sea level). Matured for 10 months in French oak casks (55 per cent new), it is full-coloured, very fragrant and supple, with an array of plum, spice, herb and nut flavours, woven with fresh acidity. An elegant, finely poised wine, it's still very youthful; open 2012+.

Vintage	10	09
WR	7	7
Drink	12-20	11-17

 DRY $55 –V

Giesen Marlborough Pinot Noir ★★★

The 2009 vintage (★★★☆) is the best yet. Matured for 11 months in French oak casks (10 per cent new), it's a supple, strongly varietal red with fresh, ripe cherry and herb flavours. Medium-bodied, it offers good, easy drinking, with some savoury, toasty complexity.

 DRY $25 –V

Giesen Marlborough The Brothers Pinot Noir ★★★☆

The 2010 vintage (★★★★) was matured for a year in French oak barriques and puncheons (26 per cent new). A graceful wine with obvious potential, it is generous and supple, with sweet-fruit characters and excellent depth of cherryish, nutty flavours, finely textured and harmonious.

DRY $34 –V

Gladstone Vineyard Pinot Noir ★★★★

The 2009 vintage (★★★★☆) was hand-picked in the Wairarapa and matured for 10 months in French oak casks (30 per cent new). Ruby-hued, it is mouthfilling, with strawberry and spice aromas and flavours, fresh and strong, a subtle oak influence and very good complexity. Savoury and supple, it builds well across the palate; drink now or cellar.

 DRY $45 –V

Glasnevin Limited Release Waipara Valley Pinot Noir   ★★★★☆

From Fiddler's Green, the 2009 vintage (★★★★☆) was matured for 18 months in French oak barriques (50 per cent new). Deeply coloured, with a floral, finely scented bouquet, it is still very youthful, with fresh, rich plum and cherry flavours that have lapped up the new oak effortlessly. Vibrantly fruity and supple, it's well worth cellaring; open 2013+.

Vintage	09
WR	6
Drink	11-18

 DRY $43 AV

Glazebrook Hand Picked Gladstone Pinot Noir   ★★★☆

From the Ngatarawa winery, in Hawke's Bay, this wine was formerly labelled 'Regional Reserve' and grown at Te Muna, near Martinborough. The 2009 vintage (★★★★), grown further north in the Wairarapa, at Gladstone, is arguably the best yet. Mouthfilling, warm and savoury, it has cherry and spice flavours, showing excellent concentration and complexity, and good supporting tannins. Best drinking mid-2012+.

Vintage	09	08	07
WR	6	6	NM
Drink	11-15	11-14	NM

DRY $27 AV

Goldridge Estate Marlborough Pinot Noir   ★★☆

The 2009 vintage (★★★) was grown at three sites in the Wairau Valley and barrique-aged. Ruby-hued, it offers decent depth of cherry, plum, herb and spice flavours, showing some savoury complexity. Priced right.

 DRY $19 –V

Goldridge Estate Premium Reserve Marlborough Pinot Noir   ★★★

The 2008 vintage (★★★) was hand-picked in the Wairau Valley and matured in oak barriques (25 per cent new). Light ruby, it's a middleweight style with moderately concentrated, ripe cherry, spice and nut flavours.

 DRY $22 AV

Goldwater Wairau Valley Marlborough Pinot Noir   ★★★☆

The 2010 vintage (★★★★) is a fleshy, generous red, matured for nine months in French oak barriques (30 per cent new). Ruby-hued, with mouthfilling body and excellent depth of ripe cherry and spice flavours, it is a finely balanced, complex, smooth wine, very skilfully crafted for early appeal.

Vintage	10
WR	7
Drink	11-15

 DRY $26 AV

Grass Cove Marlborough Pinot Noir (★★☆)

From an Auckland-based company, the 2008 vintage (★★☆) is lightish and developed, with strawberryish, spicy, leafy flavours that lack real richness but offer pleasant, easy drinking.

DRY $22 –V

Grasshopper Rock Earnscleugh Vineyard Central Otago Pinot Noir ★★★★

Estate-grown in Alexandra, the 2009 vintage (★★★☆) was matured in French oak barrels (30 per cent new). Mouthfilling and full-coloured, with cherry and herb flavours, seasoned with nutty oak, and firm tannins, it shows good concentration, vibrancy and complexity, in a slightly crisper, less ripe style than the 2008 (★★★★★).

Vintage	09	08	07	06
WR	7	7	7	6
Drink	11-18	11-17	11-17	11-14

DRY $30 AV

Greenhough Hope Vineyard Pinot Noir ★★★★★

One of Nelson's greatest reds, at its best powerful, rich and long-lived. It is estate-grown on an elevated terrace of the south-eastern Waimea Plains, where the vines, planted in gravelly loam clays, range up to 29 years old. Yields are very low – 4 to 5 tonnes of grapes per hectare – and the wine is matured for a year in French oak barrels (25 to 50 per cent new). The 2008 vintage (★★★★★) is a lovely wine, deeply coloured, powerful and concentrated. It has deep, ripe flavours of plums and spices, unusually savoury and complex, and the structure to age well.

Vintage	08	07	06	05	04
WR	6	7	6	7	5
Drink	11-15	11-14	11-13	11-13	11-12

DRY $45 AV

Greenhough Nelson Pinot Noir ★★★☆

This wine is handled in a similar way to its Hope Vineyard stablemate (above), but without the contribution of as much new oak or fruit from the oldest vines. It is hand-picked from a range of sites and matured for a year in French oak casks (25 per cent new). Drinking well now, the 2009 vintage (★★★☆), grown at Hope and Upper Moutere, shows good 'pinosity', with cherry/plum flavours, a herbal thread, some savoury complexity and gentle tannins.

Vintage	09	08	07	06	05	04	03
WR	6	6	7	6	5	5	6
Drink	11-15	11-13	11-13	11-12	11-12	P	P

DRY $26 AV

Greylands Ridge Central Otago Pinot Noir ★★★☆

Grown at Alexandra, the 2009 vintage (★★★☆) is a single-vineyard red, matured for 10 months in French oak casks (30 per cent new). Ruby-hued, floral and supple, it is moderately concentrated, with fresh, ripe cherry, spice and herb flavours. It's drinking well now.

Vintage	09	08
WR	7	5
Drink	11-16	11-14

DRY $35 –V

Greystone Waipara Pinot Noir   ★★★☆

The deeply coloured, sturdy 2009 (★★★☆) has highly concentrated cherry/plum flavours and a distinctly herbal streak, in a vibrant, smooth style with some aging potential. The 2010 vintage (★★★★) is the best yet. Matured for 11 months in French oak casks (30 per cent new), it is dark and purple-flushed, with dense, plummy flavours, hints of herbs and spices, and the power and structure to age for several years.

Vintage	10	09	08	07	06
WR	6	7	5	6	5
Drink	11-16	11-17	P	11-12	11-12

 DRY $39 –V

Greywacke Marlborough Pinot Noir   (★★★★)

The debut 2009 vintage (★★★★) from Kevin Judd was grown at elevated sites (mostly the Yarrum Vineyard) on the south side of the Wairau Valley. Hand-picked and fermented with indigenous yeasts, it was matured for over a year in French oak barriques (45 per cent new). Ruby-hued, it is silky-textured and richly varietal, in a 'feminine', gentle style with moderately concentrated, ripe plum, cherry and spice flavours, showing good complexity.

Vintage	09
WR	5
Drink	11-14

 DRY $47 –V

Grove Mill Grand Reserve
Seventeen Valley Vineyard Marlborough Pinot Noir   (★★★★)

Built to last, the 2009 vintage (★★★★) is a single-vineyard red, hand-picked and matured for 10 months in French oak barriques. Vibrantly fruity and full-coloured, with a floral, berryish fragrance, it offers strong cherry, plum and spice flavours, ripe and supple, showing excellent depth and harmony.

 DRY $43 –V

Growers Mark Anderson Marlborough Pinot Noir   (★★★★)

The 2009 vintage (★★★★) is a sturdy red (14.9 per cent alcohol), fragrant and savoury, with sweet-fruit delights, fresh, concentrated cherry, plum and spice flavours, and lots of drink-young charm.

 DRY $26 V+

Hans Herzog Marlborough Pinot Noir   ★★★★★

This powerful wine needs at least a couple of years to reveal its class. The 2008 vintage (★★★★☆) was fermented with indigenous yeasts, matured for a year in French oak puncheons (10 per cent new), and bottled unfined and unfiltered. Full-coloured, it is rich, savoury and complex, with ripe cherry, plum and spice flavours, a hint of dark chocolate, and a firm backbone of tannin. It's a finely scented wine with an almost raisiny richness.

Vintage	08	07
WR	7	7
Drink	11-20	11-19

DRY $49 AV

Harris Estate Waipara Pinot Noir

The 2006 vintage (★★☆) is a light, green-edged wine, now slightly past its best. There is no 2007 or 2008. Already enjoyable, the 2009 (★★★☆) is a significant step up. Full-coloured, it is vibrantly fruity, sweet-fruited and supple, with very good depth of fresh cherry, plum and spice flavours.

DRY $43 –V

Harwood Hall Central Otago Pinot Noir

Drinking well now, the 2009 vintage (★★★☆) was grown at several sites, fermented with indigenous yeasts and matured in French oak barrels for 10 months. It's a full-bodied wine (14.5 per cent alcohol), with generous cherry, herb and spice flavours, showing considerable complexity.

Vintage	09	08
WR	6	5
Drink	12-15	11-13

DRY $25 AV

Hawkdun Rise Central Otago Pinot Noir

This is a single-vineyard, Alexandra red. The ripe-tasting 2008 (★★★★) is deeply coloured and mouthfilling (14.2 per cent alcohol), with generous cherry, plum and spice flavours, and the structure to mature well.

DRY $38 –V

Hawkshead Bannockburn Central Otago Pinot Noir

The deeply coloured 2008 vintage (★★★★) was made for this Gibbston-based producer by Steve Davies, using grapes from his vineyard at Bannockburn. Hand-picked at 24.2 to 25.5 brix, it was fermented with indigenous yeasts, matured in French oak barriques (33 per cent new), and bottled unfined and unfiltered. Mouthfilling, warm and supple, it's a deliciously sweet-fruited wine, packed with cherryish, plummy flavour, showing good complexity.

DRY $48 –V

Hawkshead Central Otago Pinot Noir

The 2008 vintage (★★★☆) is a ruby-hued, regional blend of Lowburn (Cromwell Basin) and Gibbston grapes, matured for 11 months in French oak barrels (40 per cent new). It has moderately rich cherry/plum flavours, hints of herbs and tamarillos, well-integrated oak and a very smooth finish.

DRY $39 –V

Hawkshead First Vines Central Otago Pinot Noir

Grown at Gibbston, this wine is based on the oldest vines. Harvested at 24 brix and matured for 11 months in French oak casks (40 per cent new), the 2008 (★★★☆) is a spicy, vibrant, slightly herbal red, with fresh acidity and very good flavour depth. The 2009 vintage (★★★☆) is ruby-hued, with a slightly earthy, rustic bouquet. The palate is fresh and moderately concentrated, with good drive and complexity, and a silky texture giving drink-young charm.

DRY $45 –V

Hell or Highwater Central Otago Pinot Noir   (★★★)

Grown in the Cromwell Basin, the 2009 vintage (★★★) is enjoyable young. Ruby-hued, it is mouthfilling and smooth, with ripe, berryish fruit flavours, hints of herbs and spices, a touch of complexity and gentle tannins.

 DRY $22 AV

Highfield Marlborough Pinot Noir   ★★★★☆

The 2008 (★★★★★) is a top vintage. Highly scented, with full colour, it is very generous, savoury and sweet-fruited, with deep cherry, plum and spice flavours, seasoned with nutty oak, gentle acidity, and a soft, rich finish. The 2009 vintage (★★★★) is ruby-hued, mouthfilling and savoury, with cherry, plum, herb and spice flavours, showing good complexity and harmony, fairly firm tannins, and a fragrant bouquet. Drink now or cellar.

Vintage	09	08	07	06	05	04
WR	6	5	6	5	7	6
Drink	11-15	11-15	11-14	P	P	P

 DRY $38 V+

Homer Marlborough Pinot Noir   ★★★

From Odyssey, this wine is hand-picked in the Brancott Valley and matured in seasoned oak casks. The 2009 vintage (★★★) is enjoyable young. Mouthfilling, it is ruby-hued, with cherry, plum and slight herb flavours, showing a touch of complexity, gentle tannins and a smooth finish.

Vintage	09	08
WR	5	5
Drink	11-13	11-12

 DRY $20 AV

Hoppers Crossing Central Otago Pinot Noir   ★★★

From an Auckland-based company, the 2010 vintage (★★★) is a youthful, vibrantly fruity wine, with good depth of cherry and plum flavours and a touch of toasty oak. The 2009 (★★★) is similar – ruby-hued and mouthfilling, with moderately concentrated plum/spice flavours and fairly firm tannins. Priced right.

DRY $19 AV

Hudson John Henry Pinot Noir   ★★★

The 2008 vintage (★★★) is a Martinborough red with cherryish, slightly spicy and herbal flavours. It's a middleweight style with good depth, gentle tannins and an attractively perfumed bouquet.

Vintage	08
WR	7
Drink	11-15

 DRY $31 –V

Huia Marlborough Pinot Noir   ★★★★

The very youthful 2010 vintage (★★★★) has dark, purple-flushed colour in a vibrant, fruit-packed style with fresh, deep plum/spice flavours, and a subtle seasoning of oak. Supple and age-worthy, it's best opened 2013+. The 2009 (★★★★) is sturdy and savoury, with very satisfying depth of ripe plum, cherry and spice flavours, seasoned with nutty oak, good tannin support and the potential to mature well.

DRY $36 AV

Hunky Dory Marlborough Pinot Noir   (★★★☆)

From Huia, the 2010 vintage (★★★☆) is a deeply coloured, bold style with strong, ripe cherry, plum and spice flavours, quite nutty and savoury. It's a more complex style than most Pinot Noirs in this price range.

DRY $23 V+

Huntaway Reserve Central Otago Pinot Noir   (★★★☆)

The 2008 vintage (★★★☆) is a single-vineyard red, grown at Bendigo, in the Cromwell Basin. Ruby-hued, it is mouthfilling and sweet-fruited, with strong cherry, herb and spice flavours, gentle tannins, and some savoury complexity. Ready.

DRY $24 V+

Hunter's Marlborough Pinot Noir   ★★★

Typically a supple, charming red. Recent vintages reflect a change in grape source from Rapaura to the more clay-based soils on the south side of the Wairau Valley. The 2009 (★★★) was matured for 10 months in French oak barriques. Ruby-hued, it's a moderately concentrated wine with ripe cherry, plum and spice flavours, fresh acidity, a touch of complexity, and some development showing. Drink 2012.

Vintage	09	08
WR	5	5
Drink	11-13	11-13

DRY $26 –V

Hyperion Eos Pinot Noir   ★★

Estate-grown at Matakana, north of Auckland, and barrel-matured for a year, this is one of New Zealand's northernmost Pinot Noirs. The 2008 vintage (★★) has slightly developed colour. Mouthfilling and smooth, it is spicy, with hints of herbs and raisins, but lacks real ripeness and richness.

Vintage	08	07	06	05
WR	7	5	7	6
Drink	11-14	11-12	P	P

DRY $31 –V

Incognito Pinot Noir   (★★★★)

From Gibbston Highgate, the 2008 vintage (★★★★) was grown at Gibbston, in Central Otago, fermented with indigenous yeasts, matured for 11 months in French oak barrels (30 per cent new), and bottled unfined and unfiltered. Floral and ruby-hued, it's a sweet-fruited, supple wine with much more body and depth than its colour suggests. Delicious young, it has rich plum and cherry flavours, subtle oak and gentle tannins. Slightly savoury, with lots of charm and a persistent finish, it's fragrant and finely textured.

DRY $23 V+

Instinct Marlborough Pinot Noir (★★☆)

From C.J. Pask, the 2008 vintage (★★☆) was hand-picked and French oak-aged for 10 months. It's an easy-drinking wine, light ruby, with fresh strawberry and spice aromas and flavours, and a rounded finish.

DRY $20 –V

Invivo Central Otago Pinot Noir ★★★★

From an Auckland-based company, the 2010 vintage (★★★★☆) was grown at Lowburn, in the Cromwell Basin. Hand-picked, it's an instantly attractive wine, bursting with rich plum, spice and slight liquorice flavours. Very youthful, boldly coloured and sweet-fruited, it should be at its best mid-2012+. The 2009 (★★★☆) was fermented with indigenous yeasts and matured in French oak barriques (35 per cent new). It's a fragrant, supple wine with cherry, spice and herb flavours, savoury and supple, and good personality. It's drinking well now.

Vintage	10	09	08
WR	6	5	5
Drink	12-17	11-15	11-13

DRY $35 AV

Isabel Marlborough Pinot Noir ★★★☆

This multi-site blend, grown partly in the original vineyard near Renwick, also includes fruit from the company's Elevation Vineyard in the Waihopai Valley, 300 metres above sea level. It is matured for 10 to 12 months in French oak barriques (15 to 20 per cent new), and bottled without fining or filtering. The 2008 vintage (★★★) is ruby-hued, with some raisiny notes amid its ripe cherry, plum and spice flavours.

DRY $38 –V

Jack's Canyon Waipara Pinot Noir (★★)

The 2009 vintage (★★) was grown in North Canterbury and matured in an even split of tanks and barrels. Ruby-hued, it's an easy-drinking, slightly rustic quaffer, with moderate flavour depth and a smooth finish.

DRY $17 –V

Jackson Estate Gum Emperor Marlborough Pinot Noir ★★★★★

The 2008 vintage (★★★★★) was estate-grown in the Gum Emperor Vineyard, in the Waihopai Valley. Hand-picked, it was fermented with indigenous yeasts, matured in French oak barriques, and bottled without fining or filtering. Richly coloured, it is ripely scented, mouthfilling and supple, with very deep cherry and plum flavours, and hints of liquorice and nuts. Very generous, sweet-fruited and finely textured, with lovely flow across the palate, it's a drink-now or cellaring proposition.

Vintage	08	07	06	05
WR	7	7	NM	6
Drink	11-20	11-18	NM	11-15

DRY $43 V+

Jackson Estate Vintage Widow Marlborough Pinot Noir ★★★★☆

The quality of Jackson Estate's Pinot Noir has shot up since the 2005 (★★★★), the first to be labelled 'Vintage Widow' – a reference to 'our families, often forgotten at vintage'. The 2009 (★★★★★), hand-picked, fermented with indigenous yeasts, and matured in French oak barriques, is deeply coloured, with a fragrant, complex bouquet. Beautifully rich and sweet-fruited, it has dense cherry, plum and spice flavours and ripe, supple tannins. A powerful, generous wine, with obvious cellaring potential, it's already delicious.

Vintage	10	09	08	07	06	05	04
WR	7	6	5	6	5	6	5
Drink	12-25	11-20	11-15	11-18	11-12	P	P

DRY $35 V+

Johanneshof Maybern Single Vineyard Reserve Marlborough Pinot Noir (★★☆)

Estate-grown on a steep, north-facing slope at Koromiko, between Picton and Blenheim – cool and wet by Marlborough standards – the 2008 vintage (★★☆) was matured for 18 months in French oak casks (30 per cent new). Light and slightly developed in colour, it has vibrant strawberry, spice and herb flavours, woven with crisp acidity, and some savoury complexity. Don't expect a fruit bomb.

DRY $36 –V

John Forrest Collection Bannockburn Central Otago Pinot Noir ★★★★

The 2009 vintage (★★★★), estate-grown, is deeply coloured, with rich cherry, plum and spice flavours. It's a very elegant, fresh and youthful wine, with obvious potential.

DRY $60 –V

Johner Estate Gladstone Pinot Noir ★★★

Grown in the northern Wairarapa, and French oak-aged for a year (20 per cent new), the 2009 vintage (★★☆) is a drink-young style, ruby-hued, with cherry and spice flavours, a distinct herbal thread, and some savoury complexity.

Vintage	09	08
WR	6	5
Drink	14-17	13-15

DRY $34 –V

Johner Estate Gladstone Reserve Pinot Noir ★★★★

The 2009 vintage (★★★★) is a single-vineyard Wairarapa red, French oak-aged (30 per cent new). Full-coloured, with a hint of development, it is mouthfilling, with strong cherry, spice and herb flavours, showing good complexity, and a soft, well-rounded finish. Drink now onwards.

Vintage	09
WR	6
Drink	11-20

DRY $50 –V

Johner Estate Moonlight Pinot Noir ★★☆

The 2009 vintage (★★★) is a lightly oaked style, grown in the Wairarapa. Full-bodied and savoury, it has a slightly leafy bouquet, but also plenty of flavour and some complexity. Best drinking 2011.

Vintage	09
WR	4
Drink	P

 DRY $22 –V

John Forrest Collection Waitaki Valley North Otago Pinot Noir ★★★★☆

Only 1400 bottles were produced of the 2009 vintage (★★★★★). Deep and youthful in colour, it is beautifully scented, with highly concentrated, youthful plum and spice flavours, showing excellent complexity.

 DRY $75 –V

Judge Rock Central Otago Pinot Noir ★★★★

This single-vineyard red is grown at Alexandra. The 2009 vintage (★★★☆) is a scented, supple wine with cherry, plum, spice and herb flavours, showing some complexity. The deep ruby 2010 (★★★★), harvested at over 25 brix and matured in French oak casks (one-third new), is poised and elegant, with good intensity of plum, spice and nutty oak flavours, savoury and complex, fresh acidity and the structure to age.

Vintage	09	08	07	06	05
WR	5	6	6	6	6
Drink	11-15	11-15	11-14	11-13	11-12

 DRY $39 AV

Judge Rock Venus Central Otago Pinot Noir ★★★☆

The 2008 vintage (★★★☆) from this Alexandra producer is a floral, single-vineyard wine with cherry, spice and herb flavours, showing some complexity, elegance and charm. The 2009 (★★★) is ruby-hued, juicy and spicy, with moderately ripe flavours and firm tannins.

Vintage	.09	08	07
WR	5	6	6
Drink	11-12	11-12	P

 DRY $25 AV

Jules Taylor Marlborough Pinot Noir (★★★★)

Floral and full of charm, the 2010 vintage (★★★★) was hand-harvested in the Awatere and Brancott valleys. Ruby-hued and finely scented, with gentle tannins, it has a subtle seasoning of oak and generous, vibrant cherry and plum flavours.

DRY $30 AV

Julicher 99 Rows Martinborough Pinot Noir   ★★★★☆

The 2009 vintage (★★★★☆) is a typically great buy. Estate-grown at Te Muna, it was hand-picked at 23 to 26 brix and matured for 10 months in French oak casks (20 per cent new). A robust wine (14.5 per cent alcohol), it is very generous, warm and savoury, with deep cherry, plum and spice flavours and ripe, supple tannins. Showing good complexity, it's already delicious.

Julicher Martinborough Pinot Noir   ★★★★☆

Estate-grown at Te Muna, the 2008 (★★★★★) was hand-picked at 23 to 24 brix and matured for 11 months in French oak casks (20 per cent new). Rich and savoury, it has lovely concentration and flow, with brambly, spicy flavours, a hint of herbs, and notable ripeness, depth and complexity. Already drinking well, the 2009 vintage (★★★★☆) is full-coloured, fleshy and rich, in a robust style (14.8 per cent alcohol), very ripe, spicy and savoury.

Vintage	09	08	07	06	05
WR	6	7	6	7	6
Drink	11-15	11-16	11-14	11-13	11-13

Jumper, The, Marlborough Pinot Noir   ★★☆

From Spring Creek Estate, the 2008 vintage (★★★) was matured for a year in seasoned French oak barriques. Medium-bodied, it's a slightly rustic wine, but shows some flavour depth and complexity. Priced right.

Junction Body and Soul Pinot Noir   (★★★★☆)

Grown on the Takapau Plains, Central Hawke's Bay, and matured in all-new French oak casks, the finely poised 2010 vintage (★★★★☆) is boldly coloured, youthful and fragrant. Still a baby, it shows excellent richness, texture and complexity, with vibrant cherry and plum flavours, slightly herbal and nutty, fresh acidity, ripe, supple tannins, and a long finish. Best drinking 2013+.

Junction Possession Pinot Noir   (★★★☆)

The deeply coloured 2010 vintage (★★★☆) was grown on the Takapau Plains of Central Hawke's Bay. Rich and supple, it is vibrantly fruity, with strong, cherryish, distinctly herbal flavours, woven with fresh acidity. It's a very youthful wine; drink 2013+.

Kaikoura Kaikoura-Marlborough Pinot Noir   (★★☆)

Hand-picked at Kaikoura, the 2009 vintage (★★☆) was matured for eight months in seasoned French oak barriques. Light in colour and body, it is smooth, with gentle strawberry and spice flavours. A pleasant, drink-young style.

DRY $25 –V

Kaimira Estate Brightwater Vintner's Selection Pinot Noir   ★★★

Is a vintner a wine merchant or a winemaker? Setting that aside, the 2009 vintage (★★★) was grown in Nelson and matured for 10 months in French oak barriques (17 per cent new). Ruby-hued, it is drinking well now, with cherry, plum and herb flavours, and a smooth finish.

Vintage	09
WR	6
Drink	11-16

 DRY $29 –V

Kaituna Valley Canterbury The Kaituna Vineyard Pinot Noir   ★★★★★

This arresting Canterbury red flows from a warm and sheltered site on Banks Peninsula, south of Christchurch. Of the total area of Pinot Noir vines, a third was planted between 1977 and 1979; the rest was established in 1997. The wine is matured for over a year in Burgundy oak casks (50 to 70 per cent new). The 2007 vintage (★★★★★) is classy. Deeply coloured, with a ripely scented, slightly peppery bouquet, it has sweet-fruit delights and striking depth of cherry, plum, spice and nut flavours, rich and supple.

DRY $45 AV

Kalex Wines Central Otago Pinot Noir   (★★★)

The 2009 vintage (★★★) was matured in French oak casks (75 per cent new). Full and bright in colour, it lacks fragrance, but is mouthfilling, sweet-fruited and supple, with cherry, plum and spice flavours, showing good depth.

Vintage	09
WR	7
Drink	12-17

DRY $35 –V

Karikari Estate Calypso Martinborough Pinot Noir   (★★★)

The 2009 vintage (★★★) is from 'a small vineyard with a long history of producing some of the finest New Zealand Pinots'. Harvested at 24.2 to 25.6 brix and French oak-aged for a year, it has slightly developed colour. Silky and savoury, but with some tamarillo and herb notes, it shows a lack of full ripeness, but considerable complexity, and is drinking well now.

DRY $24 AV

Kate Radburnd Vine Velvet Wairarapa Pinot Noir   (★★☆)

From C.J. Pask, the 2009 vintage (★★☆) is light in colour and flavour, with cherry and herb characters, offering pleasant, easy drinking.

DRY $17 AV

Kawarau Estate Central Otago Pinot Noir

Estate-grown organically at Lowburn, the 2008 vintage (★★) was hand-picked and matured for 10 months in French oak barriques (mostly seasoned). Ruby-hued, it offers light plum and herb flavours. The 2009 vintage (★★) is similar – ruby-hued, with fruity, crisp berry, spice and herb flavours, lacking richness and roundness.

DRY $30 –V

Kawarau Estate Reserve Pinot Noir

Grown organically at Pisa Flats, in Central Otago, at its best this is a classy, powerful and complex wine. The 2008 vintage (★★★☆) is ruby-hued, mouthfilling, vibrant and supple, with cherry and spice flavours, showing moderate concentration and good complexity.

Vintage	08	07	06	05
WR	6	7	7	5
Drink	11-14	11-13	11-12	P

DRY $43 –V

Kemp Road Marlborough Pinot Noir   (★★★★)

Drinking well now, the 2007 vintage (★★★★) from wine distributor Kemp Rare Wines is very savoury, with rich cherry and spice flavours, ripe and rounded.

DRY $30 AV

Kennedy Point Marlborough Pinot Noir   (★★★☆)

From a Waiheke Island-based producer, the 2008 vintage (★★★☆) was fermented with indigenous yeasts and matured in French oak for 16 months. It's a supple, fruity wine with ripe plum and spice flavours, showing good varietal character, and some savoury complexity.

DRY $35 –V

Kerner Estate Marlborough Pinot Noir

Already past its best, the disappointing 2009 vintage (★★) has lightish, developed colour and green-edged, fading flavours.

Vintage	09
WR	5
Drink	11-13

DRY $20 –V

Kim Crawford Marlborough Pinot Noir

The 2008 vintage (★★☆), aged in tanks and barrels, is a pleasant, easy-drinking red, but lacks the richness you'd expect at its price.

DRY $23 –V

Kina Beach Vineyard Reserve Pinot Noir

Estate-grown at Tasman, on the Nelson coast, the 2008 vintage (★★★☆) was matured for 14 months in French oak barriques (a third new). Still youthful, it is brightly coloured, warm and spicy, with ripe cherry, plum and spice flavours, a slightly earthy streak, and firm tannins.

DRY $45 –V

Kina Cliffs Nelson Pinot Noir (★★☆)

Estate-grown overlooking Ruby Bay, the 2009 vintage (★★☆) was hand-harvested and French oak-aged for 11 months. Ruby-hued, with a hint of development, it is cherryish, savoury and green-edged, with a distinct herbal thread, but full-bodied, clearly varietal and smooth. Drink young.

Vintage	09
WR	6
Drink	11-16

DRY $30 –V

Kina Cliffs Reserve Nelson Pinot Noir (★★★☆)

Grown near the Kina Peninsula, the 2009 vintage (★★★☆) was hand-picked at over 24 brix from very low-cropping vines (2 tonnes/hectare), and matured for 11 months in French oak casks. Mouthfilling, generous, savoury and supple, with very good flavour depth, spicy and slightly herbal, it's a moderately ripe-tasting wine with strong personality, offering good drinking from now onwards.

Vintage	09
WR	7
Drink	11-19

DRY $45 –V

Kingsmill Tippet's Dam Central Otago Pinot Noir ★★★★☆

A single-vineyard Bannockburn red, the 2008 vintage (★★★★) is less compelling than the finely scented and flowing 2007 (★★★★★), but still rewarding. Ruby-hued, with a complex bouquet, it is mouthfilling and savoury, with strong cherry, plum, spice and nut flavours and ripe, supple tannins. Drink now or cellar.

Vintage	08	07	06
WR	5	6	5
Drink	11-14	11-14	11-12

DRY $45 –V

Konrad Marlborough Pinot Noir ★★★

The 2009 vintage (★★★☆) was estate-grown in the Waihopai Valley and at Foxes Island, in the Wairau Valley. Barrel-aged for 10 months, it is floral and mouthfilling, in a sturdy, sweet-fruited style with ripe plum and spice flavours, showing some savoury complexity.

Vintage	09	08	07
WR	6	4	4
Drink	11-15	11-14	P

DRY $29 –V

Koru Pinot Noir ★★★★☆

(The Koru brand was purchased recently by Kemp Rare Wines.) This rare, distinguished wine has flowed from a tiny vineyard at the foot of the Wither Hills, Marlborough. The intensely varietal 2007 vintage (★★★★★) was French oak-matured and bottled unfined and unfiltered. Retasted in 2011, it is full-coloured, with lots of fungal complexity on the nose and palate, in a sweet-fruited, generous style, with heaps of character. Ready.

Vintage	07	06	05	04
WR	7	7	7	6
Drink	11-22	11-20	11-18	11-15

 DRY $78 –V

Koura Bay Whalesback Marlborough Pinot Noir (★★☆)

The 2009 vintage (★★☆) was grown in the Awatere and Wairau valleys. Light ruby, it is showing considerable development, with cherry and herb flavours, light and smooth.

 DRY $19 –V

Kumeu River Estate Pinot Noir ★★★☆

This West Auckland red is different to the floral, buoyant reds grown in the south – less overtly varietal, more savoury and 'red-winey'. The 2008 vintage (★★★☆) is lightish in colour, with earthy, 'forest floor' aromas. Mouthfilling and supple, it is cherryish, slightly spicy, earthy and nutty, with a smooth finish. It's enjoyable now.

Vintage	09	08	07	06	05
WR	7	6	7	7	5
Drink	11-16	11-15	11-15	11-13	P

 DRY $36 –V

Kumeu River Village Pinot Noir ★★★

Estate-grown at Kumeu, in West Auckland, the 2009 vintage (★★★) is bright ruby, fresh, plummy and spicy, in a medium-bodied style, slightly savoury and earthy, with firm tannins. Drink now.

 DRY $18 V+

Kurow Village Waitaki Valley Reserve Pinot Noir (★★★)

Grown in North Otago, the 2009 vintage (★★★) is full-coloured, with strong plum and herb aromas and flavours. It's an easy-drinking wine, generous and supple.

 DRY $39 –V

Lake Chalice Marlborough Pinot Noir ★★★☆

The 2009 vintage is a good buy. Mouthfilling and savoury, with youthful cherry and spice flavours, warm and complex, it is weighty and firm, with good concentration and length.

DRY $25 AV

Lake Hayes Central Otago Pinot Noir   ★★★★

From Amisfield, the 2010 vintage (★★★★) was matured in French oak casks (30 per cent new). Boldly coloured, it is rich and supple, with loads of cherryish, plummy flavour, hints of herbs and spices, and a fresh, well-rounded finish. It's drinking well from the start.

Vintage	10	09	08	07	06
WR	7	6	6	6	6
Drink	11-14	11-13	11-12	P	P

DRY $30 AV

Latitude 41 New Zealand Pinot Noir   ★★☆

From Spencer Hill, the 2008 vintage (★★☆) is a blend of Marlborough and Nelson grapes, fermented with indigenous yeasts and aged 'on' oak (meaning not barrel-aged). Light and slightly developed in colour, it has cherry, spice and slight herb flavours, with a touch of complexity and firm tannins, but leafy notes detract.

 DRY $21 –V

Lawson's Dry Hills Marlborough Pinot Noir   ★★★☆

The 2008 vintage (★★★) was hand-picked in the Potez Vineyard, overlooking the Brancott Valley, and matured for nine months in French oak barriques (25 per cent new). Ruby-hued, it has moderately concentrated cherry, plum and spice flavours, seasoned with nutty oak, a hint of herbs, and firm tannins.

Vintage	08	07	06
WR	6	7	5
Drink	11-12	11-12	P

DRY $27 AV

Leaning Rock Central Otago Pinot Noir   ★★★☆

Estate-grown at Alexandra, the 2008 vintage (★★★☆) is full-bodied and sweet-fruited, with plummy, spicy flavours, showing some savoury, nutty complexity, and fairly firm tannins. Drink 2012.

DRY $35 –V

Lil Rippa Central Otago Bannockburn Pinot Noir   (★★★☆)

From a Blenheim-based producer, the 2009 vintage (★★★☆) is ruby-hued, mouthfilling, ripe and supple, with generous plum and cherry flavours, fresh and lively. A fleshy, sweet-fruited wine with easy tannins, it's a drink-young charmer.

DRY $25 AV

Lime Rock Central Hawke's Bay Pinot Noir   ★★★☆

Grown near Waipawa, hand-picked and barrel-aged, the 2009 (★★★☆) is mouthfilling (14.5 per cent alcohol) and fleshy, with cherryish, plummy, herbal flavours, showing good depth and roundness. It's a forward vintage, enjoyable now.

 DRY $29 AV

Limestone Creek Waipara Pinot Noir   (★★☆)

From Greystone, the 2009 vintage (★★☆) is ruby-hued, full-flavoured and smooth, but green-edged and leafy.

DRY $20 –V

Lobster Reef Marlborough Pinot Noir   (★★★)

The 2009 vintage (★★★) is a medium-bodied style, light ruby, with smooth, ripe cherry and plum flavours, showing decent depth, and a touch of savoury, spicy complexity. Drink young.

DRY $19 AV

Locharburn Central Otago Pinot Noir   ★★★☆

Hand-picked in the Cromwell Basin and matured in French oak casks, the 2009 vintage (★★★) is full-coloured, with moderately ripe cherry, plum and herb flavours, showing good density.

Vintage	09	08	07	06
WR	6	5	6	5
Drink	11-17	11-13	11-13	11-12

DRY $35 –V

Loopline Pinot Noir   ★★★

Grown at Opaki, near Masterton, in the northern Wairarapa, the 2008 vintage (★★★☆) is fragrant, with good colour depth and fresh cherry, spice and plum flavours, showing good complexity.

DRY $26 –V

Lowburn Ferry Central Otago Pinot Noir   ★★★★

Estate-grown at Lowburn, in the Cromwell Basin, the 2008 vintage (★★★★) was matured for 10 months in French oak barriques (20 per cent new). Full-flavoured and firmly structured, it is deeply coloured, with rich, ripe, cherryish fruit flavours and a spicy, savoury complexity.

Vintage	08	07	06	05
WR	7	6	5	6
Drink	11-14	11-14	11-12	P

DRY $41 –V

Lowburn Ferry Reserve The Ferryman Pinot Noir   (★★★★★)

Estate-grown at Lowburn, in Central Otago, this is the producer's flagship red, made only in top vintages. Hand-harvested at over 25 brix from low-cropped vines, and matured for nine months in French oak barriques (25 per cent new), the debut 2010 (★★★★★) is deeply coloured, fragrant and supple, in a very elegant, 'feminine' style with beautifully poised cherry, plum, spice and nut flavours, graceful, savoury and silky-textured. A stylish wine, it's full of potential.

Vintage	10
WR	7
Drink	13-17

DRY $79 AV

Lowburn Ferry Single Vineyard Home Block Pinot Noir ★★★★☆

The 2010 vintage (★★★★★) is a highly concentrated, single-vineyard red, hand-picked at Lowburn, in Central Otago, and matured for nine months in French oak casks (30 per cent new). Deeply coloured, it is fleshy, ripe and supple, with intense plum, cherry and slight liquorice flavours and a lovely, silky texture.

Vintage	10	09
WR	6	7
Drink	12-16	12-17

DRY $48 –V

Lowburn Ferry Skeleton Creek Central Otago Pinot Noir (★★★★☆)

The 2009 vintage (★★★★☆) is not estate-grown, but made from Lowburn grapes harvested at 25 brix. Matured for 10 months in French oak barriques (30 per cent new), it is deeply coloured, rich and sweet-fruited, warm and savoury, with strong cherry, plum and spice flavours, showing good complexity, and the structure to mature well.

Vintage	09
WR	5
Drink	12-16

DRY $35 V+

Lynfer Estate Wairarapa Pinot Noir (★★☆)

Grown at Gladstone, the 2009 vintage (★★☆) is a single-vineyard red, hand-picked and matured in seasoned barrels. Ruby-hued, it is smooth, with fresh, simple berry/plum flavours in a pleasant, drink-young style.

DRY $23 –V

MacKenzie's Pardon Free Flow Pinot Noir (★★☆)

Grown in Waipara, the 2008 vintage (★★☆) is a light style, with moderate depth of spicy, slightly leafy flavour. Ready.

DRY $21 –V

Mahi Marlborough Pinot Noir (★★★★)

Savoury and complex, rather than 'fruity', the 2010 vintage (★★★★) is a multi-site blend, hand-harvested, fermented with indigenous yeasts, and matured for 11 months in French oak casks. Full ruby, it is sweet-fruited, with strong cherry, plum, spice and nut flavours, earthy, mushroomy notes, substantial body and good tannin backbone. It's worth cellaring; open 2013+.

Vintage	10
WR	6
Drink	11-16

DRY $30 AV

Mahi Rive Vineyard Marlborough Pinot Noir ★★★★

The 2008 vintage (★★★★) was hand-picked at a relatively warm site at Rapaura, fermented with indigenous yeasts, barrel-aged for 15 months, and bottled unfiltered. Deeply coloured, it is slightly less rich than the highly concentrated 2007 (★★★★☆), but shows good complexity and texture, with mouthfilling body and strong, ripe cherry/plum flavours, smooth and savoury.

Vintage	08	07
WR	6	6
Drink	11-17	11-16

 DRY $45 –V

Main Divide Canterbury Pinot Noir ★★★★

A consistently rewarding, drink-young style from Pegasus Bay. The 2009 vintage (★★★★) was fermented with indigenous yeasts and matured for 18 months in French oak barriques (15 per cent new). Delicious now, it is a top buy, with loads of body, colour and flavour. Mouthfilling and supple, it is generous and fruit-packed, with cherry, plum, herb and nut flavours, fresh and strong.

Vintage	09	08	07	06	05	04
WR	7	7	6	7	7	7
Drink	11-17	11-13	11-12	11-12	P	P

 DRY $25 V+

Main Divide Tehau Reserve Waipara Valley Pinot Noir ★★★★☆

From Pegasus Bay, the 2008 vintage (★★★★) was matured for 18 months in French oak barriques (30 per cent new). A floral, deeply coloured red, it is sturdy, generous and sweet-fruited, with ripe cherry, plum and spice flavours, slightly nutty and savoury, and good complexity.

Vintage	08	07	06
WR	7	6	5
Drink	11-15	11-15	11-13

 DRY $33 V+

Main Divide Tipinui Selection Marlborough Pinot Noir ★★★★

From Pegasus Bay, the 2008 vintage (★★★★☆) was grown on clay slopes in the Brancott Valley, hand-picked, and matured for 18 months in French oak barriques (30 per cent new). A fleshy, big-bodied red, it is fragrant and full-coloured, with generous, ripe cherry and plum flavours, a spicy, nutty complexity and lots of personality. The 2009 (★★★☆) was matured for 18 months in old French oak barriques. Deeply coloured, it is generous and supple, with fresh, youthful plum, herb and nut flavours and a rounded finish. Verging on four stars.

Vintage	09	08	07	06
WR	7	7	6	7
Drink	12-15	11-16	11-15	11-13

DRY $33 AV

Ma Maison Martinborough Pinot Noir   ★★★★☆

This rare wine from Leung Estate is based on close-planted, low-cropped vines planted in 1995. The 2008 vintage (★★★★★) is outstanding. Deep in colour, it is very rich and sweet-fruited, with a wealth of plum, spice and nut flavours. Sturdy and finely textured, it's well worth cellaring. The 2009 (★★★★) is a forward vintage, with strong, plummy, spicy flavours in a complex, savoury style with gentle tannins and good harmony. It's drinking well now.

DRY $35 V+

Ma Maison Martinborough Pinot Noir Cuvée Sabrina   (★★★★☆)

Made from clone 5 Pinot Noir, matured in seasoned French oak barriques, and bottled unfined and unfiltered, the 2007 vintage (★★★★☆) is deeply coloured and fragrant, with very rich, vibrant cherry, plum, herb and slight liquorice flavours, threaded with fresh acidity. It's a classy, very graceful wine, lovely now.

DRY $70 –V

Ma Maison Martinborough Pinot Noir Cuvée Saffron   (★★★★)

Based on the 10/5 clone, the 2007 vintage (★★★★) was matured for 11 months in French oak barriques of mixed ages, and bottled without fining or filtering. It's a concentrated, supple wine, deep in colour, with plum and slight herb flavours, showing good complexity.

DRY $70 –V

Manu Marlborough Pinot Noir   ★★★

From Steve Bird, the 2009 vintage (★★★) was hand-picked on the south side of the Wairau Valley, fermented with indigenous yeasts, and barrel-aged for 10 months. Ruby-hued, floral and supple, with vibrant cherry/plum flavours, hints of herbs and spices, and a light oak seasoning, it's a drink-young charmer.

Vintage	09	08
WR	6	4
Drink	11-14	11-12

DRY $25 –V

Maori Point Central Otago Pinot Noir   ★★★★

This single-vineyard wine is grown at Tarras, north of Lake Dunstan. The 2008 vintage (★★★★) was fermented with indigenous yeasts and matured for 10 months in French oak barriques (33 per cent new). Maturing well, it is floral, with concentrated, cherryish, spicy flavours and a well-rounded finish. It's a finely textured wine, with some barnyard notes adding complexity. The 2010 (★★★★) is savoury, earthy and full-coloured, with good density of cherry, plum and spice flavours and a firm backbone of tannin.

Vintage	10	09	08
WR	7	6	6
Drink	12-20	11-15	11-14

DRY $30 AV

Map Maker Marlborough Pinot Noir   (★★★)

From Staete Landt, the 2009 vintage (★★★) was hand-harvested at Rapaura and matured in French oak barriques (15 per cent new). An easy-drinking style, light ruby, it is rounded and ready, with ripe, cherryish flavours, showing some savoury, nutty complexity.

DRY $29 –V

Marble Point Hanmer Springs Pinot Noir   ★★★★

From a high-altitude site in North Canterbury, the 2009 (★★★★) was matured in French oak casks (25 per cent new). Showing good richness and stuffing, it is youthful and full-coloured, with very ripe flavours of plums, cherries, spices and liquorice, oak complexity, and a firm backbone of tannin. Well worth cellaring, the 2010 vintage (★★★★) is deeply coloured and mouthfilling, with strong plum and spice flavours, hints of liquorice and nuts, and good complexity. Fine value.

Vintage	10	09	08
WR	6	6	6
Drink	12-17	12-16	11-13

DRY 25 V+

Margrain Home Block Martinborough Pinot Noir   ★★★★

Typically an impressive red, based on 'vines from our original plantings which surround the winery'. Matured for 10 months in French oak barriques, the 2009 vintage (★★★★) is ruby-hued, with fresh cherry, plum, herb and spice aromas. An intensely varietal wine with good complexity, it builds across the palate to a strong, sweet-fruited, well-rounded finish.

Vintage	08	07	06	05	04
WR	6	7	7	7	7
Drink	11-16	11-17	11-15	11-14	11-12

DRY $52 –V

Margrain River's Edge Martinborough Pinot Noir   ★★★

Designed for early drinking, this wine is 'barrel selected for its smoothness and charm'. The 2009 vintage (★★☆) is ruby-hued, with cherry, spice and herb flavours, showing moderate ripeness and depth. Ready.

Vintage	09	08
WR	6	5
Drink	11-14	11-13

DRY $28 –V

Martinborough Vineyard 30th Anniversary Pinot Noir   (★★★★)

Celebrating 30 years since the first vines were planted, the 2005 vintage (★★★★) is a rare wine – only 756 bottles were produced. Based on old clone 5 and clone 10/5 vines, it shows considerable development, in a very savoury, herbal, nutty style. It's a rich, complex wine, probably at its best now.

DRY $100 –V

Martinborough Vineyard Marie Zelie Reserve Pinot Noir ★★★★★

Only 984 bottles exist of the hedonistic 2006 vintage (★★★★★), the first since the arrestingly rich 2003 (★★★★★). From vines up to 26 years old (in 2006), it is a selection of the four best barrels, which were blended in January 2007, returned to older oak casks for a further eight months' aging, and bottled unfined and unfiltered. A very powerful wine, it is also full of charm, with deep colour and great ripeness and richness. Notably concentrated, with an array of plum, strawberry, liquorice and nut flavours, it is silky-textured, inviting current drinking, but still fresh and lively, with obvious potential. (The next vintage of Marie Zelie is 2008.)

Martinborough Vineyard Pinot Noir ★★★★★

This was the first consistently distinguished Pinot Noir made in New Zealand. An intensely varietal wine, it is typically fragrant, with sweet-tasting fruit and cherryish, spicy, complex flavours. In the past, it impressed principally with fragrance and finesse, rather than sheer scale, but in recent years the wine has become markedly bolder. Grown on the shingly Martinborough Terrace, it is made from vines ranging from young to over 30 years old, fermented with indigenous yeasts, matured in French oak barriques (33 per cent new), and bottled unfined and unfiltered. Already quite open and expressive, the 2008 (★★★★) is a fragrant, concentrated wine with cherry and spice flavours, some herb and olive notes, and a savoury, 'forest floor' complexity. The 2009 (★★★★) is full-coloured, with spice and dried-herb flavours showing sweet fruit and good, savoury complexity. It impresses as a 'forward' vintage, already drinking well.

Vintage	09	08	07	06	05	04	03
WR	5	6	7	7	7	6	7
Drink	11-17	11-19	11-18	11-17	11-15	11-12	P

Martinborough Vineyard Te Tera Pinot Noir ★★★★

Te Tera ('the other') is made for earlier drinking than its famous big brother. Based on 'predominantly younger' vines on the Martinborough Terrace, it is hand-harvested, fermented with indigenous yeasts and matured for eight months in French oak casks (5 per cent new in 2010). The full-coloured 2010 vintage (★★★★) is very graceful and supple, with cherry, plum and dried-herb flavours, showing good complexity and harmony. Already highly approachable, it's a top drink-young style.

Vintage	10	09	08	07	06
WR	7	7	7	7	7
Drink	11-14	11-13	11-12	P	P

Martinus Estate Martinborough Pinot Noir ★★★★☆

The 2007 (★★★★), released in 2010, was matured for 11 months in French oak casks (25 per cent new). Deeply coloured, it is full-bodied and concentrated, with cherry, herb and spice flavours, showing good, savoury complexity. The 2008 vintage (★★★★☆) is mouthfilling and sweet-fruited, with deep colour and cherry, plum and spice flavours, showing excellent complexity and richness.

DRY $40 AV

Matahiwi Estate Holly Wairarapa Pinot Noir ★★★★

The 2009 vintage (★★★★) was grown in the northern Wairarapa and matured in French oak casks (35 per cent new). A generous, full-coloured red, it is deep and sweet-fruited, with plum and spice flavours, savoury and complex.

Vintage	09	08
WR	6	6
Drink	11-15	11-13

Matahiwi Estate Wairarapa Pinot Noir ★★★☆

The 2009 vintage (★★★☆) is a fresh, lively wine, matured in a mix of tanks and barrels. Ruby-hued, it is mouthfilling and supple, with good depth of cherry, herb and spice flavours and some savoury notes adding complexity. Drink now or cellar.

Vintage	09
WR	5
Drink	11-13

Matakana Estate Marlborough Pinot Noir ★★★☆

The 2009 vintage (★★★☆) was matured for 10 months in mostly French oak barriques (one-third new). A mouthfilling, ruby-hued, moderately concentrated wine, it's already drinking well, with ripe cherry, plum and spice flavours, savoury and supple.

Matua Valley Marlborough Pinot Noir ★★★

The 2009 vintage (★★★) is ruby-hued, floral and sweet-fruited, with fresh, vibrant cherry and plum flavours, showing good depth, gentle tannins, and lots of drink-young charm.

DRY $19 AV

Matua Valley Reserve Release Central Otago Pinot Noir ★★★

The 2010 vintage (★★★) is ruby-hued, scented, fruity and smooth, in a very easy-drinking style with some substance. Cherryish and plummy, with hints of herbs and spices, it's ready to roll.

DRY $22 AV

Maude Central Otago Pinot Noir ★★★★

The 2009 vintage (★★★★☆) is a blend of grapes from four sub-regions, matured for a year in French oak casks (35 per cent new). Delicious from the start, it is full-coloured, floral and supple, with concentrated plum and spice flavours, sweet-fruited and finely textured. A savoury, very harmonious wine with a silky charm, it's a drink-now or cellaring proposition.

Vintage	09	08	07	06
WR	6	5	6	5
Drink	11-16	11-14	11-16	11-15

Maude Mount Maude Vineyard Reserve Pinot Noir   ★★★★☆

Developing well, the 2007 (★★★★☆) was estate-grown at Wanaka. Dark, with plum and spice flavours, it shows excellent density. A 'serious', savoury, tightly structured wine, starting to round out, it's revealing impressive complexity with bottle-age and drinking well now. The 2009 vintage (★★★★☆), from vines planted in 1994, was matured for 18 months in French oak casks (50 per cent new). Bold and youthful in colour, it has deep, vibrant plum and spice flavours, woven with fresh acidity, and firm tannins. A powerful young wine, it's built for the long haul; open 2013+.

Vintage	09	08	07
WR	6	NM	6
Drink	13-18	11-16	11-16

DRY $49 –V

Maven Marlborough Pinot Noir   ★★★

The 2008 vintage (★★☆) was grown at Rapaura and in the Wairau's southern valleys. Lightish in colour, with a hint of development, it's an easy-drinking style with solid depth of cherry and spice flavours and gentle tannins. Ready.

DRY $24 AV

Michelle Richardson Central Otago Pinot Noir   ★★★★☆

The 2009 vintage (★★★★☆) was grown at sites in the Cromwell Basin, fermented with indigenous yeasts, matured for 16 months in French oak barriques, and bottled unfined and unfiltered. Full-coloured, fresh and vibrant, it's a youthful wine, highly scented and savoury, with concentrated, cherryish, plummy flavours, slightly herbal and spicy, and excellent complexity and length. Already delicious, it's well worth cellaring.

DRY $45 –V

Millton Clos de Ste Anne Naboth's Vineyard Pinot Noir –
see Clos de Ste Anne Naboth's Vineyard Pinot Noir

Misha's Vineyard The High Note Central Otago Pinot Noir   ★★★★

(The first 2007 vintage was labelled 'The Audition'.) Estate-grown at Bendigo, the 2009 vintage (★★★★) was hand-picked at 23.5 to 24.8 brix, fermented with indigenous yeasts and matured in French oak hogsheads (27 per cent new). It's a very elegant and supple wine, floral and ruby-hued, with strong, ripe cherry, herb and spice flavours, showing good complexity. Drink now or cellar.

Vintage	09	08	07
WR	7	6	7
Drink	11-17	11-16	11-15

DRY $45 –V

Misha's Vineyard Verismo Central Otago Pinot Noir   (★★★★☆)

The finely poised 2008 vintage (★★★★☆) was estate-grown at Bendigo and matured for 15 months in French oak hogsheads (62 per cent new). Ruby-hued, it is vibrantly fruity, plummy and savoury, very sweet-fruited and supple, in a notably elegant style, worth cellaring to 2012+.

Vintage	08
WR	6
Drink	11-16

DRY $60 –V

Mission Reserve Central Otago Pinot Noir   ★★★☆

The 2009 vintage (★★★☆) was hand-picked at Pisa, in the Cromwell Basin, and matured in French oak barrels. It's a scented, youthful, firmly structured wine, with fresh plum, herb and spice flavours, showing good complexity. Open mid-2012+.

Vintage	09	08	07
WR	6	6	5
Drink	12-18	11-18	11-16

DRY $28 AV

Mitre Rocks Central Otago Pinot Noir   ★★★★☆

Estate-grown at Parkburn, in the Cromwell Basin, and matured in French oak barriques, the 2009 vintage (★★★★★) is a rich, finely structured red, deeply coloured and fragrant, with concentrated cherry, spice and nut flavours, firm and savoury, complex and sweet-fruited, with great persistence.

Vintage	09	08	07	06
WR	7	7	7	6
Drink	12-19	11-17	11-15	11-14

DRY $38 V+

Moana Park Hawke's Bay Pinot Noir   (★★☆)

Grown at Te Awanga and barrel-aged for six months, the 2010 vintage (★★☆) is light in colour and body, with gentle cherry and spice flavours, a hint of herbs, and a fairly firm finish.

DRY $19 –V

Moana Park Vineyard Tribute Altitude Pinot Noir   (★★★)

Grown in Central Hawke's Bay, the 2009 vintage (★★★) was matured in French oak casks (45 per cent new). It's a supple wine with cherry and herb flavours, showing good, savoury complexity.

DRY $30 –V

Momo Marlborough Pinot Noir ★★★

From Seresin, the 2009 vintage (★★★) was hand-picked at four sites, fermented with indigenous yeasts and matured for 11 months in French oak barriques. A light style with drink-young appeal and some complexity, it is ruby-hued, with decent depth of cherry, herb and spice flavours, slightly nutty and savoury. Ready.

Vintage	09	08	07	06
WR	7	5	7	6
Drink	11-15	11-13	11-15	P

 DRY $27 –V

Moncellier Central Otago Pinot Noir (★★★)

The softly mouthfilling 2008 vintage (★★★) was harvested at over 24 brix, fermented with indigenous yeasts and matured for 10 months in barrels (25 per cent new). Ruby-hued, it's a very easy-drinking style, with moderately concentrated cherry, plum and spice flavours, ripe and supple.

Vintage	08
WR	5
Drink	11-14

 DRY $29 –V

Mondillo Central Otago Pinot Noir ★★★★★

A rising star. The enticingly floral 2010 vintage (★★★★☆) was estate-grown at Bendigo, in the Cromwell Basin, and matured for 10 months in French oak barriques (30 per cent new). Enticingly floral and smooth, it is full-coloured and weighty, with strong, fresh cherry, plum and spice flavours, rich, intensely varietal and harmonious. It's still unfolding; open mid-2012+.

Vintage	10	09	08	07	06	05
WR	6	7	7	7	6	6
Drink	12-15	11-15	11-14	11-13	11-12	11-12

 DRY $40 V+

Monowai Crownthorpe Pinot Noir ★★★☆

The 2010 vintage (★★★) was estate-grown in inland Hawke's Bay and matured for 10 months in French (90 per cent) and American oak barrels. It's a fresh, youthful wine with strawberry and spice flavours, showing some nutty, savoury complexity, and a tight finish.

Vintage	10
WR	5
Drink	11-16

DRY $25 AV

Montana Living Land Series Marlborough Pinot Noir (★★★★)

The debut 2009 vintage (★★★★) is a wonderful buy. From vines in conversion to organic production, it was grown on the south side of the Wairau Valley, barrel-matured for nine months (in French and Hungarian oak) and bottled unfined. Fragrant and full-bodied, it has sweet-fruit delights, ripe plum and spice flavours, gentle tannins, and more complexity than you'd expect at its modest price. (The 2010 vintage is branded Brancott Estate.)

 DRY $20 V+

Montana South Island Pinot Noir

Since 2006, this multi-region blend has replaced the former Montana Marlborough Pinot Noir. Grown in Marlborough, Waipara and Central Otago, it is matured in stainless steel tanks, large oak cuves and French and European oak barriques. The 2008 vintage (★★★) is enjoyable young, with gentle tannins and good depth of fresh, smooth plum and slight herb flavours.

DRY $21 AV

Morton Estate Black Label Marlborough Pinot Noir

The 2010 vintage (★★★★), from the Stone Creek Vineyard, is boldly coloured, mouthfilling and smooth, with fresh, deep cherry/plum flavours and finely integrated oak. A weighty wine with ripe, supple tannins, it's approachable now, but well worth cellaring.

DRY $34 –V

Morton Estate White Label Marlborough Pinot Noir

The 2008 vintage (★★☆) has lightish, slightly developed colour. It's an easy-drinking red with plum, spice and herb flavours, fresh and smooth. Ready.

Vintage	08	07
WR	6	7
Drink	11-12	11-12

DRY $19 –V

Mountain Road Single Barrique Taranaki Pinot Noir

From vines planted near Waitara in 2004, the 2010 vintage (★★★) is a rare wine – just one barrel was made. Light ruby, it is fresh and supple, with cherry and strawberry flavours, showing some savoury, spicy complexity, and drink-young appeal.

DRY $25 –V

Mount Brown Waipara Valley Pinot Noir

The 2009 vintage (★★★), matured in French oak casks (22 per cent new), has generous cherry and spice flavours, a distinctly herbal thread and considerable complexity. The 2010 (★★☆) has developed colour and herbal, nutty, slightly rustic flavours.

DRY $23 –V

Mount Dottrel Central Otago Pinot Noir ★★★★

Estate-grown at Parkburn, in the Cromwell Basin, this is the second label of Mitre Rocks. The 2009 vintage (★★★★) is floral and finely textured, rich and supple, with deep, bright colour, fresh acidity and strong cherry, spice, olive and dried-herb flavours.

Vintage	09	08	07	06	05
WR	7	6	7	6	5
Drink	11-16	11-14	11-15	11-12	P

DRY $30 AV

Mount Edward Central Otago Pinot Noir ★★★★☆

The 2008 vintage (★★★★☆) was grown at Lowburn and Bannockburn (in the Cromwell Basin), and also at Gibbston, fermented with indigenous yeasts, and matured for a year in French oak casks (28 per cent new). The goal is 'a refined style of wine, as opposed to the fruit bomb'. Deep and youthful in colour, it is rich, sweet-fruited and supple, with deep cherry and plum flavours, a subtle oak influence, fresh acidity, gentle tannins, and impressive elegance and harmony. The 2009 (★★★★★) is deeply coloured, finely scented and supple, with rich cherry, plum, dried-herb and nut flavours, oak complexity and a lovely, velvety texture. It's maturing really well.

DRY $47 –V

Mount Edward Morrison Vineyard Pinot Noir ★★★★★

Estate-grown at Lowburn and bottled unfined and unfiltered, the 2008 vintage (★★★★☆) of this Central Otago red is mouthfilling, with strong, plummy, spicy, nutty flavours, showing excellent complexity, and a firm backbone of tannin. It's still youthful. The lovely 2009 (★★★★★) is deeply coloured, weighty and supple, very generous and sweet-fruited, with rich, plummy, cherryish, complex flavours, finely textured and long. Open 2013+.

DRY $65 –V

Mount Edward Muirkirk Pinot Noir ★★★★★

From vines planted in 1997 at Bannockburn, in Central Otago, the 2008 vintage (★★★★★) is mouthfilling, richly coloured, layered and supple, with very sweet fruit characters and strong cherry, plum and spice flavours, showing lovely texture, complexity and harmony. Savoury and seamless, it's delicious now, but also well worth cellaring. The 2009 (★★★★★) is rare – only 79 cases were produced. Deep ruby, it is a powerful, sturdy wine with very generous, lush cherry, spice, liquorice and nut flavours, ripe, supple tannins, and strong potential.

DRY $68 AV

Mount Edward Stevens Vineyard Pinot Noir (★★★★)

Grown at Gibbston, this wine was formerly called 'Susan's Vineyard' (the site is owned by Susan and Terry Stevens). The 2009 vintage (★★★★) is an elegant, strongly varietal red with good concentration of cherry, plum, spice and herb flavours, fresh acidity and ripe, supple tannins.

DRY $65 –V

Mount Fishtail Marlborough Pinot Noir ★★★

From Konrad, the 2009 vintage (★★★) was French oak-aged for 10 months. Floral, fruity, ripe and supple, it is ruby-hued, with plum, berry and spice flavours, a touch of savoury complexity and drink-young charm.

Vintage	09	08
WR	5	3
Drink	11-13	11-14

DRY $20 AV

Mountford Estate Waipara Pinot Noir ★★★★

The 2008 vintage (★★★★) is lightish in colour and delicately scented, with cherryish, nutty flavours in a 'feminine' style, subtle, complex, savoury and long. It's not highly concentrated, but gently seductive; drink now.

`DRY $65 –V`

Mountford Liaison Waipara Pinot Noir (★★★☆)

The 'big brother of the Village', the 2008 vintage (★★★☆), grown at two neighbouring sites, is ruby-hued, with cherry, spice, herb and nut flavours, showing good but not great depth, and lots of current-drinking appeal.

`DRY $50 –V`

Mountford The Gradient Waipara Pinot Noir (★★★★★)

The 2008 vintage (★★★★★) is a majestic wine, revealing great personality. Estate-grown and hand-harvested in three 'passes', it was fermented and matured in French oak barriques. Deep and youthful in colour, it is enticingly perfumed, concentrated, very savoury and complex, with deep, ripe cherry, plum, spice and nut flavours, and a firm backbone of tannin. An arresting, thought-provoking wine, it should flourish for a decade.

`DRY $150 AV`

Mountford Village Waipara Pinot Noir ★★★☆

The 2008 vintage (★★★☆) was chosen for its 'fruity and easy-drinking qualities that are appealing to beginning Pinot Noir drinkers…' Probably at its peak, it is lightish in colour, with a highly scented, savoury, herbal bouquet. Mouthfilling and supple, it's a finely textured wine, drinking well now.

`DRY $32 –V`

Mount Riley Limited Release Marlborough Pinot Noir (★★★★)

The 2008 vintage (★★★★) was hand-picked, fermented with indigenous yeasts, and matured in French oak casks (30 per cent new). Sweet-fruited, scented and silky, with cherry, spice and herb flavours, it shows good concentration, complexity and charm.

`DRY $25 V+`

Mount Riley Marlborough Pinot Noir ★★★

The 2009 vintage (★★★) was matured for nine months in French oak casks. Ruby-hued, it is fresh and supple, with cherry and plum flavours, not concentrated, but offering good varietal character and drink-young appeal.

`DRY $22 AV`

Mount Riley Seventeen Valley Marlborough Pinot Noir ★★★

Hand-picked in the company's Seventeen Valley Vineyard, south of Blenheim, the 2007 (★★★) is full-bodied, spicy, savoury and supple, with a seasoning of nutty French oak. It's a complex style, but green-edged, with considerable development showing. The 2009 vintage (★★★) is firmly structured, fresh, ripe and lively, with good flavour depth and some savoury complexity.

`DRY $35 –V`

Mt Beautiful Cheviot Hills Pinot Noir ★★★

The 2009 vintage (★★★) was hand-picked in North Canterbury and matured for a year in French oak barriques (30 per cent new). Light ruby, it's a mid-weight wine, with gentle cherry, plum, spice and herb flavours, seasoned with toasty oak, and a firm, savoury, spicy finish.

Vintage	09
WR	6
Drink	11-14

 DRY $30 –V

Mt Campbell Nelson Pinot Noir (★★☆)

From Anchorage, the 2009 vintage (★★☆) is a ruby-hued red with fresh cherry, spice and plum flavours. Slightly leafy, with moderate depth, it's a pleasant, early-drinking style.

 DRY $18 AV

Mt Difficulty Central Otago Pinot Noir ★★★★

This popular red is grown entirely at Bannockburn. The 2009 vintage (★★★★), matured for nearly a year in French oak barriques, is deeply coloured and savoury, with a floral bouquet and strong, cherryish, spicy flavours, woven with fresh acidity. It's still developing; open mid-2012+.

Vintage	09	08	07	06
WR	6	6	7	7
Drink	14-19	11-16	11-16	11-14

 DRY $45 –V

Mt Difficulty Roaring Meg Pinot Noir ★★★☆

Grown in the Cromwell Basin (but not entirely at Bannockburn, unlike its stablemate, above) and French oak-aged for nine months, the 2008 vintage (★★★☆) is floral, supple and sweet-fruited, with ripe cherry/plum flavours, gently seasoned with toasty oak, and some savoury complexity. It's a delicious drink-young style.

Vintage	08	07	06
WR	6	7	7
Drink	11-13	11-13	P

 DRY $28 AV

Mt Difficulty Single Vineyard Long Gully Central Otago Pinot Noir ★★★★☆

From a vineyard that supplies core fruit for the Mt Difficulty Central Otago Pinot Noir label, this is promoted as a more 'feminine' style than its Pipeclay Terrace stablemate. The 2009 vintage (★★★★☆), matured for 14 months in French oak barriques, is dark and highly concentrated, with a savoury, complex bouquet, very youthful cherry, plum and spice flavours, and firm tannins beneath. Drink 2013+.

Vintage	09
WR	6
Drink	14-25

DRY $90 –V

Mt Difficulty Single Vineyard Pipeclay Terrace Pinot Noir   ★★★★★

A powerful, lush Central Otago red with densely packed, cherryish, plummy flavours, spicy and long. It is grown on a steep, relatively hot slope at Bannockburn, with bony, gravelly soils. The full-coloured 2009 (★★★★★) was matured for 14 months in French oak barriques. Deep in colour, with an intensely floral bouquet, it is still a baby – fresh and youthful, with impressive weight and very strong, vibrant plum, cherry and spice flavours. Crying out for cellaring, it is richly scented and built to last, with a real sense of 'brooding' potential.

Vintage	09
WR	6
Drink	14-25

 DRY $90 AV

Mt Difficulty Single Vineyard Target Gully Pinot Noir   ★★★★★

Likely to flourish for a decade, the 2009 vintage (★★★★★) is from an elevated, late-ripening block at Bannockburn, in Central Otago. Barrel-matured for over a year, it is a distinctly masculine style, dark and rich, with layers of cherry, plum, spice and nut flavours, firm and very 'complete'.

Vintage	09
WR	6
Drink	14-25

 DRY $90 AV

Mt Hector Wairarapa Pinot Noir   (★★★)

From Matahiwi, the 2009 vintage (★★★) is a very attractive, drink-young style. Fragrant and supple, it has fresh, ripe plum and slight herb flavours, showing good depth, and a well-rounded finish.

 DRY $17 V+

Mt Rosa Central Otago Pinot Noir   ★★★☆

Grown at Gibbston, the 2009 vintage (★★★) is a single-vineyard red, French oak-matured. Showing full, slightly developed colour, it has a distinctly leafy streak, but also offers plenty of flavour.

DRY $31 –V

Muddy Water Hare's Breath Pinot Noir   ★★★★☆

From 'a block on limestone slopes at the back of the property', the 2009 (★★★★★) was hand-picked at Waipara, fermented with indigenous yeasts, and matured for over a year in French oak barriques (30 per cent new). Crying out for cellaring, it is a deeply coloured, powerful, fruit-crammed red with deep plum and spice flavours. Very savoury and complex, it's built to last; open 2013+.

Vintage	09	08	07	06
WR	7	7	7	7
Drink	11-19	11-24	11-15	11-12

 DRY $60 –V

Muddy Water Slowhand Waipara Pinot Noir   ★★★★★

Since 2006 (★★★★★), this label has replaced Mojo as the Waipara winery's top red. Based on the oldest vines (clone 10/5), 'tended by slow hands', it always reveals outstanding personality. Matured for 14 months in French oak barriques (30 per cent new), the 2009 vintage (★★★★★) is a stunner. Lush and lovely, it is rich, fruit-packed and complex, with dense plum/spice flavours and even a hint of chocolate. Finely textured, with good tannin backbone, it's a very 'complete' wine, likely to reward long cellaring.

Vintage	09
WR	7
Drink	11-22

DRY $70 AV

Muddy Water Waipara Pinot Noir   ★★★★☆

The 2009 vintage (★★★★) was hand-picked, fermented with indigenous yeasts and matured for 16 months in French oak barriques (30 per cent new). Still very youthful, it is a very generous wine with rich cherry/plum flavours, showing good, spicy complexity. Full, bright ruby, it should be at its best from mid-2012+.

Vintage	09	08	07
WR	7	7	7
Drink	11-17	11-21	11-15

DRY $40 AV

Mud House Central Otago Pinot Noir   ★★★☆

The 2009 vintage (★★★☆), grown at Bendigo and partly oak-aged, is a fruit-driven style with fresh cherry/herb flavours, not complex but showing good depth and drink-young charm. The 2010 (★★★☆) is similar – ruby-hued, fresh and supple, with vibrant cherry and plum flavours, a hint of herbs, and fungal notes adding a touch of complexity.

DRY $25 AV

Mud House Marlborough Pinot Noir   (★★★)

The 2008 vintage (★★★) is a fruit-driven style with vibrant cherry and spice flavours, fresh and supple.

DRY $27 –V

Mud House Swan Central Otago Pinot Noir   ★★★★

Grown at Bendigo, in the Cromwell Basin, the fruit-packed, supple 2009 vintage (★★★★) was hand-picked and matured in French oak casks (30 per cent new). Deeply coloured, it has good weight and strong, ripe, youthful flavours of plums and spices.

DRY $35 AV

Murdoch James Blue Rock Martinborough Pinot Noir   ★★★★

Estate-grown south of the township, the 2010 (★★★★☆) is an excellent vintage of this single-vineyard red. Deeply coloured and mouthfilling, with a floral, finely perfumed bouquet, it is a fruit-driven style, sweet-fruited and supple, with a subtle seasoning of French oak, gentle tannins and fresh, concentrated cherry/plum flavours. It's already delicious. The 2009 (★★★) is a powerful (15 per cent alcohol), bold wine with strong, herbal flavours, but lacks the finesse of the 2010.

 DRY $39 AV

Murdoch James Fraser Pinot Noir   ★★★☆

Earlier vintages were a single-vineyard red, grown on the Martinborough Terrace, but the 2008 (★★★) is a blend of the 'very best barrels'. Matured in French oak casks (80 per cent new), it is full-coloured, with mouthfilling body and plenty of spicy, nutty, slightly leafy flavour.

 DRY $65 –V

Murdoch James Martinborough Pinot Noir   ★★★

The 2010 vintage (★★★☆) has lots of drink-young charm. Matured for 10 months in French oak casks (30 per cent new), it is deeply coloured, freshly scented and supple, in a mouthfilling, fruit-driven style with good depth of cherry and plum flavours.

 DRY $30 –V

Murrays Road Marlborough Pinot Noir   (★★★)

Showing some development, the 2008 vintage (★★★) was barrel-aged for 10 months. A fruity, ruby-hued red, it has plum, spice and slight herb flavours, a touch of complexity and a firm finish.

Vintage	08
WR	5
Drink	11-12

 DRY $30 –V

Nanny Goat Vineyard Central Otago Pinot Noir   ★★★☆

The 2009 vintage (★★★☆) was grown at Gibbston (in what is claimed to be 'the highest and most southerly' vineyard in the country). Ruby-hued, it is a floral, intensely varietal red, moderately concentrated, with fresh, vibrant cherry and plum flavours, gently seasoned with oak, and supple tannins.

DRY $36 –V

Nautilus Four Barriques Marlborough Pinot Noir   ★★★★★

The 2007 vintage (★★★★★) was made from four casks chosen from over 120 for 'that special magic'. A blend of three barrels, estate-grown in the Clay Hills Vineyard in the Omaka Valley, and one barrel from the company-owned Kaituna Vineyard, on the north side of the Wairau River, it is richly coloured, beautifully scented and supple, with lovely fruit sweetness, dense cherry and plum flavours, and great harmony. The 2009 (★★★★★) was matured for 18 months in French oak casks (50 per cent new). Highly perfumed, it is deliciously sweet-fruited, with smooth cherry, plum and nut flavours showing excellent richness, complexity and harmony. Already delicious, it should be in full stride mid-2012+.

Vintage	09	08	07	06	05
WR	7	NM	7	7	7
Drink	12-18	NM	11-16	11-16	11-15

 DRY $65 AV

Nautilus Marlborough Pinot Noir   ★★★★

The 2009 vintage (★★★★☆) was sourced mostly from clay slopes on the south side of the Wairau Valley. Hand-picked and matured for 11 months in French oak barriques (30 per cent new), it is deep ruby, savoury and supple, with strong, ripe cherry, spice and nut flavours, showing good complexity and texture. Sweet-fruited and concentrated, it's built to last; open 2012+.

Vintage	10	09	08	07	06	05	04
WR	7	7	6	7	6	7	6
Drink	12-16	11-15	11-14	11-13	11-12	P	P

 DRY $42 –V

Nest, The, Marlborough Pinot Noir   (★★☆)

From Lake Chalice, the debut 2008 vintage (★★☆) was estate-grown in the Wairau and lower Waihopai valleys, and matured for eight months in French oak barrels. Ruby-hued, it's a lightweight style, fruity and supple, with drink-young appeal.

DRY $20 –V

Neudorf Moutere Home Vineyard Pinot Noir   ★★★★★

Neudorf's flagship red is based principally on a block of clone 5 Pinot Noir vines, over 20 years old, in the original estate vineyard at Upper Moutere, in Nelson. The wine is fermented with indigenous yeasts, matured in French oak barriques (usually 35 to 40 per cent new), and is bottled without fining or filtration. The superb 2009 vintage (★★★★★) is finely scented and highly complex, with full, youthful colour and deep strawberry and spice flavours. Very sweet-fruited, with gentle acidity and tannins, it is deliciously savoury, ripe and rounded, with great presence.

Vintage	09	08	07	06	05	04	03	02	01
WR	6	NM	NM	6	7	NM	7	6	7
Drink	11-16	NM	NM	11-15	11-14	NM	11-14	11-12	P

 DRY $80 AV

Neudorf Moutere Pinot Noir ★★★★★

Typically a very classy Nelson red. It is hand-picked at Upper Moutere, in the Neudorf home vineyard and the tiny Pomona Vineyard, where the AM 10/5 vines are over 20 years old. The wine is fermented with indigenous yeasts, matured for about 10 months in French oak barriques (20 to 40 per cent new), and is usually bottled without fining or filtering. The 2009 vintage (★★★★★) is deeply coloured, with a full-bloomed, very savoury and spicy bouquet. Highly concentrated, it is savoury, sweet-fruited and supple, and already quite open and expressive. Drink now or cellar.

Vintage	09	08	07	06	05	04	03
WR	6	6	6	7	7	6	7
Drink	11-17	11-17	11-16	11-15	11-14	11-12	11-13

 DRY $50 AV

Neudorf Tom's Block Nelson Pinot Noir ★★★★☆

This regional blend is typically good value. The 2009 vintage (★★★★) was hand-harvested, fermented with indigenous yeasts, matured for 10 months in French oak barriques (25 per cent new), and bottled unfined and unfiltered. Ruby-hued, it has a floral, slightly herbal bouquet, leading into a mouthfilling and supple wine, intensely varietal, with cherry, plum, herb and nut flavours showing good complexity.

Vintage	09	08	07	06	05
WR	6	6	6	7	7
Drink	11-15	11-15	11-14	11-13	11-13

DRY $30 V+

Nevis Bluff Central Otago Pinot Noir ★★★☆

The attractively perfumed 2008 vintage (★★★★) was matured in French oak barriques (25 per cent new). A generous wine, with full colour and strong plum and spice flavours, it is sweet-fruited, savoury and finely textured, with good complexity and harmony.

Vintage	08
WR	5
Drink	11-15

DRY $48 –V

Ngatarawa Stables Reserve Hawke's Bay Pinot Noir (★★★)

The 2010 vintage (★★★) is enjoyable young. Light in colour, it is sweet-fruited, with cherry, herb and spice flavours showing some savoury complexity and ripe, supple tannins.

Vintage	10
WR	6
Drink	11-15

DRY $25 –V

Nga Waka Martinborough Pinot Noir ★★★★

The latest vintages are the best yet. The instantly attractive 2009 (★★★★☆) is full-bodied, vibrant and sweet-fruited, with lovely depth and texture. Full-coloured, it is very generous and smooth-flowing. The 2010 (★★★★) is deeply coloured and fresh-scented, with a subtle seasoning of oak, gentle tannins and loads of vibrant, cherryish, plummy flavour.

Vintage	10	09
WR	7	6
Drink	12+	11+

Night Owl Central Otago Pinot Noir (★★★)

A drink-young style, the 2008 vintage (★★★) is vibrantly fruity and supple, with fresh cherry and herb flavours, showing satisfying depth, a touch of complexity and a well-rounded finish.

Nobilo Icon Marlborough Pinot Noir ★★★☆

Grown mostly in the Awatere Valley and matured in French oak casks (25 per cent new), the 2009 vintage (★★★☆) is a fragrant, savoury red, ruby-hued, medium-bodied and supple, with fresh cherry, plum and spice flavours, showing good ripeness and complexity.

Northburn Station Bill's Blend Lot 2 Pinot Noir (★★★☆)

The 2008 vintage (★★★☆), grown at Bendigo, in Central Otago, was matured in French oak barrels (15 per cent new). A fruity, drink-young charmer, it shows good depth of very ripe cherry/plum flavours, gentle tannins and a well-rounded finish.

Northburn Station Central Otago Pinot Noir ★★★★

Grown at Bendigo, the 2008 vintage (★★★★☆) was matured in French oak barriques (35 per cent new). It is full-coloured and fragrant, ripe, spicy and savoury, with a firm backbone of tannin and excellent complexity and density.

Vintage	08	07	06
WR	5	6	6
Drink	11-14	11-13	11-12

Northfield Home Creek Vineyard Waipara Pinot Noir ★★★

Matured for 10 months in French oak barriques (25 per cent new), the 2009 vintage (★★★☆) is ripely fragrant and mouthfilling, with plum and spice flavours showing good depth, fairly firm tannins and considerable complexity.

DRY $25 –V

Odyssey Marlborough Pinot Noir ★★★★

This single-vineyard red is estate-grown and hand-picked in the Brancott Valley, fermented with indigenous yeasts, and matured in French oak barriques (30 per cent new in 2008). The 2009 vintage (★★★★☆) is the best yet. The bouquet is highly scented; the palate is concentrated, sweet-fruited and savoury, with rich, vibrant plum and spice flavours, seasoned with oak, a hint of herbs, and good tannin support. It's a complex style, for drinking now or cellaring.

Vintage	09	08
WR	6	5
Drink	11-16	11-15

 DRY $29 V+

Old Coach Road Nelson Pinot Noir ★★☆

From Seifried, the 2009 vintage (★★☆) was matured for eight months in French oak barriques (new to three years old). Ruby-hued, it has moderate depth of cherry, plum and herb flavours. The 2010 (★★☆) is bright ruby, with fresh berry and spice flavours, simple but pleasant. A drink-young style, priced right.

Vintage	10
WR	5
Drink	11-14

DRY $17 AV

Olssens Jackson Barry Pinot Noir ★★★★

This is the Central Otago winery's middle-tier red, usually impressive. Estate-grown at Bannockburn, the 2009 vintage (★★★★) was matured in French oak barriques (39 per cent new). Deeply coloured, it is concentrated, with ripe cherry and spice flavours, showing excellent texture, complexity and harmony.

Vintage	09	08	07	06
WR	6	5	6	6
Drink	11-20	11-15	11-17	11-17

 DRY $46 –V

Olssens Nipple Hill Central Otago Pinot Noir ★★★☆

Bright ruby, the 2010 vintage (★★★★) is an elegant, fruit-driven style, designed for early consumption (only 30 per cent barrel-aged). Finely textured, it has some savoury complexity and excellent flavour depth.

 DRY $25 AV

Olssens Slapjack Creek Reserve Pinot Noir ★★★★★

The top label from the longest-established Bannockburn, Central Otago winery is 'made from a careful selection of barrels in those years when the wine is of distinctly superior quality'. The 2009 vintage (★★★★★), from vines planted in 1991 (60 per cent) and 2002 (40 per cent), was matured in French oak barriques (38 per cent new). Full-coloured, it is a powerful wine with concentrated plum and spice flavours, notably dense, savoury and complex. It should mature well for a decade.

DRY $85 –V

Omaka Springs Estates Falveys Marlborough Pinot Noir   ★★☆

French oak-aged for 10 months, the 2009 vintage (★★☆) is a gutsy, full-bodied (14.5 per cent) wine, with spicy, herbal flavours, strong and developed. Priced right.

Vintage	09	08
WR	6	6
Drink	11-13	11-12

DRY $18 AV

Omihi Road Waipara Pinot Noir   ★★★☆

From Torlesse, the 2009 vintage (★★★☆) is a barrique-matured wine, ruby-hued, with a hint of development. The bouquet is savoury, herbal and spicy, with considerable complexity; the palate is green-edged but its cherry, plum and olive flavours show good 'pinosity' and length.

Vintage	09
WR	5
Drink	12-15

DRY $30 –V

Opawa Marlborough Pinot Noir   ★★★☆

From Nautilus, the delicious 2010 vintage (★★★★) is a drink-young style, full of charm. Matured partly in tanks (20 per cent), but mostly in French oak barriques (8 per cent new), it is floral, full-bodied and buoyantly fruity, with generous cherry and plum flavours, very ripe and smooth.

DRY $28 AV

Opihi Vineyard South Canterbury Pinot Noir   ★★☆

The 2009 vintage (★★☆) was French oak-aged. Estate-grown and hand-picked, it is light ruby, with smooth, gentle strawberry, herb and spice flavours, and drink-young appeal.

DRY $26 –V

Ostler Blue House Vines Waitaki Valley Pinot Noir   (★★★★)

Part of Ostler's 'grower selection' (meaning it is not estate-grown), the 2010 vintage (★★★★) was matured entirely in old French oak barrels. Fresh and buoyantly fruity, it has good concentration of cherry/plum flavours, with a gentle seasoning of nutty oak, and immediate appeal. Drink now or cellar.

Vintage	10
WR	6
Drink	11-15

DRY $35 AV

Ostler Caroline's Waitaki Valley Pinot Noir   ★★★★☆

Grown in the Waitaki Valley of North Otago, the 2010 vintage (★★★★★) is outstanding. Matured in French oak casks (25 per cent), it is deeply coloured, highly scented and mouthfilling, with a strong surge of plum, cherry, spice and nut flavours. Densely packed and supple, with excellent complexity and vibrancy, this concentrated, silky-textured wine is arguably the valley's finest red to date.

Vintage	10	09	08	07
WR	7	6	6	NM
Drink	11-18	11-17	11-16	NM

DRY $50 –V

Overstone Marlborough Pinot Noir   (★★☆)

From Sileni, the 2008 vintage (★★☆) is ruby-hued, with ripe flavours of cherries and plums. Floral, fresh and supple, it's a fruity, uncomplicated style, with drink-young appeal.

DRY $16 AV

Oyster Bay Marlborough Pinot Noir   ★★★☆

From Delegat's, this is typically a ruby-hued, floral wine, moderately concentrated, with fresh, ripe plum/spice flavours, finely textured, with some complexity and plenty of drink-young charm.

DRY $25 AV

Palliser Estate Martinborough Pinot Noir   ★★★★★

This enticingly perfumed, notably elegant, rich and harmonious red is attractively priced, reflecting its relatively large volume. Most but not all of the grapes come from the company's own vineyards – Palliser, Om Santi, Clouston, Pinnacles and East Base – where the vines range up to over 20 years old. Maturation is for a year in French oak barriques (partly new). The 2008 vintage (★★★★★) is powerful, with full, bright colour, still youthful, and a floral bouquet. A concentrated, generous wine, it has masses of sweet, ripe fruit, well balanced by oak, fresh acidity and firm tannins. The very graceful 2009 (★★★★★) is deeply coloured, highly scented and supple, in a voluptuous, fruit-driven style with loads of cherryish, plummy flavour. Slightly spicy and nutty, silky-textured and long, it should be at its best 2013+.

DRY $42 V+

Vintage	09	08	07	06	05	04
WR	7	7	6	7	7	4
Drink	11-17	11-16	11-15	11-14	11-14	P

Palliser Pencarrow Martinborough Pinot Noir – see Pencarrow Martinborough Pinot Noir

Pandora Martinborough Pinot Noir   (★★★)

From Coney, the 2009 vintage (★★★) is a good buy. Ruby-hued, it has strawberry, herb and spice flavours, showing some savoury, fungal complexity, and a rounded finish. Ready.

DRY $15 V+

Paritua Central Otago Pinot Noir

The 2008 vintage (★★★★) is a regional blend, grown mostly at Lowburn and blended with grapes from Alexandra and Gibbston. Very scented and supple, it's an intensely varietal wine, ruby-hued, with ripe cherry, plum and spice flavours, showing good complexity.

DRY $37 AV

Parr & Simpson Limestone Bay Pinot Noir

A single-vineyard Nelson red, grown at Pohara, Golden Bay, the 2009 vintage (★★★★) was hand-picked and matured for 10 months in French oak barrels (30 per cent new). Ruby-hued, with some fungal, earthy notes in the bouquet, it's an elegant, savoury, intensely varietal wine with strawberry, herb, spice and nut flavours, showing good complexity, and a well-rounded finish.

DRY $27 V+

Partington Upper Moutere Pinot Noir (★★★★)

The powerful, concentrated 2008 vintage (★★★★), certified by BioGro, was matured for a year in French oak barriques and bottled unfiltered. Deeply coloured, it is sturdy and tightly structured, with dense plum and spice flavours and a firm backbone of tannin.

Vintage	08	07
WR	6	5
Drink	11-15	11-13

DRY $49 –V

Pasquale Hakataramea Valley Pinot Noir (★★★☆)

Grown in South Canterbury, the 2008 vintage (★★★☆) was fermented with indigenous yeasts, oak-aged for a year, and bottled without fining. It's a medium-bodied red, fresh and vibrant, with cherry, plum, spice and herb flavours, showing good complexity and depth. It's leafier than its Waitaki Valley stablemate (below), but more concentrated.

DRY $27 AV

Pasquale Waitaki Valley Pinot Noir (★★★☆)

The 2008 vintage (★★★☆) was barrel-aged for a year and bottled without fining. Full-coloured, it has a floral, spicy, attractive bouquet, leading into a youthful wine with moderately concentrated cherry, plum and slight herb flavours, fresh and supple.

DRY $27 AV

Paua Marlborough Pinot Noir ★★★☆

From Highfield, the 2010 vintage (★★★☆) was harvested at 24–26 brix and matured for nine months in French oak casks. An excellent drink-young style, it is ruby-hued, fresh and soft, with very satisfying depth of cherry, plum and spice flavours, showing some savoury complexity. Fine value.

DRY $23 V+

Paulownia Pinot Noir   (★★★☆)

Grown in the northern Wairarapa, the 2009 vintage (★★★☆) is a lightly oaked style. Full of promise, it is sweet-fruited, with very good flavour depth and some savoury complexity.

Vintage	09
WR	6
Drink	11-15

 DRY $23 V+

Pegasus Bay Pinot Noir   ★★★★★

This Waipara red is one of Canterbury's greatest Pinot Noirs, typically very rich in body and flavour. The close-planted vines, planted in stony, sandy soils, range from 11 to 25 years old. The juice is fermented with indigenous yeasts and the wine is matured for 16 to 18 months in Burgundy oak barrels (40 per cent new). The 2008 vintage (★★★★☆) is deeply coloured and rich. Still youthful, it is tightly structured, with fresh acidity woven through its generous plum and spice flavours, good complexity and a highly scented bouquet.

Vintage	09	08	07	06
WR	7	6	6	7
Drink	11-17	11-16	11-14	11-14

 DRY $47 AV

Pegasus Bay Prima Donna Pinot Noir   ★★★★★

For its reserve Waipara Pinot Noir, Pegasus Bay wants 'a heavenly voice, a shapely body and a velvety nose'. Only made in favourable vintages (about one in two), it is based on the oldest vines – well over 20 years old – and matured for up to two years in Burgundy barrels (40 to 50 per cent new). The 2009 vintage (★★★★★) is gently seductive. Notably sweet-fruited, it is very savoury and silky-textured, in a subtle, 'feminine' style that caresses the palate with an array of cherry, plum, spice and nut flavours, rich and rounded.

Vintage	09	08	07	06	05
WR	7	NM	NM	7	6
Drink	11-17	NM	NM	11-18	11-16

 DRY $84 AV

Pencarrow Martinborough Pinot Noir   ★★★★

This is Palliser Estate's second-tier label, but in top years it is an impressive wine, better than some companies' top reds, and is typically a great buy. The 2009 (★★★★★) is a star vintage. Full-coloured, it is rich and supple, with concentrated plum, cherry and olive flavours that linger well, and great texture for early drinking.

DRY $23 V+

People's, The, Pinot Noir   (★★★)

From Constellation NZ, the 2008 vintage (★★★) was grown in Alexandra, Central Otago. Ruby-hued, it is smooth, with ripe strawberry and spice flavours, gentle tannins, and a touch of savoury complexity. Drink now.

DRY $22 AV

Peregrine Central Otago Pinot Noir   ★★★★★

This typically outstanding red is also a good buy. Grown principally in the Cromwell Basin, but also at Gibbston, it is matured for about 10 months in Burgundy oak barrels (25 to 40 per cent new). The goal is 'power with elegance', showing 'ripe-fruit characters, without overt oak, and a silky texture'. The 2009 (★★★★★) is mouthfilling and highly scented, with rich cherry, plum and spice flavours, showing good, savoury complexity, and lovely harmony.

Vintage	09	08	07	06	05	04
WR	6	5	6	6	6	5
Drink	11-16	11-14	11-14	11-13	11-12	P

 DRY $40 V+

Peter Yealands Marlborough/Central Otago Pinot Noir   ★★★

The 2010 vintage (★★★☆) is a very good, drink-young style, mouthfilling and supple, with cherry, strawberry, plum and spice flavours, fresh and strong.

 DRY $25 –V

Pete's Shed Pinot Noir   (★★★☆)

From Yealands, the debut 2009 vintage (★★★☆) was harvested in Alexandra at 24 brix and matured in French oak barriques (35 per cent new). Bright ruby, it is mouthfilling and savoury, with fresh acidity and moderately concentrated cherry, plum and herb flavours, fresh, vibrant and firm.

 DRY $25 AV

Petit Clos by Clos Henri Marlborough Pinot Noir   ★★★☆

Based on relatively young vines, the gently oaked 2010 vintage (★★★☆) is full-coloured and fleshy, with generous, ripe, plummy, cherryish, nutty flavours, finely balanced tannins, and lots of drink-young appeal. Good value.

Vintage	10
WR	6
Drink	11-14

 DRY $23 V+

Pheasant Plucker Martinborough Pinot Noir   (★★★)

From mature vines, the 2008 vintage (★★★) was matured in French oak casks (25 per cent new). Bright ruby, with good depth of plummy, spicy flavours, showing fresh acidity, it has a hint of herbs and some complexity.

 DRY $28 –V

Pick & Shovel Central Otago Pinot Noir   ★★★

From Dry Gully, at Alexandra, the lightly oaked 2009 vintage (★★★) is a drink-young style. Freshly scented and supple, it has fresh, light plum and herb flavours, with a Beaujolais-like charm.

DRY $20 AV

Picnic by Two Paddocks Pinot Noir   ★★★☆

A Central Otago regional blend, the 2009 vintage (★★★) tastes like a second-tier Two Paddocks Pinot Noir, rather than a sort of picnic Beaujolais. Matured in French oak barrels (25 per cent new), it is full ruby, with strong plum, herb and spice flavours, showing some savoury complexity, and fairly firm tannins.

DRY $28 AV

Pied Stilt Nelson Pinot Noir   (★★☆)

Grown at Motueka, the 2010 vintage (★★☆) is a single-vineyard wine, matured for 10 months in French oak. Ruby-hued, it's a light, simple style with fresh, raspberryish scents and flavours, offering drink-young appeal.

DRY $22 –V

Pisa Range Estate Black Poplar Block Pinot Noir   ★★★★★

Estate-grown at Pisa Flats, north of Cromwell, in Central Otago, this consistently classy, enticingly scented wine is well worth discovering. Hand-picked and matured for a year in French oak barriques (one-third new), the 2009 vintage (★★★★★) is dark, powerful and fruit-packed, with dense cherry and plum flavours. Weighty, savoury and supple, it shows lovely richness and harmony. The 2010 (★★★★★) is outstanding. Densely coloured, it is highly concentrated and complex, yet also supple and silky, with arrestingly rich plum, cherry and spice flavours. It should be long-lived.

Vintage	10	09	08	07	06	05	04	03
WR	6	7	7	7	7	6	6	6
Drink	13-23	11-18	11-17	11-15	11-14	11-13	11-12	P

DRY $49 AV

Pond Paddock Te Muna Martinborough Pinot Noir   ★★★☆

The 2009 vintage (★★★★), matured in French oak barrels (30 per cent new), is an elegant, intensely varietal wine, mouthfilling, with fresh, ripe cherry and spice flavours, gentle tannins and some savoury complexity. It's well worth cellaring.

DRY $32 –V

Porter's Martinborough Pinot Noir   ★★★★

Based on vines over 15 years old and matured in French oak casks (33 per cent new), the 2009 vintage (★★★★) is floral and vibrantly fruity, with ripe plum, strawberry, herb and spice flavours, showing some savoury complexity. Still very fresh, with good texture and concentration, it's well worth cellaring.

Vintae	09	08	07	06
WR	7	6	6	7
Drink	11-15	11-14	11-13	11-13

DRY $60 –V

Prophet's Rock Central Otago Pinot Noir   ★★★★☆

The 2009 vintage (★★★★★) was estate-grown at Bendigo, in the Cromwell Basin, hand-picked, fermented with indigenous yeasts, and matured for 18 months in French oak barriques (35 per cent new). Ruby-hued, it is sweet-fruited and supple, with moderately concentrated cherry and spice flavours, showing good, savoury complexity, and a deliciously soft texture. Drink now or cellar.

Vintage	09	08	07	06	05
WR	6	NM	7	6	6
Drink	11-16	NM	11-18	11-15	11-13

DRY $45 –V

Pruner's Reward, The, Waipara Valley Pinot Noir   (★★)

From Bellbird Spring, the 2009 vintage (★★) is green-edged and spicy, with developed colour and flavours, lacking real ripeness and freshness.

DRY $24 –V

Pukeora Estate Pinot Noir   ★★★

The 2010 (★★★) was hand-picked at altitude at Waipukurau, in Central Hawke's Bay, and matured for nine months in French oak barriques. Showing drink-young appeal, it is ruby-hued and mouthfilling, with gentle tannins and good depth of ripe strawberry and spice flavours, fresh and smooth.

Vintage	10	09
WR	5	5
Drink	11-15	11-14

DRY $22 AV

Pukeora Estate Ruahine Range Pinot Noir   (★★★)

Estate-grown in Central Hawke's Bay, the 2010 vintage (★★★) was matured for 10 months in French oak barriques (61 per cent new). It is full-bodied and supple, with fresh strawberry and spice flavours, showing some savoury complexity.

Vintage	10
WR	5
Drink	11-15

DRY $25 –V

Pyramid Valley Growers Collection Calvert
Vineyard Central Otago Pinot Noir   (★★★★★)

The delicious 2008 vintage (★★★★★) was grown in a Bannockburn vineyard managed, but not owned, by Felton Road. Hand-harvested, it was fermented with indigenous yeasts, matured for 14 months in French oak barriques (25 per cent new), and bottled without fining or filtering. Richly coloured, it is robust, with highly concentrated, beautifully ripe cherry, plum and spice flavours, and a hint of liquorice. A powerful, lush red, it should flourish with cellaring.

DRY $52 AV

Pyramid Valley Vineyards Angel Flower Pinot Noir (★★★★☆)

Only 22 cases were produced of the 2007 vintage (★★★★☆). Estate-grown at altitude at Waikari, in North Canterbury, it was matured for a year in a one-year-old French oak barrique, and bottled unfined and unfiltered. Deeply coloured, it is mouthfilling, savoury and complex, with generous cherry, plum and spice flavours, fresh and supple. A very graceful wine, harmonious and finely scented, it's still youthful; open 2012+.

DRY $75 –V

Pyramid Valley Vineyards Earth Smoke Pinot Noir ★★★★

Estate-grown on an elevated, east-facing clay slope at Waikari, in North Canterbury, the 2007 vintage (★★★★) is a rare wine – only 22 cases were made. Matured for a year in a single, one-year-old French oak barrique, and bottled unfined and unfiltered, it's a floral, medium-bodied wine (11.8 per cent alcohol), with gentle acidity and strawberry, spice and herb flavours, very savoury and mellow. Ready.

DRY $75 –V

Quartz Reef Bendigo Estate Vineyard Pinot Noir ★★★★★

An emerging Central Otago star. Designed for cellaring, it is estate-grown on a steep, north-facing, 'seriously warm' site at the north-east end of Lake Dunstan, at Bendigo Station. The 2008 (★★★★★) is deeply coloured, with dense cherry and spice flavours and ripe, supple tannins giving it early approachability. The 2010 vintage (★★★★★) is a dark, authoritative wine, combining power with approachability. Likely to flourish for a decade, it is very savoury and nutty, with layers of very ripe plum, cherry and spice flavours, fine-grained tannins and a rich, rounded finish.

Vintage	10	09	08
WR	6	NM	7
Drink	13-16	NM	12-16

DRY $77 AV

Quartz Reef Central Otago Bendigo Pinot Noir ★★★★★

A bold, fleshy, generous red. The 2008 vintage (★★★★☆) was estate-grown at Bendigo, hand-picked and matured in French oak barriques. Deeply coloured, it is rich and sweet-fruited, with fresh, strong plum and cherry flavours, a hint of liquorice, subtle oak and fine, supple tannins. The 2010 (★★★★★) is deeply coloured and beautifully scented, in a powerful style with concentrated cherry, plum and spice flavours. Sweet-fruited and savoury, it is still very fresh and youthful, with good tannin backbone and obvious cellaring potential; open 2013+.

Vintage	10
WR	6
Drink	12-15

DRY $40 V+

Rabbit Ranch Central Otago Pinot Noir ★★★

The early vintages from Chard Farm set out to introduce a 'new breed of Pinot Noir from Central Otago – affordable, early-drinking, fruit-driven'. It is typically a light, buoyantly fruity red with fresh, smooth plum, herb and spice flavours, finely balanced for enjoyable, no-fuss drinking.

DRY $22 AV

Ra Nui Marlborough Pinot Noir   ★★★

The 2009 vintage (★★★) was hand-picked and matured for nine months in seasoned French oak barriques. It's an easy-drinking style, ruby-hued, with good depth of cherryish, spicy flavour, fresh, ripe and smooth.

Rapaura Springs Marlborough Pinot Noir   ★★★☆

The 2010 vintage (★★★★) is the best yet. Fully barrel-aged, it is mouthfilling and generous, with good muscle and depth of strong, ripe cherry, plum and spice flavours, youthful, nutty and complex. Concentrated and firm, it's an age-worthy wine; open 2013+.

Rapaura Springs Reserve Central Otago Pinot Noir   ★★★☆

The 2009 vintage (★★★★), French oak-aged, is drinking well now. Savoury and silky, it is full-coloured, with generous cherry, plum and slight herb flavours, rich and well-rounded.

Red Tussock Central Otago Pinot Noir   ★★★

Grown in the Cromwell Basin, the 2009 vintage (★★★) is a floral and supple, ruby-hued red with good depth of fresh cherry/plum flavours, savoury notes adding a touch of complexity and ripe, smooth tannins.

DRY $27 –V

Redwood Pass by Vavasour Marlborough Pinot Noir   (★★★)

Floral, mouthfilling and supple, the 2008 vintage (★★★) is ruby-hued, with decent depth of ripe cherry, red-berry, herb and spice flavours, and some savoury notes adding a touch of complexity.

Vintage	08
WR	5
Drink	11-12

Renato Nelson Pinot Noir   ★★★

The 2009 (★★★) was grown on the coast, at Kina, and on the Waimea Plains. Hand-picked at 24 brix, fermented with indigenous yeasts and matured for 10 months in French oak barriques (40 per cent new), it's ruby-hued, with good but not great depth of vibrant cherry/plum flavours, threaded with fresh acidity, and some leafy notes. The 2010 vintage (★★☆) is ruby-hued, with strawberry and spice flavours, hints of herbs and tamarillos, and fresh acidity. It's still very youthful, with some savoury complexity, but shows a slight lack of ripeness and roundness.

Vintage	10	09	08	07
WR	6	6	NM	7
Drink	12-14	11-13	NM	11-13

DRY $27 –V

Ribbonwood Marlborough Pinot Noir   ★★★☆

The 2010 vintage (★★★☆) is an excellent, drink-young style. Ruby-hued and sweet-fruited, it offers very good depth of cherry and plum flavours, with ripe, supple tannins and lots of youthful charm. (From Framingham.)

Vintage	10	09
WR	6	5
Drink	11-13	11-12

 DRY $25 AV

Richmond Plains Nelson Pinot Noir   ★★★

Certified organic, the 2010 vintage (★★★) was matured in French oak barrels (25 per cent new). Ruby-hued, it is floral and supple, with ripe, moderately concentrated strawberry and spice flavours, balanced for easy drinking.

Vintage	10	09	08	07	06
WR	6	6	5	6	5
Drink	11-16	11-13	11-12	11-12	P

 DRY $23 AV

Rimu Grove Nelson Pinot Noir   ★★★★

Estate-grown near Mapua, on the Nelson coast, this is typically a rich wine with loads of personality. The 2007 vintage (★★★★) is maturing well – deeply coloured, with a savoury, earthy bouquet and tight, concentrated, sweet-fruited flavours. The 2009 (★★★☆) was matured for 11 months in French oak barriques. Ruby-hued, it is vibrantly fruity, with moderately concentrated cherry, plum and herb flavours, showing good complexity. Worth cellaring.

Vintage	09	08	07	06	05	04
WR	6	6	·7	7	7	6
Drink	12-23	11-22	11-21	11-20	11-15	P

 DRY $45 –V

Rippon Emma's Block Mature Vine Pinot Noir   ★★★★☆

The debut 2008 vintage (★★★★☆) is from an east-facing, lakefront block at Lake Wanaka, in Central Otago. Matured for 17 months in French oak barrels and bottled unfined and unfiltered, it's a very 'feminine', graceful style of Pinot Noir, spicy and supple, with hints of herbs, and excellent complexity and drive. Very subtle and savoury, the 2009 (★★★★☆) is deeply coloured and complex, with strong cherry, plum, spice and nut flavours, fine-grained tannins and a tight, youthful finish. Open 2013+.

 DRY $82 –V

Rippon Jeunesse Pinot Noir   ★★★★

Made from vines in their youth ('jeunesse'), defined as 'under 12 years old', at Lake Wanaka, in Central Otago, the 2009 vintage (★★★☆) was fermented with indigenous yeasts, matured in seasoned French oak barrels, and bottled unfined and unfiltered. Bright ruby, it is a virile young red, medium-bodied, with strawberry, plum and spice flavours, light and lively, and considerable complexity. Drink now or cellar.

DRY $39 AV

Rippon Mature Vine Central Otago Pinot Noir

This Lake Wanaka red (labelled 'Mature Vine' since 2008) has a long, proud history and is an elegant, 'feminine' style, not a blockbuster. Hand-picked from ungrafted vines planted between 1985 and 1991, the 2009 vintage (★★★★☆) was French oak-aged for 16 months and bottled unfined and unfiltered. Ruby-hued and finely scented, it is intensely varietal, with strawberry, spice and nut flavours, coupling complexity and charm, in a deliciously refined and harmonious style. Best drinking mid-2012+.

DRY $55 –V

Rippon Tinker's Field Mature Vine Pinot Noir

★★★★★

From 'the oldest vines on the property', the 2008 vintage (★★★★★) was estate-grown on a north-facing slope at Lake Wanaka, in Central Otago, matured for 17 months in French oak barriques, and bottled without fining or filtering. Described by Rippon as displaying 'unforced masculinity', it is sturdy and full-coloured, with a fragrant, spicy bouquet and generous, ripe, spicy flavours, braced by firm tannins. A powerful, complex wine with strong personality, it's set for a long life. The 2009 (★★★★★) has deep, youthful colour. It's a sturdy, notably complex wine, sweet-fruited, with strong, ripe cherry, plum, spice and nut flavours, buried tannins, and the power and structure to flourish long-term.

DRY $95 AV

Ripponvale Central Otago Pinot Noir

(★★)

The 2009 vintage (★★), grown in the Cromwell Basin, is developed, with berryish, slightly spicy flavours, light and ready.

DRY $19 –V

Riverby Estate Marlborough Pinot Noir

★★★

The 2009 vintage (★★★) is a single-vineyard wine, grown in the heart of the Wairau Valley and matured for a year in French oak casks (20 per cent new). Fruity and supple, it's a ruby-hued, moderately rich style with cherry and slight herb flavours, showing some savoury complexity. The 2010 (★★★☆) is fleshy and smooth, with very good depth of ripe cherry, plum and spice flavours. Finely balanced for early drinking, it shows considerable complexity and should reward cellaring.

DRY $28 –V

River Farm Godfrey Road Marlborough Pinot Noir

(★★★☆)

The mouthfilling 2009 vintage (★★★☆) was hand-picked in the Wairau Valley at 24.6 brix, fermented with indigenous yeasts, and matured for 11 months in French oak barriques. Sturdy (14.5 per cent alcohol), it is scented and supple, with moderately concentrated cherry/plum flavours and some nutty complexity. It's quite open and expressive; drink now onwards.

Vintage	09
WR	6
Drink	11-15

DRY $29 AV

Roaring Meg Pinot Noir – see Mt Difficulty Roaring Meg Pinot Noir

Rockburn Central Otago Pinot Noir   ★★★★☆

This consistently stylish blend of Parkburn, Cromwell Basin (principally) and Gibbston grapes is matured in French oak barriques (30 to 40 per cent new). It typically offers concentrated cherry, plum and herb flavours, very finely textured and silky. The 2010 vintage (★★★★★) is a generous, layered wine, already delicious. It reveals dense plum and spice flavours, showing good, savoury complexity, ripe, supple tannins and an attractively floral, smoky and savoury bouquet.

Vintage	10	09	08	07
WR	7	7	5	7
Drink	12-20	11-18	11-13	11-16

 DRY $45 –V

Rockburn Twelve Barrels Central Otago Pinot Noir   -   (★★★★★)

The 2009 vintage (★★★★★) is a single-vineyard red, estate-grown at Parkburn and matured in French oak casks (50 per cent new). Selected from 234 barrels, and bottled unfined and unfiltered, it is deeply coloured and sweet-fruited, with a compelling density of cherry, plum and nut flavours, very supple and finely poised. A youthful, very elegant wine, it should be in peak form mid-2012+.

Vintage	09
WR	7
Drink	11-20

 DRY $85 AV

Rock Face Waipara Pinot Noir   ★★☆

From Bishop's Head, the 2009 vintage (★★) is very developed, with green-edged, rustic flavours.

 DRY $22 –V

Rock Ferry Central Otago Pinot Noir   (★★★★☆)

The savoury, unusually complex 2009 vintage (★★★★☆) is a single-vineyard red from Bendigo, in the Cromwell Basin, fermented with indigenous yeasts. Deeply coloured, with concentrated, ripe plum and spice flavours, it's built to last; best drinking 2013+.

 DRY $39 V+

Rock N Pillar Central Otago Pinot Noir   (★★★★)

From the Moffitt family, of Dry Gully, the 2008 vintage (★★★★) was grown in the Rock N Pillar Vineyard, overlooking the Dunstan Basin at Alexandra. Fermented with indigenous yeasts and matured in French oak casks (30 per cent new), it's a delicious wine, full-coloured, ripe, savoury and supple, with finely textured cherry and spice flavours showing good complexity.

Vintage	08
WR	5
Drink	11-18

DRY $26 V+

Rocky Point Central Otago Pinot Noir ★★★☆

From Prophet's Rock, the youthful 2010 vintage (★★★☆) was estate-grown at Bendigo and matured in French oak casks (20 per cent new). Deep and youthful in colour, it's a fruit-driven style, packed with cherryish, plummy, slightly herbal flavour, fresh, strong and smooth.

Vintage	10	09	08	07	06
WR	7	6	6	7	6
Drink	12-15	12-15	11-14	11-14	11-13

DRY $28 AV

Rongopai Marlborough Pinot Noir (★★☆)

From Babich, the 2009 vintage (★★☆) is full-bodied, with cherry, plum, spice and nut flavours, showing some complexity, and a firm, slightly grippy finish.

DRY $18 AV

Rua Central Otago Pinot Noir – see Akarua Rua Central Otago Pinot Noir

Russian Jack Pinot Noir ★★★

From Martinborough Vineyard, the 2010 vintage (★★★) is a good, drink-young style with a spicy, slightly herbal bouquet and plenty of smooth, vibrant, cherryish, plummy, spicy flavour.

DRY $22 AV

St Jacques Nelson Pinot Noir ★★☆

From Blackenbrook, the 2008 vintage (★★★) was estate-grown, hand-picked and matured for a year in seasoned French oak barrels. Drinking well in its youth, it has good depth of berry, spice and herb flavours, with a hint of oak adding complexity.

Vintage	08
WR	6
Drink	P

DRY $23 –V

Sacred Hill Halo Marlborough Pinot Noir ★★★☆

Showing lots of drink-young appeal, the 2009 vintage (★★★☆) was mostly estate-grown and hand-picked in the Waihopai Valley, and 'blended with a touch of Central Otago Pinot for complexity'. French oak-aged, it is full-bodied (14.5 per cent), scented and supple, with fresh strawberry/spice flavours, showing good depth and some savoury complexity.

Vintage	09
WR	6
Drink	11-14

DRY $26 AV

Sacred Hill Marlborough Pinot Noir ★★★

The 2010 vintage (★★★) was matured 'with' French oak for nine months. Fresh-scented, it is buoyantly fruity and supple, with gentle acidity and lots of drink-young charm.

DRY $21 AV

Sacred Hill Prospector Central Otago Pinot Noir ★★★★

Grown in a single vineyard at Bannockburn, the 2009 vintage (★★★★) was matured for 16 months in French oak casks. Well worth cellaring, it is deeply coloured, concentrated and savoury, with elegant, sweet-fruit flavours, good complexity, and a firm foundation of tannin.

Vintage	09
WR	6
Drink	11-16

DRY $60 –V

Sacred Hill The Wine Thief Series Dry Run Central Otago Pinot Noir (★★★☆)

Offering drink-young charm, the 2008 vintage (★★★☆) is a single-vineyard red, grown at Lowburn, hand-picked and matured for a year in French oak casks (25 per cent new). Bright ruby, it is floral, fresh, vibrantly fruity and supple, with moderately concentrated cherry and plum flavours, finely integrated oak and gentle tannins.

Vintage	08
WR	6
Drink	P

DRY $30 –V

Saddleback Central Otago Pinot Noir ★★★☆

From Peregrine, the 2008 vintage (★★★☆) is a skilfully crafted, drink-young style, hand-picked and matured in French oak casks (20 per cent new). Ruby-hued and floral, with very good body and depth of ripe strawberry and spice flavours, showing some savoury complexity and gentle tannins, it's verging on four-star quality.

DRY $25 AV

Saint Clair Marlborough Pinot Noir ★★★☆

The 2009 (★★★☆), French oak-aged for nine months, is a supple red with considerable elegance. It has cherry, plum and slight herb flavours, showing good ripeness, in a light to medium-bodied style, enjoyable young. The 2010 vintage (★★★☆), matured in tanks and barrels, is ruby-hued, fruity and supple, with lively cherry/spice flavours, a touch of complexity, and lots of drink-young appeal.

DRY $25 AV

Saint Clair Omaka Reserve Marlborough Pinot Noir ★★★★

This is Saint Clair's top Pinot Noir. The 2007 vintage (★★★★) was grown mostly in the company's vineyards in the Omaka Valley, and matured for 10 months in French oak barriques (68 per cent new). Deep ruby, it is fresh, vibrant, flowing and supple, with sweet-fruit characters, cherry, plum and olive flavours, gentle tannins and good complexity. There is no 2008.

Vintage	08	07	06
WR	NM	6	NM
Drink	NM	P	NM

DRY $37 AV

Saint Clair Pioneer Block 4 Sawcut Pinot Noir   ★★★★

Grown in Marlborough's Ure Valley, 40 kilometres south of the Wairau Valley, the Pinot Noirs from this site are deeply coloured and flavoursome, although sometimes a bit leafy. The 2009 vintage (★★★★), matured in French oak casks (53 per cent new), is richly floral, vibrantly fruity and youthful, with pure, ripe, sweet-fruit flavours of cherries and plums, seasoned with French oak. An elegant, intensely varietal wine with fresh, lively acidity, it's well worth cellaring.

DRY $33 AV

Saint Clair Pioneer Block 5 Bull Block Marlborough Pinot Noir   ★★★★☆

From clay soils on the south side of the Omaka Valley, the 2009 vintage (★★★★☆) was matured for 10 months in French oak casks (31 per cent new). Still youthful and built to last, it is deeply coloured, with strong, ripe cherry, plum and spice flavours, savoury and complex. Woven with fresh acidity, it is finely textured and weighty.

DRY $33 V+

Saint Clair Pioneer Block 10 Twin Hills Marlborough Pinot Noir   (★★★☆)

From the Omaka Valley, the 2010 vintage (★★★☆) was matured in French oak barriques (78 per cent new). Floral, supple and very youthful, it is vibrantly fruity, with cherryish, plummy flavours, showing very good depth, a seasoning of toasty oak and fresh acidity. Open 2013+.

DRY $33 –V

Saint Clair Pioneer Block 12 Lone Gum Pinot Noir   ★★★★☆

The 2010 vintage (★★★★☆), grown in the Omaka Valley and matured in French oak casks (25 per cent new), could easily be mistaken for a Central Otago wine, it's so vibrantly fruity and floral. Fleshy and richly coloured, it's very full-bodied and sweet-fruited, with finely integrated oak and good density of cherry, plum and spice flavours. The 2009 (★★★★★) is a beautifully rich, densely packed and flowing red.

DRY $33 V+

Saint Clair Pioneer Block 14 Doctor's Creek Pinot Noir   ★★★★☆

Formerly sold under a Reserve label, the 2009 vintage (★★★★★) was estate-grown in the Doctor's Creek Vineyard, south-west of Blenheim. A fragrant, dense, sweet-fruited wine with deep colour and generous plum and spice flavours, it has concentration right through the palate, structured tannins and good length. The 2010 (★★★★), which includes some Ure Valley fruit, was matured for 10 months in French oak barriques (36 per cent new). Deeply coloured, mouthfilling and fresh, with strong, plummy, spicy flavours, it is sweet-fruited, with excellent concentration and complexity.

DRY $33 V+

Saint Clair Pioneer Block 15 Strip Block Pinot Noir   ★★★★☆

From the lower reaches of the Waihopai Valley, the 2010 vintage (★★★★☆) was matured for 10 months in French oak barriques (37 per cent new). A powerful, very ripe-tasting red, deeply coloured, rich and rounded, it is soft and generous, with plum, cherry and spice flavours, showing good complexity. Already approachable, it's well worth cellaring.

DRY $33 V+

Saint Clair Pioneer Block 16 Awatere Pinot Noir ★★★★☆

Grown at a north-facing hill site overlooking the Awatere Valley, the 2010 vintage (★★★★☆) is an elegant red, matured for 10 months in French oak casks (54 per cent new). A very youthful wine, powerful and poised, it is deeply coloured, vibrantly fruity, rich and flowing, with deep cherry, plum and spice flavours, fresh acidity and a long finish.

 DRY $33 V+

Saint Clair Pioneer Block 22 Barn Block Pinot Noir (★★★★★)

Grown on the southern edge of the Wairau Valley, at the base of the Wither Hills, the 2010 vintage (★★★★★) is Pinot Noir on steroids – but it retains varietal character and freshness. Notably dark, it is a strapping wine (14.5 per cent alcohol), fruit-packed, with dense cherry, plum and spice flavours, very rich and lush. A real 'wow!' factor.

 DRY $33 V+

Saint Clair Vicar's Choice Marlborough Pinot Noir ★★☆

Designed as Saint Clair's 'entry-level' Pinot Noir, the 2009 vintage (★★☆) was partly barrel-aged. It's a light, green-edged wine, lacking real richness.

 DRY $19 –V

Satellite Marlborough Pinot Noir ★★★

From Spy Valley, the 2010 vintage (★★★) is a fruit-driven style, bright ruby, with good depth of plummy flavour, fresh, vibrant and smooth.

 DRY $19 AV

Saveé Sea Marlborough Pinot Noir (★★☆)

The 2008 vintage (★★☆) is a light to medium-bodied style with pleasant cherry, spice and herb flavours, green-edged, but with a touch of complexity. It's a forward, well-rounded wine, for no-fuss, early drinking.

 DRY $18 AV

Scott Base Central Otago Pinot Noir ★★★☆

From Allan Scott, the 2009 vintage (★★★☆) is a single-vineyard red, grown at Cromwell and matured for a year in French oak casks (25 per cent new). It's a moderately rich wine, ruby-hued, with fresh, vibrant cherry and plum flavours, showing considerable complexity.

Vintage	09	08
WR	6	6
Drink	12-17	11-13

DRY $35 –V

Secret Stone Marlborough Pinot Noir ★★★

From Foster's Group, owner of Matua Valley, the 2009 vintage (★★★☆) was released at less than a year old. Bright ruby, it is mouthfilling and sweet-fruited, with very satisfying depth of plum and spice flavours, showing some oak complexity, gentle tannins, and drink-young appeal.

 DRY $22 AV

Seifried Nelson Pinot Noir ★★☆

Matured for 10 months in French oak barriques (new to two years old), the 2009 vintage (★★☆) is ruby-hued, with pleasant, light strawberry and spice flavours, a hint of oak and drink-young charm. The 2010 (★★☆) is gutsy (14.5 per cent alcohol), with mouthfilling body and firm, slightly leafy flavours.

Vintage	10	09	08	07	06
WR	5	6	6	6	6
Drink	11-15	11-15	11-14	11-12	P

DRY $21 –V

Seifried Winemakers Collection Pinot Noir ★★★

The 2009 vintage (★★★) was grown in Nelson and matured for nine months in new and one-year-old French oak barriques. Still youthful, it is ruby-hued and supple, with ripe plum and spice flavours, showing some savoury complexity. (The 2010 vintage is branded Aotea – see that wine.)

Vintage	09	08	07	06
WR	5	7	6	6
Drink	11-16	11-15	11-14	P

DRY $35 –V

Selaks Winemaker's Favourite Central Otago Pinot Noir ★★★☆

The 2009 vintage (★★★☆) was grown at Bendigo. A fruit-driven style, it is deeply coloured, with vibrant cherry, plum and spice flavours, showing very good depth, a subtle seasoning of oak, and gentle tannins. Drink now.

DRY $26 AV

Seresin Home Marlborough Pinot Noir ★★★★☆

The 2008 vintage (★★★★) was estate-grown near Renwick, in the central Wairau Valley, hand-picked, fermented with indigenous yeasts, matured for 15 months in French oak barriques (35 per cent new), and bottled unfined and unfiltered. Full and slightly developed in colour, with an earthy bouquet, it is rich and flowing, with cherry, plum, spice and nut flavours, savoury and firm.

Vintage	08	07
WR	6	7
Drink	11-17	11-18

DRY $50 –V

Seresin Leah Pinot Noir ★★★★

Unlike the single-vineyard reds, this immediately appealing, lower-priced wine is grown at three sites – the Home Vineyard, Raupo Creek and Tatou – and is less new oak-influenced. The 2009 vintage (★★★★☆) was hand-picked, fermented with indigenous yeasts, matured for 11 months in French oak barriques (25 per cent new), and bottled without fining and filtering. Delicious now, it is a very 'feminine' style of Pinot Noir, finely scented, savoury and supple, with strong strawberry, cherry and spice flavours, and loads of personality.

Vintage	09	08	07	06	05	04
WR	7	6	7	6	6	7
Drink	11-15	11-15	11-15	11-12	P	P

DRY $38 AV

Seresin Rachel Marlborough Pinot Noir   ★★★★

From three company-owned sites, the 2009 vintage (★★★★☆) was hand-harvested, fermented with indigenous yeasts, matured for nine months in French oak barriques (35 per cent new), followed by another six months in barrels, and then bottled unfined and unfiltered. Ruby-hued (and not entirely clear), with a savoury bouquet, it's an unusually complex style, sweet-fruited, with rich plum, cherry, spice and nut flavours. A wine of strong personality, it's already approachable; drink now or cellar.

Vintage	09
WR	7
Drink	11-18

 DRY $57 –V

Seresin Raupo Creek Pinot Noir   ★★★★

Grown on clay slopes in the Omaka Valley, the 2008 vintage (★★★★) is a single-vineyard wine, fermented with indigenous yeasts, matured for 15 months in French oak barriques (30 per cent new), and bottled unfined and unfiltered. Deeply coloured, with fresh, strong flavours of plums, cherries, spices and herbs, it shows good complexity, but needs time; open mid-2012+.

Vintage	08	07	06	05	04
WR	6	7	6	7	6
Drink	11-17	11-18	11-15	11-12	P

 DRY $55 –V

Seresin Sun & Moon Marlborough Pinot Noir   ★★★★☆

Only 732 bottles were made of the 2008 vintage (★★★★☆), 'the very best expression of Pinot Noir we can make'. From the hillside Raupo Creek Vineyard, in the Omaka Valley, it was fermented with indigenous yeasts, matured for 17 months in French oak barriques, and bottled unfined and unfiltered. Built to last, it is deep ruby, mouthfilling and sweet-fruited, in a 'masculine' style with firm, spicy, nutty flavours, showing excellent concentration. Still fresh and youthful, it's a wine to ponder.

Vintage	08	07
WR	6	7
Drink	11-20	11-18

 DRY $125 –V

Seresin Tatou Pinot Noir   ★★★★☆

Grown in deep gravels at the upper end of the Wairau Valley, the 2008 vintage (★★★★☆) is certified organic. Hand-picked, it was fermented with indigenous yeasts and matured for 15 months in French oak barriques (30 per cent new). Deep and youthful in colour, it is fleshy, with rich plum/spice flavours woven with fresh acidity, and finely poised, with ripe, supple tannins. Open mid-2012+.

Vintage	08	07	06	05	04
WR	6	7	6	7	7
Drink	11-17	11-18	11-17	11-14	P

DRY $55 –V

Shaky Bridge Central Otago Pinot Noir   ★★★☆

Grown at Alexandra, the 2009 vintage (★★★☆) is full-coloured, with a subtle seasoning of oak. It's a slightly herbal style, with very good depth of flavour, cherryish and spicy.

Vintage	09
WR	5
Drink	12-15

DRY $35 –V

Shaky Bridge Pioneer Series Central Otago Pinot Noir   (★★★☆)

The 2010 vintage (★★★☆), barrel-aged for 11 months, is a fresh, youthful Alexandra red with very good depth of plum and spice flavours, showing a distinct herbal streak. Slightly earthy and gamey, it has fine-grained tannins and some cellaring potential.

Vintage	10
WR	6
Drink	11-12

 DRY $25 AV

Shingle Peak New Zealand Pinot Noir   ★★☆

In the past labelled as Matua Valley Shingle Peak Marlborough Pinot Noir, this is now a country-wide blend. The 2009 vintage (★★☆) is ruby-hued and mouthfilling, with solid depth of cherryish, plummy flavours, slightly spicy and smooth.

DRY $18 AV

Shingle Peak Reserve Release Marlborough Pinot Noir   (★★★)

Made in a 'fruit-driven' style, the 2010 vintage (★★★) is ruby-hued, with lots of fresh, ripe, cherryish, plummy, slightly nutty flavour, offering good, easy drinking.

 DRY $23 AV

Sileni Cellar Selection Hawke's Bay Pinot Noir   ★★★

Top vintages work well as a drink-young proposition. On the market within six months of the harvest, it's a Beaujolais-style red, made with 'minimal' oak handling. The 2010 (★★★) is buoyantly fruity, with ripe, cherryish, strawberryish flavours, and gentle acidity and tannins giving a soft, easy finish.

DRY $20 AV

Sileni Exceptional Vintage Pinot Noir   ★★★★

Grown in the company's elevated, inland vineyard between Maraekakaho and Mangatahi, the 2009 vintage (★★★★) is a youthful Hawke's Bay red with full, ruby colour. Mouthfilling, it has vibrant cherry and spice flavours, fresh and generous, and a nutty, savoury complexity.

Vintage	09
WR	5
Drink	12-15

DRY $60 –V

Sileni Springstone Hawke's Bay Pinot Noir   (★★☆)

Grown mostly in the Springstone Vineyard, at Mangatahi, the 2010 vintage (★★☆) was barrel-aged for 10 months. Cherryish and slightly herbal, with some oak complexity, it's an attractive wine, but shows a slight lack of concentration.

DRY $32 –V

Sileni The Plateau Hawke's Bay Pinot Noir   ★★★☆

Estate-grown in the inland, elevated Plateau Vineyard at Maraekakaho, and barrel-aged for 10 months, the strongly varietal, ruby-hued 2009 vintage (★★★☆) shows very good depth of vibrant plum and spice flavours, fresh and smooth.

Vintage	09	08	07
WR	6	6	5
Drink	11-15	11-14	11-13

DRY $30 –V

Sisters Ridge North Canterbury Pinot Noir   (★★★☆)

From the owners of Mt Beautiful, the 2009 vintage (★★★☆) was grown in the Cheviot Hills, hand-picked and matured for 10 months in French oak casks. Ruby-hued, it is mouthfilling, with ripe cherry, spice and herb flavours, showing some savoury complexity. Drink now or cellar.

DRY $23 V+

Sliding Hill Marlborough Pinot Noir   (★★★)

The 2009 vintage (★★★) is ruby-hued, scented and supple, with red-berry, plum and spice flavours, in a drink-young style with a touch of complexity. Ready.

DRY $25 –V

Soderberg Home Block Single Vineyard Marlborough Pinot Noir   (★★★★)

Not scheduled for release until March/April 2012 (and with no price available at the time of publication), the 2010 vintage (★★★★) is from a tiny, 1-hectare vineyard at the base of the Wither Hills that previously supplied the grapes for Koru. Matured in French oak casks (20 per cent new), it is full-coloured and finely scented, with rich, ripe cherry, plum and spice flavours, gentle tannins, and a silky, well-rounded finish. Drink now onwards.

DRY $? V?

Soho Marlborough Pinot Noir   ★★★☆

From an Auckland-based company, the 2010 vintage (★★★★) was bottled unfined and unfiltered. A full-flavoured, complex wine, already drinking well, it is sturdy and richly coloured, with excellent depth of cherry, plum and spice flavours, a hint of herbs and fine-grained tannins.

DRY $34 –V

Soho McQueen Central Otago Pinot Noir   ★★★★

The 2009 vintage (★★★★) was grown at Gibbston and Bannockburn, and matured in French oak casks (35 per cent new). Richly scented and deeply coloured, it has cherry, plum and slight herb flavours, vibrant and supple, showing excellent complexity and concentration. The 2010 (★★★★☆) is boldly coloured, fleshy and supple, with strong plum/spice flavours, seasoned with quality oak, and good, savoury complexity. It's a rich, youthful wine; open 2013+.

Vintage	10	DRY $40 –V
WR	7	
Drink	11-20	

Soho White Marlborough Pinot Noir   (★★★☆)

The 2010 vintage (★★★☆) is full-coloured, mouthfilling and sweet-fruited, with very good depth of plum and spice flavours, fresh acidity, and drink-young appeal.

Vintage	10	DRY $25 AV
WR	7	
Drink	11-18	

Soljans Barrique Reserve Marlborough Pinot Noir   ★★★

The 2010 vintage (★★☆) is developed for its age, with cherry, plum and spice flavours, quite savoury and leathery. Drink now.

Vintage	10	DRY $30 –V
WR	6	
Drink	11-16	

Soma Nelson Pinot Noir   ★★★☆

The 2008 vintage (★★★) was hand-picked in the Avery Vineyard at Hope and matured for 10 months in French oak barrels (one year old). Ruby-hued, it is full-bodied, with cherry and herb flavours showing decent depth, some savoury complexity, and a fairly firm finish.

Vintage	08	DRY $25 AV
WR	6	
Drink	11-15	

Southern Cross Hawke's Bay Pinot Noir   ★★

From One Tree Hill Vineyards, a division of Morton Estate, the 2009 vintage (★★) is a drink-young quaffer, with lightish, slightly developed colour. Full-bodied, it has cherry, nut and herb flavours, showing moderate depth. Priced right.

Vintage	09	DRY $13 AV
WR	6	
Drink	11-13	

Southern Lighthouse Nelson Pinot Noir   (★★☆)

Offering light, easy drinking, the 2010 vintage (★★☆) is a ruby-hued, medium-bodied red, fresh, plummy and smooth, with a Beaujolais-like appeal.

DRY $17 AV

Spinyback Nelson Pinot Noir   ★★☆

From Waimea Estates, the 2009 vintage (★★☆) is light ruby, with very satisfying depth of plum and herb flavours. It shows a slight lack of ripeness and roundness, but also some savoury complexity, and is priced right. Verging on three stars.

Vintage	09	08	07
WR	7	6	7
Drink	11-12	11-12	P

DRY $18 AV

Sprig by Bouldevines Marlborough Pinot Noir   (★★★☆)

Estate-grown in the Bouldevines Vineyard and matured for 10 months in French oak barrels (10 per cent new), the 2009 vintage (★★★☆) is a fleshy, generous red, full-coloured, with ripe, plummy flavours, showing moderate complexity, and a smooth finish. Fine value.

Vintage	09
WR	6
Drink	11-15

DRY $20 V+

Spring Creek Estate Marlborough Pinot Noir   ★★★

Grown at Rapaura, on the north side of the Wairau Valley, the 2009 vintage (★★★) was matured for 10 months in French oak barriques. Ruby-hued, it is mouthfilling and sweet-fruited, with very satisfying depth of cherry and spice flavours, ripe and smooth. Priced sharply.

Vintage	09	08
WR	5	4
Drink	11-14	P

DRY $18 V+

Spy Valley Envoy Marlborough Pinot Noir   ★★★★☆

The 2009 vintage (★★★★☆) was matured for 18 months in French oak barriques (60 per cent new). Estate-grown in the lower Waihopai Valley, it is deeply coloured and very mouthfilling (14.5 per cent alcohol), with deep cherry/plum flavours, finely integrated oak, and a rich, rounded finish. It's a powerful, but very graceful and youthful wine; open 2013+.

Vintage	09	08	07	06	05
WR	6	6	7	6	7
Drink	11-15	11-14	11-13	11-12	P

DRY $56 –V

Spy Valley Envoy Outpost Marlborough Pinot Noir   (★★★★☆)

More 'feminine' and 'funky' than its Envoy stablemate from the same season, the 2008 vintage (★★★★☆) was sourced from hill-grown vines in the Omaka Valley (5 kilometres from the Waihopai Valley estate vineyard), and French oak-matured for 18 months. Full ruby, it is mouthfilling and youthful, with fresh, vibrant cherry and spice flavours, showing good concentration, and some 'forest floor' notes adding complexity.

Vintage	08
WR	6
Drink	11-14

 DRY $56 –V

Spy Valley Marlborough Pinot Noir   ★★★★

The 2010 vintage (★★★★) was hand-picked at 23.5–26.7 brix, fermented with indigenous yeasts and matured for eight months in French oak casks. Youthful, fruit-packed and supple, with substantial body and strong plum/spice flavours, delicately seasoned with oak, it is deliciously smooth, with plenty of potential.

Vintage	10	09	08	07	06	05	04
WR	6	7	6	7	6	6	6
Drink	11-15	11-13	11-12	11-12	P	P	P

 DRY $32 AV

Squealing Pig Central Otago Pinot Noir   (★★★☆)

From Matua Valley, the 2010 (★★★☆) was French oak-aged for 10 months. Bright ruby, it is invitingly floral and sweet-fruited, with fresh, moderately complex cherry and plum flavours, showing good depth, and ripe, supple tannins. It's still very youthful; open mid-2012+.

 DRY $28 AV

Staete Landt Marlborough Pinot Noir   ★★★☆

This single-vineyard red is typically very fragrant and supple. The 2008 vintage (★★★★) was grown at Rapaura, hand-picked at 24.9 to 26.4 brix, and matured for 18 months in French oak casks (20 per cent new). An elegant wine, ruby-hued, it has ripe plum/spice flavours, showing some nutty complexity. Fresh and tight-knit, it is finely textured, with good aging potential.

Vintage	08
WR	7
Drink	11-17

 DRY $39 –V

Stafford Lane Nelson Pinot Noir   ★★☆

The 2008 vintage (★★) was hand-harvested at 23 brix and not barrel-aged. It's a simple, drink-young style, with light strawberry and spice flavours and a smooth finish.

DRY $20 –V

Stockmans Station Central Otago Pinot Noir ★★★☆

From Wild Earth, the 2009 vintage (★★★★) is a delicious, finely crafted, drink-young style. Ruby-hued, with an invitingly scented, floral bouquet, it is buoyantly fruity, with fresh, ripe cherry, plum and spice flavours, and offers greater density and complexity than you'd expect at this price.

DRY $25 AV

Stoneburn Marlborough Pinot Noir (★★★)

From Hunter's, the 2008 vintage (★★★) is mouthfilling, with a ripe, slightly earthy bouquet. Bright ruby, it is fresh and plummy, with a touch of spicy complexity and decent depth.

DRY $20 AV

Stoneleigh Latitude Marlborough Pinot Noir (★★★☆)

Celebrating the 'Golden Mile' along Rapaura Road, on the stony north side of the Wairau Valley, the debut 2010 vintage (★★★☆) was matured for eight months in French oak casks (30 per cent new). Full-coloured, it is sweet-fruited and smooth, in a vibrantly fruity style with very good depth of fresh plum/spice flavours and lots of drink-young charm.

DRY $28 AV

Stoneleigh Marlborough Pinot Noir ★★★

The 2009 vintage (★★★☆) from Pernod Ricard NZ was grown on the relatively warm, north side of the Wairau Valley, picked at 23.5 to 24.5 brix, matured in French oak casks, and bottled unfined. Floral and supple, it is ruby-hued, with cherry, plum and spice flavours, showing some savoury complexity. The 2010 (★★★) is similar, with good depth of fresh, ripe, plummy, spicy flavours, a subtle seasoning of oak adding complexity, gentle tannins, and drink-young appeal.

Vintage	10	09	08	07	06
WR	6	6	6	6	6
Drink	11-13	11-12	P	P	P

DRY $24 AV

Stoneleigh Vineyards Rapaura Series Marlborough Pinot Noir ★★★★

French oak-matured for 10 months, the 2009 vintage (★★★★) is a sturdy (14.5 per cent alcohol), concentrated, ripe and spicy red, showing a strong oak influence in its youth, with excellent texture and richness. It should mature well. The 2010 (★★★★) has deep cherry, plum and spice flavours, nutty and savoury, good complexity and ripe, supple tannins. Best drinking 2013+.

Vintage	10	09	08	07	06	05
WR	6	6	6	6	6	5
Drink	11-13	11-12	P	P	P	P

DRY $32 AV

Stone Paddock Central Otago Pinot Noir ★★★

From Paritua, the 2009 vintage (★★☆) was grown at Lowburn, in the Cromwell Basin, and oak-aged. Medium-bodied, it's a smooth, green-edged wine with plummy, herbal flavours, showing decent depth.

DRY $25 –V

Stonewall Marlborough Pinot Noir (★★)

From Forrest, the 2008 vintage (★★) is light, simple and smooth, lacking any real depth or appeal.

DRY $19 –V

Summerhouse Marlborough Pinot Noir ★★★☆

The 2009 vintage (★★★☆) is a single-vineyard red, hand-picked and matured for 11 months in French oak barriques. It's a moderately concentrated wine, ruby-hued and supple, with cherry, plum and nut flavours showing good varietal character and some savoury complexity.

DRY $32 –V

Surveyor Thomson Central Otago Pinot Noir ★★★☆

The 2007 vintage (★★★☆) from this Lowburn-based producer is a moderately mature red with a nutty, spicy bouquet, leading into a firm and savoury palate. It shows a slight lack of softness and charm, but also very good depth and complexity. The 2008 (★★★★) is a generous red with excellent ripeness, complexity and depth. It's a graceful, savoury wine, showing good 'pinosity', and likely to be long-lived.

DRY $42 –V

Takutai Nelson Pinot Noir ★★☆

The 2009 vintage (★★★) from Waimea Estates is a great buy. It has a spicy, slightly herbal bouquet, leading into a gutsy wine with spice and green-olive flavours, earthy and chewy.

Vintage	09
WR	5
Drink	11-13

DRY $12 V+

Tarras Vineyards Central Otago Pinot Noir ˙ (★★★★)

The deeply coloured 2008 vintage (★★★★) is an elegant red, grown in The Steppes and The Canyon vineyards. Matured in French oak barriques (30 per cent new), it's a mouthfilling wine with excellent depth of warm, spicy flavour and a backbone of firm, ripe tannins.

Vintage	08
WR	7
Drink	11-16

DRY $32 AV

Tarras Vineyards The Canyon Pinot Noir ★★★★☆

Grown at Bendigo, in Central Otago, and matured in French oak barriques (30 per cent new), the 2008 vintage (★★★★☆) is deeply coloured and beautifully scented. Rich and very vibrant, it has strong, ripe, cherryish flavours, finely integrated oak and supple tannins. A graceful wine, it should reward cellaring.

Vintage	08	07
WR	7	7
Drink	11-18	11-17

DRY $42 AV

Tarras Vineyards The Steppes Pinot Noir   ★★★★☆

The 2008 vintage (★★★★☆) is a single-vineyard red, grown at Tarras (a much cooler site than Bendigo, 10 kilometres away), and matured in French oak barriques (30 per cent new). Deeply coloured, it is sweet-fruited, with strong cherry/spice flavours, warm and savoury. It's a dense, rich Central Otago wine with good presence.

Vintage	08
WR	7
Drink	11-17

DRY $42 AV

Tasman Bay New Zealand Pinot Noir   ★★

The 2008 vintage (★★☆) was grown in Nelson and Marlborough, and aged 'on' French oak (meaning not barrel-aged). Ruby-hued, it is enjoyable young, with cherry, herb and spice flavours, light and smooth.

DRY $19 –V

Te Henga Premium The Westie Marlborough Pinot Noir   (★★☆)

From Babich, the 2008 vintage (★★☆) is pale ruby, in a light style with smooth, cherryish, spicy flavours, balanced for easy, early drinking.

DRY $17 AV

Te Kairanga Estate Martinborough Pinot Noir   ★★★☆

The 2009 vintage (★★★☆) is a good-value, drink-young style, oak-matured for eight months. Ruby-hued and floral, it has fresh, strong berry/spice flavours, a hint of herbs and some savoury complexity.

Vintage	09	08
WR	7	7
Drink	11-13	11-12

DRY $21 V+

Te Kairanga John Martin Reserve Martinborough Pinot Noir   ★★★★

The 2009 vintage (★★★★) was hand-harvested and matured for 20 months in French oak barriques (50 per cent new). Deeply coloured and sturdy (14.5 per cent alcohol), it's a firm, very ripe-tasting wine with concentrated plum/spice flavours, hints of liquorice and nuts, and good complexity. It shows some maturity; drink now or cellar.

Vintage	09	08	07	06	05
WR	7	NM	7	6	5
Drink	11-18	NM	11-16	11-15	11-14

DRY $49 –V

Te Kairanga Runholder Martinborough Pinot Noir   ★★★☆

This is the middle-tier label. The 2008 vintage (★★★☆), matured for 10 months in French oak barriques (25 per cent new), is drinking well now. Full-coloured, it is mouthfilling, with an array of plum, herb, spice and nut flavours, fresh acidity, and very good complexity and depth.

Vintage	08	07	06	05
WR	7	6	6	5
Drink	11-15	11-13	11-12	P

 DRY $29 AV

Te Mania Nelson Pinot Noir   ★★☆

The 2009 vintage (★★★), matured in a mix of tanks and barrels, is a slightly herbal wine, but firm, spicy, savoury and full-flavoured.

Vintage	09	08	07	06	05
WR	6	5	7	6	7
Drink	11-14	11-13	11-12	11-12	P

DRY $22 –V

Te Mania Reserve Nelson Pinot Noir   ★★★★

Hand-harvested and matured for 10 months in French oak barrels (30 per cent new), the 2009 vintage (★★★★) is full-flavoured and finely textured, with ripe plum, spice and dried-herb characters, gently seasoned with toasty oak, and a floral bouquet. It shows good complexity and richness.

Vintage	09	08	07	06
WR	6	5	7	6
Drink	11-14	11-13	11-14	11-12

 DRY $35 AV

Te Mara Central Otago Pinot Noir   ★★★☆

The 2008 vintage (★★★☆) is a scented, supple, mid-weight style. The bouquet is spicy and savoury; the palate is cherryish and plummy, with a hint of herbs and gentle tannins.

 DRY $36 –V

Terrace Edge Waipara Valley Pinot Noir   ★★★☆

The 2009 vintage (★★★☆) was hand-picked, fermented with indigenous yeasts and matured in French oak barriques. A moderately complex style, it is ruby-hued and attractively floral, with mouthfilling body and vibrant cherry, plum and spice flavours, fresh, ripe and supple.

DRY $25 AV

Terrace Heights Estate Marlborough Pinot Noir   ★★★☆

The 2010 vintage (★★★★), matured in French oak casks, is deeply coloured, concentrated and supple, with fresh, strong plum, herb and spice flavours, seasoned with fine-quality oak, and a finely balanced, long finish. Well worth cellaring.

Vintage	10	09
WR	5	6
Drink	11-15	11-15

 DRY $30 –V

Terravin Cowley Vineyard Pinot Noir   (★★★★☆)

Still a baby, the 2010 vintage (★★★★☆) was grown in the Southern Valleys, Marlborough, hand-picked at 23.5 brix, fermented with indigenous yeasts, French oak-matured for 11 months, and bottled unfined and unfiltered. A very graceful wine, it is full-coloured, savoury and complex, with intense, youthful cherry/spice flavours, woven with fresh acidity, a nutty oak influence, and good tannin backbone. Open mid-2013+.

DRY $60 –V

Terravin Eaton Family Vineyard Pinot Noir   ★★★★☆

Estate-grown in Marlborough, the 2009 vintage (★★★★☆) was hand-picked at 23.5 brix, fermented with indigenous yeasts, matured for 11 months in French oak casks (40 per cent new), and bottled unfined and unfiltered. It's a very 'feminine' style, floral and supple, with sweet-fruit delights. Highly perfumed, with ripe cherry, plum and spice flavours, woven with fresh acidity, and good, savoury complexity, it's a graceful wine, still very youthful. Open 2012+. The 2010 (★★★★★) is a beautiful, very 'complete' wine. Deep and youthful in colour, it is powerful and finely poised, with rich cherry, plum and spice flavours, showing excellent complexity, and silky tannins. Already delicious, it should be long-lived; open 2013+.

DRY $78 –V

Terravin Hillside Reserve Marlborough Pinot Noir   ★★★★★

Grown on clay slopes in the Omaka Valley, this exceptional red (until recently labelled Hillside Selection) is harvested from the centre of the slope, fermented with indigenous yeasts, matured for 16 to 20 months in French oak barriques (40 to 70 per cent new), and bottled without fining or filtering. The 2008 vintage (★★★★★) is a deeply coloured, masculine style of Pinot Noir, but not tough. Generous, rich and opulent, with a fragrant, warm and spicy bouquet, it is powerful yet supple, with deep, ripe flavours of cherries, plums and spices, and a hint of liquorice. Notably sweet-fruited and complex, it should be long-lived. (The 2009 vintage was grown at two sites – the Eaton and Cowley vineyards.)

Vintage	09	08	07	06	05
WR	7	6	NM	7	6
Drink	12-16	11-15	NM	11-13	11-13

DRY $56 AV

Terravin Pinot Noir   ★★★★☆

The 2009 vintage (★★★★) was grown in Marlborough and matured for 11 months in French oak barriques (35 per cent new). Finely scented, it is full-coloured and mouthfilling, with fresh, vibrant plum, spice and slight liquorice flavours, and supple tannins. The 2010 (★★★★★) is the best yet. Harvested at over 24 brix, French oak-aged for 11 months, and bottled unfined and unfiltered, it is beautifully scented. Already delicious, it is complex, savoury and supple, with lovely colour and depth of plum, cherry and spice flavours, finely textured and harmonious. A real standout.

DRY $39 V+

Thornbury Central Otago Pinot Noir   ★★★★☆

Typically a great buy. The 2010 vintage (★★★★☆) from Villa Maria was hand-picked at
Bannockburn and matured in French oak barriques (25 per cent new). It's an instantly appealing
wine, perfumed, rich and silky, with deep cherry and plum flavours, finely integrated oak and
ripe, supple tannins. Drink now or cellar.

Vintage	10	09	08	07	06	05
WR	6	6	7	6	7	6
Drink	11-15	11-15	11-15	11-14	11-13	P

DRY $33 V+

Three Miners Central Otago Pinot Noir   ★★★☆

This single-vineyard red is grown in the Earnscleugh Valley, between Alexandra and Clyde,
and matured in French oak barriques (25 per cent new). The 2010 vintage (★★★★) is richly
coloured, with bold, vibrant cherry and plum flavours to the fore. It's an elegant wine, with
concentrated, ripe sweet-fruit characters and a subtle seasoning of oak.

Vintage	10
WR	6
Drink	12-16

DRY $30 –V

Three Paddles Martinborough Pinot Noir   ★★★☆

From Nga Waka, this second-tier red is a rewarding drink-young style. The 2010 vintage
(★★★☆) is full-coloured and scented, with generous, plummy, cherryish, spicy flavours, ripe
and rounded. Best drinking mid-2012+.

Vintage	10
WR	7
Drink	11+

DRY $25 AV

Tiki Central Otago Pinot Noir   (★★★★)

The 2008 vintage (★★★★) is enjoyable now. Bright ruby, it is fresh, sweet-fruited and finely
balanced, with rich cherry, plum, spice and slight herb flavours, good, savoury, nutty complexity
and ripe, supple tannins.

DRY $45 –V

Tinpot Hut Marlborough Pinot Noir   (★★★)

The lively, youthful 2009 vintage (★★★) is a fresh, medium-bodied style with a light ruby hue
and cherry, plum and spice flavours, showing moderate concentration.

DRY $28 –V

Tohu Marlborough Pinot Noir   ★★★☆

The 2009 vintage (★★★★), grown in the Awatere and Waihopai valleys, was hand-picked and
matured in French oak casks (new to two years old). Full-bodied, with generous cherry, plum
and spice flavours and ripe, supple tannins, it has very good texture and length.

DRY $28 AV

Tohu Rore Reserve Marlborough Pinot Noir ★★★★☆

The 2009 vintage (★★★★) is firmly structured, with cherry, spice and dried-herb aromas and rich, ripe flavours, finely balanced, complex and long. The 2010 (★★★★☆), estate-grown in the Awatere Valley, is a barrel selection from two blocks. Deep ruby, it is full-bodied (14.5 per cent alcohol), very elegant and supple, with strong, cherryish, plummy, spicy flavours, ripe and savoury. Best drinking mid-2012+. (There is also a single block, 'Limited Release' version from 2010, very deep, ripe, nutty, savoury and age-worthy.)

Vintage	10	DRY $39 V+
WR	7	
Drink	11-20	

Tohu Single Vineyard Marlborough Pinot Noir (★★★★)

The 2010 vintage (★★★★), estate-grown and hand-picked in the Awatere Valley, is full-coloured, rich and supple, with deep strawberry, cherry and plum flavours, finely textured and already delicious.

Vintage	10	DRY $28 V+
WR	7	
Drink	11-15	

Tohu Young Vine Nelson Pinot Noir (★★★)

Enjoyable from the start, the 2010 vintage (★★★) is a simple but charming red, estate-grown at Upper Moutere. Light ruby, it is fresh, fruity and smooth, with lively strawberry/spice flavours, a touch of oak, and some elegance.

DRY $22 AV

Toi Toi Central Otago Reserve Single Vineyard Pinot Noir (★★★★)

Still a baby, the 2010 vintage (★★★★) is a full-coloured red, fermented with indigenous yeasts and barrel-aged for over a year. Sturdy and supple, it is fruit-packed, with excellent density of plum and spice flavours. Open 2013+.

DRY $41 –V

Torea Marlborough Pinot Noir ★★★☆

Offering good value, the 2010 vintage (★★★☆) is a single-vineyard red from Fairhall Downs, hand-picked in the Brancott Valley and French oak-aged for 10 months. Deeply coloured, it's a fruit-packed wine with generous, ripe plum/spice flavours, delicious young.

DRY $20 V+

Torlesse Waipara Pinot Noir ★★☆

The 2009 (★★☆), barrel-aged for a year, is light, cherryish and slightly leafy. The 2010 vintage (★★★☆) is by far the best yet. Drinking well in its youth, it is ruby-hued and mouthfilling, with strong cherry, herb and nut flavours, woven with lively acidity. Vibrantly fruity, it is fresh and generous.

DRY $20 –V

Torrent Bay Nelson Pinot Noir   ★★☆

From Anchorage, the 2010 vintage (★★★) was grown at Motueka and gently oaked. A floral, charming, drink-young style, it has gentle tannins and fresh, buoyant cherry and plum flavours.

DRY $21 –V

Tranquillity Bay Nelson Pinot Noir   (★★☆)

The 2009 vintage (★★☆) is a light style, ruby-hued, with moderate depth of plum and herb flavours.

DRY $18 AV

Trinity Hill Hawke's Bay Pinot Noir   ★★★

The 2009 vintage (★★★) was grown at two sites in the cooler hill country to the south and barrel-aged for seven months. Ruby-hued and floral, it has plenty of vibrant, plummy, spicy flavour, some savoury notes and fresh acidity. The 2010 (★★★), oak-aged for six months, is a ruby-hued, vibrantly fruity wine, with ripe cherry/plum flavours, some savoury complexity, and good tannin support.

Vintage	10
WR	5
Drink	12-13

DRY $20 AV

Trinity Hill High Country Pinot Noir   ★★★★

This impressive wine proves that Hawke's Bay *can* make fine Pinot Noir. Sourced from vineyards in the relatively cool hill country, south of the Heretaunga Plains, it is picked by hand and matured in French oak (with a high percentage of new barriques). The 2009 vintage (★★★★☆) is deeply coloured, mouthfilling and very rich, with highly concentrated cherry and plum flavours, still youthful. It's a powerful wine, full of promise.

Vintage	09	08	07	06	05	04
WR	7	6	6	6	6	5
Drink	11-16	11-15	11-14	P	P	P

DRY $39 AV

Triplebank Awatere Valley Marlborough Pinot Noir   ★★★☆

From Pernod Ricard NZ, the 2009 vintage (★★★) is mouthfilling (14.5 per cent alcohol), with mature colour and cherry, herb and spice flavours, surprisingly developed. Drink now. The 2010 (★★★★) is more promising, with strong, fresh cherry, plum and spice flavours, showing some savoury complexity.

Vintage	09	08	07	06
WR	6	6	6	6
Drink	11-12	P	P	P

DRY $27 AV

Tukipo River Fat Duck Pinot Noir   ★★★☆

Grown on a steep bank at Takapau, in Central Hawke's Bay, the 2008 vintage (★★★☆) is very supple and savoury, with good harmony and complexity.

DRY $35 –V

Tukipo River Fat Pheasant Pinot Noir   (★★☆)

Barrel-aged, the 2009 vintage (★★☆) is light and smooth, with berry, herb and spice flavours, offering easy drinking. As the owners say: 'it's a Wednesday, rather than Saturday, night red'.

DRY $20 –V

Turning Point New Style Pinot Noir   (★★)

From Spencer Hill, the 2008 vintage (★★), grown in Marlborough and Nelson, is based on Pinot Noir (90 per cent), blended with Merlot (5 per cent) and Malbec (5 per cent), to give the 'new style'. Aged 'on' French oak (meaning not barrel-aged), it's a smooth, light dry red with cherry, plum and herb flavours, offering easy, no-fuss drinking.

DRY $16 –V

Tussock Nelson Pinot Noir   ★★☆

From Woollaston, the 2009 vintage (★★★) is an enjoyable drink-young style, ruby-hued, fresh and fruity, with cherryish, spicy, slightly herbal flavours, showing some savoury complexity.

DRY $24 –V

Twin Islands Marlborough Pinot Noir   ★★☆

Negociants' red is a drink-young style. The 2009 vintage (★★☆) is light ruby, with ripe, berryish fruit flavours. A pleasant quaffer.

DRY $18 AV

Two Paddocks Pinot Noir   ★★★★

The 2008 vintage (★★★★) is a blend of Alexandra (70 per cent) and Gibbston (30 per cent) fruit, matured in French oak barriques (30 per cent new). Full-coloured, it has strong cherry, plum, herb and spice flavours, showing excellent complexity. The ruby-hued 2009 (★★★★) is supple and savoury, with good richness and complexity. Scented, it's a mouthfilling wine with deep cherry and herb flavours, vibrantly fruity and flowing.

Vintage	08	07	06
WR	6	7	6
Drink	12-16	12-18	12-14

DRY $50 –V

Two Rivers Marlborough Awatere Selection Pinot Noir   ★★★★

Grown in the upper Awatere Valley, hand-picked, fermented with indigenous yeasts and French oak-aged for 11 months, the 2010 vintage (★★★★) is a 'feminine' style of Pinot Noir, floral, sweet-fruited and supple. Full-coloured, it is vibrantly fruity, with good density of cherry and plum flavours, a herbal twist and a lingering finish. Drink now or cellar.

DRY $30 AV

Two Rivers Marlborough Pinot Noir   ★★★☆

Grown and hand-picked at high altitude in the Awatere Valley (333 metres above sea level), the 2009 vintage (★★★☆) was fermented with indigenous yeasts and matured for 11 months in French oak barrels. It's a graceful, ruby-hued, medium-bodied red with fresh, supple cherry and plum flavours, showing very good vibrancy, harmony and drinkability.

DRY $29 AV

Two Tracks Marlborough Pinot Noir   (★★★)

A drink-young style from Wither Hills, the 2008 vintage (★★★) is a ruby-hued red with decent depth of cherry, plum and slight herb flavours, showing good varietal character, and a silky-smooth finish.

Vintage	08
WR	6
Drink	11-12

DRY $24 AV

Urlar Gladstone Pinot Noir   ★★★★☆

The 2009 vintage (★★★★★) is a rich, instantly appealing wine, estate-grown in the northern Wairarapa, hand-picked and matured in French oak barriques (25 per cent new). Full-coloured and generous, deep and finely textured, it is very ripe and savoury, with concentrated, sweet fruit and lovely weight, harmony and length.

DRY $37 V+

Valli Bannockburn Vineyard Otago Pinot Noir   ★★★★☆

The 2009 vintage (★★★★☆) was French oak-matured for 11 months. Deeply coloured, it is powerful, with concentrated cherry, herb and nut flavours in a masculine, but supple and harmonious, style with obvious cellaring potential.

Vintage	09	08	07	06	05
WR	7	7	7	7	6
Drink	12-18	11-17	11-16	11-16	11-14

DRY $55 –V

Valli Gibbston Vineyard Otago Pinot Noir   ★★★★☆

The 2009 vintage (★★★★☆) is deeply coloured, with lovely flavour richness. It shows the more herbal nature of Gibbston (high-altitude) fruit, in a savoury, spicy, complex style, very generous and silky.

Vintage	09	08	07	06	05
WR	7	7	7	7	5
Drink	12-18	11-18	11-17	11-16	11-12

DRY $55 –V

Valli Waitaki Vineyard Otago Pinot Noir   ★★★★

Grown in North Otago, the 2009 vintage (★★★★) was French oak-matured for 11 months and bottled unfined and unfiltered. Ruby-hued, it is intensely varietal and supple, with cherry, plum, herb and spice flavours, showing good, savoury complexity. Delicious drinking now onwards.

Vintage	09	08	07	06
WR	6	6	4	5
Drink	12-16	11-15	11-14	11-12

 DRY $55 –V

Vavasour Awatere Valley Marlborough Pinot Noir   ★★★★

The 2009 vintage (★★★☆) was hand-picked and matured for 11 months in French oak casks. A supple, savoury, moderately rich red, ruby-hued, with cherryish, plummy, slightly spicy flavours, showing good texture and depth, and some complexity, it tastes ready.

Vintage	10	09	08	07
WR	7	6	5	6
Drink	11-15	11-14	11-13	11-12

 DRY $32 AV

Vidal Marlborough Pinot Noir   ★★★★

The 2009 vintage (★★★★) was matured in French oak barrels (21 per cent new). It's a refined, very appealing wine, fragrant and supple, with strong, vibrant, cherryish, plummy flavours.

Vintage	09	08	07	06	05
WR	7	6	7	6	6
Drink	11-14	P	P	P	P

 DRY $26 V+

Vidal Reserve Hawke's Bay Pinot Noir   ★★★★

One of the region's best Pinot Noirs, in the past labelled 'Stopbank'. The 2008 vintage (★★★★) was hand-picked in the Keltern Vineyard, at Maraekakaho, and matured in French oak barriques (38 per cent new). It is mouthfilling and concentrated, with rich, ripe plum and spice flavours, showing good complexity. The 2009 (★★★★) is rich and ripe, savoury and complex, in a sturdy, firmly structured style, well worth cellaring.

Vintage	09	08	07	06	05	04
WR	7	7	6	6	6	6
Drink	11-15	11-13	11-12	P	P	P

 DRY $32 AV

Vidal Reserve Series Marlborough Pinot Noir   ★★★★

Grown and hand-picked in the Wairau and Awatere valleys, the 2009 vintage (★★★★) was matured in French oak casks (21 per cent new). It's a 'feminine', very graceful style with good texture, complexity and concentration. The 2010 (★★★★) is fleshy and sweet-fruited, with cherry and plum flavours, showing good, savoury complexity, and ripe, supple tannins.

Vintage	10	09
WR	7	6
Drink	11-15	11-14

DRY $31 AV

Villa Maria Cellar Selection Marlborough Pinot Noir ★★★★★

Typically a delightful wine, this is often New Zealand's best-value Pinot Noir. Grown in the Awatere and Wairau valleys, it is hand-picked, fermented partly with indigenous yeasts, and matured in French oak barriques (15 per cent new in 2010). Densely coloured, the 2009 vintage (★★★★★) is weighty, vibrant and sweet-fruited, with concentrated, ripe cherry and plum flavours and a subtle seasoning of oak. A tight, youthful wine, it is firm and spicy, with fresh acidity, good intensity and length. Tasted prior to bottling (and so not rated), the 2010 is highly scented, with sweet-fruit delights and finely textured plum/spice flavours, fresh and strong.

Vintage	10	09	08	07	06
WR	6	6	6	6	7
Drink	11-16	11-14	11-14	11-13	11-12

DRY $33 V+

Villa Maria Private Bin Central Otago Pinot Noir   NR

The 2010 vintage (like the 2009) was tasted prior to bottling, so is not rated. Matured in French oak barriques (5 per cent new), it is deeply coloured, with strong, vibrant plum and spice flavours.

Vintage	10
WR	6
Drink	11-15

DRY $27 V?

Villa Maria Private Bin Marlborough Pinot Noir ★★★☆

The 2008 vintage (★★★) was grown in the Awatere and Wairau valleys, and matured for 10 months in French oak barriques (10 per cent new). Ruby-hued, it is vibrantly fruity, with fairly light cherry and plum flavours and a smooth finish.

Vintage	10	09	08	07
WR	6	6	6	6
Drink	11-14	11-13	11-12	P

DRY $26 AV

Villa Maria Reserve Marlborough Pinot Noir ★★★★★

Launched from the 2000 vintage, this label swiftly won recognition as one of the region's boldest, lushest reds. Based on ultra low-yielding vines (2.5 tonnes/hectare) in the Awatere and Wairau valleys, it is matured for over a year in French oak barriques (25 per cent new in 2010), and bottled with minimal fining and filtration. The powerful 2009 vintage (★★★★★) is a commanding wine, very fleshy, dark and rich, with dense, ripe cherry, plum and spice flavours that retain vibrancy and suppleness, and notable complexity. Tasted prior to bottling (and so not rated), the 2010 vintage is powerful, rich and silky, with lovely density of cherry and plum flavours.

Vintage	10	09	08	07
WR	7	7	6	7
Drink	11-19	11-18	11-18	11-17

DRY $51 AV

Villa Maria Single Vineyard Seddon Pinot Noir ★★★★★

From an Awatere Valley site even further inland and higher than its stablemate (below), the 2009 vintage (★★★★★) was matured in French oak barriques (17 per cent new). Weighty and dark, it is vibrantly fruity, with rich plum/spice flavours, deliciously concentrated, savoury and supple. The 2010 (tasted prior to bottling, and so not rated) is still very youthful, with vibrant, plummy, spicy, toasty flavours, showing good complexity and roundness.

Vintage	10	09	08	07	06	05
WR	7	7	NM	7	7	7
Drink	11-19	11-17	NM	11-17	11-19	11-16

DRY $57 AV

Villa Maria Single Vineyard Southern Clays Pinot Noir ★★★★★

Hand-harvested in the Ben Morven foothills, on the south side of the Wairau Valley, the richly coloured 2008 vintage (★★★★★) is a lovely, generous red with bold, sweet-fruit characters and plum/spice flavours showing excellent complexity and density. The 2009 (★★★★★) was matured in French oak barriques (24 per cent new). Deeply coloured, it's an intensely varietal wine, with fresh, densely packed cherry, plum and spice flavours, very refined, supple and long. Tasted prior to bottling (and so not rated), the 2010 vintage is a powerful wine with highly concentrated plum, spice and liquorice flavours, very ripe and rich.

Vintage	10	09	08
WR	7	7	7
Drink	11-19	11-18	11-18

DRY $57 AV

Villa Maria Single Vineyard Taylors Pass Pinot Noir ★★★★☆

Estate-grown in the upper Awatere Valley, the 2010 vintage was matured in French oak barriques (28 per cent new). Tasted prior to bottling (and so not rated), it is vibrantly fruity, plummy and rich, in a very elegant style, woven with fresh acidity.

Vintage	10
WR	7
Drink	10-17

DRY $57 –V

Volcanic Hills Central Otago Pinot Noir (★★★☆)

Showing very good depth and complexity, the 2010 vintage (★★★☆) is full-coloured, with mouthfilling body, strong, ripe plum/spice flavours and finely balanced tannins. Best drinking mid-2012+.

Vintage	10
WR	6
Drink	11-15

DRY $27 AV

Voss Martinborough Pinot Noir ★★★★☆

Voss is a small winery with a big, instantly likeable Pinot Noir. The 2009 vintage (★★★★) was hand-picked on the Martinborough Terrace from vines up to 22 years old, matured for a year in French oak barriques (15 per cent new), and bottled unfined and unfiltered. Ruby-hued, it is sweet-fruited and finely textured, with fresh cherry, plum, spice and nut flavours, showing good complexity. It's already delicious.

Vintage	09	08	07	06	05
WR	7	6	7	6	7
Drink	11-15	11-14	11-14	11-13	11-13

Vynfields Martinborough Pinot Noir ★★★☆

The 2008 vintage (★★★★★), certified BioGro, is a great buy. Hand-picked and matured in French oak barriques (40 per cent new), it is ruby-hued, with an invitingly floral bouquet. Vibrantly fruity, warm and supple, it is notably concentrated, with hints of coffee and spices, and great charm. It should be a five to 10-year wine; open 2012+.

Waimea Barrel Selection Nelson Pinot Noir ★★★☆

The 2008 vintage (★★★☆) was harvested at 24 brix and matured for nine months in French and American oak barrels (partly new). A generous wine, it has full, slightly developed colour and firm, spicy, herbal flavours, savoury and concentrated.

Vintage	08	07
WR	6	7
Drink	11-13	11-12

Waimea Nelson Pinot Noir ★★☆

The 2009 vintage (★★☆) is ruby-hued and sturdy (over 14 per cent alcohol), with plum, spice and herb flavours, fresh and crisp, that lack real ripeness and richness.

Vintage	10	09
WR	7	6
Drink	11-14	11-14

Waipara Downs Waipara Pinot Noir ★★☆

The 2008 vintage (★★) of this estate-grown, North Canterbury red is disappointing, with slightly developed colour and green-edged flavours.

Waipara Hills Central Otago Pinot Noir (★★★★☆)

Seductively scented and supple, the 2009 vintage (★★★★☆) is a very graceful wine. Ruby-hued, with strong, fresh cherry and plum flavours to the fore, deft oak handling adding a savoury, nutty complexity and gentle tannins, it is a floral, 'feminine' style with good immediacy, but also considerable cellaring potential.

DRY $30 V+

Waipara Hills Equinox Waipara Pinot Noir (★★★★☆)

Estate-grown in the Mound Vineyard, the 2009 vintage (★★★★☆) is a very harmonious wine, enticingly floral, sweet-fruited, savoury and supple, with good complexity. Mouthfilling, it is intensely varietal, with cherry, plum, herb and spice flavours that build well across the palate.

 DRY $30 V+

Waipara Hills Waipara Pinot Noir ★★★

The 2009 vintage (★★★), partly oak-aged, is ruby-hued, with buoyantly fruity flavours of plums and spices, woven with fresh acidity, and some savoury complexity.

 DRY $21 AV

Waipara Springs Premo Pinot Noir ★★★★☆

Hand-picked from Waipara's oldest Pinot Noir vines, the 2009 vintage (★★★★☆) was fermented with indigenous yeasts and matured for 15 months in French oak barriques (20 per cent new). Full ruby, it is mouthfilling and sweet-fruited, with strong, vibrant cherry, plum and spice flavours, a hint of liquorice, and ripe, supple tannins. It's still youthful, but already delicious.

 DRY $36 V+

Waipara Springs Waipara Pinot Noir (★★★☆)

A very charming, drink-young style, the 2009 vintage (★★★☆) was matured in an even split of tanks and French oak casks (10 per cent new). Ruby-hued, it is mouthfilling, with fresh, vibrant flavours of cherries, plums and spices and gentle tannins.

 DRY $22 V+

Waipipi Henry Wairarapa Pinot Noir ★★☆

The 2008 vintage (★★★) was grown at Opaki and French oak-aged. Sweet oak aromas lead into a cherry and plum-flavoured wine, moderately concentrated, with some savoury complexity, gentle tannins, and plenty of drink-young appeal.

Vintage	08
WR	6
Drink	11-13

DRY $25 –V

Wairau River Home Block Marlborough Pinot Noir ★★★☆

The 2008 vintage (★★★☆) is full-bodied, with vibrant cherry, plum and spice flavours, seasoned with savoury oak, and very good ripeness, depth and harmony.

 DRY $32 –V

Wairau River Marlborough Pinot Noir ★★★☆

Estate-grown on the north side of the Wairau Valley, the 2009 vintage (★★★☆) was harvested at over 24 brix and matured for eight months in tanks (30 per cent) and French oak barrels (70 per cent). Enjoyable young, it is mouthfilling, ruby-hued and supple, with fresh cherry, plum and spice flavours, showing a touch of complexity, and a smooth finish.

 DRY $25 AV

Wairau River Reserve Marlborough Pinot Noir   ★★★★

The 2009 vintage (★★★★) was estate-grown at Rapaura and matured for 10 months in French oak barriques and puncheons. Savoury and supple, it is ruby-hued, with ripe plum and spice flavours, seasoned with toasty oak, and good complexity. The 2010 (★★★★) is deeply coloured, with loads of plummy, spicy flavour. Sweet-fruited and savoury, it's approachable now, but best opened mid-2012+.

Vintage	10
WR	7
Drink	12-16

 DRY $40 –V

Waitaki Braids Waitaki Valley Pinot Noir   ★★★★

The 2008 vintage (★★★★☆), grown in the Otago Station Vineyard, was hand-harvested, fermented with indigenous yeasts and matured for a year in French oak barriques. Very fragrant, savoury and supple, it is full-coloured, rich and complex, with ripe, sweet-fruit flavours, lovely flow across the palate and a long finish. It's a feminine, graceful style, with lots of class.

 DRY $60 –V

Waitaki Valley Wines Grants Road Vineyard Pinot Noir   (★★★☆)

The 2008 vintage (★★★☆) has a floral bouquet, fresh, ripe, moderately concentrated plum and spice flavours, gentle tannins and lots of drink-young charm.

 DRY $40 –V

Waitiri Creek Central Otago Pinot Noir   ★★★★

This label has leapt in quality in recent vintages. Grown at Gibbston and Bannockburn, the 2007 vintage (★★★★) was matured in French oak barriques (33 per cent new). It is rich and elegant, with deep colour, strong, plummy, spicy flavours, finely integrated oak and considerable complexity. The 2008 (★★★★☆) is very fragrant and rich, with impressive texture, ripeness, complexity and depth.

 DRY $45 –V

Walnut Block Collectables Marlborough Pinot Noir   ★★☆

The 2009 vintage (★★☆) is light and developed, with gentle cherry, herb and nut flavours, offering easy, early drinking.

 DRY $24 –V

Walnut Block Single Vineyard Marlborough Pinot Noir   ★★★★☆

Estate-grown and hand-picked in the Wairau Valley, the 2008 vintage (★★★★☆) was fermented with indigenous yeasts, and matured for 16 months in French oak casks. Full-coloured, it is mouthfilling and supple, with ripe cherry, plum and spice flavours showing excellent complexity and depth.

DRY $32 V+

Weaver Estate Central Otago Pinot Noir   (★★★★)

Grown at Alexandra and matured in French oak casks (35 per cent new), the ruby-hued, elegant 2009 vintage (★★★★) is a youthful, tightly structured red with good colour depth and strong, vibrant plum, cherry and spice flavours, showing considerable complexity. Well worth cellaring.

Vintage	09
WR	6
Drink	12-16

 DRY $35 AV

West Brook Marlborough Pinot Noir   ★★★★

The 2009 vintage (★★★★★) is a single-vineyard wine, matured in French oak casks (30 per cent new). Full-bodied, it is savoury and silky, with an array of cherry, plum, herb and spice flavours, showing excellent complexity. Dense, ripe, finely balanced and long, it's priced sharply.

 DRY $27 V+

West Brook Waimauku Pinot Noir   ★★★

Here's proof that you *can* make good Pinot Noir in Auckland. Estate-grown, hand-picked and matured in French oak casks, the 2008 vintage (★★★) is a ruby-hued, medium-bodied wine with ripe plum/spice flavours, good texture and toasty oak adding complexity.

 DRY $26 –V

Whitehaven Greg Marlborough Pinot Noir   ★★★★☆

From 'the very best barrels', the 2009 vintage (★★★★☆) was grown in the Wairau and Awatere valleys and matured in French oak barriques (50 per cent new). A complex wine, it is mouthfilling and savoury, with strong cherry, plum, spice and nut flavours. It's already drinking well.

 DRY $40 AV

Whitehaven Marlborough Pinot Noir   ★★★★

The 2009 vintage (★★★☆) was matured in French oak casks (25 per cent new). Floral and ruby-hued, it's a very supple red with moderately concentrated strawberry, herb and spice flavours, showing some savoury complexity. A middleweight style, it's drinking well now. The 2010 (★★★★) is deeply coloured and richly scented, in a fruit-driven style with ripe plum and cherry flavours, a subtle seasoning of oak (French, 25 per cent new), good concentration, and strong drink-young appeal.

Vintage	10	09
WR	7	7
Drink	11-17	11-17

DRY $30 AV

Wild Earth Central Otago Pinot Noir   ★★★★☆

The latest vintages are impressive. Grown in the Bannockburn and Lowburn districts, hand-picked and matured in French oak barriques, the 2009 vintage (★★★★☆) is still very youthful, but full of promise. Full-coloured, mouthfilling and rich, it has cherry, plum, herb and spice flavours woven with fresh acidity and excellent density. Open 2013+.

 DRY $42 AV

Wild Irishman Bannockburn Central Otago Pinot Noir   (★★★★)

From pioneer winemaker Alan Brady, the 2008 vintage (★★★★) is from a block of young vines in the Desert Heart Vineyard, at Bannockburn. Fermented with indigenous yeasts, matured in French oak casks (30 per cent new), and bottled unfiltered, it is ruby-hued, scented and supple, with ripe cherry, plum and spice flavours. It's a buoyantly fruity, lively wine with some muscle and instant appeal.

DRY $32 AV

Wild Irishman Three Colleens Central Otago Pinot Noir   (★★★☆)

The 2008 vintage (★★★☆) is from young vines, grown high on the slopes of Mt Rosa, at Gibbston. Fermented with indigenous yeasts, matured for 10 months in French oak barrels (30 per cent new), and bottled unfiltered, it is floral, fruity and soft, with moderately concentrated cherry and herb flavours, showing some savoury, nutty complexity, and a seductively silky texture.

DRY $32 –V

Wild Rock Cupid's Arrow Central Otago Pinot Noir   ★★★☆

From Craggy Range, the 2008 vintage (★★★☆) was harvested at 24 brix and matured in seasoned French oak casks. It's a ruby-hued red with a fragrant bouquet of spices and dried herbs. Savoury and spicy, it shows good flavour depth and complexity, with a fairly firm finish.

DRY $25 AV

Wild Rock Struggler's Flat Pinot Noir   ★★★☆

From a subsidiary of Craggy Range, the 2009 vintage (★★★☆) was grown in Martinborough and matured for eight months in French oak casks (10 per cent new). Full-bodied, it has ripe cherry, plum and spice flavours, generous, savoury and softly textured.

Vintage	09	08
WR	6	7
Drink	11-15	11-13

DRY $24 V+

Wild South Marlborough Pinot Noir   ★★★☆

From Sacred Hill, the 2010 vintage (★★★☆) was grown in the Waihopai and Awatere valleys. A generous, sweet-fruited wine, it is bright ruby, with very good depth of ripe, cherryish, plummy flavour and a well-rounded finish. A delicious drink-young style, it offers fine value.

DRY $18 V+

Wingspan Nelson Pinot Noir   ★★

From Woollaston Estates, the 2009 vintage (★★) is light in colour, body and flavour, with berry and herb characters, showing some development. A pleasant, drink-young quaffer, it's priced right.

DRY $13 AV

Wither Hills Wairau Valley Marlborough Pinot Noir   ★★★★

The 2008 vintage (★★★★) is fragrant and full-coloured, with strong cherry, plum and spice flavours, showing considerable complexity. The 2009 (★★★★) is ruby-hued, richly fruity and very smooth-flowing. Sweet-fruited and finely textured, it has nutty, spicy, fungal notes adding complexity. Drink now to 2013.

DRY $30 AV

Wooing Tree Beetle Juice Central Otago Pinot Noir   ★★★★

A great buy. The 2010 vintage (★★★★) is a single-vineyard Cromwell red, hand-picked and matured for 11 months in French oak barriques (21 per cent new). Full-coloured, it has strong, ripe plum and spice flavours, showing good complexity and length.

DRY $28 V+

Wooing Tree Central Otago Pinot Noir   ★★★★★

The 2009 vintage (★★★★☆) of this single-vineyard Cromwell red was hand-picked at over 25 brix and matured for 11 months in French oak barriques (40 per cent new). Fragrant and deeply coloured, it is powerful (14.5 per cent alcohol), fresh and vibrant, with highly concentrated, ripe flavours of cherries, plums, herbs and liquorice, and a strong new oak influence. The 2010 (★★★★☆) is deeply coloured, with excellent richness, complexity and poise. Still very fresh, it has strong cherry, plum and spice flavours, tight and youthful; open 2013+.

DRY $45 AV

Wooing Tree Sandstorm Reserve Central Otago Pinot Noir   ★★★★★

Estate-grown at Cromwell, this wine is hand-picked from low-yielding vines and given extended oak-aging. All silky charm, the 2008 vintage (★★★★☆) was harvested at nearly 26 brix and matured for 18 months in French oak casks (40 per cent new). Ruby-hued, it is rich, supple and flowing, with an array of cherry, plum, herb, spice and nut flavours, in a very elegant, 'feminine' style. The 2009 (★★★★★) is deeply coloured, with lovely richness of plum, cherry, liquorice and nut flavours. Finely textured, it is very sweet-fruited and highly concentrated; drink now or cellar.

DRY $85 –V

Woollaston Estates Nelson Pinot Noir   ★★★

The 2010 vintage (★★★), oak-matured for nearly a year, is a ruby-hued, vibrantly fruity wine with good depth of cherry, plum, spice and herb flavours, offering smooth, easy drinking.

Vintage	10
WR	6
Drink	11-15

DRY $32 –V

Wycroft Forbury Pinot Noir ★★★

Grown near Masterton, in the Wairarapa, the 2008 vintage (★★★) was hand-picked and matured for 10 months in French oak casks (30 per cent new). Ruby-hued, it is fresh, fruity and smooth, with good varietal character and moderate depth of cherry/plum flavours, enjoyable young. The 2009 (★★★) is fresh, berryish and supple, with lively acidity and a touch of complexity.

Wycroft Pinot Noir (★★★☆)

Grown in the northern Wairarapa, the 2009 vintage (★★★☆) is scented and vibrantly fruity, with good depth of cherry, herb and plum flavours, fresh acidity and some savoury complexity.

Yealands Estate Awatere Valley Marlborough Pinot Noir ★★★☆

The 2010 vintage (★★★★) is a generous, savoury, silky red with full, bright colour and substantial body. Already enjoyable but well worth cellaring, it has strong, plummy, slightly spicy flavours, gentle tannins and good complexity.

DRY $29 AV

St Laurent

This Austrian variety is known for its deeply coloured, silky-smooth reds. It buds early, so is prone to frost damage, but ripens well ahead of Pinot Noir. Judge Rock imported the vine in 2001.

Judge Rock Central Otago St Laurent   (★★★)

The 2009 vintage (★★★) is New Zealand's first commercial release of St Laurent. Grown at Alexandra, it's a gutsy, full-coloured red, fresh and fruity, with ripe, berryish, pruney, slightly rustic flavours and firm tannins.

DRY $35 –V

Sangiovese

Sangiovese, Italy's most extensively planted red-wine variety, is a rarity in New Zealand. Cultivated as a workhorse grape throughout central Italy, in Tuscany it is the foundation of such famous reds as Chianti and Brunello di Montalcino. Here, Sangiovese has sometimes been confused with Montepulciano and its plantings are not expanding – the 2012 area of 6 hectares of bearing vines (mostly in Auckland) will be slightly less than in 2006.

Black Barn Hawke's Bay Sangiovese ★★★★

This Havelock North producer has been producing estate-grown Sangiovese for almost a decade. The 2009 vintage (★★★★) *tastes* like Sangiovese, with its full colour, floral bouquet and fresh, concentrated cherry and plum flavours. It's less compelling than Black Barn's 2009 Montepulciano, but still worth discovering.

DRY $32 –V

Hitchen Road Vineyard Pokeno Sangiovese (★★★☆)

Estate-grown in the northern Waikato and oak-matured for 10 months, the 2010 vintage (★★★☆) is an auspicious debut. A wine of some substance, it is deeply coloured and vibrantly fruity, with strong plum and cherry flavours, a gentle seasoning of oak and a fresh, smooth finish. Priced sharply.

Vintage	10
WR	6
Drink	11

DRY $18 V+

Matariki Hawke's Bay Sangiovese (★★★☆)

The 2007 vintage (★★★☆), grown in the Gimblett Gravels, was blended with Cabernet Sauvignon (9 per cent), and matured for 17 months in French oak casks (37 per cent new). It's a fruity, spicy, plummy, savoury and nutty red, showing very good flavour depth, although not obviously varietal, in the sense of displaying clear-cut Sangiovese characters.

Vintage	07
WR	6
Drink	11-12

DRY $30 –V

Syrah

Hawke's Bay and the upper North Island (especially Waiheke Island) have a hot new red-wine variety. At the *Decanter* World Wine Awards 2011, judged in the UK, the trophy for 'Best Rhône Varietal Over £10' was awarded to Elephant Hill Hawke's Bay Syrah 2009.

The classic 'Syrah' of the Rhône Valley, in France, and Australian 'Shiraz' are in fact the same variety. On the rocky, baking slopes of the upper Rhône Valley, and in several Australian states, this noble grape yields red wines renowned for their outstanding depth of cassis, plum and black-pepper flavours.

Syrah was well known in New Zealand a century ago. Government viticulturist S.F. Anderson wrote in 1917 that Shiraz was being 'grown in nearly all our vineyards [but] the trouble with this variety has been an unevenness in ripening its fruit'. For today's winemakers, the problem has not changed: Syrah has never favoured a too-cool growing environment (wines that are not fully ripe show distinct tomato or tamarillo characters). It needs sites that are relatively hot during the day and retain the heat at night, achieving ripeness in Hawke's Bay late in the season, at about the same time as Cabernet Sauvignon. To curb its natural vigour, stony, dry, low-fertility sites or warm hillside sites are crucial.

The latest national vineyard survey showed that 300 hectares of Syrah will be bearing in 2012 – a steep rise from 62 hectares in 2000. Syrah is now New Zealand's fourth most widely planted red-wine variety, behind Pinot Noir, Merlot and Cabernet Sauvignon, but well ahead of Malbec and Cabernet Franc. Over two-thirds of the vines are in Hawke's Bay, with other significant pockets in Auckland and Northland.

Syrah's potential in this country's warmer vineyard sites is finally being tapped.

The top wines possess rich, vibrant blackcurrant, plum and black-pepper flavours, with an enticingly floral bouquet, and are winning growing international applause.

Could Syrah replace Bordeaux-style Merlot and Cabernet Sauvignon-based blends over the next decade as the principal red-wine style from Hawke's Bay and the upper North Island? Don't rule it out.

Alpha Domus The Barnstormer Hawke's Bay Syrah ★★★☆

The 2010 vintage (★★★★), French oak-aged, is deeply coloured, with a fragrant bouquet of plums and spices. Supple, sweet-fruited and vibrant, it has strong plum and black-pepper flavours, gently seasoned with nutty oak, and a good backbone of tannin. Drink now or cellar.

Vintage	10	DRY $27 –V
WR	6	
Drink	11-16	

Arrow Junction Hawke's Bay Syrah (★★★★)

From distributor Federal Geo, the 2009 vintage (★★★★) is a classy, fruit-packed Gimblett Gravels red, French oak-matured. Floral, rich and supple, with deep, bright colour, it has fresh blackcurrant, plum and spice flavours, a subtle seasoning of nutty oak, and excellent concentration.

DRY $31 –V

Ash Ridge Cardoness Vineyard Hawke's Bay Syrah   (★★★)

From second-crop vines, the 2008 vintage (★★★) was matured in seasoned French oak casks. Full and bright in colour, it is fresh and youthful, with peppery aromas and flavours, showing good depth, and gentle tannins.

Vintage	09	08
WR	7	5
Drink	12-17	11-15

DRY $29 –V

Askerne Hawke's Bay Syrah   (★★☆)

Estate-grown, hand-harvested and oak-aged, the 2009 vintage (★★☆) has full, fairly youthful colour and mouthfilling body. It offers smooth, early drinking, with fresh, slightly herbal flavours.

Vintage	09
WR	5
Drink	12-15

DRY $20 –V

Aurora Vineyard, The, Bendigo Syrah   ★★★★

Syrah is still largely unproven in Central Otago, but this Cromwell Basin red shows what can be achieved. The 2008 vintage (★★★★) was harvested at 24.5 brix and matured for 10 months in French oak casks (40 per cent new). Dark and dense, it has very concentrated blackcurrant, plum, spice and nut flavours. A powerful, rich wine, it is finely structured, with considerable elegance and finesse.

DRY $38 –V

Aurora Vineyard, The, Legacy Syrah   (★★★★)

Here's further proof Central Otago is not too cool for Syrah. The 2008 vintage (★★★★), matured for 18 months in French oak puncheons, is a deeply coloured, spicy red with concentrated plum, spice and nut flavours, not too peppery, and an inviting, floral bouquet.

DRY $60 –V

Babich Gimblett Gravels Syrah   ★★★

The 2009 vintage (★★☆) was grown in Hawke's Bay and French oak-aged. Ruby-hued, it's an easy-drinking, medium-bodied style with plummy, slightly spicy flavours and a smooth finish.

DRY $20 –V

Babich Winemakers' Reserve Hawke's Bay Syrah   ★★★☆

Estate-grown in Gimblett Road and matured in French and American oak casks, the 2008 vintage (★★★☆) was co-fermented with Viognier (5 per cent). A harmonious wine, it offers generous plum and black-pepper flavours, but herbal notes are emerging with bottle-age.

Vintage	10	09	08	07	06
WR	7	6	5	7	6
Drink	12-18	11-16	11-16	11-15	11-12

DRY $27 –V

Bilancia La Collina Syrah ★★★★★

la collina ('the hill') is grown at the company's steep, early-ripening site on the northern slopes of Roy's Hill, overlooking the Gimblett Gravels, Hawke's Bay, co-fermented with Viognier skins (but not their juice, giving a tiny Viognier component in the final blend), and matured for up to 22 months in all new (but 'low-impact') French oak barriques. A majestic red, it ranks among the country's very finest Syrahs. The 2009 vintage (★★★★★) is impossible to criticise. Deeply coloured, with commanding mouthfeel – but not heavy – it is highly fragrant, with blackcurrant, black-pepper and new oak flavours, ripe, rich and silky-textured. Powerful, with layers of flavour, great harmony and a sense of latent power, it should flourish for a decade.

Vintage	09	08	07	06	05	04
WR	7	6	7	7	7	7
Drink	15-20	13-18	12-16	11-18	11-17	11-16

 DRY $95 AV

Bilancia Syrah/Viognier ★★★★

This Hawke's Bay red is blended from sites in the Gimblett Gravels (85 per cent in 2008) and the company's own block, *la collina*, on Roy's Hill (15 per cent). Co-fermented with Viognier (6 per cent) and matured in French oak barriques (40 per cent new), the 2008 vintage (★★★★) has youthful, purple-flushed colour. Concentrated and vibrantly fruity, with ripe, peppery aromas, it is fresh, savoury and earthy, with lively acidity and good complexity. Drink 2012+.

Vintage	08	07	06
WR	6	7	7
Drink	11-15	11-15	11-12

 DRY $35 –V

Black Barn Vineyards Hawke's Bay Syrah (★★★★)

The graceful, finely textured 2008 vintage (★★★★) is deeply coloured, floral and fruity, with ripe plum, black-pepper and slight liquorice flavours, showing some savoury complexity. Fragrant and supple, it's highly enjoyable from the start.

 DRY $32 –V

Bloody Bay Hawke's Bay Syrah (★★★)

From Federal Geo, a wine distributor, the 2008 vintage (★★★) is full-coloured, with a peppery bouquet. Light but attractive, it's a fruit-driven style with plenty of plummy, spicy flavour, a hint of herbs, and a smooth finish.

 DRY $20 –V

Boundary Vineyards Lake Road Gisborne Syrah ★★☆

From Pernod Ricard NZ, the 2008 vintage (★★☆) is strongly peppery, but lacks real richness and roundness. The 2009 (★★★) is a riper style with satisfying depth of plum and spice flavours and a well-rounded finish.

 DRY $23 –V

Brookfields Back Block Syrah ★★★☆

Grown in Hawke's Bay, the 2010 vintage (★★★☆), barrel-aged for eight months, is full-coloured, mouthfilling, fresh and vibrantly fruity, with plum and black-pepper flavours, spicy, slightly nutty and well-rounded. Drink now or cellar.

Vintage	10	09
WR	7	7
Drink	13-18	11-19

DRY $20 AV

Brookfields Hillside Syrah ★★★★☆

This distinguished red is grown on a sheltered, north-facing slope between Maraekakaho and Bridge Pa in Hawke's Bay (described by winemaker Peter Robertson as 'surreal – a chosen site'). The 2009 vintage (★★★★☆), matured for 15 months in 'predominantly' new oak casks, is deep and youthful in colour, with rich blackcurrant, plum, spice and pepper flavours, ripe, sweetly oaked, supple and lingering. Finely balanced, it's delicious now.

Vintage	09	NM	07	06
WR	7	NM	7	7
Drink	13-20	NM	11-18	11-16

DRY $44 –V

Cable Bay Reserve Waiheke Island Syrah ★★★★★

The 2009 vintage (★★★★★), grown at Church Bay, was co-fermented with Viognier (3 per cent) and matured for over a year in French oak barriques. Dark and fragrant, with a well-spiced bouquet, it is mouthfilling and rich, with plum, spice, liquorice and black-pepper flavours, seasoned with toasty oak, and fine-grained tannins. It should be long-lived, but is already delicious.

Vintage	09
WR	7
Drink	11-17

DRY $56 AV

Cable Bay Waiheke Island Syrah ★★★★☆

The weighty (14.5 per cent alcohol), very floral and supple 2010 vintage (★★★★★) was matured for 14 months in French oak casks. Co-fermented with a small percentage of Viognier, it has dense, inky colour and lovely freshness, texture and richness. Still a baby, it offers deep blackcurrant and black-pepper flavours, finely integrated oak and excellent weight, complexity, suppleness and fragrance. It should flourish for a decade.

Vintage	10	09
WR	7	7
Drink	11-20	11-16

DRY $39 AV

Church Road Hawke's Bay Syrah   (★★★★☆)

The debut 2009 vintage (★★★★☆) offers great value. Grown in the Gimblett Gravels (75 per cent) and Pernod Ricard NZ's Redstone Vineyard in The Triangle (25 per cent), it was hand-picked and matured for over a year in French oak barriques (45 per cent new). Weighty and deeply coloured, it has a floral, peppery bouquet. The palate is powerful, with fresh, concentrated plum and spice flavours, savoury, complex and supple. Drink now or cellar.

DRY $27 V+

Church Road Reserve Hawke's Bay Syrah   ★★★★★

The 2008 (★★★★☆) was estate-grown and hand-harvested in the Redstone Vineyard, in The Triangle, and matured for 16 months in French oak barriques. A powerful, densely coloured red, with concentrated flavours of blackcurrants, plums, dark chocolate and black pepper, seasoned with toasty oak, it's a stylish, complex, rich wine, well worth cellaring. The 2009 vintage (★★★★★) is even finer, with bold blackcurrant, spice and black-pepper flavours, very fresh and youthful, and an enticingly floral bouquet.

DRY $37 V+

C.J. Pask Declaration Syrah   ★★★★

The 2009 vintage (★★★★), estate-grown in the Gimblett Gravels of Hawke's Bay, has a fragrant, complex bouquet with savoury oak aromas. Deeply coloured, it has excellent density of plum, blackcurrant and spice flavours, ripe and nutty, fresh acidity and a long finish.

DRY $49 –V

C.J. Pask Gimblett Road Syrah   ★★★☆

Top vintages of this Hawke's Bay red offer fine value. Estate-grown, the 2009 (★★★☆) is a fruit-driven style, full-coloured, fresh, vibrantly fruity and supple. A strongly varietal wine with ripe plum, cherry and black-pepper flavours, and a subtle seasoning of oak, it has lots of drink-young charm.

DRY $19 V+

Clearview Reserve Hawke's Bay Syrah   (★★★★★)

An outstanding debut, the 2009 vintage (★★★★★) was made from hand-harvested Gimblett Gravels grapes and French oak-matured for 18 months. Deeply coloured, powerful and sweet-fruited, with vibrant plum and black-pepper flavours, it has notable density and complexity, and supple, finely textured tannins.

DRY $51 AV

Clevedon Hills Syrah ★★★★

Grown at Clevedon, in South Auckland, the 2008 vintage (★★★★) is deep and still youthful in colour, with a fresh bouquet of plums and pepper. Building up well with bottle-age, it's concentrated, with ripe, supple tannins and strong, savoury, spicy, nutty flavours. The 2010 (tasted prior to bottling, and so not rated) is potentially outstanding. Deep and purple-flushed in colour, it is vibrant, with fine-grained tannins and very dense, ripe blackcurrant, plum, pepper and liquorice flavours.

 DRY $45 –V

Clos de Ste Anne Syrah The Crucible ★★★★★

A majestic red, the 2009 vintage (★★★★★) was grown organically in Millton's elevated Clos de Ste Anne Vineyard in Gisborne, co-fermented with Viognier (5 per cent) and matured in large, seasoned French oak casks. It's a very 'complete', Rhône-like wine, deeply coloured, with an arrestingly complex bouquet – earthy, spicy and nutty. Powerful (14.5 per cent alcohol), highly concentrated and firmly structured, it's clearly Gisborne's greatest Syrah to date, likely to flourish for a decade.

Vintage	09	08	07	06	05
WR	7	6	7	6	6
Drink	11-19	11-17	11-17	11-15	P

 DRY $55 AV

Coney Martinborough Que Sera Syrah ★★★☆

The 2009 vintage (★★★☆) is full-coloured, vibrantly fruity and supple, with generous, ripe flavours of plums, spices and liquorice, gentle tannins and plenty of personality.

DRY $32 –V

Contour Estate Reserve Syrah ★★★★

Launched from the 2007 vintage (★★★★), this rewarding wine has been grown at Matakana, north of Auckland, but the 2009 is the last to be estate-grown – future releases will be made from grapes purchased from Hawke's Bay. Matured in French and American oak barriques, the 2009 (★★★☆) is deeply coloured, with toasty oak aromas leading into a full-flavoured palate, fresh, vibrant and plummy, showing very good depth.

 DRY $38 –V

Coopers Creek Hawke's Bay Syrah ★★★

Enjoyable young, the 2010 vintage (★★★☆) was French oak-aged for a year. Deeply coloured, with a lifted, peppery fragrance, it has fresh, strong blackcurrant, plum and black-pepper flavours, seasoned with toasty oak, and a very smooth finish.

Vintage	10
WR	7
Drink	11-13

 DRY $19 AV

Coopers Creek Reserve Hawke's Bay Syrah   (★★★★☆)

From Chalk Ridge Vineyard, in the Havelock North hills, the 2010 vintage (★★★★☆) was French oak-matured for a year. It's a classy wine, very finely textured, with deep, youthful colour, substantial body, and rich plum and spice flavours, showing excellent complexity and flow. Sweet-fruited, with good tannin support and a long, spicy finish, it's already delicious, but best cellared to 2013+.

Vintage	10
WR	7
Drink	11-14

 DRY $45 –V

Coopers Creek SV Chalk Ridge Hawke's Bay Syrah   ★★★★

The 2009 vintage (★★★★) was blended with a splash of Viognier and matured for over a year in French oak casks (50 per cent new). Full-coloured, it is mouthfilling and supple, with ripe plum and spice flavours, showing some savoury, nutty complexity, in a very harmonious style with drink-young appeal.

Vintage	10	09	08	07	06
WR	7	6	7	7	6
Drink	12-14	11-14	11-13	11-12	P

 DRY $28 AV

Corazon Single Vineyard Syrah   ★★★★

The 2010 vintage (★★★★) was grown in Hawke's Bay and matured in French oak casks (20 per cent new). Deeply coloured, it is mouthfilling (14.5 per cent alcohol) and youthful, with dense, ripe plum and black-pepper flavours, slightly nutty and well-spiced. A richly varietal wine, it's drinking well already, but likely to be at its best 2013+.

Vintage	10
WR	7
Drink	12-18

DRY $27 AV

Corbans Cottage Block Hawke's Bay Syrah   ★★★★☆

Grown and hand-picked in Pernod Ricard NZ's Redstone Vineyard, in The Triangle, the 2007 vintage (★★★★★) was matured for 18 months in French oak barriques (40 per cent new), and bottled unfined and unfiltered. Dark, powerful and concentrated, it is intensely varietal, with complex plum, black-pepper and toasty oak flavours, tight-knit, strong and youthful, with powerful tannins. The 2008 (★★★★☆) is deeply coloured and scented, with good weight and fresh, intense plum and black-pepper varietal flavours, showing real immediacy.

DRY $39 AV

Couper's Shed Hawke's Bay Syrah   ★★★☆

The 2009 (★★★) is a charming, drink-young style from Pernod Ricard NZ. Full-coloured, vibrantly fruity and supple, it has fresh berry and black-pepper flavours, with a distinctly spicy finish, and a peppery, perfumed bouquet. The 2010 (★★★☆) is similar – deeply coloured, with strong, peppery aromas and ripe plum/spice flavours, showing some complexity, and well-defined varietal characters.

 DRY $23 AV

Craggy Range Gimblett Gravels Vineyard Syrah   ★★★★★

This label (up to and including the 2007 vintage labelled 'Block 14') is overshadowed by the reputation of its stablemate, Le Sol, but proves the power, structure and finesse that can be achieved with Syrah grown in the Gimblett Gravels of Hawke's Bay. The 2009 (★★★★☆) is a tight, youthful wine, matured in French oak barriques (31 per cent new). Deeply coloured, with an enticing fragrance of plums, black pepper and spices, it is floral, rich and savoury, with fresh, intensely varietal plum/spice flavours, firm tannins and good harmony. Open 2013+.

Vintage	09	08	07	06	05	04
WR	6	6	7	6	7	6
Drink	11-18	11-18	11-22	11-20	11-12	P

 DRY $32 V+

Craggy Range Le Sol Syrah – see Craggy Range Le Sol
in the Branded and Other Red Wines section

Crater Rim, The, Waipara Syrah   (★★☆)

Grown on the valley floor, the 2009 vintage (★★☆) was blended with Viognier (5 per cent) and matured in seasoned French oak puncheons. Fullish and slightly developed in colour, it has a leafy bouquet and good depth of slightly nutty, rounded but green-edged flavour.

DRY $30 –V

Crossroads Hawke's Bay Syrah   ★★☆

The 2010 vintage (★★★) was grown in the Gimblett Gravels and matured in seasoned French oak barriques. It's a drink-young style, full-coloured, with vibrant plum and spice flavours, fresh, ripe and smooth.

Vintage	10
WR	5
Drink	11-18

 DRY $19 –V

Crossroads Vineyard Selection Elms Vineyard Gimblett Gravels Syrah   (★★★★)

The elegant, supple 2009 vintage (★★★★) is a single-vineyard red, hand-picked and matured for over a year in French oak barriques (30 per cent new). A medium to full-bodied style with floral, plum and black-pepper aromas, it is full-coloured, with strongly varietal flavours and a finely textured, distinctly spicy finish.

DRY $45 –V

Cypress Hawke's Bay Syrah   ★★★☆

Estate-grown in the Gimblett Gravels, the 2009 vintage (★★★☆) was aged in seasoned French oak casks. A drink-now or cellaring proposition, it is full-coloured and supple, with gentle tannins and good depth of fresh plum and black-pepper flavours, showing some savoury, nutty complexity.

Vintage	09	08	07
WR	6	6	6
Drink	11-13	11-12	P

DRY $26 –V

Cypress Terraces Hawke's Bay Syrah ★★★★☆

Estate-grown at an elevated, terraced site on Roy's Hill, in the Gimblett Gravels, the 2008 vintage (★★★★☆) was matured for 19 months in French oak casks (50 per cent new). It's a very savoury, full-coloured wine with strong, firm blackcurrant, plum and spice flavours, showing good density and structure.

Vintage	08	07
WR	6	7
Drink	11-14	11-13

 DRY $42 –V

Dry River Lovat Vineyard Martinborough Syrah ★★★★

Some vintages of this red have been strikingly concentrated and tight-knit, but others are less convincing. The 2009 (★★★☆), matured in French oak casks (25 per cent new), is boldly coloured, fleshy and supple, with deep plum, herb and nut flavours, woven with fresh acidity. A leafy note detracts, suggesting a lack of full ripeness, but the wine is highly concentrated and finely textured. Best drinking 2013+.

Vintage	09	08	07	06	05	04
WR	7	7	6	7	7	6
Drink	12-23	11-22	11-21	11-20	11-15	11-14

 DRY $64 –V

Elephant Hill Hawke's Bay Syrah ★★★★

The 2009 vintage (★★★★☆) is a delicious drink-young style. Hand-picked and matured for 11 months in French oak casks (30 per cent new), it is deeply coloured, with a floral, spicy bouquet, concentrated plum, pepper and spice flavours, showing good complexity, and very supple, ripe tannins. It has great drink-young appeal, but should also age gracefully.

 DRY $29 AV

Elephant Hill Reserve Hawke's Bay Syrah ★★★☆

Grown at Te Awanga, the 2008 vintage (★★★☆) was blended with Viognier (1 per cent) and matured for 15 months in French oak casks (100 per cent new). Deeply coloured, it is full-bodied and generous, with concentrated plum and pepper flavours, some herbal and jammy notes, and a rounded finish.

 DRY $45 –V

Esk Valley Hawke's Bay Syrah ★★★★

The 2009 vintage (★★★★) was hand-harvested and matured for 18 months in French oak barrels (30 per cent new). Deeply coloured, it is perfumed, rich and finely balanced, with fresh, strong red-berry and spice flavours, fine-grained tannins and a long finish.

Vintage	09	08	07	06	05
WR	6	6	6	7	6
Drink	12-18	11-12	11-12	11-12	P

DRY $24 V+

Esk Valley Winemakers Reserve Gimblett Gravels Syrah · ★★★★★

The 2007 vintage (★★★★★) is the first to be labelled 'Winemakers Reserve' (past releases were sold as 'Reserve'). Grown in the Cornerstone Vineyard, Hawke's Bay, it was matured for 21 months in French oak barriques (35 per cent new). Boldly coloured, it's a powerful wine with deliciously deep, ripe flavours of blackcurrants, plums and spices, showing lovely richness, roundness and harmony. There is no 2008, due to frost.

Vintage	09	08	07	06	05
WR	6	NM	7	7	7
Drink	12-20	NM	11-17	11-18	11-15

DRY $60 AV

Fromm La Strada Marlborough Syrah (★★★★)

A 'fruit-driven' style – with style. The 2009 vintage (★★★★) was blended with Viognier (3 per cent) and matured for 14–16 months in French oak casks (10 to 20 per cent new). A top example of South Island Syrah, it is mouthfilling and spicy, with a fresh, peppery, fragrant bouquet and strong, well-spiced, slightly nutty flavours, smooth and sustained. Drink now or cellar.

Vintage	09	08	07	06	05
WR	7	6	7	7	6
Drink	11-15	11-14	11-13	11-12	P

DRY $35 –V

Fromm Syrah Fromm Vineyard ★★★★☆

The 2009 vintage (★★★★☆) was estate-grown in the Wairau Valley, Marlborough, blended with Viognier (4 per cent) and matured for 16–18 months in French oak barriques (10–20 per cent new). Bold and youthful in colour, it is powerful, sturdy and firmly structured, with rich blackcurrant, plum, spice and nut flavours, showing excellent ripeness and density. It's built for the long haul; open 2013+.

Vintage	09	08	07	06	05	04	03	02	01
WR	7	NM	7	6	7	7	6	6	7
Drink	13-19	NM	11-19	11-16	11-17	11-16	11-13	11-12	11-16

DRY $65 –V

Georges Michel La Reserve Marlborough Syrah ★★★

The youthful, full-coloured 2009 vintage (★★★) was matured for over a year in French oak barrels (50 per cent new). Fresh, fruity and supple, it has blackcurrant, spice and nut flavours, some funky, slightly rustic notes, decent depth and a smooth finish.

Vintage	09	08
WR	6	5
Drink	11-19	11-17

DRY $30 –V

Glazebrook Handpicked Hawke's Bay Syrah   (★★★☆)

(Previously 'Regional Reserve'.) Drinking well now, the 2009 vintage (★★★☆) is deeply coloured and mouthfilling, with fresh blackcurrant, plum and nut flavours, showing some herbal notes, very good depth and a smooth finish.

Vintage	09	08	07
WR	7	NM	7
Drink	11-16	NM	11-13

DRY $27 –V

Golden Hills Estates Nelson Syrah   (★★★★)

The seductive 2009 vintage (★★★★) is a single-vineyard red (except for the addition of 7 per cent Viognier, not estate-grown), matured for nearly a year in American oak casks (42 per cent new). Full-coloured, it is delicious in its youth, with a floral bouquet and strong, ripe, plummy, spicy flavours, savoury and supple.

DRY $35 –V

Goldridge Estate Premium Reserve Matakana Syrah   (★★☆)

The 2008 vintage (★★☆) is solid, showing some spicy, savoury complexity, but also green-edged, lacking a bit of ripeness and roundness.

DRY $19 –V

Greystone Waipara Syrah   ★★★

Estate-grown in North Canterbury, the 2009 vintage (★★★) is a sturdy, high-alcohol red (14.5 percent), matured for a year in French oak casks (40 per cent new). Fullish and slightly developed in colour, it has leafy, green-edged aromas and flavours, some savoury, nutty complexity and good depth. Ready.

Vintage	09
WR	7
Drink	11-15

DRY $55 –V

Grower's Mark Hawke's Bay Syrah   (★★★)

Deeply coloured, the 2010 vintage (★★★) has a slightly rustic bouquet, but also very good depth of vibrant blackcurrant, plum and black-pepper flavours, fresh and smooth. (From Farmers Market Wine Co.)

DRY $25 –V

Harvest Man Syrah   ★★★★☆

From The Hay Paddock, on Waiheke Island, the 2008 vintage (★★★★) was barrel-aged for a year. It's distinctly Rhône Valley-like, with plum and black-pepper flavours, ripe, slightly earthy and savoury, and fine-grained tannins giving early appeal.

Vintage	08	07
WR	5	6
Drink	11-16	11-14

DRY $35 AV

Harwood Hall Marlborough Syrah   ★★★☆

Matured for 10 months in seasoned oak barriques, the 2009 vintage (★★★☆) is deeply coloured, floral and supple, in a vibrantly fruity style with good depth of fresh plum and black-pepper flavours. It's a charming, drink-young style, with earthy, savoury notes adding interest.

Vintage	09
WR	6
Drink	11-15

 DRY $24 AV

Hyperion Asteria Matakana Syrah   (★★☆)

The 2009 vintage (★★☆) was hand-harvested and matured for a year in European oak barriques. Full and youthful in colour, it is mouthfilling, fruity and smooth, with plum and spice flavours, woven with fresh acidity, and a hint of herbs. Moderately ripe-tasting, it shows a slight lack of stuffing and roundness.

Vintage	09
WR	6
Drink	11-18

 DRY $32 –V

Johner Gladstone Syrah   ★★★☆

The dark 2009 vintage (★★★☆) was estate-grown in the northern Wairarapa and French oak-aged. It's a sturdy red (14.5 per cent alcohol) with concentrated plum, herb and spice flavours, fresh and strong, and a fragrant, slightly leafy bouquet.

DRY $50 –V

John Forrest Collection Syrah   ★★★★☆

John Forrest views Syrah as Hawke's Bay's 'premier varietal'. Grown in the Cornerstone Vineyard, in the Gimblett Gravels, the 2007 vintage (★★★★☆) is still very youthful. Boldly coloured, it is sturdy (14.5 per cent alcohol), with loads of fresh, spicy flavour, highly concentrated and firm. Best drinking 2013+.

Vintage	07	06	05
WR	7	7	6
Drink	11-17	11-15	11-12

DRY $75 –V

Jurassic Ridge Syrah   ★★★★

The 2008 vintage (★★★★) was grown at Church Bay, on Waiheke Island. It's a distinctly savoury and earthy style with good density of blackcurrant and spice flavours and ripe, supple tannins.

Vintage	08
WR	7
Drink	11-14

 DRY $35 –V

Kaimira Estate Brightwater Syrah/Viognier   (★★☆)

Made in 'tiny' quantities, the 2009 vintage (★★☆) is a blend of Syrah (90 per cent) and Viognier (10 per cent), matured for 15 months in French oak casks (50 per cent new). Fullish and slightly developed in colour, it is berryish and spicy, with some savoury complexity, but shows a slight lack of ripeness and roundness.

Vintage	09	DRY $34 –V
WR	5	
Drink	11-16	

Kaipara Estate Syrah/Malbec/Cabernet Franc   (★★★)

Grown on the South Head Peninsula of the Kaipara Harbour, the 2009 vintage (★★★) is a blend of Syrah (40 per cent), Malbec (20 per cent) and Cabernet Franc (20 per cent), with minor portions of Cabernet Sauvignon, Petit Verdot and Tannat. Matured for over a year in French and American oak barrels (new and second fill), it is fullish in colour, with good depth of spicy, moderately ripe flavours, showing some savoury complexity and firm tannins. Priced right. Best drinking mid-2012+.

Vintage	09	DRY $19 AV
WR	5	
Drink	11-16	

Karikari Estate Syrah   ★★★☆

The impressive 2010 vintage (★★★★) was estate-grown on the Karikari Peninsula, in the Far North, hand-picked at over 23 brix, and matured for 10 months in new French oak puncheons. Deeply coloured, it is fragrant and rich, with plenty of muscle, fresh, strong blackcurrant, plum and spice flavours, and fine-grained tannins. It's a youthful, supple wine; drink now or cellar.

Vintage	10	DRY $26 –V
WR	6	
Drink	13-16	

Kennedy Point Waiheke Island Syrah   ★★★★★

A rising star. The dark, finely scented 2008 (★★★★★) is powerful, yet very elegant and supple, with a complex array of cassis, spice, liquorice and nut flavours, rich, ripe and flowing. A 'serious' yet seductive wine, it's already delicious, but should mature well for a decade. I have not tasted the 2009. The 2010 vintage (★★★★★), which includes a splash of Viognier (2 per cent), was matured for over a year in French oak casks. Densely coloured, it is beautifully fragrant, with ripe aromas of black pepper, spices and dark chocolate. Still very youthful, it is highly concentrated, with densely packed cassis, plum, spice and liquorice flavours, well-ripened, complex and finely structured. It's a potentially great wine; open 2015+.

Vintage	08	07	06	DRY $49 AV
WR	7	7	7	
Drink	11-16	11-18	11-18	

Kidnapper Cliffs Hawke's Bay Syrah   (★★★★★)

From Te Awa, the boldly coloured 2009 vintage (★★★★★) is very elegant, finely poised and age-worthy. Estate-grown in the Gimblett Gravels, it's not a blockbuster, but youthful and tightly structured, with fresh, highly concentrated plum and black-pepper flavours, deeply spicy, supple and long. Potentially very complex, it's well worth cellaring to 2014+.

DRY $55 AV

Lake Chalice Hawke's Bay Syrah   (★★★)

Barrel-aged for 10 months, the 2010 vintage (★★★) is a floral, supple, fruit-driven style with vibrant cherry, plum and spice flavours, showing good depth, gentle tannins and lots of drink-young charm.

DRY $20 –V

Lil Rippa Hawke's Bay Syrah   (★★★☆)

From Shoestring Wines, in Marlborough, the 2010 vintage (★★★☆) is mouthfilling and generous, with full, bright colour and fresh plum, pepper and spice flavours, seasoned with toasty oak. It's a moderately complex wine, with upfront appeal.

DRY $25 –V

Mahurangi River Winery Companions Syrah/Viognier   ★★

The 2009 vintage (★★☆), matured briefly in French oak casks (50 per cent new), is fullish in colour, in a middleweight style with a spicy, peppery bouquet and fresh, supple, green-edged flavours.

Vintage	09
WR	6
Drink	11-13

DRY $39 –V

Maimai Creek Hawke's Bay Syrah   ★★★

The 2009 vintage (★★★) is deeply coloured, with bold, peppery flavours in a fresh, fruit-driven style, vibrant and smooth.

DRY $25 –V

Man O' War Waiheke Island Dreadnought Syrah   ★★★★★

Estate-grown at the eastern end of the island, the 2009 vintage (★★★★★) was hand-harvested at 24.5 to 26 brix and matured in French oak casks (25 per cent new). Deeply coloured, with a highly floral bouquet, it has concentrated plum, spice and black-pepper flavours, a hint of dark chocolate, and ripe, supple tannins. Rich, vibrantly fruity and supple, it's already delicious.

Vintage	09	08
WR	7	6
Drink	11-18	11-18

DRY $50 –V

Man O' War Waiheke Island Syrah   ★★★★

The 2008 (★★★★) was matured in French and American oak casks. It's a densely packed wine with plum, blackcurrant and spice flavours, a hint of sweet oak, and a firm finish. A powerful red, it should reward cellaring. (This is the last vintage of this label.)

Vintage	08	07
WR	6	5
Drink	11-15	P

DRY $28 AV

Marsden Bay of Islands Syrah   ★★★☆

The 2009 vintage (★★★★), grown at Kerikeri, in Northland, was matured for 15 months in oak casks. Vibrantly fruity, with full, bright colour, it's a sweet-fruited wine with ripe plum/pepper flavours, now developing a savoury, spicy complexity.

Vintage	09
WR	6
Drink	11-14

DRY $35 –V

Marsden Bay of Islands Vigot Syrah   (★★★★☆)

Already delicious, the 2010 vintage (★★★★☆) of this Northland red was oak-matured for 16 months. Boldly coloured, with a fragrant, perfumed bouquet and mouthfilling body, it is concentrated and supple, with rich blackcurrant, plum and spice flavours, seasoned with sweet oak, ripe tannins and excellent complexity. Drink now or cellar.

Vintage	10
WR	7
Drink	12-18

DRY $38 AV

Martinborough Vineyard Limited Edition Syrah/Viognier   (★★★★☆)

From vines planted in 2000 in the Moy Hall Vineyard, the 2009 vintage (★★★★☆) includes 4 per cent Viognier and was matured for 16 months in French oak casks (25 per cent new). Finely textured, it is drinking well now, with concentrated, plummy, peppery, complex flavours, very savoury, supple and harmonious.

DRY $48 –V

Matakana Estate Hawke's Bay Syrah   (★★★)

The 2009 vintage (★★★) is full-coloured, mouthfilling and supple, with toasty French oak aromas. Berryish, plummy and peppery, with a firmly structured, distinctly spicy finish, it has some aging potential.

DRY $35 –V

Matua Valley Reserve Release Hawke's Bay Syrah   ★★★

The 2009 vintage (★★★) is mouthfilling and full-coloured, with good depth of fresh spice and plum flavours, a hint of liquorice, firm tannins and some savoury complexity. Drink now or cellar.

DRY $22 –V

Mills Reef Elspeth Syrah ★★★★★

In top vintages, this has been one of Hawke's Bay's greatest Syrahs. The 2009 (★★★★☆), estate-grown and hand-picked in the Mere Road Vineyard, in the Gimblett Gravels, was matured for 16 months in large (300L and 400L) French oak casks (96 per cent new), which give 'a more refined style of Syrah'. Highly perfumed and supple, it has fresh, deep plum and black-pepper flavours, with a subtle seasoning of oak, and good tannin support. Does it have the complexity to be a great Syrah? Time will tell.

Vintage	09	08	07	06	05	04
WR	7	NM	7	7	7	7
Drink	11-18	NM	11-17	11-15	11-16	11-15

 DRY $43 AV

Mills Reef Elspeth Trust Vineyard Syrah ★★★★☆

The 2009 vintage (★★★★) is an estate-grown, single-vineyard Hawke's Bay red, hand-picked in the Gimblett Gravels, fermented with indigenous yeasts, and matured for 15 months in American (two-thirds) and French oak casks (18 per cent new). Full and bright in colour, it is medium to full-bodied, fresh and elegant, with blackcurrant, plum, spice and nut flavours, finely textured and harmonious.

Vintage	09
WR	7
Drink	11-18

 DRY $43 –V

Mills Reef Reserve Gimblett Gravels Hawke's Bay Syrah ★★★☆

The very charming 2009 vintage (★★★☆) was estate-grown in the Trust and Mere Road vineyards. Deeply coloured, it is flowing and supple, with a floral bouquet and vibrant plum/spice flavours, slightly toasty and strong. The 2010 (★★★), matured for over a year in large oak casks, American (mostly) and French, is a 'fruit-driven' style, fruity and smooth, with fresh plum/spice flavours and a touch of complexity.

Vintage	10
WR	7
Drink	11-15

 DRY $24 AV

Miro Syrah/Viognier ★★★★☆

Grown on Waiheke Island, the 2009 vintage (★★★★) is a blend of Syrah (95 per cent) and Viognier (5 per cent). Matured in French oak casks (mostly seasoned), it has rich, sweet-fruit flavours of plums and spices, a gentle oak influence and ripe, supple tannins. Delicious young.

 DRY $45 –V

Mission Hawke's Bay Syrah ★★★☆

The 2010 vintage (★★★★) is a 'lightly oaked' wine, supple and intensely varietal, with deep colour and an attractively floral, peppery bouquet. Mouthfilling and finely textured, with rich plum and spice flavours and silky tannins, it offers fine value. (The 2009 vintage, matured in tanks 'to retain primary fruit', won three gold medals.)

DRY $19 V+

Mission Huchet Syrah   (★★★★★)

Named in honour of its nineteenth-century winemaker, Cyprian Huchet, the Mission sees the debut 2007 vintage (★★★★★) as 'the greatest wine we have ever produced in our proud 160-year history'. Harvested at 24.6 to 25.2 brix, and matured for 15 months in French oak casks (new and one year old), it's a youthful, powerful wine with deep blackcurrant, spice, liquorice and nut flavours, complex and lasting. A 'serious', highly concentrated wine, set for the long haul, it's best opened 2013+.

Vintage	07
WR	6
Drink	11-20

 DRY $100 AV

Mission Jewelstone Syrah   ★★★★☆

The 2009 vintage (★★★★★) is a classy, single-vineyard red, estate-grown in Mere Road, in the Gimblett Gravels of Hawke's Bay. Matured in French oak casks (40 per cent new), it has bold, almost black colour. Very fragrant and smooth-flowing, it has fine-grained tannins and notably dense blackcurrant, plum, liquorice, spice and nut flavours, yet remains highly approachable.

Vintage	09	08	07
WR	6	5	7
Drink	12-20	11-20	12-20

 DRY $35 AV

Mission Reserve Hawke's Bay Syrah   ★★★★

The 2009 vintage (★★★★) is a blend of Gimblett Gravels (89 per cent) and Ohiti Road grapes, matured in French oak casks (17 per cent new). Dense and tightly structured, with obvious potential, it has a fragrant, peppery bouquet leading into a dark, youthful wine with blackcurrant, plum and black-pepper flavours, fresh and strong.

Vintage	09	08	07	06
WR	5	5	7	5
Drink	11-16	11-12	11-15	P

 DRY $26 AV

Mission Vineyard Selection Hawke's Bay Syrah   ★★★☆

Grown in 'several vineyards', the 2010 vintage (★★★☆) is deeply coloured and vibrantly fruity, with plum and spice flavours woven with fresh acidity, and ripe, supple tannins giving a soft texture. If you like Pinot Noir, try this.

 DRY $20 AV

Moana Park Hawke's Bay Syrah   (★★★)

The 2010 vintage (★★★) is a drink-young style, grown in Gimblett Road and the Dartmoor Valley. Full-coloured, with gentle tannins and fresh, strongly varietal plum and black-pepper flavours, it is supple, with a Pinot Noir-ish appeal.

DRY $19 AV

Moana Park Limited Edition Syrah/Viognier   (★★☆)

The 2009 vintage (★★☆), which includes 6 per cent Viognier, was grown in Gimblett Road, Hawke's Bay, and matured for 18 months in oak casks (30 per cent new). Full-coloured, it is fresh and full-flavoured, plummy and spicy, with some savoury complexity, but also shows a slight lack of ripeness, roundness and harmony.

DRY $29 –V

Moana Park Vineyard Selection Gimblett Road Syrah   ★★★

The 2009 vintage (★★★) was grown in the Gimblett Gravels and French oak-aged. Full-coloured, it is fruity and smooth, with vibrant, berryish flavours, gentle tannins and a spicy finish.

DRY $22 –V

Moana Park Vineyard Tribute Syrah/Viognier   ★★★★

Very rich and soft, the 2008 vintage (★★★★☆) is a dark, powerful Gimblett Road, Hawke's Bay red. Harvested at over 24 brix, matured for a year in French oak barriques (45 per cent new), and bottled unfined and unfiltered, it is perfumed and spicy, with an earthy streak and highly concentrated plum, black-pepper and nut flavours. Worth cellaring.

DRY $32 –V

Morton Estate Black Label Hawke's Bay Syrah   ★★★

The 2007 vintage (★★★☆) is full-flavoured, plummy and spicy. It shows good density and complexity, with a fairly firm finish, but some herbal and rustic notes detract slightly.

Vintage	07
WR	7
Drink	11-16

DRY $35 –V

Morton Estate White Label Hawke's Bay Syrah   ★★★

The 2009 vintage (★★★☆) is the best yet. Deeply coloured, it is mouthfilling, with fresh, vibrant blackcurrant, plum and spice flavours, slightly nutty and strong. A gutsy, generous red, it's drinking well now.

DRY $18 AV

Mountain Landing Syrah   (★★★☆)

The 2009 vintage (★★★☆) was grown at the Bay of Islands, in Northland. It's a savoury, ripe-tasting wine with concentrated, brambly, plummy, spicy flavours, a hint of liquorice, balanced tannins, and the power to age.

DRY $35 –V

Mount Riley Marlborough Limited Release Syrah   (★★★☆)

Grown in the sheltered, warm Seventeen Valley Vineyard, south of Blenheim, the 2009 vintage (★★★☆) was hand-picked and co-fermented with Viognier. Full-coloured, it is mouthfilling (14.5 per cent alcohol) and intensely varietal, with fresh plum, black-pepper, spice and nutty oak flavours, showing good concentration, and supple tannins. Drink now or cellar.

DRY $30 –V

Mount Tamahunga Matakana Syrah   (★★★☆)

Grown at the property previously called The Antipodean, the 2008 vintage (★★★☆) was matured for 15 months in French oak casks (two-thirds new). Full-coloured, it is mouthfilling, with very good depth of plum and spice flavours, fresh acidity and considerable complexity. Worth cellaring.

Vintage	08
WR	6
Drink	11-16

DRY $39 –V

Mudbrick Vineyard Reserve Syrah   ★★★★★

Grown on Waiheke Island, the outstanding 2008 vintage (★★★★★) was matured in American oak casks (50 per cent new). Hand-picked, it is finely scented, with deep, purple-flushed colour, mouthfilling body (14.4 per cent alcohol), a core of sweet fruit, lovely density of blackcurrant, plum and black-pepper flavours, nutty and complex, and fine-grained tannins. The 2009 (★★★★★), grown at Church Bay and Onetangi, is powerful (15 per cent alcohol) but caresses the mouth, with deliciously concentrated plum, black-pepper and toasty oak flavours, impressive complexity and ripe, velvety tannins. Well worth cellaring.

DRY $52 –V

Mudbrick Vineyard Shepherds Point Syrah   ★★★★☆

A single-vineyard red, grown at Onetangi, on Waiheke Island, the 2009 vintage (★★★★) is an elegant, finely textured wine with good density of plum and black-pepper flavours, ripe and smooth. The 2010 (★★★★☆) is already delicious, with deep colour, sweet-fruit delights and rich plum, chocolate and spice flavours, ripe and silky-textured.

Vintage	10	09	08
WR	7	6	7
Drink	11-14	11-12	11-12

DRY $42 –V

Murdoch James Saleyards Syrah   ★★★

The 2008 vintage (★★★), matured in all-new oak, is a Martinborough red, ruby-hued, with a peppery bouquet and silky-smooth palate, showing a hint of herbs and some nutty complexity.

DRY $39 –V

Ngatarawa Stables Reserve Syrah   ★★★☆

The debut 2009 vintage (★★★☆) has deep, purple-red colour and fresh cassis, plum and pepper flavours, showing some earthy, savoury notes. It's a well-balanced, vibrantly fruity wine with very satisfying depth. The 2010 (★★★) is similar – deeply coloured, with fresh blackcurrant, spice and herb flavours, showing a touch of savoury complexity, and good depth.

 DRY $22 AV

Obsidian Waiheke Island Syrah   ★★★★★

The 2009 vintage (★★★★★) is a beauty. Co-fermented with Viognier (2.5 per cent), it was matured for 10 months in French oak barriques (40 per cent new). Floral, rich and supple, it is very elegant, with deep plum, spice and nut flavours, gentle tannins and a finely poised, silky-smooth finish. It's already delicious, but has obvious cellaring potential.

Vintage	09	08
WR	7	7
Drink	11-20	11-20

 DRY $54 AV

Omaha Bay Vineyard Huapai Syrah   ★★☆

The 2007 vintage (★★) was grown in the Papa Vineyard at Huapai, in West Auckland. Retasted in 2011, it has full, developed colour, with rustic plum and green-leaf flavours, earthy, smoky and leathery. It's clearly overshadowed by its Matakana stablemate (below).

Vintage	07
WR	5
Drink	11-15

 DRY $27 –V

Omaha Bay Vineyard Matakana Syrah   ★★★★

The 2008 vintage (★★★★) was matured for a year in French oak casks (one-third new). Full-coloured, it is mouthfilling, ripe and supple, with precise varietal characters and good density of blackcurrant, spice and black-pepper flavours. Drink now or cellar.

Vintage	08
WR	6
Drink	12-18

 DRY $32 –V

Paritua Hawke's Bay Syrah   ★★★★

Intensely varietal, the 2009 vintage (★★★★) was estate-grown at Maraekakaho, hand-picked and matured in French oak barriques (50 per cent new). Full and youthful in colour, with a fragrant, spicy and earthy bouquet, it has strong plum, herb and black-pepper flavours, in a complex, savoury style, for drinking now or cellaring.

DRY $32 –V

Passage Rock Reserve Syrah ★★★★★

Waiheke Island's most awarded wine of late is partly estate-grown at Te Matuku Bay, on the south side of the island, supplemented by fruit from Oneroa. Matured in American and French oak barriques, mostly new, it is typically a powerful, opulent red, rich and well-rounded. There is no 2009. The 2010 (★★★★★) is densely coloured, with beautifully rich cassis, black-pepper and nut flavours, and gentle tannins giving instant appeal. Finely textured and supple, it has lovely depth and a powerful presence.

DRY $60 AV

Passage Rock Syrah ★★★★★

This Waiheke Island red is consistently rewarding. Partly estate-grown and fully matured in American (mostly) and French oak barriques, the 2010 vintage (★★★★★) has dense, youthful colour. A star wine, it has substantial body and lovely, dense flavours of blackcurrants, plums, chocolate and spices, ripe and rich.

DRY $35 V+

Pukeko Vineyard Bay of Islands Blue Bird on Red Stilts Syrah (★★☆)

Grown and barrel-aged at Kerikeri, the 2010 vintage (★★☆) is deeply coloured and vibrantly fruity, with plummy, peppery flavours, light and slightly short of full ripeness. A pleasant, drink-young style.

DRY $25 –V

Pukeora Estate Ruahine Range Syrah (★★)

From Central Hawke's Bay, the debut 2010 vintage (★★) was matured for almost a year in French and American oak barriques (one-third new). Purple-flushed, it has very fresh, crisp, berryish flavours, lacking real ripeness and roundness.

Vintage	10
WR	5
Drink	12-15

DRY $25 –V

Ransom K Syrah ★★★☆

The 2008 vintage (★★★), grown at Matakana and French and American oak-aged, is full and slightly developed in colour, with a nutty, slightly herbal bouquet. It's green-edged, but shows some leathery complexity and good depth.

DRY $36 –V

Richmond Plains Hawke's Bay Syrah   (★★☆)

Certified organic, the 2010 vintage (★★☆) was partly barrel-aged. Full-coloured, it's a slightly under-ripe style, with plummy, herbal flavours showing very good freshness and depth, but also a slight lack of warmth and roundness.

Vintage	10
WR	6
Drink	11-15

DRY $20 –V

Runner Duck Estate Matakana Syrah   ★★★

An elegant wine, drinking well now, the 2007 vintage (★★★★) was harvested at 24 brix and matured for 20 months in French and American oak casks. Savoury, rather than vibrantly fruity, with impressive complexity and personality, it is spicy and plummy, with a hint of herbs, and very good body, texture and harmony. The 2009 (★★☆) has full, youthful colour. It is mouthfilling, fruity, plummy and spicy, but lacks real fragrance and finesse.

DRY $40 –V

Sacred Hill Deer Stalkers Syrah   ★★★★★

The 2009 vintage (★★★★★), estate-grown and hand-picked in the Gimblett Gravels, Hawke's Bay, was matured for 16 months in French oak barriques. A powerful, silky red, with dense, inky colour, it has notably rich, brambly, plummy, peppery flavours, a lovely silky texture and a lasting finish. It should flourish for a decade.

Vintage	09	08	07	06
WR	7	6	7	7
Drink	11-18	11-16	11-15	11-16

DRY $60 AV

Sacred Hill Halo Hawke's Bay Syrah   ★★★☆

The boldly coloured 2009 vintage (★★★★) is a Gimblett Gravels red with fragrant, lifted aromas of black pepper and plums. A youthful, elegant wine, with good density of ripe blackcurrant/plum flavours, spicy and long, it's already quite expressive. Drink now or cellar.

Vintage	10
WR	6
Drink	11-15

DRY $25 –V

Sacred Hill Hawke's Bay Syrah   (★★★☆)

The 2010 vintage (★★★☆), grown in the Gimblett Gravels, is a blend of Syrah (90 per cent) and Malbec (10 per cent), 'aged with a percentage of French oak'. The bouquet is fresh, aromatic and peppery; the palate is mouthfilling and vibrant, with strong plum and spice flavours, gentle tannins, and lots of drink-young appeal.

DRY $22 AV

Saint Clair Pioneer Block 17 Bay Block Hawke's Bay Syrah ★★★★

The dark, mouthfilling, supple 2010 vintage (★★★★) was grown in the Gimblett Gravels. Matured for 10 months in French oak casks (half new), it is a rich wine with strong blackcurrant and plum flavours, distinctly spicy, and a seasoning of toasty oak. Worth cellaring.

 DRY $33 –V

Seifried Nelson Syrah ★★★

Grown at Brightwater, on the Waimea Plains, and matured in French oak barriques, the 2010 vintage (★★★☆) is the finest yet. Ruby-hued, it is mouthfilling, vibrantly fruity and supple, with generous plum, herb, black-pepper and prune flavours, and gentle tannins. A very good, drink-young style.

Vintage	10
WR	6
Drink	11-15

 DRY $21 –V

Selaks Winemaker's Favourite Hawke's Bay Syrah ★★★☆

Grown mostly in the Gimblett Gravels, but also in the company's Corner 50 Vineyard, in The Triangle, the 2009 vintage (★★★☆) is deeply coloured, with ripe, spicy, slightly earthy flavours, showing some complexity.

 DRY $21 AV

Serine Syrah ★★★☆

From Iron Hills Vineyards at Kerikeri, in Northland, the 2010 vintage (★★★☆) is a promising, very youthful wine, full-coloured, with an earthy, rather than obviously peppery, bouquet. A savoury style with ripe plum and spice flavours, showing good complexity, it's worth cellaring; open 2013+.

Vintage	10
WR	7
Drink	11-16

 DRY $35 –V

Sileni Cellar Selection Hawke's Bay Syrah ★★☆

The easy-drinking 2009 vintage (★★☆) was French and American oak-aged. Medium-bodied, it has moderately ripe berry, herb and spice flavours, showing a touch of savoury complexity, and a smooth finish. Ready.

 DRY $20 –V

Sileni The Peak Hawke's Bay Syrah (★★★☆)

A single-vineyard red, grown in The Triangle and French and American oak-matured for over a year, the 2007 vintage (★★★☆) is full-coloured, plummy and supple, with gentle black-pepper notes and good fruit sweetness, complexity and depth. It's drinking well now.

Vintage	07
WR	5
Drink	11-14

DRY $30 –V

Soho Valentino Waiheke Island Syrah   (★★★★)

The 2009 vintage (★★★★) is deeply coloured, with a nutty, spicy bouquet. It's a rich, ripe, concentrated red with plum, spice and liquorice flavours, strongly seasoned with toasty oak. Showing good warmth and density, it's worth cellaring.

Vintage 09
WR 7
Drink 11-14

DRY $38 –V

Spy Valley Marlborough Syrah   (★★★)

Hand-picked from the 'warmest vineyard block', fermented with indigenous yeasts, matured for 18 months in French oak casks, and bottled unfiltered, the debut 2009 vintage (★★★) is a full-bodied, fresh and supple red with good depth of plummy, spicy, toasty flavours, a slightly rustic streak and a smooth finish.

Vintage 09
WR 5
Drink 11-15

DRY $29 –V

Squawking Magpie The Stoned Crow Syrah   ★★★★★

A distinguished, single-vineyard red, grown in the Gimblett Gravels of Hawke's Bay and French oak-aged, the 2009 vintage (★★★★★) should mature well for a decade. Dark and purple-flushed, it is deliciously rich and supple, with very dense blackcurrant and spice flavours, woven with fresh acidity, and lovely concentration and texture. The 2008 (★★★★★) is deeply coloured and powerful, with strong cassis, plum, black-pepper and liquorice flavours, seasoned with toasty oak, a firm backbone of tannin and a long, spicy finish.

DRY $40 AV

Staete Landt Marlborough Syrah   ★★★☆

The 2008 vintage (★★★☆) was hand-harvested at Rapaura and matured for 17 months in French oak barriques (40 per cent new). Full-coloured, it is sturdy and firm, with plum and spice flavours, showing a hint of tamarillo, lots of toasty oak, and good concentration and complexity.

Vintage 08
WR 6
Drink 11-17

DRY $55 –V

Stonecroft Gimblett Gravels Reserve Syrah   ★★★★★ ·

The 2009 vintage (★★★★★) was estate-grown in Mere Road and at Roy's Hill and matured for 18 months in French oak casks (30 per cent new). Deeply coloured, it is finely fragrant, with plum, pepper and floral notes. A very graceful and supple wine, it is lithe, finely poised and youthful, with pure plum, black-pepper and liquorice flavours that build to a tight-knit, lasting finish. Best drinking 2013+.

Vintage 09
WR 6
Drink 14-22

DRY $60 AV

Stonecroft Gimblett Gravels Serine Syrah ★★★★

Estate-grown and barrel-aged for 18 months, the 2009 vintage (★★★★) of this Hawke's Bay red is unusually savoury. It's not boldly fruity but finely textured, with a floral bouquet and spicy, nutty flavours. Still youthful, with underlying tannins, it's enjoyable young, but well worth cellaring.

Vintage	09	08	07	06
WR	7	6	5	5
Drink	12-16	11-15	11-15	11-15

 DRY $25 AV

Stonecroft The Original Hawke's Bay Syrah (★★★★★)

The rare – only 210 bottles were produced – 2009 vintage (★★★★★) was made from the two surviving rows of original Syrah vines planted at Stonecroft in 1984. A lovely, generous wine, it is deeply coloured and highly fragrant, with concentrated, plummy, spicy flavours, very vibrant, supple and sustained. One for the cellar.

 DRY $80 AV

Stone Paddock Hawke's Bay Syrah ★★☆

From Paritua, the 2008 vintage (★★☆), matured for nine months in barrels (30 per cent new), is fullish in colour, with spicy, slightly earthy and leafy flavours.

Vintage	08
WR	6
Drink	11-14

DRY $23 –V

Stonyridge Pilgrim Syrah/Mourvedre/Grenache ★★★★★

This distinguished Rhône-style blend is estate-grown at Onetangi, on Waiheke Island, and matured for a year in French oak barriques. The 2009 (★★★★★) is fleshy, dark, rich and supple, with sweet-fruit delights and deep blackcurrant, plum and spice flavours. A muscular wine with real power and complexity, it's well worth cellaring. Still a baby, the 2010 vintage (★★★★★) is Syrah-based (90 per cent), with minor portions of Mourvedre (6 per cent), Grenache (2 per cent), Cinsaut (1 per cent) and Viognier (1 per cent). Deeply coloured, it is very floral, sweet-fruited and supple, with dense plum and spice flavours, a hint of liquorice, and fine-grained tannins. It should develop for many years.

Vintage	10	09
WR	7	7
Drink	12-20	11-18

 DRY $80 AV

Te Awa Left Field Hawke's Bay Syrah (★★★☆)

Designed for early drinking, the 2009 vintage (★★★☆) was estate-grown in the Gimblett Gravels, blended with a small amount of Viognier, and matured for nine months in old oak hogsheads. It's a fruit-driven style, deeply coloured, with very good depth of strongly varietal, plummy, peppery flavour, fresh, vibrant and youthful.

DRY $26 –V

Te Awa Syrah ★★★★

The boldly coloured 2009 vintage (★★★★) of this estate-grown Gimblett Gravels, Hawke's Bay red is mouthfilling and sweet-fruited, with rich plum and black-pepper flavours, and a hint of liquorice. Finely textured and vibrantly fruity, it's likely to be at its best 2012+.

DRY $35 –V

Te Kairanga Runholder Syrah (★★★☆)

The debut 2008 vintage (★★★☆) was grown in Hawke's Bay and matured for 17 months in French oak casks (42 per cent new). Richly coloured, with a spicy bouquet, it is mouthfilling, with plum, spice and black-pepper flavours, showing some savoury complexity, and good tannin backbone. Drink now or cellar.

Vintage	08
WR	7
Drink	11-18

DRY $29 –V

Te Mania Big Balls Syrah (★★★★)

The impressive 2010 vintage (★★★★) doesn't state Nelson on the label – but that's where the grapes were grown. Full and bright in colour, it is mouthfilling, with fresh, deep plum and black-pepper flavours, and hints of dark chocolate and spices. A youthful wine, it is firm, savoury and complex, with obvious cellaring potential.

DRY $22 V+

Te Mania Nelson Syrah ★★★

The 2010 vintage (★★★☆) is the best yet. Full-coloured, it is vibrantly fruity, with ripe, plummy, spicy, peppery flavours, showing clear-cut varietal character and very good depth. Drink now or cellar.

DRY $22 –V

Te Mata Estate Bullnose Syrah ★★★★★

Grown in the Bullnose Vineyard, in The Triangle inland from Hastings, in Hawke's Bay, this classy red is based on 13 to 21-year-old vines, hand-picked and matured for 15 to 16 months in French oak barriques (35 per cent new). Unlike its Woodthorpe stablemate (below), it is not blended with Viognier, and the vines for the Bullnose label are cropped lower. The 2009 (★★★★★) is a top vintage. It's a very graceful wine, dark and concentrated, with beautifully rich, ripe plum and black-pepper flavours, good tannin backbone and a long, finely textured finish. Well worth cellaring.

Vintage	10	09	08	07	06	05	04
WR	7	7	7	7	7	7	7
Drink	13-19	11-19	11-16	11-17	11-16	11-15	11-12

DRY $44 AV

Te Mata Estate Woodthorpe Syrah　　★★★☆

The good-value 2009 vintage (★★★☆) was made by co-fermenting Syrah, estate-grown and hand-picked in the Woodthorpe Vineyard, in Hawke's Bay, with a splash (4 per cent) of Viognier. French oak-aged for 13 months, it has a floral, peppery bouquet, leading into a fresh, supple wine with very good depth of plum/spice flavours, a touch of complexity and lots of drink-young appeal.

Vintage	09
WR	7
Drink	11-13

Te Puna Mountain Landing Syrah　　(★★★)

Grown on the Purerua Peninsula, in Northland, the 2009 vintage (★★★) was picked at over 25 brix from first-crop vines and matured for a year in seasoned oak casks. Full-coloured, it has a peppery fragrance, with plummy, spicy, slightly raisiny flavours and substantial body.

Terrace Edge Waipara Valley Syrah　　★★★☆

The 2009 vintage (★★★★), the best to date, was hand-picked at 24.9 to 26 brix, fermented with indigenous yeasts and matured for 14 months in French oak barriques (25 per cent new). A powerful, peppery red, it is full-coloured and mouthfilling, with strong plum, spice and nut flavours, an earthy streak, gentle tannins and good complexity.

Te Whau Vineyard Waiheke Island Syrah　　★★★★★

This rare wine is hand-picked from hill-grown vines, fermented with indigenous yeasts and matured in French oak barrels. The 2009 vintage (★★★★☆) has a fragrant bouquet of spices, earth and olives. The palate is full-bodied, firm, savoury and complex, with deep spice, plum, herb and dark chocolate flavours. The 2010 (★★★★☆) is similar – deeply coloured, fragrant, highly concentrated and supple, with an array of blackcurrant, plum, herb, spice and nut flavours, showing impressive complexity, and a rich, well-rounded finish.

Vintage	10	09	08	07
WR	7	7	7	7
Drink	11-16	11-15	11-15	11-13

Tinpot Hut Hawke's Bay Syrah　　★★★

The 2008 vintage (★★☆) , from two sites, is a fresh, medium-bodied red with spicy, leafy, green-edged flavours and a fairly firm finish. It's a solid wine but lacks real richness.

Ti Point Hawke's Bay Syrah　　(★★★☆)

The 2008 vintage (★★★☆) is a buoyantly fruity Gimblett Gravels red, hand-picked and French oak-aged for a year, with very good depth of plum and black-pepper flavours. It's a deeply coloured, mouthfilling wine with gentle tannins.

DRY $22 AV

Ti Point Matriarch Matakana Coast Syrah   (★★★★)

Estate-grown north of Auckland and matured in one and two-year-old French oak casks, the youthful 2010 vintage (★★★★) is an excellent debut. Deeply coloured, it is mouthfilling, very fresh and vibrant, with concentrated cassis, plum and spice flavours and a finely textured, long finish. Open 2013+.

Vintage	10
WR	7
Drink	12-25

 DRY $39 –V

Trinity Hill Gimblett Gravels Syrah   ★★★★★

Winemakers John Hancock and Warren Gibson are pursuing a 'savoury, earthy Rhône style'. Grown in the Gimblett Gravels, the 2009 (★★★★★) was hand-picked, co-fermented with Viognier (3 per cent), and matured for over a year in French oak barriques (25 per cent new). A beautifully rich, harmonious red, it is deeply coloured, with strong plum, spice, black-pepper and nut flavours and a foundation of ripe, supple tannins. A top vintage, it shows lovely mouthfeel, texture and depth. The 2010 (★★★★★) is also a star. Almost entirely Syrah-based (0.5 per cent Viognier), it is inky-hued. The palate is notably bold, rich and flowing, with beautifully ripe cassis, plum and black-pepper flavours. Sweet-fruited, concentrated and harmonious, it should mature gracefully for many years.

Vintage	10	09	08	07	06	05	04
WR	6	7	6	6	6	5	6
Drink	12-20	13-21	12-20	11-17	11-18	11-15	11-12

 DRY $35 V+

Trinity Hill Hawke's Bay Syrah   ★★★☆

The 2010 vintage (★★★☆) was grown in the Gimblett Gravels, blended with Viognier (5 per cent), and barrel-aged for a year. A finely textured, drink-young style, it is deeply coloured, with very good depth of plum and black-pepper flavours, supported by fine tannins.

Vintage	10
WR	6
Drink	12-15

 DRY $20 AV

Trinity Hill Homage Gimblett Gravels Hawke's Bay Syrah   ★★★★★

One of the country's most distinguished – and expensive – reds. Harvested by hand from ultra low-cropped, mature vines, and matured in French oak barriques (mostly new), the 2009 vintage (★★★★★) was blended with Viognier (2 per cent). Densely coloured and floral, it has lovely mouthfeel and harmony, with substantial body, concentrated blackcurrant, plum, spice, liquorice and pepper flavours, gentle tannins, and a flowing, finely textured finish.

Vintage	09	08	07	06	05	04	03	02
WR	7	NM	6	7	NM	5	NM	6
Drink	11-20	NM	11-17	11-17	NM	11-14	NM	11-14

 DRY $120 –V

Two Gates Gimblett Gravels Hawke's Bay Syrah   ★★★★☆

Certified organic, the 2008 vintage (★★★★★) of this single-vineyard, French oak-aged red is deeply coloured and highly fragrant, with lovely depth, complexity and texture. Packed with well-ripened cassis, spice, plum and nut flavours, it is supple, savoury and deeply satisfying, with powerful tannins beneath and a long life ahead.

DRY $55 –V

Unison Hawke's Bay Syrah   ★★★★☆

The 2008 vintage (★★★★) was hand-picked in the Gimblett Gravels and barrel-aged for 16 months. Deeply coloured, with a peppery fragrance, it is youthful, with fresh plum, spice and dark chocolate flavours, showing good concentration. Open 2012+.

DRY $39 AV

Vidal Legacy Series Gimblett Gravels Syrah   ★★★★★

(This replaces the former 'Reserve' label, last produced in 2007. It was typically a dark, opulent wine with dense plum, spice and liquorice flavours, lush and long.) The debut 2009 vintage (★★★★★) was matured for 18 months in French oak casks (33 per cent new). It's a densely packed wine, fleshy and layered, with delicious depth of fresh plum and black-pepper flavours, and fine-grained tannins.

Vintage	09	08	07	06	05
WR	7	NM	7	7	7
Drink	11-20	NM	11-15	11-13	11-15

DRY $57 AV

Vidal Reserve Series Gimblett Gravels Syrah   (★★★★)

The debut 2009 vintage (★★★★) of this classy, second-tier red was grown in the company's Omahu Gravels and Twyford Gravels vineyards, and matured for 20 months in French oak casks (25 per cent new). Bold and very youthful, with dark, purple-flushed colour, it has strong, well-ripened flavours of blackcurrants, plums and spices, silky tannins and an inviting perfume.

Vintage	09
WR	7
Drink	11-16

DRY $31 –V

View East Syrah   (★★★★)

The instantly appealing 2008 vintage (★★★★) was grown on Waiheke Island, hand-picked at 23.7 brix and oak-aged for 10 months. It has strong, ripe plum/spice flavours, seasoned with sweet American oak, and a well-rounded finish. Ready to roll.

DRY $39 –V

Villa Maria Cellar Selection Hawke's Bay Syrah   ★★★★★

A great buy. The 2009 vintage (★★★★★) is a highly perfumed blend of Gimblett Gravels (65 per cent) and Dartmoor Valley (35 per cent) grapes, hand-picked and matured for 18 months in French oak barriques (35 per cent new). Dark, fresh and richly varietal, with substantial body, it has concentrated plum/spice flavours, leathery, savoury notes adding complexity, and silky tannins.

Vintage	09	08	07	06	05	04
WR	7	7	7	6	6	7
Drink	11-16	11-15	11-15	11-16	11-12	11-12

 DRY $33 V+

Villa Maria Private Bin Hawke's Bay Syrah   ★★★☆

The 2009 vintage (★★★) was based mostly (87 per cent) on estate-grown grapes from the Joseph Soler Vineyard, blended with Petite Syrah (10 per cent) and 'other' fruit. Mostly handled in tanks (20 per cent of the blend was barrel-aged), it has a peppery, slightly earthy bouquet, leading into a full-coloured, plummy, slightly herbal red, firm and moderately ripe-tasting, with some richness.

Vintage	09	08
WR	6	6
Drink	11-15	11-12

 DRY $27 –V

Villa Maria Reserve Hawke's Bay Syrah   ★★★★★

The 2009 vintage (★★★★★), grown in the Gimblett Gravels, was matured for 20 months in French oak barriques (60 per cent new). It's a powerful, concentrated, finely textured wine with dense, beautifully ripe plum, pepper and nut flavours, complex and savoury. Built for the long haul.

Vintage	09
WR	7
Drink	12-20

 DRY $61 AV

Waimarie Muriwai Valley Syrah   ★★★

Estate-grown in West Auckland, the 2008 vintage (★★☆) was French oak-aged for 18 months. Slightly developed in colour, it's a lightish red with herbal, slightly smoky flavours that lack real ripeness and richness.

 DRY $35 –V

Waimarie Waimauku Syrah   (★★)

The 2009 vintage (★★), estate-grown in West Auckland, was French oak-matured for 14 months. Lightish and developed in colour, it is green-edged, with leafy, nutty flavours that lack ripeness and stuffing.

DRY $20 –V

Waimea Nelson Syrah ★★★

The 2008 vintage (★★★) is a single-vineyard red, American oak-aged. It's savoury, slightly nutty and herbal, with some peppery notes and good balance and depth.

Vintage	08	07
WR	6	6
Drink	11-12	P

DRY $25 –V

Waitapu Estate Reef Point Syrah (★★★)

The full-coloured 2008 vintage (★★★) was grown at Ahipara, in Northland. Vibrantly fruity, with plenty of plummy, spicy flavour, seasoned with cedary French oak, it is floral and supple, with some aging potential.

DRY $28 –V

Weeping Sands Waiheke Island Syrah ★★★★☆

From Obsidian, the 2010 vintage (★★★★☆) was grown at Onetangi and matured in French (principally) and American oak casks (25 per cent new). Deep and purple-flushed in colour, it is rich, savoury and flowing, with deep plum, black-pepper and spice flavours, showing excellent complexity and concentration. An elegant wine, it's approachable now, but should be at its best 2013+.

Vintage	10	09	08	07	06
WR	7	6	7	6	5
Drink	11-16	11-18	11-16	11-15	11-12

DRY $31 AV

Tempranillo

The star grape of Rioja, Tempranillo is grown extensively across northern and central Spain, where it yields strawberry, spice and tobacco-flavoured reds, full of personality. Barrel-aged versions mature well, developing great complexity. The great Spanish variety is starting to spread into the New World, but is still very rare in New Zealand, with 7 hectares of bearing vines in 2012 (mostly in Hawke's Bay).

Black Barn Hawke's Bay Tempranillo (★★★★☆)

Hand-picked at Havelock North, the 2009 vintage (★★★★☆) is deeply coloured, generous, full-bodied (14.5 per cent alcohol) and supple, with deep plum and spice flavours, hints of raisins and liquorice, power through the palate and good, savoury complexity. Full of personality.

DRY $48 –V

Hans Herzog Marlborough Tempranillo (★★★☆)

Promising, rather than convincing, the debut 2009 vintage (★★★☆) was estate-grown on the north side of the Wairau Valley and matured for 18 months in French oak barriques. Fullish and slightly developed in colour, it's a full-bodied red with leafy notes mingled with its blackcurrant, plum and spicy flavours, which show good, savoury complexity. It's drinking well now.

Vintage	09
WR	7
Drink	11-21

DRY $64 –V

Hawkes Ridge Tempranillo (★★★)

Hand-picked in Hawke's Bay, the 2008 vintage (★★★) has fullish colour, with some early development showing. Slightly leafy, it's a smooth, middleweight red with fresh acidity and cherry/plum flavours that show some savoury complexity, but it lacks real ripeness and stuffing. Drink now.

DRY $36 –V

Obsidian Young Vines Waiheke Island Tempranillo (★★★★☆)

An excellent debut, the 2010 vintage (★★★★☆) was estate-grown at Onetangi, blended with Cabernet Sauvignon (10 per cent) and matured for 10 months in seasoned American oak casks. Boldly coloured, it is rich and savoury, with fresh, well-ripened plum, strawberry and spice aromas and flavours, hints of blackcurrant and dark chocolate, and impressive density. Best drinking 2013+.

Vintage	10
WR	6
Drink	11-16

DRY $35 AV

Pete's Shed Tempranillo ★★☆

From Yealands, the 2009 vintage (★★☆) was estate-grown in the Awatere Valley, Marlborough, hand-picked at 25 brix, and matured for eight months in seasoned French oak casks. It's a lightweight style with plum/spice flavours and hints of herbs and tamarillos, but lacks any real stuffing.

DRY $23 –V

Rock Ferry Central Otago Tempranillo ★★★

Grown at Bendigo – as far from Rioja, Spain, as anyone has planted the famous red-wine grape – the 2009 vintage (★★★) is a single-vineyard red, matured for a year in French oak casks (30 per cent new). Lightish in colour, it is fresh and fruity, with strawberry and spice flavours, slightly nutty and smooth. Medium-bodied, it lacks richness, but has an almost Pinot Noir-ish charm.

Vintage	09	08
WR	5	6
Drink	12-16	12-13

 DRY $39 –V

Trinity Hill Gimblett Gravels Tempranillo ★★★★★

This is a consistently impressive red, full of personality. The 2008 vintage (★★★★★), estate-grown in the Gimblett Gravels, Hawke's Bay, was matured for 10 months in French (90 per cent) and American oak casks (25 per cent new). A blend of Tempranillo (87 per cent), Touriga Nacional (10 per cent), Malbec (2 per cent) and Viognier (1 per cent), it's a generous, serious, age-worthy red with deep plum and spice flavours, complex, savoury, finely balanced and lingering. The 2009 (★★★★☆) is deeply coloured, with a fragrant, slightly leathery bouquet. Full-bodied, it has rich blackcurrant, plum and spice flavours, still fresh and vibrant, in a generous, soft style, already drinking well.

Vintage	09	08	07	06	05	04
WR	5	6	6	6	5	5
Drink	12-16	11-14	11-14	11-14	11-12	P

 DRY $35 V+

Zinfandel

In California, where it is extensively planted, Zinfandel produces muscular, heady reds that can approach a dry port style. It is believed to be identical to the Primitivo variety, which yields highly characterful, warm, spicy reds in southern Italy. There are only 4 hectares of bearing Zinfandel vines in New Zealand, clustered in Hawke's Bay, with no expansion projected between 2004 and 2012. Alan Limmer, founder of the Stonecroft winery in Hawke's Bay, believes 'Zin' has potential here, 'if you can stand the stress of growing a grape that falls apart at the first sign of a dubious weather map!'

Stonecroft Zinfandel ★★★☆

The 2008 vintage (★★★☆) was estate-grown in the Gimblett Gravels of Hawke's Bay and matured for over 18 months in American oak casks. Ruby-hued, it's a fresh, lively, medium-bodied red with spicy, slightly peppery aromas and flavours and a firm finish, but lacks real richness.

Vintage	08	07
WR	4	7
Drink	11-15	11-20

DRY $27 –V

Zweigelt

Austria's most popular red-wine variety is a crossing of Blaufränkisch and St Laurent. It's a naturally high-yielding variety, but cropped lower can produce appealing, velvety reds, usually at their best when young. Zweigelt is extremely rare in New Zealand, with 3 hectares planted. (See also Seifried Silvia, in the Branded and Other Red Wines section.)

Hans Herzog Marlborough Zweigelt   ★★★★☆

This wine is going from strength to strength. The debut 2008 (★★★★) is boldly coloured, with fresh, concentrated, berryish flavours, and the 2009 (★★★★☆) is flavour-crammed, with great texture. The 2010 vintage (★★★★★) shows just how sophisticated Zweigelt can be. Matured for 15 months in French oak barriques (10 per cent new), and bottled unfined and unfiltered, it has dense, inky colour. Already deliciously drinkable, it is a sweet-fruited wine, overflowing with fresh blackcurrant, plum and spice flavours, complex, rich and rounded.

Vintage	10	09
WR	7	7
Drink	11-21	11-21

 DRY $53 –V

Index of Wine Brands

This index should be especially useful when you are visiting wineries as a quick way to find the reviews of each company's range of wines. It also provides links between different wine brands made by the same producer (for example, Abbey Cellars and Quail Lane).

MICHAEL COOPER'S

WINE ATLAS
of New Zealand

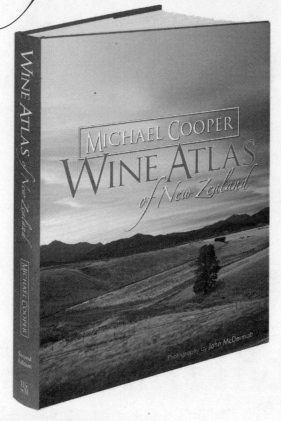

'Michael Cooper has done for New Zealand what Hugh Johnson and
Jancis Robinson did for the world.' – *New Zealand WineGrower*

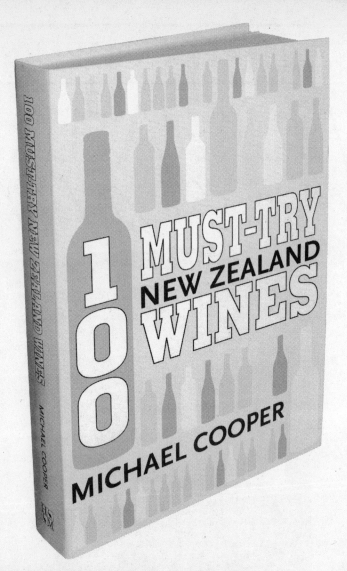

EVERYTHING YOU NEED TO KNOW

to buy the perfect bottle in an easy-to-use
book that appeals to all wine drinkers.